CONTENTS

The...™

OMNIBUS
VOLUME ONE

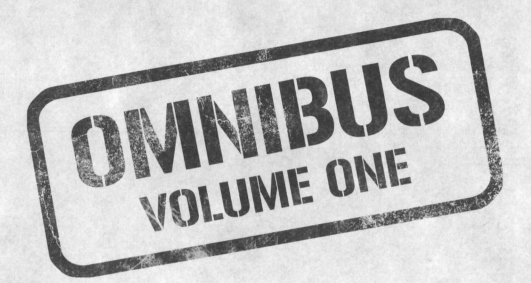

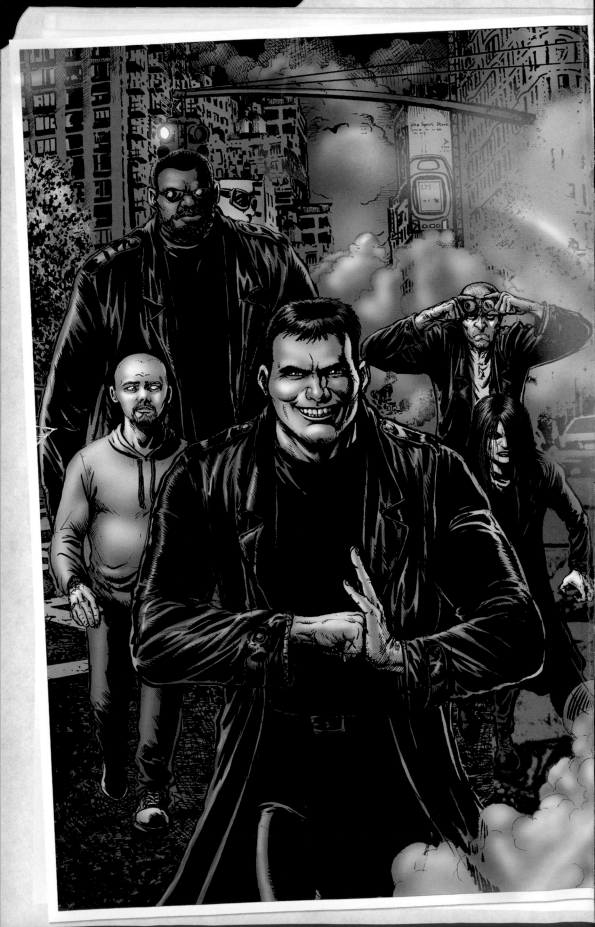

CONTENTS

The BOYS™

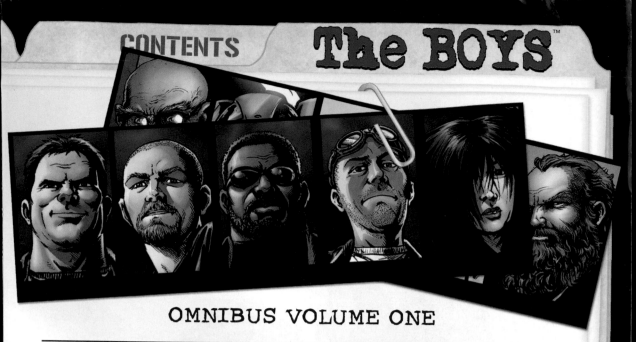

OMNIBUS VOLUME ONE

The Boys created by: GARTH ENNIS & DARICK ROBERTSON

Written by: GARTH ENNIS
Illustrated by: DARICK ROBERTSON
          & PETER SNEJBJERG #13, 14
Additional inks by: RODNEY RAMOS #11, 12
Colored by: TONY AVIÑA
Lettered by: GREG THOMPSON #1-6
          & SIMON BOWLAND #7-14
Series covers by: DARICK ROBERTSON & TONY AVIÑA
Book design by: JASON ULLMEYER
Editor (Dynamite): JOE RYBANDT
Editors (Wildstorm): BEN ABERNATHY & KRISTY QUINN

Collects issues one through fourteen of The Boys, published
by Wildstorm Productions/DC Comics (#1-6) and Dynamite (#7-14).

DYNAMITE®

Nick Barrucci, CEO / Publisher
Juan Collado, President / COO
Brandon Dante Primavera, V.P. of IT and Operations

Joe Rybandt, Executive Editor
Matt Idelson, Senior Editor

Alexis Persson, Creative Director
Rachel Kilbury, Digital Multimedia Assistant
Katie Hidalgo, Graphic Designer
Nick Pentz, Graphic Designer

Alan Payne, V.P. of Sales and Marketing
Vincent Faust, Marketing Coordinator

Jim Kuhoric, Vice President of Product Development
Jay Spence, Director of Product Development
Mariano Nicieza, Director of Research & Development

Amy Jackson, Administrative Coordinator

www.DYNAMITE.com
Instagram: /Dynamitecomics

Facebook: /Dynamitecomics
Twitter: @dynamitecomics

Standard ISBN: 978-1-5241-0859-5 | Exclusive ISBN: 978-1-5241-1190-8
Ninth Printing   10 9   Printed in Canada

For information regarding press, media rights, foreign rights, licensing, promotions, and advertising e-mail: marketing@dynamite.com

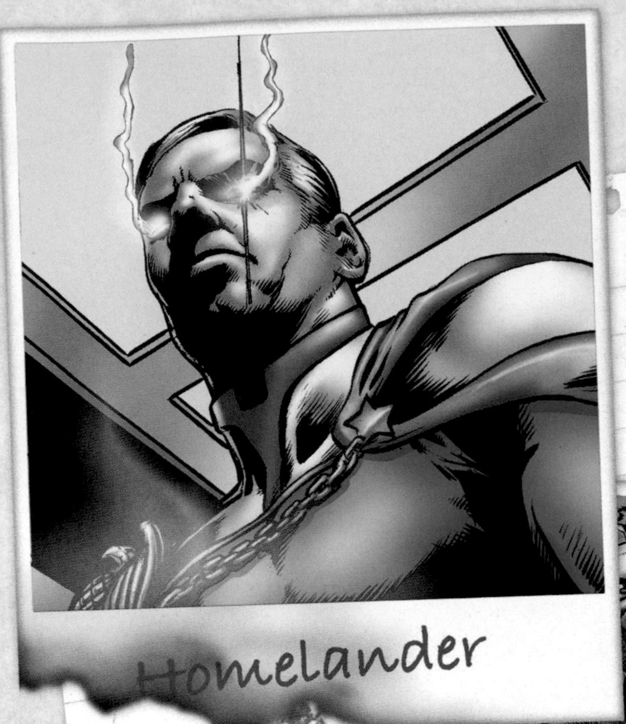
Homelander

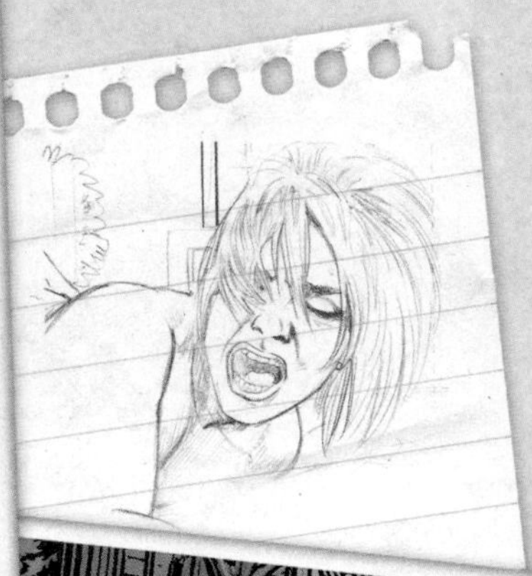

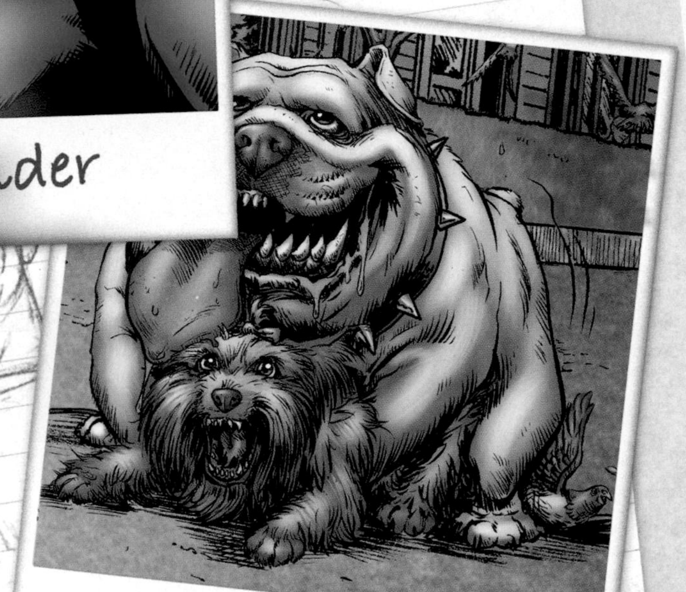

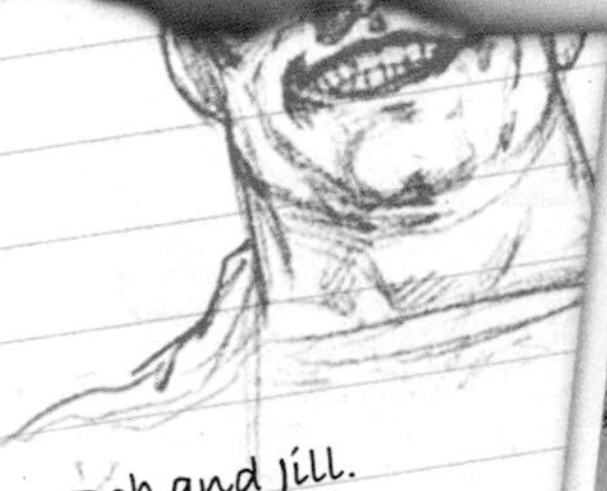

For Rob and Jill.
-Garth Ennis

For Meredith.
Special thanks
to Chad, Barbara
and Brandon
– Darick Robertson

Special thanks to Jim Lee, Scott Dunbier, Ben Abernathy,
Joe Rybandt and Nicky Barrucci.

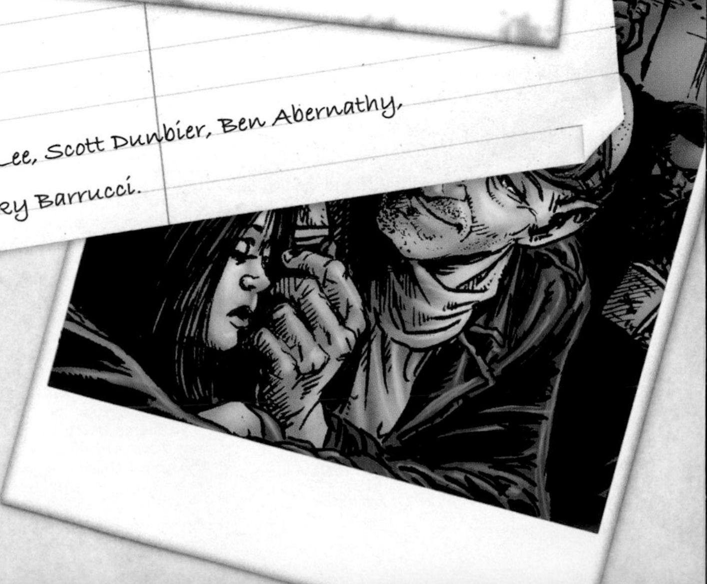

CONTENTS

BONUS MATERIALS

INTRODUCTION

I have a funny story to tell about Garth Ennis. Many of you picking this book up will know The Boys originally started out at WildStorm where, at the time, I was Executive Editor. But there's a bit of behind-the-scenes intrigue that most people don't know, and I'll have to fill in some of those blanks a bit during the telling of this story or it just won't make much sense. Now, before you get your hopes up, I'm not going to start slinging any mud around--sorry.

Okay, to set the stage, WildStorm was not the original intended home for The Boys. I first heard about the book four or five years ago from an editor at DC Comics who had received a pitch from Garth but was having trouble getting it approved. The editor, a very nice guy by the name of Pete Tomasi, told me about it over lunch when I was visiting the DC offices. Pete loved the proposal but thought it would be easier to get it going as a DC book produced out of the WildStorm offices in La Jolla, with him attached to edit. This practice wasn't so unusual, more recently I edited Darwyn Cooke's run on The Spirit. I told Pete I was open to the idea and he gave me the pitch to read.

On my flight back to San Diego I got my first real taste of The Boys. The proposal promised, on the very first line, to "out-Preacher Preacher." I want you to think about what that means, toss it around your head for a few seconds. That's a strong statement, it sets a certain tone for what's to come. But it isn't until a bit further in that we hit the real meat and potatoes of the document: The Boys, in all their glory, would co-exist with the mainstream DCU characters and inhabit the same world as Superman and Batman. Okay, now think about that.

After reading the rest of the proposal I was struck by a couple of things; the first being that this sounded like a damn entertaining book, one I would enjoy reading.

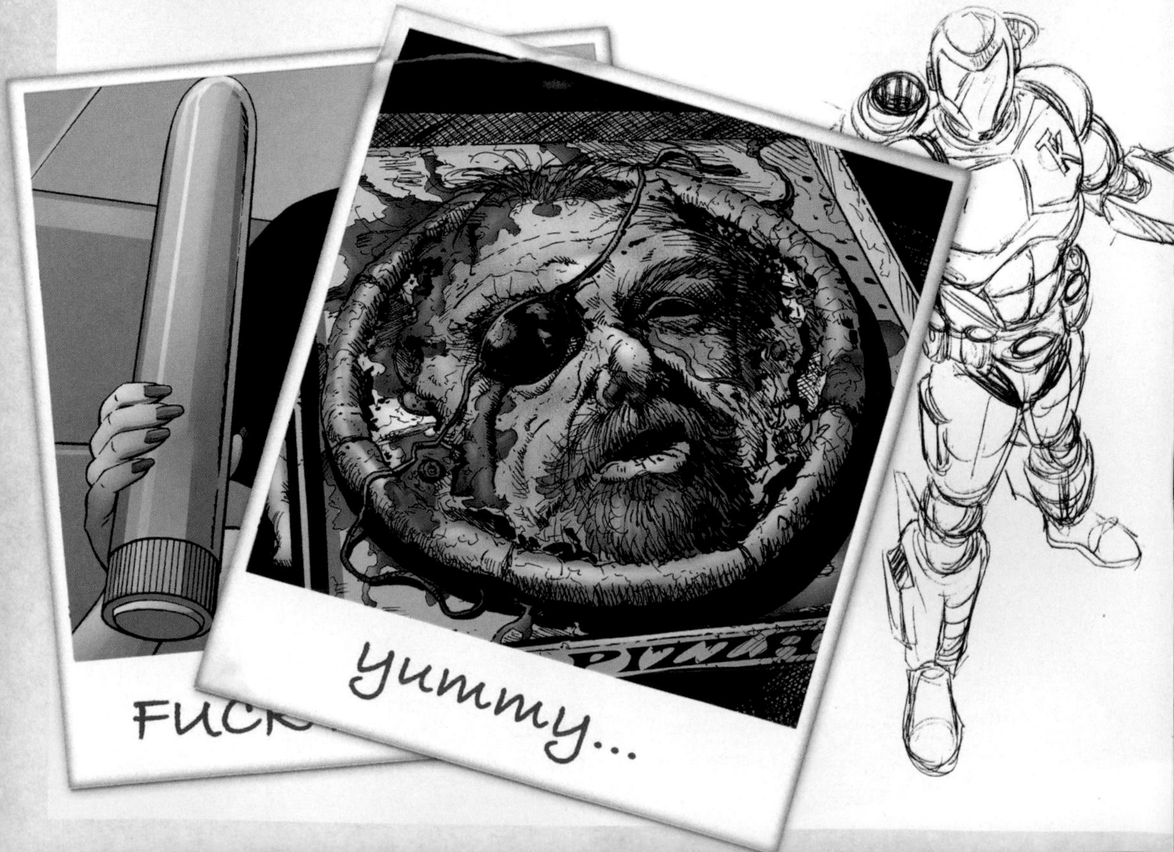
yummy...

The BOYS ™

The second was that there was no chance in Hell it would ever be published as part of the DCU. And this brings us to the punch line of the funny story I mentioned earlier—I believe that Garth, as rough as a lot of his material is, as brutal as his stories can be, is a romantic at heart. A romantic with a twisted side, sure, but still a romantic. How else do you explain his charmingly naïve belief that DC would publish The Boys as he originally intended? I really love that about Garth.

But wait, there's more--Otherwise I wouldn't have a place to write an introduction in such a fancy-pants gigantic hard cover collection like this, now would I? Around this same time Dan Didio, Executive Director or the DCU, got involved. Pete had also given the proposal to Dan, of course, and he pretty much came to the same conclusions I did—except he had an idea. Dan proposed giving the book to WildStorm and making it a creator owned, with its own set of iconic superheroes, one that wouldn't touch upon any of DC's sacred cows. So then, with that utterly simple and good idea, The Boys, as written by Garth Ennis and drawn by Darick Robertson, came over to WildStorm, where we all lived happily ever after.

Well, except for that last bit.

What happened next has been rehashed over and over so I won't add much here. Suffice to say that attempting to "out-Preacher Preacher" was just not in the cards for an imprint of the aforementioned DC Comics, even without Superman. It was a sad time for all of us who worked on and loved the book. Besides Garth and Darick, two very fine and standup guys, I felt very badly for Ben Abernathy, the line editor of the book. Ben is a very good editor who cares a lot about his books and creators; it was not an easy time for any of us. But, most importantly, The Boys came through it unscathed and has thrived.

At the end of the day all that matters is the book you now hold in your hands. It contains some of the filthiest and most absurdly funny scenes you are likely to see in a comic book. It's all classic Garth. No one tells this kind of story better or possesses a keener ear for dialogue. Darick Robertson, whose visual interpretation brought The Boys to life, continuously demonstrates his uncanny ability to incorporate exquisite detail without looking stiff. Both are at the top of their game here.

Finally, somewhere buried in this tome is a little four-pager that you should pay special attention to. It was the lead story in Liberty Comics, a benefit comic I put to-gether earlier this year for the Comic Book Legal Defense Fund. Both Garth and Darick (along with Tony Aviña and Simon Bowland) donated their time and creative energies to get it done. Please read that story and take it to heart. While I am sure the next 14 issues will be as creatively rich as the ones you are about to explore, I would prefer that the road taken to get there be a bit less bumpy.

Scott Dunbier
San Diego
September 2008 (For *The Boys Definitive Edition Vol. 1*)

Scott Dunbier is originally from New York where he was a dealer of original comic art. In 1995 he moved to San Diego to work for Jim Lee at WildStorm Productions, quickly rising to the position of Editor-in-Chief. After WildStorm was purchased by DC Comics his title changed to Group Editor, eventually becoming Executive Editor. After leaving WildStorm he joined IDW Publishing as Special Projects Editor.

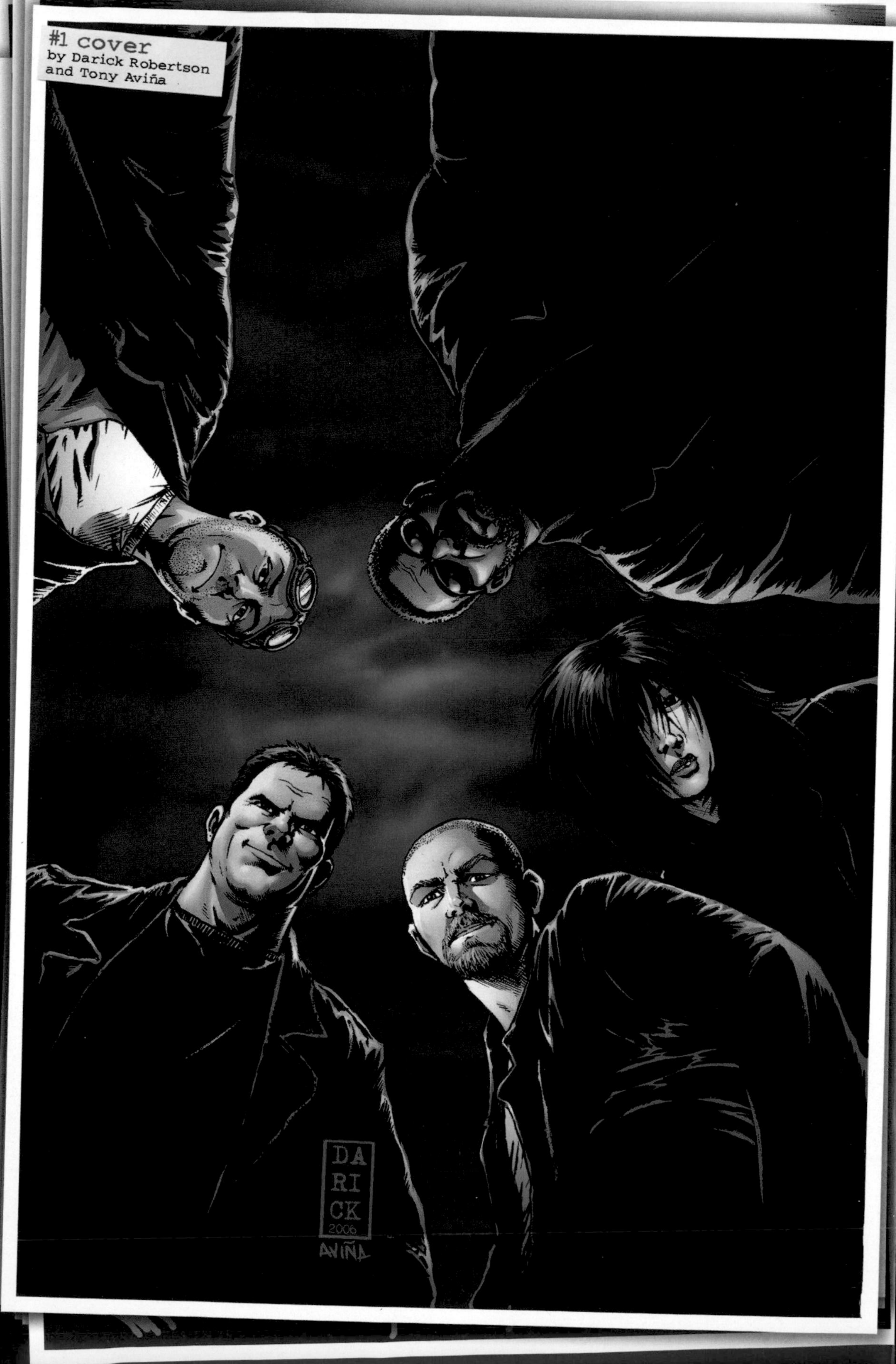
DA
RI
CK
2006
AVIÑA

#1 cover
by Darick Robertson
and Tony Aviña

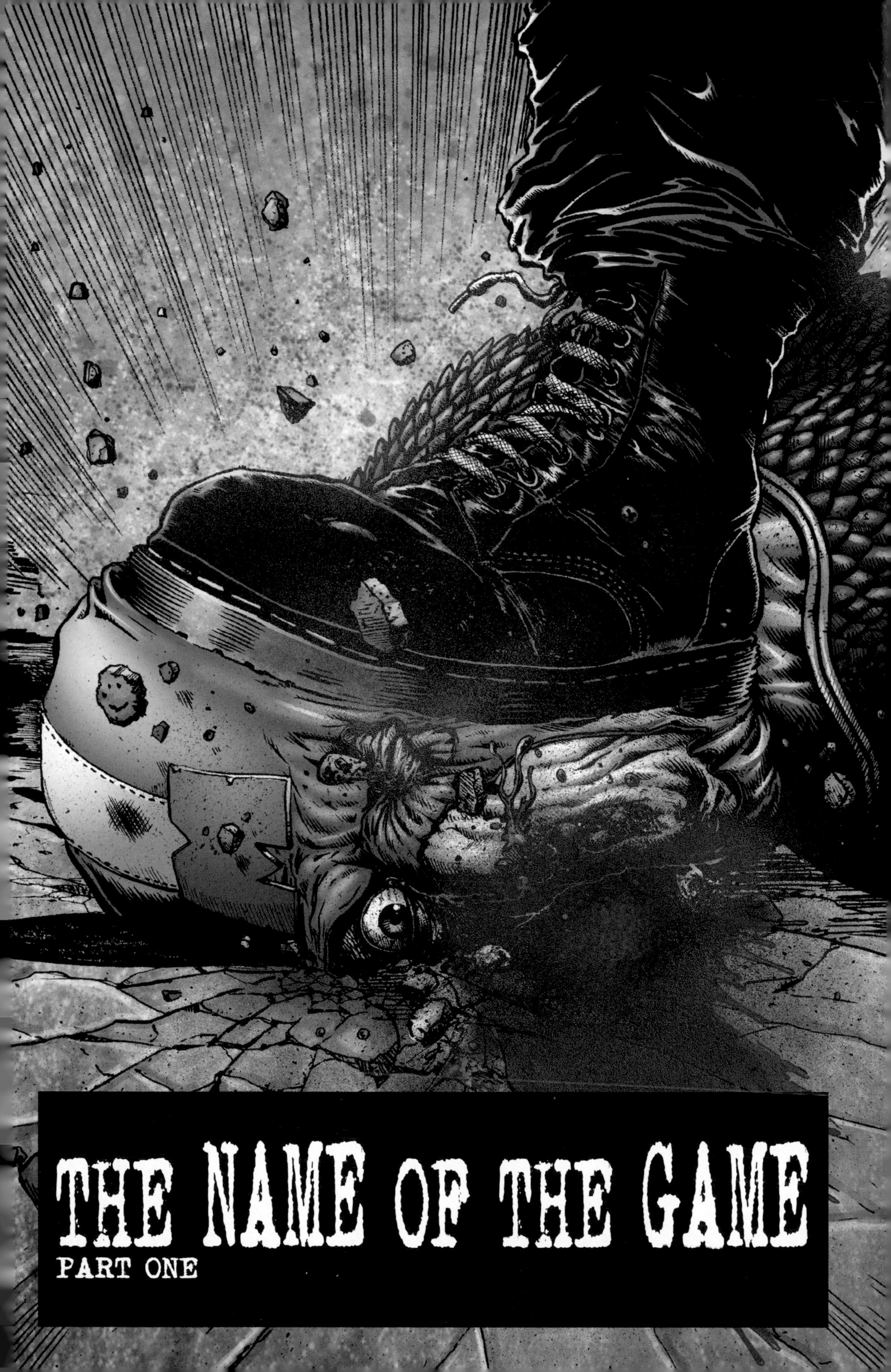
THE NAME OF THE GAME
PART ONE

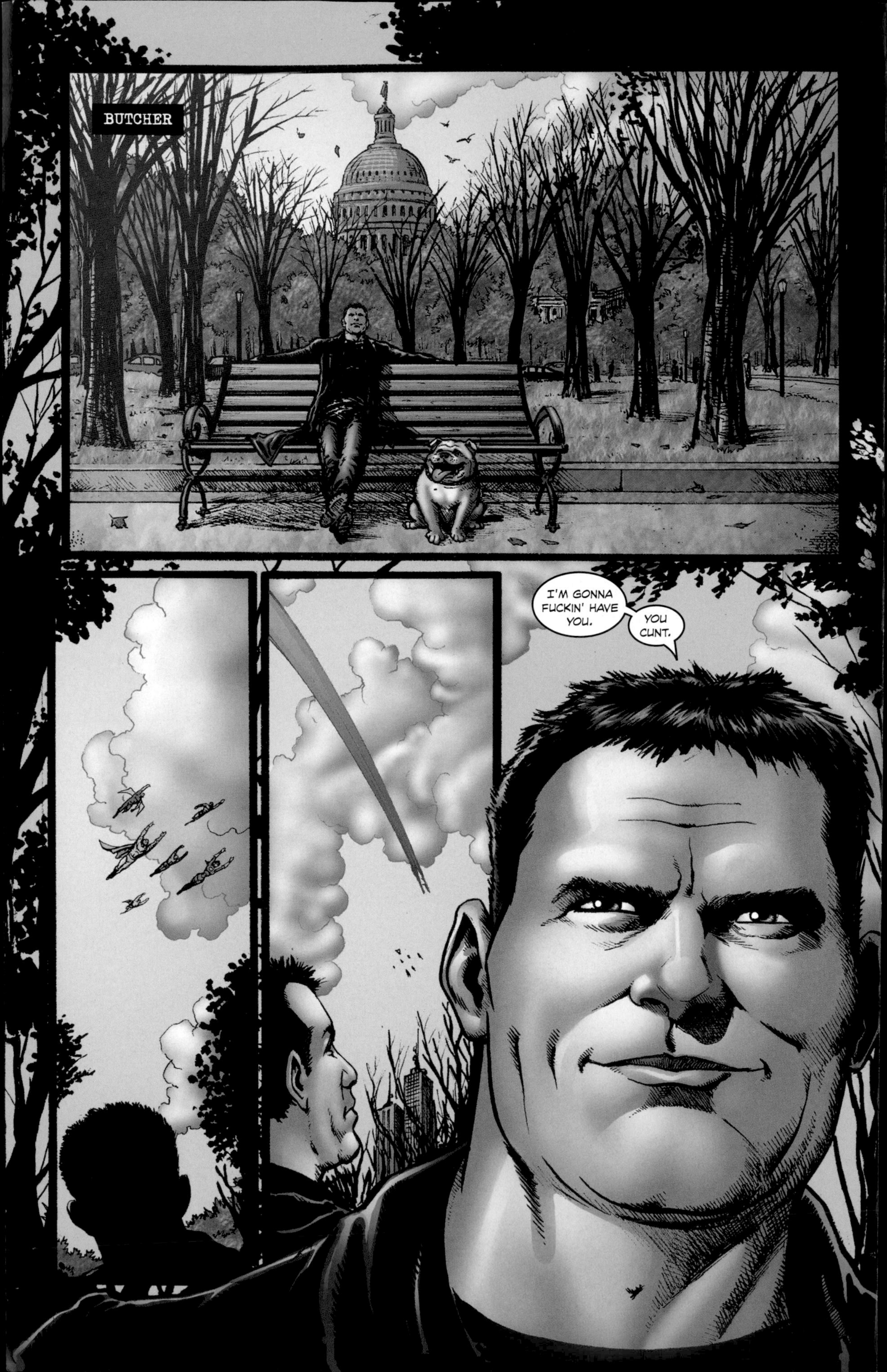
BUTCHER
I'M GONNA FUCKIN' HAVE YOU.
YOU CUNT.

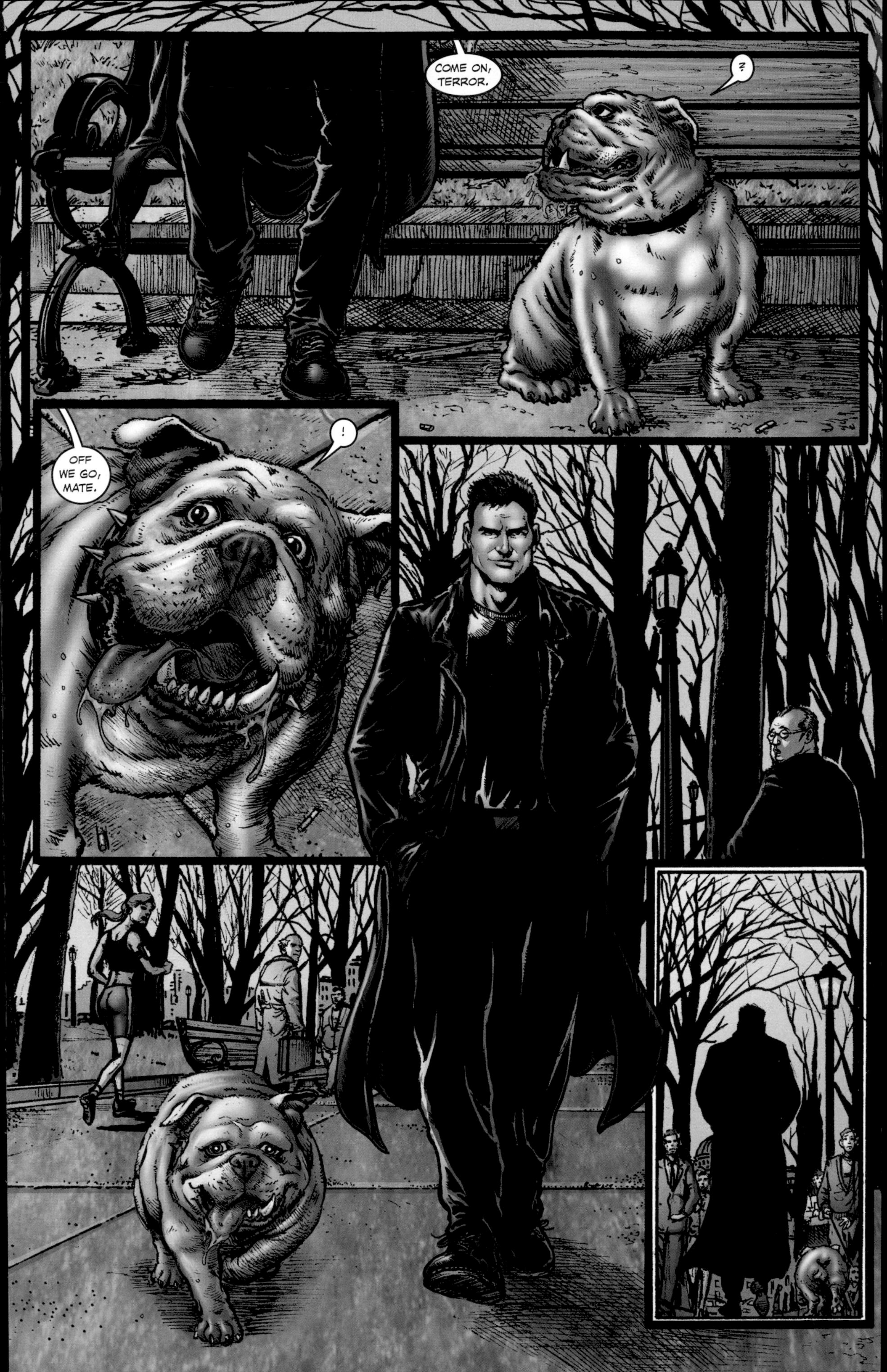
COME ON, TERROR.
?
OFF WE GO, MATE.
!

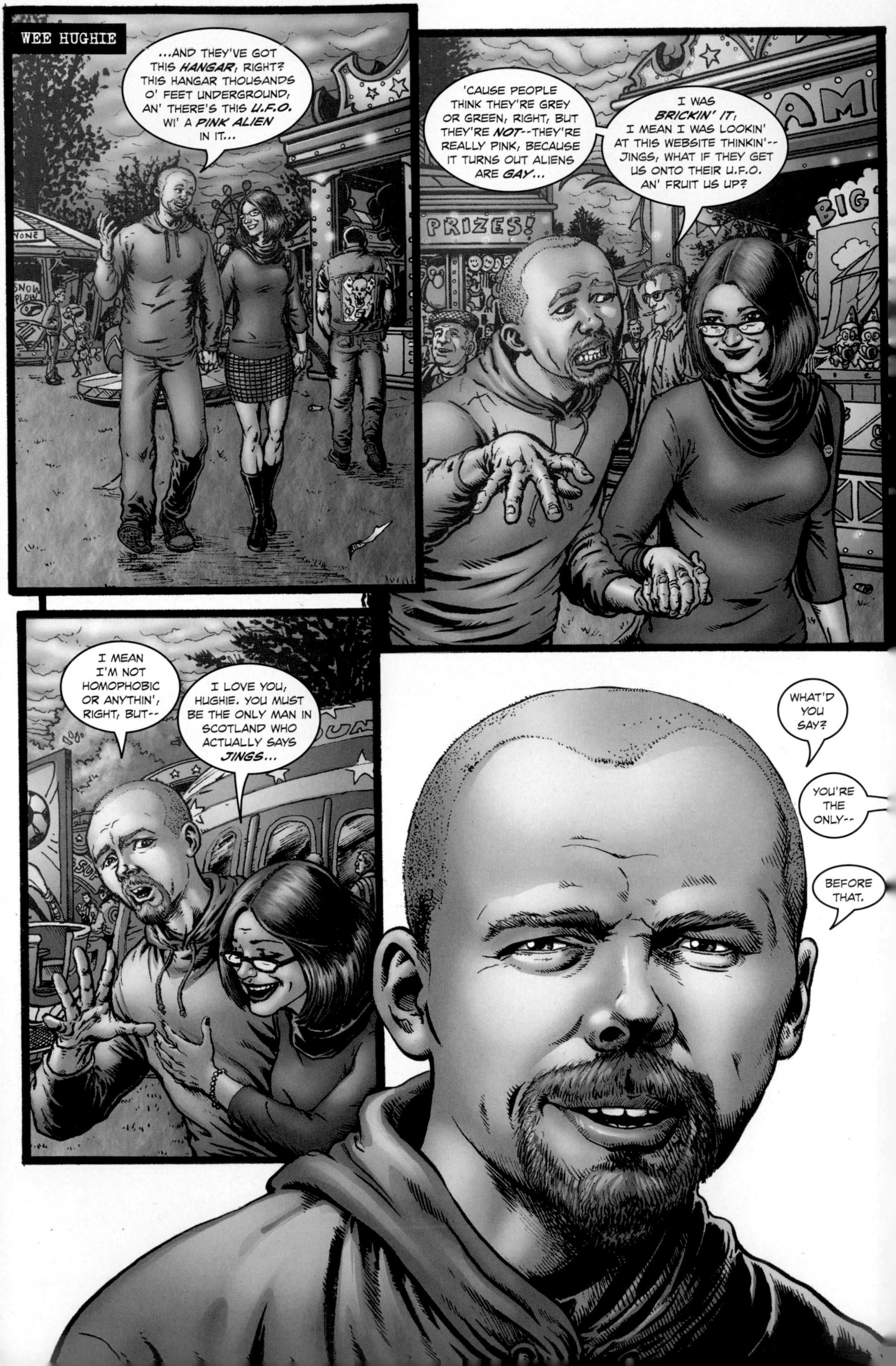
WEE HUGHIE
...AND THEY'VE GOT THIS HANGAR, RIGHT? THIS HANGAR THOUSANDS O' FEET UNDERGROUND, AN' THERE'S THIS U.F.O. WI' A PINK ALIEN IN IT...
'CAUSE PEOPLE THINK THEY'RE GREY OR GREEN, RIGHT, BUT THEY'RE NOT--THEY'RE REALLY PINK, BECAUSE IT TURNS OUT ALIENS ARE GAY...
I WAS BRICKIN' IT, I MEAN I WAS LOOKIN' AT THIS WEBSITE THINKIN'--JINGS, WHAT IF THEY GET US ONTO THEIR U.F.O. AN' FRUIT US UP?
PRIZES!
I MEAN I'M NOT HOMOPHOBIC OR ANYTHIN', RIGHT, BUT--
I LOVE YOU, HUGHIE. YOU MUST BE THE ONLY MAN IN SCOTLAND WHO ACTUALLY SAYS JINGS...
WHAT'D YOU SAY?
YOU'RE THE ONLY--
BEFORE THAT.

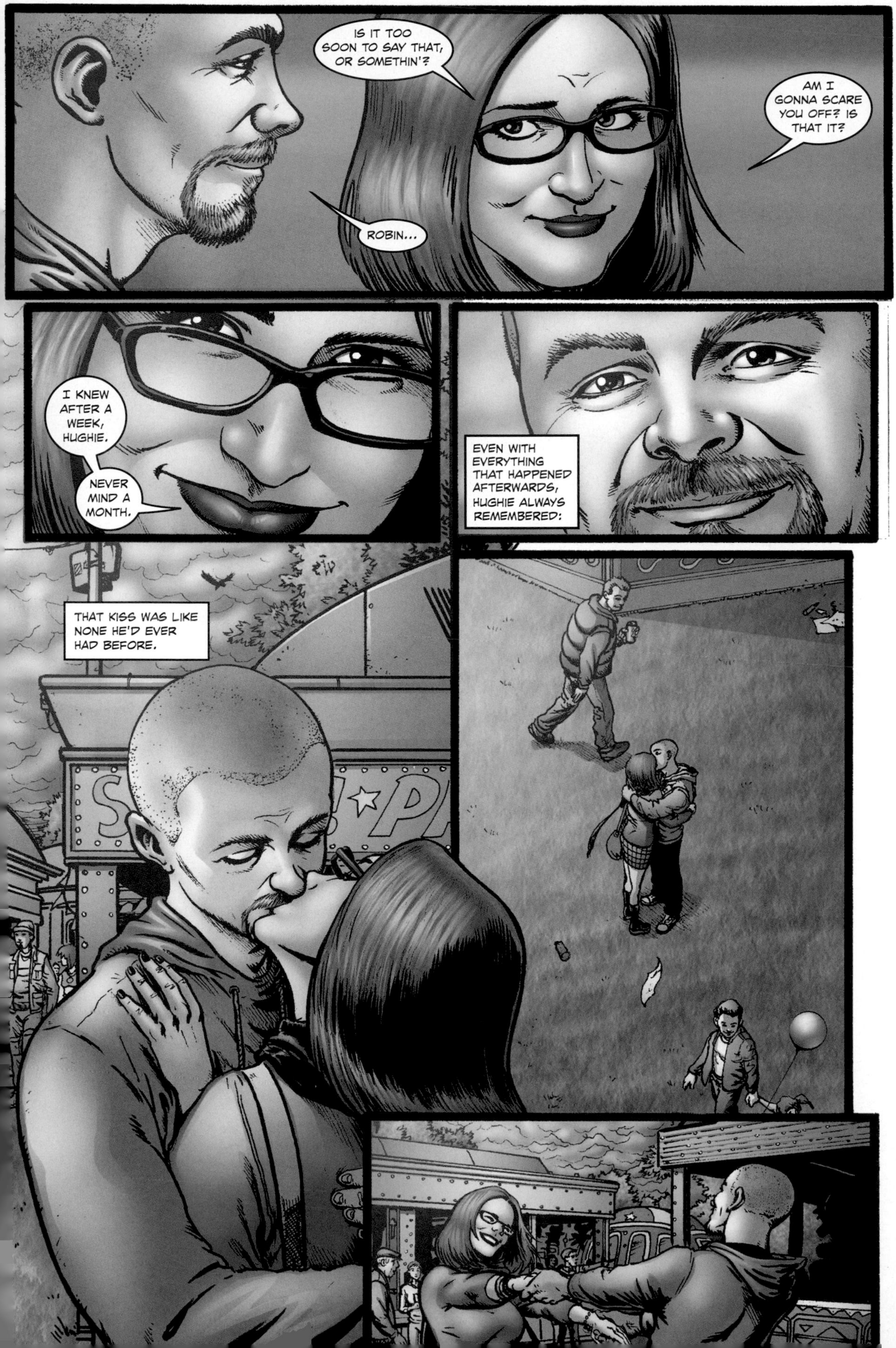
IS IT TOO SOON TO SAY THAT, OR SOMETHIN'?
ROBIN...
AM I GONNA SCARE YOU OFF? IS THAT IT?
I KNEW AFTER A WEEK, HUGHIE.
NEVER MIND A MONTH.
EVEN WITH EVERYTHING THAT HAPPENED AFTERWARDS, HUGHIE ALWAYS REMEMBERED:
THAT KISS WAS LIKE NONE HE'D EVER HAD BEFORE.

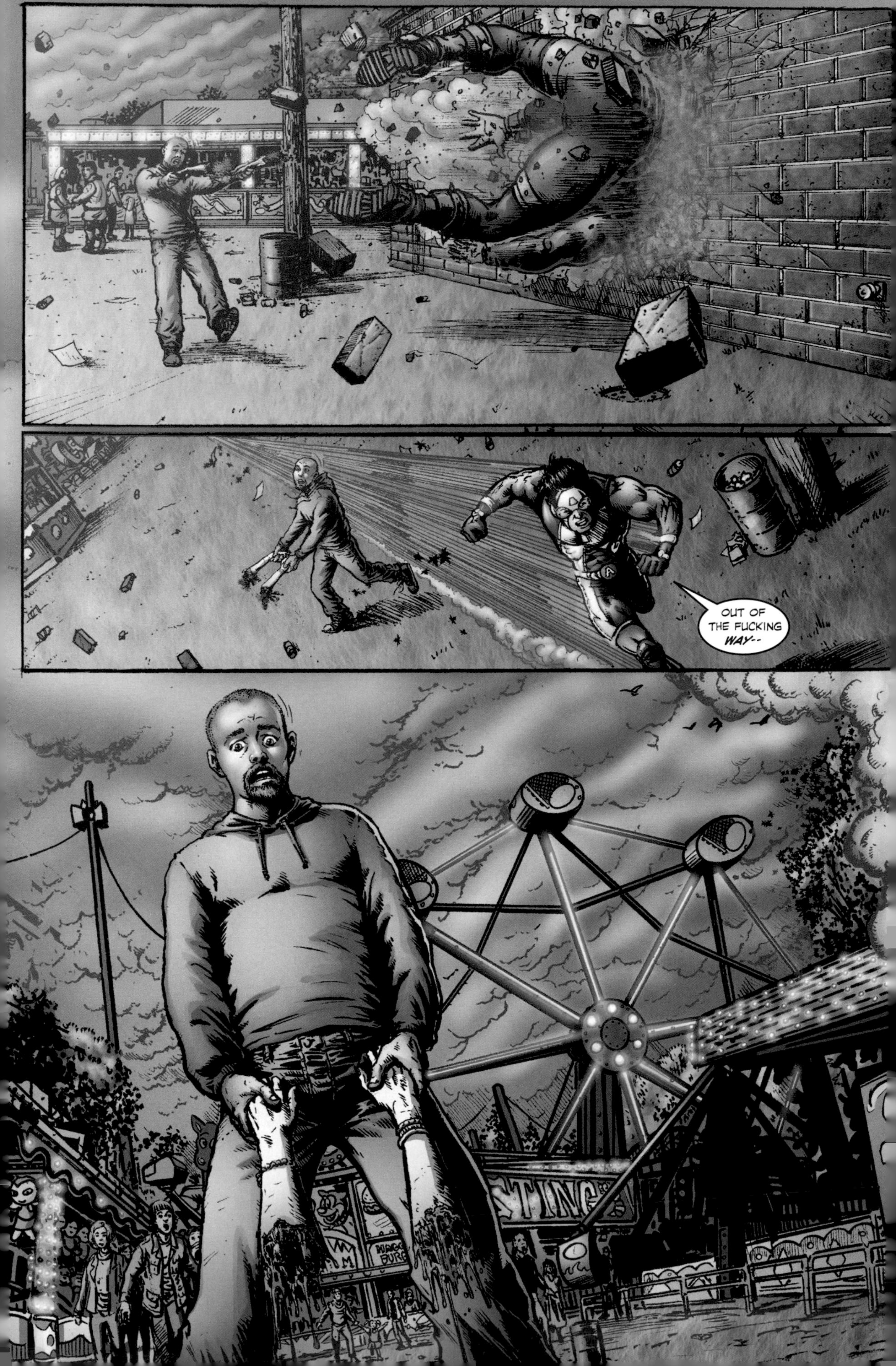
OUT OF THE FUCKING WAY--

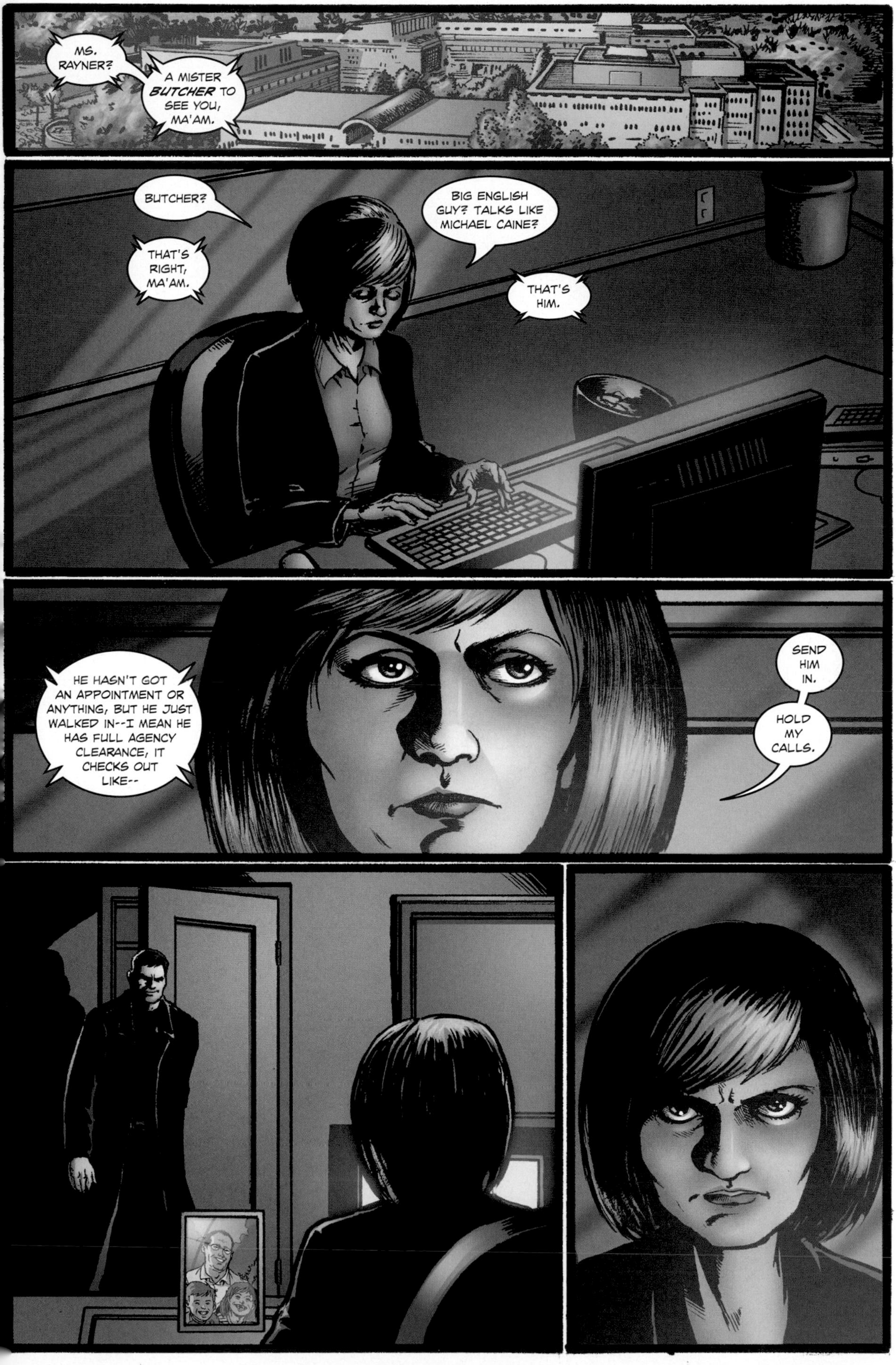
MS. RAYNER?
A MISTER BUTCHER TO SEE YOU, MA'AM.
BUTCHER?
BIG ENGLISH GUY? TALKS LIKE MICHAEL CAINE?
THAT'S RIGHT, MA'AM.
THAT'S HIM.
HE HASN'T GOT AN APPOINTMENT OR ANYTHING, BUT HE JUST WALKED IN--I MEAN HE HAS FULL AGENCY CLEARANCE, IT CHECKS OUT LIKE--
SEND HIM IN.
HOLD MY CALLS.

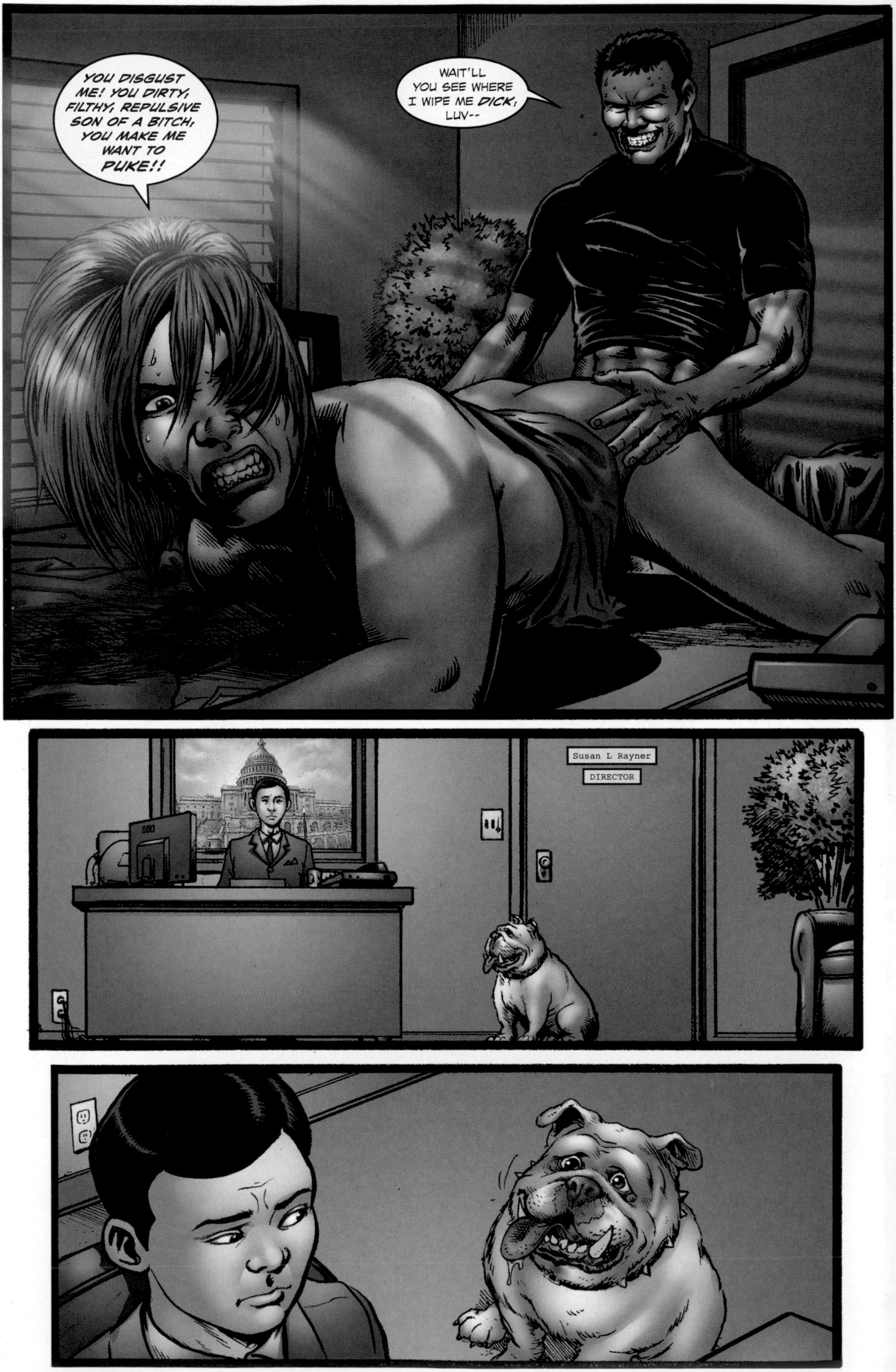
YOU DISGUST ME! YOU DIRTY, FILTHY, REPULSIVE SON OF A BITCH, YOU MAKE ME WANT TO PUKE!!
WAIT'LL YOU SEE WHERE I WIPE ME DICK, LUV--
Susan L Rayner
DIRECTOR

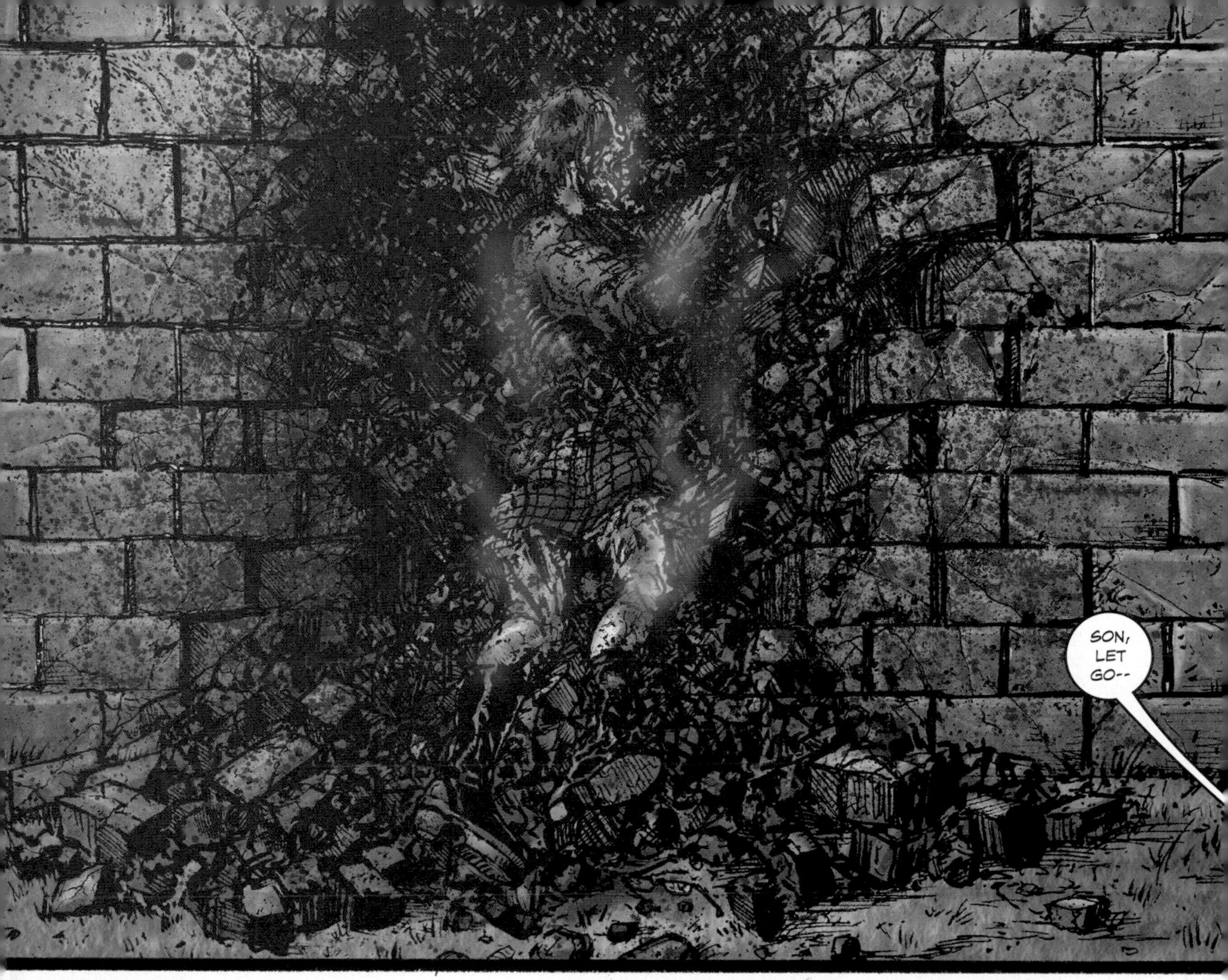
SON, LET GO--

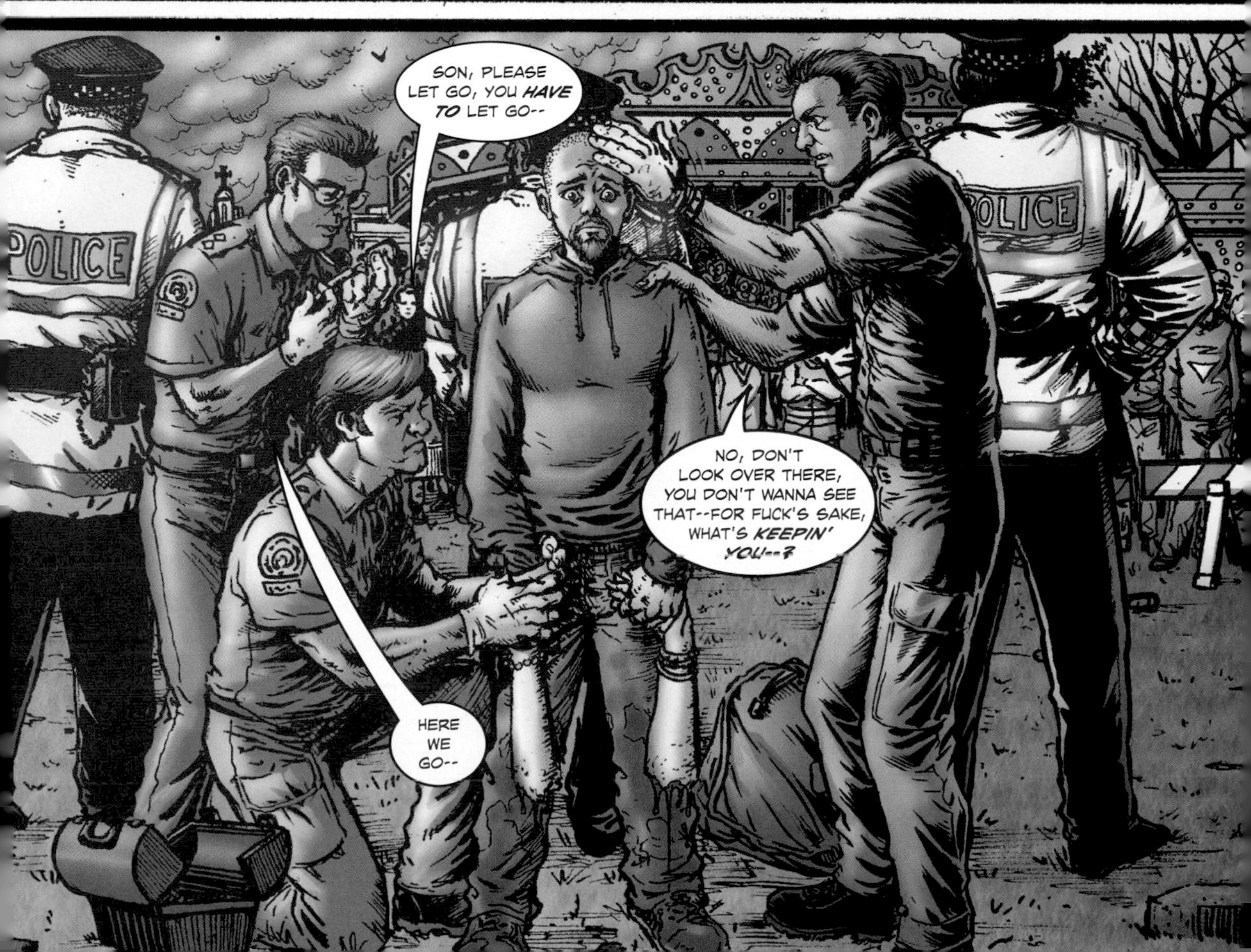
SON, PLEASE LET GO, YOU HAVE TO LET GO--
NO, DON'T LOOK OVER THERE, YOU DON'T WANNA SEE THAT--FOR FUCK'S SAKE, WHAT'S KEEPIN' YOU--?
HERE WE GO--
POLICE
POLICE

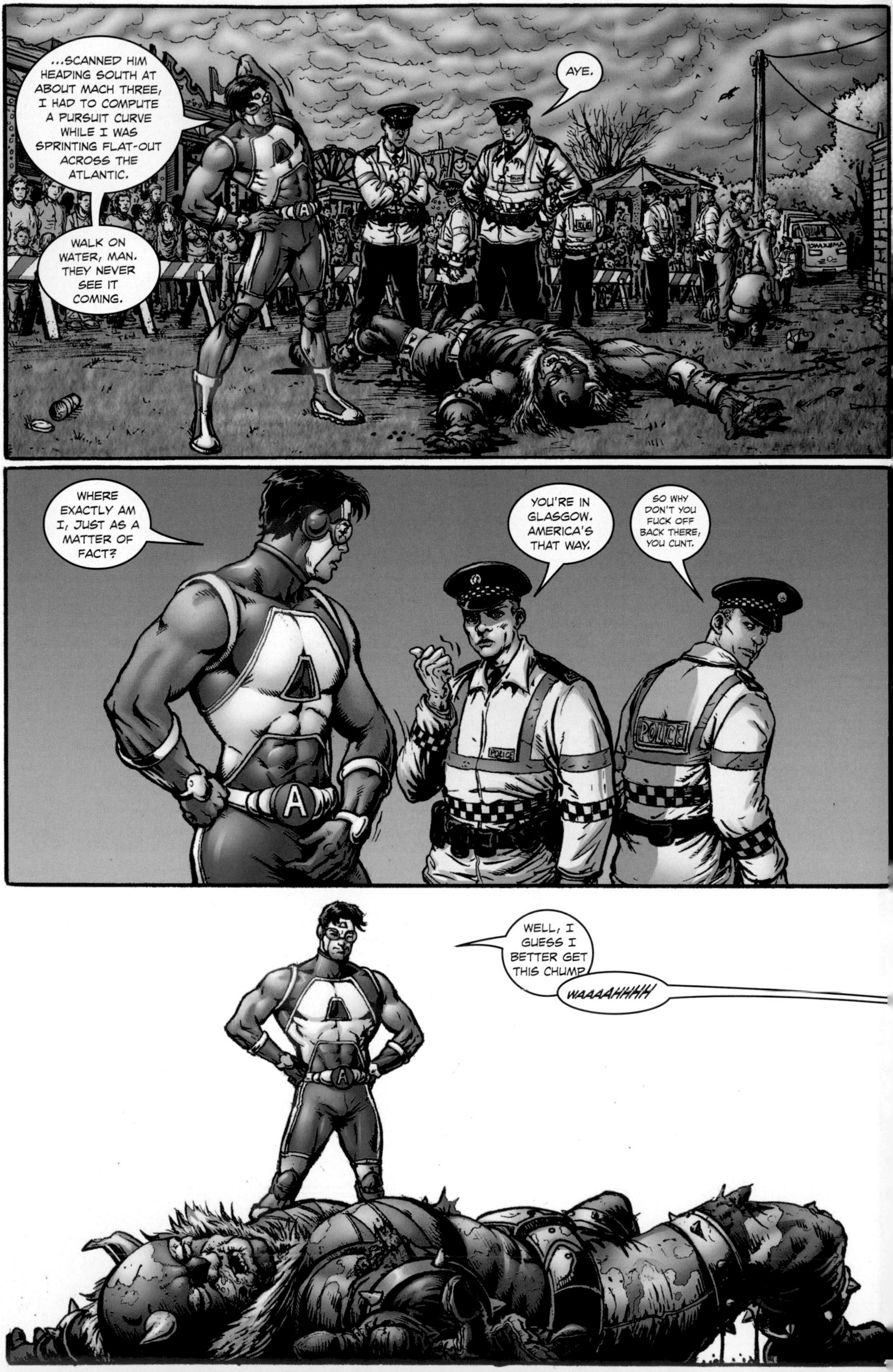
...SCANNED HIM HEADING SOUTH AT ABOUT MACH THREE, I HAD TO COMPUTE A PURSUIT CURVE WHILE I WAS SPRINTING FLAT-OUT ACROSS THE ATLANTIC.
AYE.
WALK ON WATER, MAN. THEY NEVER SEE IT COMING.
WHERE EXACTLY AM I, JUST AS A MATTER OF FACT?
YOU'RE IN GLASGOW. AMERICA'S THAT WAY.
SO WHY DON'T YOU FUCK OFF BACK THERE, YOU CUNT.
POLICE
POLICE
WELL, I GUESS I BETTER GET THIS CHUMP
WAAAAHHHH

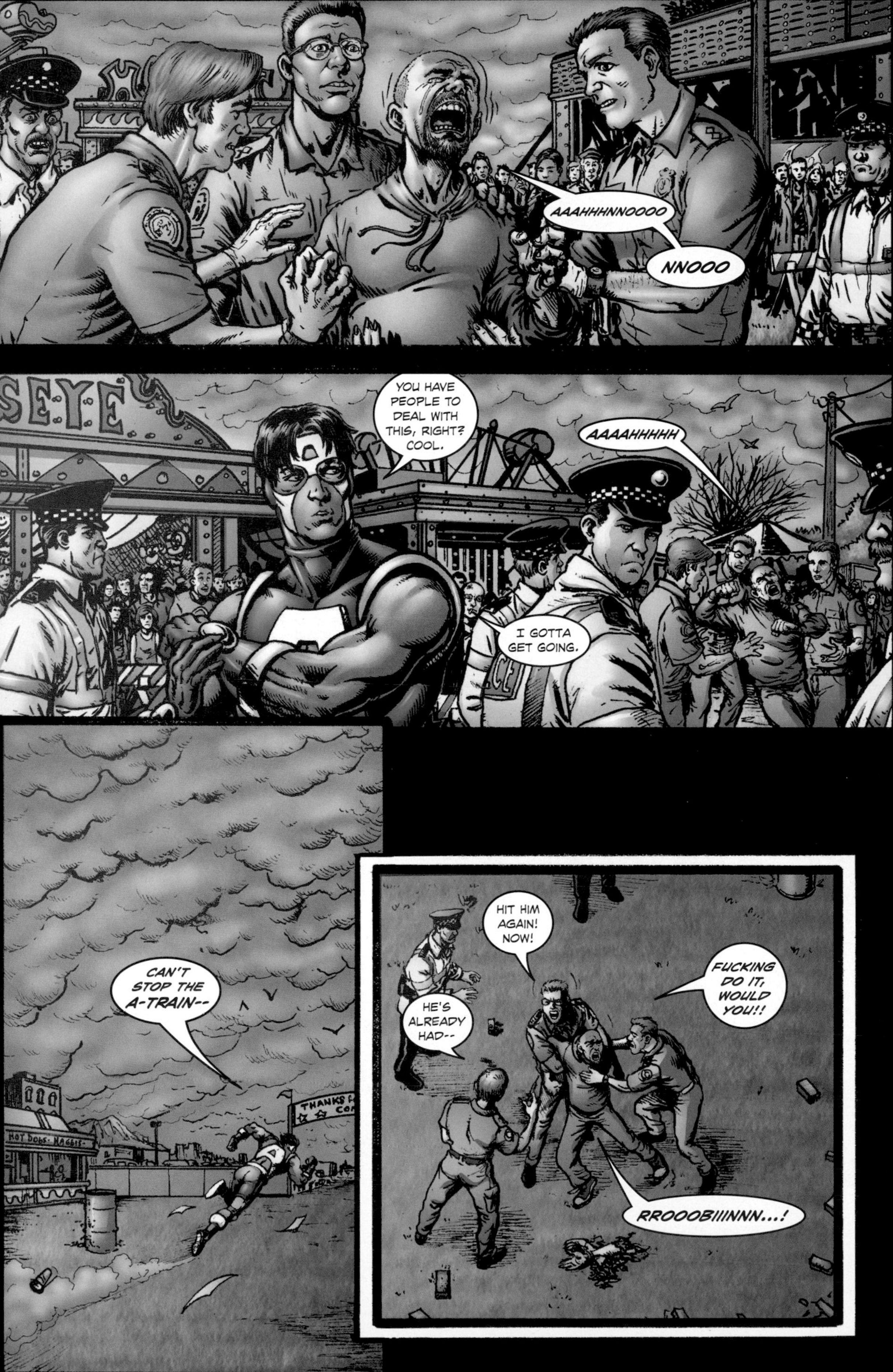
AAAHHHHNNOOOO
NNOOO
YOU HAVE PEOPLE TO DEAL WITH THIS, RIGHT? COOL.
AAAAHHHHH
I GOTTA GET GOING.
CAN'T STOP THE A-TRAIN--
HIT HIM AGAIN! NOW!
HE'S ALREADY HAD--
FUCKING DO IT, WOULD YOU!!
RROOOBIIINNN...!

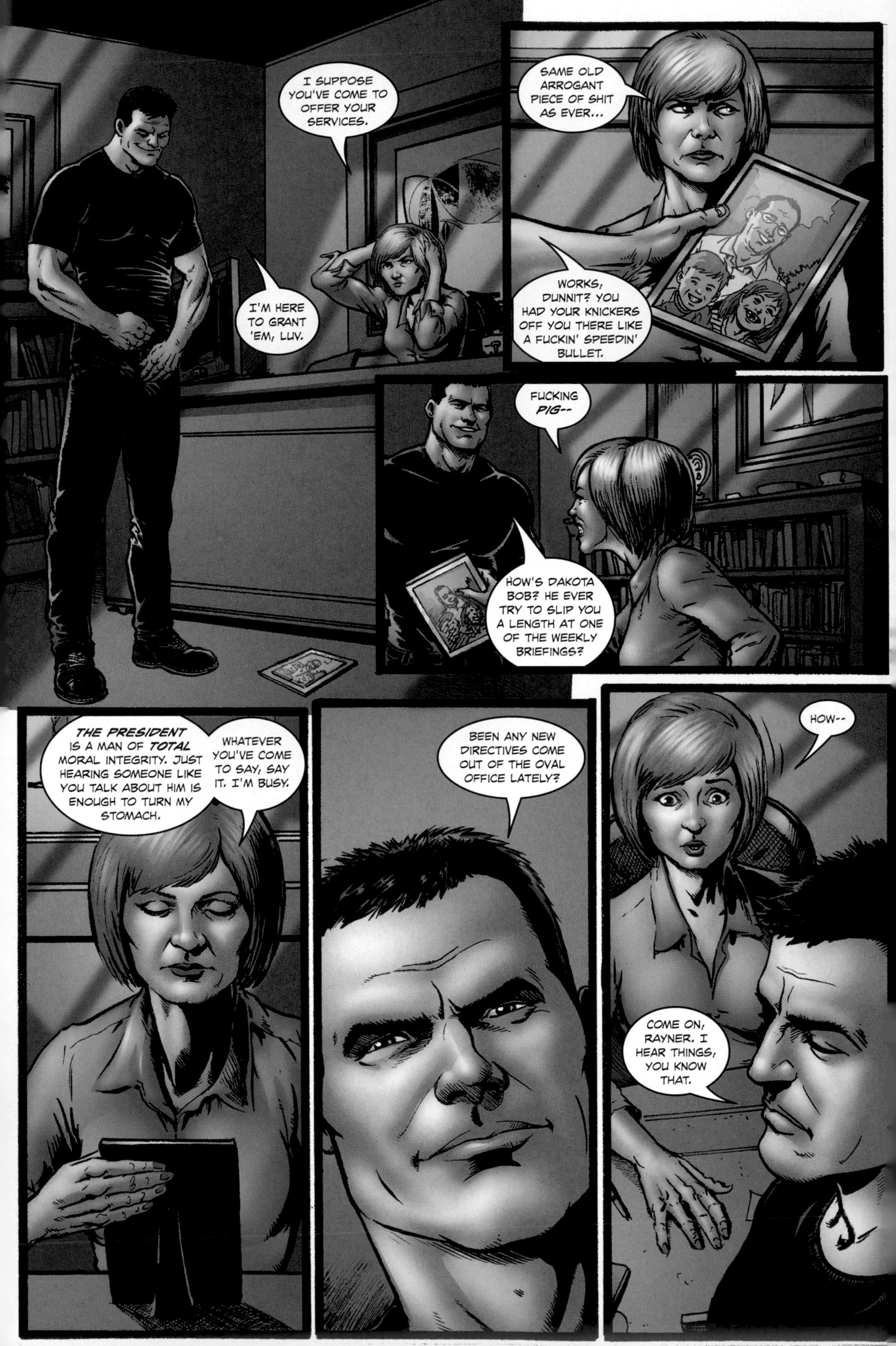
I SUPPOSE YOU'VE COME TO OFFER YOUR SERVICES.
I'M HERE TO GRANT 'EM, LUV.
SAME OLD ARROGANT PIECE OF SHIT AS EVER...
WORKS, DUNNIT? YOU HAD YOUR KNICKERS OFF YOU THERE LIKE A FUCKIN' SPEEDIN' BULLET.
FUCKING PIG--
HOW'S DAKOTA BOB? HE EVER TRY TO SLIP YOU A LENGTH AT ONE OF THE WEEKLY BRIEFINGS?
THE PRESIDENT IS A MAN OF TOTAL MORAL INTEGRITY. JUST HEARING SOMEONE LIKE YOU TALK ABOUT HIM IS ENOUGH TO TURN MY STOMACH.
WHATEVER YOU'VE COME TO SAY, SAY IT. I'M BUSY.
BEEN ANY NEW DIRECTIVES COME OUT OF THE OVAL OFFICE LATELY?
HOW--
COME ON, RAYNER. I HEAR THINGS, YOU KNOW THAT.

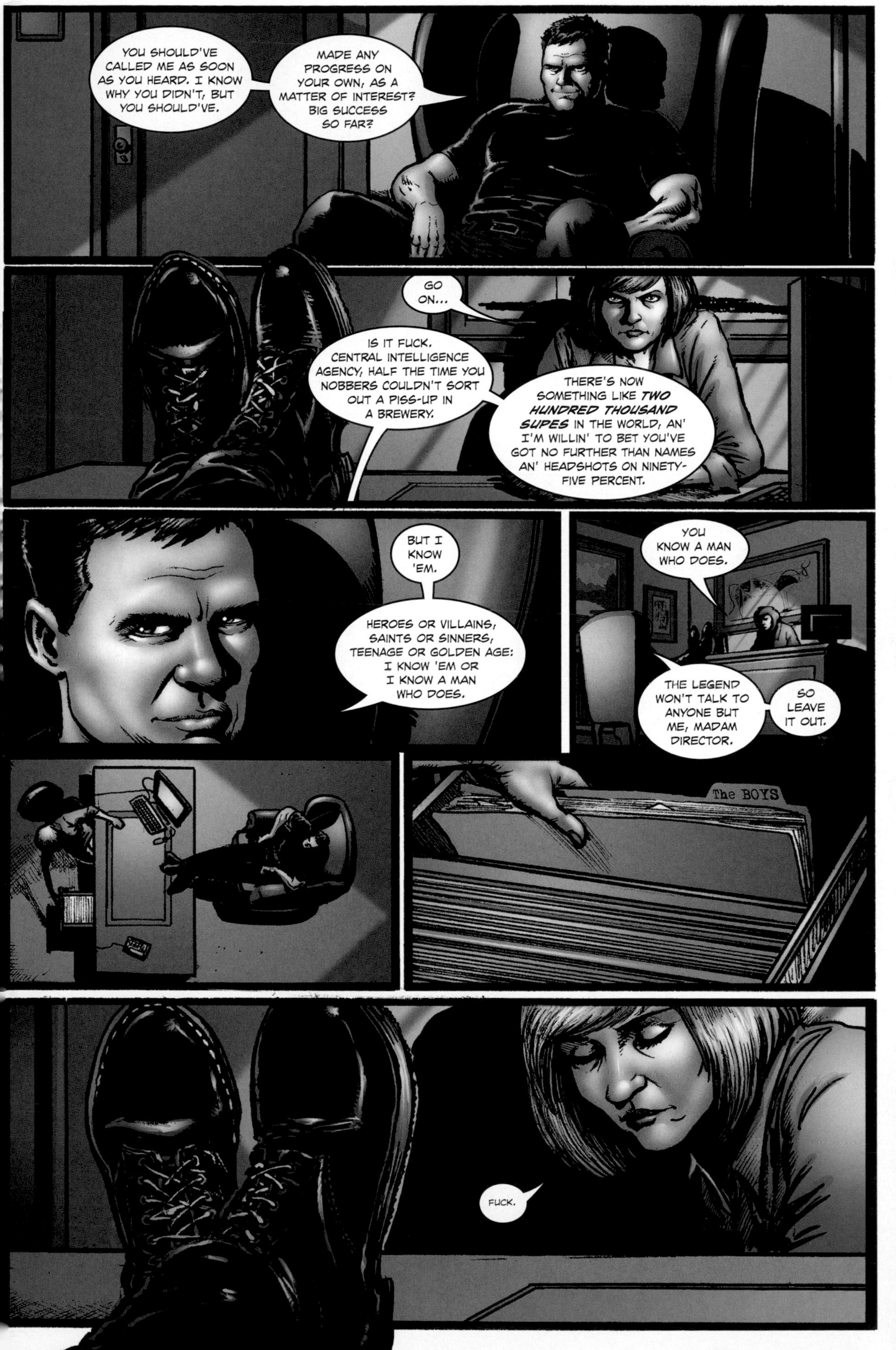
YOU SHOULD'VE CALLED ME AS SOON AS YOU HEARD. I KNOW WHY YOU DIDN'T, BUT YOU SHOULD'VE.
MADE ANY PROGRESS ON YOUR OWN, AS A MATTER OF INTEREST? BIG SUCCESS SO FAR?
GO ON...
IS IT FUCK. CENTRAL INTELLIGENCE AGENCY, HALF THE TIME YOU NOBBERS COULDN'T SORT OUT A PISS-UP IN A BREWERY.
THERE'S NOW SOMETHING LIKE TWO HUNDRED THOUSAND SUPES IN THE WORLD, AN' I'M WILLIN' TO BET YOU'VE GOT NO FURTHER THAN NAMES AN' HEADSHOTS ON NINETY-FIVE PERCENT.
BUT I KNOW 'EM.
HEROES OR VILLAINS, SAINTS OR SINNERS, TEENAGE OR GOLDEN AGE: I KNOW 'EM OR I KNOW A MAN WHO DOES.
YOU KNOW A MAN WHO DOES.
THE LEGEND WON'T TALK TO ANYONE BUT ME, MADAM DIRECTOR.
SO LEAVE IT OUT.
The BOYS
FUCK.

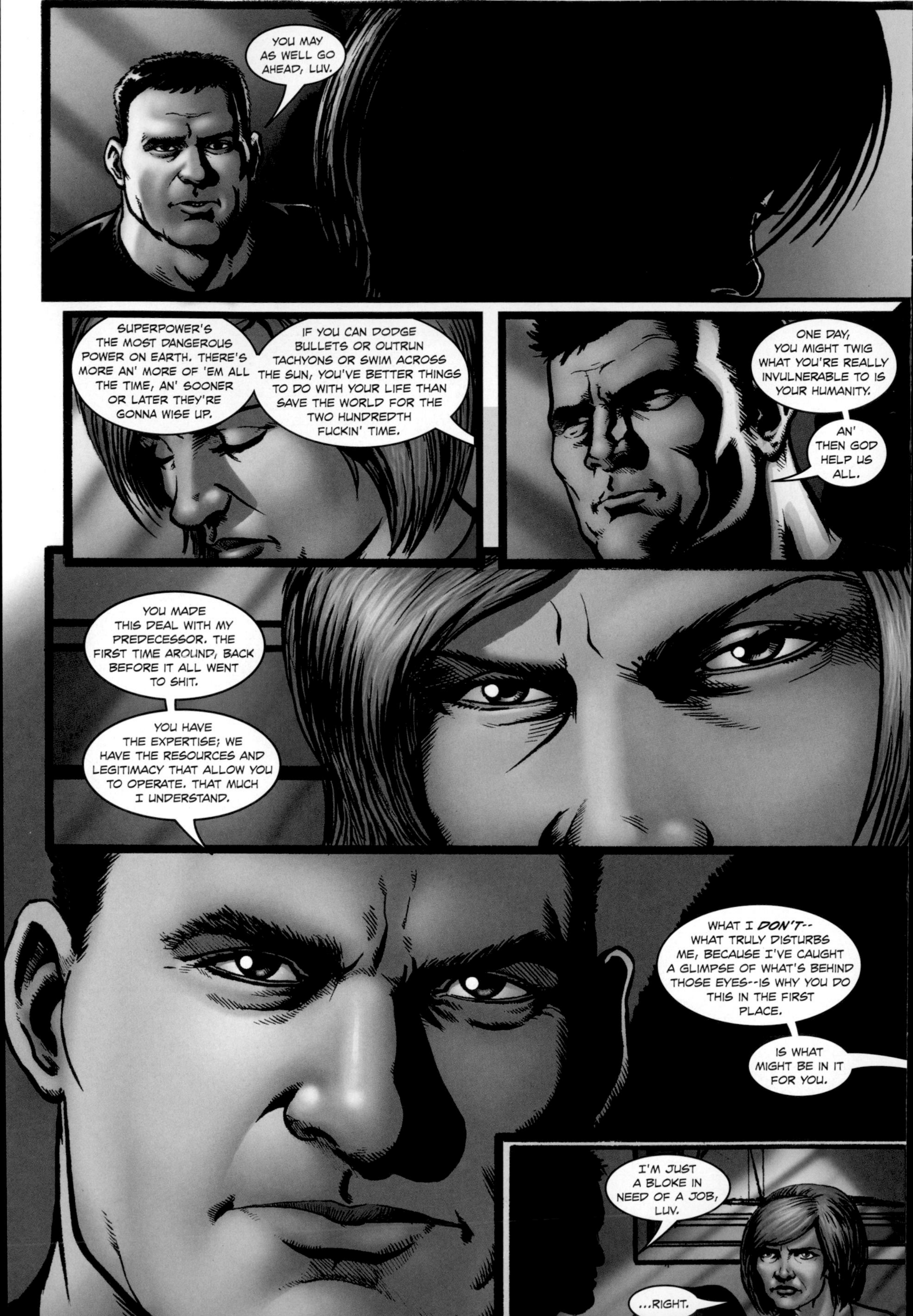
YOU MAY AS WELL GO AHEAD, LUV.
SUPERPOWER'S THE MOST DANGEROUS POWER ON EARTH. THERE'S MORE AN' MORE OF 'EM ALL THE TIME, AN' SOONER OR LATER THEY'RE GONNA WISE UP.
IF YOU CAN DODGE BULLETS OR OUTRUN TACHYONS OR SWIM ACROSS THE SUN, YOU'VE BETTER THINGS TO DO WITH YOUR LIFE THAN SAVE THE WORLD FOR THE TWO HUNDREDTH FUCKIN' TIME.
ONE DAY, YOU MIGHT TWIG WHAT YOU'RE REALLY INVULNERABLE TO IS YOUR HUMANITY.
AN' THEN GOD HELP US ALL.
YOU MADE THIS DEAL WITH MY PREDECESSOR. THE FIRST TIME AROUND, BACK BEFORE IT ALL WENT TO SHIT.
YOU HAVE THE EXPERTISE; WE HAVE THE RESOURCES AND LEGITIMACY THAT ALLOW YOU TO OPERATE. THAT MUCH I UNDERSTAND.
WHAT I *DON'T*-- WHAT TRULY DISTURBS ME, BECAUSE I'VE CAUGHT A GLIMPSE OF WHAT'S BEHIND THOSE EYES--IS WHY YOU DO THIS IN THE FIRST PLACE.
IS WHAT MIGHT BE IN IT FOR YOU.
I'M JUST A BLOKE IN NEED OF A JOB, LUV.
...RIGHT.

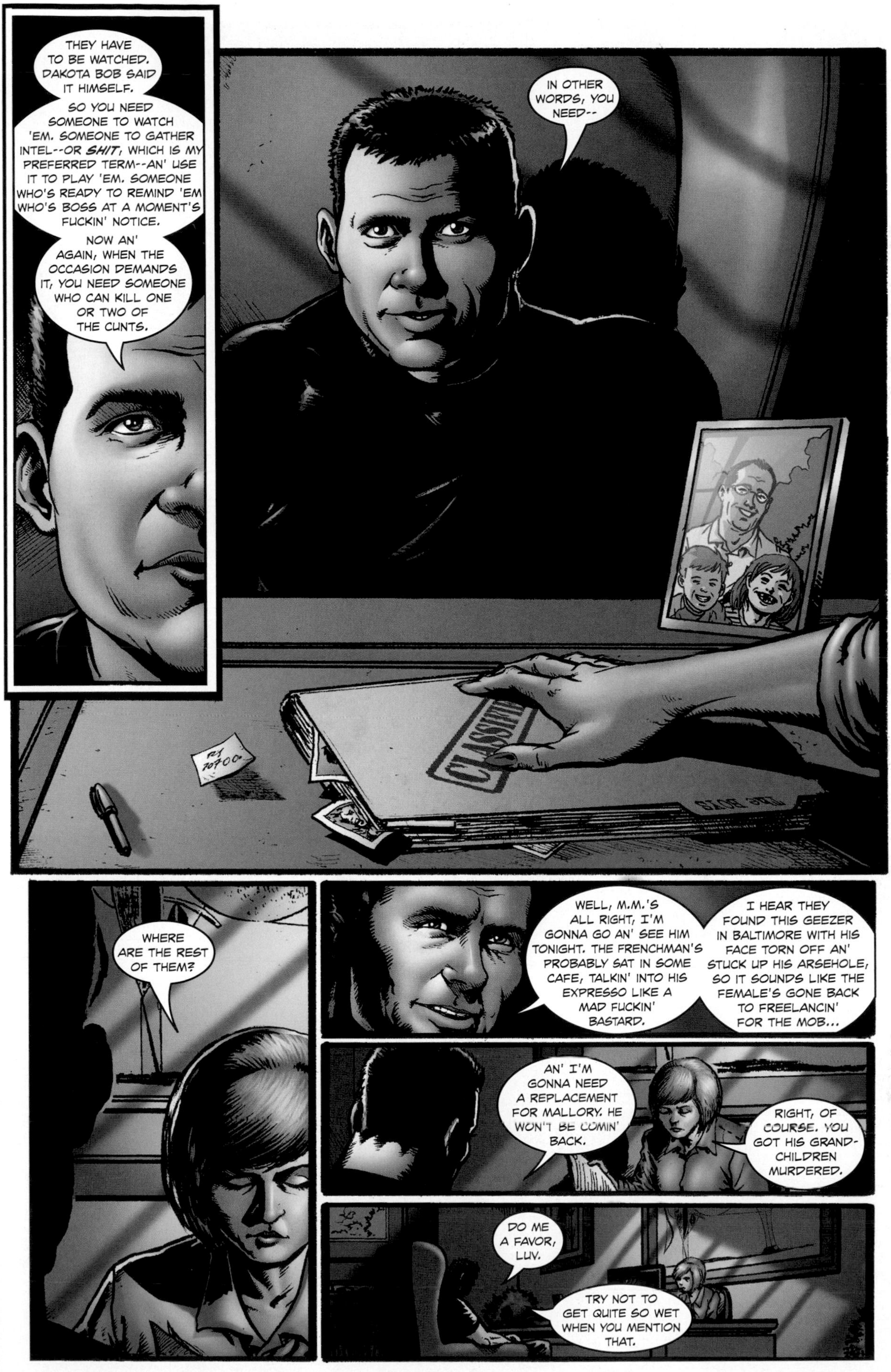
THEY HAVE TO BE WATCHED. DAKOTA BOB SAID IT HIMSELF.
SO YOU NEED SOMEONE TO WATCH 'EM. SOMEONE TO GATHER INTEL--OR *SHIT*, WHICH IS MY PREFERRED TERM--AN' USE IT TO PLAY 'EM. SOMEONE WHO'S READY TO REMIND 'EM WHO'S BOSS AT A MOMENT'S FUCKIN' NOTICE.
NOW AN' AGAIN, WHEN THE OCCASION DEMANDS IT, YOU NEED SOMEONE WHO CAN KILL ONE OR TWO OF THE CUNTS.
IN OTHER WORDS, YOU NEED--
CLASSIFIED
WHERE ARE THE REST OF THEM?
WELL, M.M.'S ALL RIGHT, I'M GONNA GO AN' SEE HIM TONIGHT. THE FRENCHMAN'S PROBABLY SAT IN SOME CAFE, TALKIN' INTO HIS EXPRESSO LIKE A MAD FUCKIN' BASTARD.
I HEAR THEY FOUND THIS GEEZER IN BALTIMORE WITH HIS FACE TORN OFF AN' STUCK UP HIS ARSEHOLE, SO IT SOUNDS LIKE THE FEMALE'S GONE BACK TO FREELANCIN' FOR THE MOB...
AN' I'M GONNA NEED A REPLACEMENT FOR MALLORY. HE WON'T BE COMIN' BACK.
RIGHT, OF COURSE. YOU GOT HIS GRAND-CHILDREN MURDERED.
DO ME A FAVOR, LUV.
TRY NOT TO GET QUITE SO WET WHEN YOU MENTION THAT.

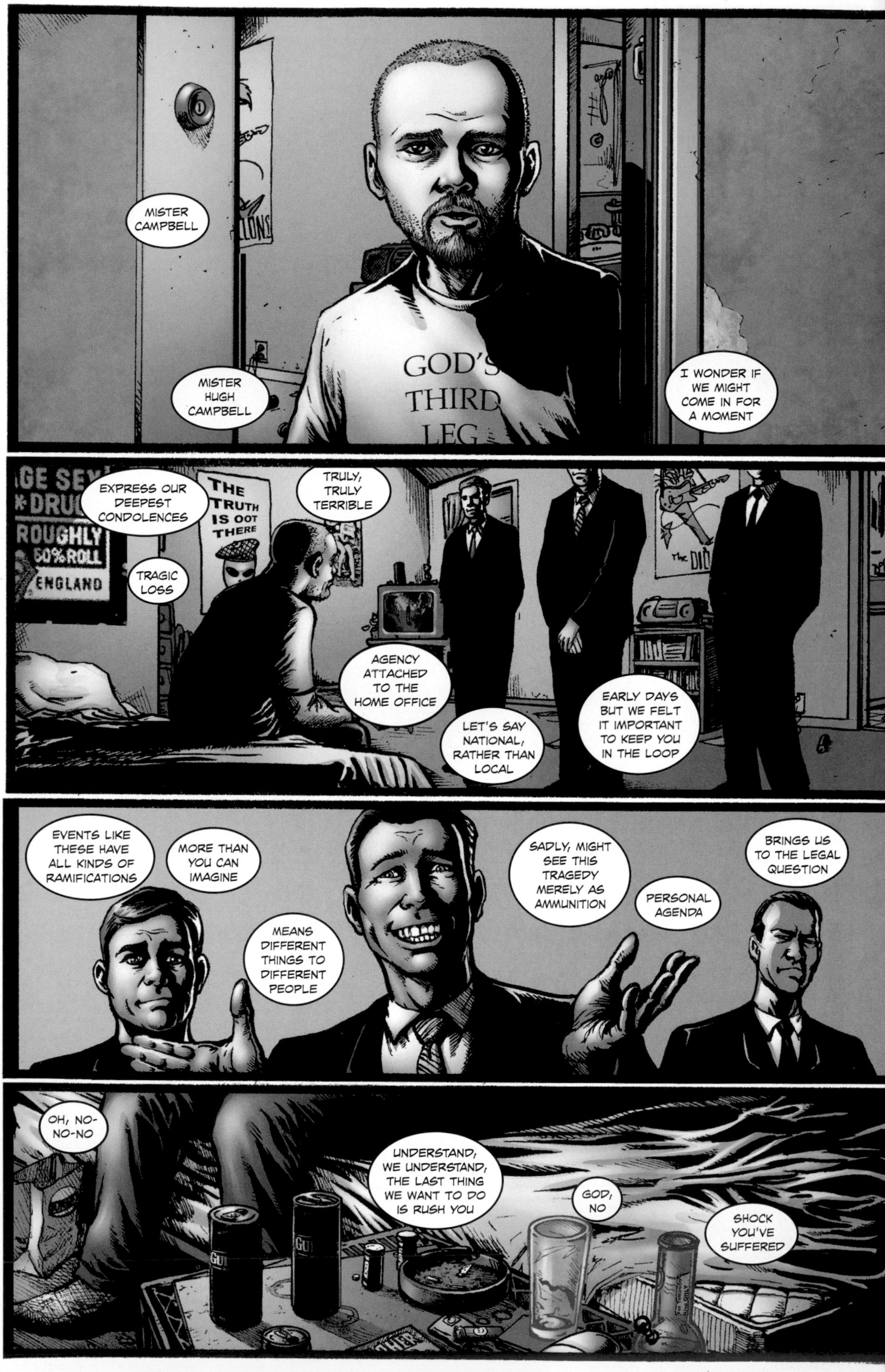
MISTER CAMPBELL
MISTER HUGH CAMPBELL
GOD'S THIRD LEG
I WONDER IF WE MIGHT COME IN FOR A MOMENT
EXPRESS OUR DEEPEST CONDOLENCES
THE TRUTH IS OOT THERE
TRULY, TRULY TERRIBLE
TRAGIC LOSS
AGENCY ATTACHED TO THE HOME OFFICE
LET'S SAY NATIONAL, RATHER THAN LOCAL
EARLY DAYS BUT WE FELT IT IMPORTANT TO KEEP YOU IN THE LOOP
EVENTS LIKE THESE HAVE ALL KINDS OF RAMIFICATIONS
MORE THAN YOU CAN IMAGINE
MEANS DIFFERENT THINGS TO DIFFERENT PEOPLE
SADLY, MIGHT SEE THIS TRAGEDY MERELY AS AMMUNITION
PERSONAL AGENDA
BRINGS US TO THE LEGAL QUESTION
OH, NO-NO-NO
UNDERSTAND, WE UNDERSTAND, THE LAST THING WE WANT TO DO IS RUSH YOU
GOD, NO
SHOCK YOU'VE SUFFERED

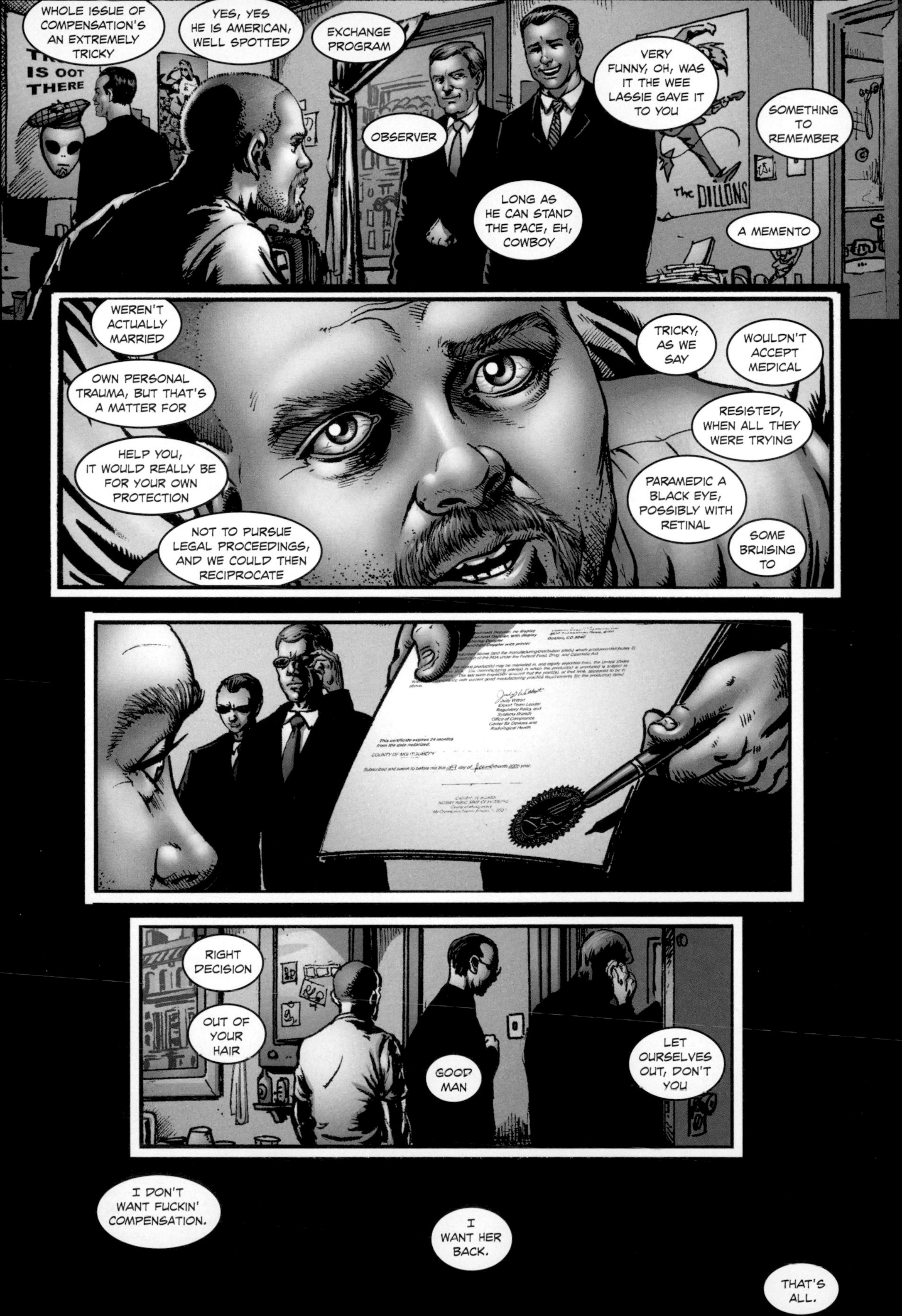
WHOLE ISSUE OF COMPENSATION'S AN EXTREMELY TRICKY
YES, YES HE IS AMERICAN, WELL SPOTTED
EXCHANGE PROGRAM
OBSERVER
VERY FUNNY, OH, WAS IT THE WEE LASSIE GAVE IT TO YOU
SOMETHING TO REMEMBER
LONG AS HE CAN STAND THE PACE, EH, COWBOY
A MEMENTO
IS OOT THERE
The DILLONS
WEREN'T ACTUALLY MARRIED
OWN PERSONAL TRAUMA, BUT THAT'S A MATTER FOR
HELP YOU, IT WOULD REALLY BE FOR YOUR OWN PROTECTION
NOT TO PURSUE LEGAL PROCEEDINGS, AND WE COULD THEN RECIPROCATE
TRICKY, AS WE SAY
WOULDN'T ACCEPT MEDICAL
RESISTED, WHEN ALL THEY WERE TRYING
PARAMEDIC A BLACK EYE, POSSIBLY WITH RETINAL
SOME BRUISING TO
RIGHT DECISION
OUT OF YOUR HAIR
GOOD MAN
LET OURSELVES OUT, DON'T YOU
I DON'T WANT FUCKIN' COMPENSATION.
I WANT HER BACK.
THAT'S ALL.

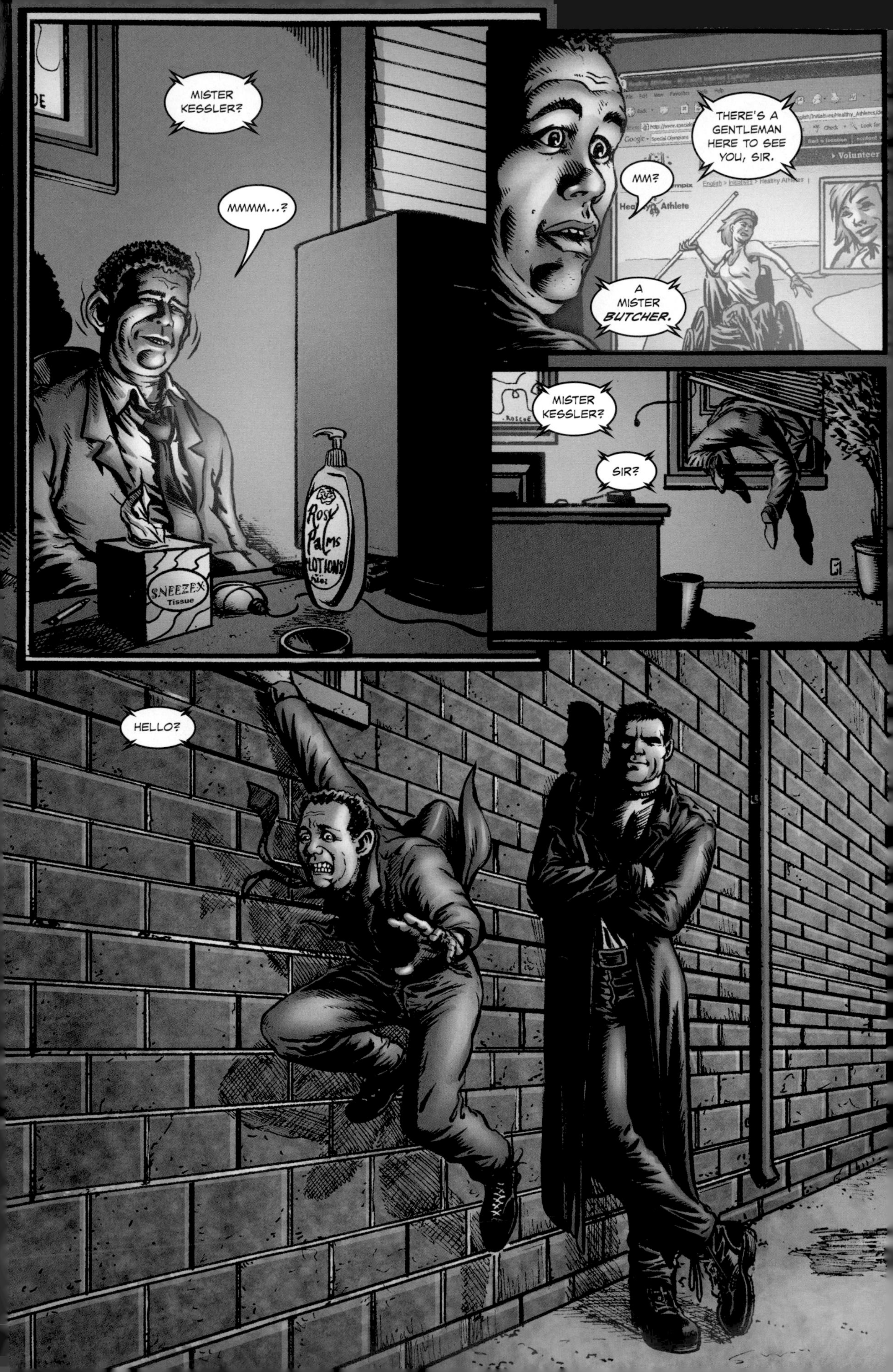
MISTER KESSLER?
MMMM...?
THERE'S A GENTLEMAN HERE TO SEE YOU, SIR.
MM?
A MISTER BUTCHER.
MISTER KESSLER?
SIR?
HELLO?

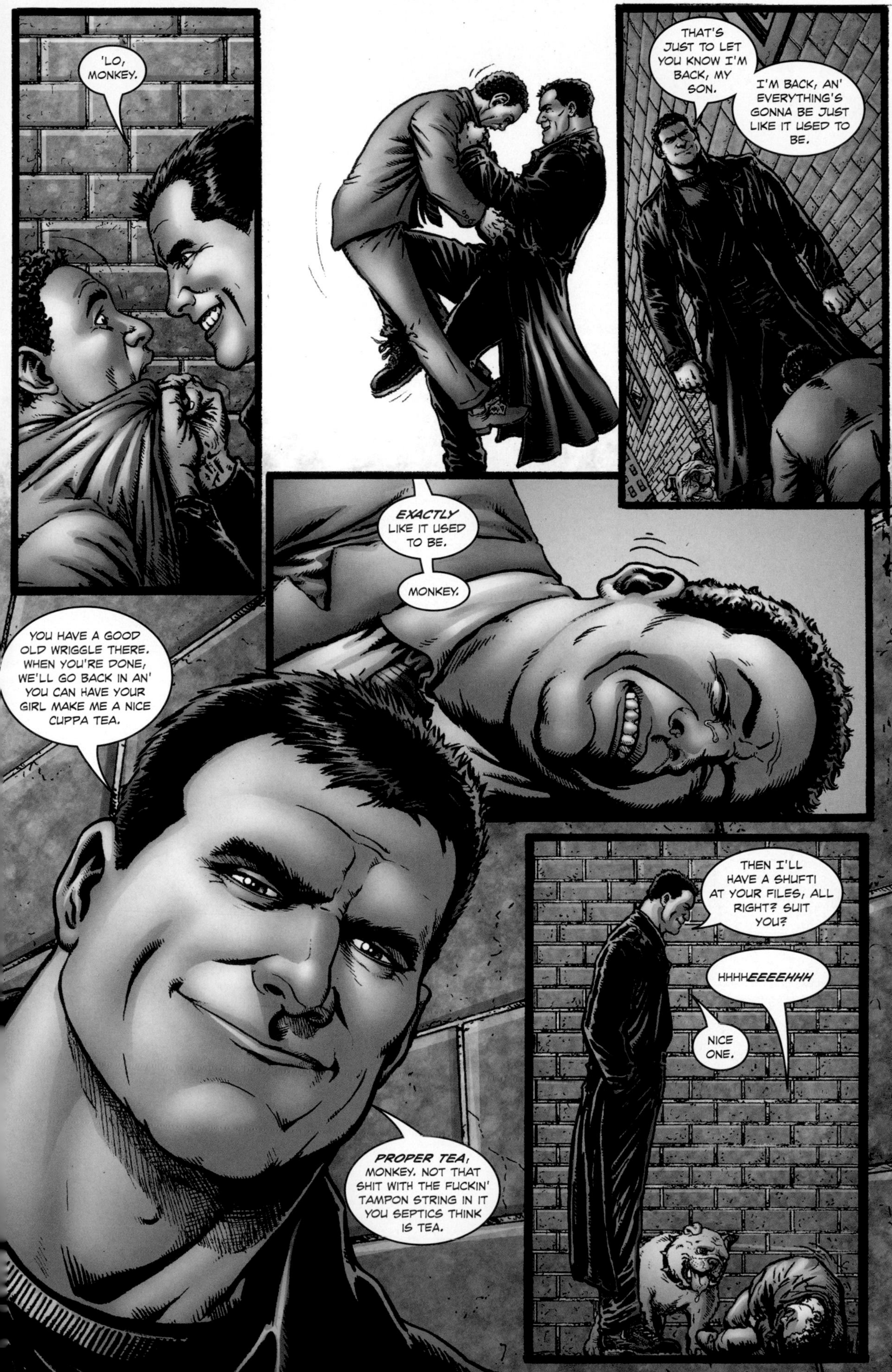
'LO, MONKEY.
THAT'S JUST TO LET YOU KNOW I'M BACK, MY SON.
I'M BACK, AN' EVERYTHING'S GONNA BE JUST LIKE IT USED TO BE.
EXACTLY LIKE IT USED TO BE.
MONKEY.
YOU HAVE A GOOD OLD WRIGGLE THERE. WHEN YOU'RE DONE, WE'LL GO BACK IN AN' YOU CAN HAVE YOUR GIRL MAKE ME A NICE CUPPA TEA.
PROPER TEA, MONKEY. NOT THAT SHIT WITH THE FUCKIN' TAMPON STRING IN IT YOU SEPTICS THINK IS TEA.
THEN I'LL HAVE A SHUFTI AT YOUR FILES, ALL RIGHT? SUIT YOU?
HHHHEEEEHHH
NICE ONE.

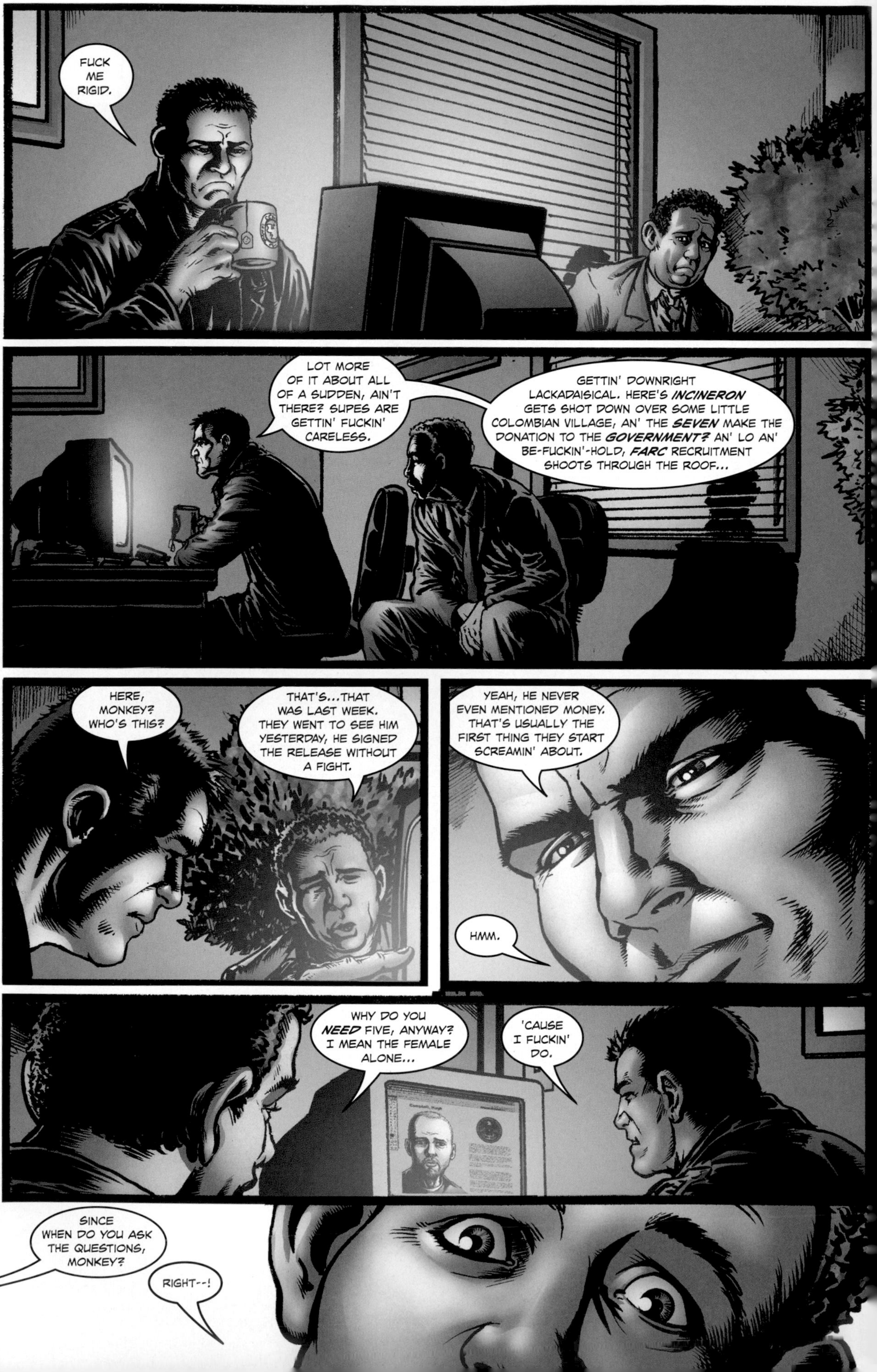

FUCK ME RIGID.
LOT MORE OF IT ABOUT ALL OF A SUDDEN, AIN'T THERE? SUPES ARE GETTIN' FUCKIN' CARELESS.
GETTIN' DOWNRIGHT LACKADAISICAL. HERE'S INCINERON GETS SHOT DOWN OVER SOME LITTLE COLOMBIAN VILLAGE, AN' THE SEVEN MAKE THE DONATION TO THE GOVERNMENT? AN' LO AN' BE-FUCKIN'-HOLD, FARC RECRUITMENT SHOOTS THROUGH THE ROOF...
HERE, MONKEY? WHO'S THIS?
THAT'S...THAT WAS LAST WEEK. THEY WENT TO SEE HIM YESTERDAY, HE SIGNED THE RELEASE WITHOUT A FIGHT.
YEAH, HE NEVER EVEN MENTIONED MONEY. THAT'S USUALLY THE FIRST THING THEY START SCREAMIN' ABOUT.
HMM.
WHY DO YOU NEED FIVE, ANYWAY? I MEAN THE FEMALE ALONE...
'CAUSE I FUCKIN' DO.
SINCE WHEN DO YOU ASK THE QUESTIONS, MONKEY?
RIGHT--!

IT'S NOT FAIR.

IT CAN'T BE.

IT WAS ALL GOIN' *RIGHT* FOR ME FOR ONCE...!

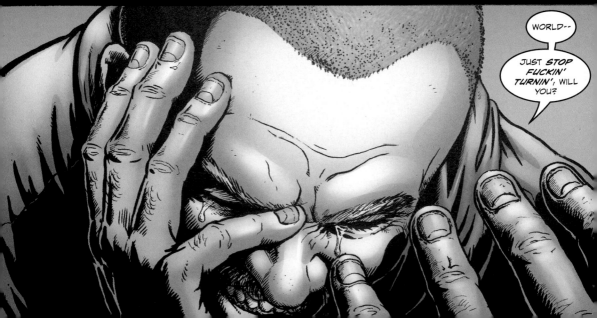

WORLD--

JUST *STOP FUCKIN' TURNIN'*, WILL YOU?

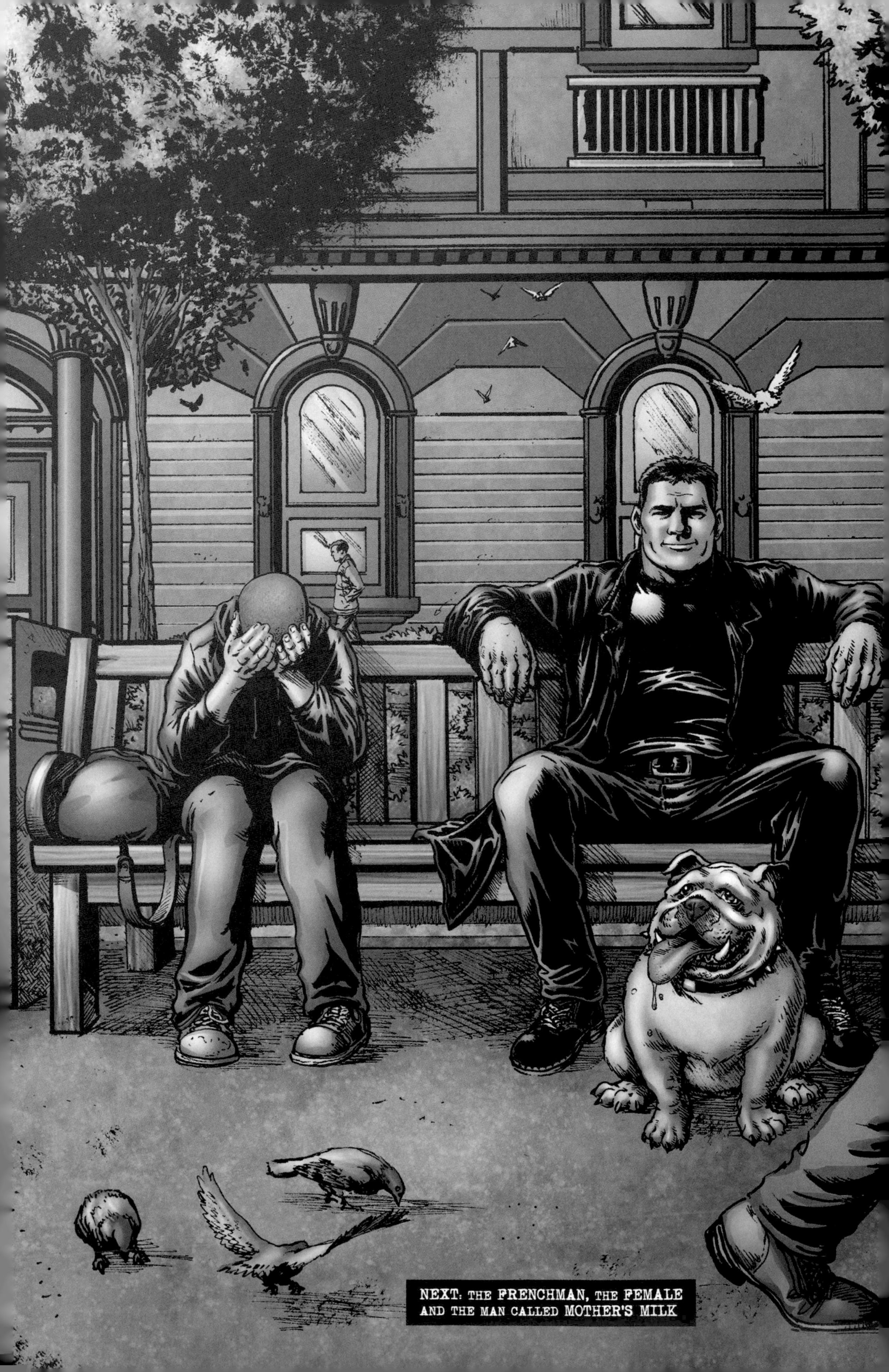
NEXT: THE FRENCHMAN, THE FEMALE AND THE MAN CALLED MOTHER'S MILK

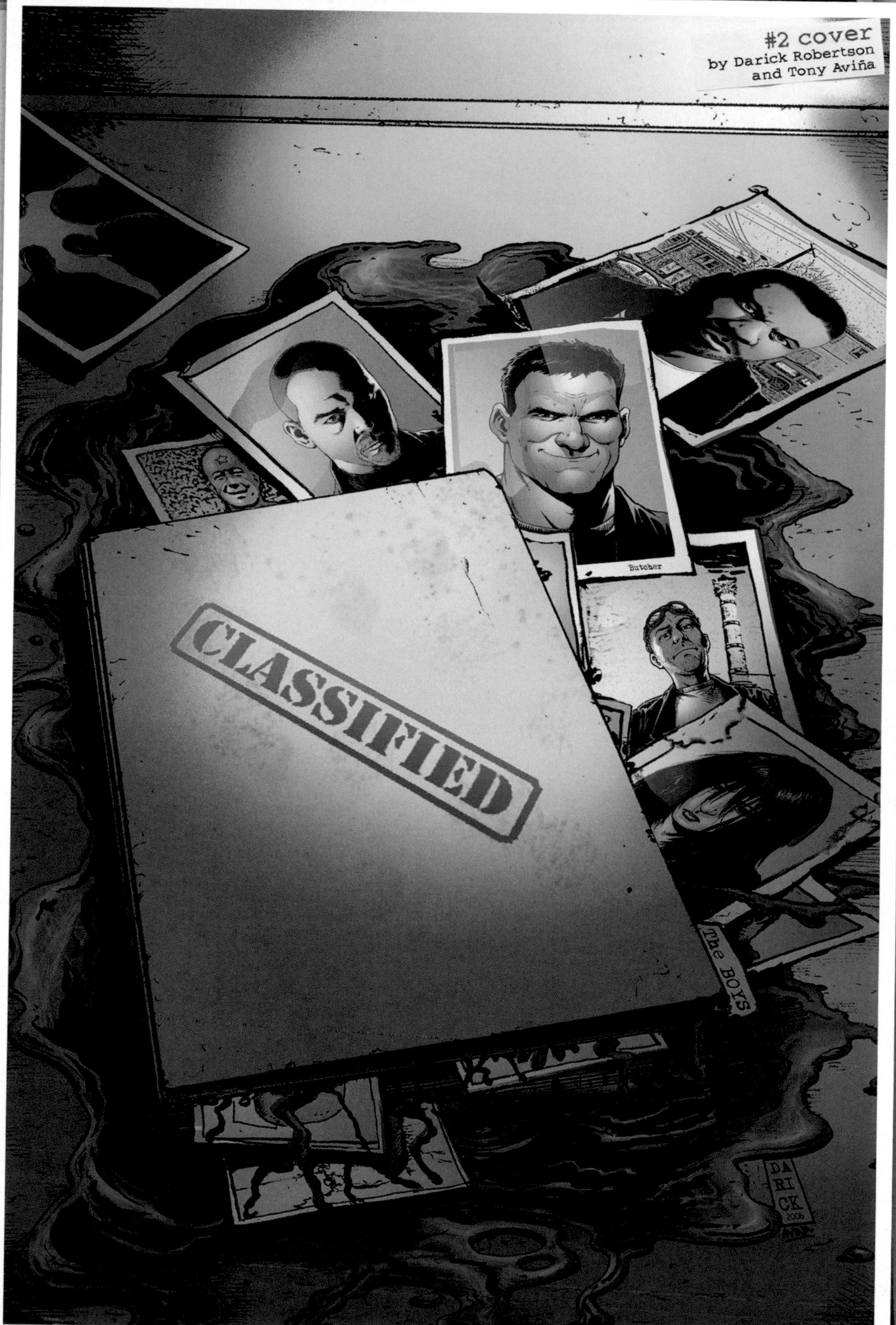
CLASSIFIED
Butcher
The BOYS
DARICK 2006

#2 cover
by Darick Robertson
and Tony Aviña

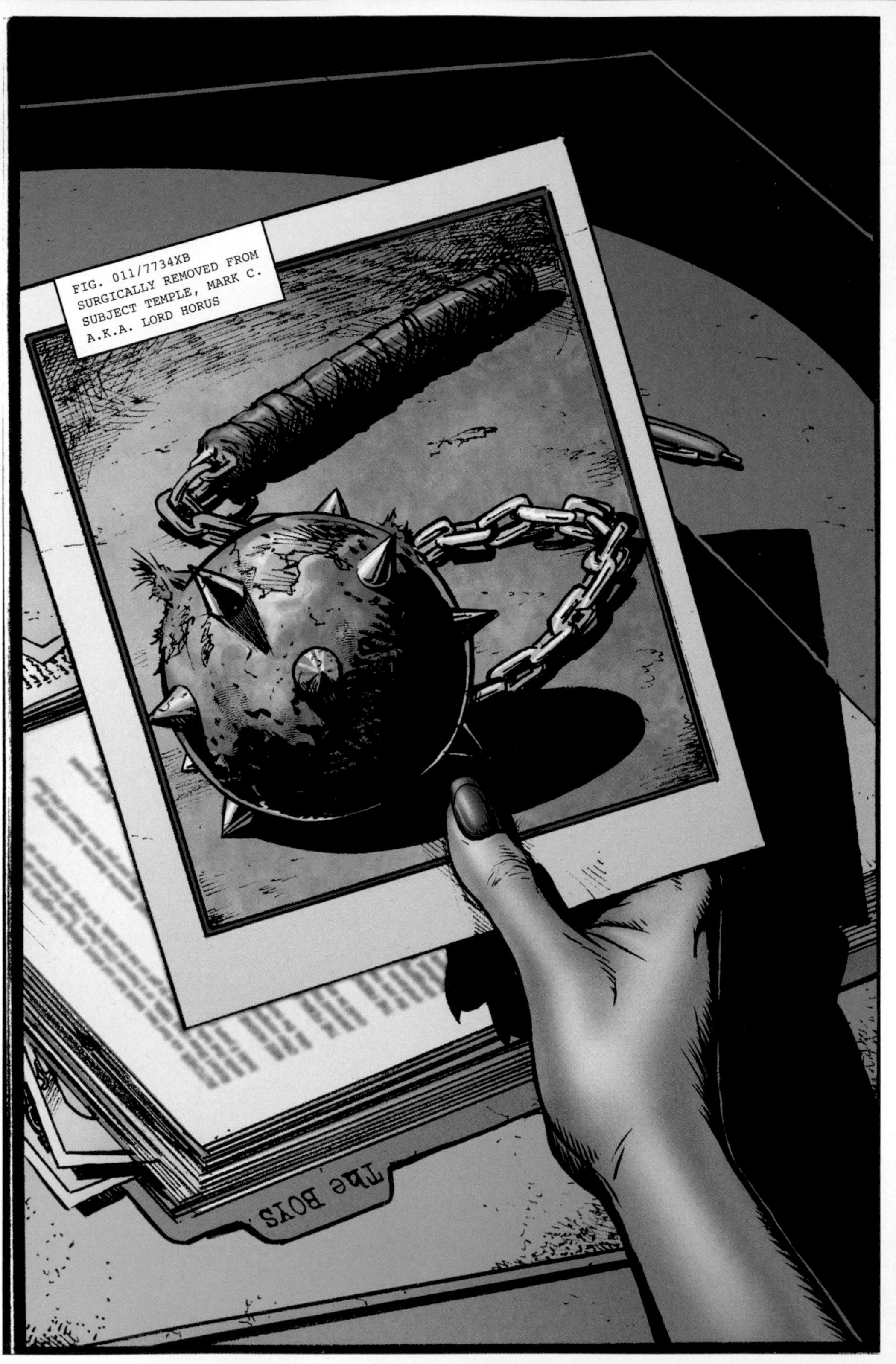
FIG. 011/7734XB
SURGICALLY REMOVED FROM
SUBJECT TEMPLE, MARK C.
A.K.A. LORD HORUS
The BOYS

THE NAME OF THE GAME

PART TWO

TRAUMATISED

TRAUMATISED

HORRIBLY TRAUMATISED

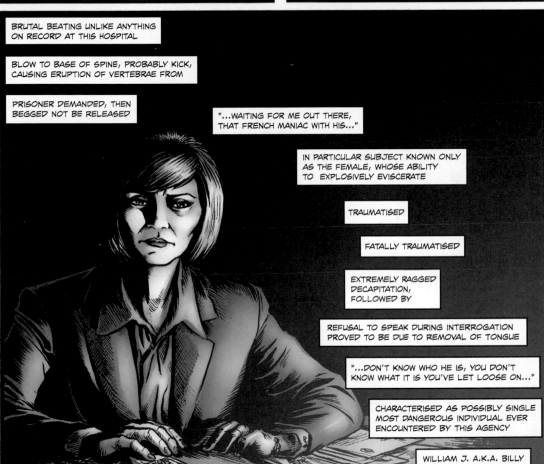

BRUTAL BEATING UNLIKE ANYTHING ON RECORD AT THIS HOSPITAL

BLOW TO BASE OF SPINE, PROBABLY KICK, CAUSING ERUPTION OF VERTEBRAE FROM

PRISONER DEMANDED, THEN BEGGED NOT BE RELEASED

"...WAITING FOR ME OUT THERE, THAT FRENCH MANIAC WITH HIS..."

IN PARTICULAR SUBJECT KNOWN ONLY AS THE FEMALE, WHOSE ABILITY TO EXPLOSIVELY EVISCERATE

TRAUMATISED

FATALLY TRAUMATISED

EXTREMELY RAGGED DECAPITATION, FOLLOWED BY

REFUSAL TO SPEAK DURING INTERROGATION PROVED TO BE DUE TO REMOVAL OF TONGUE

"...DON'T KNOW WHO HE IS, YOU DON'T KNOW WHAT IT IS YOU'VE LET LOOSE ON..."

CHARACTERISED AS POSSIBLY SINGLE MOST DANGEROUS INDIVIDUAL EVER ENCOUNTERED BY THIS AGENCY

WILLIAM J. A.K.A. BILLY

...WELL.

TOO LATE NOW.

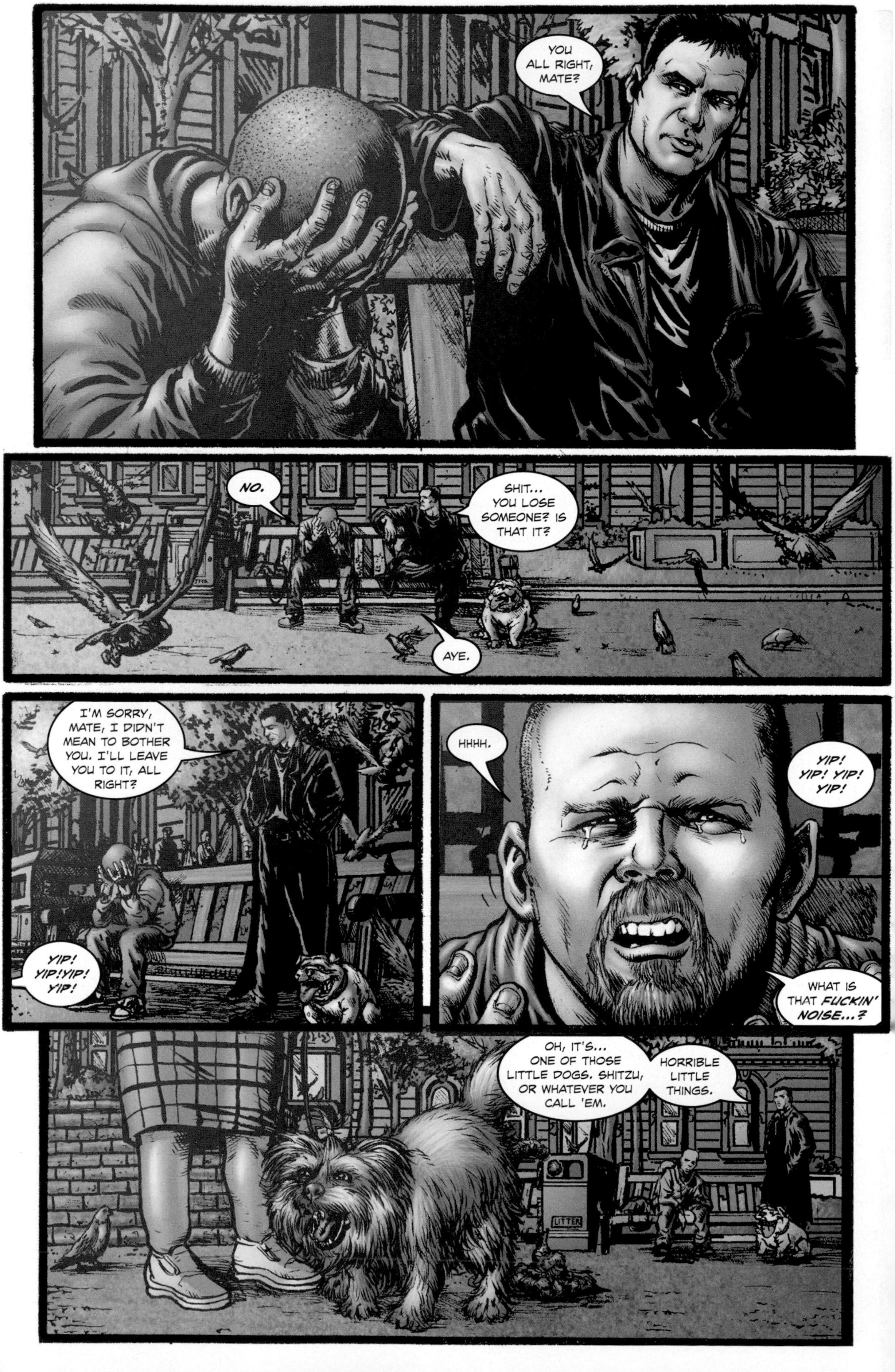
YOU ALL RIGHT, MATE?
NO.
SHIT... YOU LOSE SOMEONE? IS THAT IT?
AYE.
I'M SORRY, MATE, I DIDN'T MEAN TO BOTHER YOU. I'LL LEAVE YOU TO IT, ALL RIGHT?
YIP! YIP!YIP! YIP!
HHHH.
YIP! YIP! YIP! YIP!
WHAT IS THAT *FUCKIN'* NOISE...?
OH, IT'S... ONE OF THOSE LITTLE DOGS. SHITZU, OR WHATEVER YOU CALL 'EM.
HORRIBLE LITTLE THINGS.
LITTER

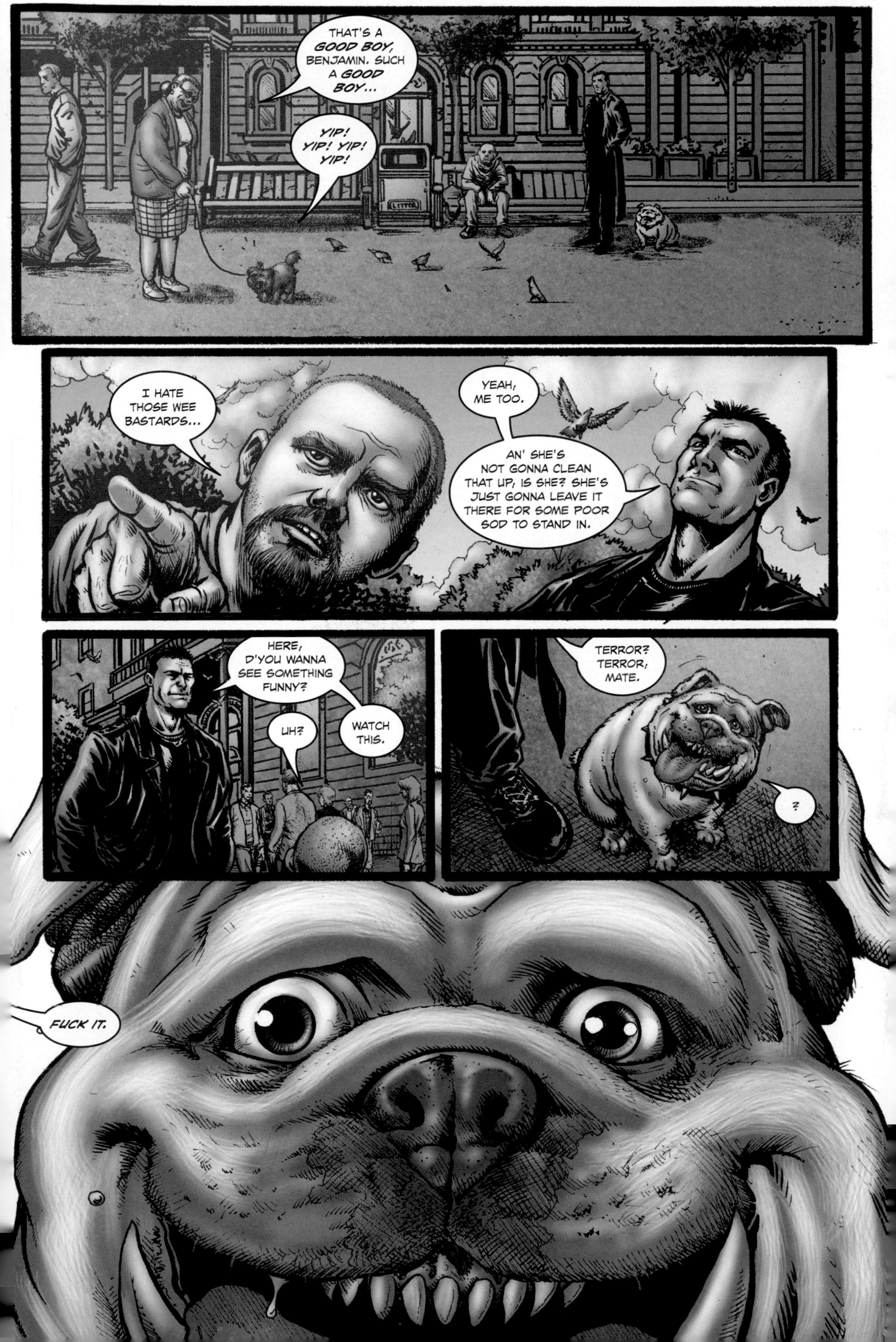
THAT'S A *GOOD BOY*, BENJAMIN. SUCH A *GOOD BOY*...
YIP! YIP! YIP! YIP!
I HATE THOSE WEE BASTARDS...
YEAH, ME TOO.
AN' SHE'S NOT GONNA CLEAN THAT UP, IS SHE? SHE'S JUST GONNA LEAVE IT THERE FOR SOME POOR SOD TO STAND IN.
HERE, D'YOU WANNA SEE SOMETHING FUNNY?
UH?
WATCH THIS.
TERROR? TERROR, MATE.
?
FUCK IT.

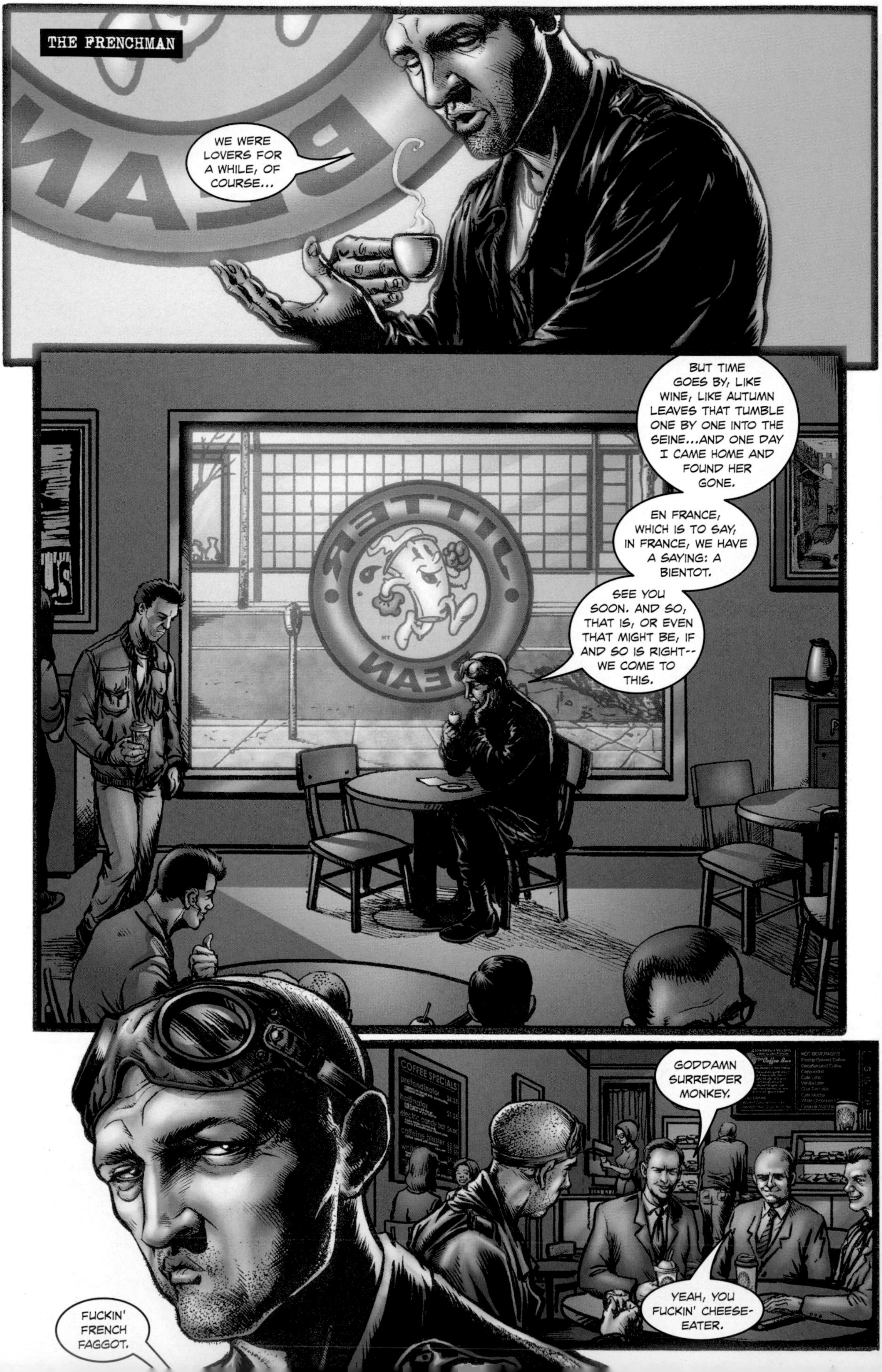
THE FRENCHMAN
WE WERE LOVERS FOR A WHILE, OF COURSE...
BUT TIME GOES BY, LIKE WINE, LIKE AUTUMN LEAVES THAT TUMBLE ONE BY ONE INTO THE SEINE...AND ONE DAY I CAME HOME AND FOUND HER GONE.
EN FRANCE, WHICH IS TO SAY, IN FRANCE, WE HAVE A SAYING: A BIENTOT.
SEE YOU SOON. AND SO, THAT IS, OR EVEN THAT MIGHT BE, IF AND SO IS RIGHT-- WE COME TO THIS.
GODDAMN SURRENDER MONKEY.
YEAH, YOU FUCKIN' CHEESE-EATER.
FUCKIN' FRENCH FAGGOT.

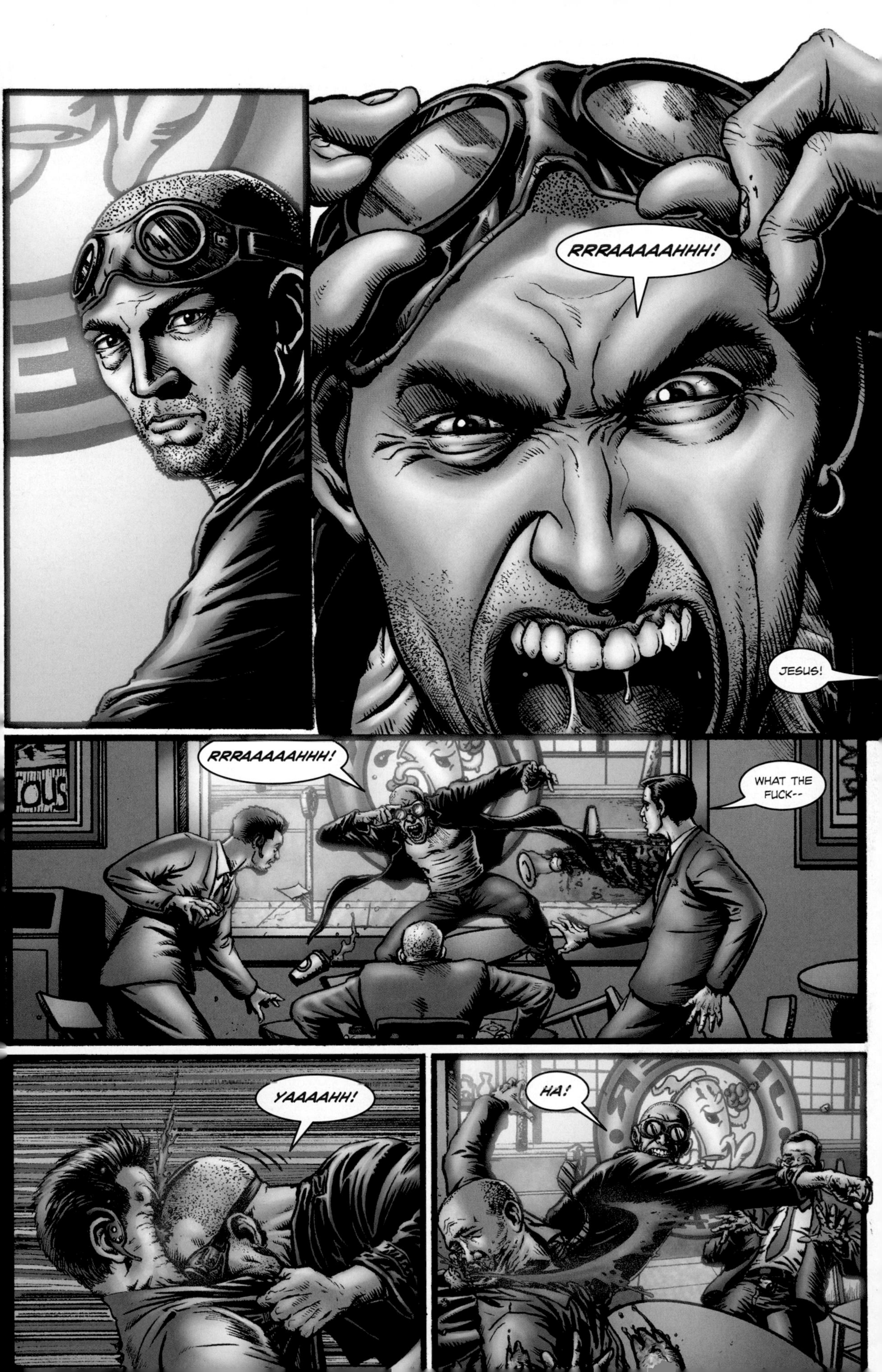
RRRAAAAAHHH!
JESUS!
RRRAAAAAHHH!
WHAT THE FUCK--
YAAAAHH!
HA!

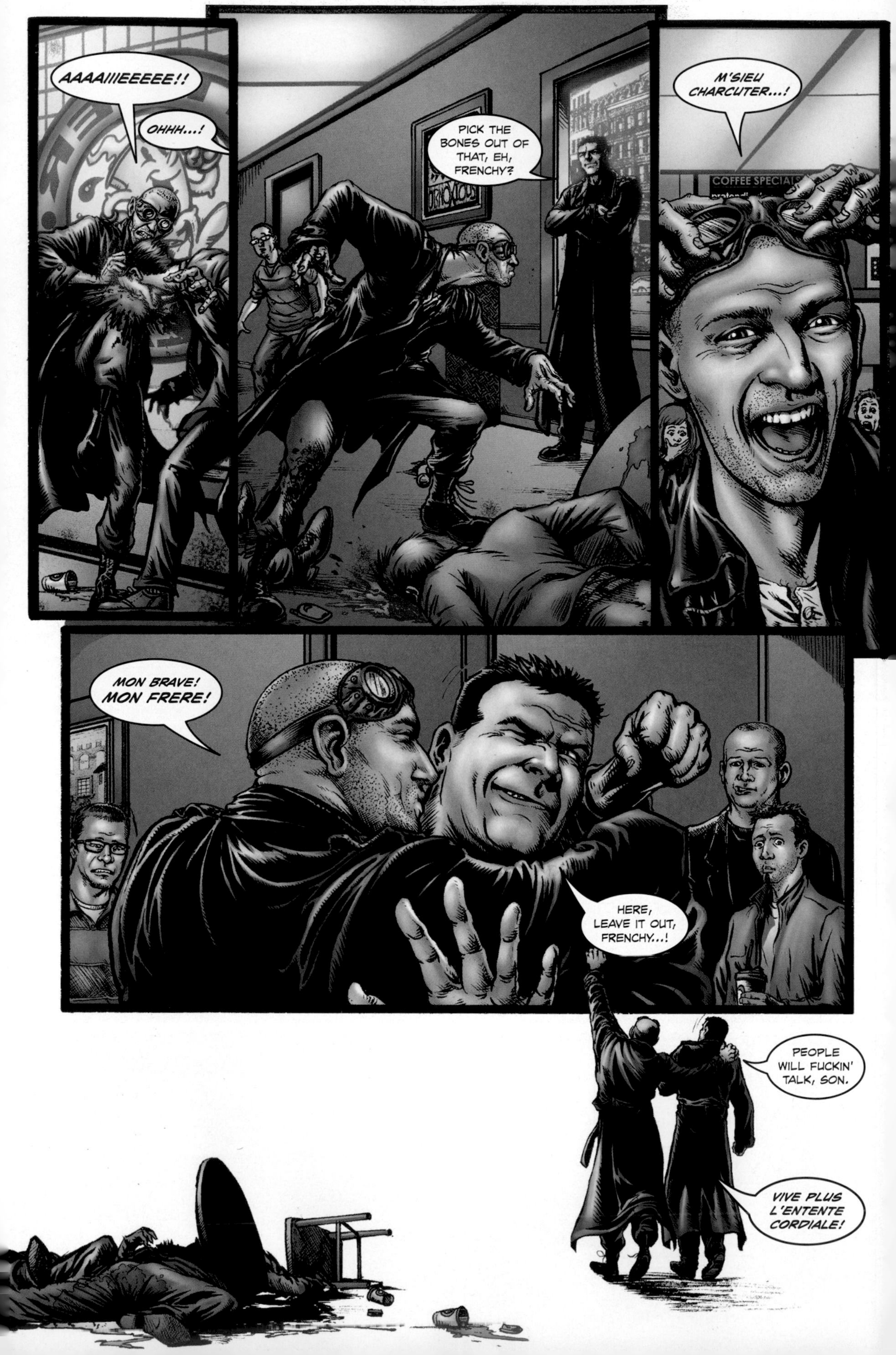
AAAAIIIEEEEE!!
OHHH...!
PICK THE BONES OUT OF THAT, EH, FRENCHY?
M'SIEU CHARCUTER...!
COFFEE SPECIALS
MON BRAVE! MON FRERE!
HERE, LEAVE IT OUT, FRENCHY...!
PEOPLE WILL FUCKIN' TALK, SON.
VIVE PLUS L'ENTENTE CORDIALE!

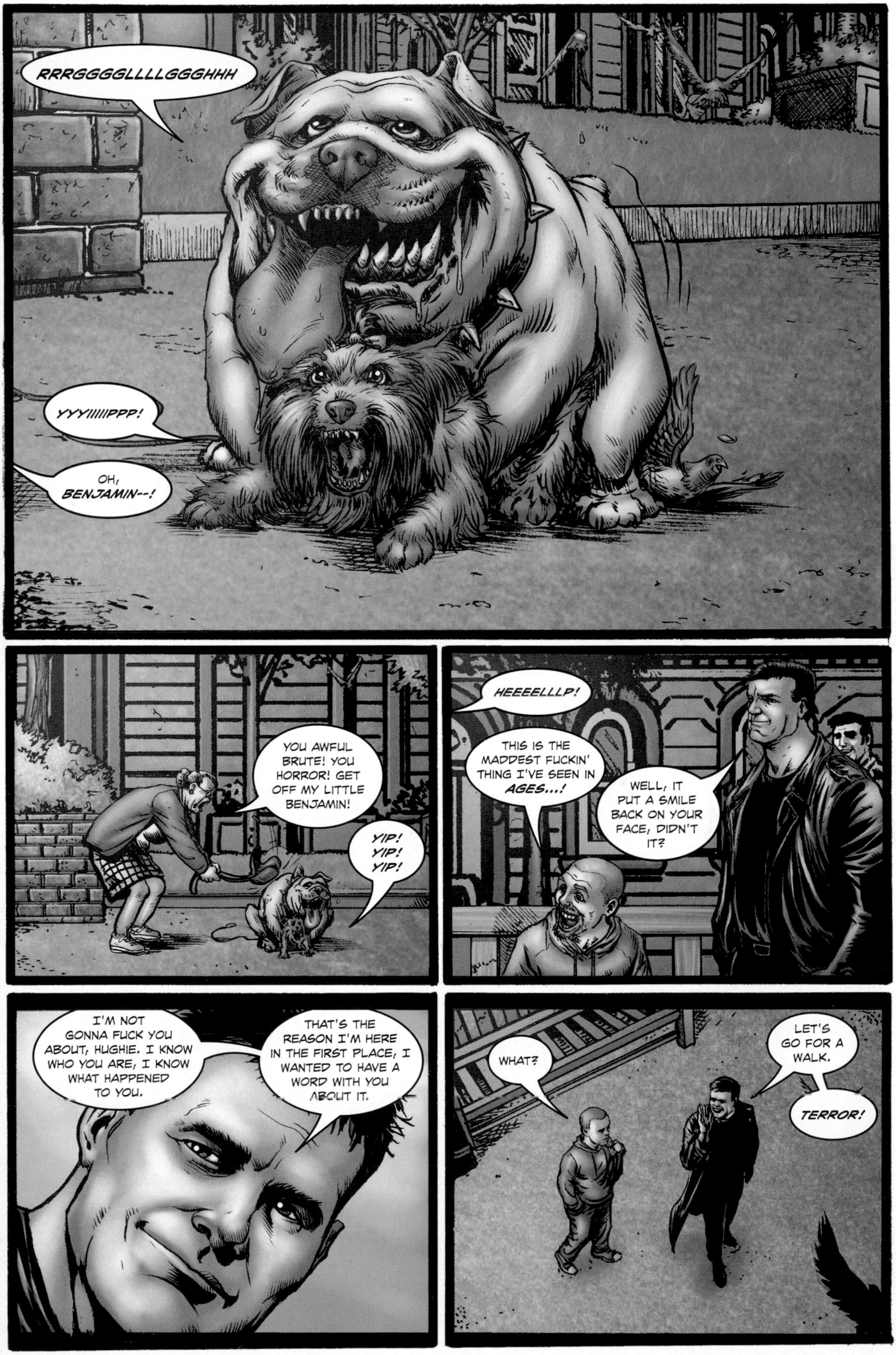
RRRGGGGLLLLGGGHHH
YYYIIIIIPPP!
OH, BENJAMIN--!
YOU AWFUL BRUTE! YOU HORROR! GET OFF MY LITTLE BENJAMIN!
YIP! YIP! YIP!
HEEEELLLP!
THIS IS THE MADDEST FUCKIN' THING I'VE SEEN IN AGES...!
WELL, IT PUT A SMILE BACK ON YOUR FACE, DIDN'T IT?
I'M NOT GONNA FUCK YOU ABOUT, HUGHIE. I KNOW WHO YOU ARE, I KNOW WHAT HAPPENED TO YOU.
THAT'S THE REASON I'M HERE IN THE FIRST PLACE, I WANTED TO HAVE A WORD WITH YOU ABOUT IT.
WHAT?
LET'S GO FOR A WALK.
TERROR!

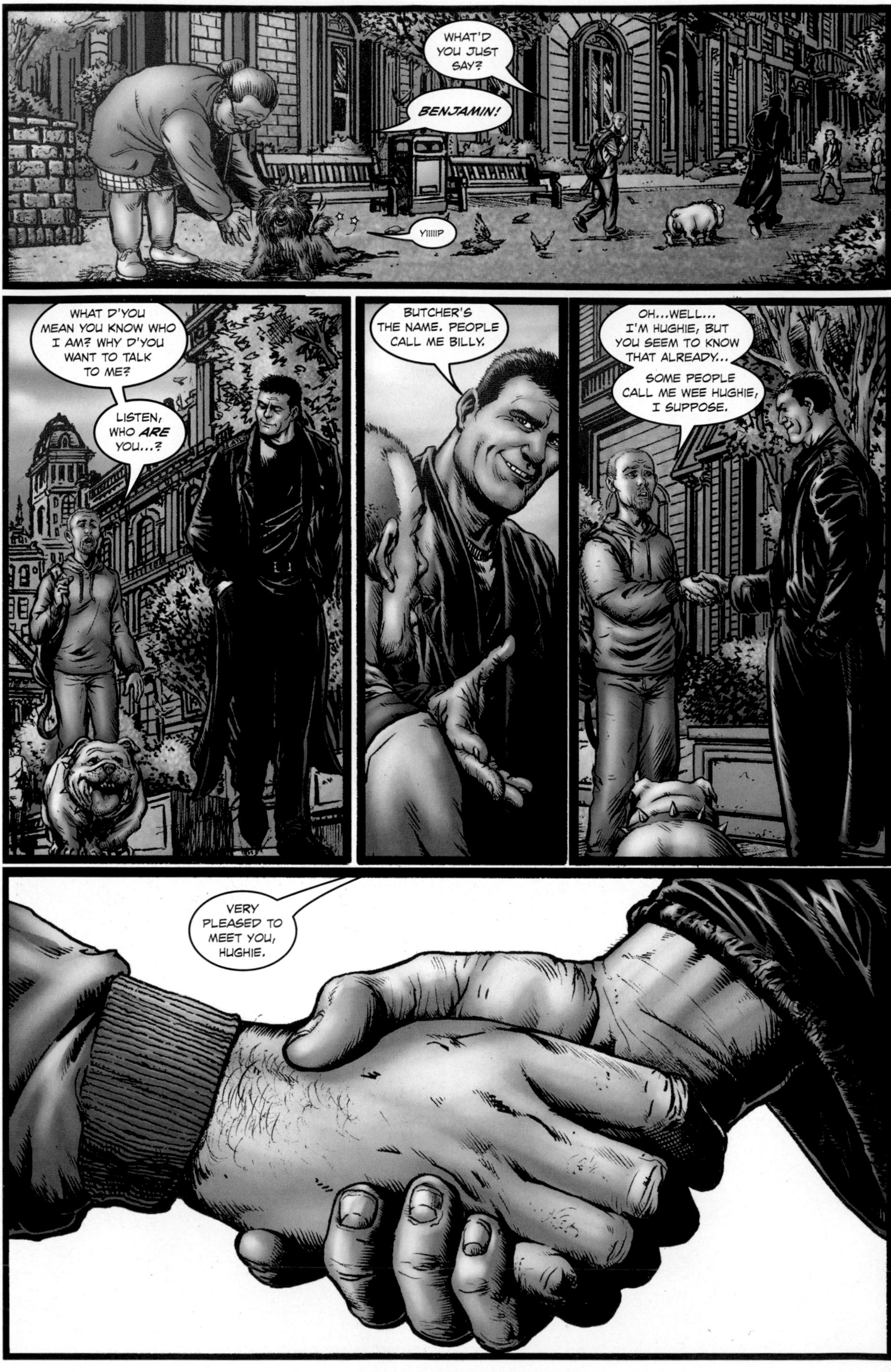
WHAT'D YOU JUST SAY?
BENJAMIN!
YIIIIIP
WHAT D'YOU MEAN YOU KNOW WHO I AM? WHY D'YOU WANT TO TALK TO ME?
LISTEN, WHO ARE YOU...?
BUTCHER'S THE NAME. PEOPLE CALL ME BILLY.
OH...WELL... I'M HUGHIE, BUT YOU SEEM TO KNOW THAT ALREADY...
SOME PEOPLE CALL ME WEE HUGHIE, I SUPPOSE.
VERY PLEASED TO MEET YOU, HUGHIE.

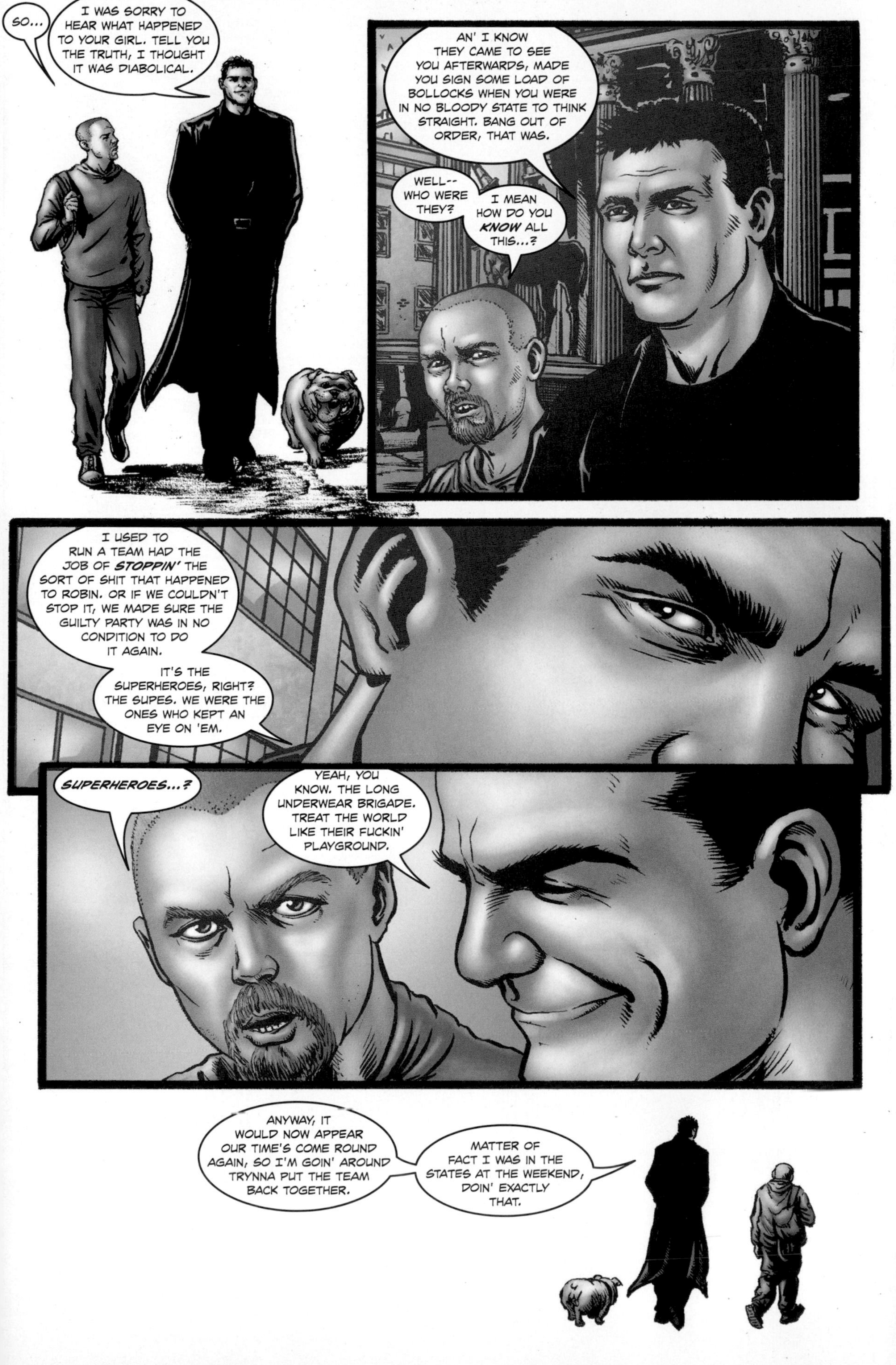
SO...
I WAS SORRY TO HEAR WHAT HAPPENED TO YOUR GIRL. TELL YOU THE TRUTH, I THOUGHT IT WAS DIABOLICAL.
AN' I KNOW THEY CAME TO SEE YOU AFTERWARDS, MADE YOU SIGN SOME LOAD OF BOLLOCKS WHEN YOU WERE IN NO BLOODY STATE TO THINK STRAIGHT. BANG OUT OF ORDER, THAT WAS.
WELL-- WHO WERE THEY?
I MEAN HOW DO YOU *KNOW* ALL THIS...?
I USED TO RUN A TEAM HAD THE JOB OF *STOPPIN'* THE SORT OF SHIT THAT HAPPENED TO ROBIN. OR IF WE COULDN'T STOP IT, WE MADE SURE THE GUILTY PARTY WAS IN NO CONDITION TO DO IT AGAIN.
IT'S THE SUPERHEROES, RIGHT? THE SUPES. WE WERE THE ONES WHO KEPT AN EYE ON 'EM.
SUPERHEROES...?
YEAH, YOU KNOW. THE LONG UNDERWEAR BRIGADE. TREAT THE WORLD LIKE THEIR FUCKIN' PLAYGROUND.
ANYWAY, IT WOULD NOW APPEAR OUR TIME'S COME ROUND AGAIN, SO I'M GOIN' AROUND TRYNNA PUT THE TEAM BACK TOGETHER.
MATTER OF FACT I WAS IN THE STATES AT THE WEEKEND, DOIN' EXACTLY THAT.

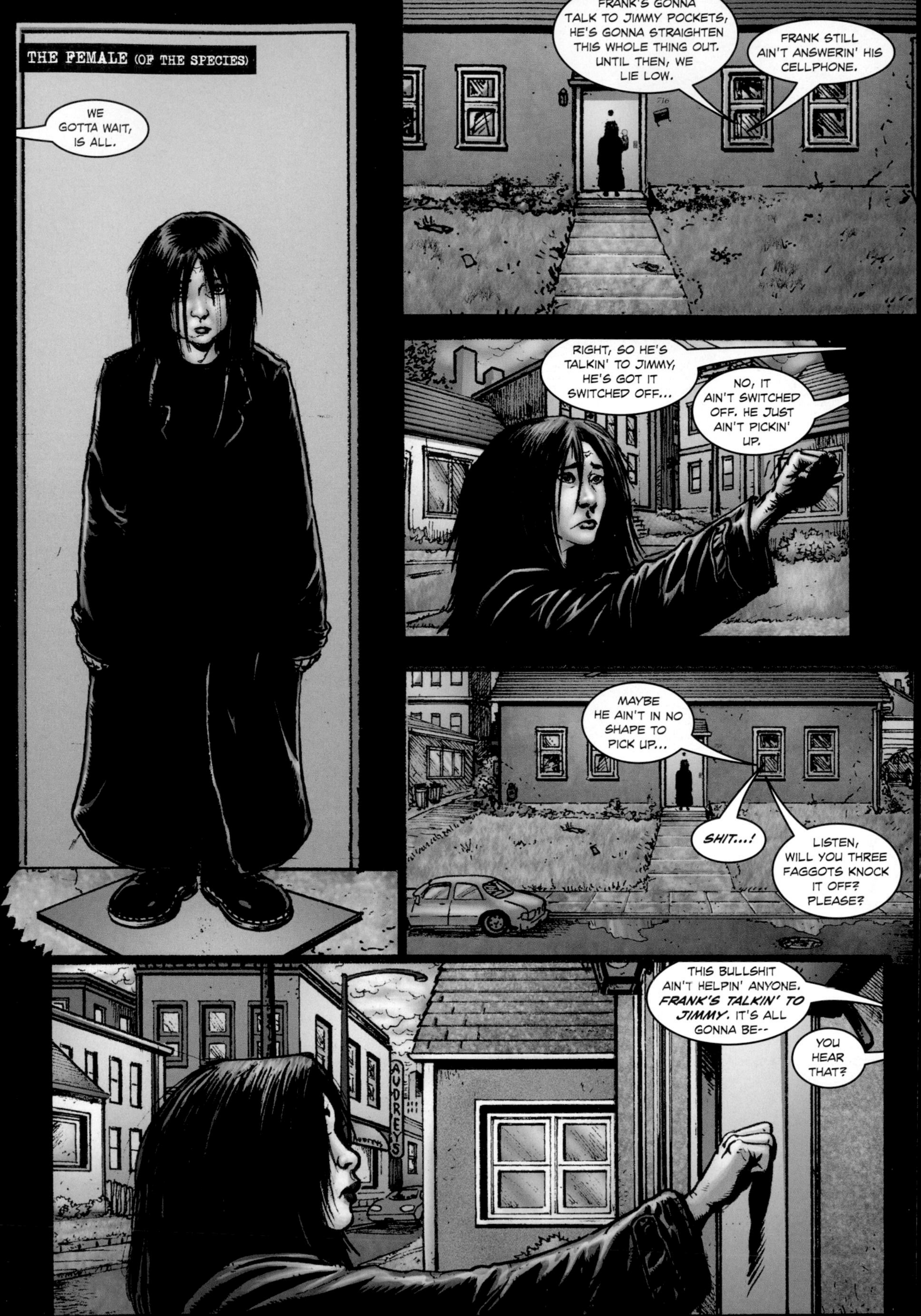
THE FEMALE (OF THE SPECIES)
WE GOTTA WAIT, IS ALL.
FRANK'S GONNA TALK TO JIMMY POCKETS, HE'S GONNA STRAIGHTEN THIS WHOLE THING OUT. UNTIL THEN, WE LIE LOW.
FRANK STILL AIN'T ANSWERIN' HIS CELLPHONE.
RIGHT, SO HE'S TALKIN' TO JIMMY, HE'S GOT IT SWITCHED OFF...
NO, IT AIN'T SWITCHED OFF. HE JUST AIN'T PICKIN' UP.
MAYBE HE AIN'T IN NO SHAPE TO PICK UP...
SHIT...!
LISTEN, WILL YOU THREE FAGGOTS KNOCK IT OFF? PLEASE?
THIS BULLSHIT AIN'T HELPIN' ANYONE. FRANK'S TALKIN' TO JIMMY. IT'S ALL GONNA BE--
YOU HEAR THAT?
AUDREY'S

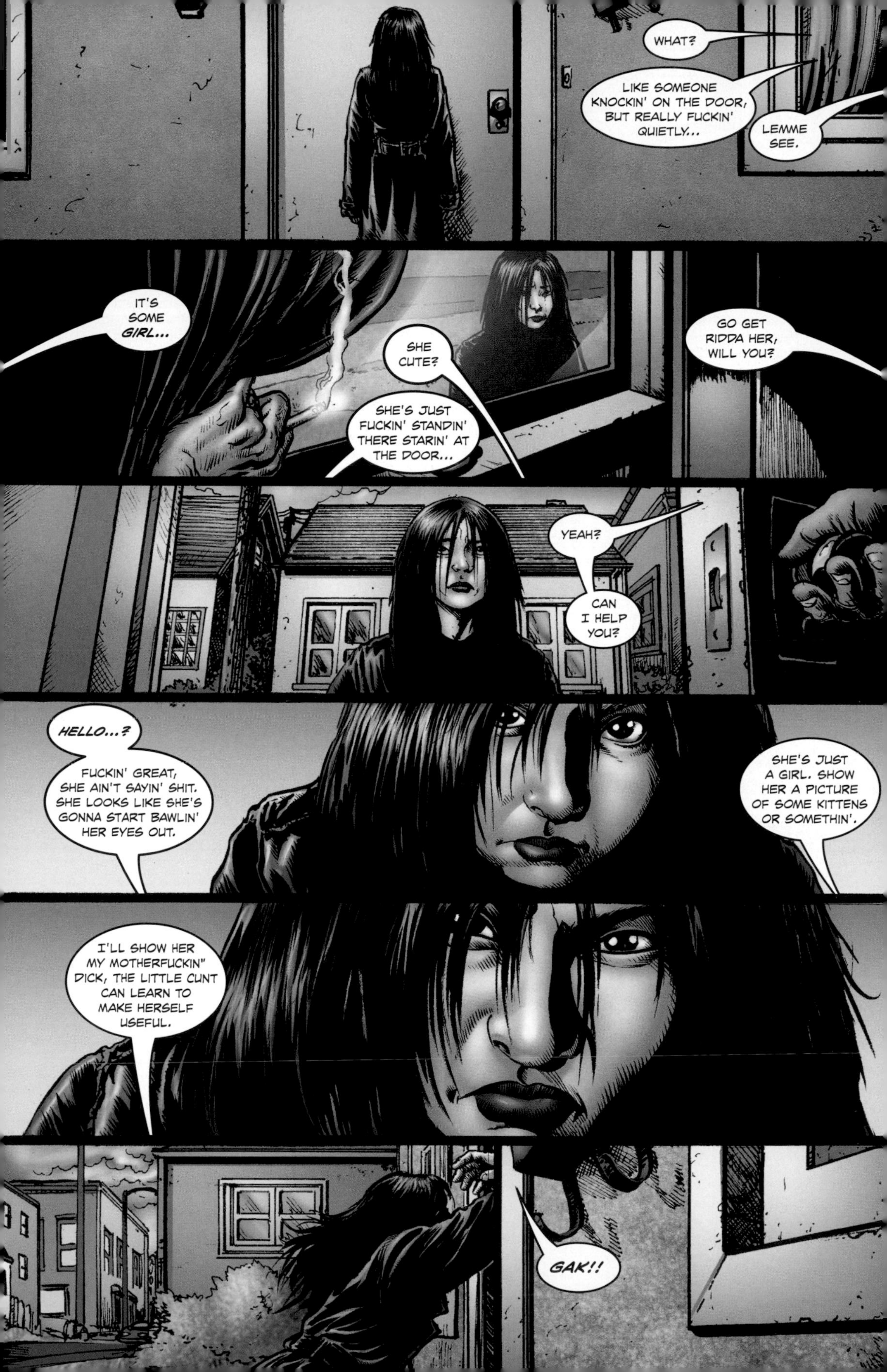

WHAT?
LIKE SOMEONE KNOCKIN' ON THE DOOR, BUT REALLY FUCKIN' QUIETLY...
LEMME SEE.
IT'S SOME GIRL...
SHE CUTE?
SHE'S JUST FUCKIN' STANDIN' THERE STARIN' AT THE DOOR...
GO GET RIDDA HER, WILL YOU?
YEAH?
CAN I HELP YOU?
HELLO...?
FUCKIN' GREAT, SHE AIN'T SAYIN' SHIT. SHE LOOKS LIKE SHE'S GONNA START BAWLIN' HER EYES OUT.
SHE'S JUST A GIRL. SHOW HER A PICTURE OF SOME KITTENS OR SOMETHIN'.
I'LL SHOW HER MY MOTHERFUCKIN" DICK, THE LITTLE CUNT CAN LEARN TO MAKE HERSELF USEFUL.
GAK!!

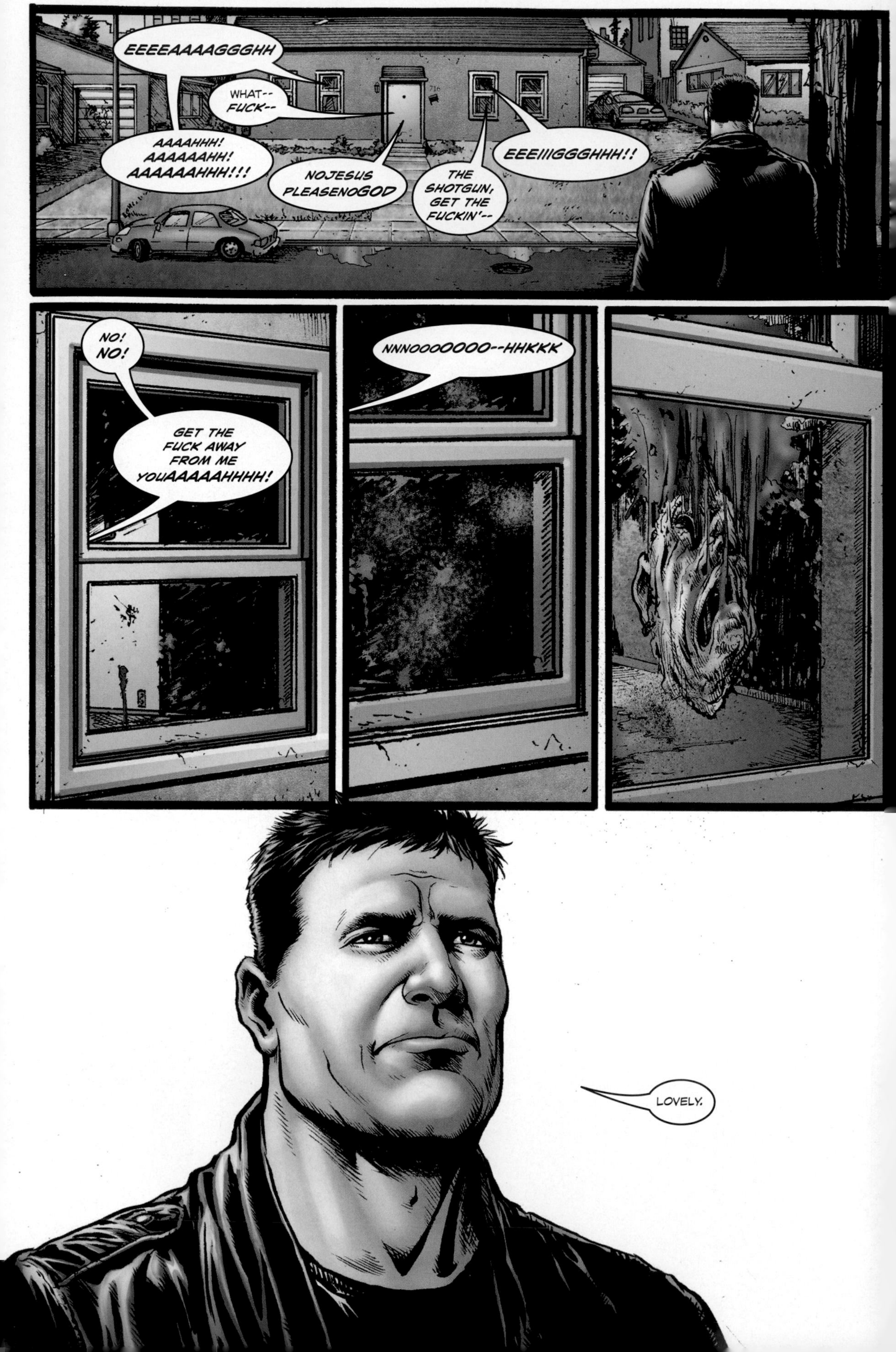

EEEEAAAAAGGGHH
WHAT-- FUCK--
AAAAHHH! AAAAAAAHH! AAAAAAAHHH!!!
NOJESUS PLEASENOGOD
THE SHOTGUN, GET THE FUCKIN'--
EEEIIIGGGHHH!!
NO! NO!
GET THE FUCK AWAY FROM ME YOUAAAAAHHHH!
NNNOOOOOOO--HHKKK
LOVELY.

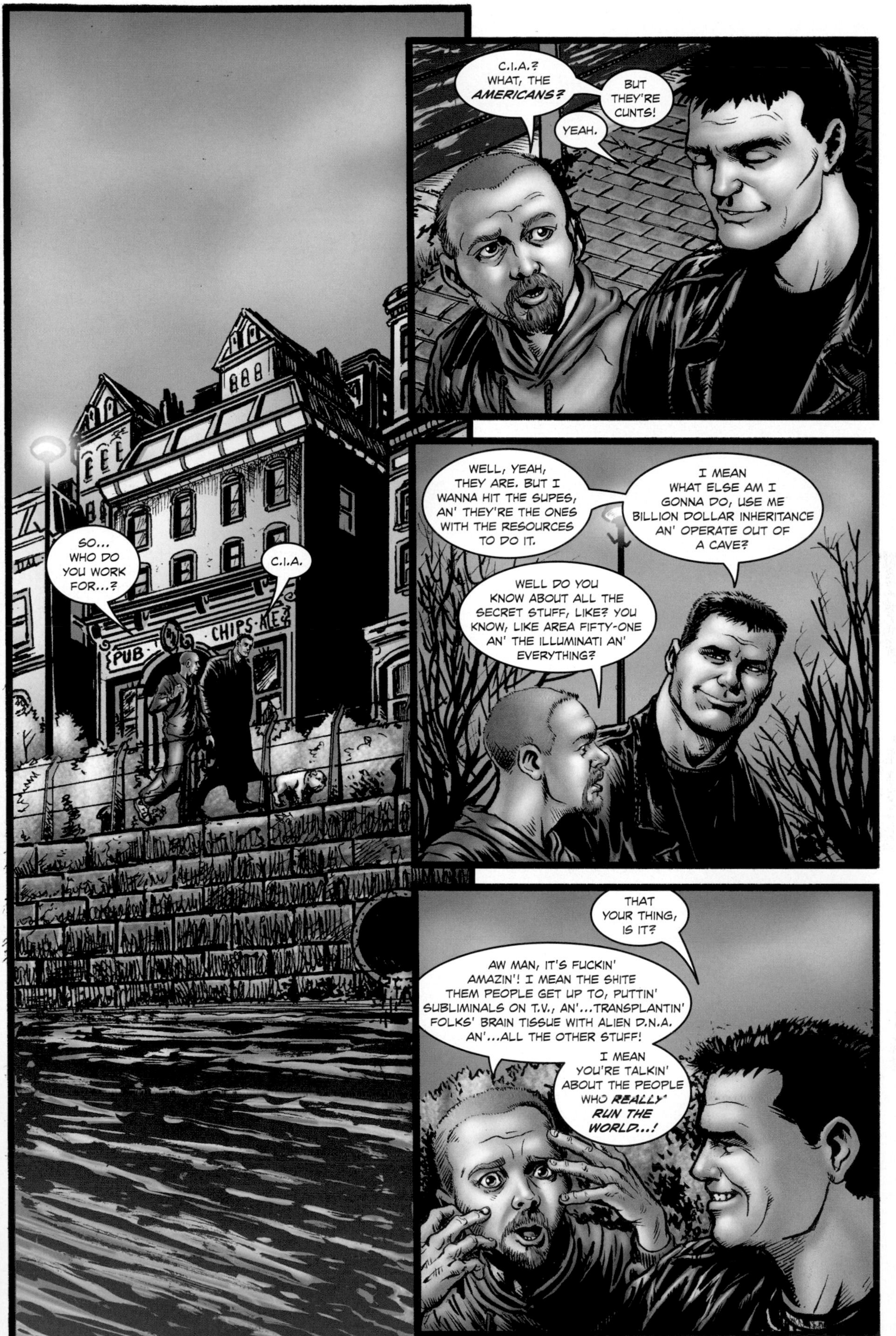
PUB
CHIPS·ALE
SO... WHO DO YOU WORK FOR...?
C.I.A.
C.I.A.? WHAT, THE AMERICANS?
YEAH.
BUT THEY'RE CUNTS!
WELL, YEAH, THEY ARE. BUT I WANNA HIT THE SUPES, AN' THEY'RE THE ONES WITH THE RESOURCES TO DO IT.
I MEAN WHAT ELSE AM I GONNA DO, USE ME BILLION DOLLAR INHERITANCE AN' OPERATE OUT OF A CAVE?
WELL DO YOU KNOW ABOUT ALL THE SECRET STUFF, LIKE? YOU KNOW, LIKE AREA FIFTY-ONE AN' THE ILLUMINATI AN' EVERYTHING?
THAT YOUR THING, IS IT?
AW MAN, IT'S FUCKIN' AMAZIN'! I MEAN THE SHITE THEM PEOPLE GET UP TO, PUTTIN' SUBLIMINALS ON T.V., AN'...TRANSPLANTIN' FOLKS' BRAIN TISSUE WITH ALIEN D.N.A. AN'...ALL THE OTHER STUFF!
I MEAN YOU'RE TALKIN' ABOUT THE PEOPLE WHO REALLY RUN THE WORLD...!

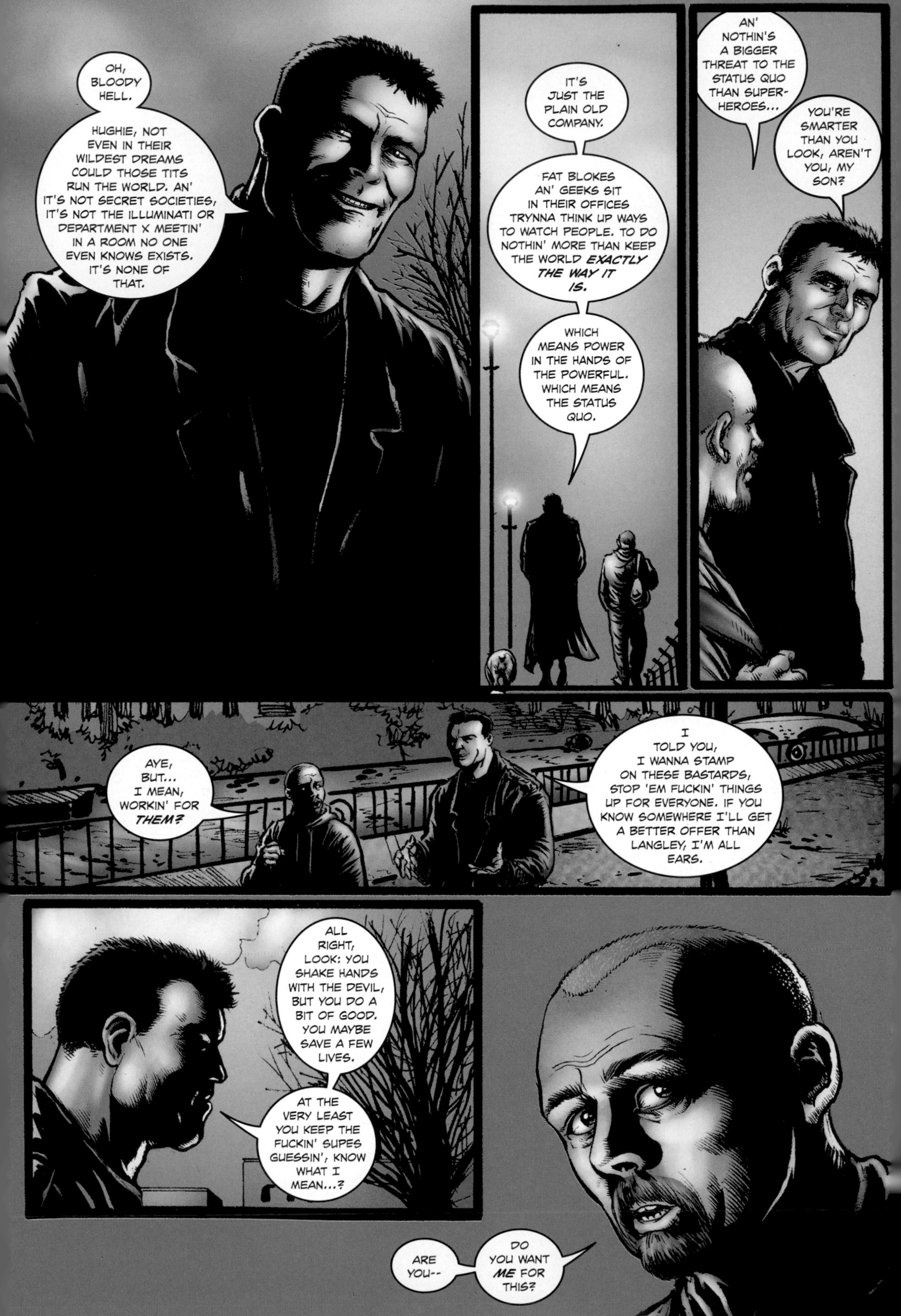
OH, BLOODY HELL.
HUGHIE, NOT EVEN IN THEIR WILDEST DREAMS COULD THOSE TITS RUN THE WORLD. AN' IT'S NOT SECRET SOCIETIES, IT'S NOT THE ILLUMINATI OR DEPARTMENT X MEETIN' IN A ROOM NO ONE EVEN KNOWS EXISTS. IT'S NONE OF THAT.
IT'S JUST THE PLAIN OLD COMPANY.
FAT BLOKES AN' GEEKS SIT IN THEIR OFFICES TRYNNA THINK UP WAYS TO WATCH PEOPLE. TO DO NOTHIN' MORE THAN KEEP THE WORLD EXACTLY THE WAY IT IS.
WHICH MEANS POWER IN THE HANDS OF THE POWERFUL. WHICH MEANS THE STATUS QUO.
AN' NOTHIN'S A BIGGER THREAT TO THE STATUS QUO THAN SUPER-HEROES...
YOU'RE SMARTER THAN YOU LOOK, AREN'T YOU, MY SON?
AYE, BUT... I MEAN, WORKIN' FOR THEM?
I TOLD YOU, I WANNA STAMP ON THESE BASTARDS, STOP 'EM FUCKIN' THINGS UP FOR EVERYONE. IF YOU KNOW SOMEWHERE I'LL GET A BETTER OFFER THAN LANGLEY, I'M ALL EARS.
ALL RIGHT, LOOK: YOU SHAKE HANDS WITH THE DEVIL, BUT YOU DO A BIT OF GOOD. YOU MAYBE SAVE A FEW LIVES.
AT THE VERY LEAST YOU KEEP THE FUCKIN' SUPES GUESSIN', KNOW WHAT I MEAN...?
ARE YOU--
DO YOU WANT ME FOR THIS?

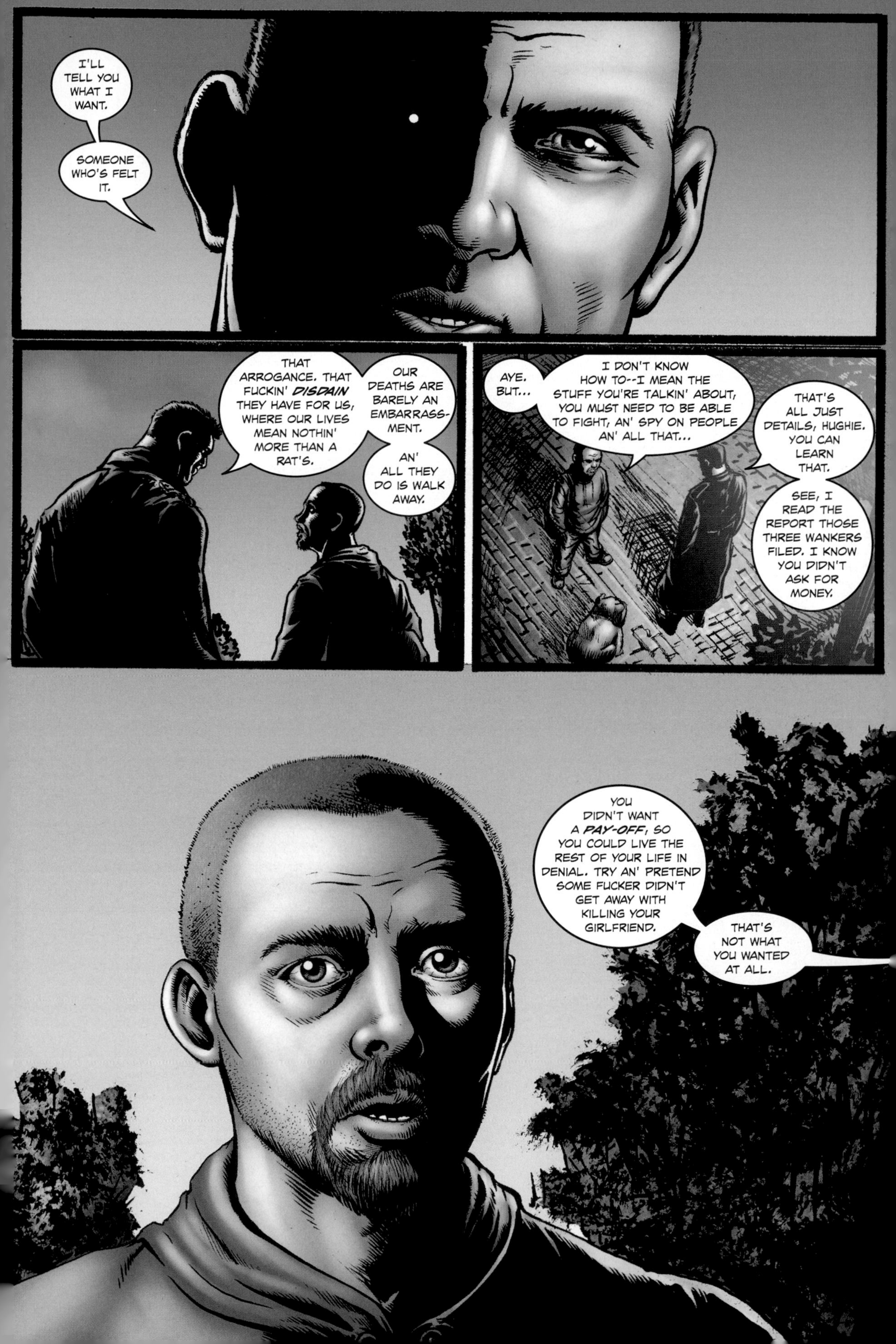
I'LL TELL YOU WHAT I WANT.
SOMEONE WHO'S FELT IT.
THAT ARROGANCE. THAT FUCKIN' *DISDAIN* THEY HAVE FOR US, WHERE OUR LIVES MEAN NOTHIN' MORE THAN A RAT'S.
OUR DEATHS ARE BARELY AN EMBARRASS-MENT.
AN' ALL THEY DO IS WALK AWAY.
AYE. BUT...
I DON'T KNOW HOW TO--I MEAN THE STUFF YOU'RE TALKIN' ABOUT, YOU MUST NEED TO BE ABLE TO FIGHT, AN' SPY ON PEOPLE AN' ALL THAT...
THAT'S ALL JUST DETAILS, HUGHIE. YOU CAN LEARN THAT.
SEE, I READ THE REPORT THOSE THREE WANKERS FILED. I KNOW YOU DIDN'T ASK FOR MONEY.
YOU DIDN'T WANT A *PAY-OFF*, SO YOU COULD LIVE THE REST OF YOUR LIFE IN DENIAL. TRY AN' PRETEND SOME FUCKER DIDN'T GET AWAY WITH KILLING YOUR GIRLFRIEND.
THAT'S NOT WHAT YOU WANTED AT ALL.

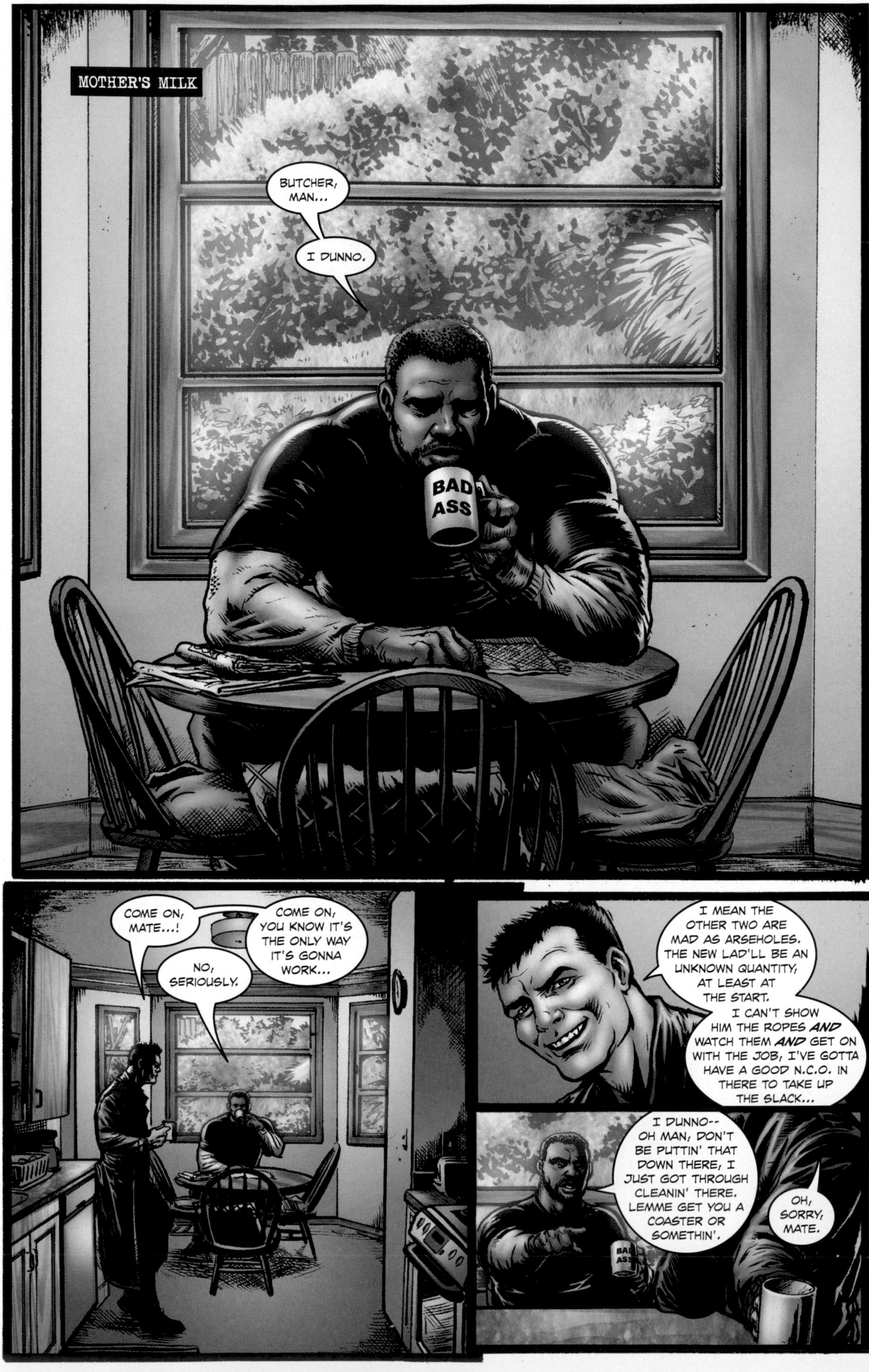
MOTHER'S MILK
BUTCHER, MAN...
I DUNNO.
BAD ASS
COME ON, MATE...!
COME ON, YOU KNOW IT'S THE ONLY WAY IT'S GONNA WORK...
NO, SERIOUSLY.
I MEAN THE OTHER TWO ARE MAD AS ARSEHOLES. THE NEW LAD'LL BE AN UNKNOWN QUANTITY, AT LEAST AT THE START.
I CAN'T SHOW HIM THE ROPES AND WATCH THEM AND GET ON WITH THE JOB, I'VE GOTTA HAVE A GOOD N.C.O. IN THERE TO TAKE UP THE SLACK...
I DUNNO-- OH MAN, DON'T BE PUTTIN' THAT DOWN THERE, I JUST GOT THROUGH CLEANIN' THERE. LEMME GET YOU A COASTER OR SOMETHIN'.
OH, SORRY, MATE.

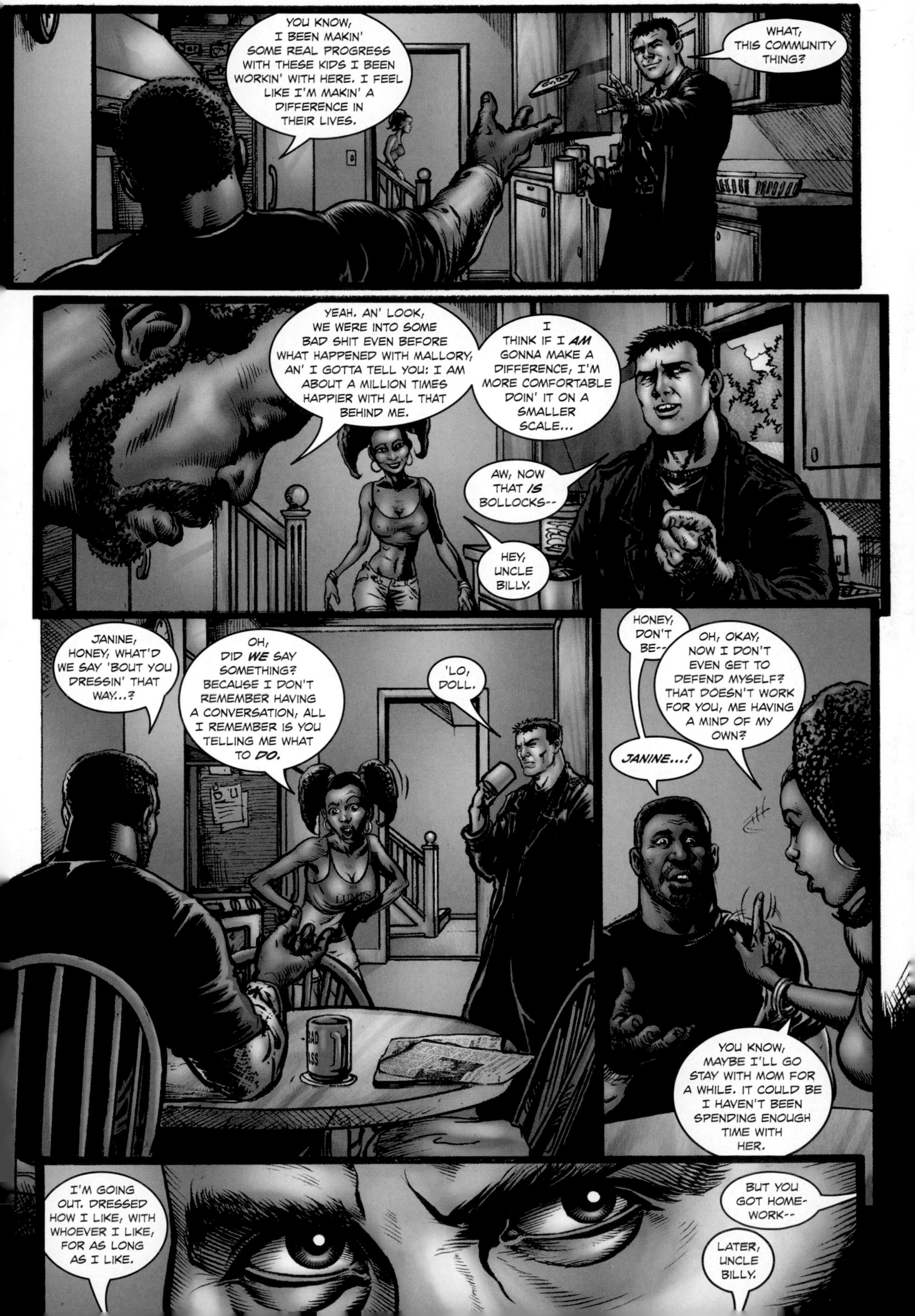

YOU KNOW, I BEEN MAKIN' SOME REAL PROGRESS WITH THESE KIDS I BEEN WORKIN' WITH HERE. I FEEL LIKE I'M MAKIN' A DIFFERENCE IN THEIR LIVES.
WHAT, THIS COMMUNITY THING?
YEAH. AN' LOOK, WE WERE INTO SOME BAD SHIT EVEN BEFORE WHAT HAPPENED WITH MALLORY, AN' I GOTTA TELL YOU: I AM ABOUT A MILLION TIMES HAPPIER WITH ALL THAT BEHIND ME.
I THINK IF I AM GONNA MAKE A DIFFERENCE, I'M MORE COMFORTABLE DOIN' IT ON A SMALLER SCALE...
AW, NOW THAT IS BOLLOCKS--
HEY, UNCLE BILLY.
JANINE, HONEY, WHAT'D WE SAY 'BOUT YOU DRESSIN' THAT WAY...?
OH, DID WE SAY SOMETHING? BECAUSE I DON'T REMEMBER HAVING A CONVERSATION, ALL I REMEMBER IS YOU TELLING ME WHAT TO DO.
'LO, DOLL.
HONEY, DON'T BE--
OH, OKAY, NOW I DON'T EVEN GET TO DEFEND MYSELF? THAT DOESN'T WORK FOR YOU, ME HAVING A MIND OF MY OWN?
JANINE...!
YOU KNOW, MAYBE I'LL GO STAY WITH MOM FOR A WHILE. IT COULD BE I HAVEN'T BEEN SPENDING ENOUGH TIME WITH HER.
I'M GOING OUT. DRESSED HOW I LIKE, WITH WHOEVER I LIKE, FOR AS LONG AS I LIKE.
BUT YOU GOT HOME-WORK--
LATER, UNCLE BILLY.

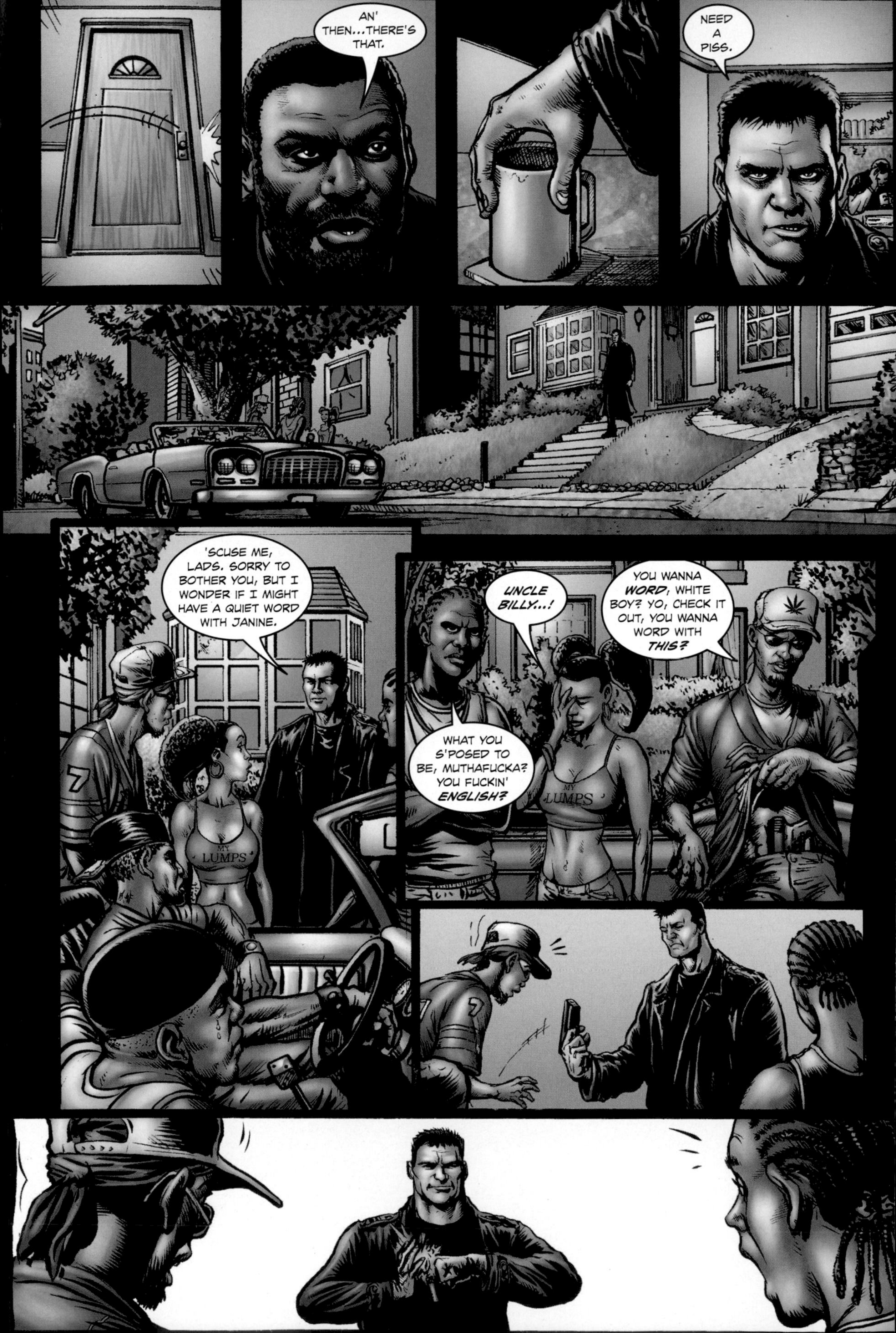
AN' THEN...THERE'S THAT.
NEED A PISS.
'SCUSE ME, LADS. SORRY TO BOTHER YOU, BUT I WONDER IF I MIGHT HAVE A QUIET WORD WITH JANINE.
MY LUMPS
UNCLE BILLY...!
WHAT YOU S'POSED TO BE, MUTHAFUCKA? YOU FUCKIN' ENGLISH?
YOU WANNA WORD, WHITE BOY? YO, CHECK IT OUT, YOU WANNA WORD WITH THIS?
MY LUMPS

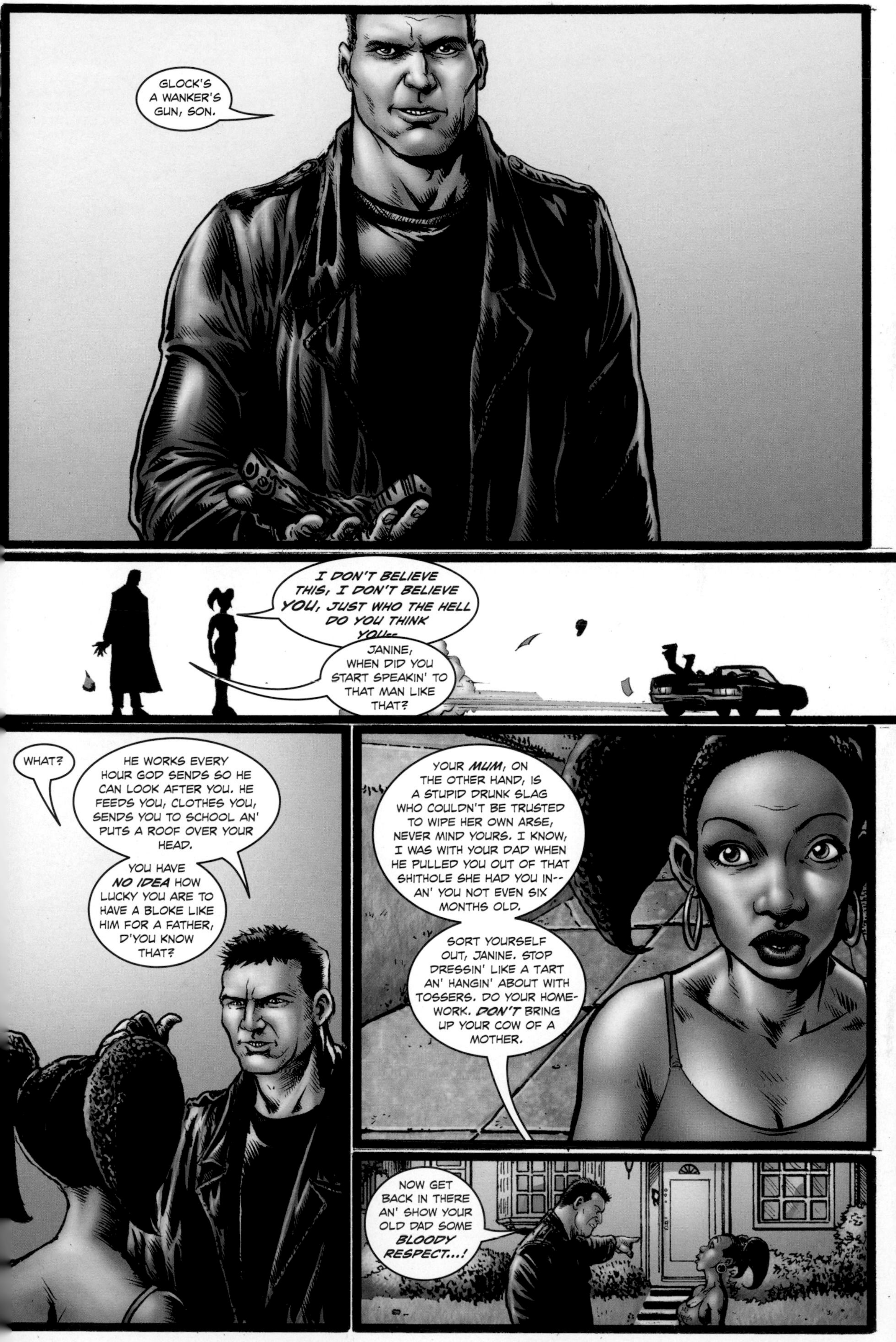
GLOCK'S A WANKER'S GUN, SON.
I DON'T BELIEVE THIS, I DON'T BELIEVE YOU, JUST WHO THE HELL DO YOU THINK YOU--
JANINE, WHEN DID YOU START SPEAKIN' TO THAT MAN LIKE THAT?
WHAT?
HE WORKS EVERY HOUR GOD SENDS SO HE CAN LOOK AFTER YOU. HE FEEDS YOU, CLOTHES YOU, SENDS YOU TO SCHOOL AN' PUTS A ROOF OVER YOUR HEAD.
YOU HAVE NO IDEA HOW LUCKY YOU ARE TO HAVE A BLOKE LIKE HIM FOR A FATHER, D'YOU KNOW THAT?
YOUR MUM, ON THE OTHER HAND, IS A STUPID DRUNK SLAG WHO COULDN'T BE TRUSTED TO WIPE HER OWN ARSE, NEVER MIND YOURS. I KNOW, I WAS WITH YOUR DAD WHEN HE PULLED YOU OUT OF THAT SHITHOLE SHE HAD YOU IN-- AN' YOU NOT EVEN SIX MONTHS OLD.
SORT YOURSELF OUT, JANINE. STOP DRESSIN' LIKE A TART AN' HANGIN' ABOUT WITH TOSSERS. DO YOUR HOME-WORK. DON'T BRING UP YOUR COW OF A MOTHER.
NOW GET BACK IN THERE AN' SHOW YOUR OLD DAD SOME BLOODY RESPECT...!

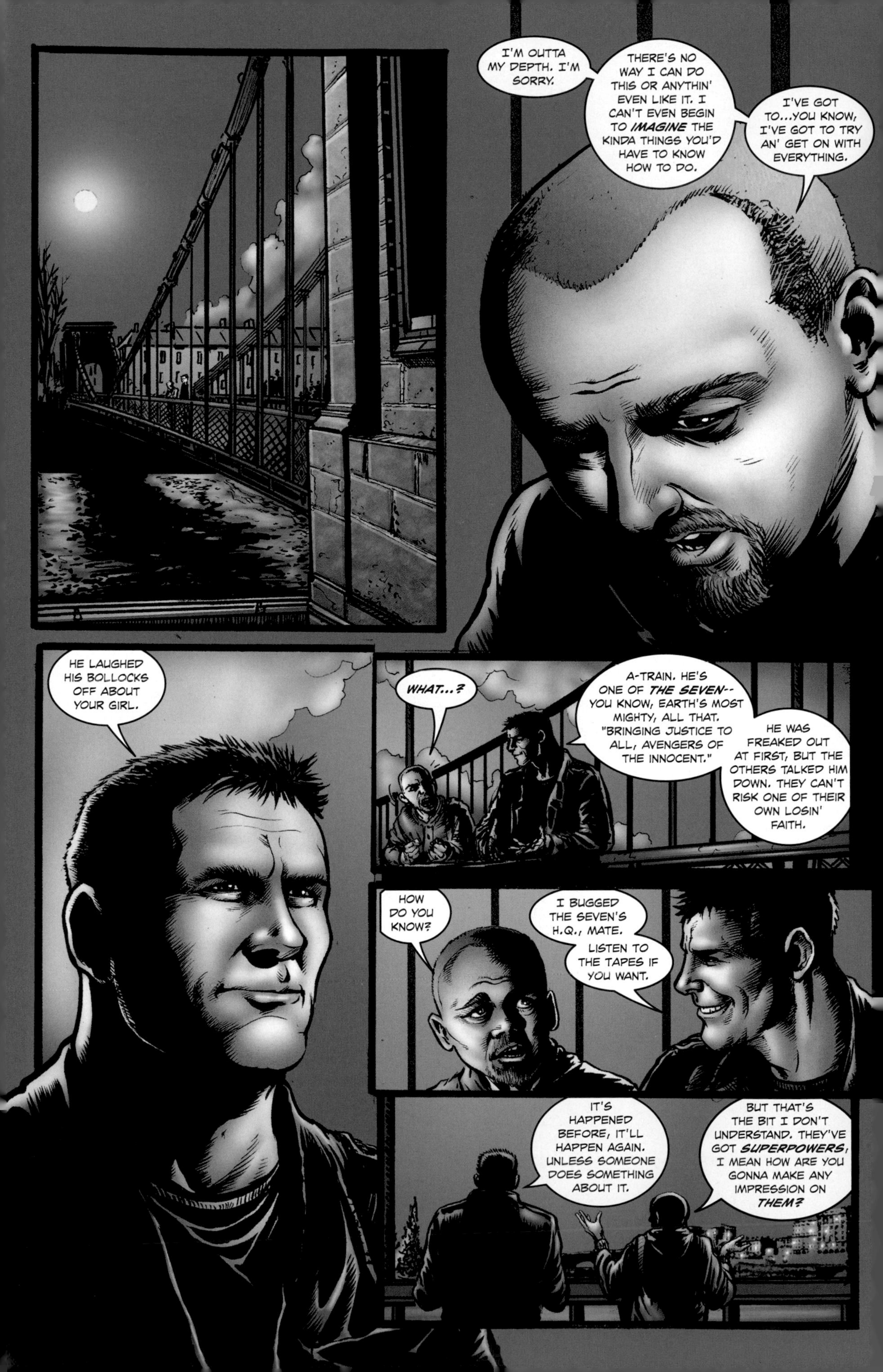
I'M OUTTA MY DEPTH. I'M SORRY.
THERE'S NO WAY I CAN DO THIS OR ANYTHIN' EVEN LIKE IT. I CAN'T EVEN BEGIN TO *IMAGINE* THE KINDA THINGS YOU'D HAVE TO KNOW HOW TO DO.
I'VE GOT TO...YOU KNOW, I'VE GOT TO TRY AN' GET ON WITH EVERYTHING.
HE LAUGHED HIS BOLLOCKS OFF ABOUT YOUR GIRL.
WHAT...?
A-TRAIN. HE'S ONE OF *THE SEVEN*--YOU KNOW, EARTH'S MOST MIGHTY, ALL THAT. "BRINGING JUSTICE TO ALL, AVENGERS OF THE INNOCENT."
HE WAS FREAKED OUT AT FIRST, BUT THE OTHERS TALKED HIM DOWN. THEY CAN'T RISK ONE OF THEIR OWN LOSIN' FAITH.
HOW DO YOU KNOW?
I BUGGED THE SEVEN'S H.Q., MATE.
LISTEN TO THE TAPES IF YOU WANT.
IT'S HAPPENED BEFORE, IT'LL HAPPEN AGAIN. UNLESS SOMEONE DOES SOMETHING ABOUT IT.
BUT THAT'S THE BIT I DON'T UNDERSTAND. THEY'VE GOT *SUPERPOWERS*, I MEAN HOW ARE YOU GONNA MAKE ANY IMPRESSION ON *THEM?*

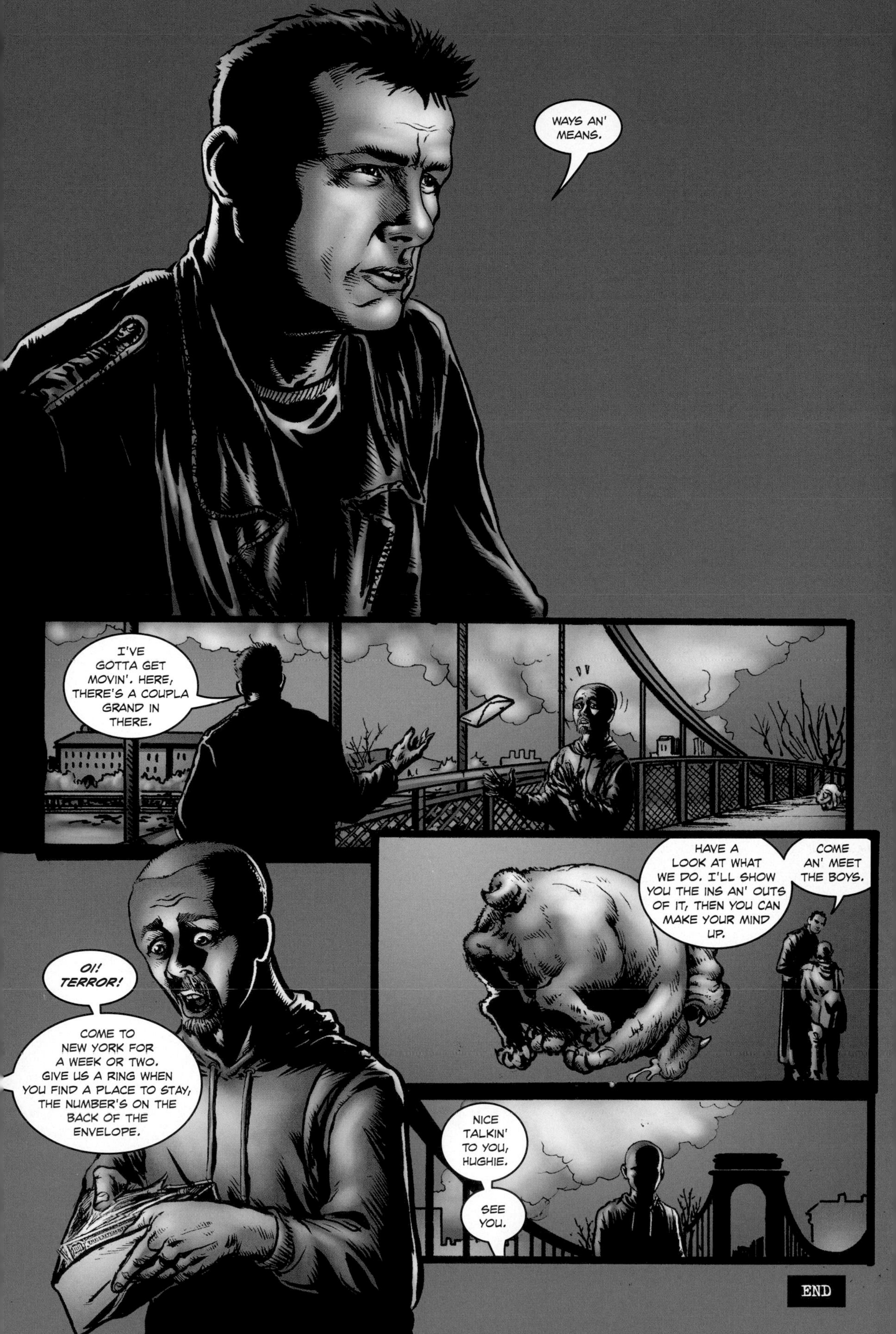
WAYS AN' MEANS.
I'VE GOTTA GET MOVIN'. HERE, THERE'S A COUPLA GRAND IN THERE.
HAVE A LOOK AT WHAT WE DO. I'LL SHOW YOU THE INS AN' OUTS OF IT, THEN YOU CAN MAKE YOUR MIND UP.
COME AN' MEET THE BOYS.
OI! TERROR!
COME TO NEW YORK FOR A WEEK OR TWO. GIVE US A RING WHEN YOU FIND A PLACE TO STAY, THE NUMBER'S ON THE BACK OF THE ENVELOPE.
NICE TALKIN' TO YOU, HUGHIE.
SEE YOU.
END

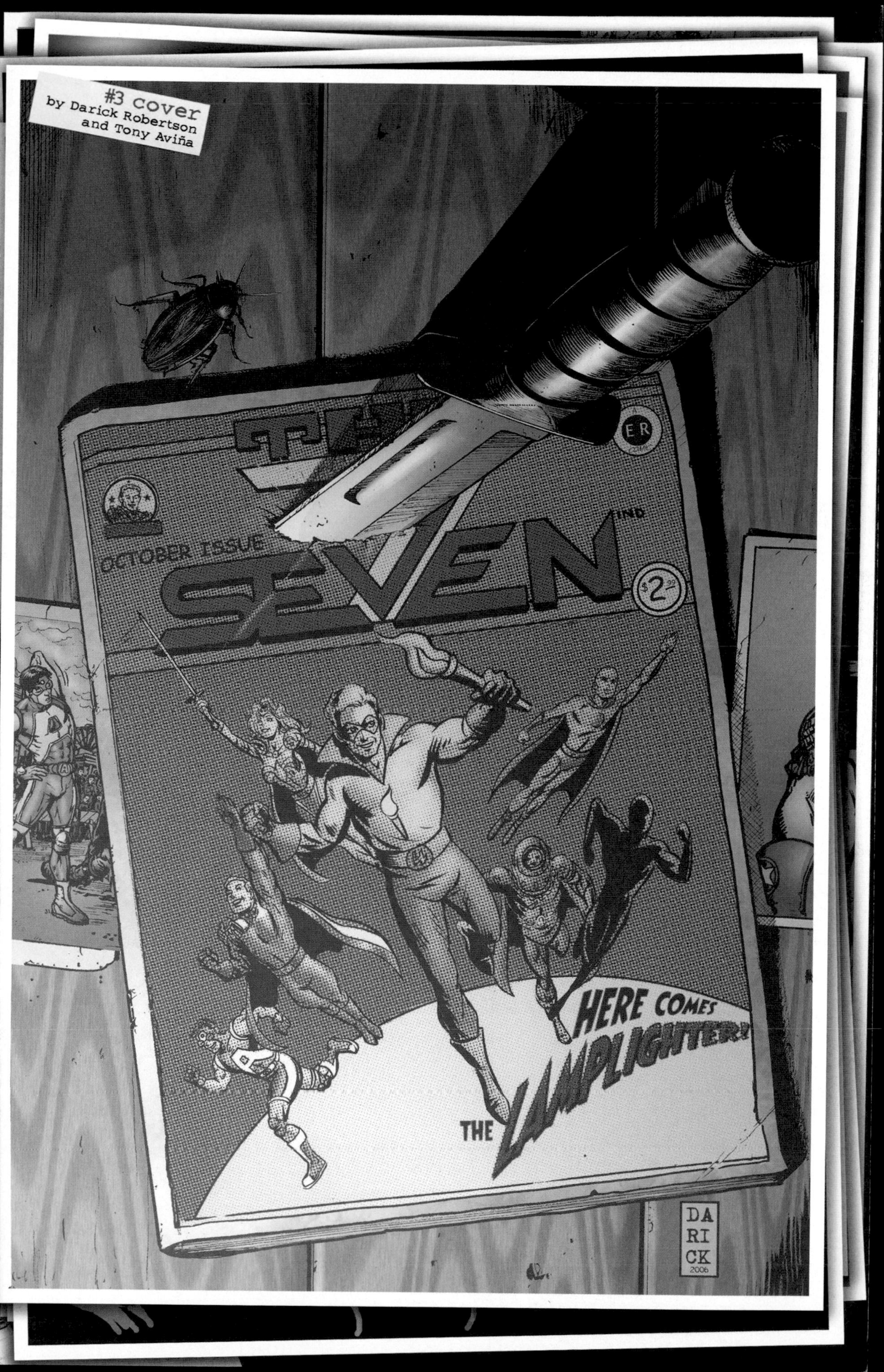
OCTOBER ISSUE
SEVEN
HERE COMES
THE LAMPLIGHTER!
DA
RI
CK
2006

#3 cover
by Darick Robertson
and Tony Aviña

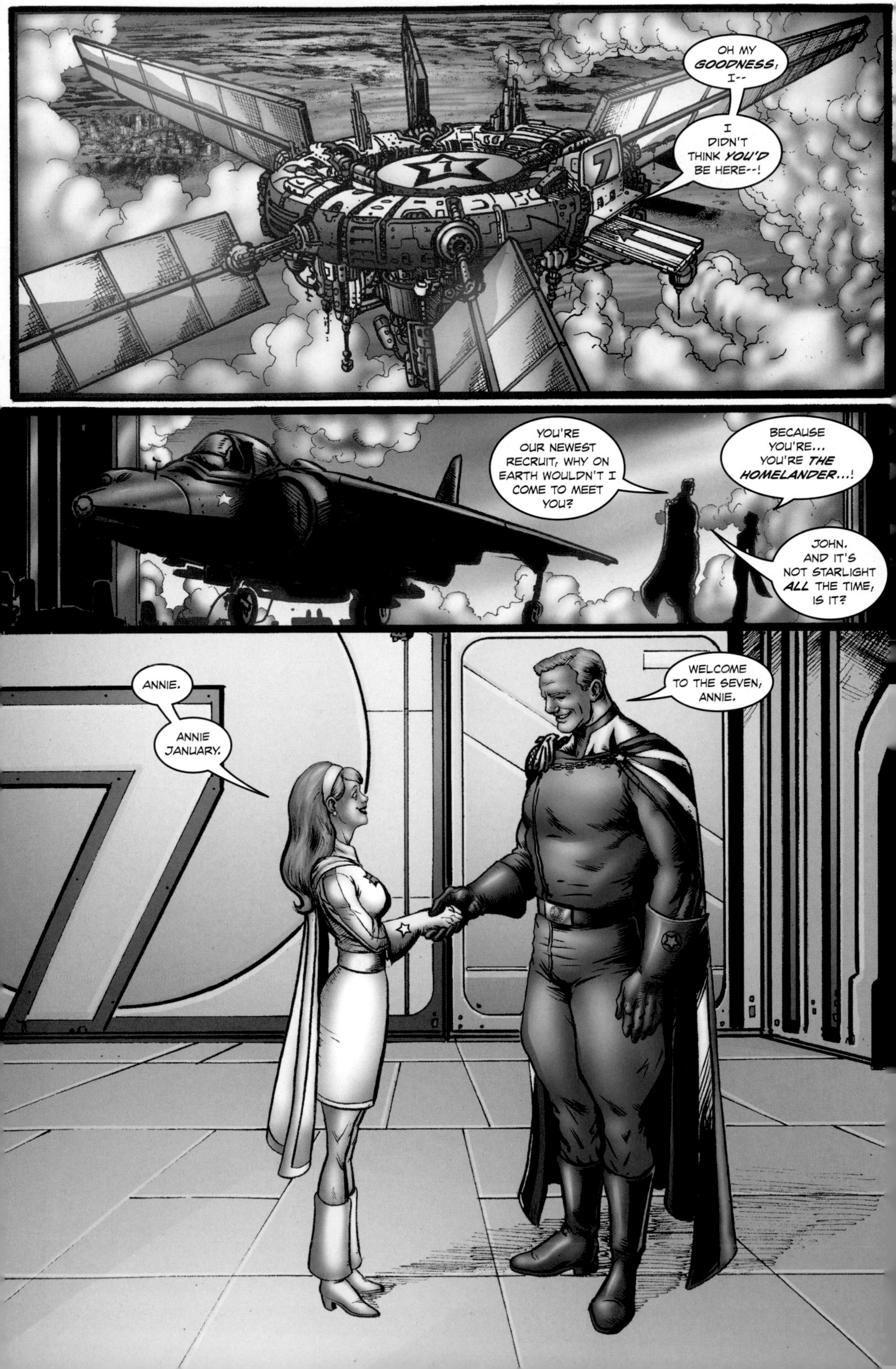
OH MY GOODNESS, I--
I DIDN'T THINK YOU'D BE HERE--!
YOU'RE OUR NEWEST RECRUIT, WHY ON EARTH WOULDN'T I COME TO MEET YOU?
BECAUSE YOU'RE... YOU'RE THE HOMELANDER...!
JOHN. AND IT'S NOT STARLIGHT ALL THE TIME, IS IT?
ANNIE.
ANNIE JANUARY.
WELCOME TO THE SEVEN, ANNIE.

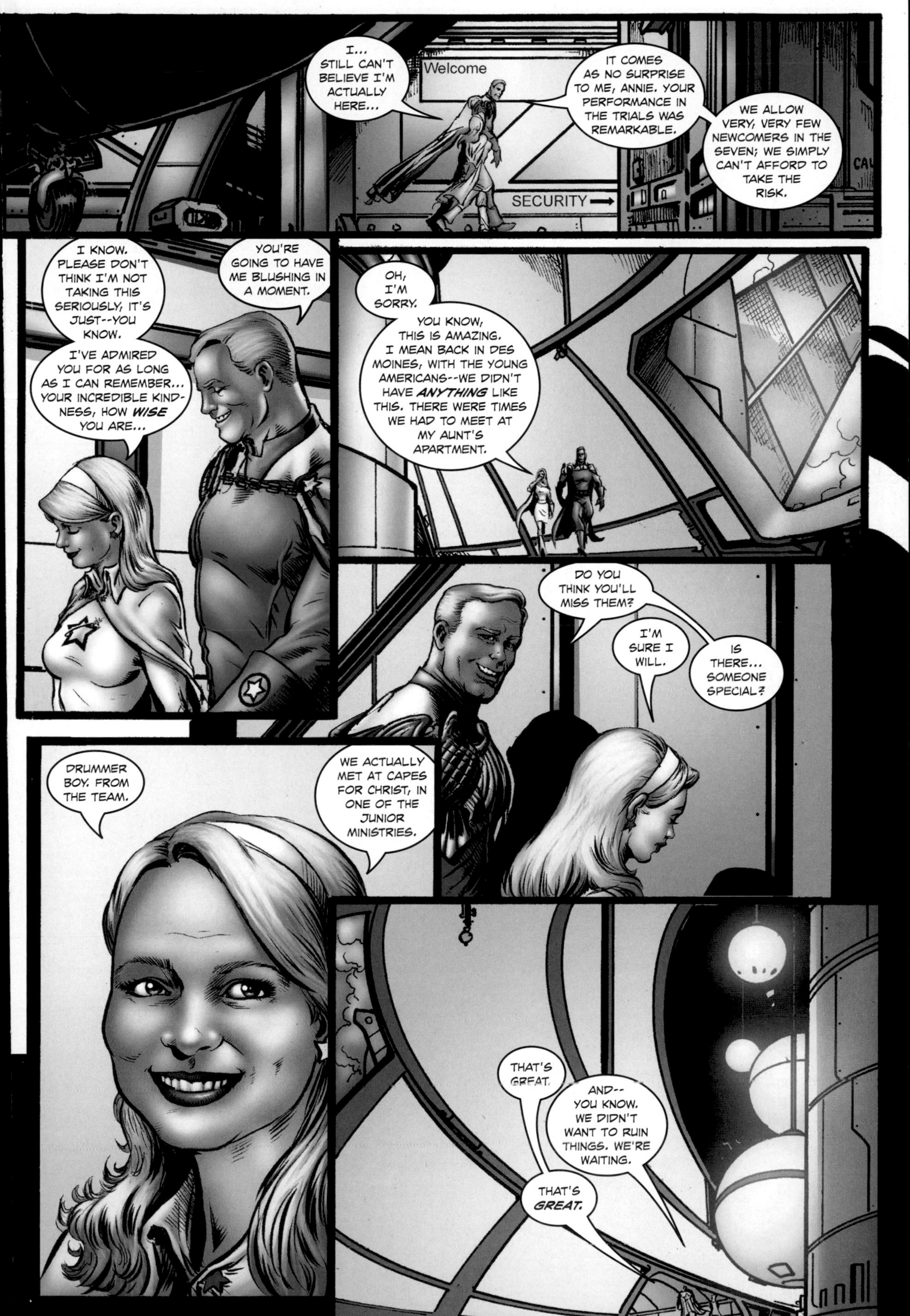
Welcome
I... STILL CAN'T BELIEVE I'M ACTUALLY HERE...
IT COMES AS NO SURPRISE TO ME, ANNIE. YOUR PERFORMANCE IN THE TRIALS WAS REMARKABLE.
WE ALLOW VERY, VERY FEW NEWCOMERS IN THE SEVEN; WE SIMPLY CAN'T AFFORD TO TAKE THE RISK.
SECURITY →
I KNOW. PLEASE DON'T THINK I'M NOT TAKING THIS SERIOUSLY, IT'S JUST--YOU KNOW.
YOU'RE GOING TO HAVE ME BLUSHING IN A MOMENT.
I'VE ADMIRED YOU FOR AS LONG AS I CAN REMEMBER... YOUR INCREDIBLE KINDNESS, HOW WISE YOU ARE...
OH, I'M SORRY.
YOU KNOW, THIS IS AMAZING. I MEAN BACK IN DES MOINES, WITH THE YOUNG AMERICANS--WE DIDN'T HAVE ANYTHING LIKE THIS. THERE WERE TIMES WE HAD TO MEET AT MY AUNT'S APARTMENT.
DO YOU THINK YOU'LL MISS THEM?
I'M SURE I WILL.
IS THERE... SOMEONE SPECIAL?
DRUMMER BOY. FROM THE TEAM.
WE ACTUALLY MET AT CAPES FOR CHRIST, IN ONE OF THE JUNIOR MINISTRIES.
THAT'S GREAT.
AND--YOU KNOW. WE DIDN'T WANT TO RUIN THINGS. WE'RE WAITING.
THAT'S GREAT.

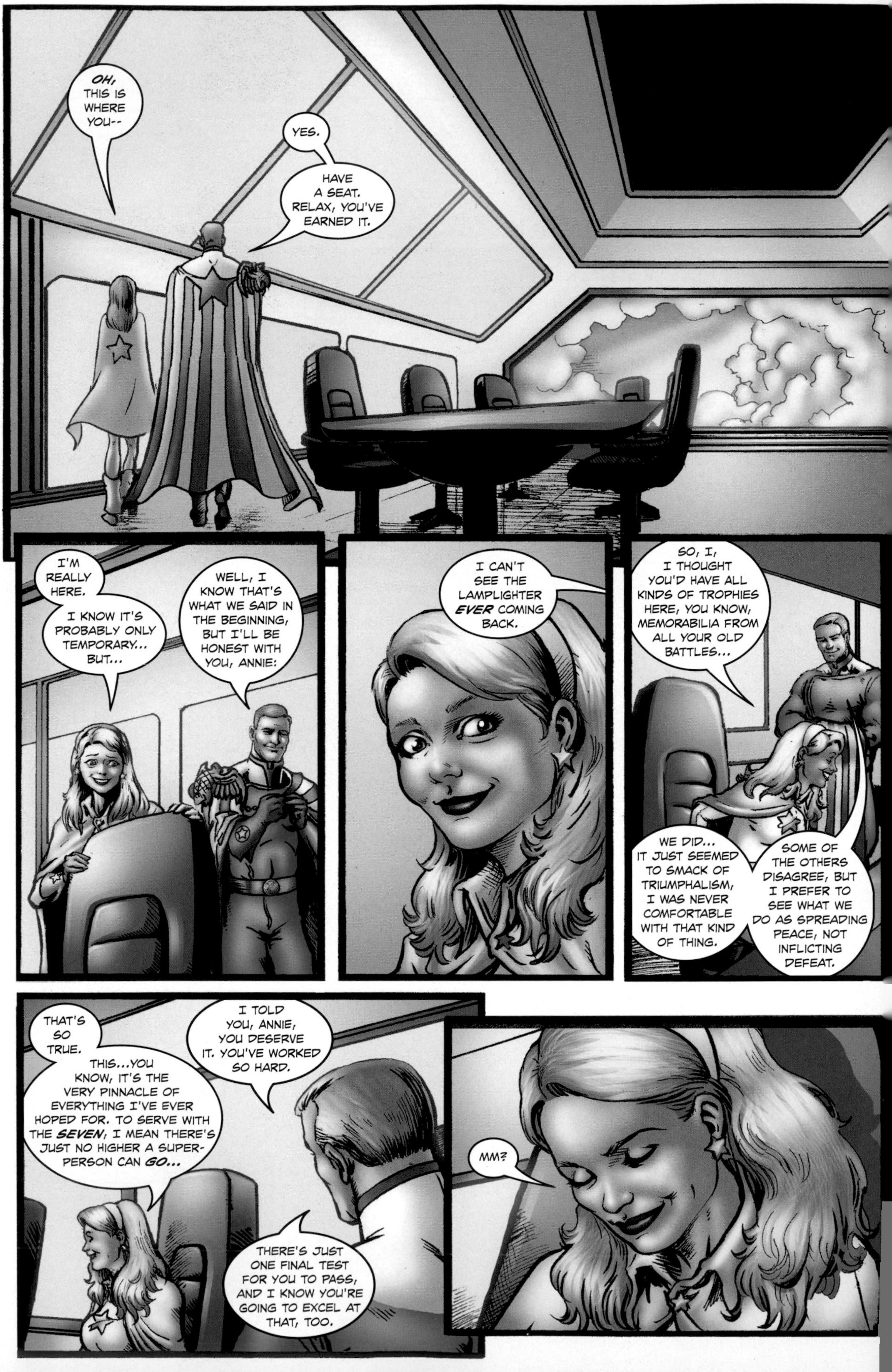
OH, THIS IS WHERE YOU--
YES.
HAVE A SEAT. RELAX, YOU'VE EARNED IT.
I'M REALLY HERE.
I KNOW IT'S PROBABLY ONLY TEMPORARY... BUT...
WELL, I KNOW THAT'S WHAT WE SAID IN THE BEGINNING, BUT I'LL BE HONEST WITH YOU, ANNIE:
I CAN'T SEE THE LAMPLIGHTER EVER COMING BACK.
SO, I, I THOUGHT YOU'D HAVE ALL KINDS OF TROPHIES HERE, YOU KNOW, MEMORABILIA FROM ALL YOUR OLD BATTLES...
WE DID... IT JUST SEEMED TO SMACK OF TRIUMPHALISM, I WAS NEVER COMFORTABLE WITH THAT KIND OF THING.
SOME OF THE OTHERS DISAGREE, BUT I PREFER TO SEE WHAT WE DO AS SPREADING PEACE, NOT INFLICTING DEFEAT.
THAT'S SO TRUE.
THIS...YOU KNOW, IT'S THE VERY PINNACLE OF EVERYTHING I'VE EVER HOPED FOR. TO SERVE WITH THE SEVEN, I MEAN THERE'S JUST NO HIGHER A SUPER-PERSON CAN GO...
I TOLD YOU, ANNIE, YOU DESERVE IT. YOU'VE WORKED SO HARD.
THERE'S JUST ONE FINAL TEST FOR YOU TO PASS, AND I KNOW YOU'RE GOING TO EXCEL AT THAT, TOO.
MM?

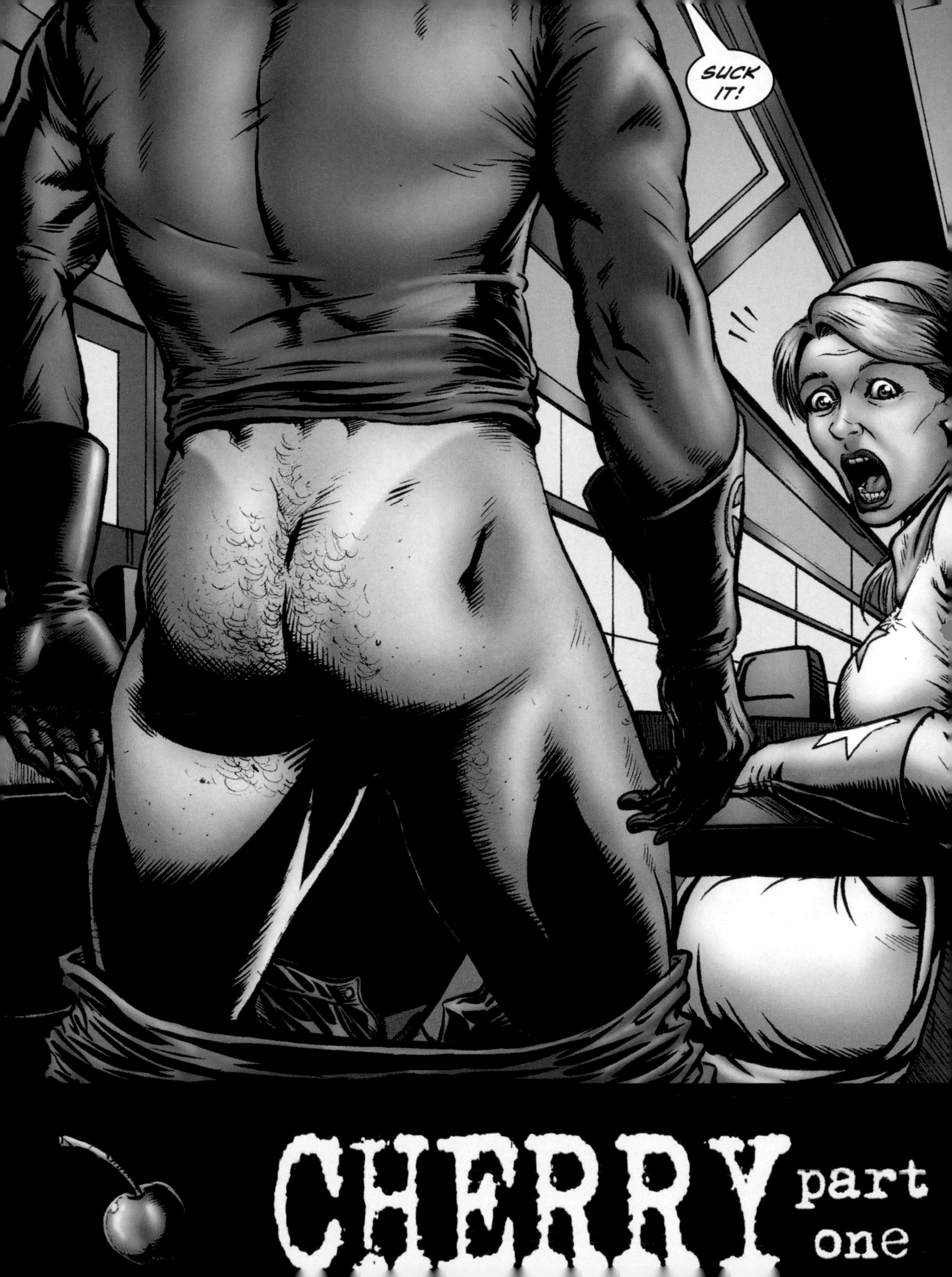
SUCK IT!

CHERRY part one

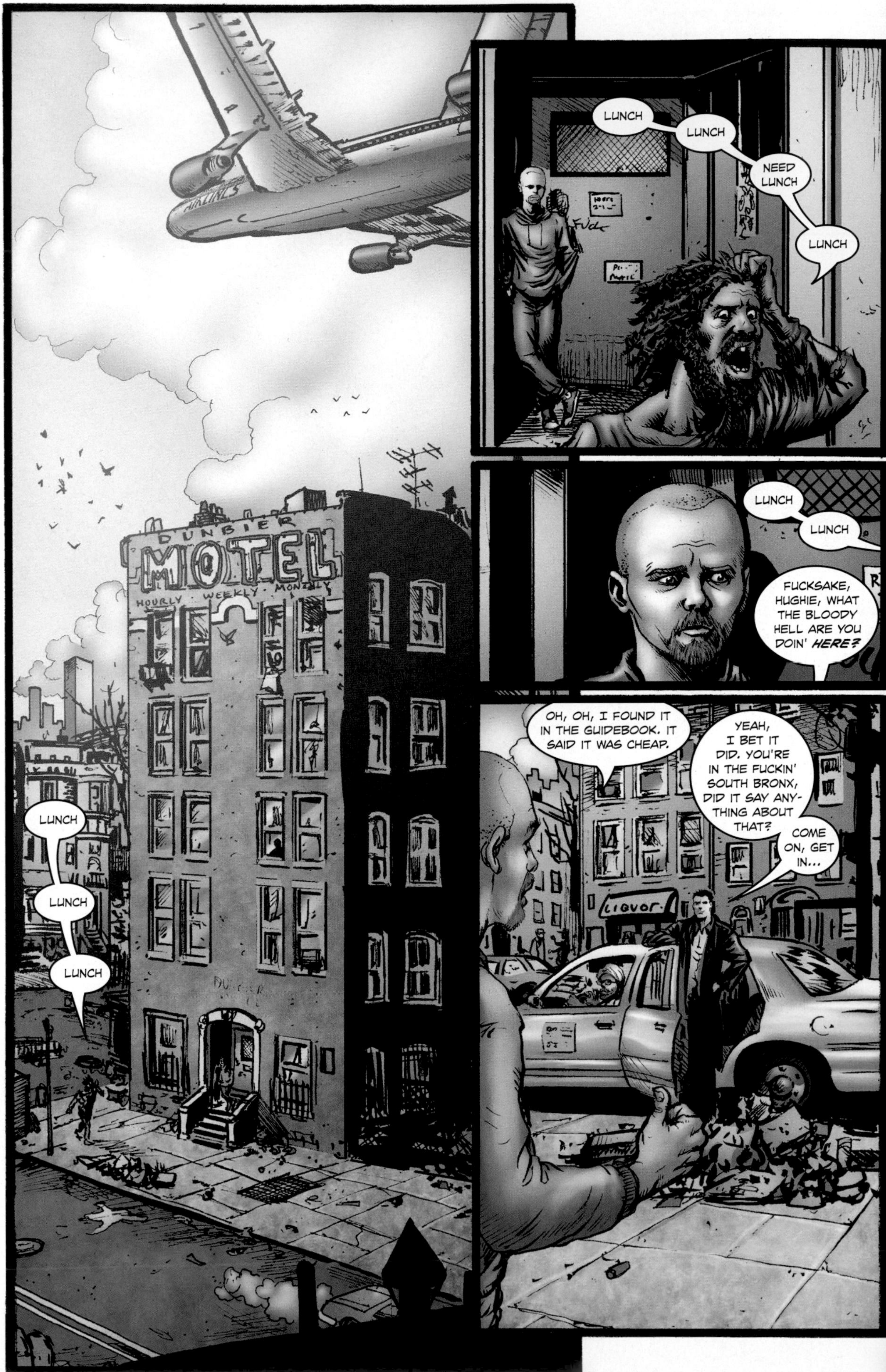
DUNBIER
MOTEL
HOURLY WEEKLY MONTHLY
LUNCH
LUNCH
LUNCH
LUNCH
LUNCH
NEED LUNCH
LUNCH
LUNCH
LUNCH
FUCKSAKE, HUGHIE, WHAT THE BLOODY HELL ARE YOU DOIN' *HERE?*
OH, OH, I FOUND IT IN THE GUIDEBOOK. IT SAID IT WAS CHEAP.
YEAH, I BET IT DID. YOU'RE IN THE FUCKIN' SOUTH BRONX, DID IT SAY ANY-THING ABOUT THAT?
COME ON, GET IN...
LIQUOR

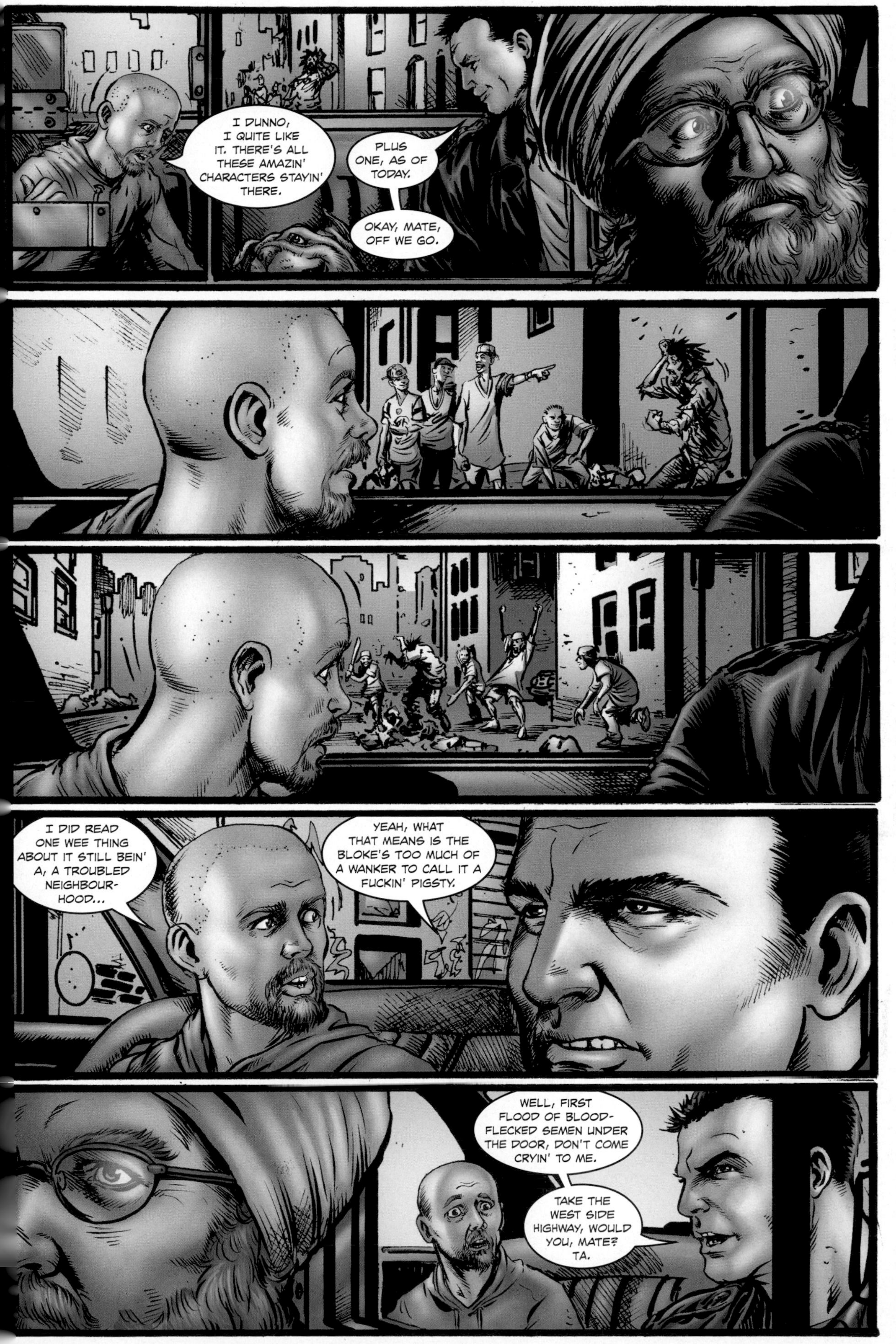
I DUNNO, I QUITE LIKE IT. THERE'S ALL THESE AMAZIN' CHARACTERS STAYIN' THERE.
PLUS ONE, AS OF TODAY.
OKAY, MATE, OFF WE GO.
I DID READ ONE WEE THING ABOUT IT STILL BEIN' A, A TROUBLED NEIGHBOURHOOD...
YEAH, WHAT THAT MEANS IS THE BLOKE'S TOO MUCH OF A WANKER TO CALL IT A FUCKIN' PIGSTY.
WELL, FIRST FLOOD OF BLOOD-FLECKED SEMEN UNDER THE DOOR, DON'T COME CRYIN' TO ME.
TAKE THE WEST SIDE HIGHWAY, WOULD YOU, MATE? TA.

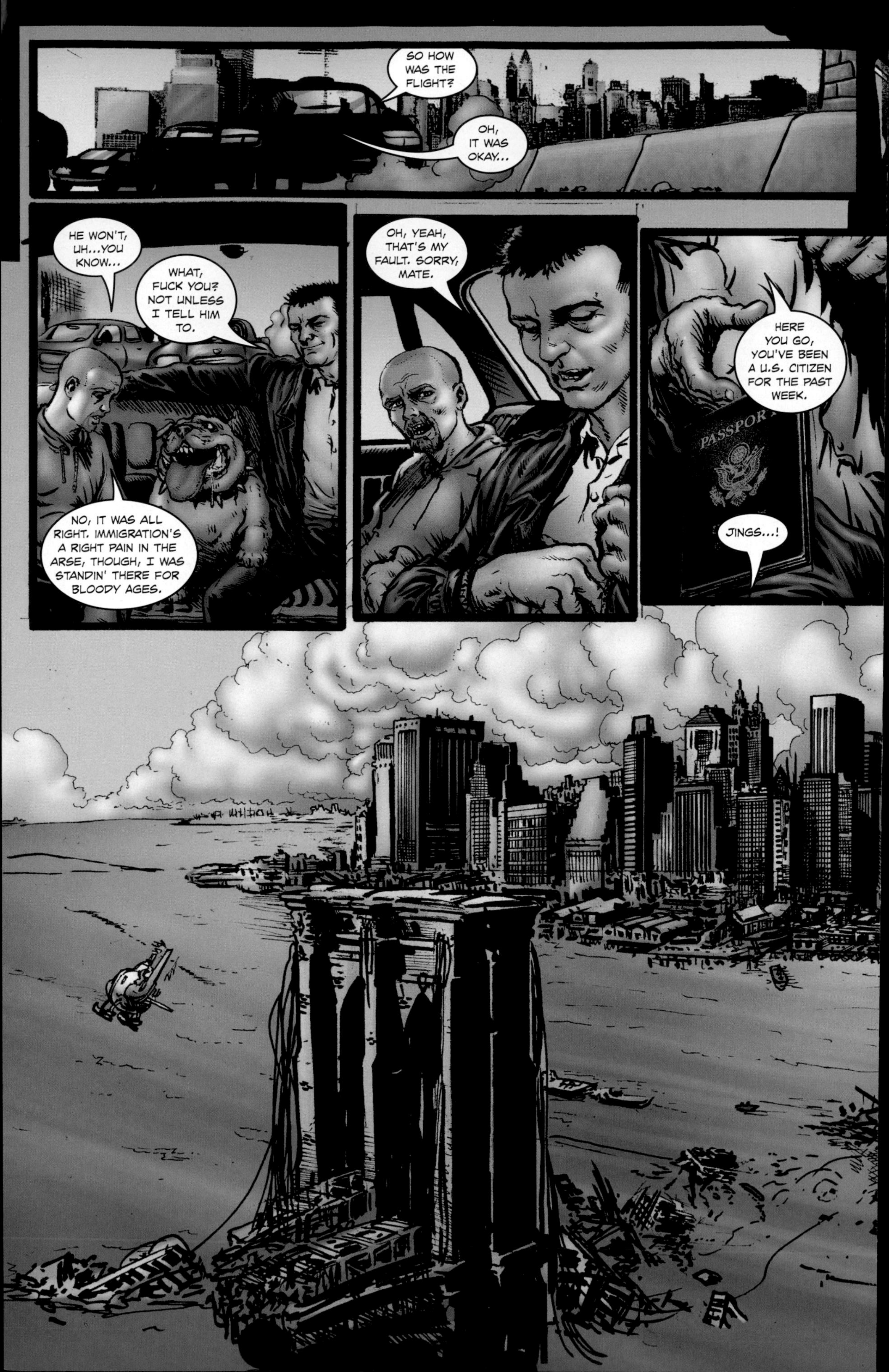
SO HOW WAS THE FLIGHT?
OH, IT WAS OKAY...
HE WON'T, UH...YOU KNOW...
WHAT, FUCK YOU? NOT UNLESS I TELL HIM TO.
NO, IT WAS ALL RIGHT. IMMIGRATION'S A RIGHT PAIN IN THE ARSE, THOUGH, I WAS STANDIN' THERE FOR BLOODY AGES.
OH, YEAH, THAT'S MY FAULT. SORRY, MATE.
HERE YOU GO, YOU'VE BEEN A U.S. CITIZEN FOR THE PAST WEEK.
JINGS...!

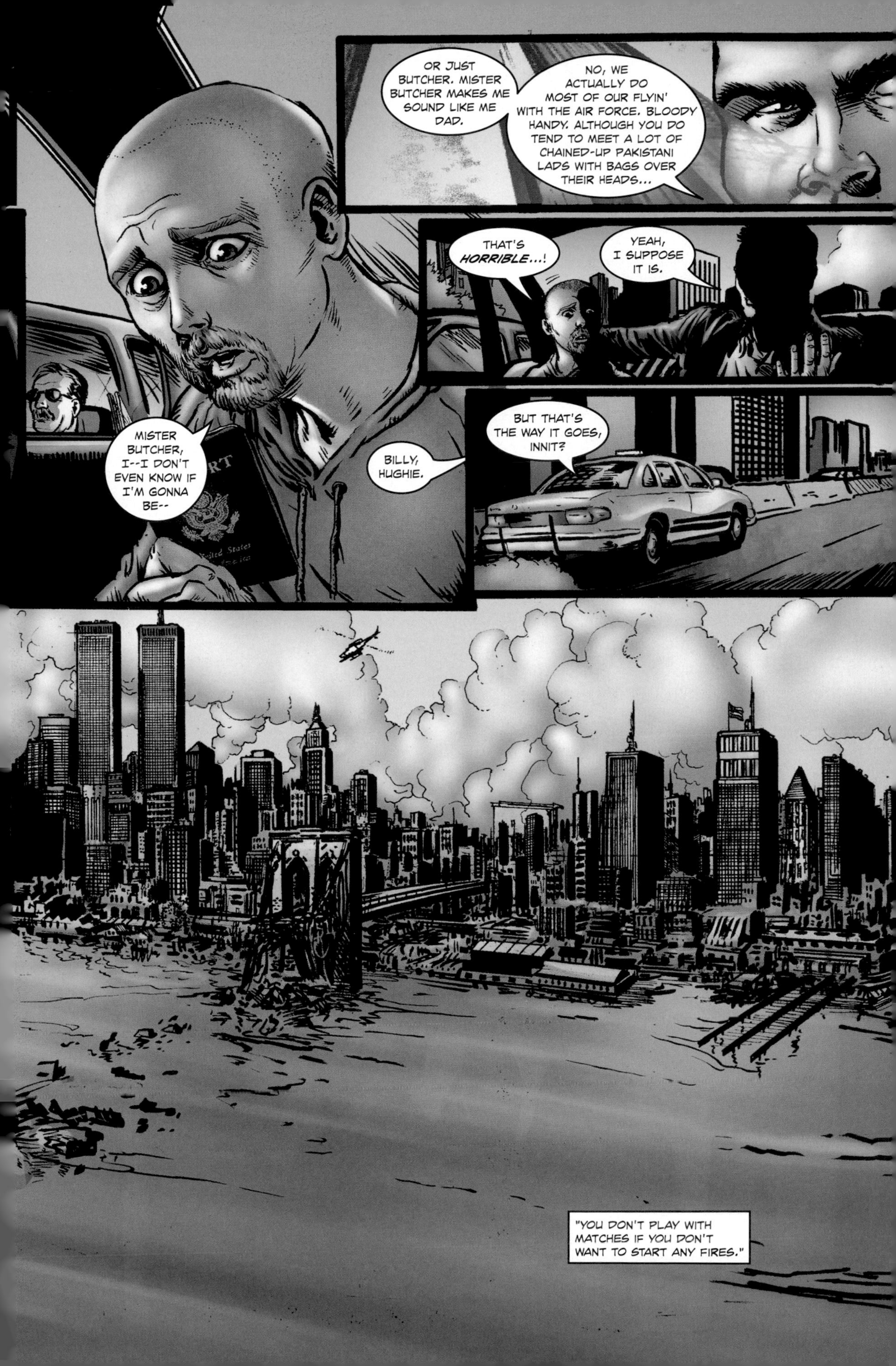
OR JUST BUTCHER. MISTER BUTCHER MAKES ME SOUND LIKE ME DAD.
NO, WE ACTUALLY DO MOST OF OUR FLYIN' WITH THE AIR FORCE. BLOODY HANDY. ALTHOUGH YOU DO TEND TO MEET A LOT OF CHAINED-UP PAKISTANI LADS WITH BAGS OVER THEIR HEADS...
THAT'S *HORRIBLE*...!
YEAH, I SUPPOSE IT IS.
MISTER BUTCHER, I--I DON'T EVEN KNOW IF I'M GONNA BE--
BILLY, HUGHIE.
BUT THAT'S THE WAY IT GOES, INNIT?
"YOU DON'T PLAY WITH MATCHES IF YOU DON'T WANT TO START ANY FIRES."

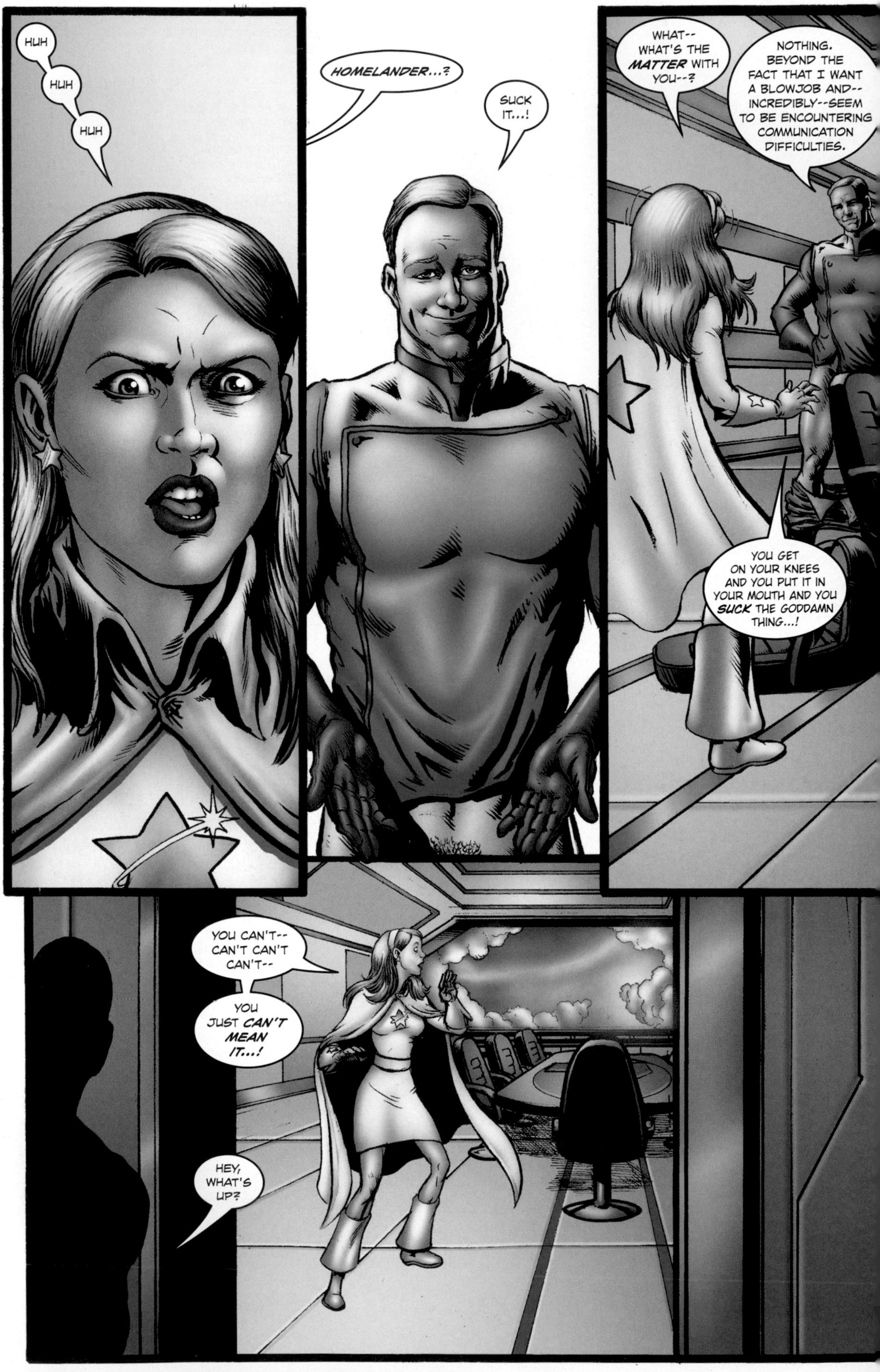
HUH
HUH
HUH
HOMELANDER...?
SUCK IT...!
WHAT-- WHAT'S THE MATTER WITH YOU--?
NOTHING. BEYOND THE FACT THAT I WANT A BLOWJOB AND-- INCREDIBLY--SEEM TO BE ENCOUNTERING COMMUNICATION DIFFICULTIES.
YOU GET ON YOUR KNEES AND YOU PUT IT IN YOUR MOUTH AND YOU SUCK THE GODDAMN THING...!
YOU CAN'T-- CAN'T CAN'T CAN'T--
YOU JUST CAN'T MEAN IT...!
HEY, WHAT'S UP?

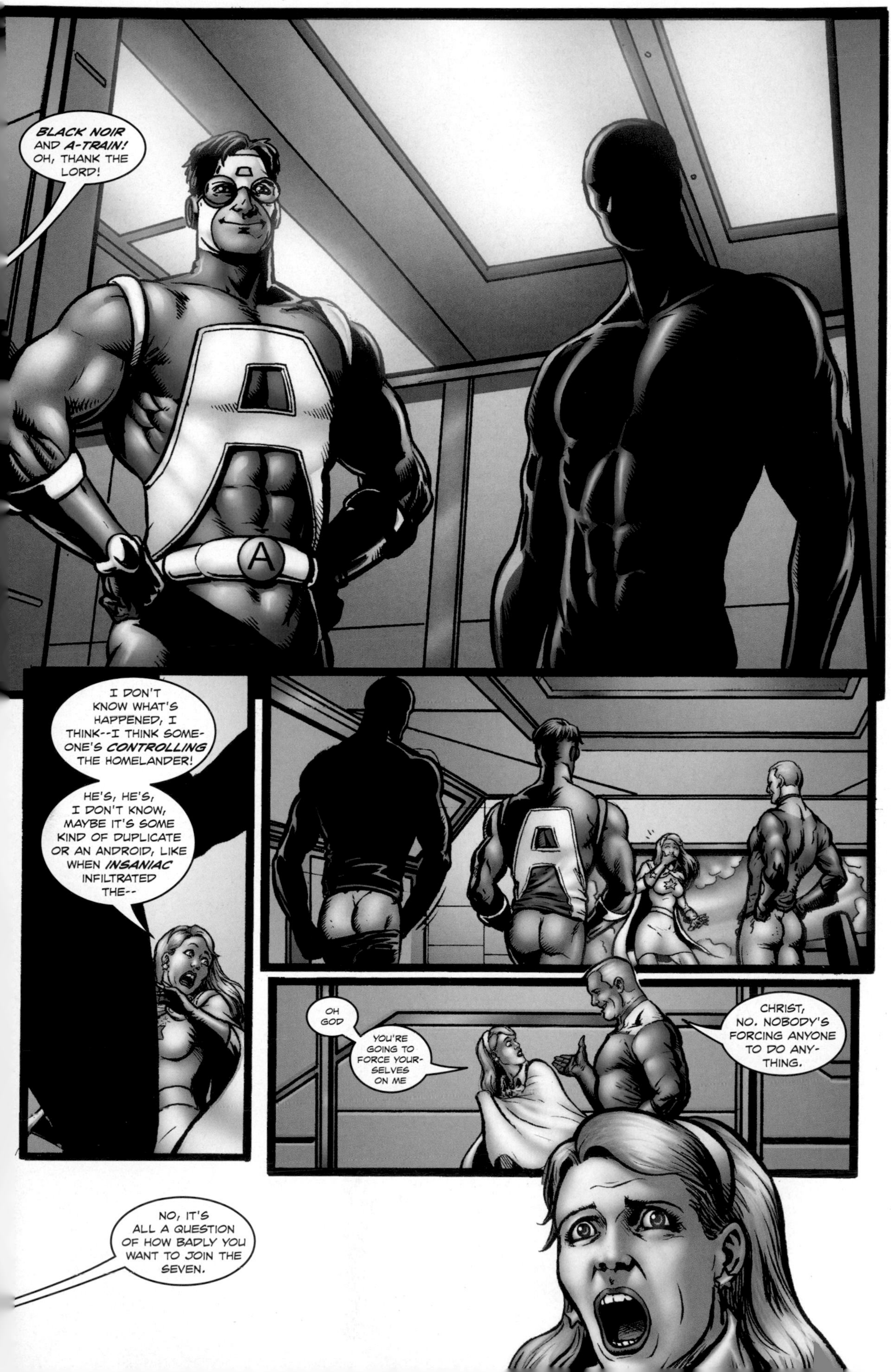
BLACK NOIR AND A-TRAIN! OH, THANK THE LORD!
I DON'T KNOW WHAT'S HAPPENED, I THINK--I THINK SOME-ONE'S CONTROLLING THE HOMELANDER!
HE'S, HE'S, I DON'T KNOW, MAYBE IT'S SOME KIND OF DUPLICATE OR AN ANDROID, LIKE WHEN INSANIAC INFILTRATED THE--
OH GOD
YOU'RE GOING TO FORCE YOUR-SELVES ON ME
CHRIST, NO. NOBODY'S FORCING ANYONE TO DO ANY-THING.
NO, IT'S ALL A QUESTION OF HOW BADLY YOU WANT TO JOIN THE SEVEN.

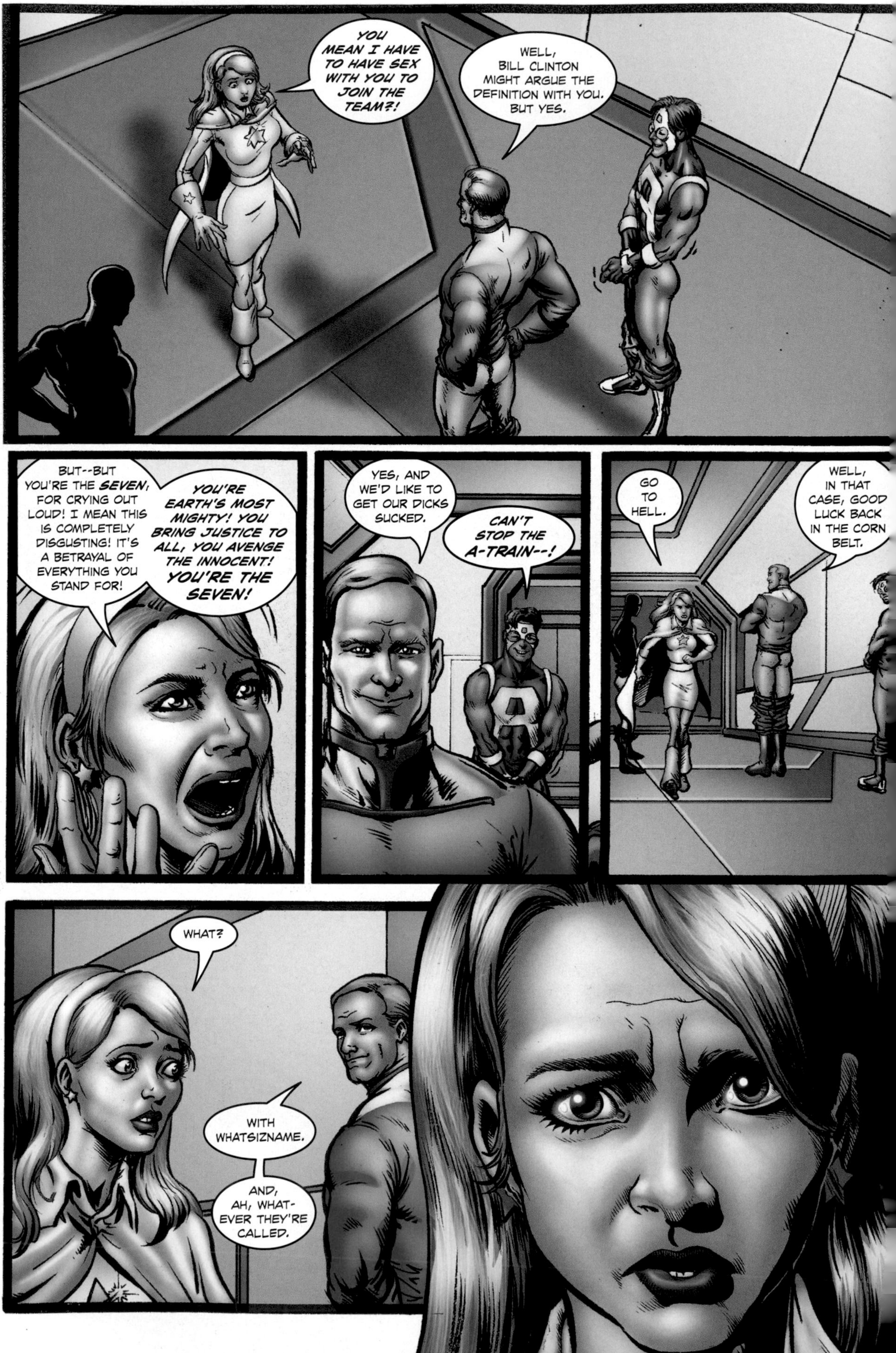
YOU MEAN I HAVE TO HAVE SEX WITH YOU TO JOIN THE TEAM?!
WELL, BILL CLINTON MIGHT ARGUE THE DEFINITION WITH YOU. BUT YES.
BUT--BUT YOU'RE THE SEVEN, FOR CRYING OUT LOUD! I MEAN THIS IS COMPLETELY DISGUSTING! IT'S A BETRAYAL OF EVERYTHING YOU STAND FOR!
YOU'RE EARTH'S MOST MIGHTY! YOU BRING JUSTICE TO ALL, YOU AVENGE THE INNOCENT! YOU'RE THE SEVEN!
YES, AND WE'D LIKE TO GET OUR DICKS SUCKED.
CAN'T STOP THE A-TRAIN--!
GO TO HELL.
WELL, IN THAT CASE, GOOD LUCK BACK IN THE CORN BELT.
WHAT?
WITH WHATSIZNAME.
AND, AH, WHAT-EVER THEY'RE CALLED.

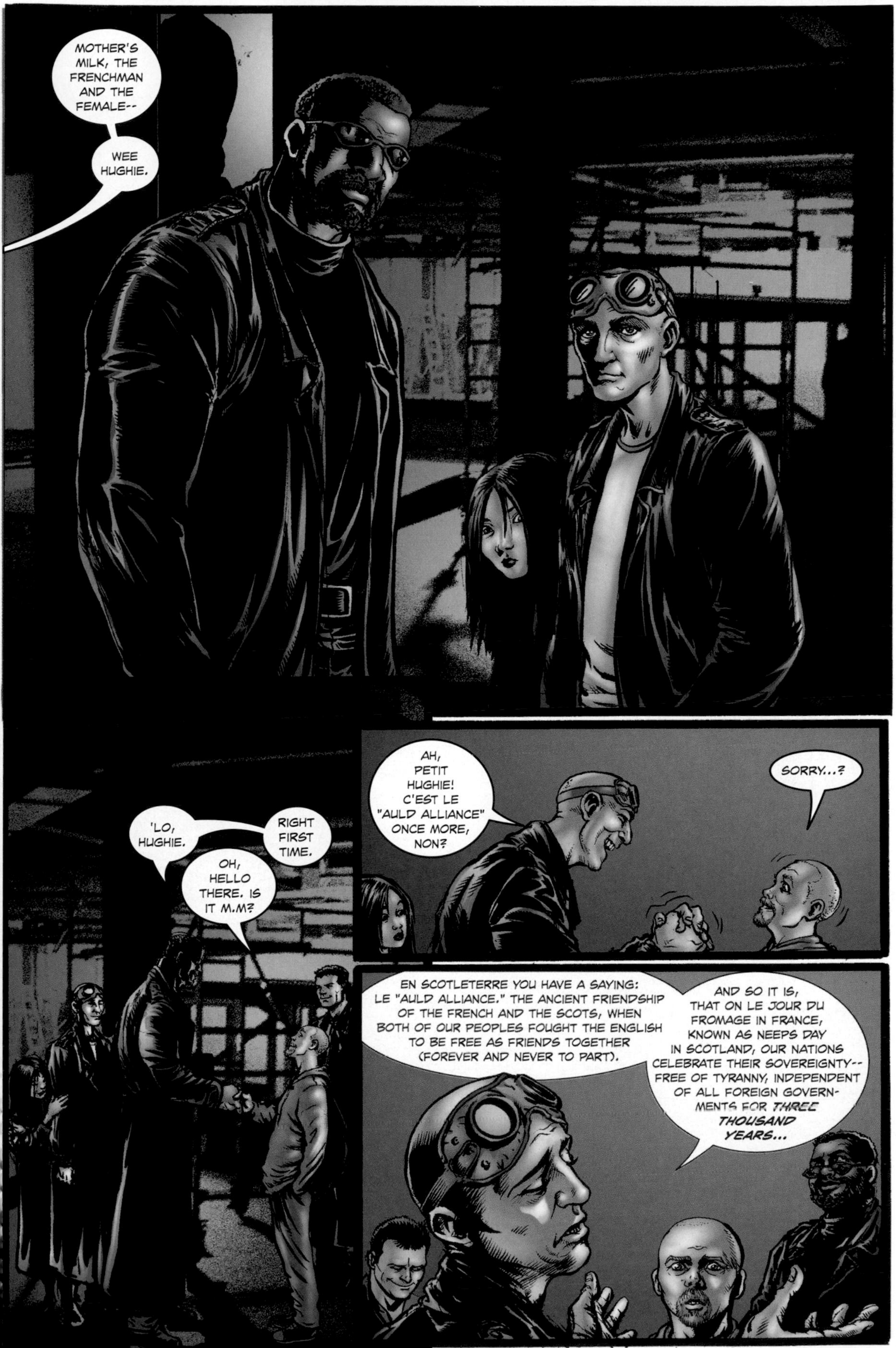
MOTHER'S MILK, THE FRENCHMAN AND THE FEMALE--
WEE HUGHIE.
'LO, HUGHIE.
RIGHT FIRST TIME.
OH, HELLO THERE. IS IT M.M?
AH, PETIT HUGHIE! C'EST LE "AULD ALLIANCE" ONCE MORE, NON?
SORRY...?
EN SCOTLETERRE YOU HAVE A SAYING: LE "AULD ALLIANCE." THE ANCIENT FRIENDSHIP OF THE FRENCH AND THE SCOTS, WHEN BOTH OF OUR PEOPLES FOUGHT THE ENGLISH TO BE FREE AS FRIENDS TOGETHER (FOREVER AND NEVER TO PART).
AND SO IT IS, THAT ON LE JOUR DU FROMAGE IN FRANCE, KNOWN AS NEEPS DAY IN SCOTLAND, OUR NATIONS CELEBRATE THEIR SOVEREIGNTY-- FREE OF TYRANNY, INDEPENDENT OF ALL FOREIGN GOVERN-MENTS FOR THREE THOUSAND YEARS...

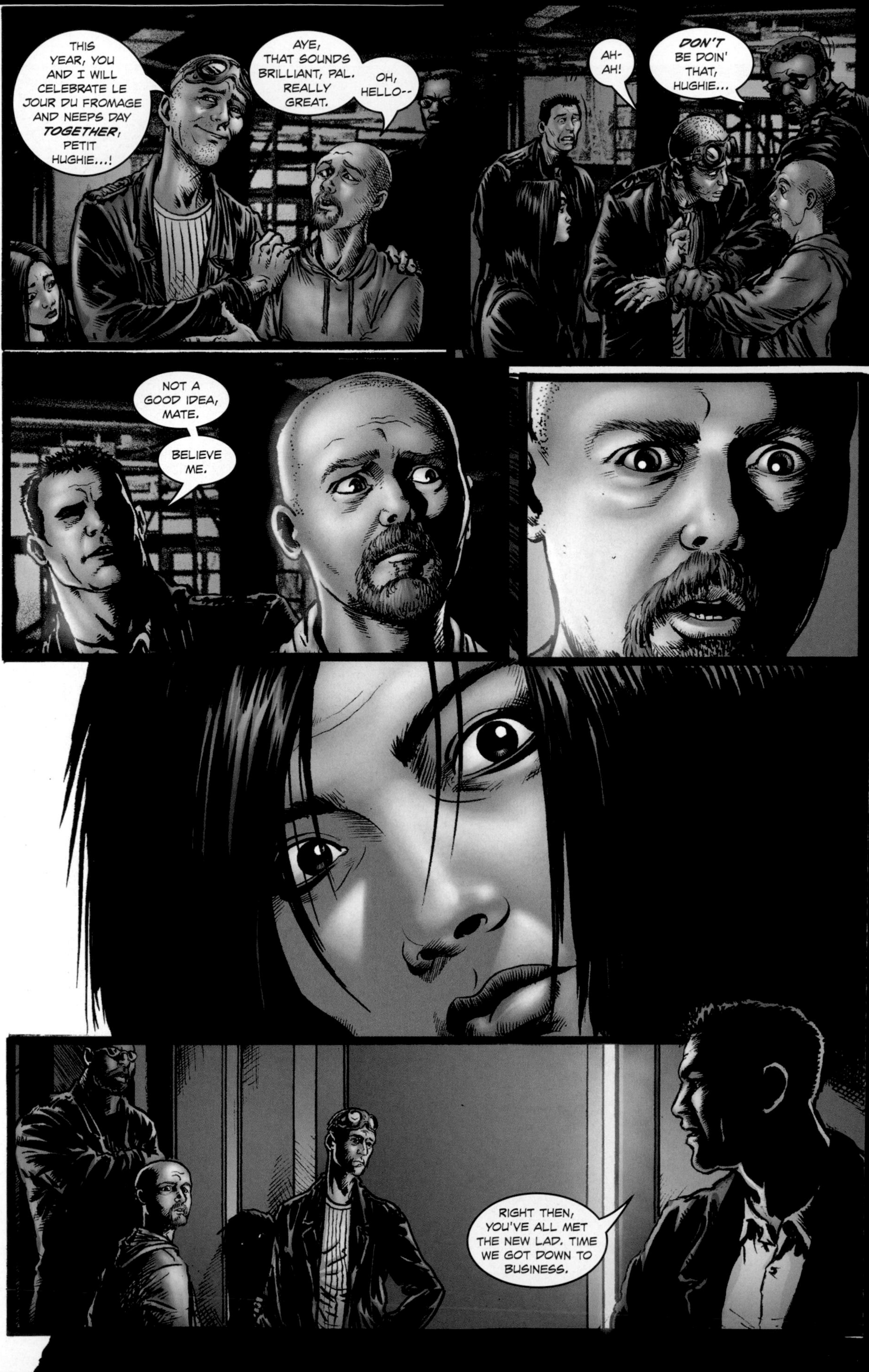

THIS YEAR, YOU AND I WILL CELEBRATE LE JOUR DU FROMAGE AND NEEPS DAY TOGETHER, PETIT HUGHIE...!
AYE, THAT SOUNDS BRILLIANT, PAL. REALLY GREAT.
OH, HELLO--
AH-AH!
DON'T BE DOIN' THAT, HUGHIE...
NOT A GOOD IDEA, MATE.
BELIEVE ME.
RIGHT THEN, YOU'VE ALL MET THE NEW LAD. TIME WE GOT DOWN TO BUSINESS.

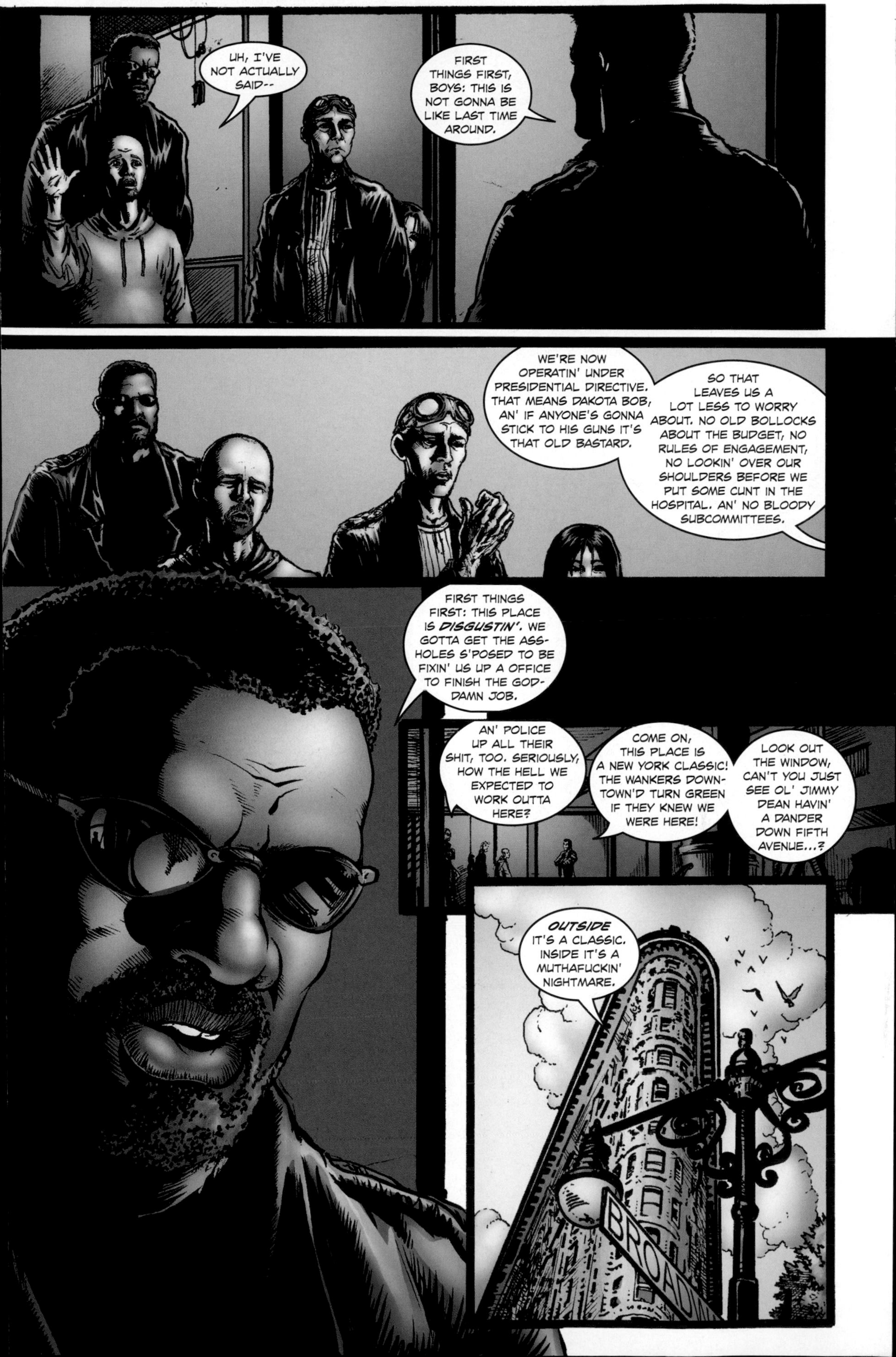
UH, I'VE NOT ACTUALLY SAID--
FIRST THINGS FIRST, BOYS: THIS IS NOT GONNA BE LIKE LAST TIME AROUND.
WE'RE NOW OPERATIN' UNDER PRESIDENTIAL DIRECTIVE. THAT MEANS DAKOTA BOB, AN' IF ANYONE'S GONNA STICK TO HIS GUNS IT'S THAT OLD BASTARD.
SO THAT LEAVES US A LOT LESS TO WORRY ABOUT. NO OLD BOLLOCKS ABOUT THE BUDGET, NO RULES OF ENGAGEMENT, NO LOOKIN' OVER OUR SHOULDERS BEFORE WE PUT SOME CUNT IN THE HOSPITAL. AN' NO BLOODY SUBCOMMITTEES.
FIRST THINGS FIRST: THIS PLACE IS *DISGUSTIN'*. WE GOTTA GET THE ASS-HOLES S'POSED TO BE FIXIN' US UP A OFFICE TO FINISH THE GOD-DAMN JOB.
AN' POLICE UP ALL THEIR SHIT, TOO. SERIOUSLY, HOW THE HELL WE EXPECTED TO WORK OUTTA HERE?
COME ON, THIS PLACE IS A NEW YORK CLASSIC! THE WANKERS DOWN-TOWN'D TURN GREEN IF THEY KNEW WE WERE HERE!
LOOK OUT THE WINDOW, CAN'T YOU JUST SEE OL' JIMMY DEAN HAVIN' A DANDER DOWN FIFTH AVENUE...?
OUTSIDE IT'S A CLASSIC. INSIDE IT'S A MUTHAFUCKIN' NIGHTMARE.
BROADW

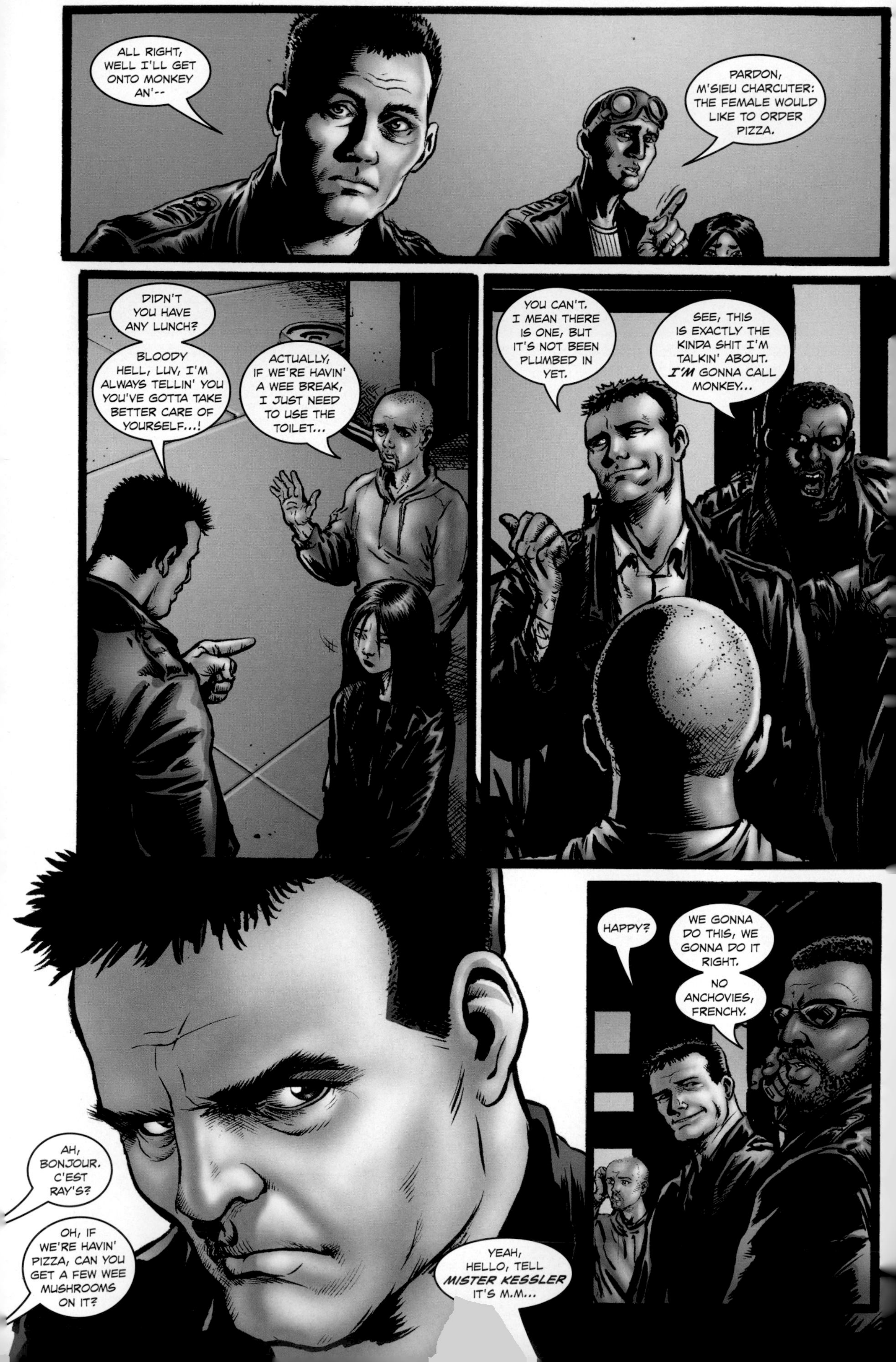
ALL RIGHT, WELL I'LL GET ONTO MONKEY AN'--
PARDON, M'SIEU CHARCUTER: THE FEMALE WOULD LIKE TO ORDER PIZZA.
DIDN'T YOU HAVE ANY LUNCH?
BLOODY HELL, LUV, I'M ALWAYS TELLIN' YOU YOU'VE GOTTA TAKE BETTER CARE OF YOURSELF...!
ACTUALLY, IF WE'RE HAVIN' A WEE BREAK, I JUST NEED TO USE THE TOILET...
YOU CAN'T. I MEAN THERE IS ONE, BUT IT'S NOT BEEN PLUMBED IN YET.
SEE, THIS IS EXACTLY THE KINDA SHIT I'M TALKIN' ABOUT. I'M GONNA CALL MONKEY...
AH, BONJOUR. C'EST RAY'S?
OH, IF WE'RE HAVIN' PIZZA, CAN YOU GET A FEW WEE MUSHROOMS ON IT?
YEAH, HELLO, TELL MISTER KESSLER IT'S M.M...
HAPPY?
WE GONNA DO THIS, WE GONNA DO IT RIGHT.
NO ANCHOVIES, FRENCHY.

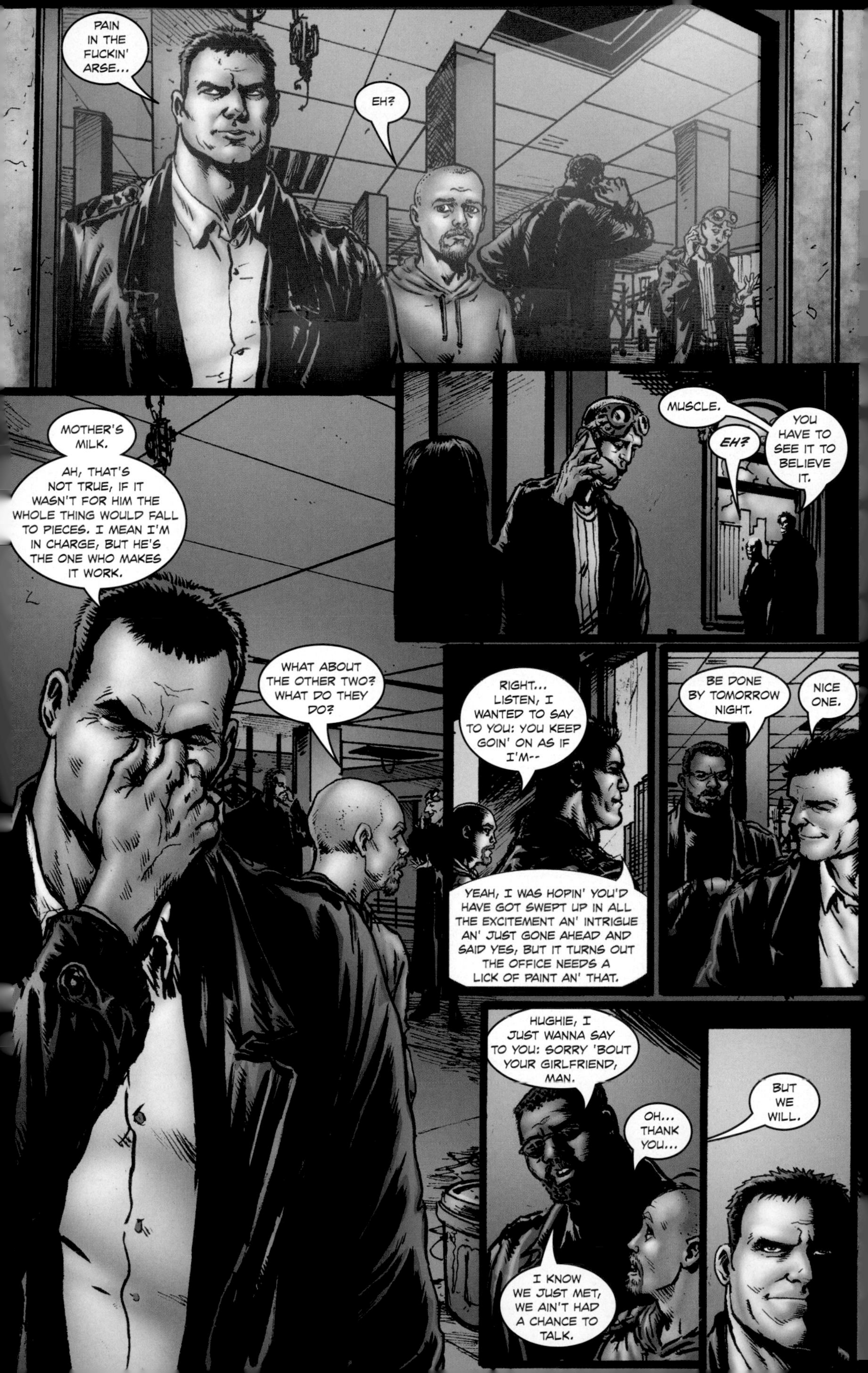
PAIN IN THE FUCKIN' ARSE...
EH?
MOTHER'S MILK.
AH, THAT'S NOT TRUE, IF IT WASN'T FOR HIM THE WHOLE THING WOULD FALL TO PIECES. I MEAN I'M IN CHARGE, BUT HE'S THE ONE WHO MAKES IT WORK.
MUSCLE.
EH?
YOU HAVE TO SEE IT TO BELIEVE IT.
WHAT ABOUT THE OTHER TWO? WHAT DO THEY DO?
RIGHT... LISTEN, I WANTED TO SAY TO YOU: YOU KEEP GOIN' ON AS IF I'M--
YEAH, I WAS HOPIN' YOU'D HAVE GOT SWEPT UP IN ALL THE EXCITEMENT AN' INTRIGUE AN' JUST GONE AHEAD AND SAID YES, BUT IT TURNS OUT THE OFFICE NEEDS A LICK OF PAINT AN' THAT.
BE DONE BY TOMORROW NIGHT.
NICE ONE.
HUGHIE, I JUST WANNA SAY TO YOU: SORRY 'BOUT YOUR GIRLFRIEND, MAN.
OH... THANK YOU...
I KNOW WE JUST MET, WE AIN'T HAD A CHANCE TO TALK.
BUT WE WILL.

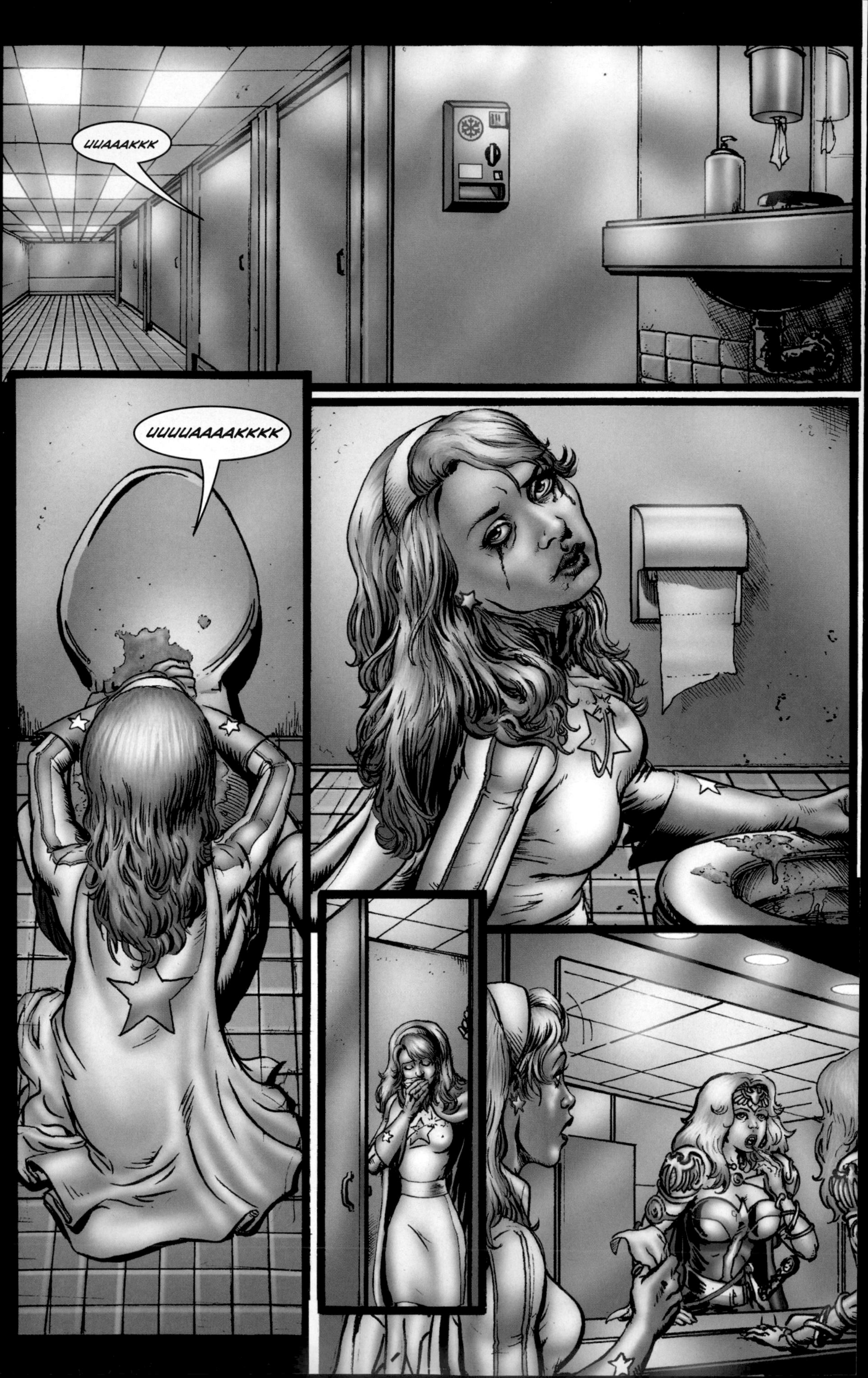
UUAAAKKK
UUUUAAAAKKKK

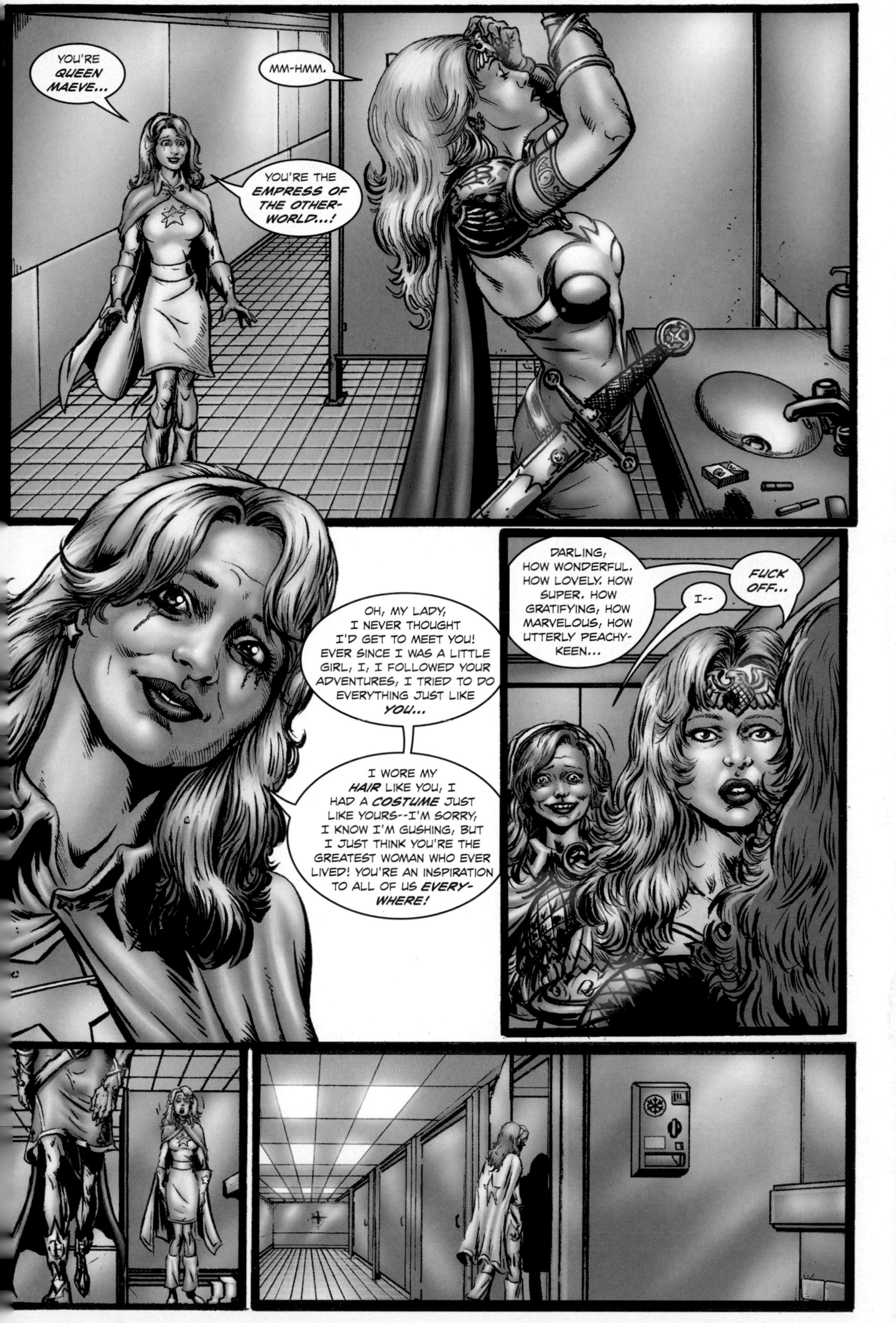
YOU'RE QUEEN MAEVE...
MM-HMM.
YOU'RE THE EMPRESS OF THE OTHER-WORLD...!
OH, MY LADY, I NEVER THOUGHT I'D GET TO MEET YOU! EVER SINCE I WAS A LITTLE GIRL, I, I FOLLOWED YOUR ADVENTURES, I TRIED TO DO EVERYTHING JUST LIKE YOU...
I WORE MY HAIR LIKE YOU, I HAD A COSTUME JUST LIKE YOURS--I'M SORRY, I KNOW I'M GUSHING, BUT I JUST THINK YOU'RE THE GREATEST WOMAN WHO EVER LIVED! YOU'RE AN INSPIRATION TO ALL OF US EVERY-WHERE!
DARLING, HOW WONDERFUL. HOW LOVELY. HOW SUPER. HOW GRATIFYING, HOW MARVELOUS, HOW UTTERLY PEACHY-KEEN...
I--
FUCK OFF...

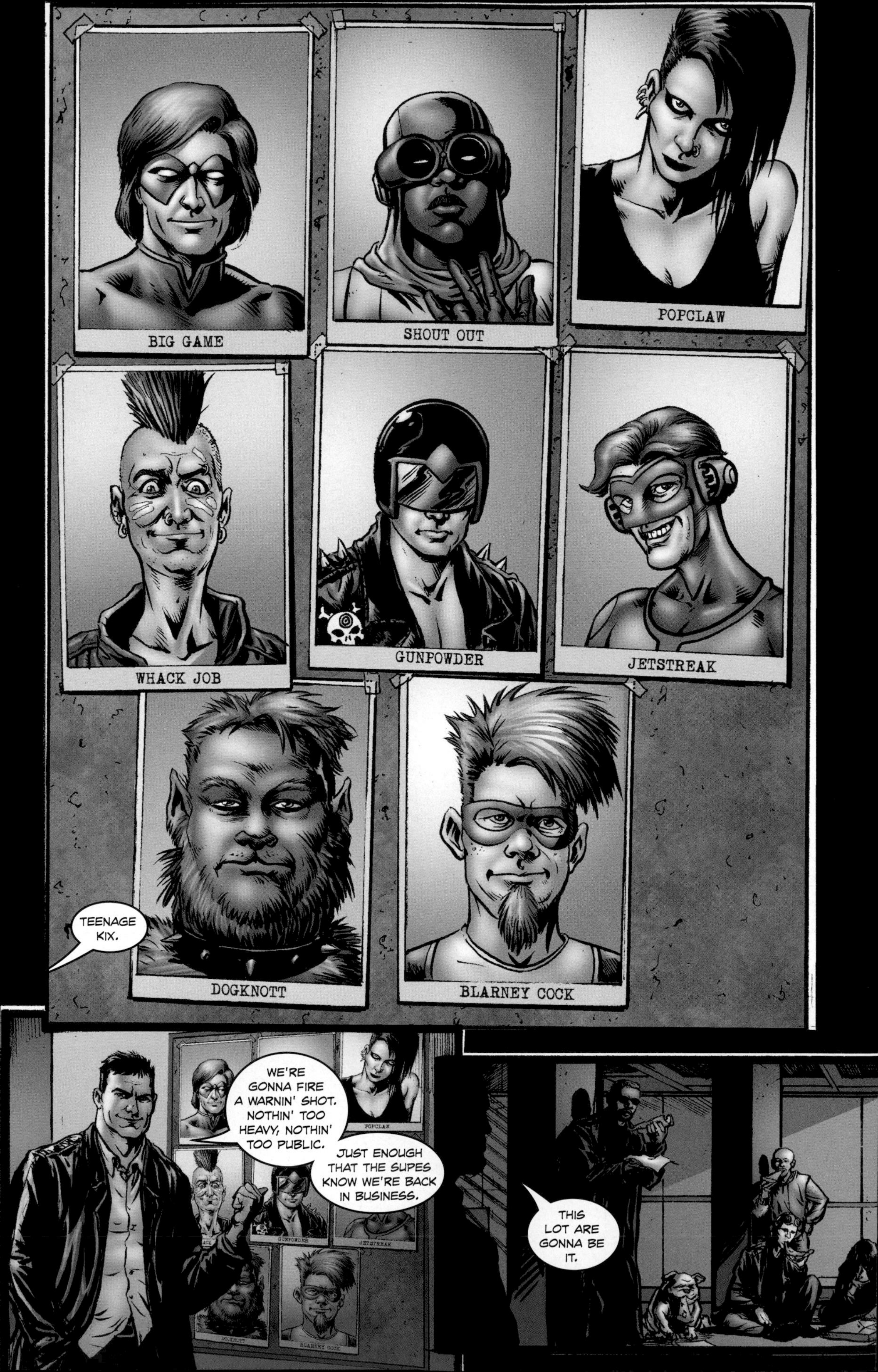
BIG GAME
SHOUT OUT
POPCLAW
WHACK JOB
GUNPOWDER
JETSTREAK
DOGKNOTT
BLARNEY COCK
TEENAGE KIX.
WE'RE GONNA FIRE A WARNIN' SHOT. NOTHIN' TOO HEAVY, NOTHIN' TOO PUBLIC.
JUST ENOUGH THAT THE SUPES KNOW WE'RE BACK IN BUSINESS.
THIS LOT ARE GONNA BE IT.

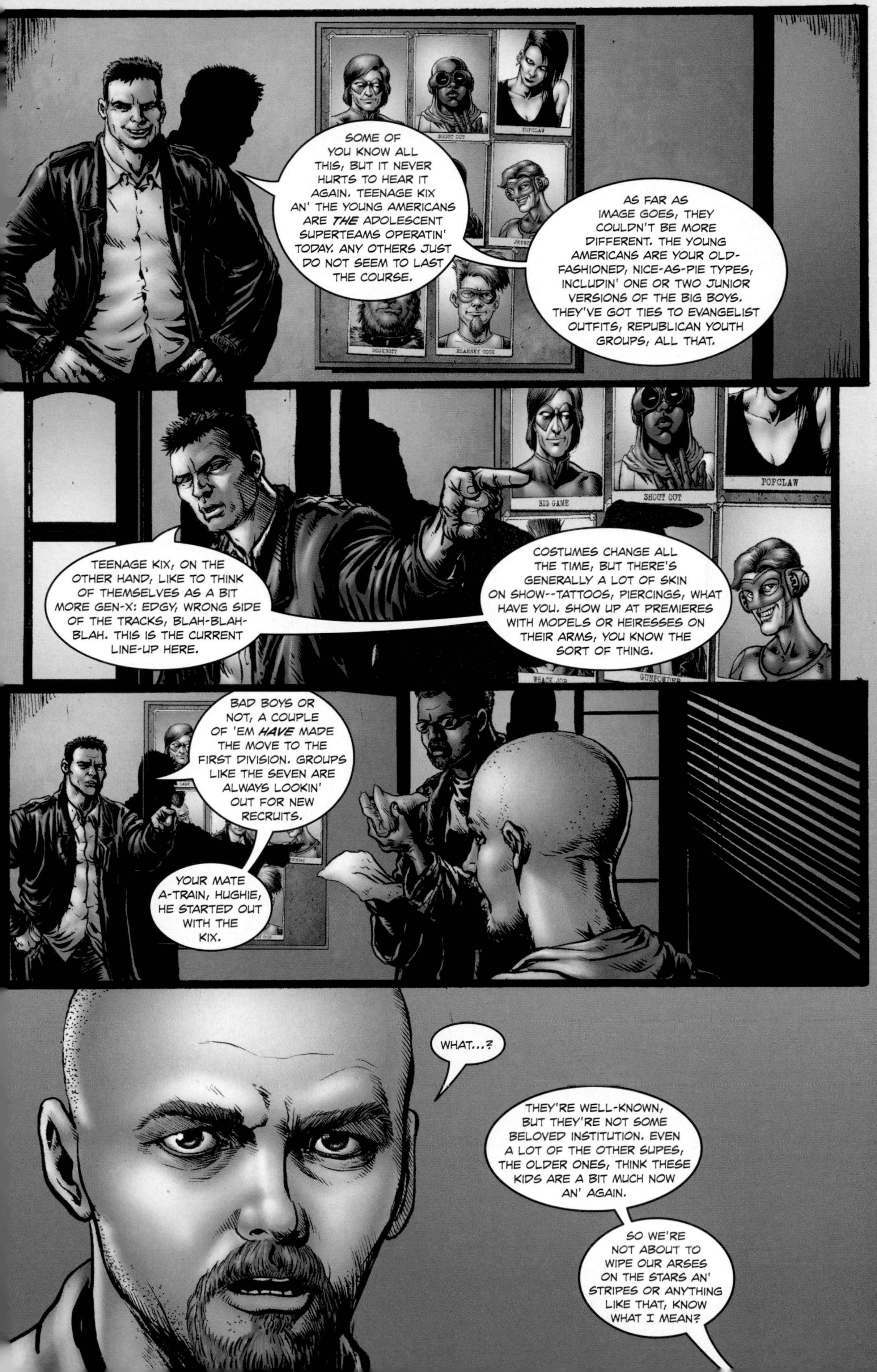
SHOUT OUT
POPCLAW
SOME OF YOU KNOW ALL THIS, BUT IT NEVER HURTS TO HEAR IT AGAIN. TEENAGE KIX AN' THE YOUNG AMERICANS ARE *THE* ADOLESCENT SUPERTEAMS OPERATIN' TODAY. ANY OTHERS JUST DO NOT SEEM TO LAST THE COURSE.
AS FAR AS IMAGE GOES, THEY COULDN'T BE MORE DIFFERENT. THE YOUNG AMERICANS ARE YOUR OLD-FASHIONED, NICE-AS-PIE TYPES, INCLUDIN' ONE OR TWO JUNIOR VERSIONS OF THE BIG BOYS. THEY'VE GOT TIES TO EVANGELIST OUTFITS, REPUBLICAN YOUTH GROUPS, ALL THAT.
DOGKNOTT
BLARNEY COCK
BIG GAME
SHOUT OUT
POPCLAW
TEENAGE KIX, ON THE OTHER HAND, LIKE TO THINK OF THEMSELVES AS A BIT MORE GEN-X: EDGY, WRONG SIDE OF THE TRACKS, BLAH-BLAH-BLAH. THIS IS THE CURRENT LINE-UP HERE.
COSTUMES CHANGE ALL THE TIME, BUT THERE'S GENERALLY A LOT OF SKIN ON SHOW--TATTOOS, PIERCINGS, WHAT HAVE YOU. SHOW UP AT PREMIERES WITH MODELS OR HEIRESSES ON THEIR ARMS, YOU KNOW THE SORT OF THING.
BAD BOYS OR NOT, A COUPLE OF 'EM *HAVE* MADE THE MOVE TO THE FIRST DIVISION. GROUPS LIKE THE SEVEN ARE ALWAYS LOOKIN' OUT FOR NEW RECRUITS.
YOUR MATE A-TRAIN, HUGHIE, HE STARTED OUT WITH THE KIX.
WHAT...?
THEY'RE WELL-KNOWN, BUT THEY'RE NOT SOME BELOVED INSTITUTION. EVEN A LOT OF THE OTHER SUPES, THE OLDER ONES, THINK THESE KIDS ARE A BIT MUCH NOW AN' AGAIN.
SO WE'RE NOT ABOUT TO WIPE OUR ARSES ON THE STARS AN' STRIPES OR ANYTHING LIKE THAT, KNOW WHAT I MEAN?

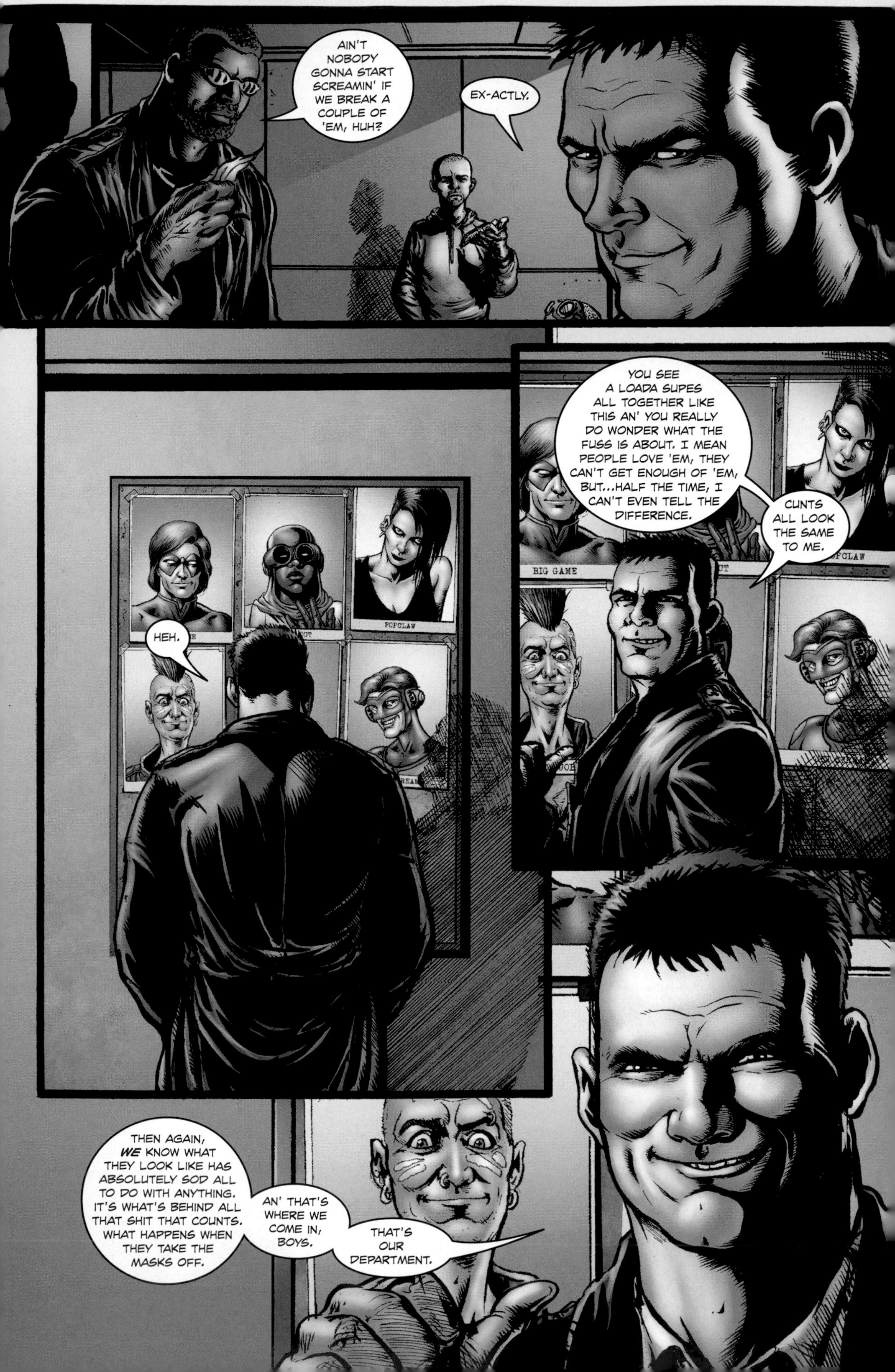

AIN'T NOBODY GONNA START SCREAMIN' IF WE BREAK A COUPLE OF 'EM, HUH?
EX-ACTLY.
POPCLAW
HEH.
YOU SEE A LOADA SUPES ALL TOGETHER LIKE THIS AN' YOU REALLY DO WONDER WHAT THE FUSS IS ABOUT. I MEAN PEOPLE LOVE 'EM, THEY CAN'T GET ENOUGH OF 'EM, BUT...HALF THE TIME, I CAN'T EVEN TELL THE DIFFERENCE.
CUNTS ALL LOOK THE SAME TO ME.
BIG GAME
THEN AGAIN, *WE* KNOW WHAT THEY LOOK LIKE HAS ABSOLUTELY SOD ALL TO DO WITH ANYTHING. IT'S WHAT'S BEHIND ALL THAT SHIT THAT COUNTS. WHAT HAPPENS WHEN THEY TAKE THE MASKS OFF.
AN' THAT'S WHERE WE COME IN, BOYS.
THAT'S OUR DEPARTMENT.

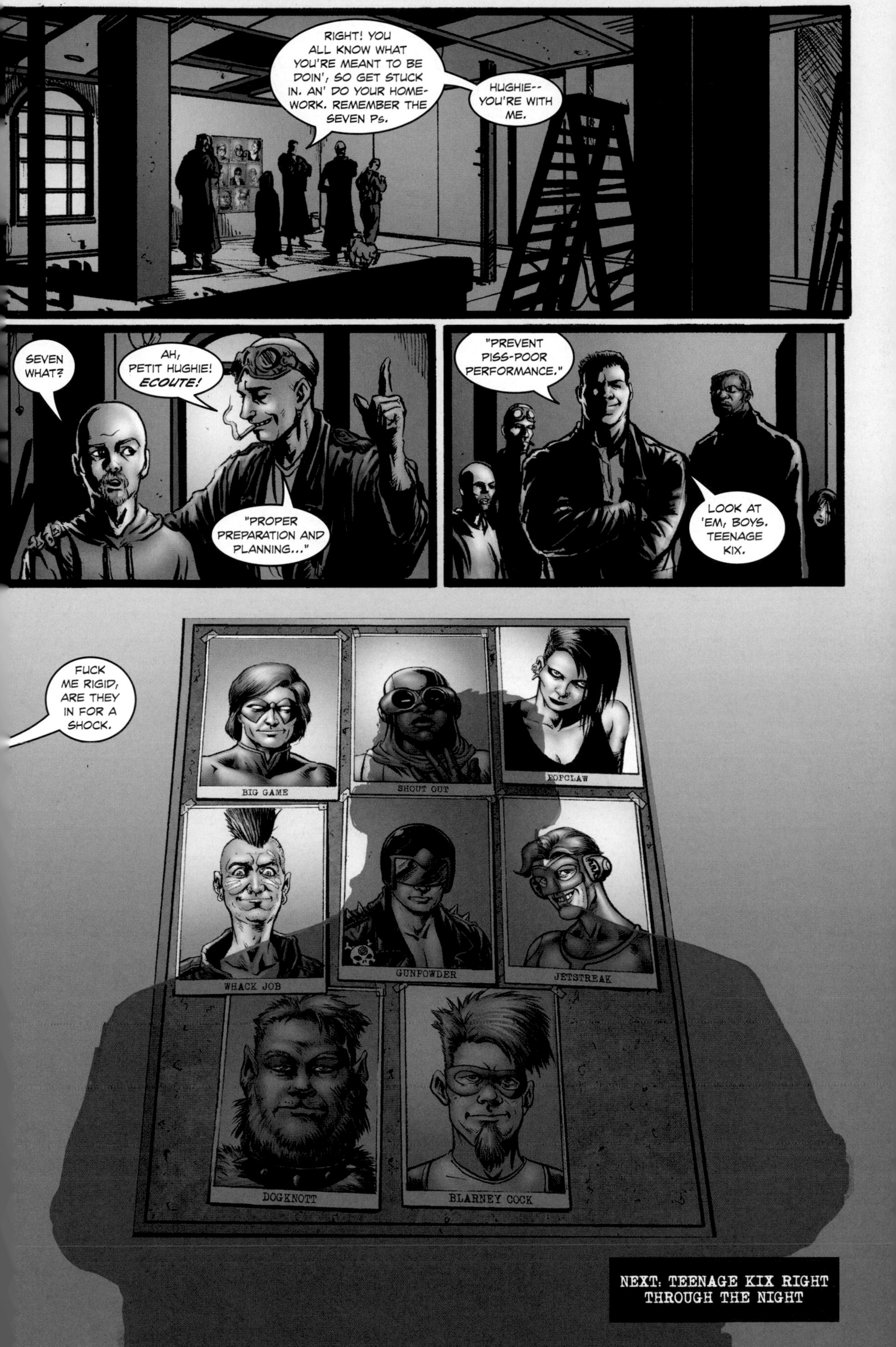
RIGHT! YOU ALL KNOW WHAT YOU'RE MEANT TO BE DOIN', SO GET STUCK IN. AN' DO YOUR HOME-WORK. REMEMBER THE SEVEN Ps.
HUGHIE-- YOU'RE WITH ME.
SEVEN WHAT?
AH, PETIT HUGHIE! *ECOUTE!*
"PROPER PREPARATION AND PLANNING..."
"PREVENT PISS-POOR PERFORMANCE."
LOOK AT 'EM, BOYS. TEENAGE KIX.
FUCK ME RIGID, ARE THEY IN FOR A SHOCK.
BIG GAME
SHOUT OUT
POPCLAW
WHACK JOB
GUNPOWDER
JETSTREAK
DOGKNOTT
BLARNEY COCK
NEXT: TEENAGE KIX RIGHT THROUGH THE NIGHT

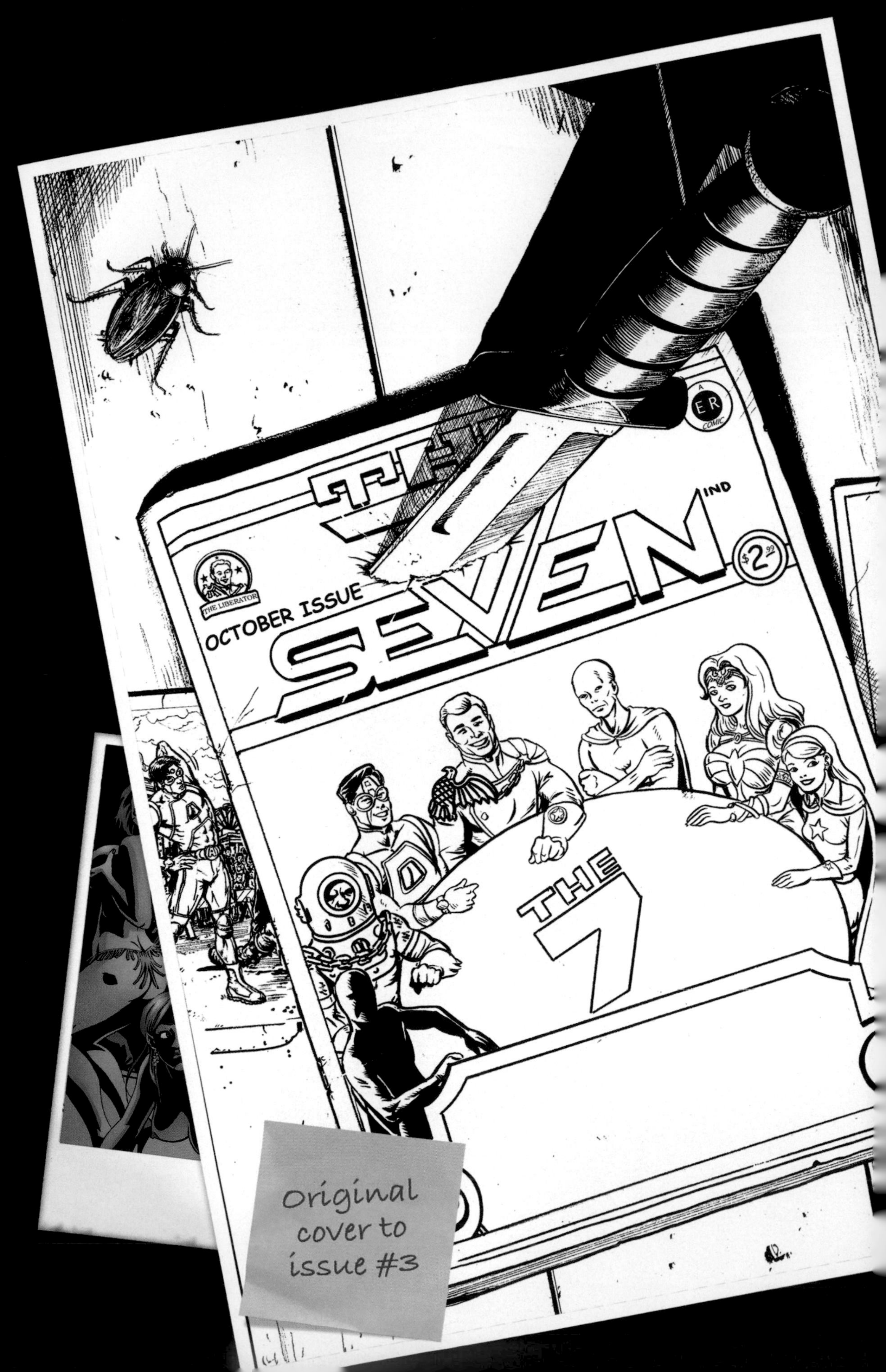
THE SEVEN
IND
$2.99
OCTOBER ISSUE
THE LIBERATOR
A ER COMIC
THE 7
original cover to issue #3

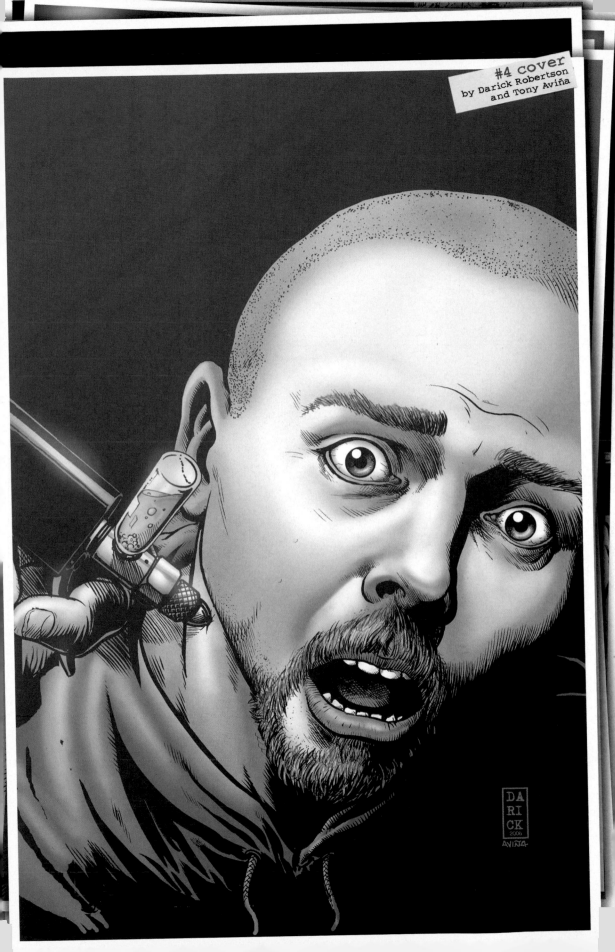

#4 COVER
by Darick Robertson
and Tony Aviña

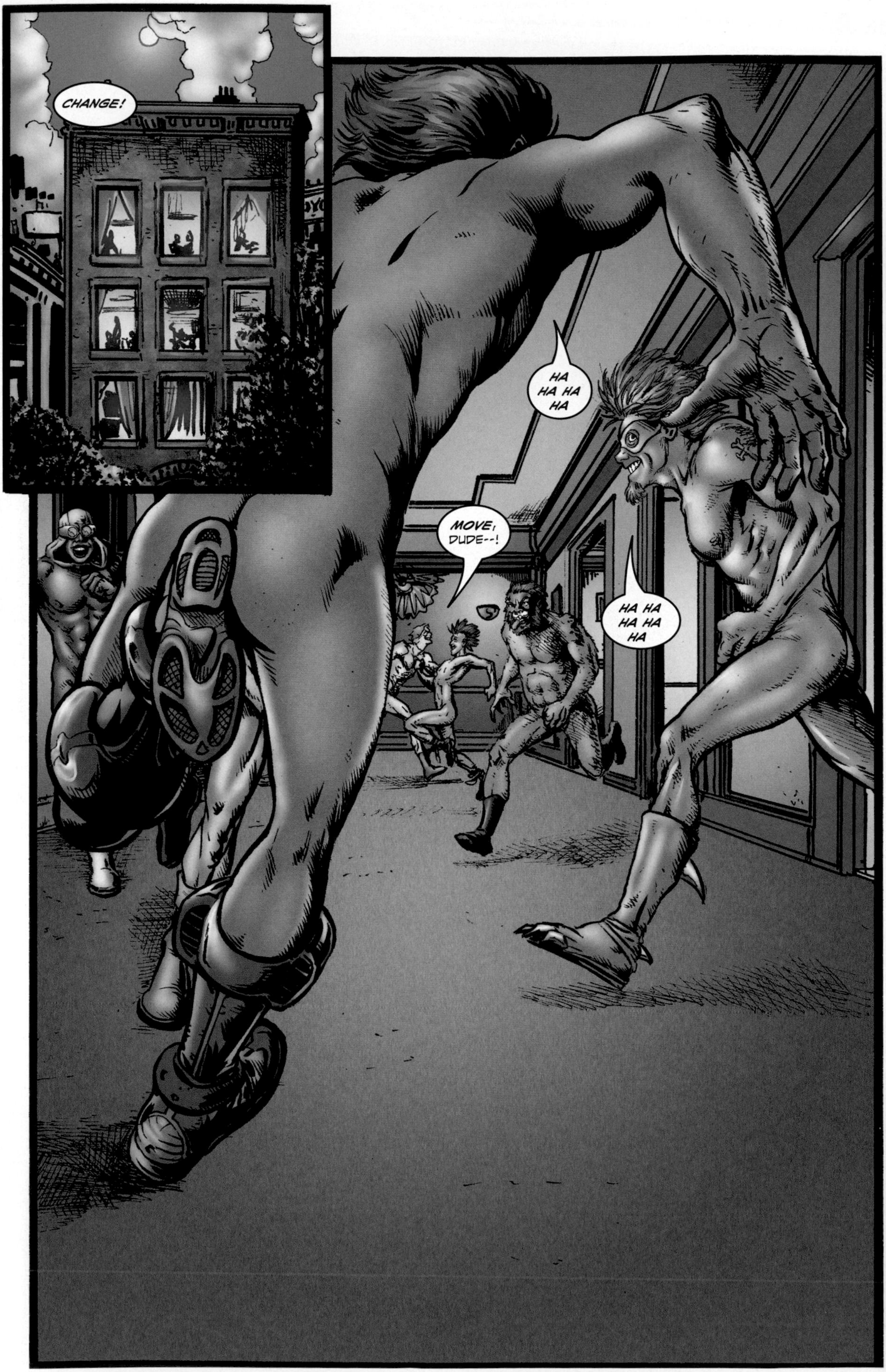
CHANGE!
HA HA HA HA
MOVE, DUDE--!
HA HA HA HA HA

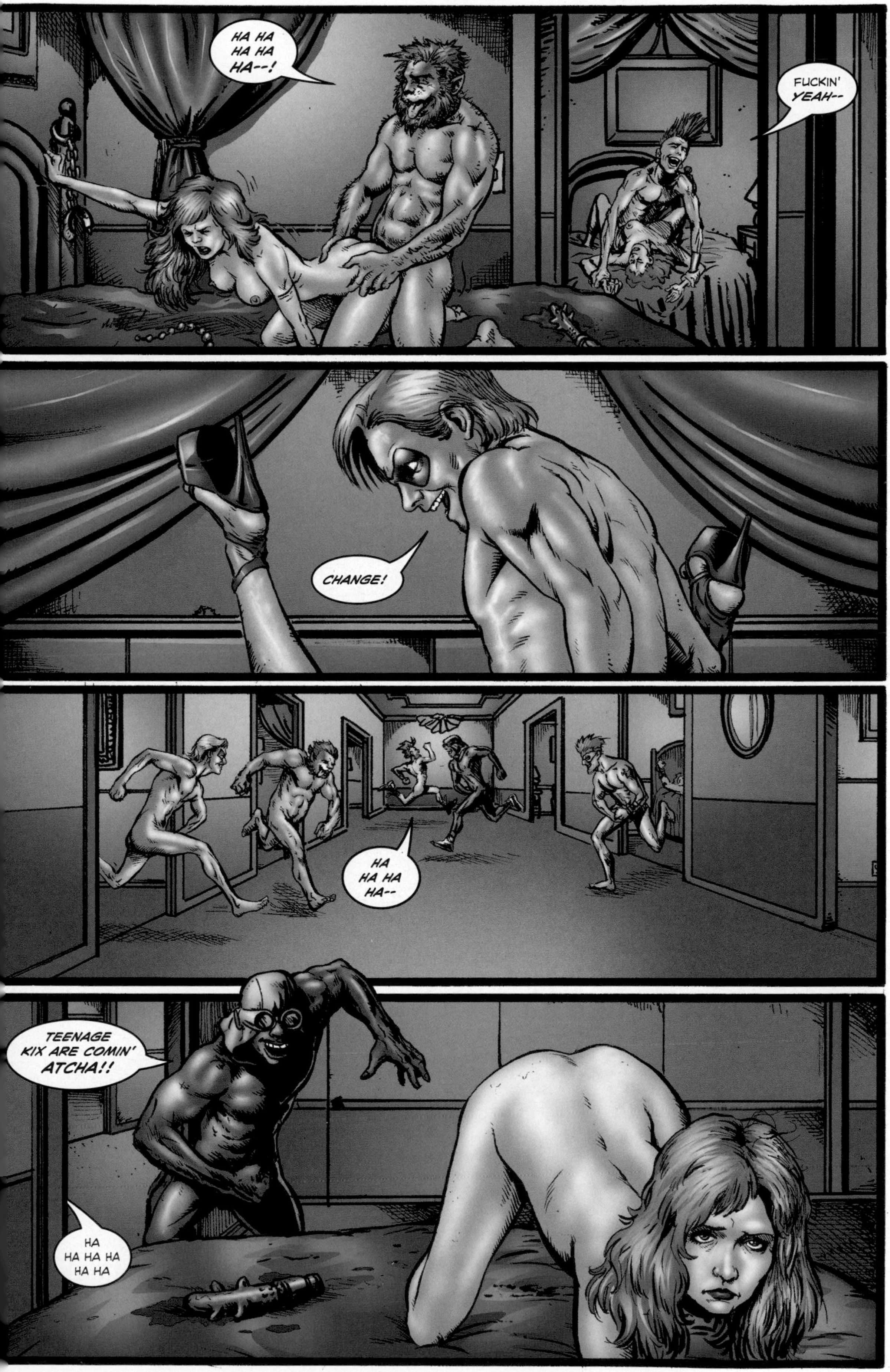
HA HA
HA HA
HA--!
FUCKIN'
YEAH--
CHANGE!
HA
HA HA HA
HA--
TEENAGE
KIX ARE COMIN'
ATCHA!!
HA
HA HA HA
HA HA

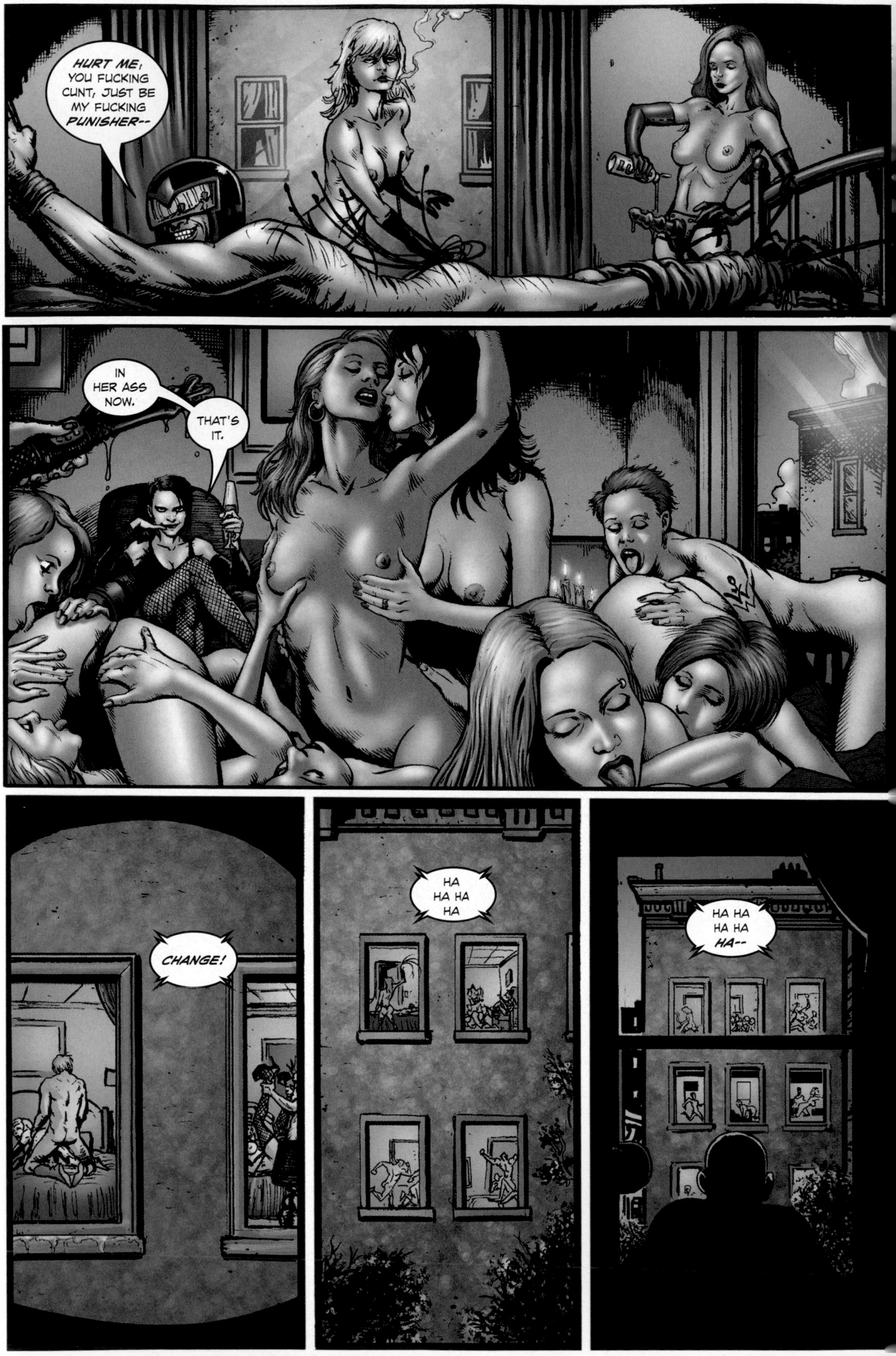
HURT ME, YOU FUCKING CUNT, JUST BE MY FUCKING PUNISHER--
IN HER ASS NOW.
THAT'S IT.
CHANGE!
HA HA HA HA HA
HA HA HA HA HA--

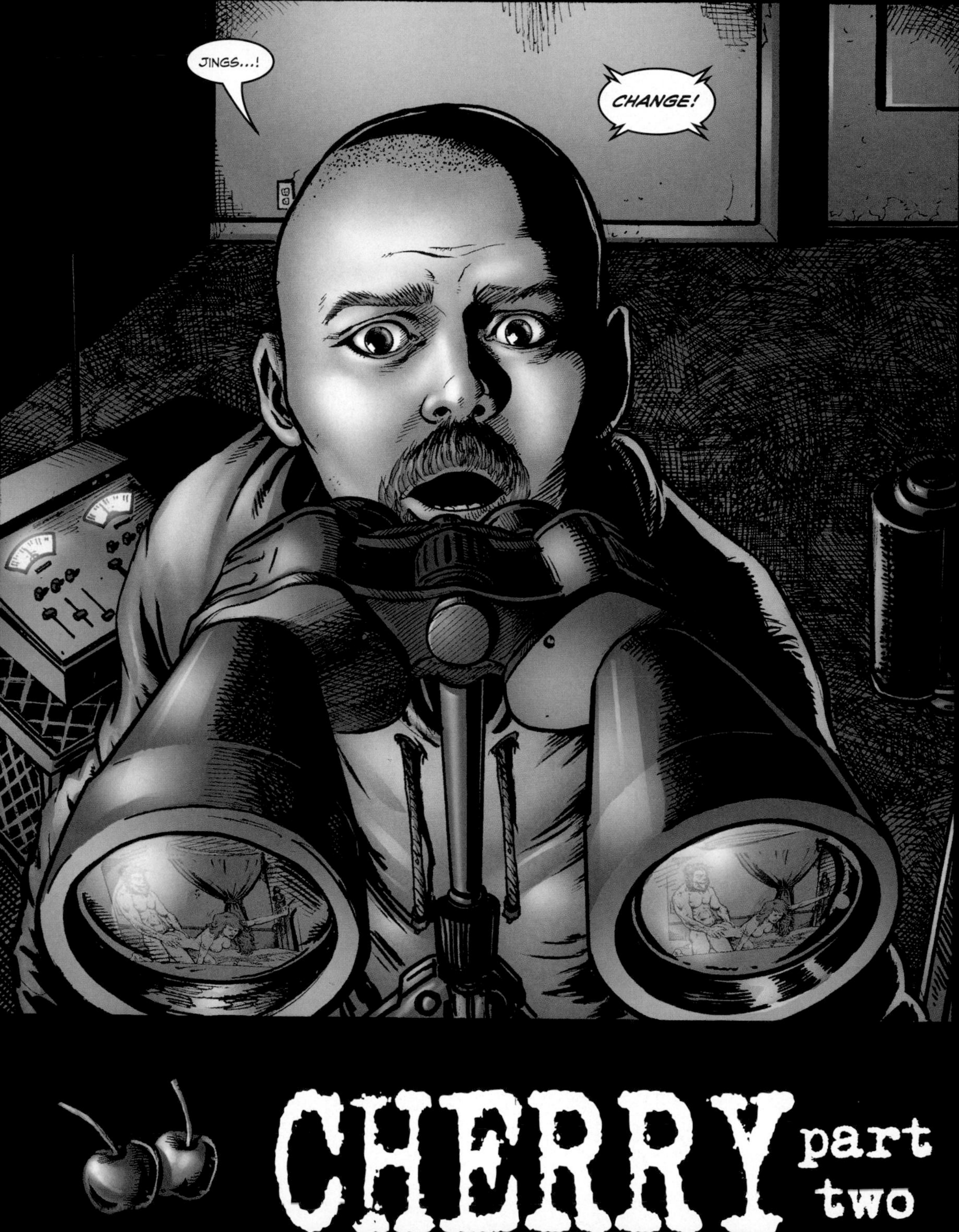
JINGS...!
CHANGE!

CHERRY part two

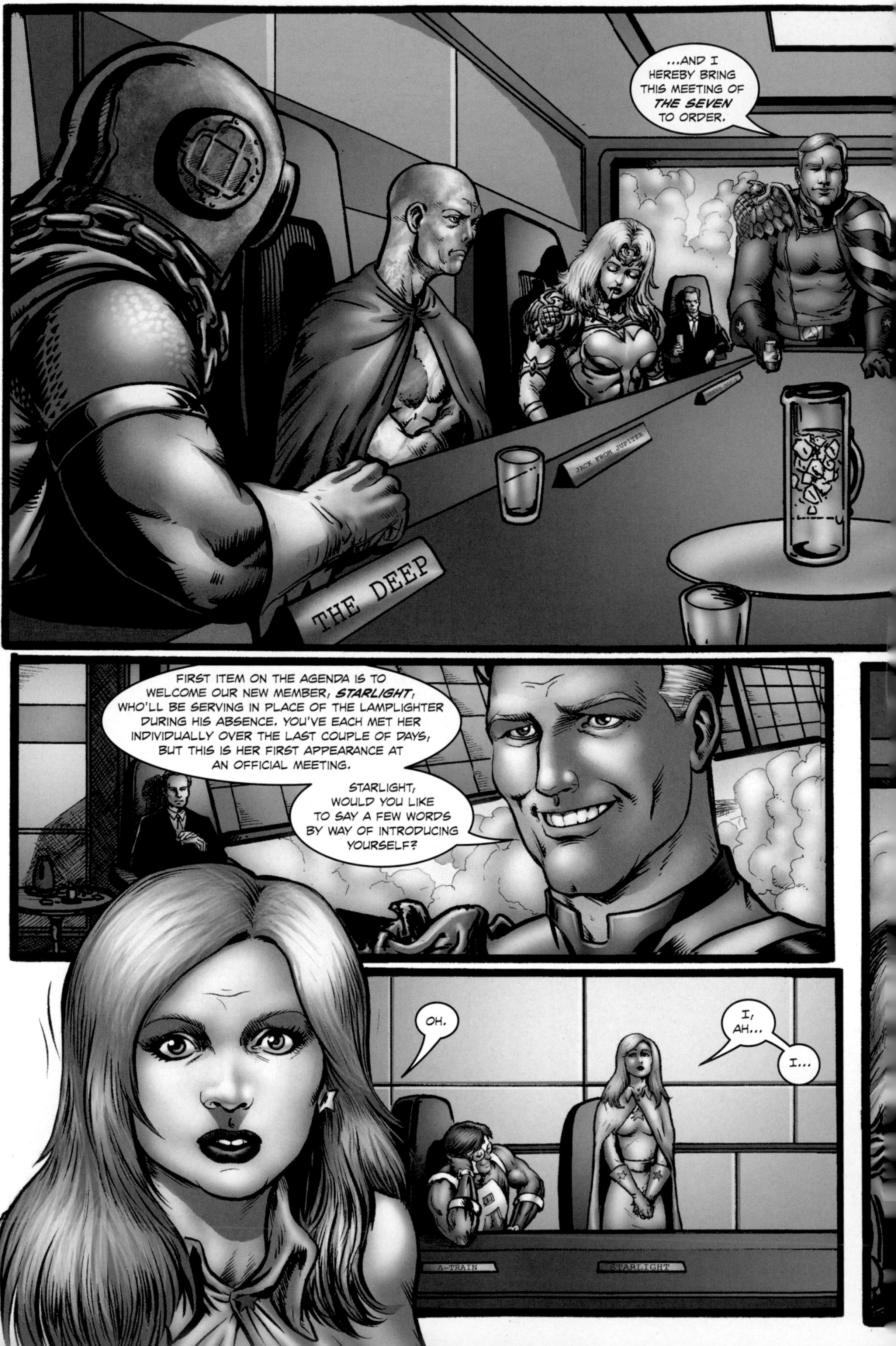
...AND I HEREBY BRING THIS MEETING OF ***THE SEVEN*** TO ORDER.
JACK FROM JUPITER
THE DEEP
FIRST ITEM ON THE AGENDA IS TO WELCOME OUR NEW MEMBER, ***STARLIGHT***, WHO'LL BE SERVING IN PLACE OF THE LAMPLIGHTER DURING HIS ABSENCE. YOU'VE EACH MET HER INDIVIDUALLY OVER THE LAST COUPLE OF DAYS, BUT THIS IS HER FIRST APPEARANCE AT AN OFFICIAL MEETING.
STARLIGHT, WOULD YOU LIKE TO SAY A FEW WORDS BY WAY OF INTRODUCING YOURSELF?
OH.
I, AH...
I...
A-TRAIN
STARLIGHT

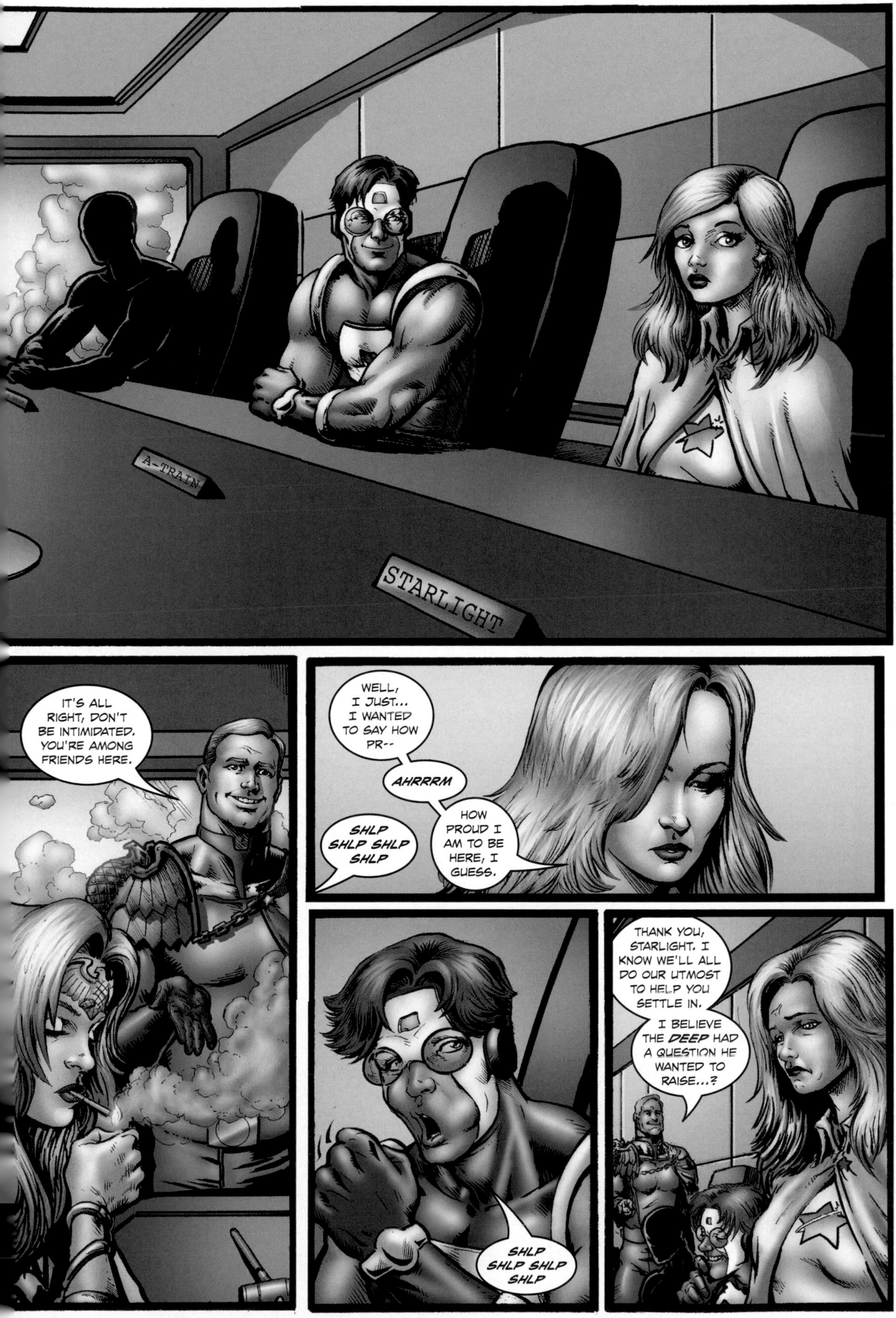
A-TRAIN
STARLIGHT
IT'S ALL RIGHT, DON'T BE INTIMIDATED. YOU'RE AMONG FRIENDS HERE.
WELL, I JUST... I WANTED TO SAY HOW PR--
AHRRRM
HOW PROUD I AM TO BE HERE, I GUESS.
SHLP SHLP SHLP SHLP
SHLP SHLP SHLP SHLP
THANK YOU, STARLIGHT. I KNOW WE'LL ALL DO OUR UTMOST TO HELP YOU SETTLE IN.
I BELIEVE THE *DEEP* HAD A QUESTION HE WANTED TO RAISE...?

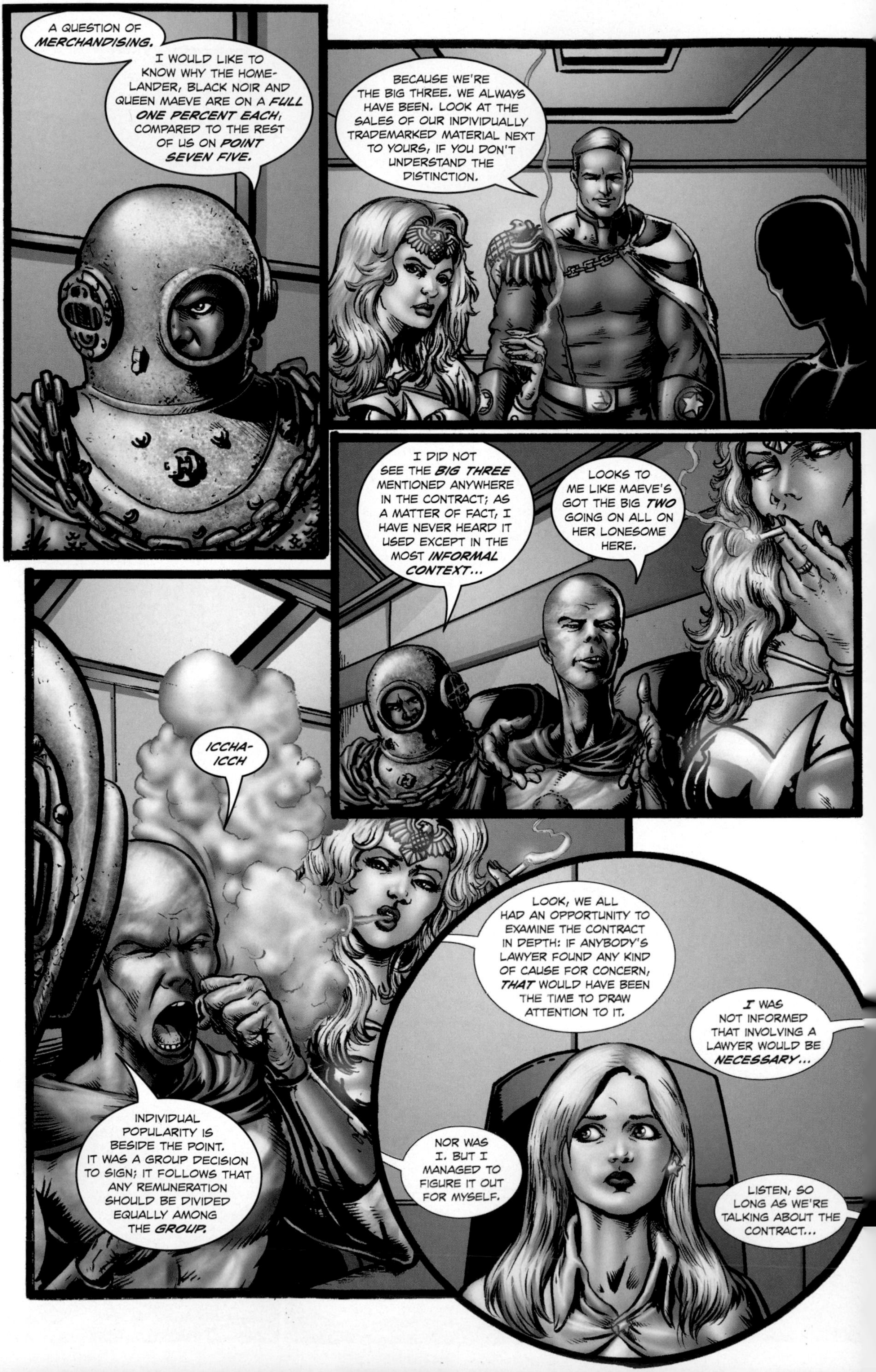

A QUESTION OF MERCHANDISING.
I WOULD LIKE TO KNOW WHY THE HOME-LANDER, BLACK NOIR AND QUEEN MAEVE ARE ON A FULL ONE PERCENT EACH; COMPARED TO THE REST OF US ON POINT SEVEN FIVE.
BECAUSE WE'RE THE BIG THREE. WE ALWAYS HAVE BEEN. LOOK AT THE SALES OF OUR INDIVIDUALLY TRADEMARKED MATERIAL NEXT TO YOURS, IF YOU DON'T UNDERSTAND THE DISTINCTION.
I DID NOT SEE THE BIG THREE MENTIONED ANYWHERE IN THE CONTRACT; AS A MATTER OF FACT, I HAVE NEVER HEARD IT USED EXCEPT IN THE MOST INFORMAL CONTEXT...
LOOKS TO ME LIKE MAEVE'S GOT THE BIG TWO GOING ON ALL ON HER LONESOME HERE.
ICCHA-ICCH
INDIVIDUAL POPULARITY IS BESIDE THE POINT. IT WAS A GROUP DECISION TO SIGN; IT FOLLOWS THAT ANY REMUNERATION SHOULD BE DIVIDED EQUALLY AMONG THE GROUP.
LOOK, WE ALL HAD AN OPPORTUNITY TO EXAMINE THE CONTRACT IN DEPTH: IF ANYBODY'S LAWYER FOUND ANY KIND OF CAUSE FOR CONCERN, THAT WOULD HAVE BEEN THE TIME TO DRAW ATTENTION TO IT.
I WAS NOT INFORMED THAT INVOLVING A LAWYER WOULD BE NECESSARY...
NOR WAS I. BUT I MANAGED TO FIGURE IT OUT FOR MYSELF.
LISTEN, SO LONG AS WE'RE TALKING ABOUT THE CONTRACT...

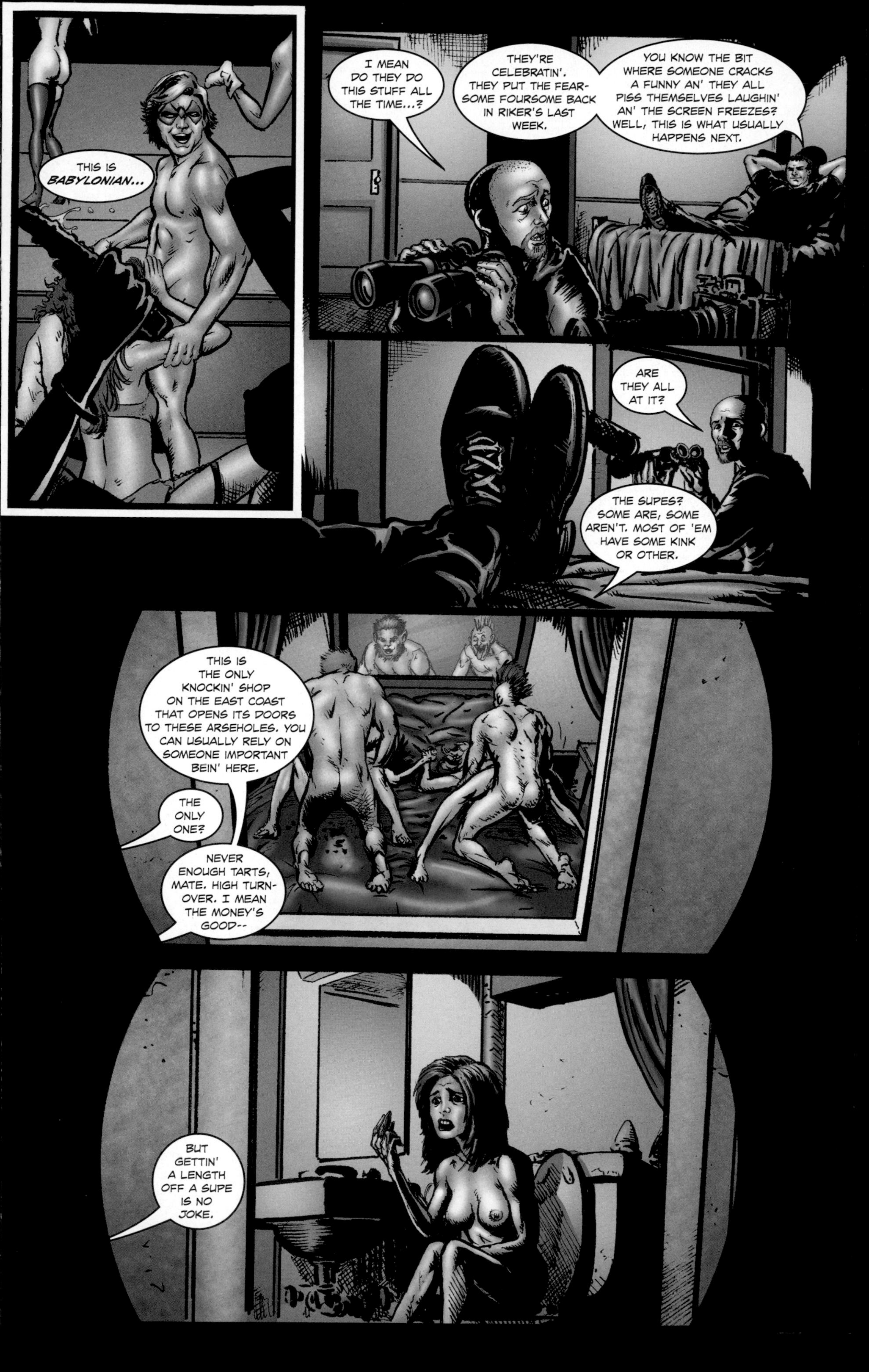

THIS IS *BABYLONIAN...*
I MEAN DO THEY DO THIS STUFF ALL THE TIME...?
THEY'RE CELEBRATIN'. THEY PUT THE FEAR-SOME FOURSOME BACK IN RIKER'S LAST WEEK.
YOU KNOW THE BIT WHERE SOMEONE CRACKS A FUNNY AN' THEY ALL PISS THEMSELVES LAUGHIN' AN' THE SCREEN FREEZES? WELL, THIS IS WHAT USUALLY HAPPENS NEXT.
ARE THEY ALL AT IT?
THE SUPES? SOME ARE, SOME AREN'T. MOST OF 'EM HAVE SOME KINK OR OTHER.
THIS IS THE ONLY KNOCKIN' SHOP ON THE EAST COAST THAT OPENS ITS DOORS TO THESE ARSEHOLES. YOU CAN USUALLY RELY ON SOMEONE IMPORTANT BEIN' HERE.
THE ONLY ONE?
NEVER ENOUGH TARTS, MATE. HIGH TURN-OVER. I MEAN THE MONEY'S GOOD--
BUT GETTIN' A LENGTH OFF A SUPE IS NO JOKE.

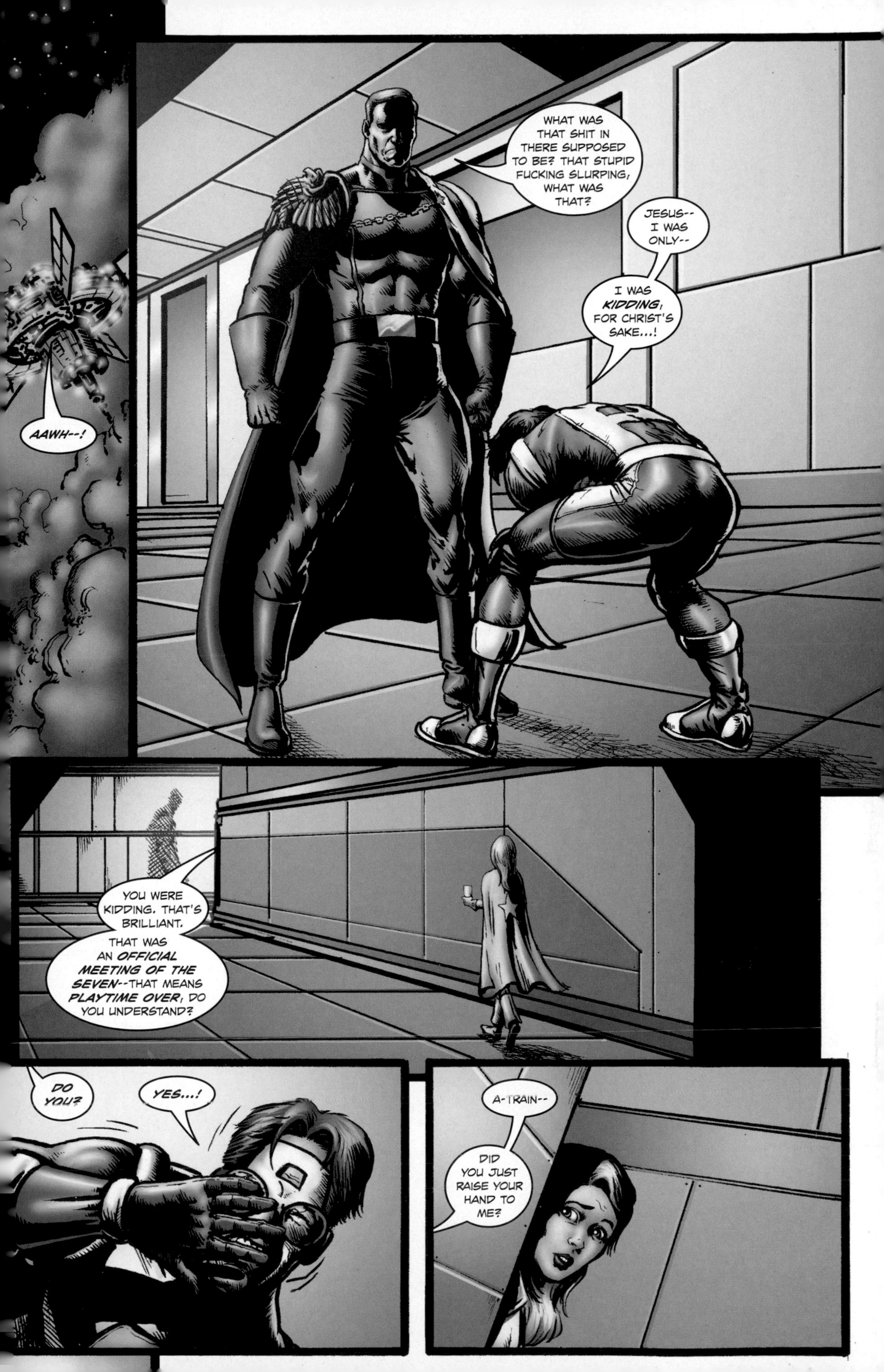
AAWH--!
WHAT WAS THAT SHIT IN THERE SUPPOSED TO BE? THAT STUPID FUCKING SLURPING, WHAT WAS THAT?
JESUS-- I WAS ONLY--
I WAS KIDDING, FOR CHRIST'S SAKE...!
YOU WERE KIDDING. THAT'S BRILLIANT.
THAT WAS AN OFFICIAL MEETING OF THE SEVEN--THAT MEANS PLAYTIME OVER, DO YOU UNDERSTAND?
DO YOU?
YES...!
A-TRAIN--
DID YOU JUST RAISE YOUR HAND TO ME?

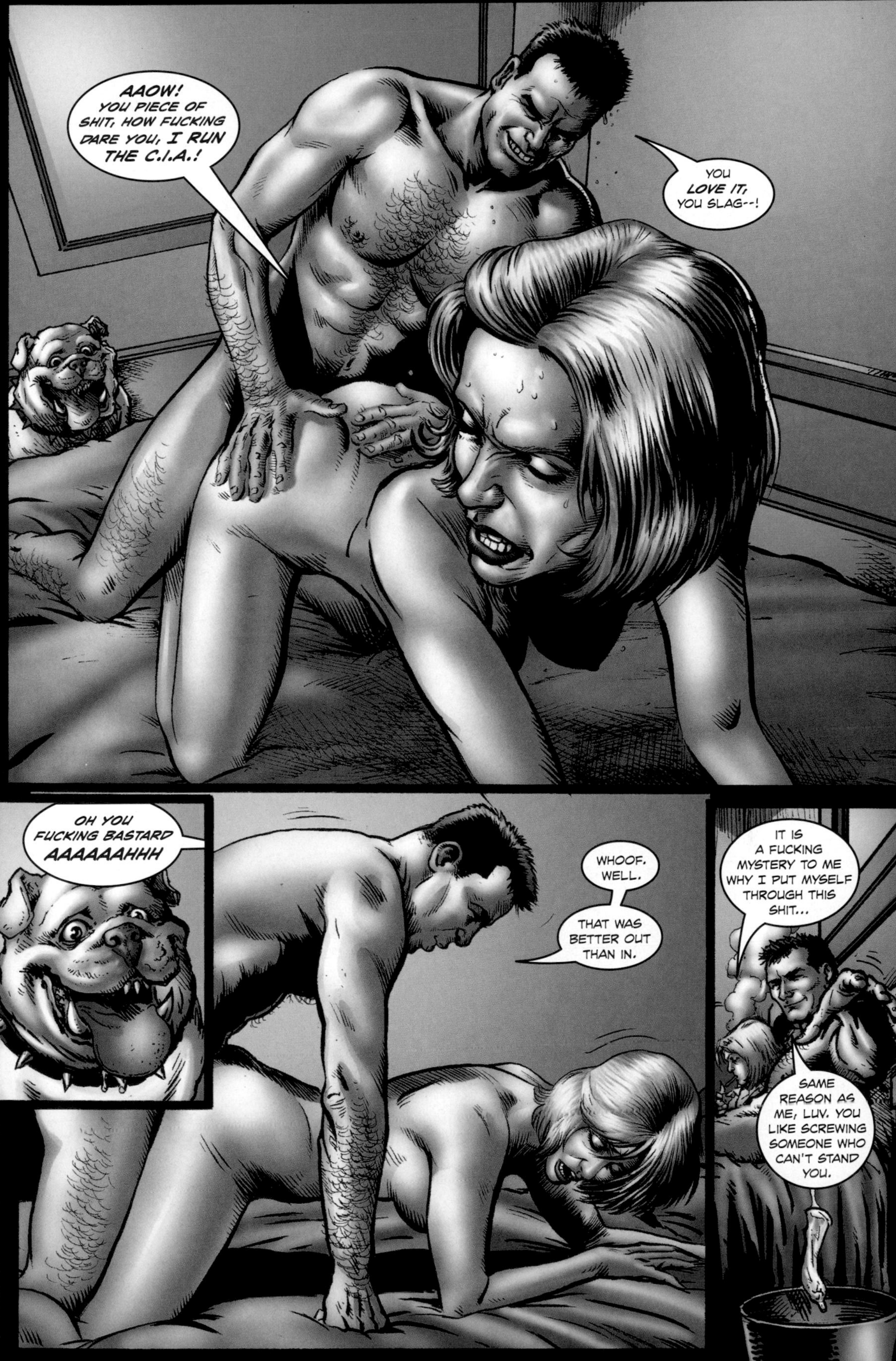
AAOW! YOU PIECE OF SHIT, HOW FUCKING DARE YOU, I RUN THE C.I.A.!
YOU LOVE IT, YOU SLAG--!
OH YOU FUCKING BASTARD AAAAAAHHH
WHOOF. WELL.
THAT WAS BETTER OUT THAN IN.
IT IS A FUCKING MYSTERY TO ME WHY I PUT MYSELF THROUGH THIS SHIT...
SAME REASON AS ME, LUV. YOU LIKE SCREWING SOMEONE WHO CAN'T STAND YOU.

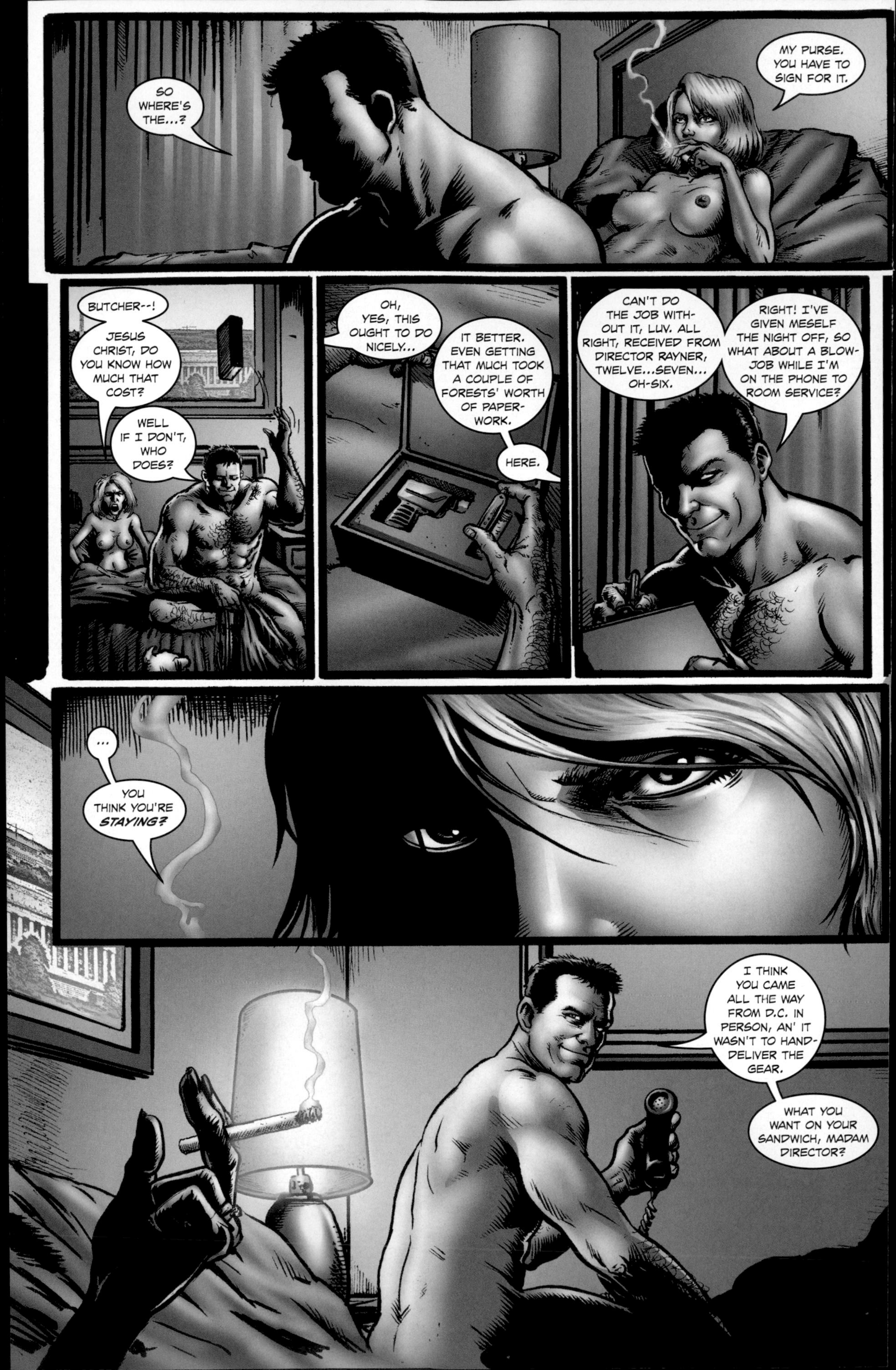
SO WHERE'S THE...?
MY PURSE. YOU HAVE TO SIGN FOR IT.
BUTCHER--!
JESUS CHRIST, DO YOU KNOW HOW MUCH THAT COST?
WELL IF I DON'T, WHO DOES?
OH, YES, THIS OUGHT TO DO NICELY...
IT BETTER. EVEN GETTING THAT MUCH TOOK A COUPLE OF FORESTS' WORTH OF PAPER-WORK.
HERE.
CAN'T DO THE JOB WITH-OUT IT, LUV. ALL RIGHT, RECEIVED FROM DIRECTOR RAYNER, TWELVE...SEVEN... OH-SIX.
RIGHT! I'VE GIVEN MESELF THE NIGHT OFF, SO WHAT ABOUT A BLOW-JOB WHILE I'M ON THE PHONE TO ROOM SERVICE?
...
YOU THINK YOU'RE *STAYING?*
I THINK YOU CAME ALL THE WAY FROM D.C. IN PERSON, AN' IT WASN'T TO HAND-DELIVER THE GEAR.
WHAT YOU WANT ON YOUR SANDWICH, MADAM DIRECTOR?

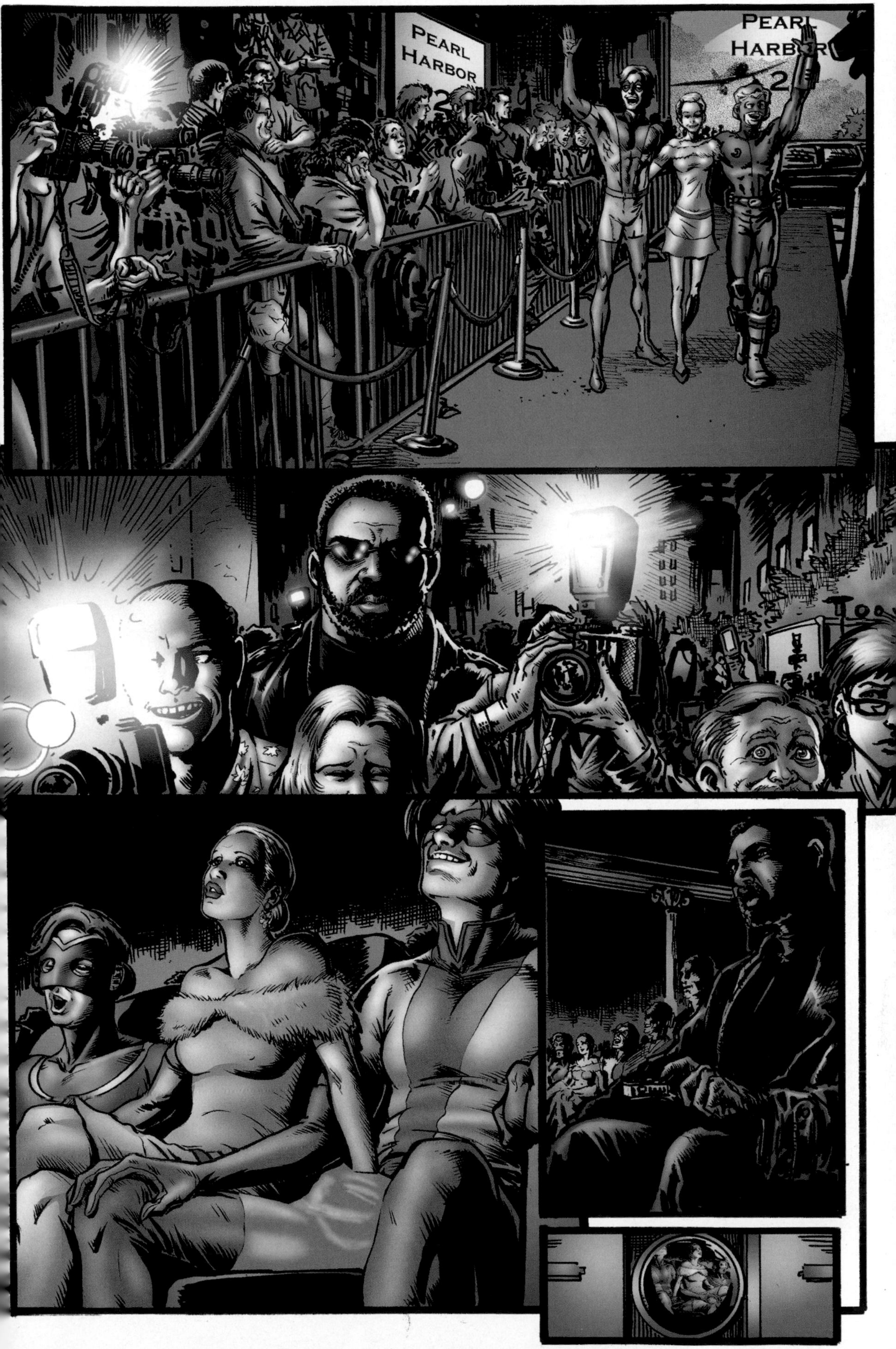
PEARL
HARBOR
2

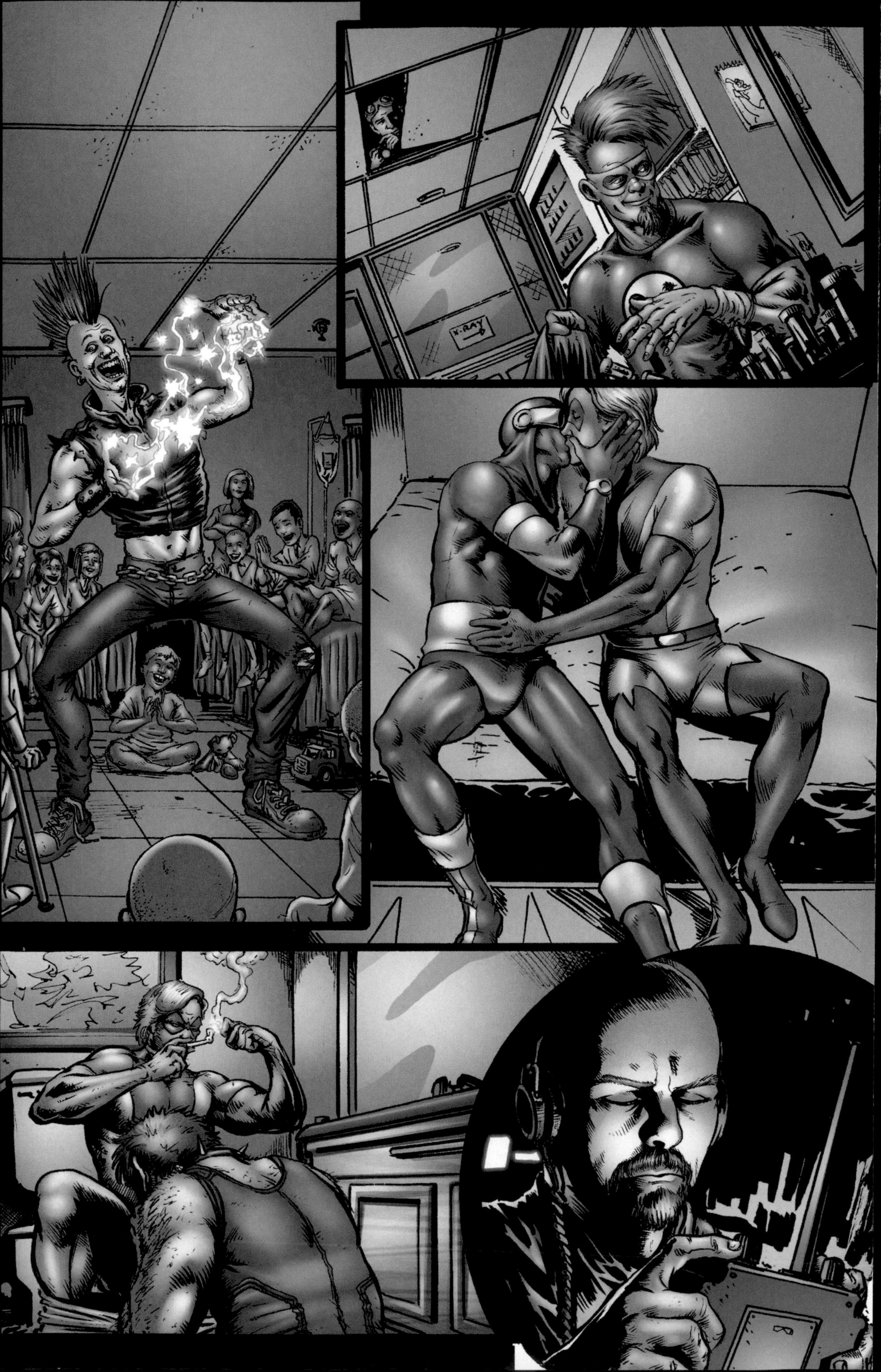
X-RAY

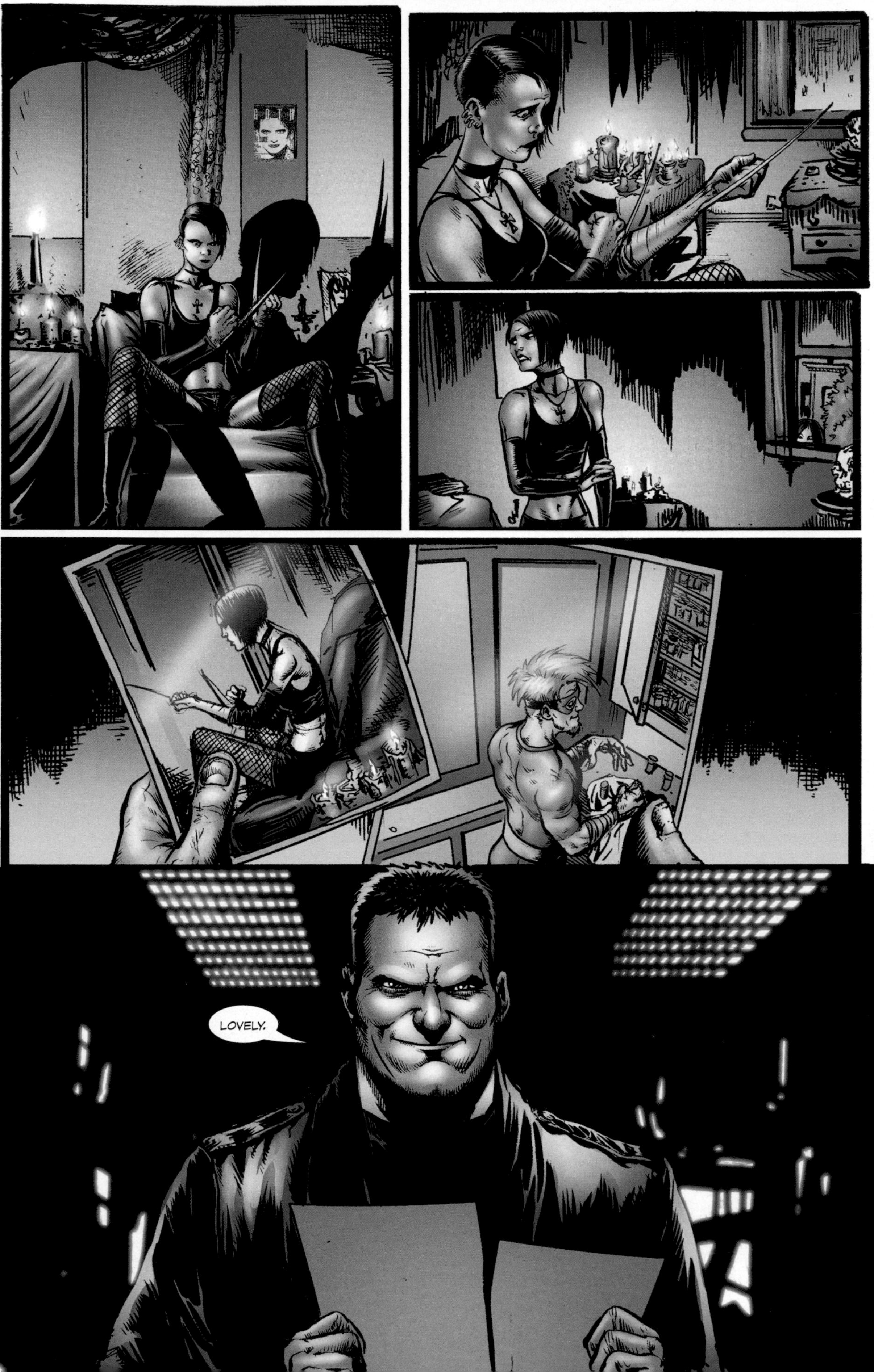
LOVELY.

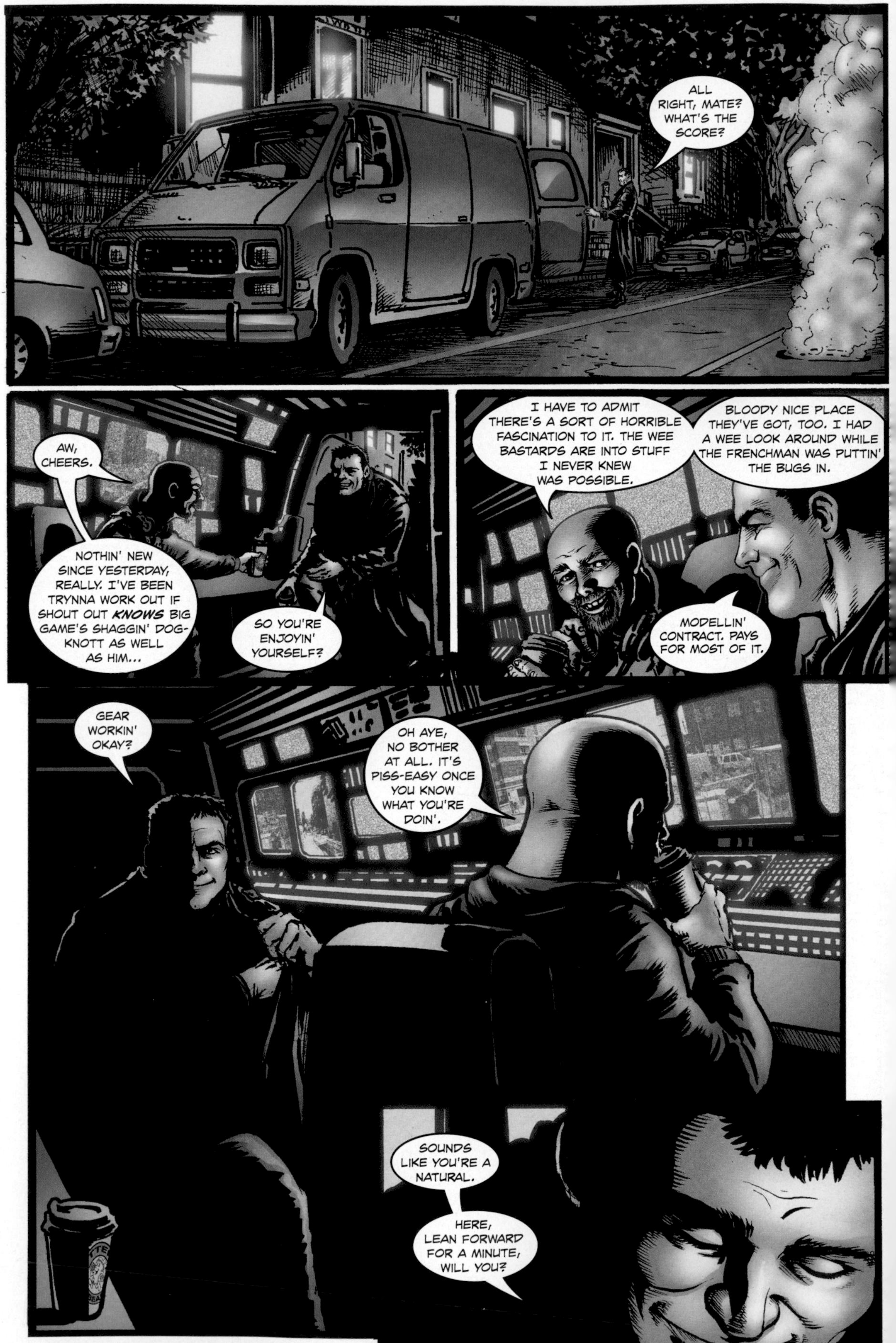
ALL RIGHT, MATE? WHAT'S THE SCORE?
AW, CHEERS.
NOTHIN' NEW SINCE YESTERDAY, REALLY. I'VE BEEN TRYNNA WORK OUT IF SHOUT OUT **KNOWS** BIG GAME'S SHAGGIN' DOG-KNOTT AS WELL AS HIM...
SO YOU'RE ENJOYIN' YOURSELF?
I HAVE TO ADMIT THERE'S A SORT OF HORRIBLE FASCINATION TO IT. THE WEE BASTARDS ARE INTO STUFF I NEVER KNEW WAS POSSIBLE.
BLOODY NICE PLACE THEY'VE GOT, TOO. I HAD A WEE LOOK AROUND WHILE THE FRENCHMAN WAS PUTTIN' THE BUGS IN.
MODELLIN' CONTRACT. PAYS FOR MOST OF IT.
GEAR WORKIN' OKAY?
OH AYE, NO BOTHER AT ALL. IT'S PISS-EASY ONCE YOU KNOW WHAT YOU'RE DOIN'.
SOUNDS LIKE YOU'RE A NATURAL.
HERE, LEAN FORWARD FOR A MINUTE, WILL YOU?

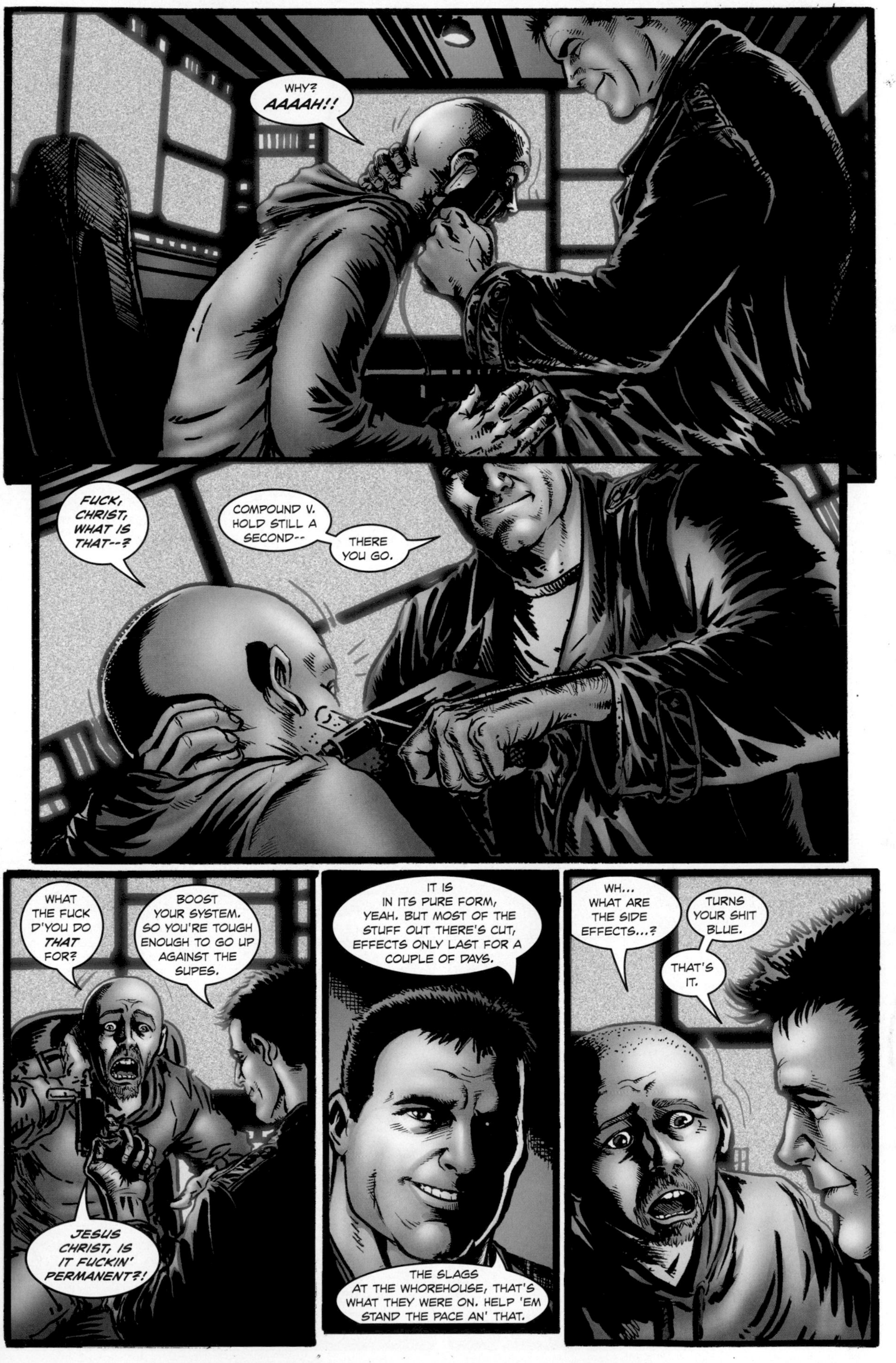
WHY? AAAAH!!
FUCK, CHRIST, WHAT IS THAT--?
COMPOUND V. HOLD STILL A SECOND--
THERE YOU GO.
WHAT THE FUCK D'YOU DO THAT FOR?
BOOST YOUR SYSTEM. SO YOU'RE TOUGH ENOUGH TO GO UP AGAINST THE SUPES.
JESUS CHRIST, IS IT FUCKIN' PERMANENT?!
IT IS IN ITS PURE FORM, YEAH. BUT MOST OF THE STUFF OUT THERE'S CUT, EFFECTS ONLY LAST FOR A COUPLE OF DAYS.
THE SLAGS AT THE WHOREHOUSE, THAT'S WHAT THEY WERE ON. HELP 'EM STAND THE PACE AN' THAT.
WH... WHAT ARE THE SIDE EFFECTS...?
TURNS YOUR SHIT BLUE.
THAT'S IT.

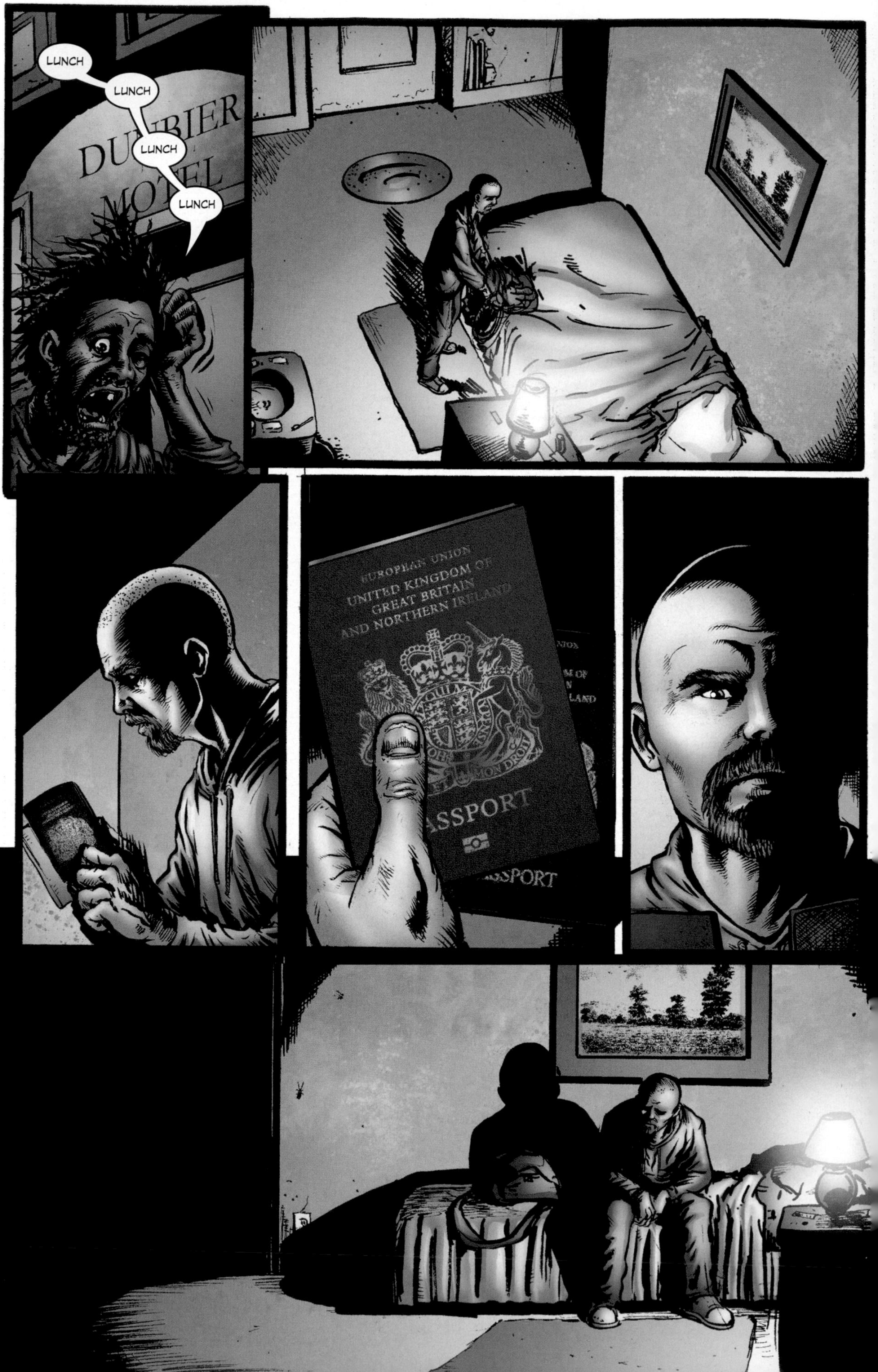
LUNCH
LUNCH
LUNCH
LUNCH
EUROPEAN UNION
UNITED KINGDOM OF
GREAT BRITAIN
AND NORTHERN IRELAND
ASSPORT

UUNNNGGHHH

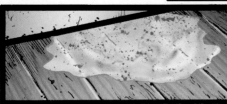

AW, NO...!

NEXT: LIFE AMONG THE SEPTICS

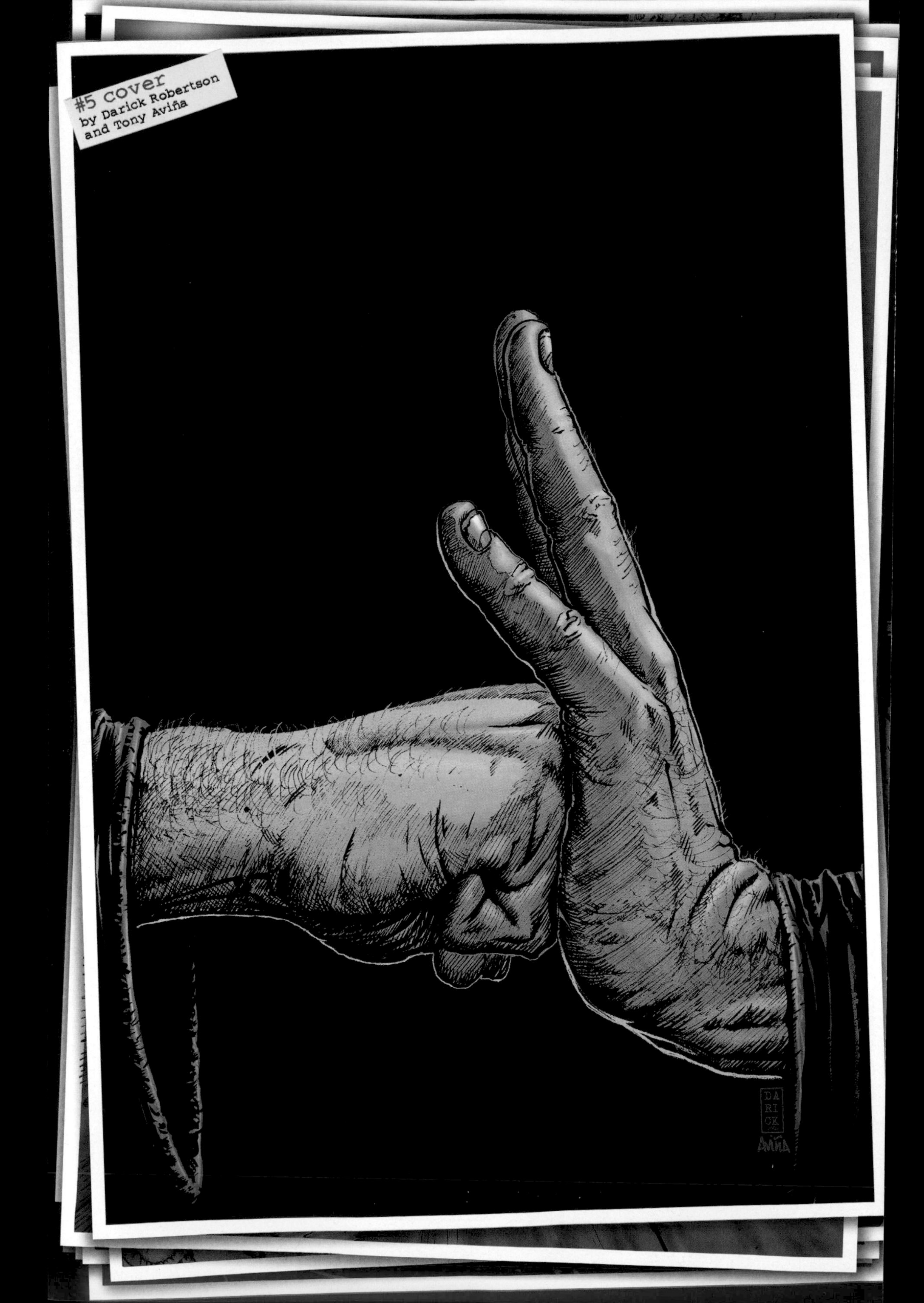
#5 cover
by Darick Robertson
and Tony Aviña
DA
RI
CK
AVIÑA

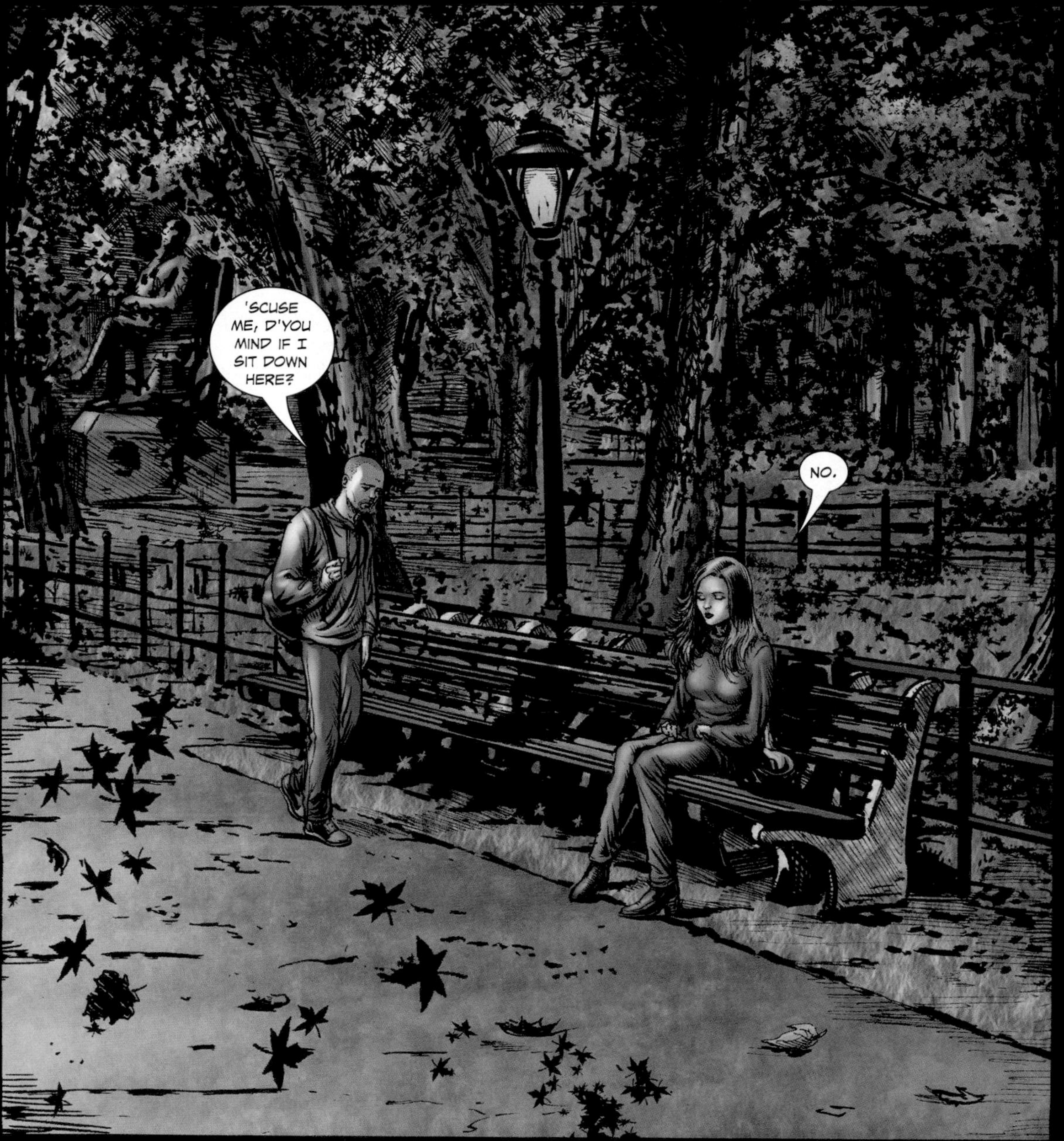
'SCUSE ME, D'YOU MIND IF I SIT DOWN HERE?
NO.

CHERRY part three

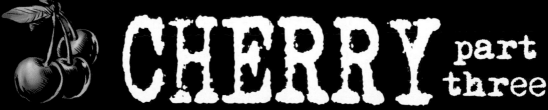

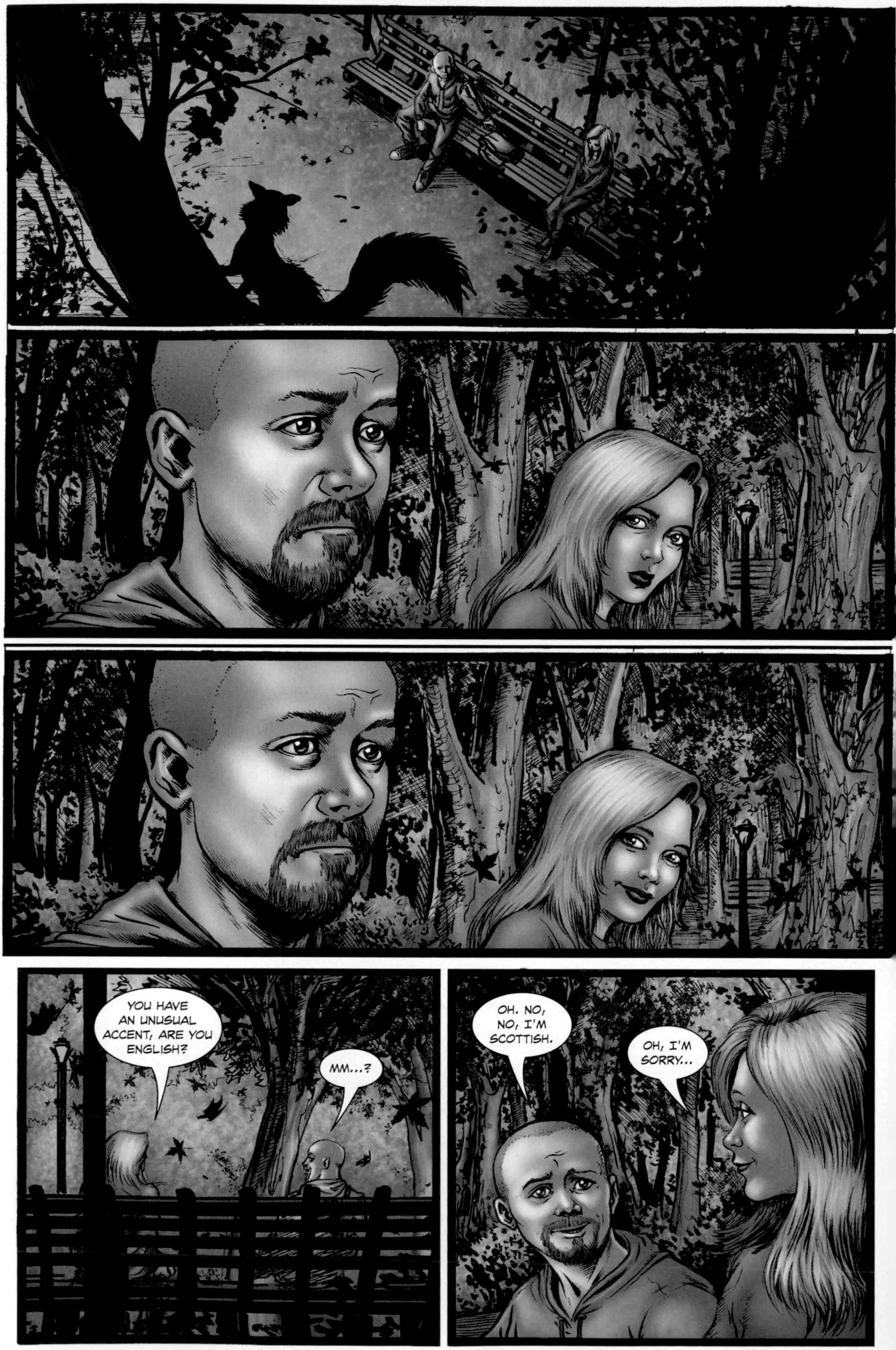
YOU HAVE AN UNUSUAL ACCENT, ARE YOU ENGLISH?
MM...?
OH. NO, NO, I'M SCOTTISH.
OH, I'M SORRY...

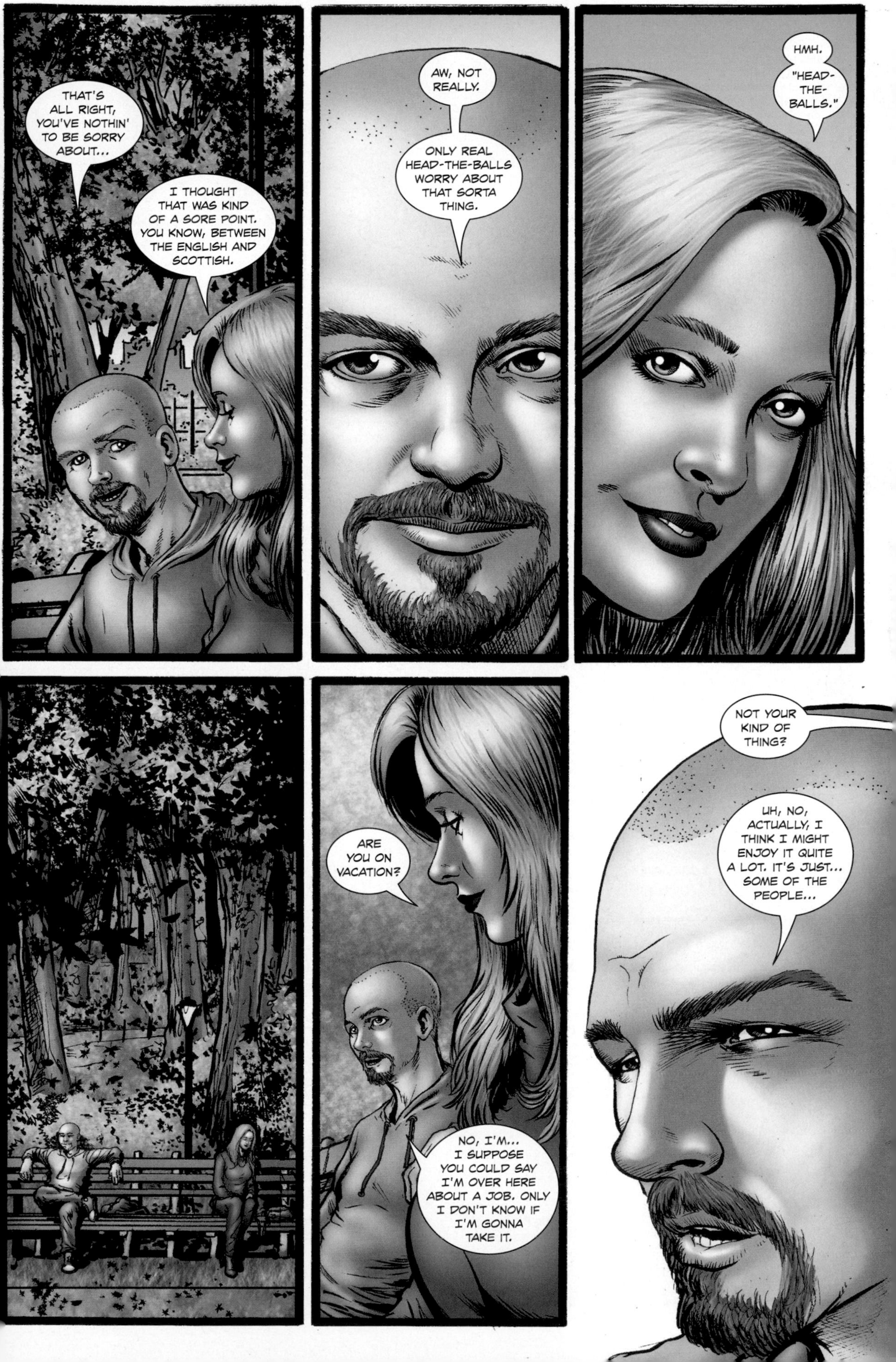
THAT'S ALL RIGHT, YOU'VE NOTHIN' TO BE SORRY ABOUT...
I THOUGHT THAT WAS KIND OF A SORE POINT. YOU KNOW, BETWEEN THE ENGLISH AND SCOTTISH.
AW, NOT REALLY.
ONLY REAL HEAD-THE-BALLS WORRY ABOUT THAT SORTA THING.
HMH.
"HEAD-THE-BALLS."
ARE YOU ON VACATION?
NO, I'M... I SUPPOSE YOU COULD SAY I'M OVER HERE ABOUT A JOB. ONLY I DON'T KNOW IF I'M GONNA TAKE IT.
NOT YOUR KIND OF THING?
UH, NO, ACTUALLY, I THINK I MIGHT ENJOY IT QUITE A LOT. IT'S JUST... SOME OF THE PEOPLE...

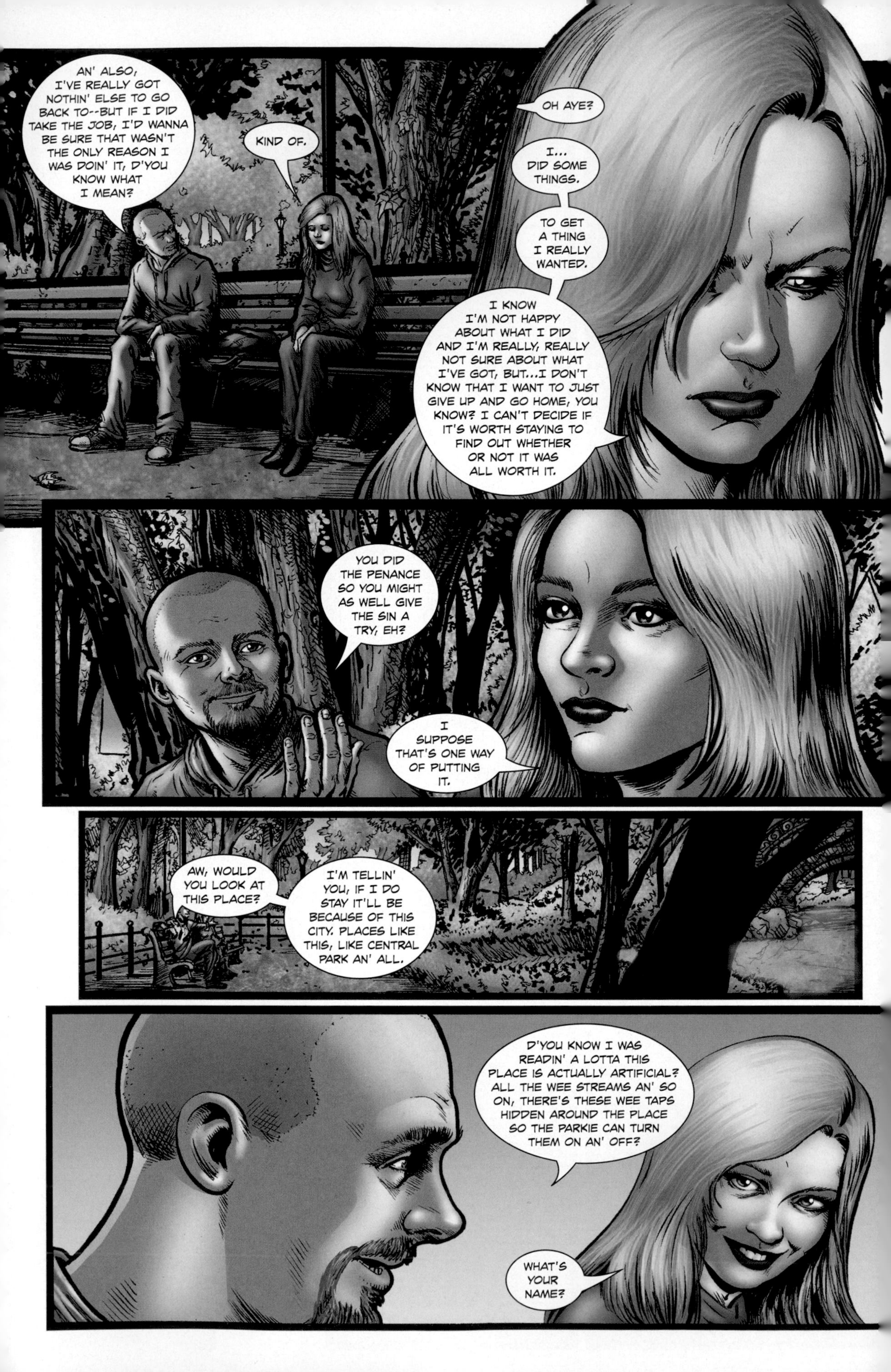
AN' ALSO, I'VE REALLY GOT NOTHIN' ELSE TO GO BACK TO--BUT IF I DID TAKE THE JOB, I'D WANNA BE SURE THAT WASN'T THE ONLY REASON I WAS DOIN' IT, D'YOU KNOW WHAT I MEAN?
KIND OF.
OH AYE?
I... DID SOME THINGS.
TO GET A THING I REALLY WANTED.
I KNOW I'M NOT HAPPY ABOUT WHAT I DID AND I'M REALLY, REALLY NOT SURE ABOUT WHAT I'VE GOT, BUT...I DON'T KNOW THAT I WANT TO JUST GIVE UP AND GO HOME, YOU KNOW? I CAN'T DECIDE IF IT'S WORTH STAYING TO FIND OUT WHETHER OR NOT IT WAS ALL WORTH IT.
YOU DID THE PENANCE SO YOU MIGHT AS WELL GIVE THE SIN A TRY, EH?
I SUPPOSE THAT'S ONE WAY OF PUTTING IT.
AW, WOULD YOU LOOK AT THIS PLACE?
I'M TELLIN' YOU, IF I DO STAY IT'LL BE BECAUSE OF THIS CITY. PLACES LIKE THIS, LIKE CENTRAL PARK AN' ALL.
D'YOU KNOW I WAS READIN' A LOTTA THIS PLACE IS ACTUALLY ARTIFICIAL? ALL THE WEE STREAMS AN' SO ON, THERE'S THESE WEE TAPS HIDDEN AROUND THE PLACE SO THE PARKIE CAN TURN THEM ON AN' OFF?
WHAT'S YOUR NAME?

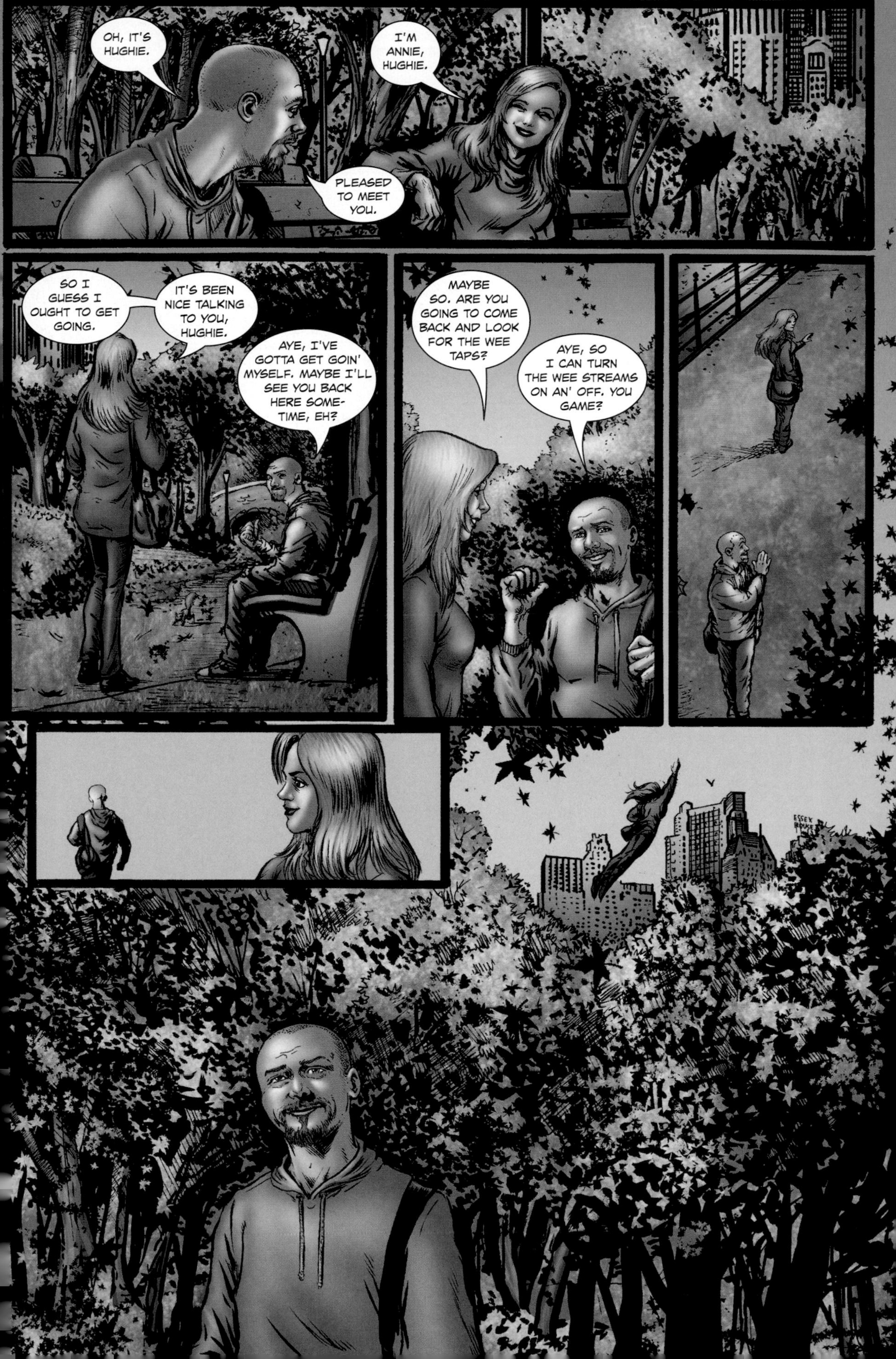
OH, IT'S HUGHIE.
I'M ANNIE, HUGHIE.
PLEASED TO MEET YOU.
SO I GUESS I OUGHT TO GET GOING.
IT'S BEEN NICE TALKING TO YOU, HUGHIE.
AYE, I'VE GOTTA GET GOIN' MYSELF. MAYBE I'LL SEE YOU BACK HERE SOME-TIME, EH?
MAYBE SO. ARE YOU GOING TO COME BACK AND LOOK FOR THE WEE TAPS?
AYE, SO I CAN TURN THE WEE STREAMS ON AN' OFF. YOU GAME?

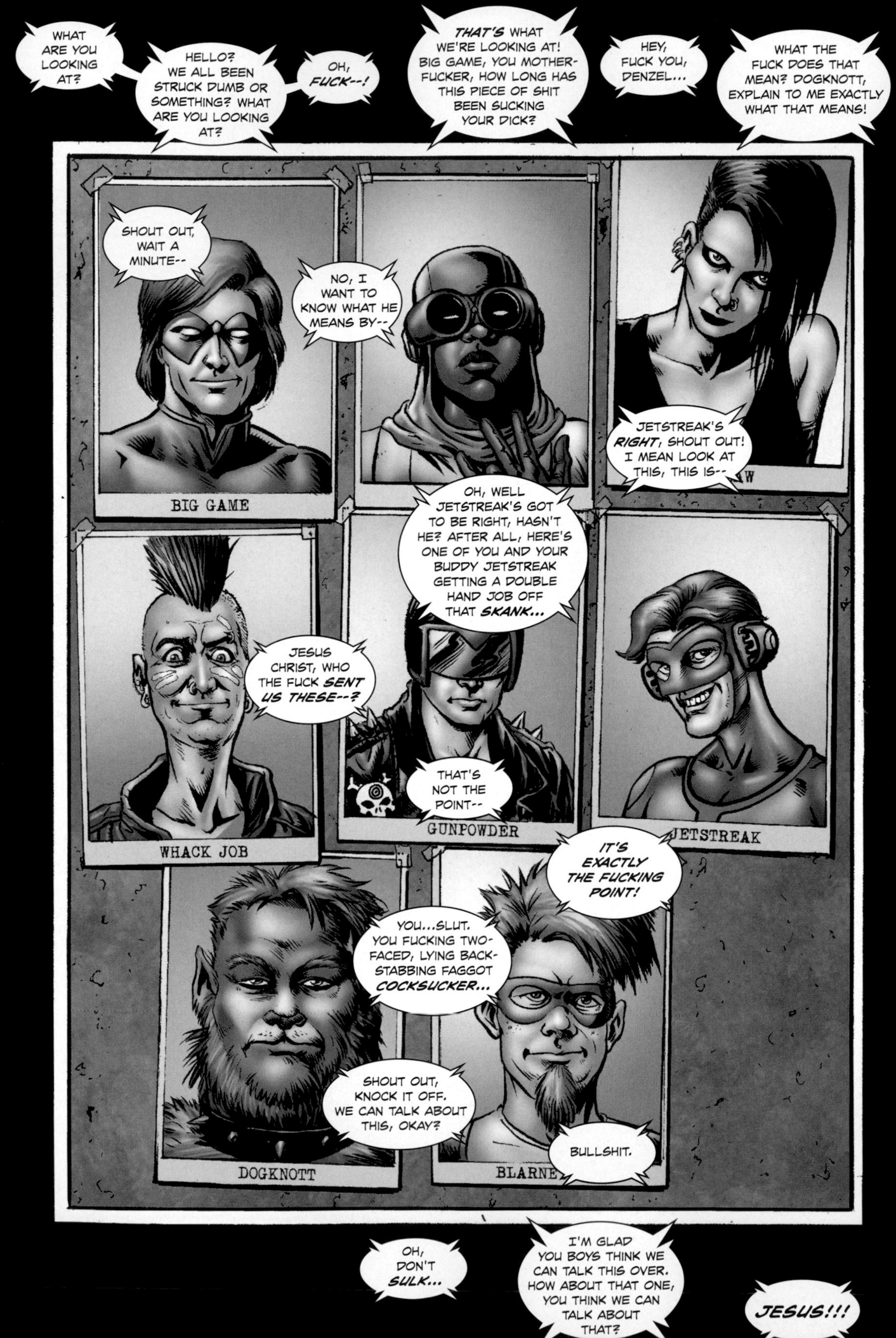
WHAT ARE YOU LOOKING AT?
HELLO? WE ALL BEEN STRUCK DUMB OR SOMETHING? WHAT ARE YOU LOOKING AT?
OH, FUCK--!
THAT'S WHAT WE'RE LOOKING AT! BIG GAME, YOU MOTHER-FUCKER, HOW LONG HAS THIS PIECE OF SHIT BEEN SUCKING YOUR DICK?
HEY, FUCK YOU, DENZEL...
WHAT THE FUCK DOES THAT MEAN? DOGKNOTT, EXPLAIN TO ME EXACTLY WHAT THAT MEANS!
SHOUT OUT, WAIT A MINUTE--
NO, I WANT TO KNOW WHAT HE MEANS BY--
JETSTREAK'S RIGHT, SHOUT OUT! I MEAN LOOK AT THIS, THIS IS--
BIG GAME
OH, WELL JETSTREAK'S GOT TO BE RIGHT, HASN'T HE? AFTER ALL, HERE'S ONE OF YOU AND YOUR BUDDY JETSTREAK GETTING A DOUBLE HAND JOB OFF THAT SKANK...
JESUS CHRIST, WHO THE FUCK SENT US THESE--?
THAT'S NOT THE POINT--
WHACK JOB
GUNPOWDER
JETSTREAK
IT'S EXACTLY THE FUCKING POINT!
YOU...SLUT. YOU FUCKING TWO-FACED, LYING BACK-STABBING FAGGOT COCKSUCKER...
SHOUT OUT, KNOCK IT OFF. WE CAN TALK ABOUT THIS, OKAY?
BULLSHIT.
DOGKNOTT
OH, DON'T SULK...
I'M GLAD YOU BOYS THINK WE CAN TALK THIS OVER. HOW ABOUT THAT ONE, YOU THINK WE CAN TALK ABOUT THAT?
JESUS!!!

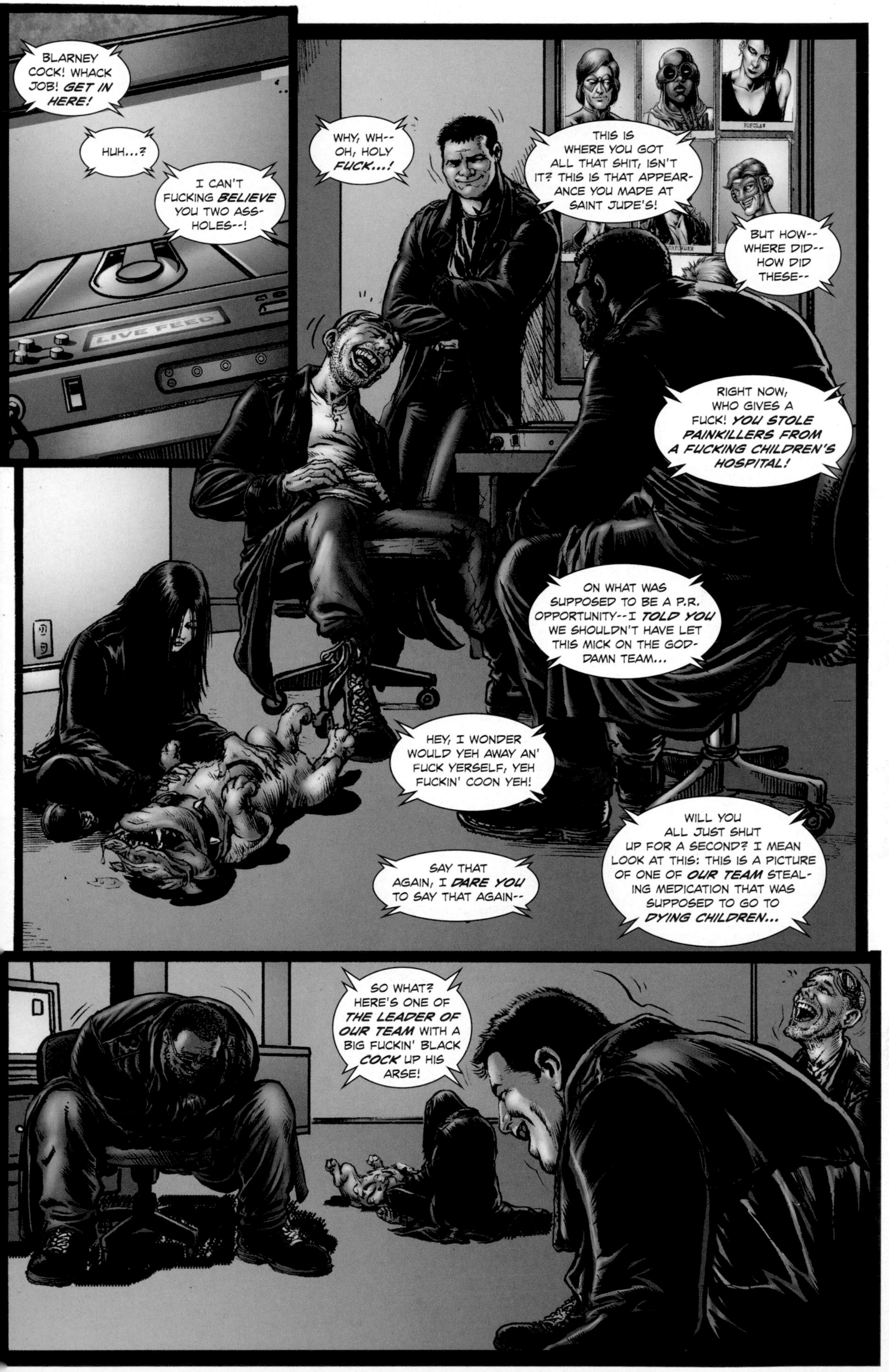
BLARNEY COCK! WHACK JOB! GET IN HERE!
HUH...?
I CAN'T FUCKING BELIEVE YOU TWO ASS-HOLES--!
LIVE FEED
WHY, WH-- OH, HOLY FUCK...!
THIS IS WHERE YOU GOT ALL THAT SHIT, ISN'T IT? THIS IS THAT APPEAR-ANCE YOU MADE AT SAINT JUDE'S!
BUT HOW-- WHERE DID-- HOW DID THESE--
RIGHT NOW, WHO GIVES A FUCK! YOU STOLE PAINKILLERS FROM A FUCKING CHILDREN'S HOSPITAL!
ON WHAT WAS SUPPOSED TO BE A P.R. OPPORTUNITY--I TOLD YOU WE SHOULDN'T HAVE LET THIS MICK ON THE GOD-DAMN TEAM...
HEY, I WONDER WOULD YEH AWAY AN' FUCK YERSELF, YEH FUCKIN' COON YEH!
SAY THAT AGAIN, I DARE YOU TO SAY THAT AGAIN--
WILL YOU ALL JUST SHUT UP FOR A SECOND? I MEAN LOOK AT THIS: THIS IS A PICTURE OF ONE OF OUR TEAM STEAL-ING MEDICATION THAT WAS SUPPOSED TO GO TO DYING CHILDREN...
SO WHAT? HERE'S ONE OF THE LEADER OF OUR TEAM WITH A BIG FUCKIN' BLACK COCK UP HIS ARSE!

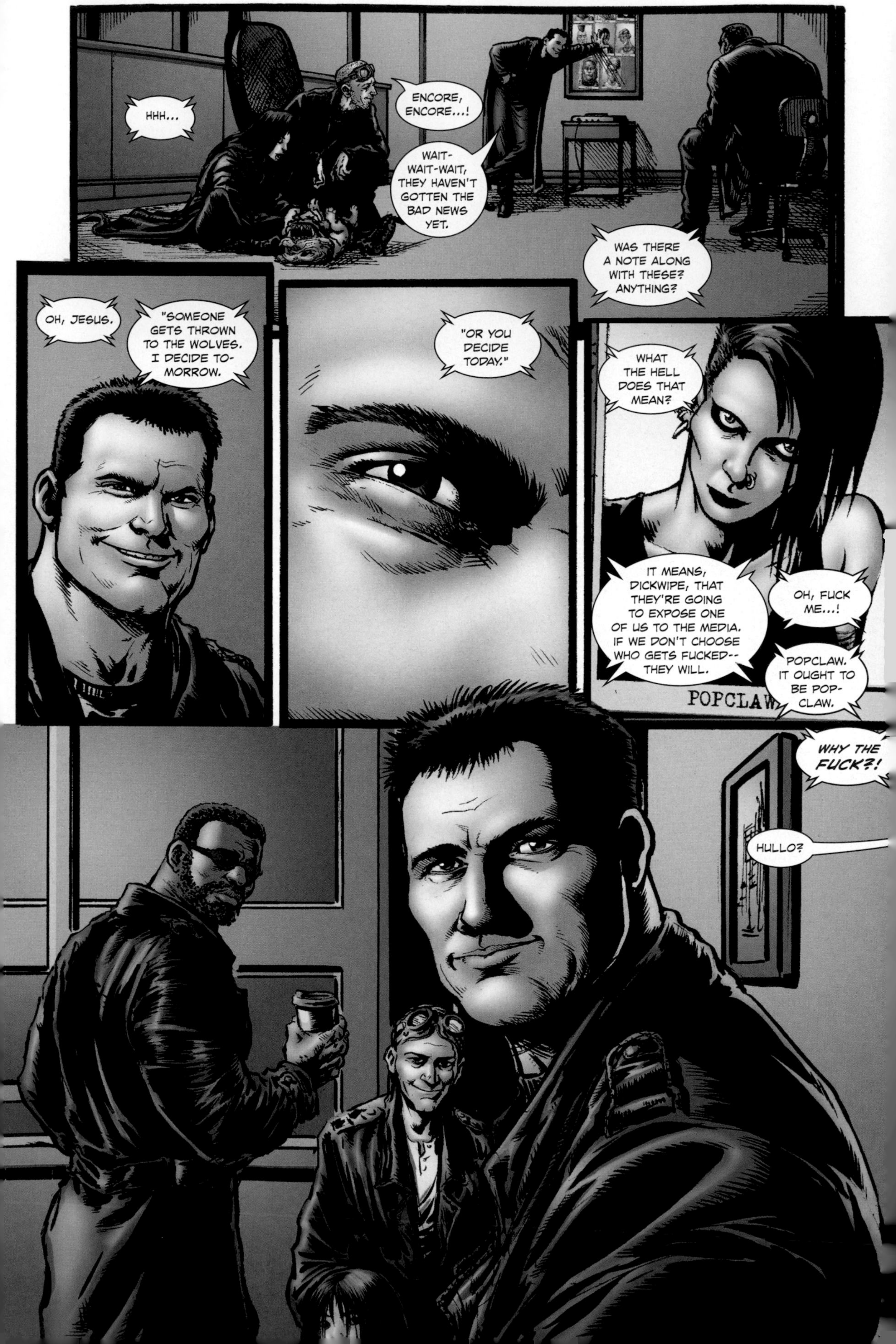
HHH...
ENCORE, ENCORE...!
WAIT-WAIT-WAIT, THEY HAVEN'T GOTTEN THE BAD NEWS YET.
WAS THERE A NOTE ALONG WITH THESE? ANYTHING?
OH, JESUS.
"SOMEONE GETS THROWN TO THE WOLVES. I DECIDE TO-MORROW.
"OR YOU DECIDE TODAY."
WHAT THE HELL DOES THAT MEAN?
IT MEANS, DICKWIPE, THAT THEY'RE GOING TO EXPOSE ONE OF US TO THE MEDIA. IF WE DON'T CHOOSE WHO GETS FUCKED-- THEY WILL.
OH, FUCK ME...!
POPCLAW. IT OUGHT TO BE POP-CLAW.
POPCLAW
WHY THE FUCK?!
HULLO?

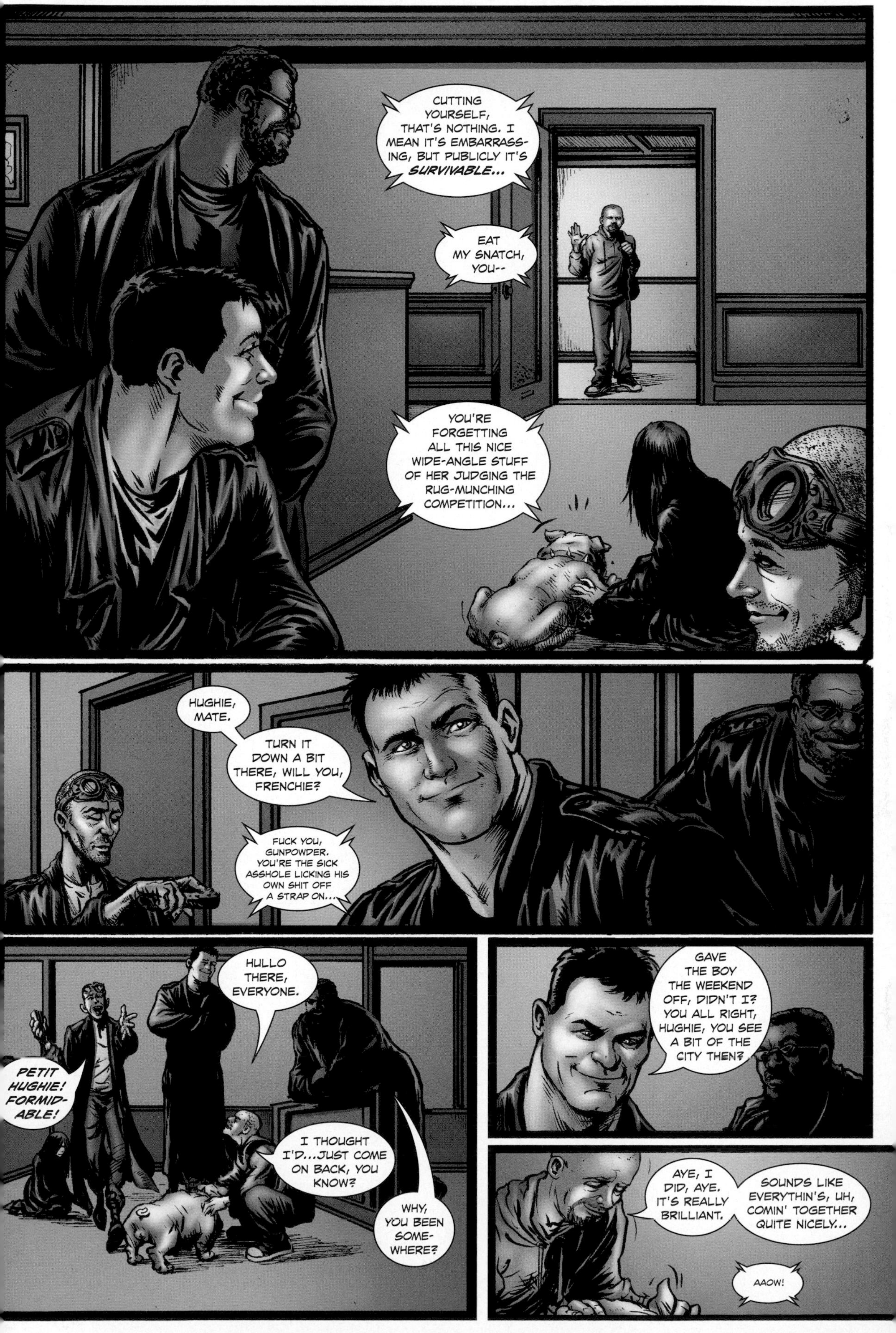
CUTTING YOURSELF, THAT'S NOTHING. I MEAN IT'S EMBARRASSING, BUT PUBLICLY IT'S *SURVIVABLE...*
EAT MY SNATCH, YOU--
YOU'RE FORGETTING ALL THIS NICE WIDE-ANGLE STUFF OF HER JUDGING THE RUG-MUNCHING COMPETITION...
HUGHIE, MATE.
TURN IT DOWN A BIT THERE, WILL YOU, FRENCHIE?
FUCK YOU, GUNPOWDER. YOU'RE THE SICK ASSHOLE LICKING HIS OWN SHIT OFF A STRAP ON...
HULLO THERE, EVERYONE.
PETIT HUGHIE! FORMIDABLE!
I THOUGHT I'D...JUST COME ON BACK, YOU KNOW?
WHY, YOU BEEN SOMEWHERE?
GAVE THE BOY THE WEEKEND OFF, DIDN'T I? YOU ALL RIGHT, HUGHIE, YOU SEE A BIT OF THE CITY THEN?
AYE, I DID, AYE. IT'S REALLY BRILLIANT.
SOUNDS LIKE EVERYTHIN'S, UH, COMIN' TOGETHER QUITE NICELY...
AAOW!

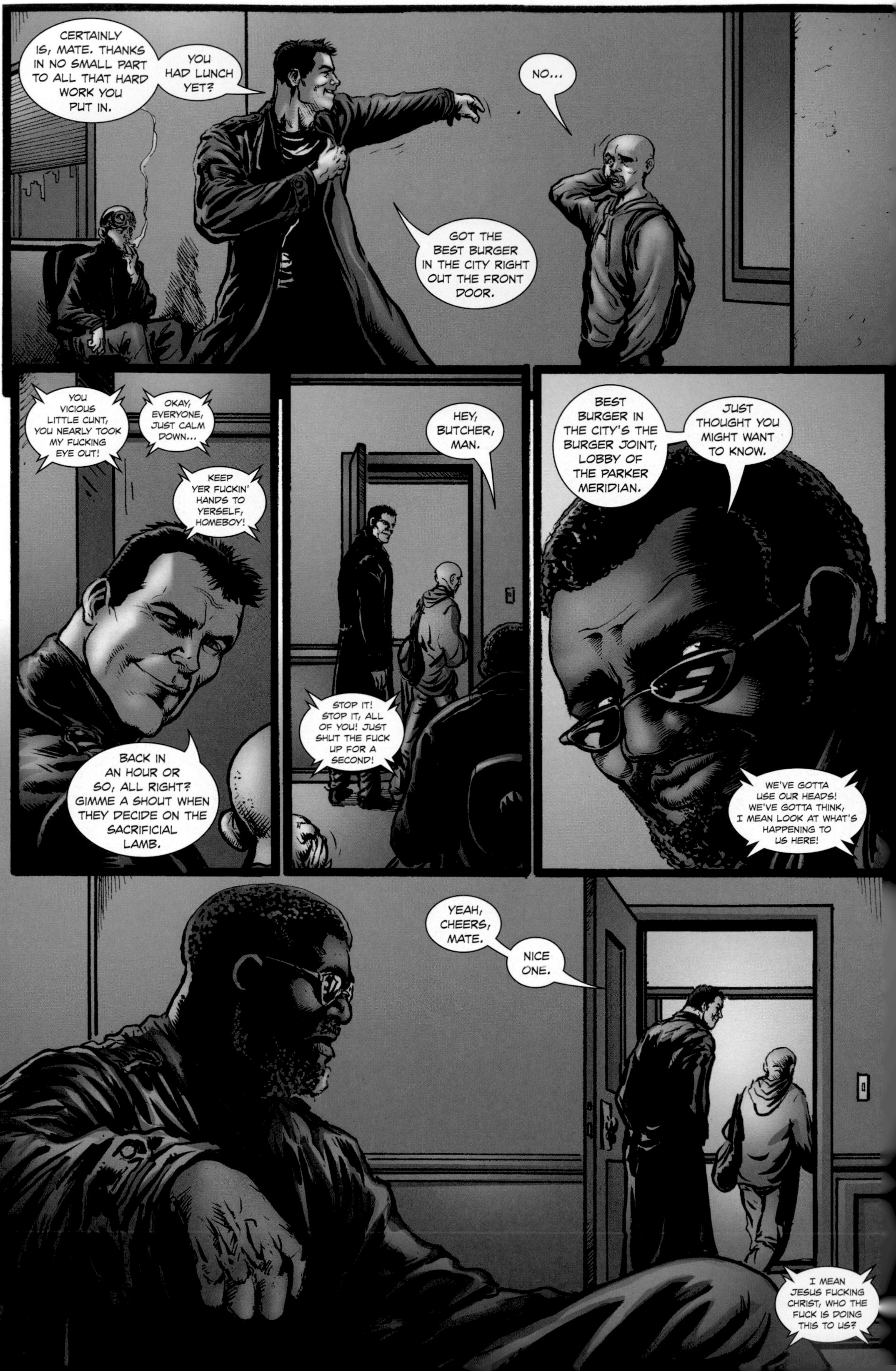

CERTAINLY IS, MATE. THANKS IN NO SMALL PART TO ALL THAT HARD WORK YOU PUT IN.
YOU HAD LUNCH YET?
NO...
GOT THE BEST BURGER IN THE CITY RIGHT OUT THE FRONT DOOR.
YOU VICIOUS LITTLE CUNT, YOU NEARLY TOOK MY FUCKING EYE OUT!
OKAY, EVERYONE, JUST CALM DOWN...
KEEP YER FUCKIN' HANDS TO YERSELF, HOMEBOY!
BACK IN AN HOUR OR SO, ALL RIGHT? GIMME A SHOUT WHEN THEY DECIDE ON THE SACRIFICIAL LAMB.
HEY, BUTCHER, MAN.
STOP IT! STOP IT, ALL OF YOU! JUST SHUT THE FUCK UP FOR A SECOND!
BEST BURGER IN THE CITY'S THE BURGER JOINT, LOBBY OF THE PARKER MERIDIAN.
JUST THOUGHT YOU MIGHT WANT TO KNOW.
WE'VE GOTTA USE OUR HEADS! WE'VE GOTTA THINK, I MEAN LOOK AT WHAT'S HAPPENING TO US HERE!
YEAH, CHEERS, MATE.
NICE ONE.
I MEAN JESUS FUCKING CHRIST, WHO THE FUCK IS DOING THIS TO US?

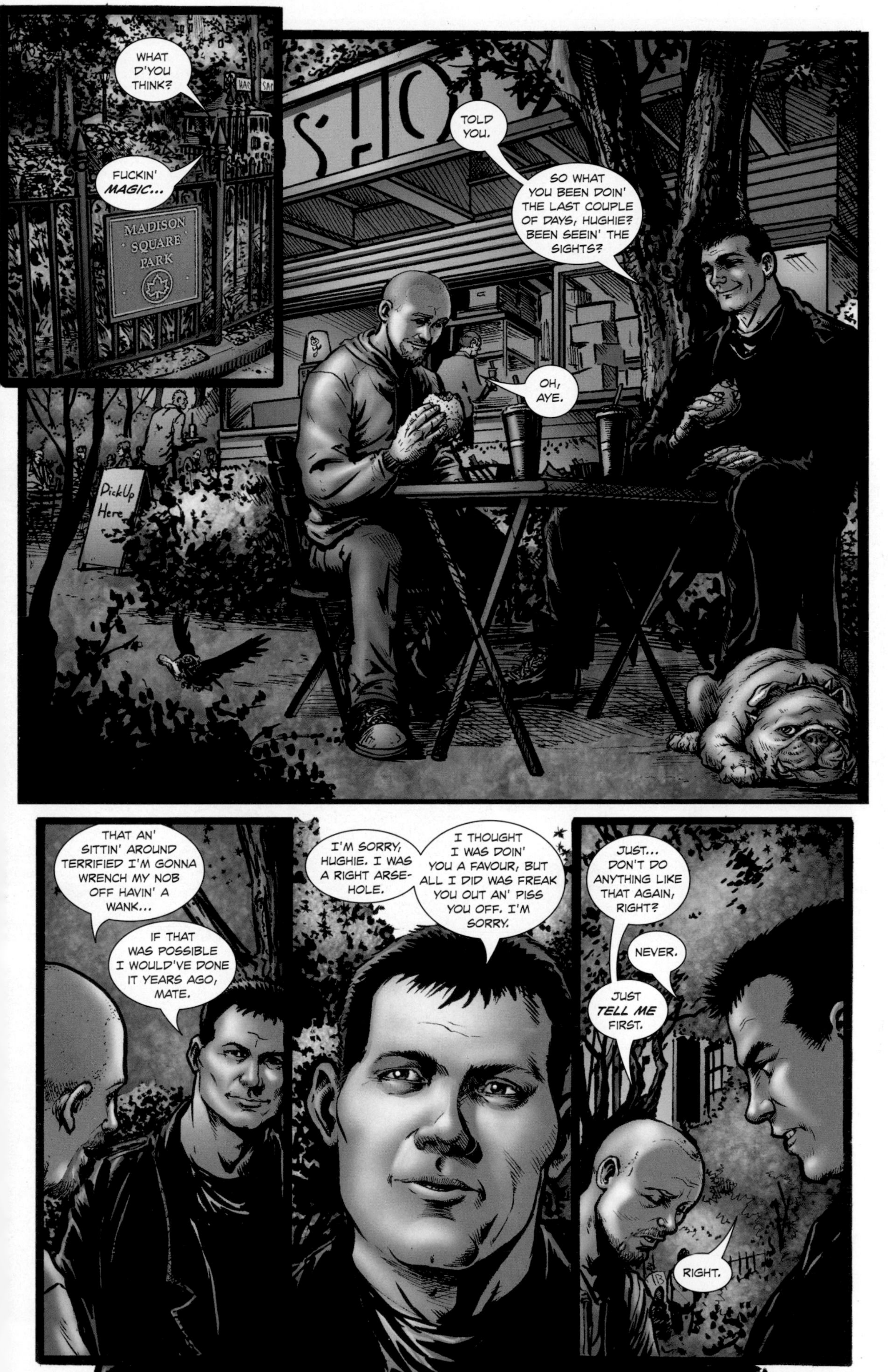
WHAT D'YOU THINK?
FUCKIN' MAGIC...
MADISON SQUARE PARK
TOLD YOU.
SO WHAT YOU BEEN DOIN' THE LAST COUPLE OF DAYS, HUGHIE? BEEN SEEIN' THE SIGHTS?
OH, AYE.
PickUp Here
THAT AN' SITTIN' AROUND TERRIFIED I'M GONNA WRENCH MY NOB OFF HAVIN' A WANK...
IF THAT WAS POSSIBLE I WOULD'VE DONE IT YEARS AGO, MATE.
I'M SORRY, HUGHIE. I WAS A RIGHT ARSE-HOLE.
I THOUGHT I WAS DOIN' YOU A FAVOUR, BUT ALL I DID WAS FREAK YOU OUT AN' PISS YOU OFF. I'M SORRY.
JUST... DON'T DO ANYTHING LIKE THAT AGAIN, RIGHT?
NEVER.
JUST TELL ME FIRST.
RIGHT.

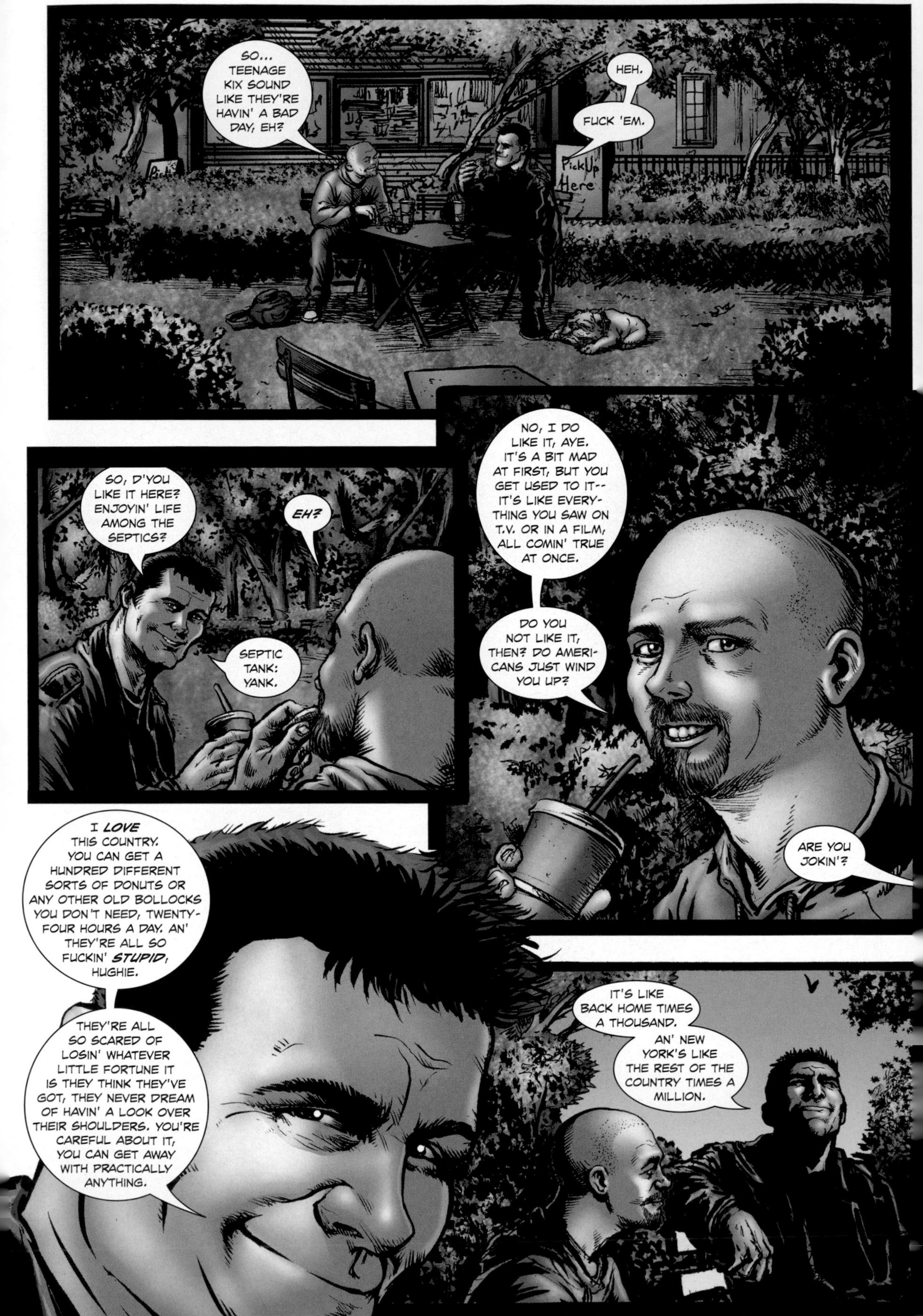
SO... TEENAGE KIX SOUND LIKE THEY'RE HAVIN' A BAD DAY, EH?
HEH.
FUCK 'EM.
PickUp Here
SO, D'YOU LIKE IT HERE? ENJOYIN' LIFE AMONG THE SEPTICS?
EH?
SEPTIC TANK: YANK.
NO, I DO LIKE IT, AYE. IT'S A BIT MAD AT FIRST, BUT YOU GET USED TO IT-- IT'S LIKE EVERY-THING YOU SAW ON T.V. OR IN A FILM, ALL COMIN' TRUE AT ONCE.
DO YOU NOT LIKE IT, THEN? DO AMERI-CANS JUST WIND YOU UP?
ARE YOU JOKIN'?
I *LOVE* THIS COUNTRY. YOU CAN GET A HUNDRED DIFFERENT SORTS OF DONUTS OR ANY OTHER OLD BOLLOCKS YOU DON'T NEED, TWENTY-FOUR HOURS A DAY. AN' THEY'RE ALL SO FUCKIN' ***STUPID***, HUGHIE.
THEY'RE ALL SO SCARED OF LOSIN' WHATEVER LITTLE FORTUNE IT IS THEY THINK THEY'VE GOT, THEY NEVER DREAM OF HAVIN' A LOOK OVER THEIR SHOULDERS. YOU'RE CAREFUL ABOUT IT, YOU CAN GET AWAY WITH PRACTICALLY ANYTHING.
IT'S LIKE BACK HOME TIMES A THOUSAND.
AN' NEW YORK'S LIKE THE REST OF THE COUNTRY TIMES A MILLION.

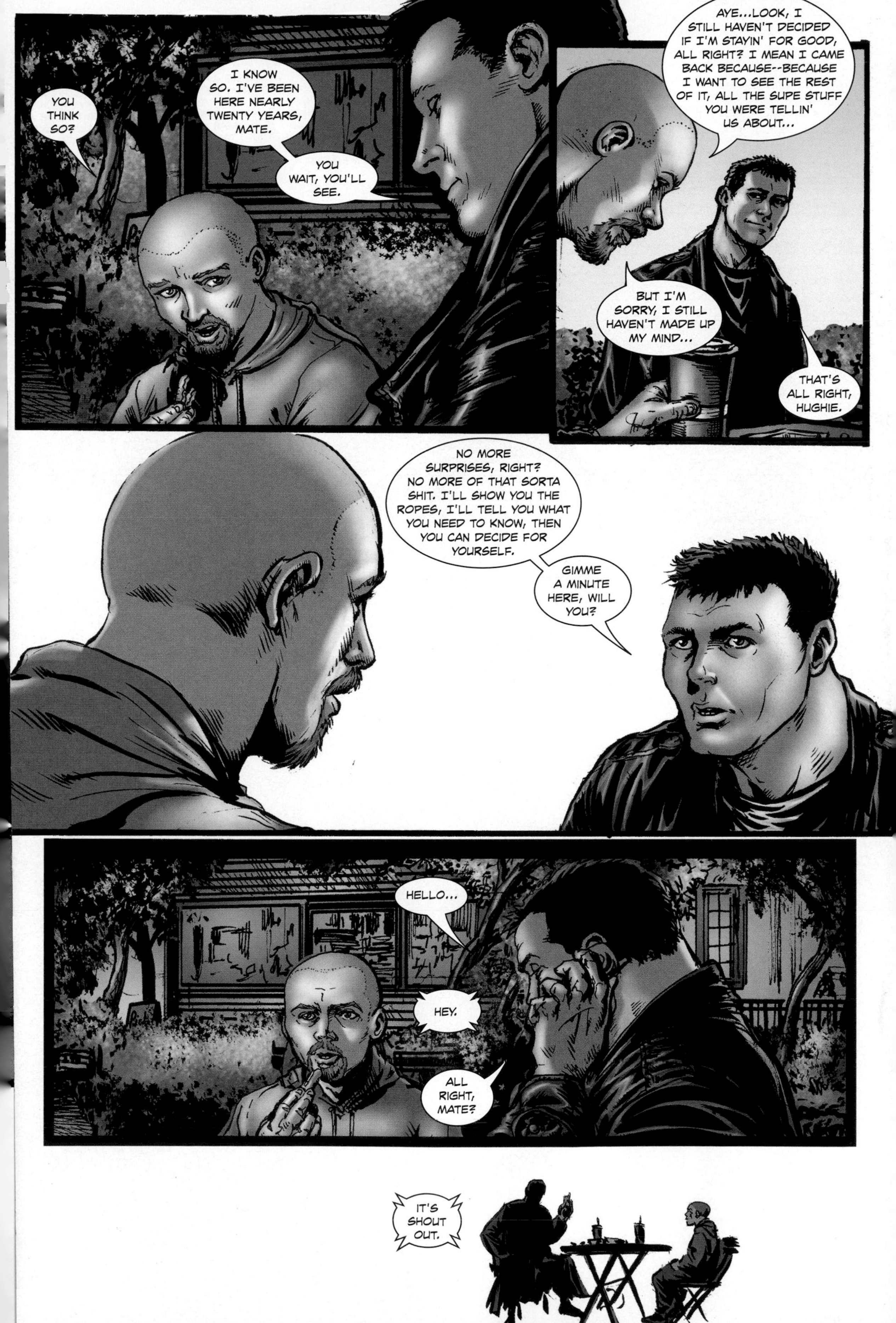
YOU THINK SO?
I KNOW SO. I'VE BEEN HERE NEARLY TWENTY YEARS, MATE.
YOU WAIT, YOU'LL SEE.
AYE...LOOK, I STILL HAVEN'T DECIDED IF I'M STAYIN' FOR GOOD, ALL RIGHT? I MEAN I CAME BACK BECAUSE--BECAUSE I WANT TO SEE THE REST OF IT, ALL THE SUPE STUFF YOU WERE TELLIN' US ABOUT...
BUT I'M SORRY, I STILL HAVEN'T MADE UP MY MIND...
THAT'S ALL RIGHT, HUGHIE.
NO MORE SURPRISES, RIGHT? NO MORE OF THAT SORTA SHIT. I'LL SHOW YOU THE ROPES, I'LL TELL YOU WHAT YOU NEED TO KNOW, THEN YOU CAN DECIDE FOR YOURSELF.
GIMME A MINUTE HERE, WILL YOU?
HELLO...
HEY.
ALL RIGHT, MATE?
IT'S SHOUT OUT.

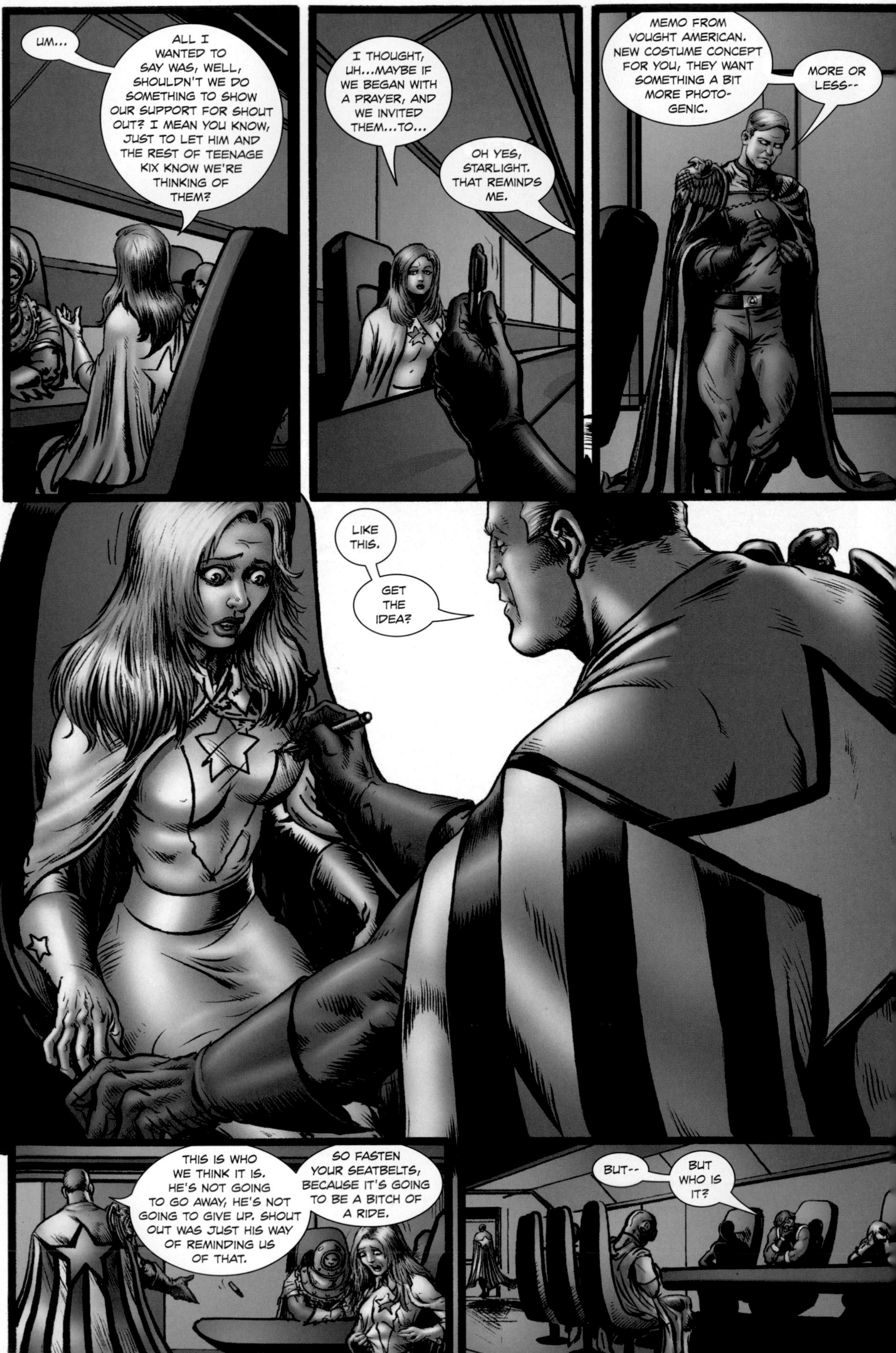
UM...
ALL I WANTED TO SAY WAS, WELL, SHOULDN'T WE DO SOMETHING TO SHOW OUR SUPPORT FOR SHOUT OUT? I MEAN YOU KNOW, JUST TO LET HIM AND THE REST OF TEENAGE KIX KNOW WE'RE THINKING OF THEM?
I THOUGHT, UH...MAYBE IF WE BEGAN WITH A PRAYER, AND WE INVITED THEM...TO...
OH YES, STARLIGHT. THAT REMINDS ME.
MEMO FROM VOUGHT AMERICAN. NEW COSTUME CONCEPT FOR YOU, THEY WANT SOMETHING A BIT MORE PHOTO-GENIC.
MORE OR LESS--
LIKE THIS.
GET THE IDEA?
THIS IS WHO WE THINK IT IS. HE'S NOT GOING TO GO AWAY, HE'S NOT GOING TO GIVE UP. SHOUT OUT WAS JUST HIS WAY OF REMINDING US OF THAT.
SO FASTEN YOUR SEATBELTS, BECAUSE IT'S GOING TO BE A BITCH OF A RIDE.
BUT--
BUT WHO IS IT?

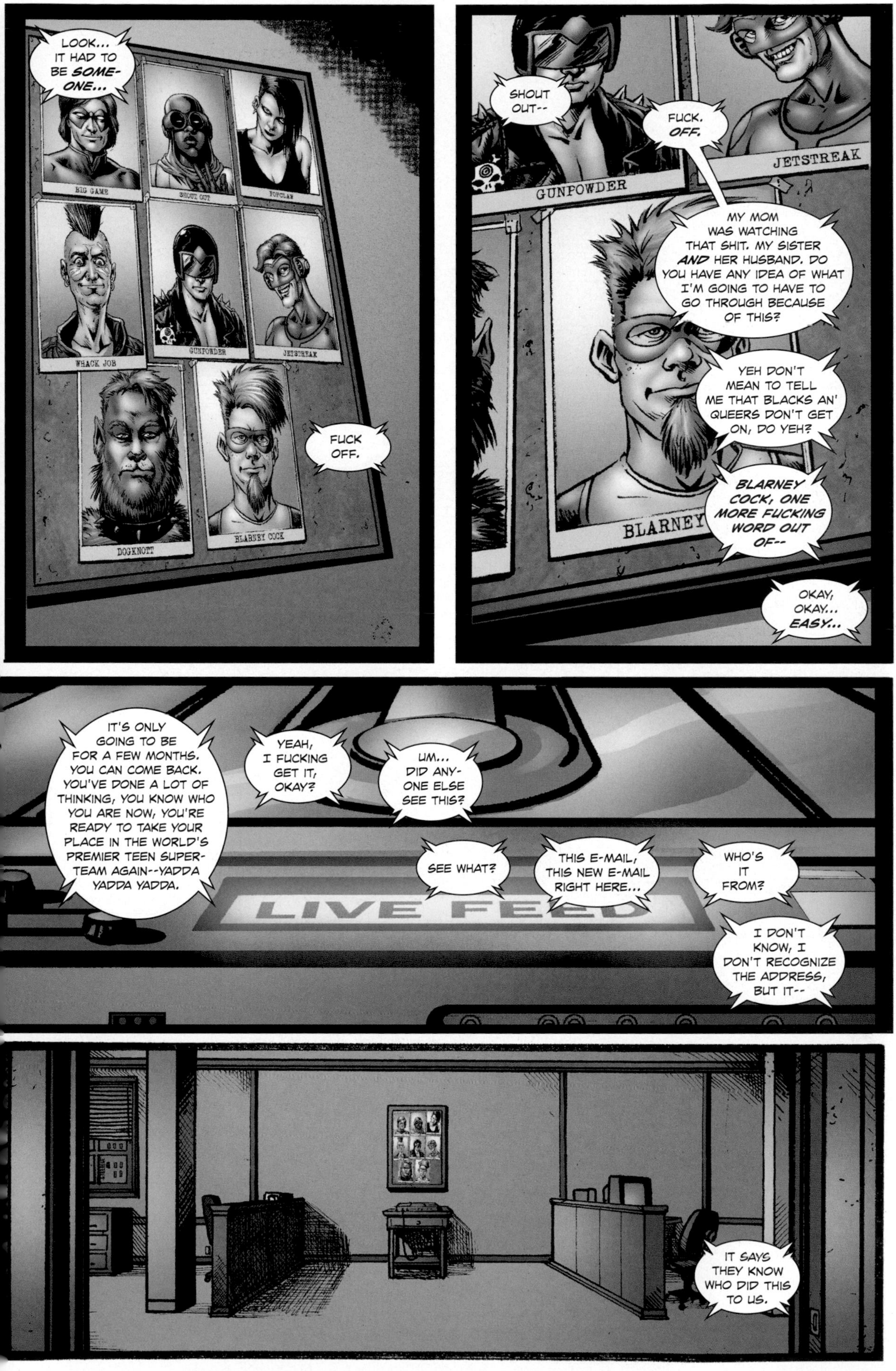
LOOK... IT HAD TO BE SOME-ONE...
BIG GAME
SHOUT OUT
POPCLAW
WHACK JOB
GUNPOWDER
JETSTREAK
DOGKNOTT
BLARNEY COCK
FUCK OFF.
SHOUT OUT--
FUCK. OFF.
GUNPOWDER
JETSTREAK
MY MOM WAS WATCHING THAT SHIT. MY SISTER AND HER HUSBAND. DO YOU HAVE ANY IDEA OF WHAT I'M GOING TO HAVE TO GO THROUGH BECAUSE OF THIS?
YEH DON'T MEAN TO TELL ME THAT BLACKS AN' QUEERS DON'T GET ON, DO YEH?
BLARNEY
BLARNEY COCK, ONE MORE FUCKING WORD OUT OF--
OKAY, OKAY... EASY...
IT'S ONLY GOING TO BE FOR A FEW MONTHS. YOU CAN COME BACK. YOU'VE DONE A LOT OF THINKING, YOU KNOW WHO YOU ARE NOW, YOU'RE READY TO TAKE YOUR PLACE IN THE WORLD'S PREMIER TEEN SUPER-TEAM AGAIN--YADDA YADDA YADDA.
YEAH, I FUCKING GET IT, OKAY?
UM... DID ANY-ONE ELSE SEE THIS?
SEE WHAT?
THIS E-MAIL, THIS NEW E-MAIL RIGHT HERE...
WHO'S IT FROM?
LIVE FEED
I DON'T KNOW, I DON'T RECOGNIZE THE ADDRESS, BUT IT--
IT SAYS THEY KNOW WHO DID THIS TO US.

HERE'S FRENCHIE NOW.

NO, IF YOU THINK ABOUT IT, IT HAD TO BE SHOUT OUT...

HEY, FRENCHIE.

LAIT DE LA MERE!

BECAUSE HE'S BLACK?

WELL YEAH, THAT DOESN'T HURT. BUT WHAT YOU'VE GOTTA THINK ABOUT, IS WHO CAN DO THE MOST DAMAGE TO THE TEAM IF THEY GO DOWN...

CAN'T BE POPCLAW. YOU CAN'T DUMP THE ONE BIRD IN A GROUP OF EIGHT. CAN'T BE GUNPOWDER, OR BANG GOES THE N.R.A. SPONSORSHIP.

CAN'T BE JETSTREAK, 'CAUSE THAT STUPID SLAG THAT WAS WANKIN' OFF HIM AN' BIG GAME COMES FROM *SERIOUS* MONEY: ONE WHIFF OF SCANDAL AN' SHE'LL FUCKIN' BURY 'EM ALL IN LEGAL SHIT.

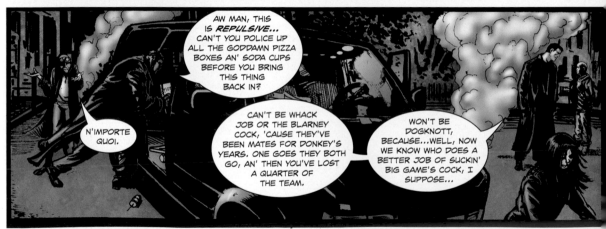

AW MAN, THIS IS *REPULSIVE*... CAN'T YOU POLICE UP ALL THE GODDAMN PIZZA BOXES AN' SODA CUPS BEFORE YOU BRING THIS THING BACK IN?

N'IMPORTE QUOI.

CAN'T BE WHACK JOB OR THE BLARNEY COCK, 'CAUSE THEY'VE BEEN MATES FOR DONKEY'S YEARS. ONE GOES THEY BOTH GO, AN' THEN YOU'VE LOST A QUARTER OF THE TEAM.

WON'T BE DOGKNOTT, BECAUSE...WELL, NOW WE KNOW WHO DOES A BETTER JOB OF SUCKIN' BIG GAME'S COCK, I SUPPOSE...

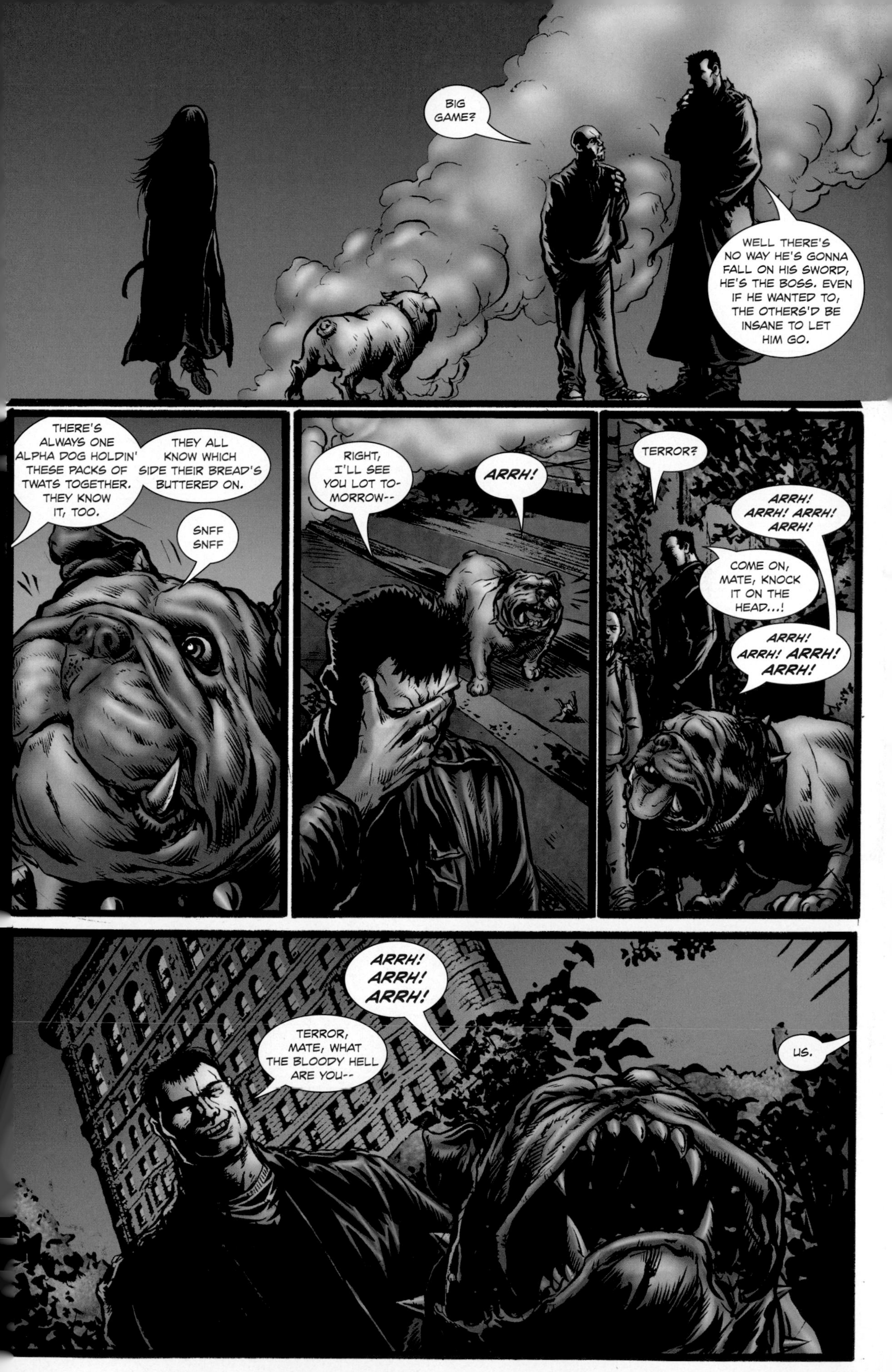
BIG GAME?
WELL THERE'S NO WAY HE'S GONNA FALL ON HIS SWORD, HE'S THE BOSS. EVEN IF HE WANTED TO, THE OTHERS'D BE INSANE TO LET HIM GO.
THERE'S ALWAYS ONE ALPHA DOG HOLDIN' THESE PACKS OF TWATS TOGETHER. THEY KNOW IT, TOO.
THEY ALL KNOW WHICH SIDE THEIR BREAD'S BUTTERED ON.
SNFF SNFF
RIGHT, I'LL SEE YOU LOT TO-MORROW--
ARRH!
TERROR?
ARRH! ARRH! ARRH! ARRH!
COME ON, MATE, KNOCK IT ON THE HEAD...!
ARRH! ARRH! ARRH! ARRH!
ARRH! ARRH! ARRH!
TERROR, MATE, WHAT THE BLOODY HELL ARE YOU--
US.

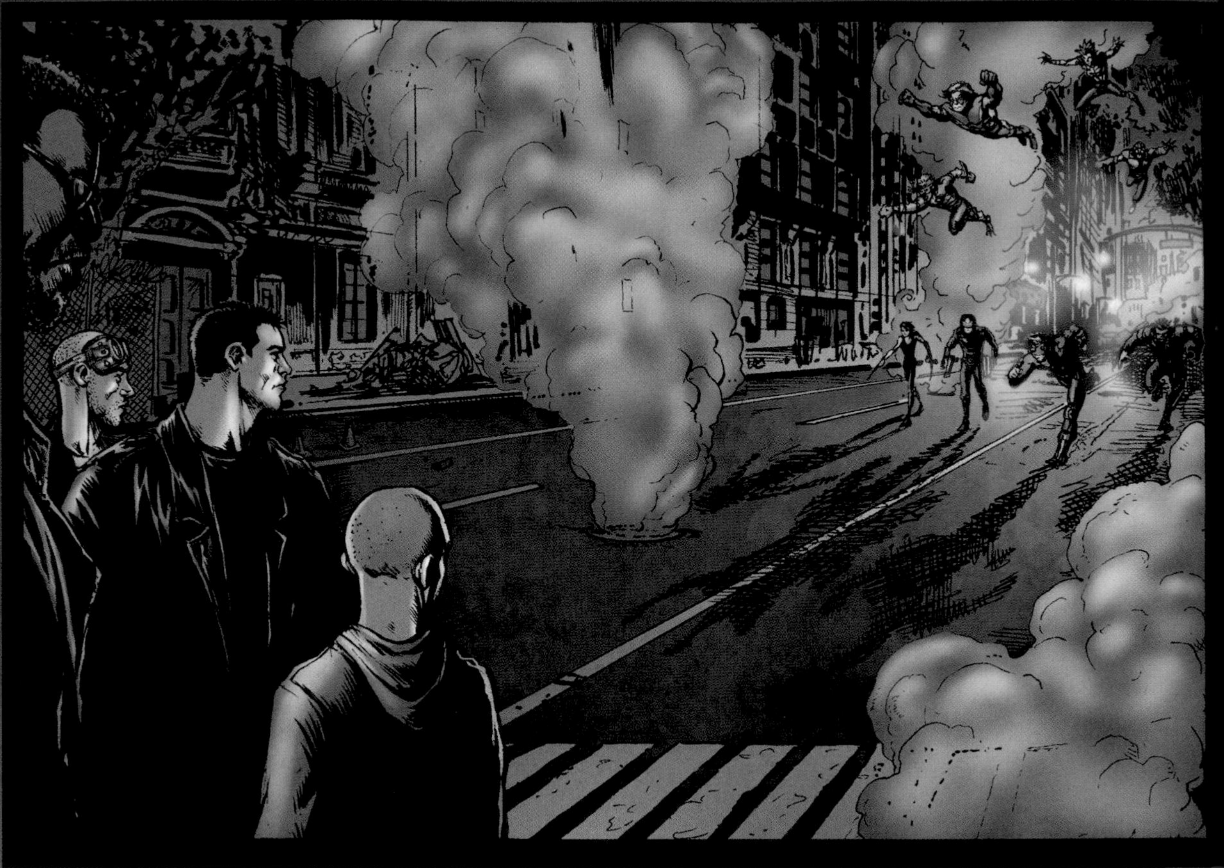

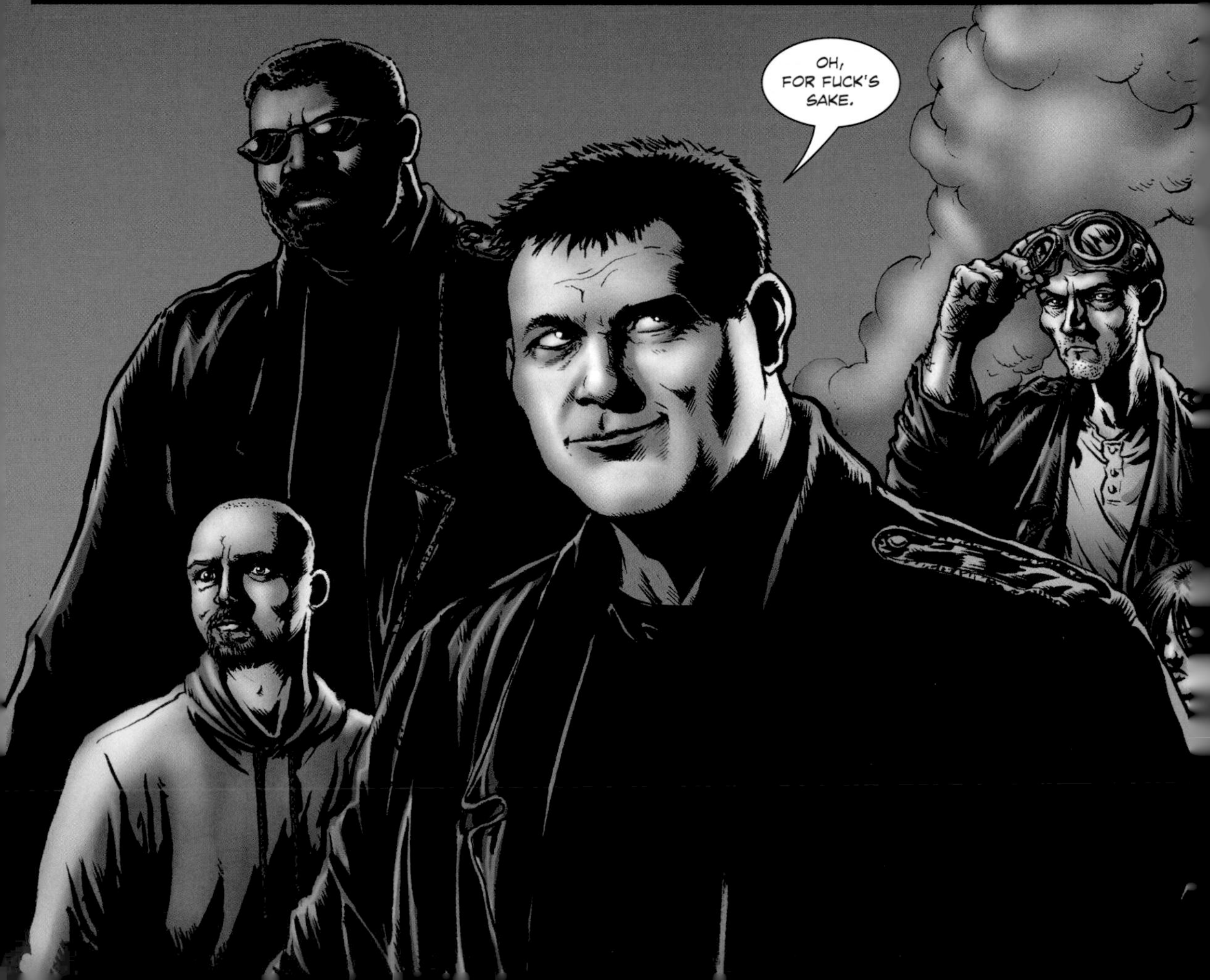
OH, FOR FUCK'S SAKE.

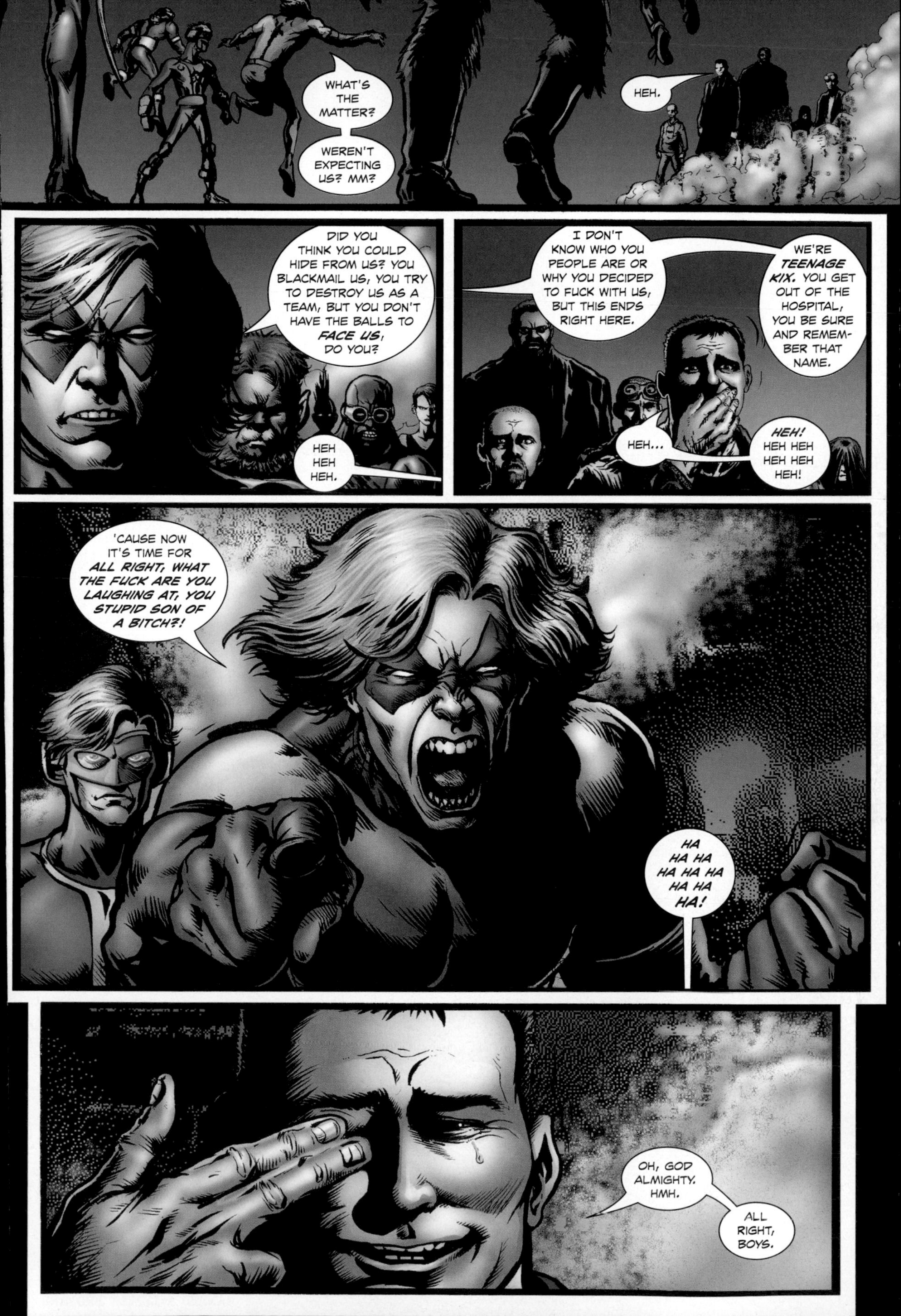
WHAT'S THE MATTER?
WEREN'T EXPECTING US? MM?
HEH.
DID YOU THINK YOU COULD HIDE FROM US? YOU BLACKMAIL US, YOU TRY TO DESTROY US AS A TEAM, BUT YOU DON'T HAVE THE BALLS TO *FACE US*, DO YOU?
HEH HEH HEH.
I DON'T KNOW WHO YOU PEOPLE ARE OR WHY YOU DECIDED TO FUCK WITH US, BUT THIS ENDS RIGHT HERE.
WE'RE *TEENAGE KIX.* YOU GET OUT OF THE HOSPITAL, YOU BE SURE AND REMEMBER THAT NAME.
HEH...
HEH! HEH HEH HEH HEH HEH!
'CAUSE NOW IT'S TIME FOR *ALL RIGHT, WHAT THE FUCK ARE YOU LAUGHING AT, YOU STUPID SON OF A BITCH?!*
HA HA HA HA HA HA HA HA HA!
OH, GOD ALMIGHTY. HMH.
ALL RIGHT, BOYS.

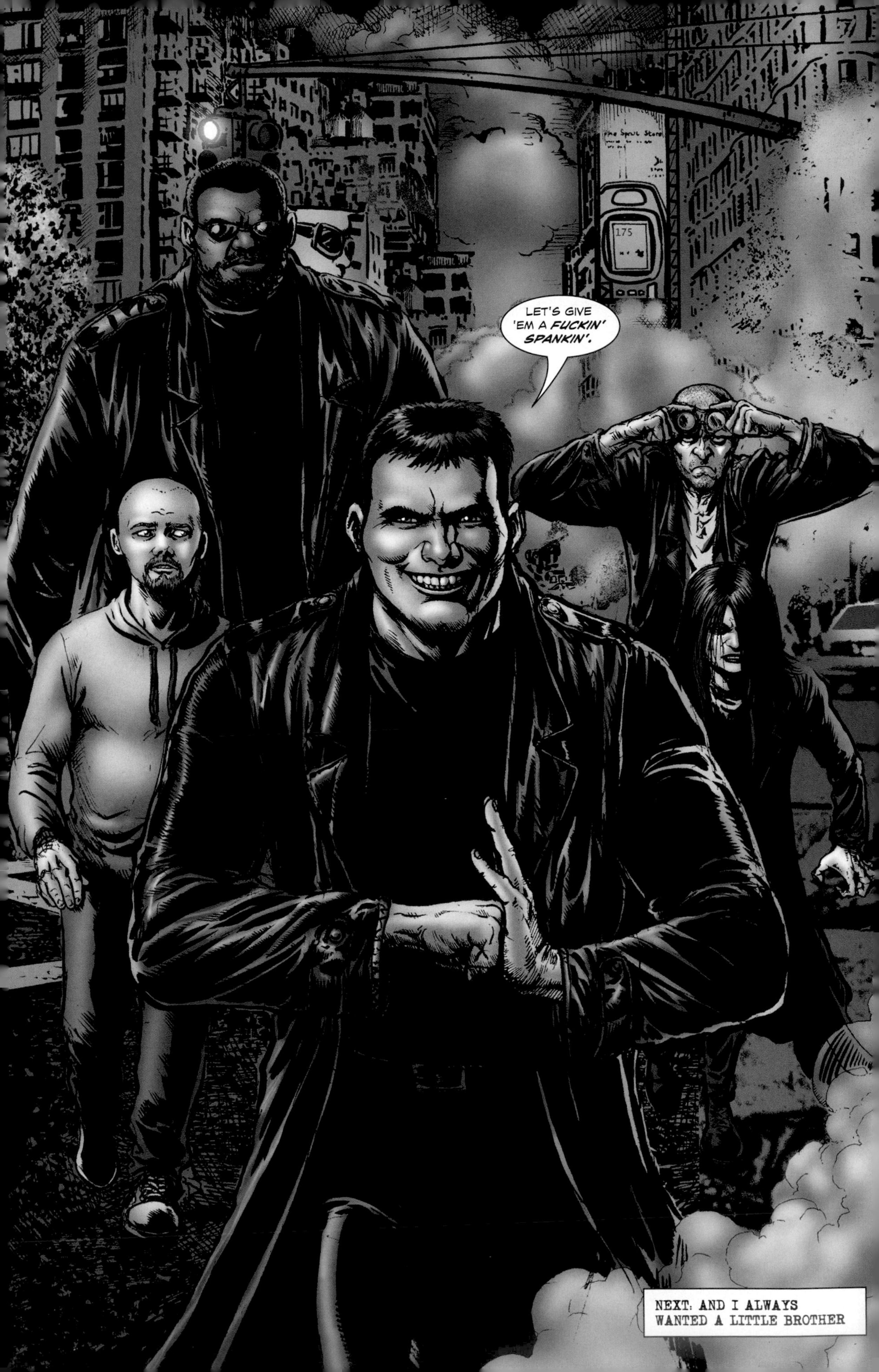
LET'S GIVE 'EM A *FUCKIN'* *SPANKIN'*.
NEXT: AND I ALWAYS WANTED A LITTLE BROTHER

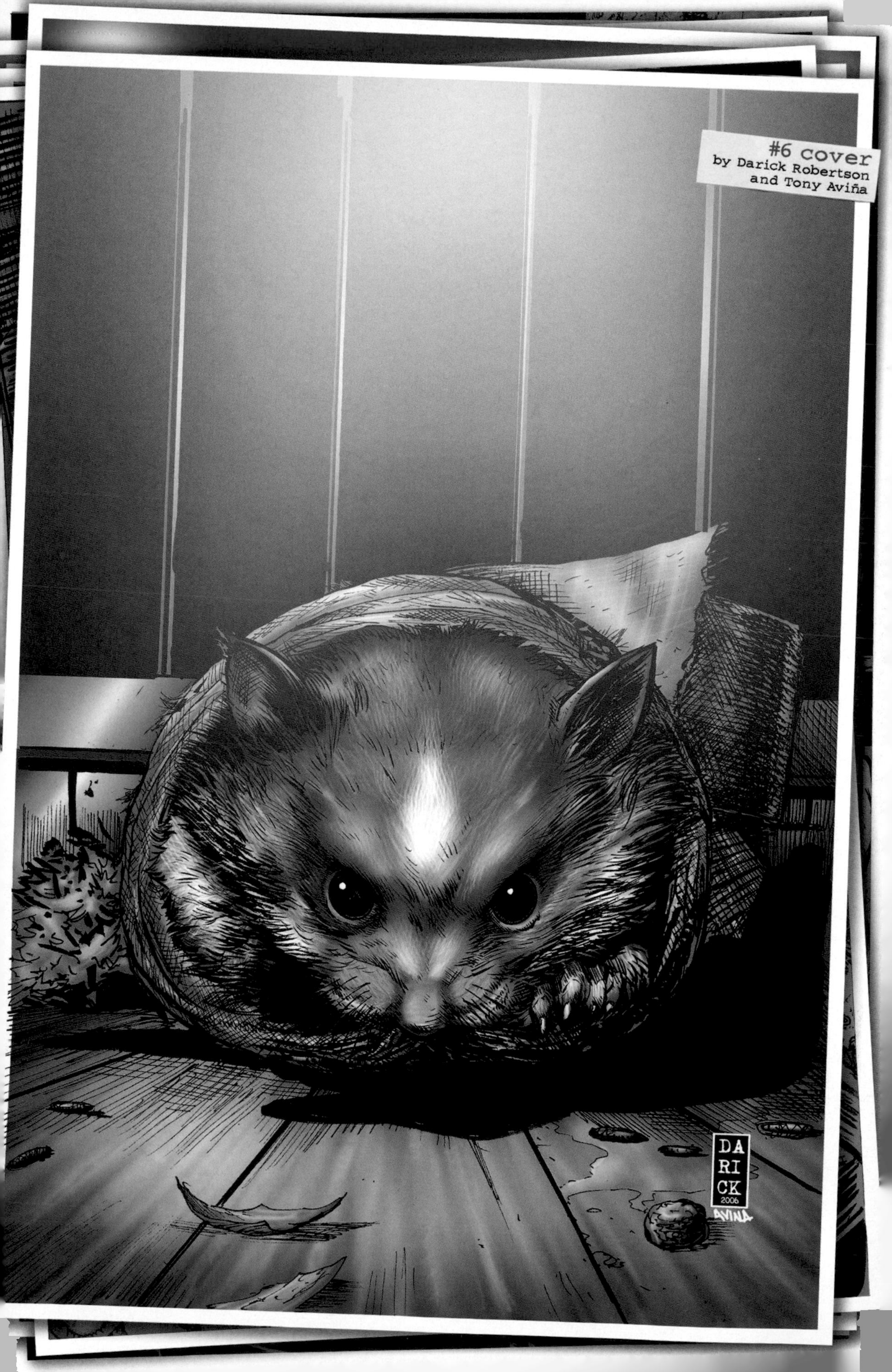
DA
RI
CK
2006
AVINA

#6 cover
by Darick Robertson
and Tony Aviña

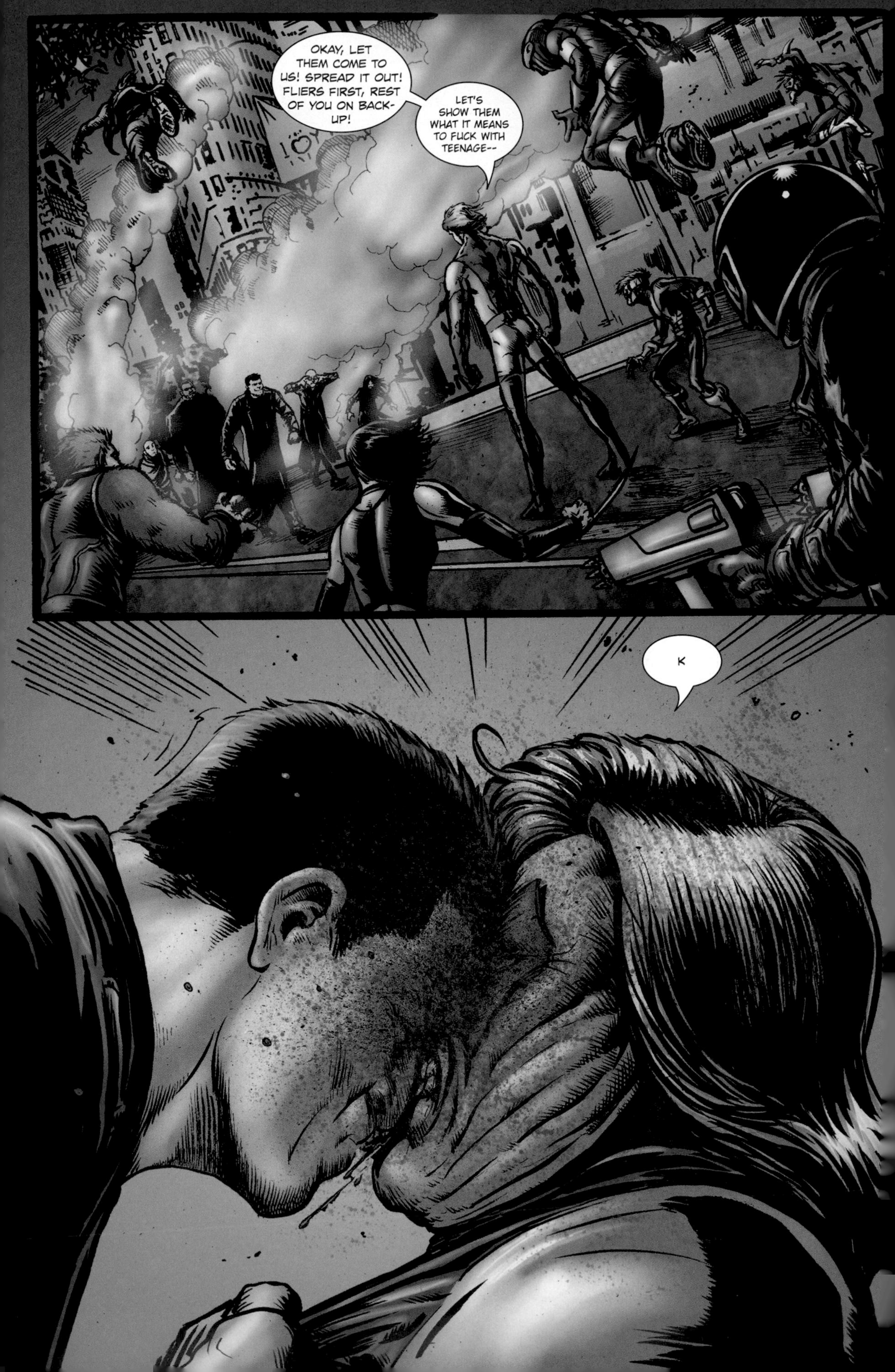
OKAY, LET THEM COME TO US! SPREAD IT OUT! FLIERS FIRST, REST OF YOU ON BACK-UP!
LET'S SHOW THEM WHAT IT MEANS TO FUCK WITH TEENAGE--
K

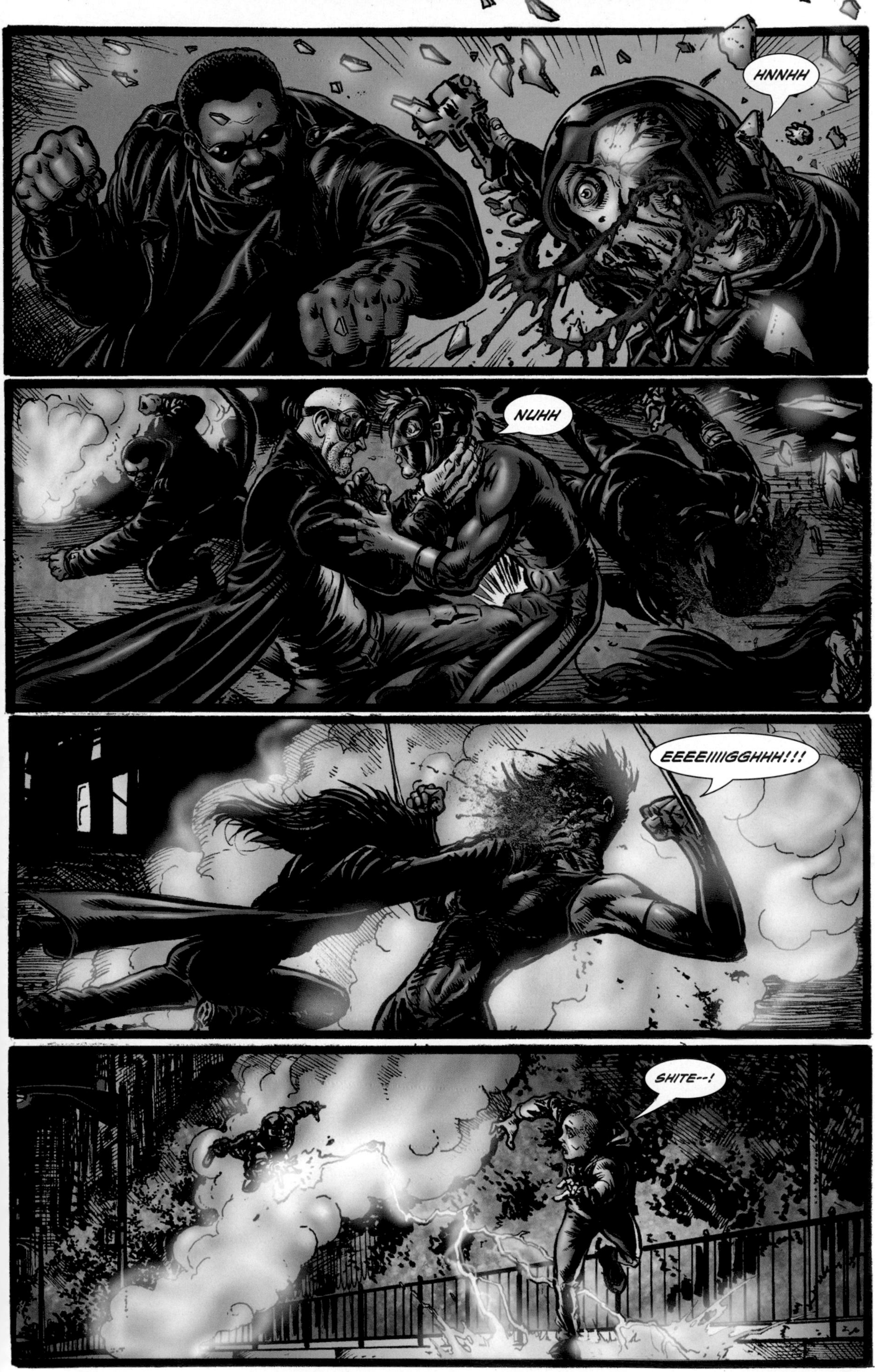

HNNHH
NUHH
EEEEIIIIGGHHH!!!
SHITE--!

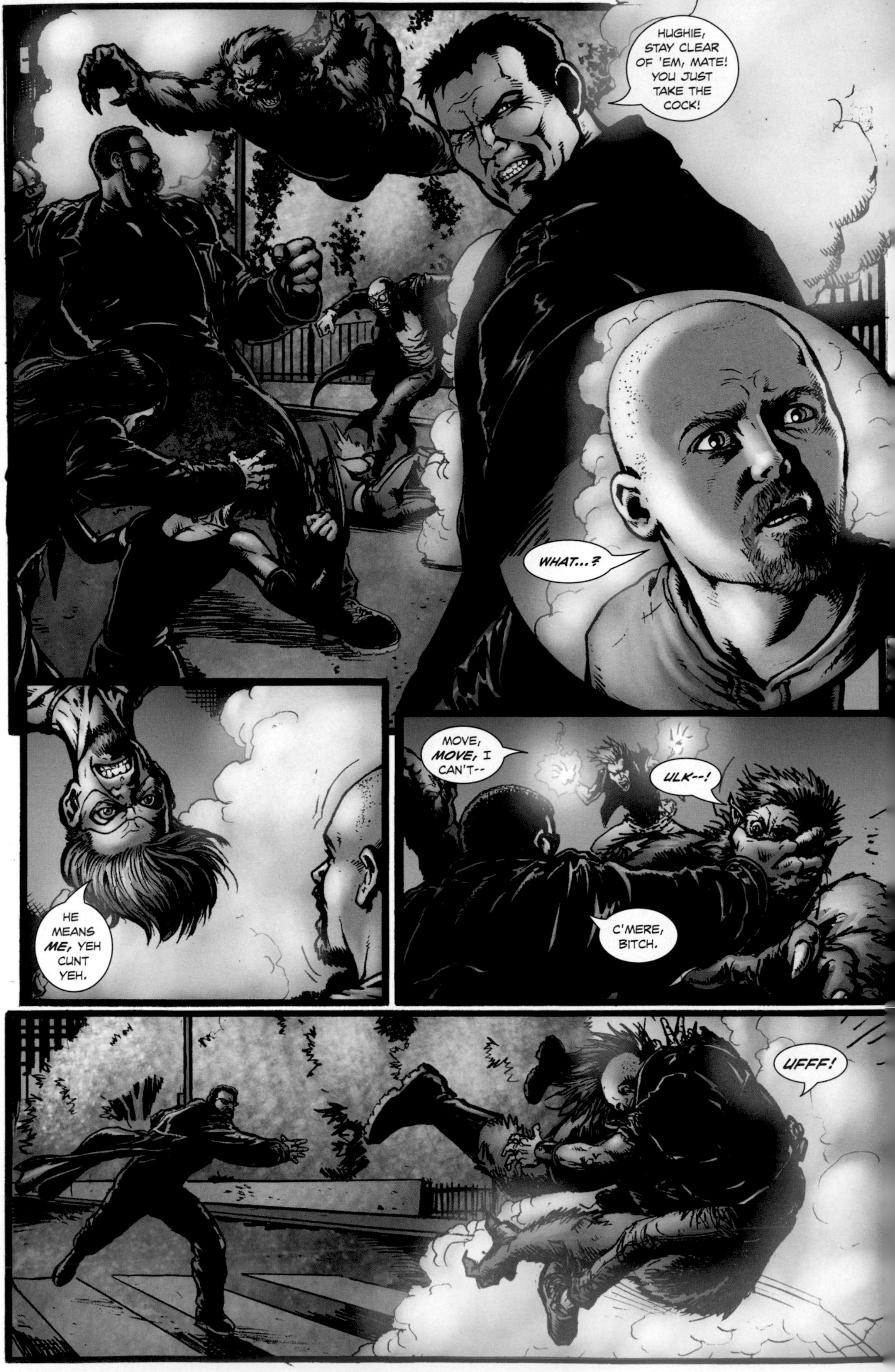
HUGHIE, STAY CLEAR OF 'EM, MATE! YOU JUST TAKE THE COCK!
WHAT...?
HE MEANS ME, YEH CUNT YEH.
MOVE, MOVE, I CAN'T--
ULK--!
C'MERE, BITCH.
UFFF!

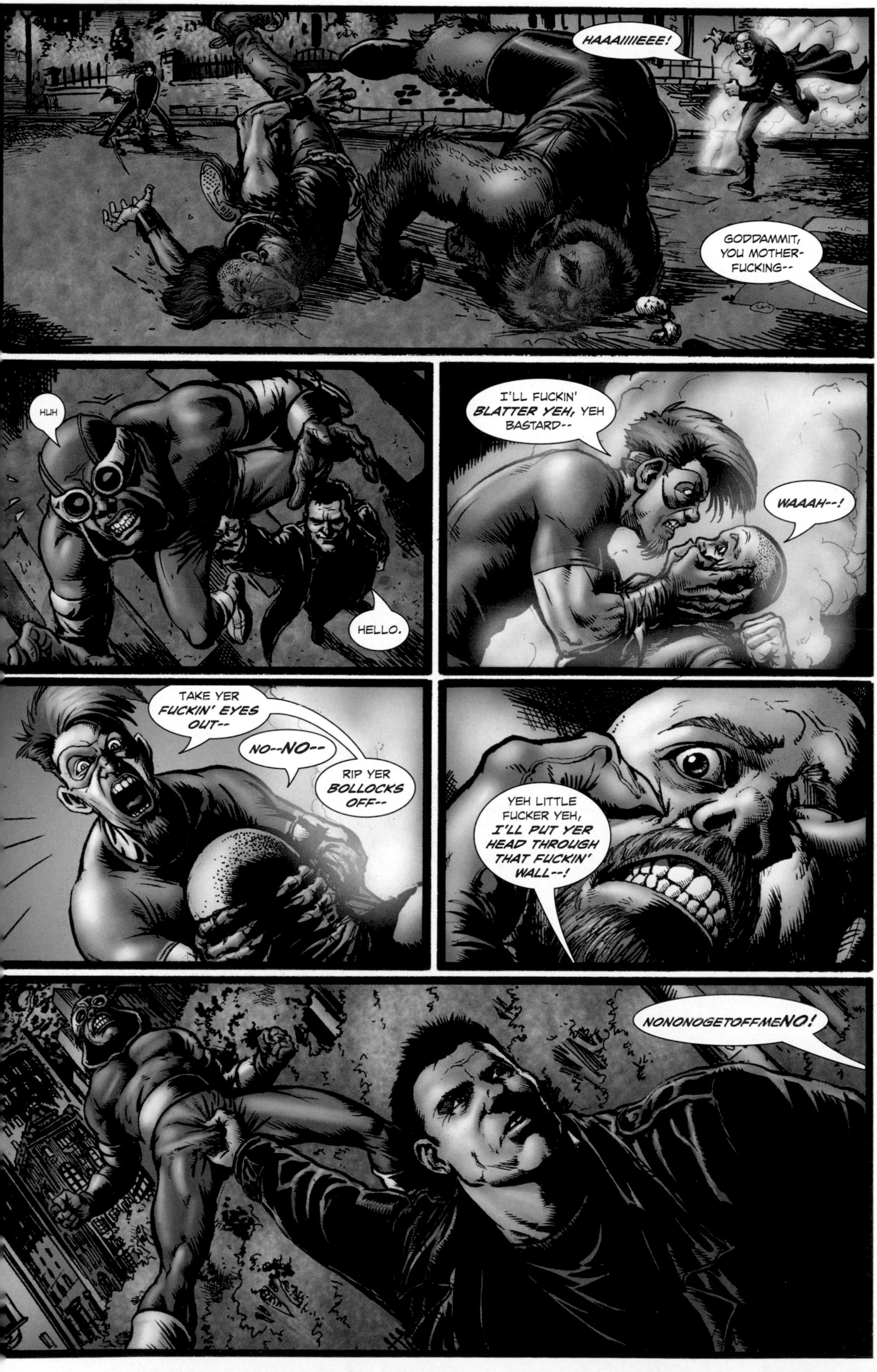
HAAAIIIIEEE!
GODDAMMIT, YOU MOTHER-FUCKING--
HUH
HELLO.
I'LL FUCKIN' BLATTER YEH, YEH BASTARD--
WAAAH--!
TAKE YER FUCKIN' EYES OUT--
NO--NO--
RIP YER BOLLOCKS OFF--
YEH LITTLE FUCKER YEH, I'LL PUT YER HEAD THROUGH THAT FUCKIN' WALL--!
NONONOGETOFFMENO!

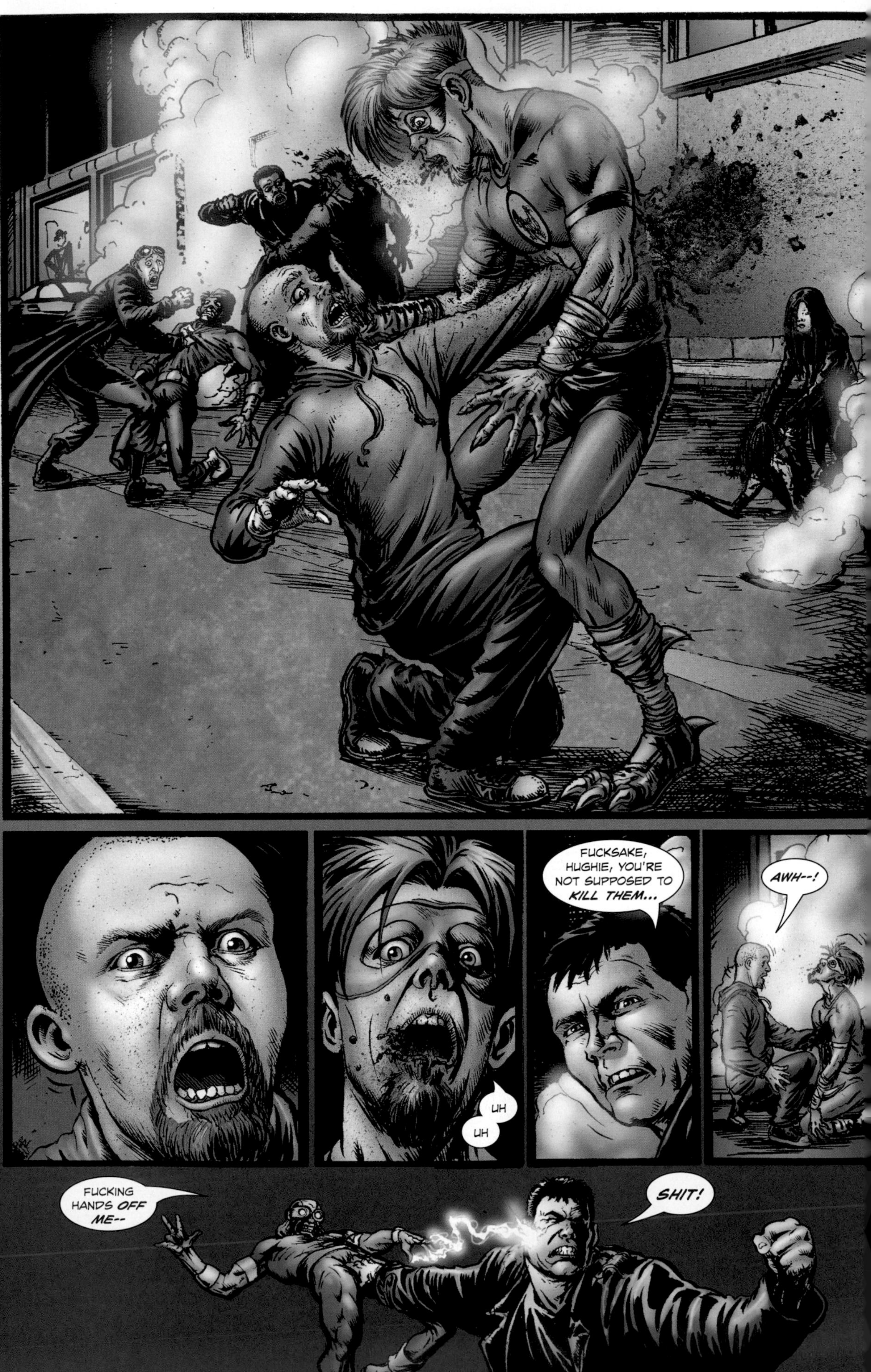
UH
UH
FUCKSAKE, HUGHIE, YOU'RE NOT SUPPOSED TO KILL THEM...
AWH--!
FUCKING HANDS OFF ME--
SHIT!

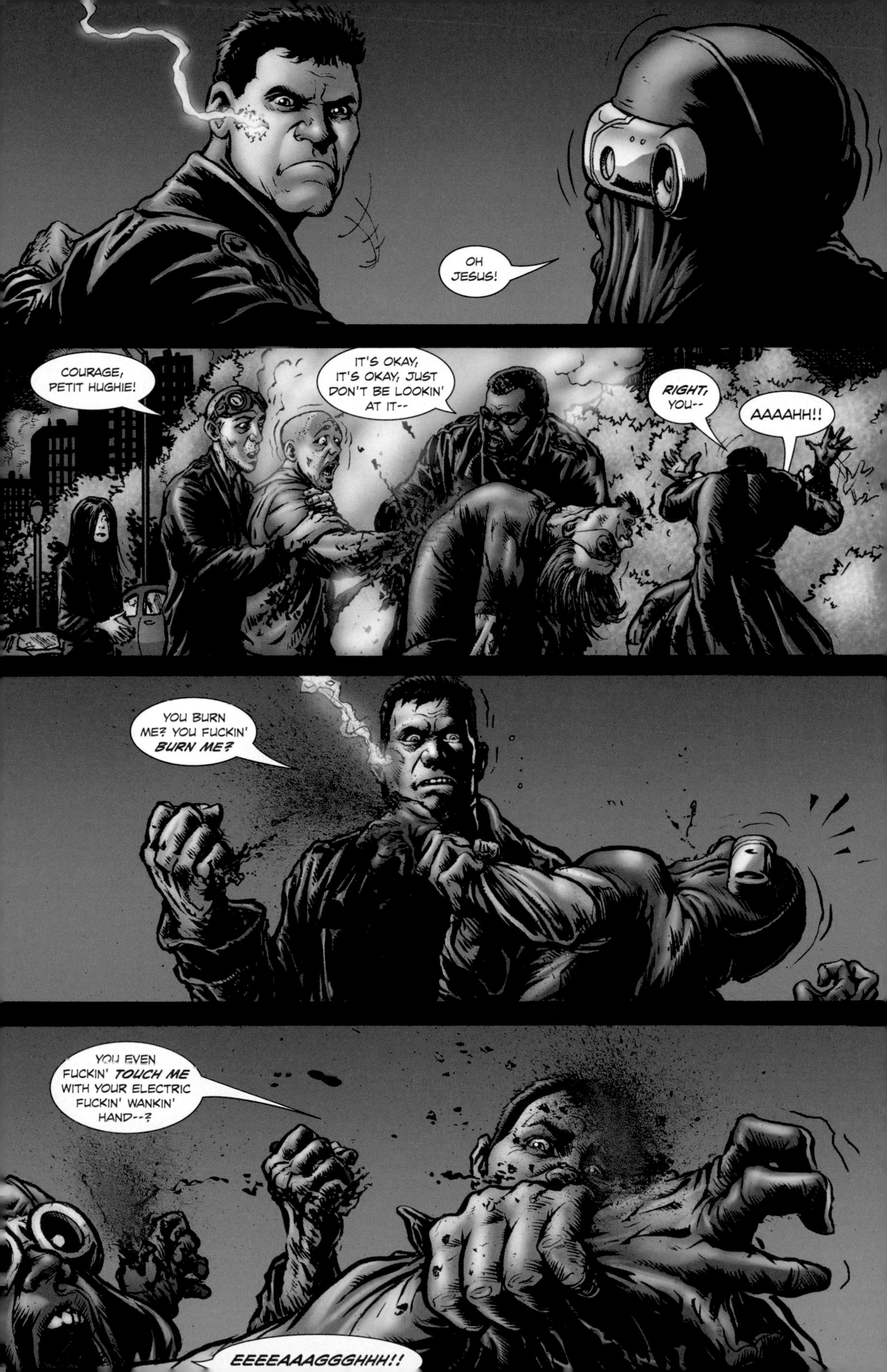
OH JESUS!
COURAGE, PETIT HUGHIE!
IT'S OKAY, IT'S OKAY; JUST DON'T BE LOOKIN' AT IT--
RIGHT, YOU--
AAAAHH!!
YOU BURN ME? YOU FUCKIN' BURN ME?
YOU EVEN FUCKIN' TOUCH ME WITH YOUR ELECTRIC FUCKIN' WANKIN' HAND--?
EEEEAAAGGGHHH!!

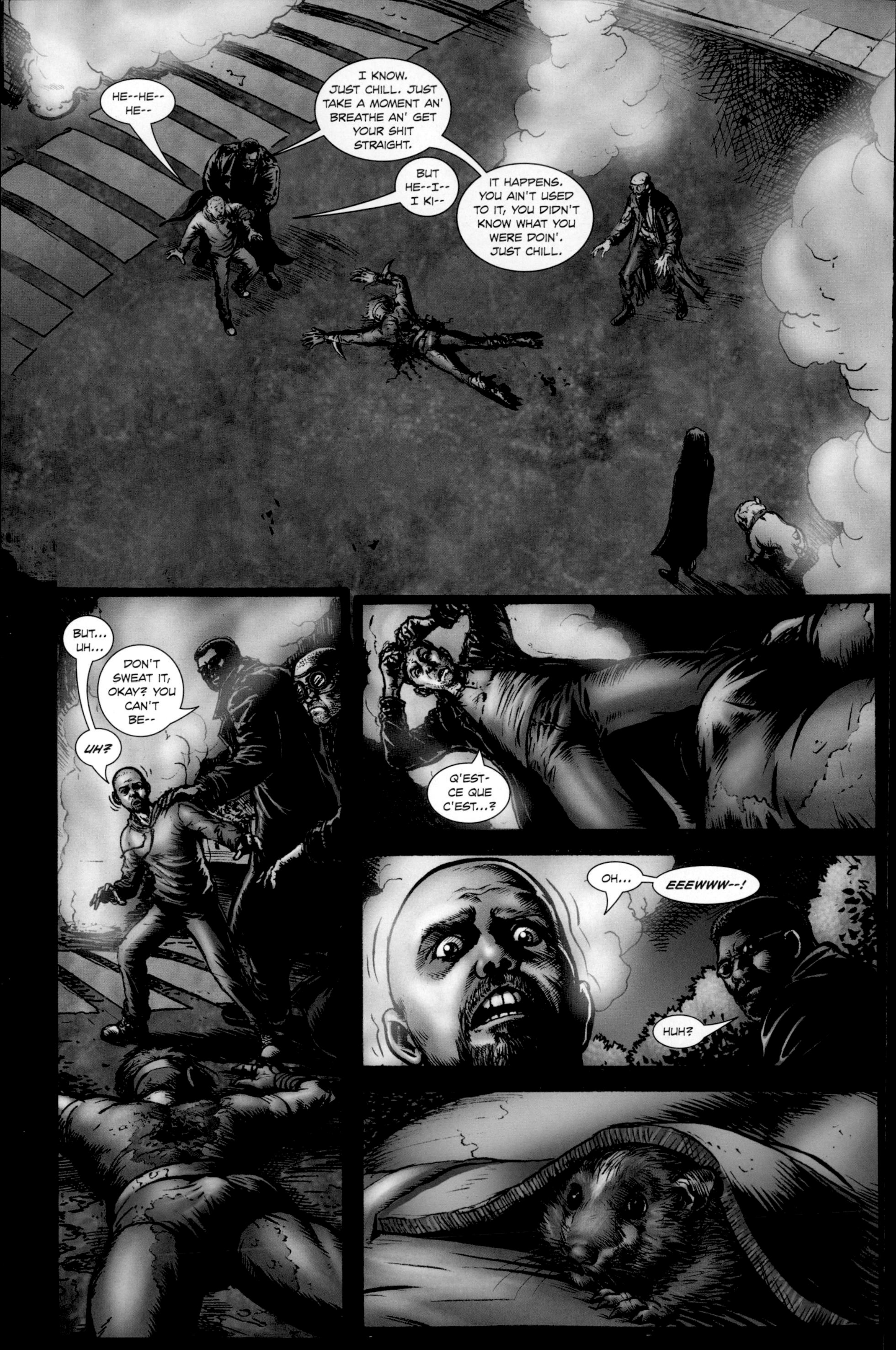
HE--HE--
HE--
I KNOW. JUST CHILL. JUST TAKE A MOMENT AN' BREATHE AN' GET YOUR SHIT STRAIGHT.
BUT HE--I--
I KI--
IT HAPPENS. YOU AIN'T USED TO IT, YOU DIDN'T KNOW WHAT YOU WERE DOIN'. JUST CHILL.
BUT... UH...
DON'T SWEAT IT, OKAY? YOU CAN'T BE--
UH?
Q'EST-CE QUE C'EST...?
OH...
EEEWWW--!
HUH?

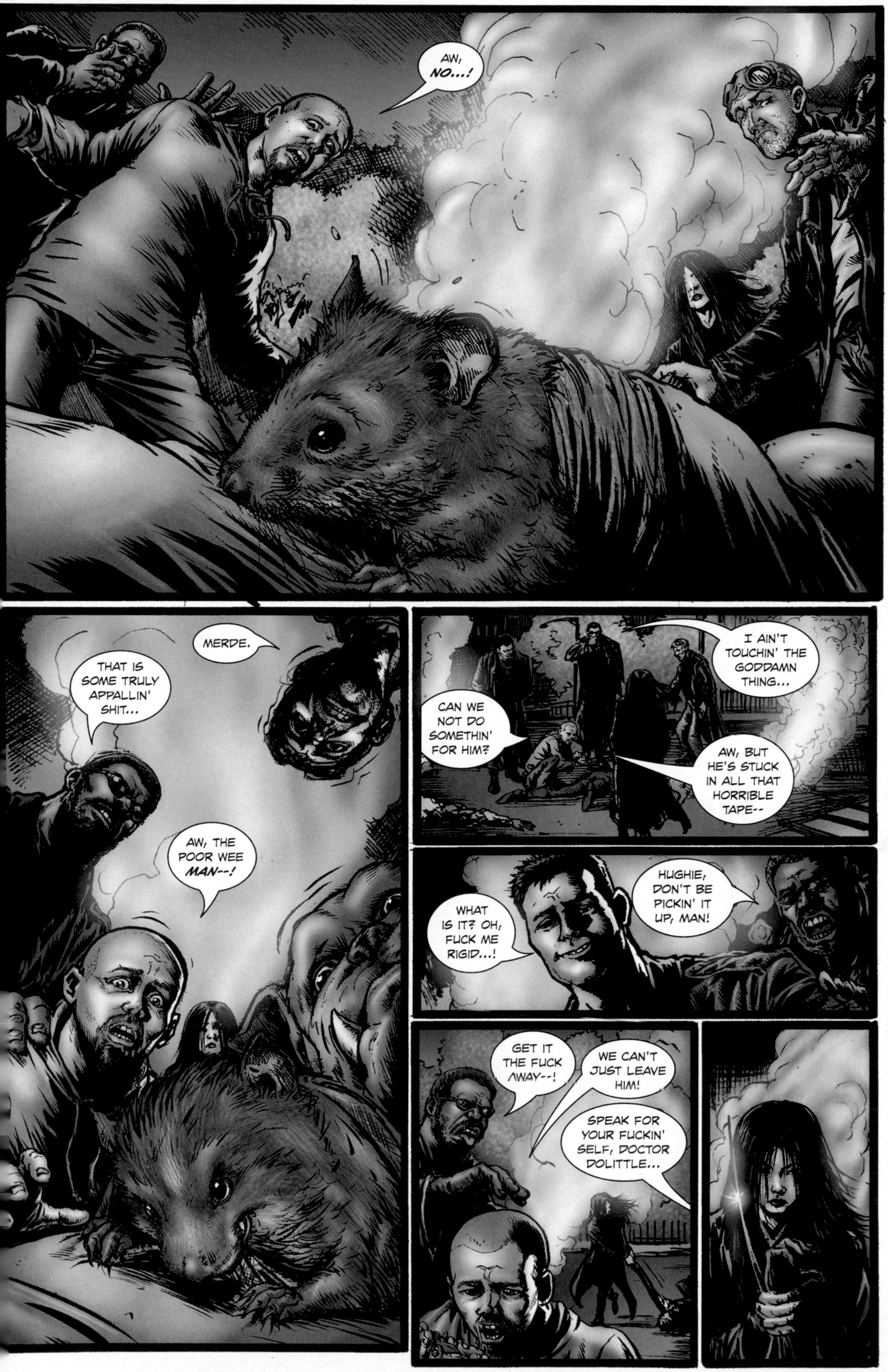
AW, NO...!
MERDE.
THAT IS SOME TRULY APPALLIN' SHIT...
AW, THE POOR WEE MAN--!
I AIN'T TOUCHIN' THE GODDAMN THING...
CAN WE NOT DO SOMETHIN' FOR HIM?
AW, BUT HE'S STUCK IN ALL THAT HORRIBLE TAPE--
HUGHIE, DON'T BE PICKIN' IT UP, MAN!
WHAT IS IT? OH, FUCK ME RIGID...!
GET IT THE FUCK AWAY--!
WE CAN'T JUST LEAVE HIM!
SPEAK FOR YOUR FUCKIN' SELF, DOCTOR DOLITTLE...

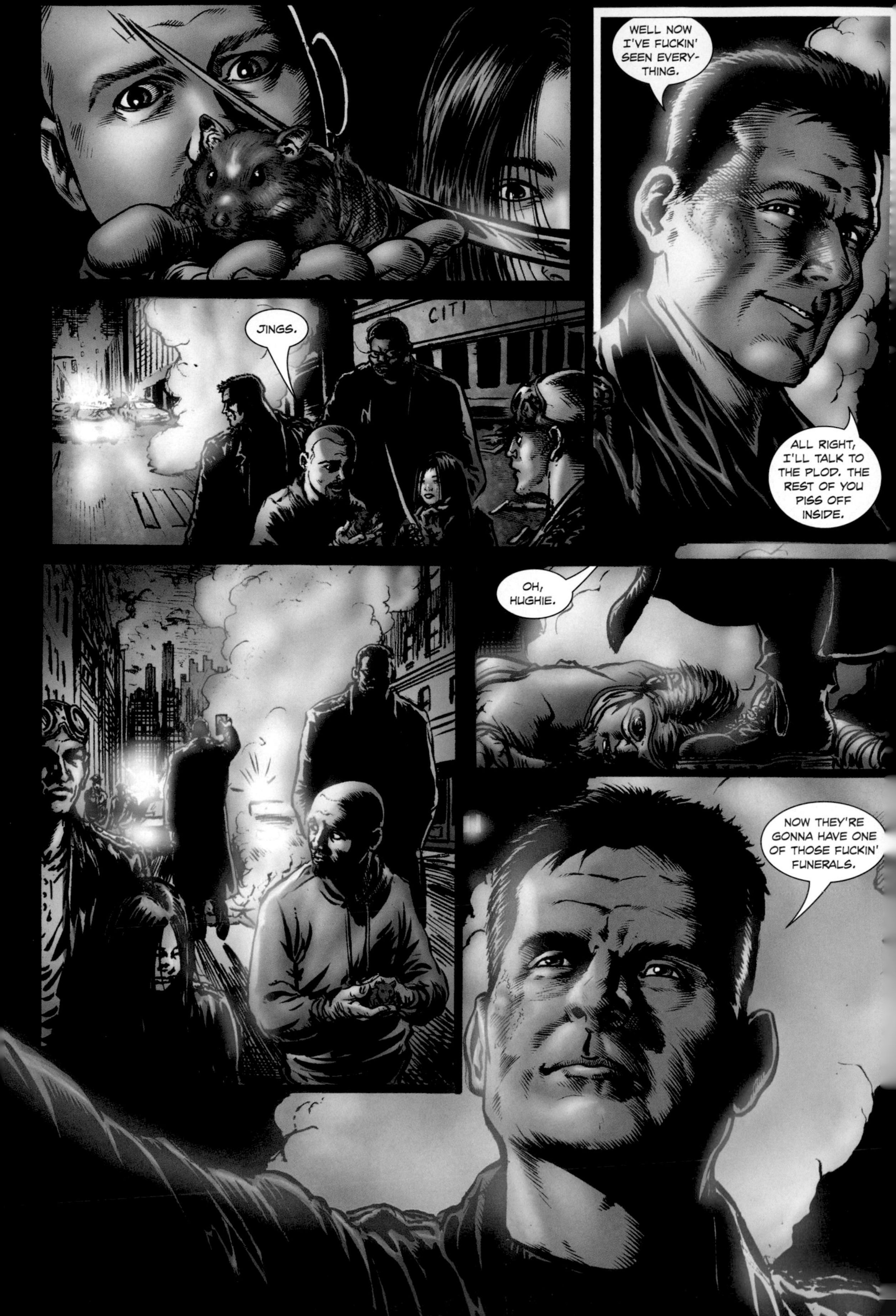
WELL NOW I'VE FUCKIN' SEEN EVERY-THING.
JINGS.
ALL RIGHT, I'LL TALK TO THE PLOD. THE REST OF YOU PISS OFF INSIDE.
OH, HUGHIE.
NOW THEY'RE GONNA HAVE ONE OF THOSE FUCKIN' FUNERALS.

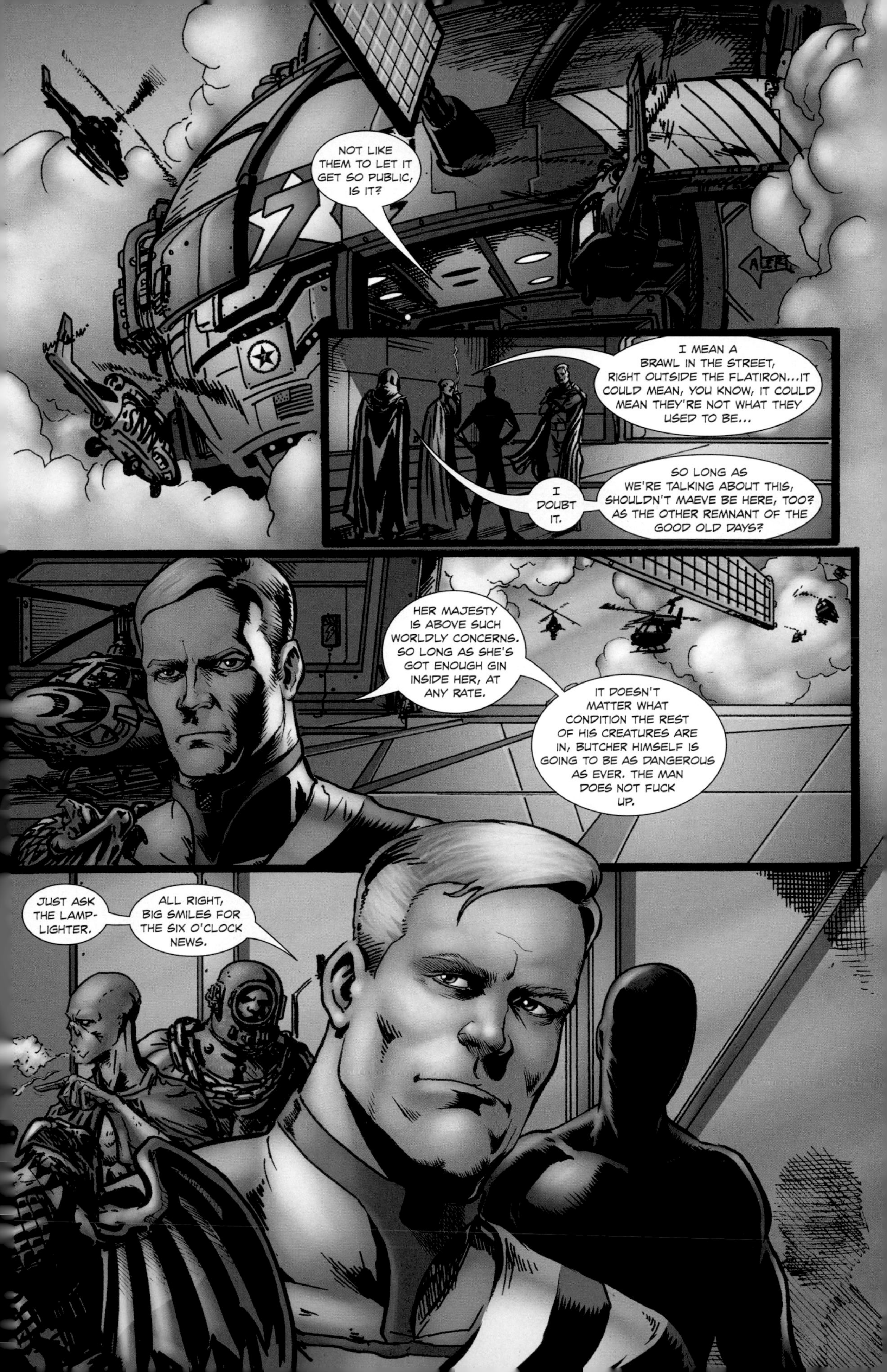

NOT LIKE THEM TO LET IT GET SO PUBLIC, IS IT?
I MEAN A BRAWL IN THE STREET, RIGHT OUTSIDE THE FLATIRON...IT COULD MEAN, YOU KNOW, IT COULD MEAN THEY'RE NOT WHAT THEY USED TO BE...
I DOUBT IT.
SO LONG AS WE'RE TALKING ABOUT THIS, SHOULDN'T MAEVE BE HERE, TOO? AS THE OTHER REMNANT OF THE GOOD OLD DAYS?
HER MAJESTY IS ABOVE SUCH WORLDLY CONCERNS. SO LONG AS SHE'S GOT ENOUGH GIN INSIDE HER, AT ANY RATE.
IT DOESN'T MATTER WHAT CONDITION THE REST OF HIS CREATURES ARE IN, BUTCHER HIMSELF IS GOING TO BE AS DANGEROUS AS EVER. THE MAN DOES NOT FUCK UP.
JUST ASK THE LAMP-LIGHTER.
ALL RIGHT, BIG SMILES FOR THE SIX O'CLOCK NEWS.

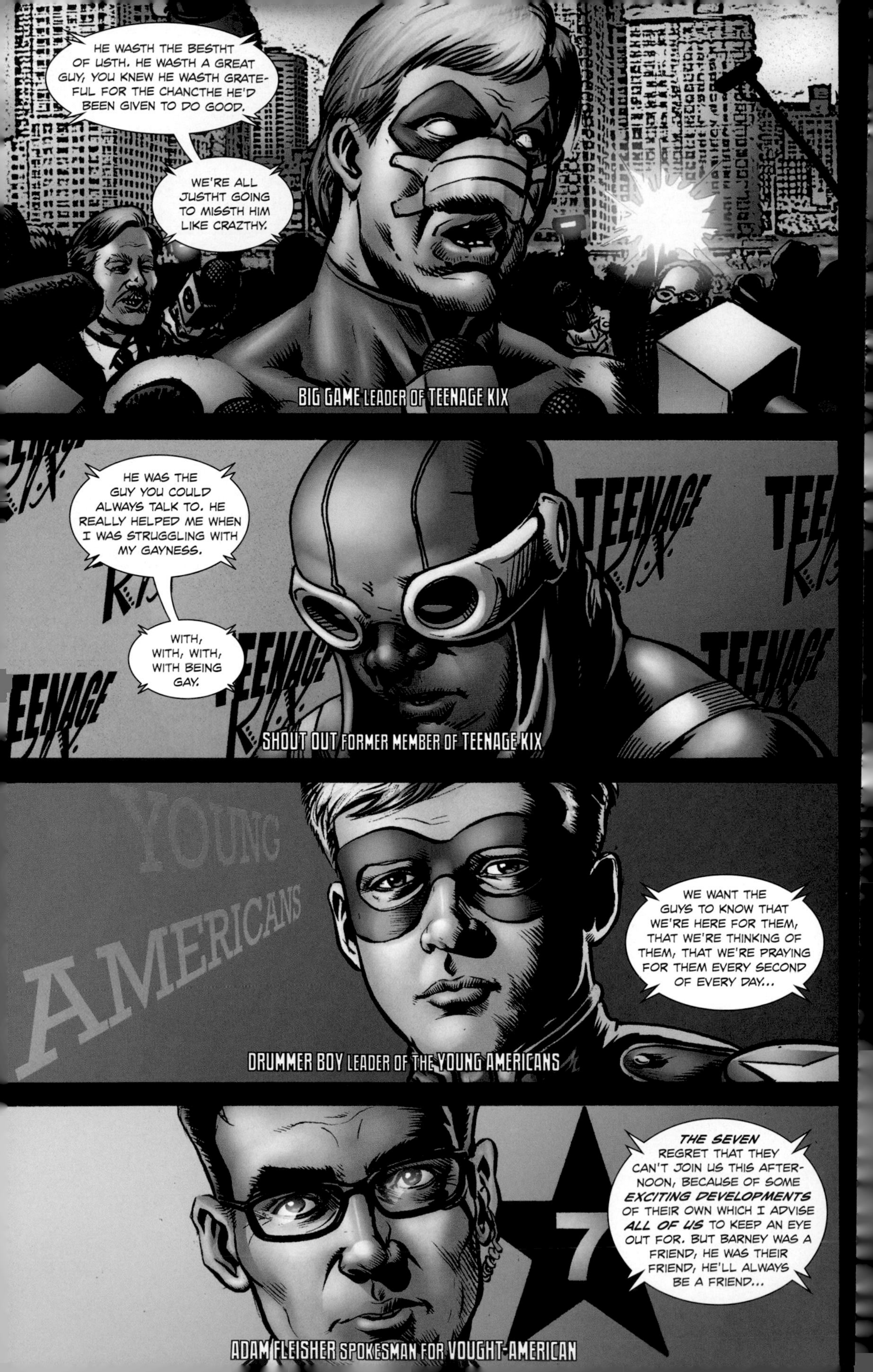

HE WASTH THE BESTHT OF USTH. HE WASTH A GREAT GUY, YOU KNEW HE WASTH GRATE-FUL FOR THE CHANCTHE HE'D BEEN GIVEN TO DO GOOD.
WE'RE ALL JUSTHT GOING TO MISSTH HIM LIKE CRAZTHY.
BIG GAME LEADER OF TEENAGE KIX
HE WAS THE GUY YOU COULD ALWAYS TALK TO. HE REALLY HELPED ME WHEN I WAS STRUGGLING WITH MY GAYNESS.
WITH, WITH, WITH, WITH BEING GAY.
SHOUT OUT FORMER MEMBER OF TEENAGE KIX
YOUNG AMERICANS
WE WANT THE GUYS TO KNOW THAT WE'RE HERE FOR THEM, THAT WE'RE THINKING OF THEM, THAT WE'RE PRAYING FOR THEM EVERY SECOND OF EVERY DAY...
DRUMMER BOY LEADER OF THE YOUNG AMERICANS
THE SEVEN REGRET THAT THEY CAN'T JOIN US THIS AFTER-NOON, BECAUSE OF SOME EXCITING DEVELOPMENTS OF THEIR OWN WHICH I ADVISE ALL OF US TO KEEP AN EYE OUT FOR. BUT BARNEY WAS A FRIEND, HE WAS THEIR FRIEND, HE'LL ALWAYS BE A FRIEND...
ADAM FLEISHER SPOKESMAN FOR VOUGHT-AMERICAN

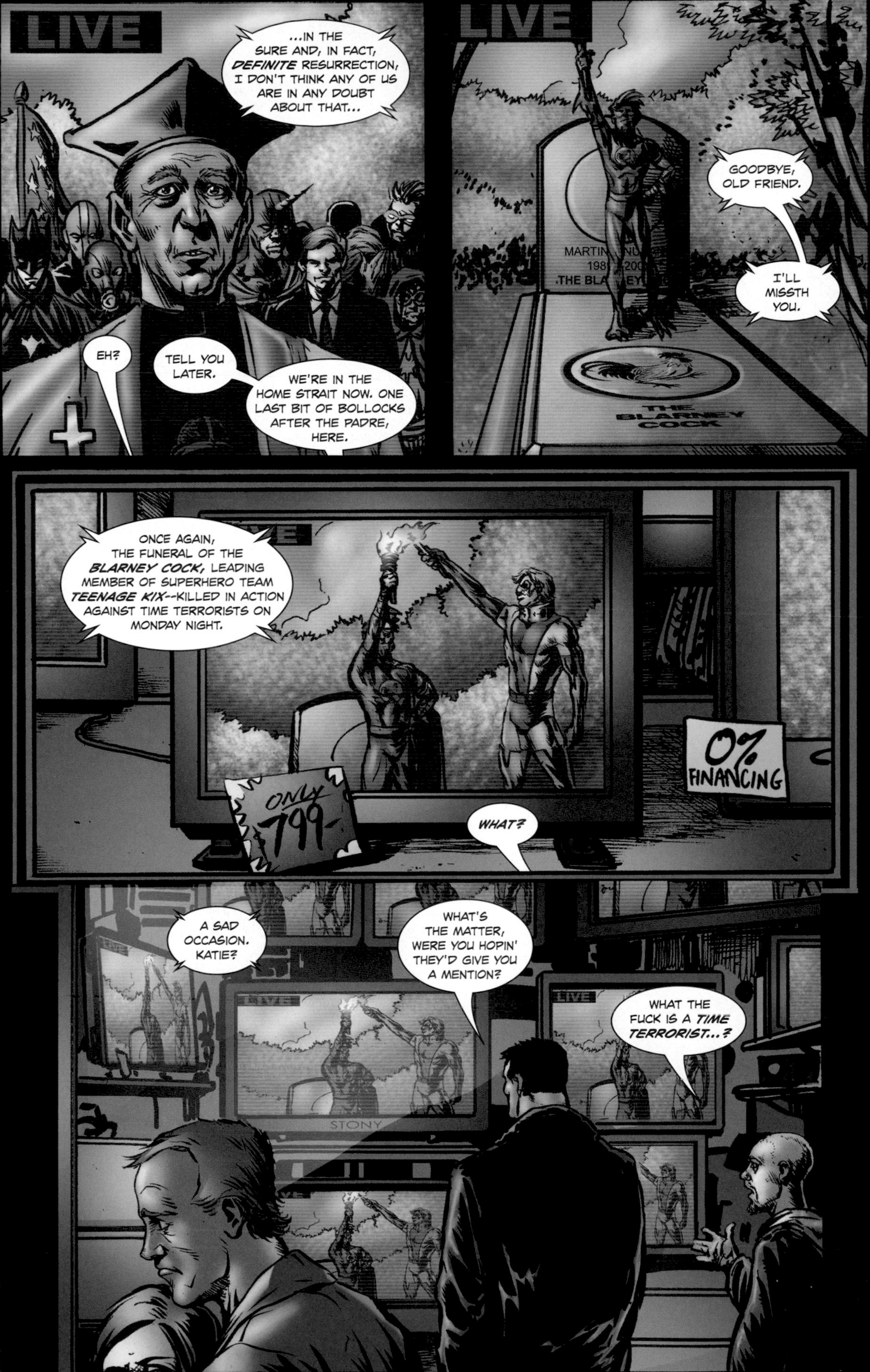
LIVE
...IN THE SURE AND, IN FACT, DEFINITE RESURRECTION, I DON'T THINK ANY OF US ARE IN ANY DOUBT ABOUT THAT...
EH?
TELL YOU LATER.
WE'RE IN THE HOME STRAIT NOW. ONE LAST BIT OF BOLLOCKS AFTER THE PADRE, HERE.
LIVE
GOODBYE, OLD FRIEND.
I'LL MISSTH YOU.
THE BLARNEY COCK
ONCE AGAIN, THE FUNERAL OF THE BLARNEY COCK, LEADING MEMBER OF SUPERHERO TEAM TEENAGE KIX--KILLED IN ACTION AGAINST TIME TERRORISTS ON MONDAY NIGHT.
0% FINANCING
ONLY 799-
WHAT?
A SAD OCCASION. KATIE?
WHAT'S THE MATTER, WERE YOU HOPIN' THEY'D GIVE YOU A MENTION?
WHAT THE FUCK IS A TIME TERRORIST...?
LIVE
STONY

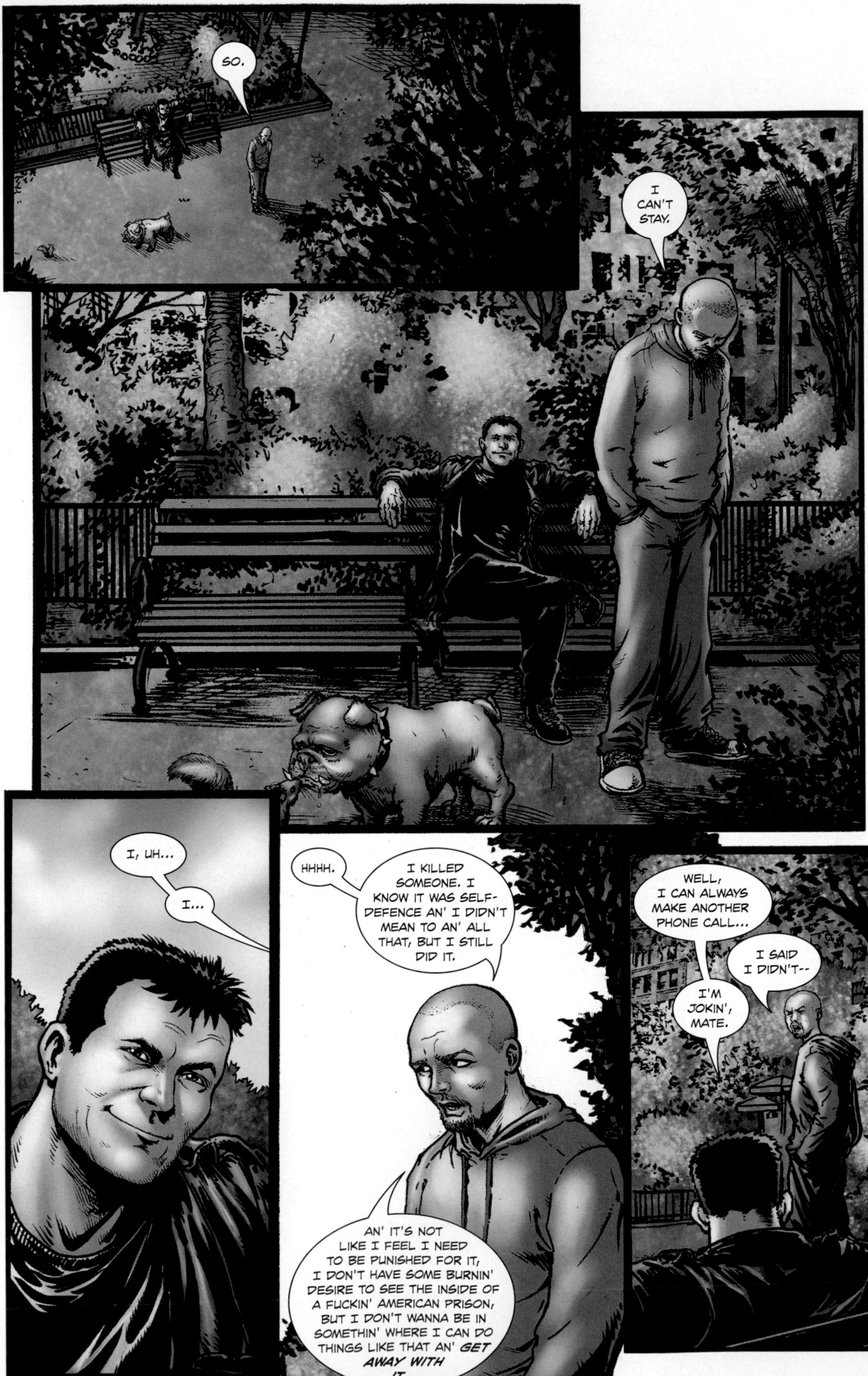
SO.
I CAN'T STAY.
I, UH...
I...
HHHH.
I KILLED SOMEONE. I KNOW IT WAS SELF-DEFENCE AN' I DIDN'T MEAN TO AN' ALL THAT, BUT I STILL DID IT.
AN' IT'S NOT LIKE I FEEL I NEED TO BE PUNISHED FOR IT, I DON'T HAVE SOME BURNIN' DESIRE TO SEE THE INSIDE OF A FUCKIN' AMERICAN PRISON, BUT I DON'T WANNA BE IN SOMETHIN' WHERE I CAN DO THINGS LIKE THAT AN' GET AWAY WITH IT...
WELL, I CAN ALWAYS MAKE ANOTHER PHONE CALL...
I SAID I DIDN'T--
I'M JOKIN', MATE.

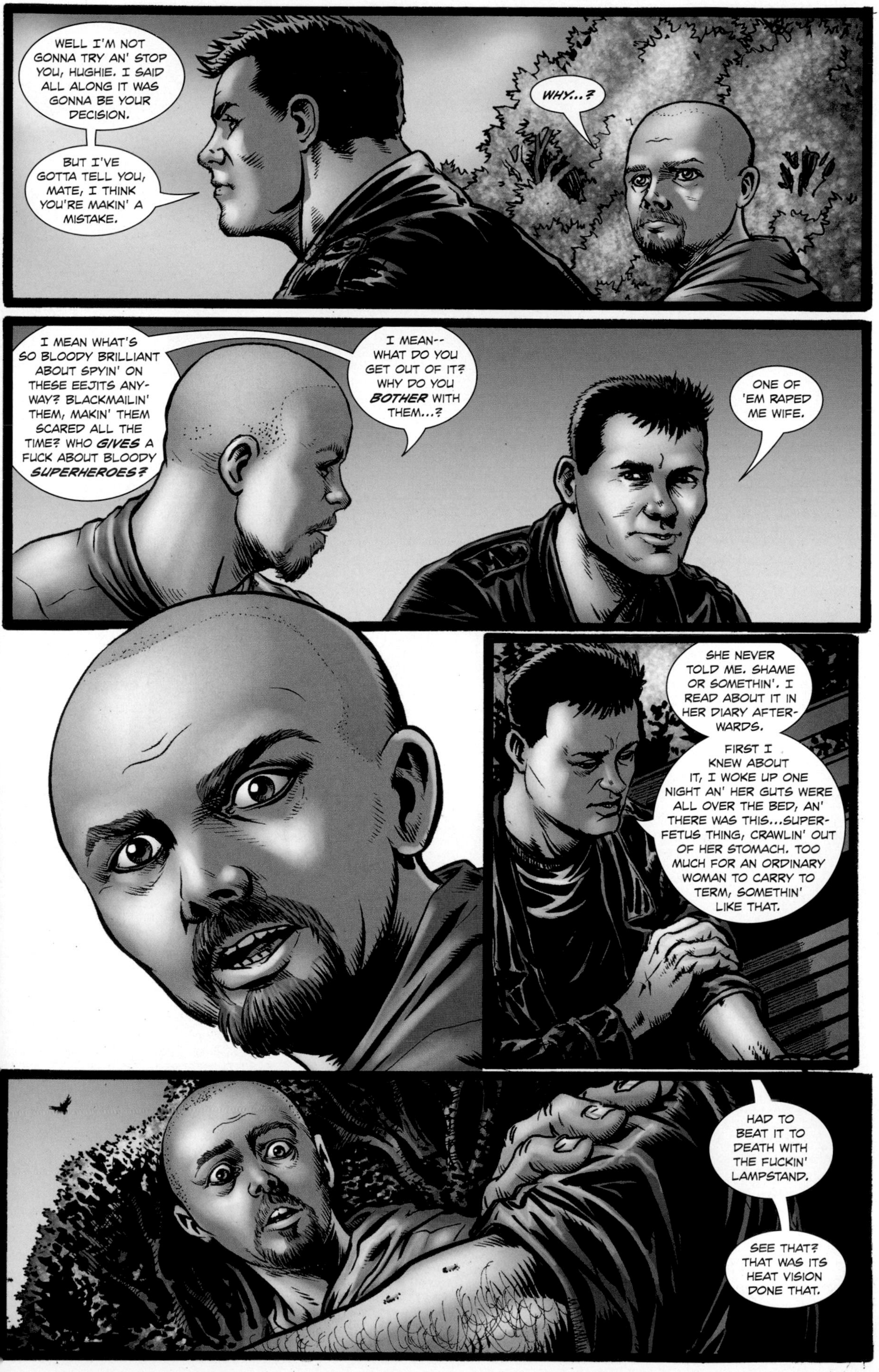
WELL I'M NOT GONNA TRY AN' STOP YOU, HUGHIE. I SAID ALL ALONG IT WAS GONNA BE YOUR DECISION.
BUT I'VE GOTTA TELL YOU, MATE, I THINK YOU'RE MAKIN' A MISTAKE.
WHY...?
I MEAN WHAT'S SO BLOODY BRILLIANT ABOUT SPYIN' ON THESE EEJITS ANY-WAY? BLACKMAILIN' THEM, MAKIN' THEM SCARED ALL THE TIME? WHO GIVES A FUCK ABOUT BLOODY SUPERHEROES?
I MEAN-- WHAT DO YOU GET OUT OF IT? WHY DO YOU BOTHER WITH THEM...?
ONE OF 'EM RAPED ME WIFE.
SHE NEVER TOLD ME. SHAME OR SOMETHIN'. I READ ABOUT IT IN HER DIARY AFTER-WARDS.
FIRST I KNEW ABOUT IT, I WOKE UP ONE NIGHT AN' HER GUTS WERE ALL OVER THE BED, AN' THERE WAS THIS...SUPER-FETUS THING, CRAWLIN' OUT OF HER STOMACH. TOO MUCH FOR AN ORDINARY WOMAN TO CARRY TO TERM, SOMETHIN' LIKE THAT.
HAD TO BEAT IT TO DEATH WITH THE FUCKIN' LAMPSTAND.
SEE THAT? THAT WAS ITS HEAT VISION DONE THAT.

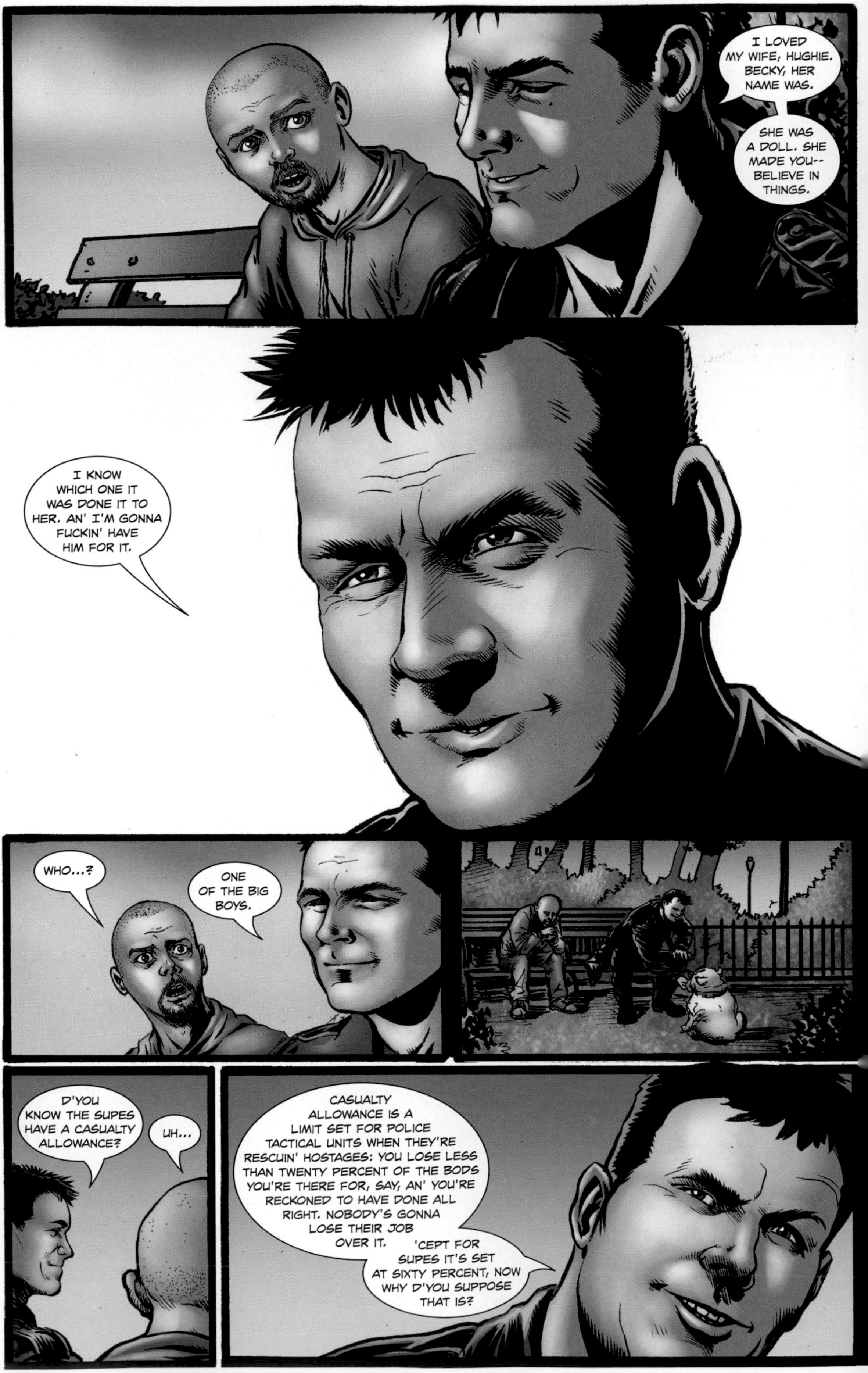
I LOVED MY WIFE, HUGHIE. BECKY, HER NAME WAS.
SHE WAS A DOLL. SHE MADE YOU-- BELIEVE IN THINGS.
I KNOW WHICH ONE IT WAS DONE IT TO HER. AN' I'M GONNA FUCKIN' HAVE HIM FOR IT.
WHO...?
ONE OF THE BIG BOYS.
D'YOU KNOW THE SUPES HAVE A CASUALTY ALLOWANCE?
UH...
CASUALTY ALLOWANCE IS A LIMIT SET FOR POLICE TACTICAL UNITS WHEN THEY'RE RESCUIN' HOSTAGES: YOU LOSE LESS THAN TWENTY PERCENT OF THE BODS YOU'RE THERE FOR, SAY, AN' YOU'RE RECKONED TO HAVE DONE ALL RIGHT. NOBODY'S GONNA LOSE THEIR JOB OVER IT.
'CEPT FOR SUPES IT'S SET AT SIXTY PERCENT, NOW WHY D'YOU SUPPOSE THAT IS?

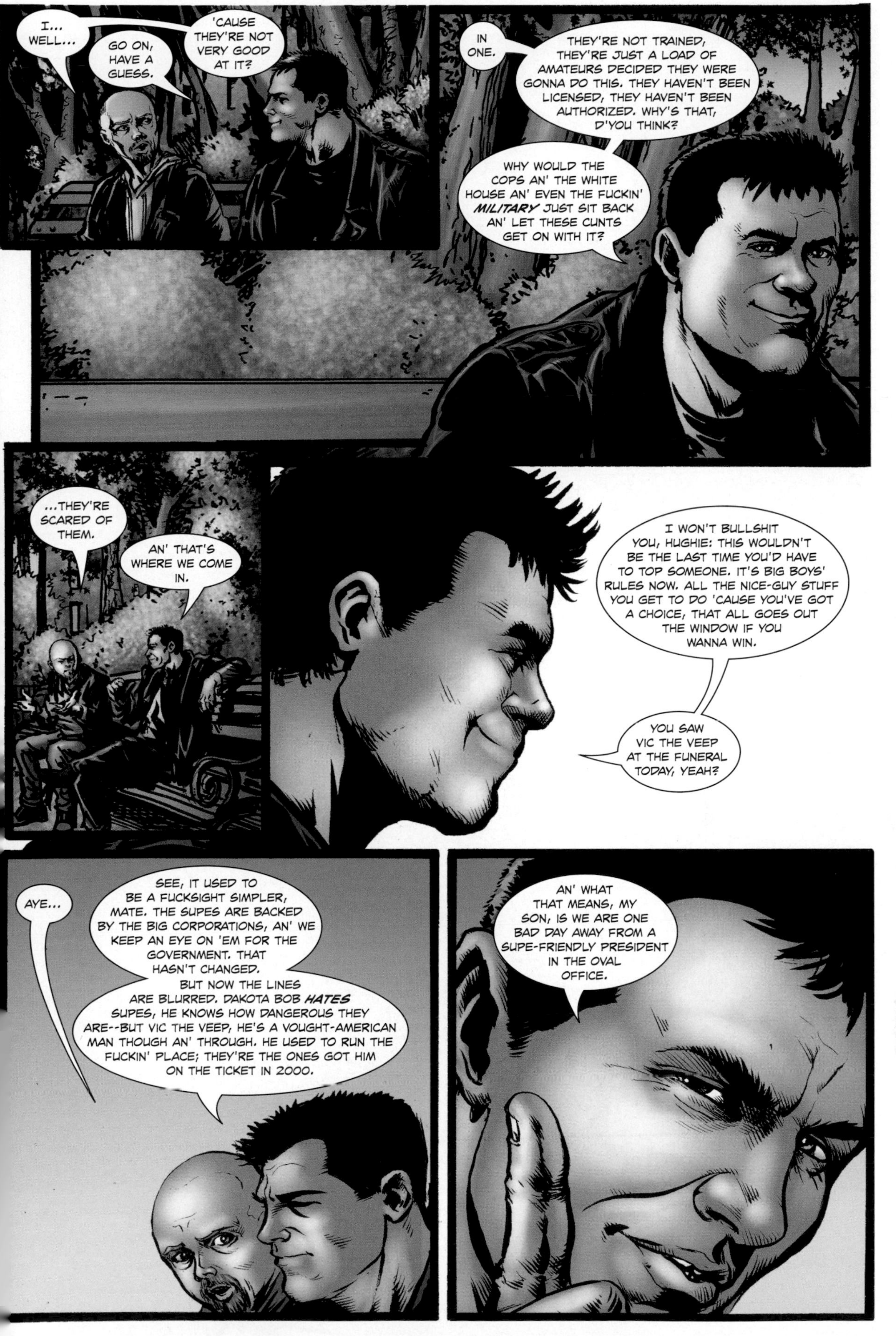
I... WELL...
GO ON, HAVE A GUESS.
'CAUSE THEY'RE NOT VERY GOOD AT IT?
IN ONE.
THEY'RE NOT TRAINED, THEY'RE JUST A LOAD OF AMATEURS DECIDED THEY WERE GONNA DO THIS. THEY HAVEN'T BEEN LICENSED, THEY HAVEN'T BEEN AUTHORIZED. WHY'S THAT, D'YOU THINK?
WHY WOULD THE COPS AN' THE WHITE HOUSE AN' EVEN THE FUCKIN' MILITARY JUST SIT BACK AN' LET THESE CUNTS GET ON WITH IT?
...THEY'RE SCARED OF THEM.
AN' THAT'S WHERE WE COME IN.
I WON'T BULLSHIT YOU, HUGHIE: THIS WOULDN'T BE THE LAST TIME YOU'D HAVE TO TOP SOMEONE. IT'S BIG BOYS' RULES NOW. ALL THE NICE-GUY STUFF YOU GET TO DO 'CAUSE YOU'VE GOT A CHOICE, THAT ALL GOES OUT THE WINDOW IF YOU WANNA WIN.
YOU SAW VIC THE VEEP AT THE FUNERAL TODAY, YEAH?
AYE...
SEE, IT USED TO BE A FUCKSIGHT SIMPLER, MATE. THE SUPES ARE BACKED BY THE BIG CORPORATIONS, AN' WE KEEP AN EYE ON 'EM FOR THE GOVERNMENT. THAT HASN'T CHANGED.
BUT NOW THE LINES ARE BLURRED. DAKOTA BOB HATES SUPES, HE KNOWS HOW DANGEROUS THEY ARE--BUT VIC THE VEEP, HE'S A VOUGHT-AMERICAN MAN THOUGH AN' THROUGH. HE USED TO RUN THE FUCKIN' PLACE; THEY'RE THE ONES GOT HIM ON THE TICKET IN 2000.
AN' WHAT THAT MEANS, MY SON, IS WE ARE ONE BAD DAY AWAY FROM A SUPE-FRIENDLY PRESIDENT IN THE OVAL OFFICE.

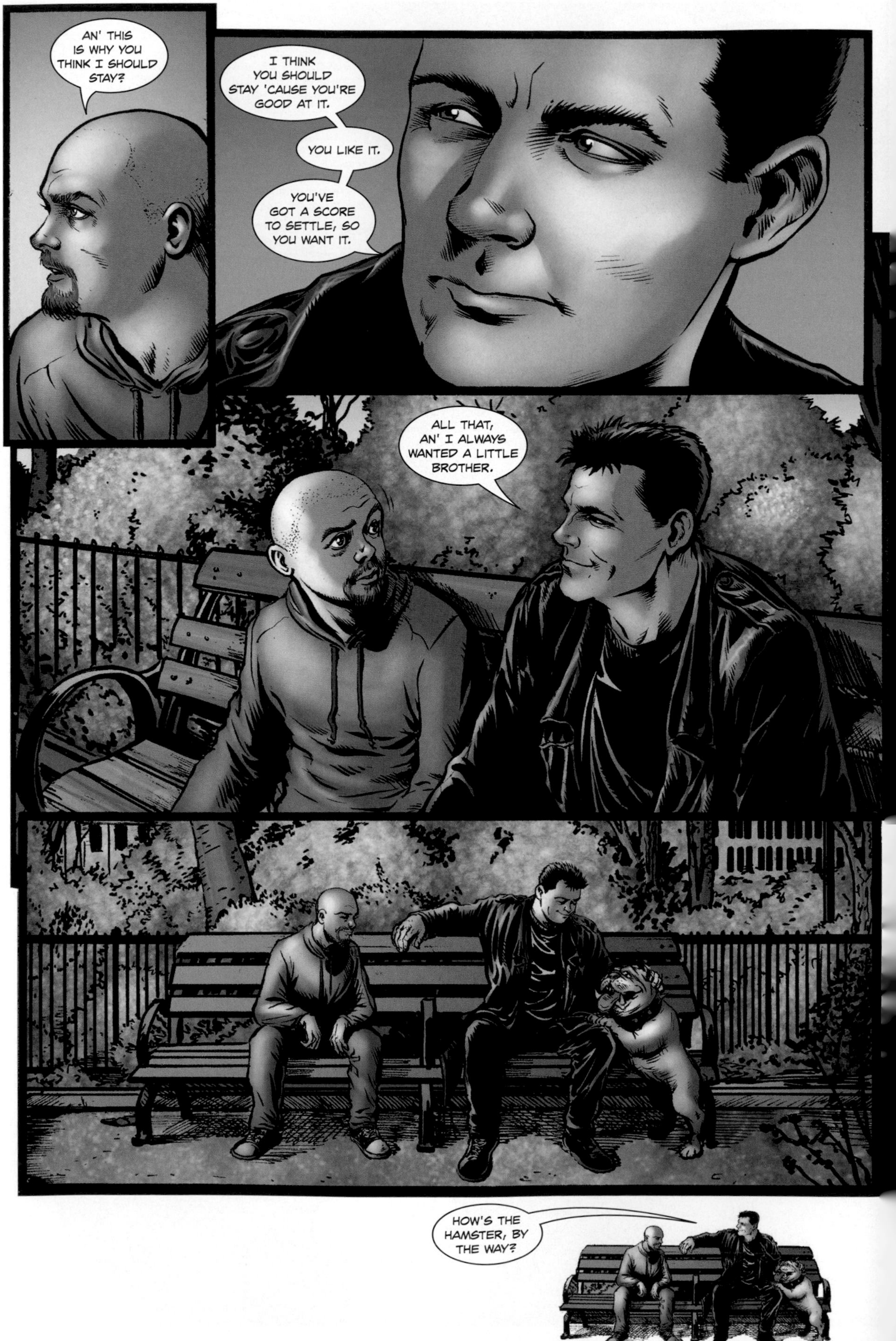
AN' THIS IS WHY YOU THINK I SHOULD STAY?
I THINK YOU SHOULD STAY 'CAUSE YOU'RE GOOD AT IT.
YOU LIKE IT.
YOU'VE GOT A SCORE TO SETTLE, SO YOU WANT IT.
ALL THAT, AN' I ALWAYS WANTED A LITTLE BROTHER.
HOW'S THE HAMSTER, BY THE WAY?

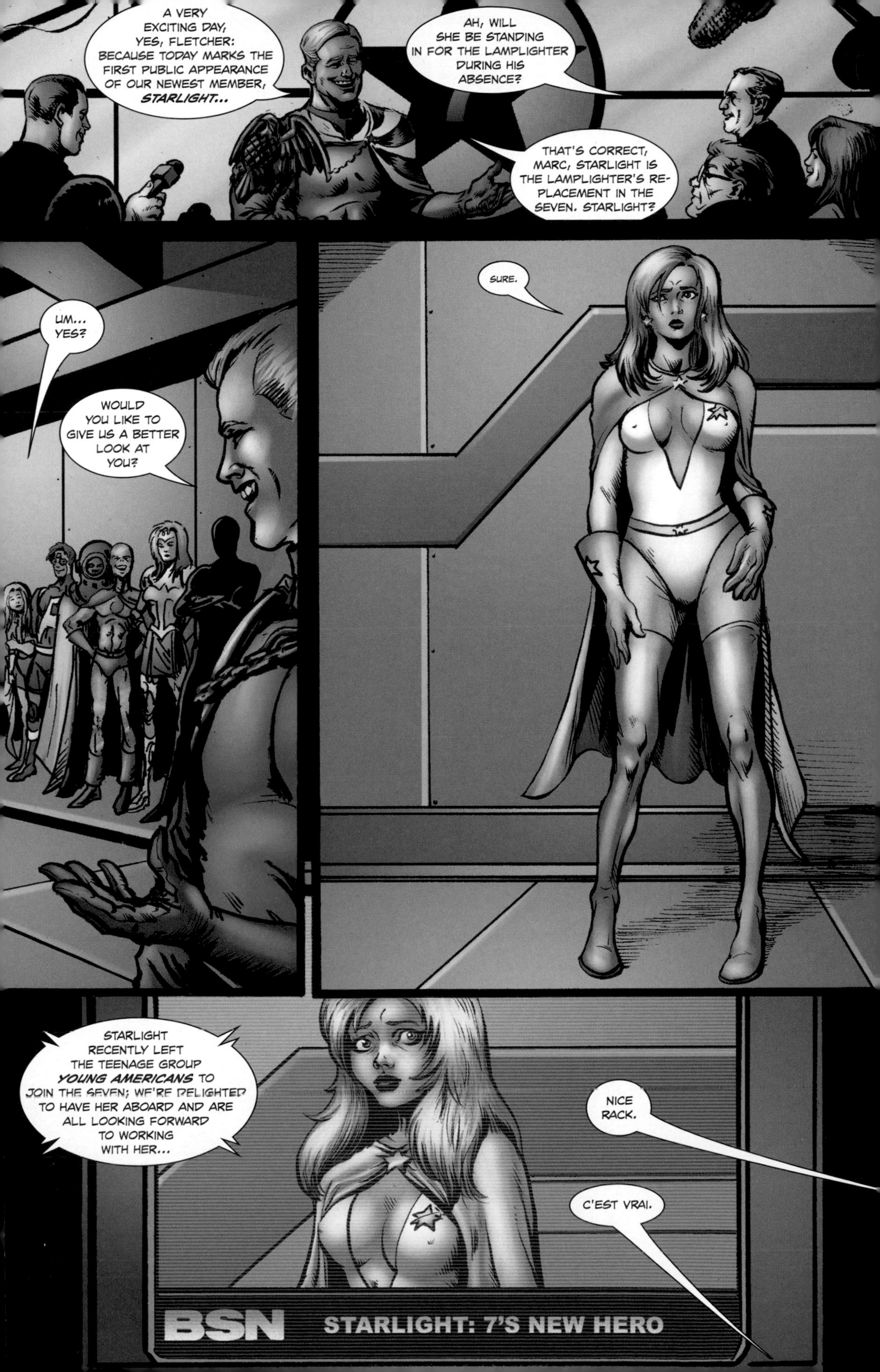
A VERY EXCITING DAY, YES, FLETCHER: BECAUSE TODAY MARKS THE FIRST PUBLIC APPEARANCE OF OUR NEWEST MEMBER, *STARLIGHT...*
AH, WILL SHE BE STANDING IN FOR THE LAMPLIGHTER DURING HIS ABSENCE?
THAT'S CORRECT, MARC, STARLIGHT IS THE LAMPLIGHTER'S RE-PLACEMENT IN THE SEVEN. STARLIGHT?
UM... YES?
WOULD YOU LIKE TO GIVE US A BETTER LOOK AT YOU?
SURE.
STARLIGHT RECENTLY LEFT THE TEENAGE GROUP *YOUNG AMERICANS* TO JOIN THE SEVEN; WE'RE DELIGHTED TO HAVE HER ABOARD AND ARE ALL LOOKING FORWARD TO WORKING WITH HER...
NICE RACK.
C'EST VRAI.
BSN
STARLIGHT: 7'S NEW HERO

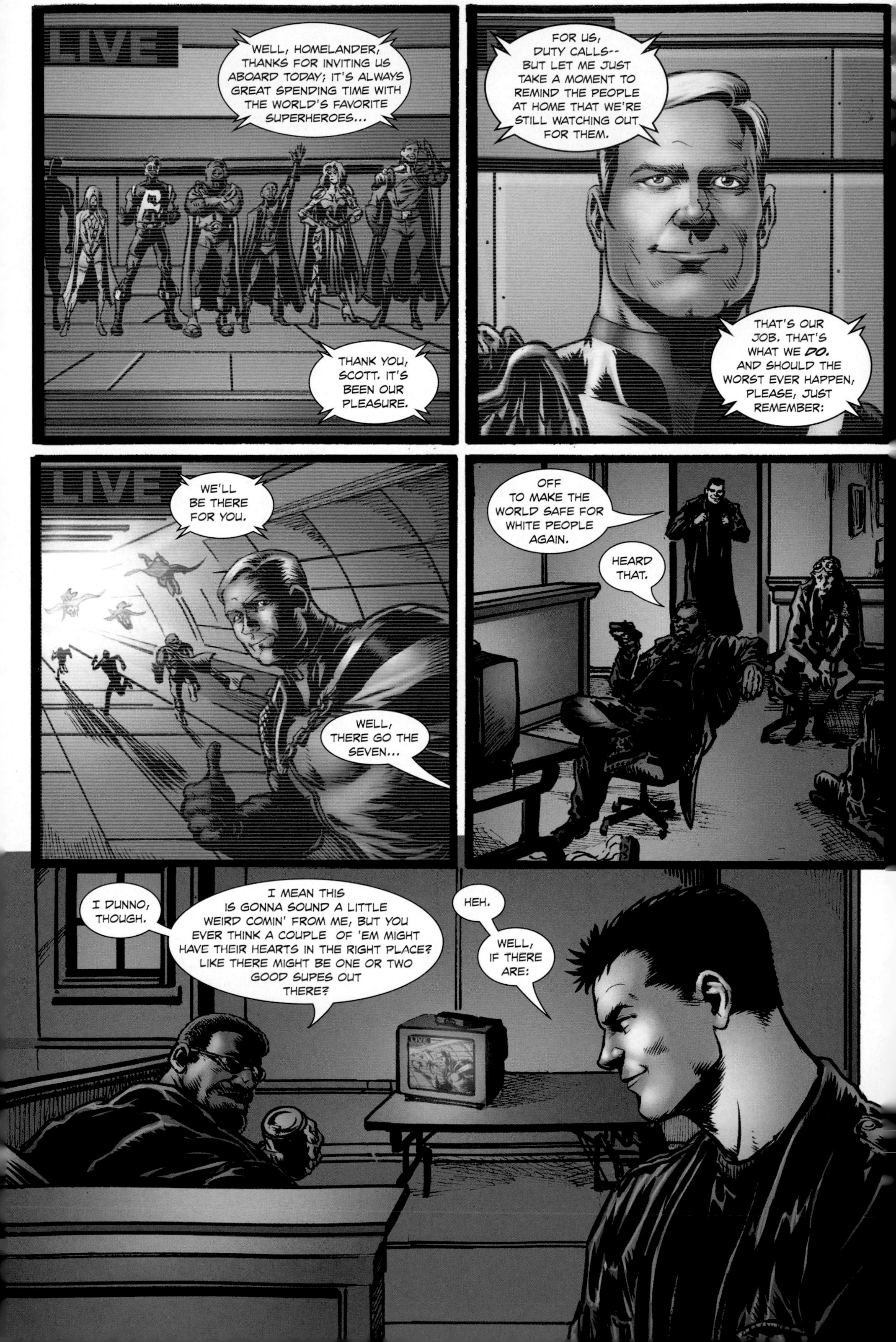
LIVE
WELL, HOMELANDER, THANKS FOR INVITING US ABOARD TODAY; IT'S ALWAYS GREAT SPENDING TIME WITH THE WORLD'S FAVORITE SUPERHEROES...
THANK YOU, SCOTT. IT'S BEEN OUR PLEASURE.
FOR US, DUTY CALLS-- BUT LET ME JUST TAKE A MOMENT TO REMIND THE PEOPLE AT HOME THAT WE'RE STILL WATCHING OUT FOR THEM.
THAT'S OUR JOB. THAT'S WHAT WE *DO.* AND SHOULD THE WORST EVER HAPPEN, PLEASE, JUST REMEMBER:
LIVE
WE'LL BE THERE FOR YOU.
WELL, THERE GO THE SEVEN...
OFF TO MAKE THE WORLD SAFE FOR WHITE PEOPLE AGAIN.
HEARD THAT.
I DUNNO, THOUGH.
I MEAN THIS IS GONNA SOUND A LITTLE WEIRD COMIN' FROM ME, BUT YOU EVER THINK A COUPLE OF 'EM MIGHT HAVE THEIR HEARTS IN THE RIGHT PLACE? LIKE THERE MIGHT BE ONE OR TWO GOOD SUPES OUT THERE?
HEH.
WELL, IF THERE ARE:

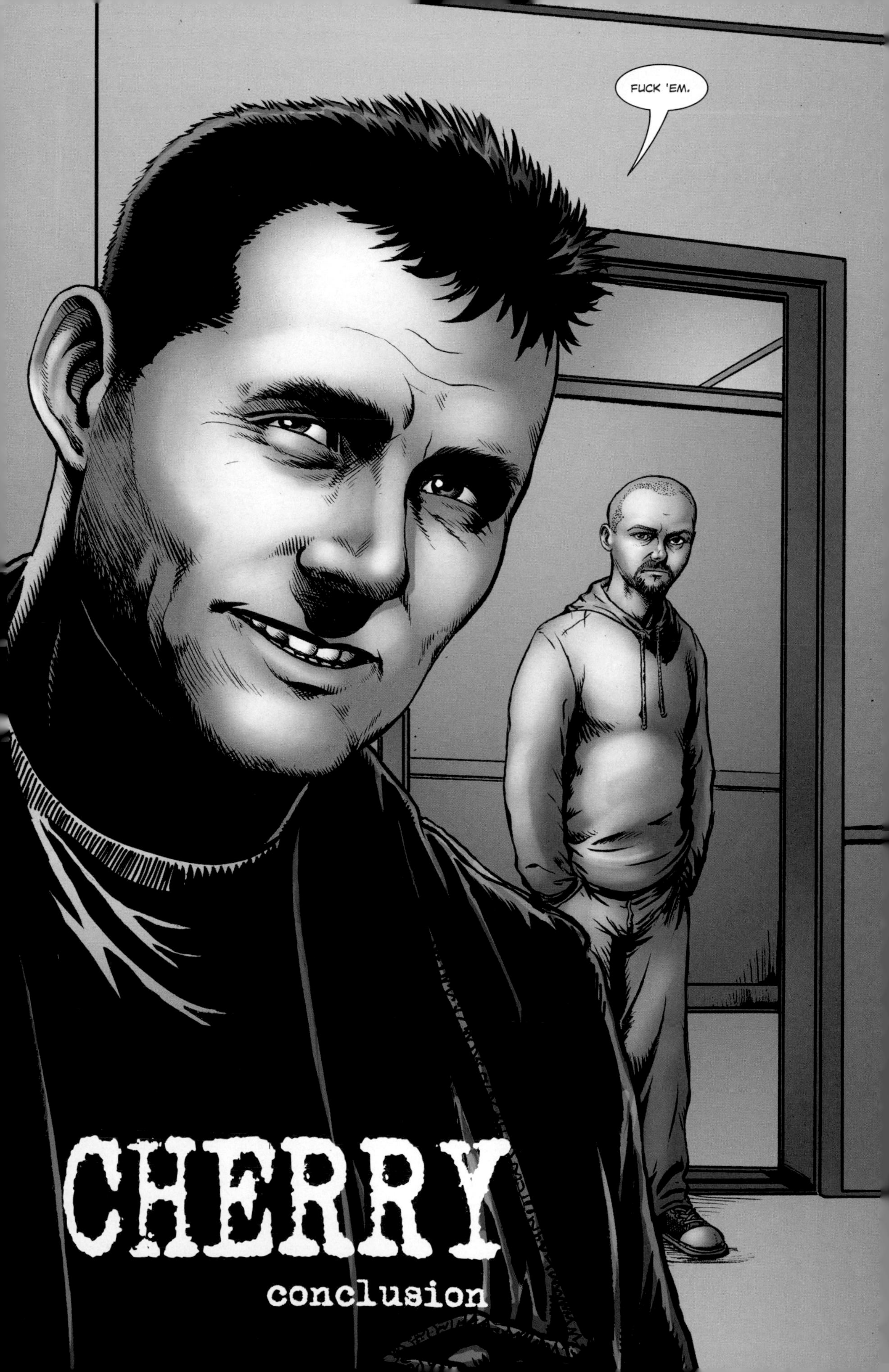
FUCK 'EM.
CHERRY
conclusion

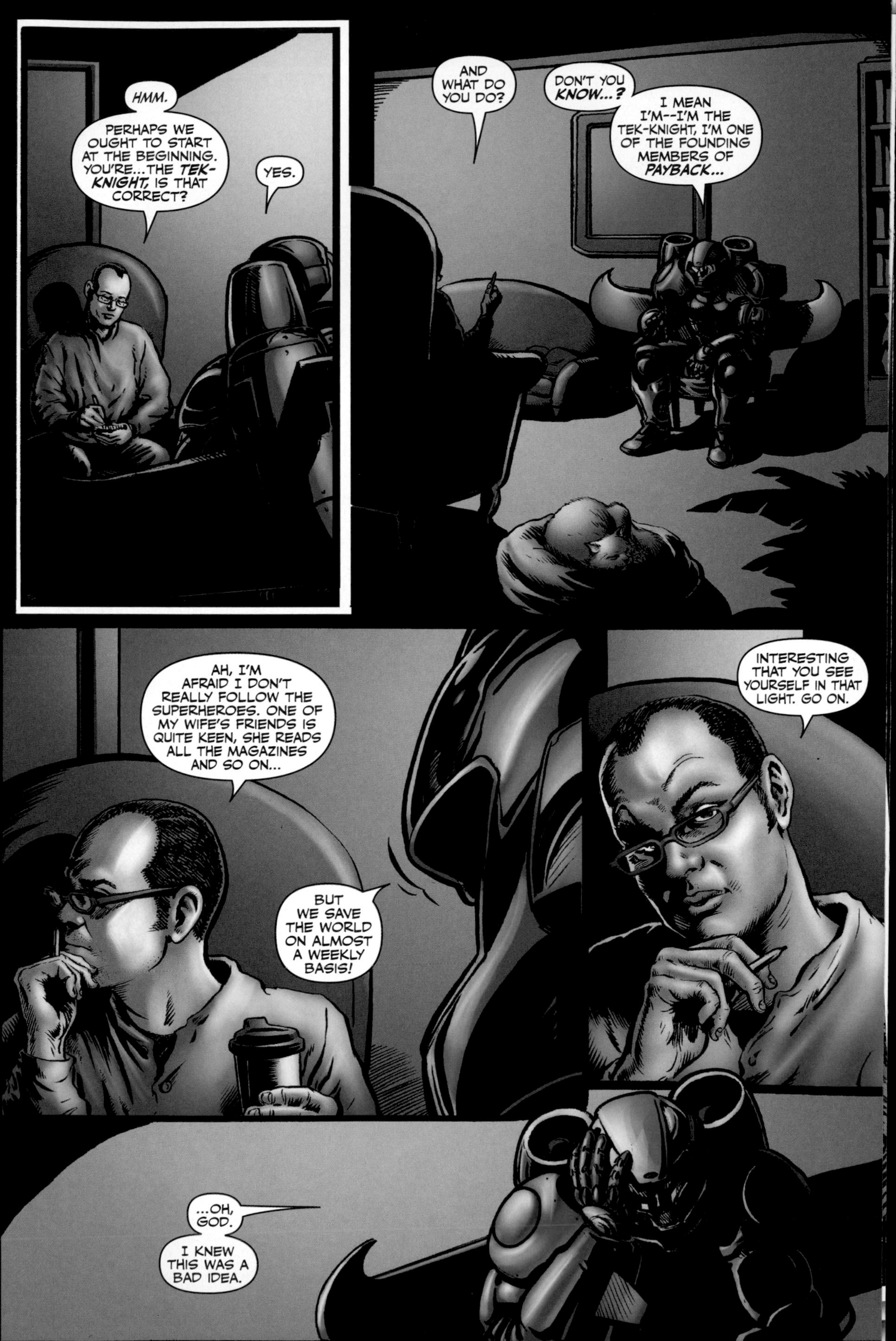
HMM.
PERHAPS WE OUGHT TO START AT THE BEGINNING. YOU'RE...THE TEK-KNIGHT, IS THAT CORRECT?
YES.
AND WHAT DO YOU DO?
DON'T YOU KNOW...?
I MEAN I'M--I'M THE TEK-KNIGHT, I'M ONE OF THE FOUNDING MEMBERS OF PAYBACK...
AH, I'M AFRAID I DON'T REALLY FOLLOW THE SUPERHEROES. ONE OF MY WIFE'S FRIENDS IS QUITE KEEN, SHE READS ALL THE MAGAZINES AND SO ON...
BUT WE SAVE THE WORLD ON ALMOST A WEEKLY BASIS!
INTERESTING THAT YOU SEE YOURSELF IN THAT LIGHT. GO ON.
...OH, GOD.
I KNEW THIS WAS A BAD IDEA.

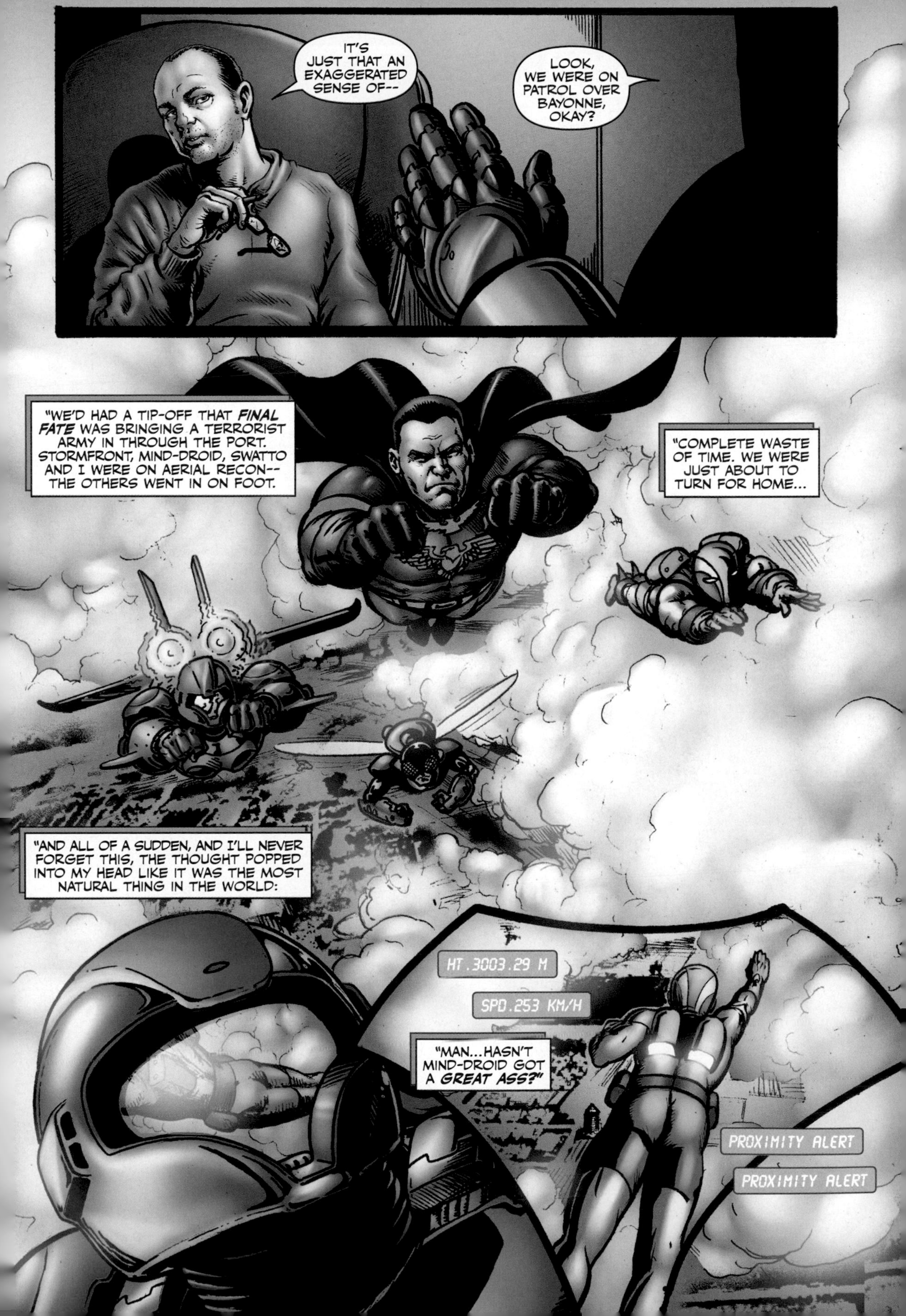
IT'S JUST THAT AN EXAGGERATED SENSE OF--
LOOK, WE WERE ON PATROL OVER BAYONNE, OKAY?
"WE'D HAD A TIP-OFF THAT FINAL FATE WAS BRINGING A TERRORIST ARMY IN THROUGH THE PORT. STORMFRONT, MIND-DROID, SWATTO AND I WERE ON AERIAL RECON-- THE OTHERS WENT IN ON FOOT.
"COMPLETE WASTE OF TIME. WE WERE JUST ABOUT TO TURN FOR HOME...
"AND ALL OF A SUDDEN, AND I'LL NEVER FORGET THIS, THE THOUGHT POPPED INTO MY HEAD LIKE IT WAS THE MOST NATURAL THING IN THE WORLD:
HT. 3003.29 M
SPD. 253 KM/H
"MAN...HASN'T MIND-DROID GOT A GREAT ASS?"
PROXIMITY ALERT
PROXIMITY ALERT

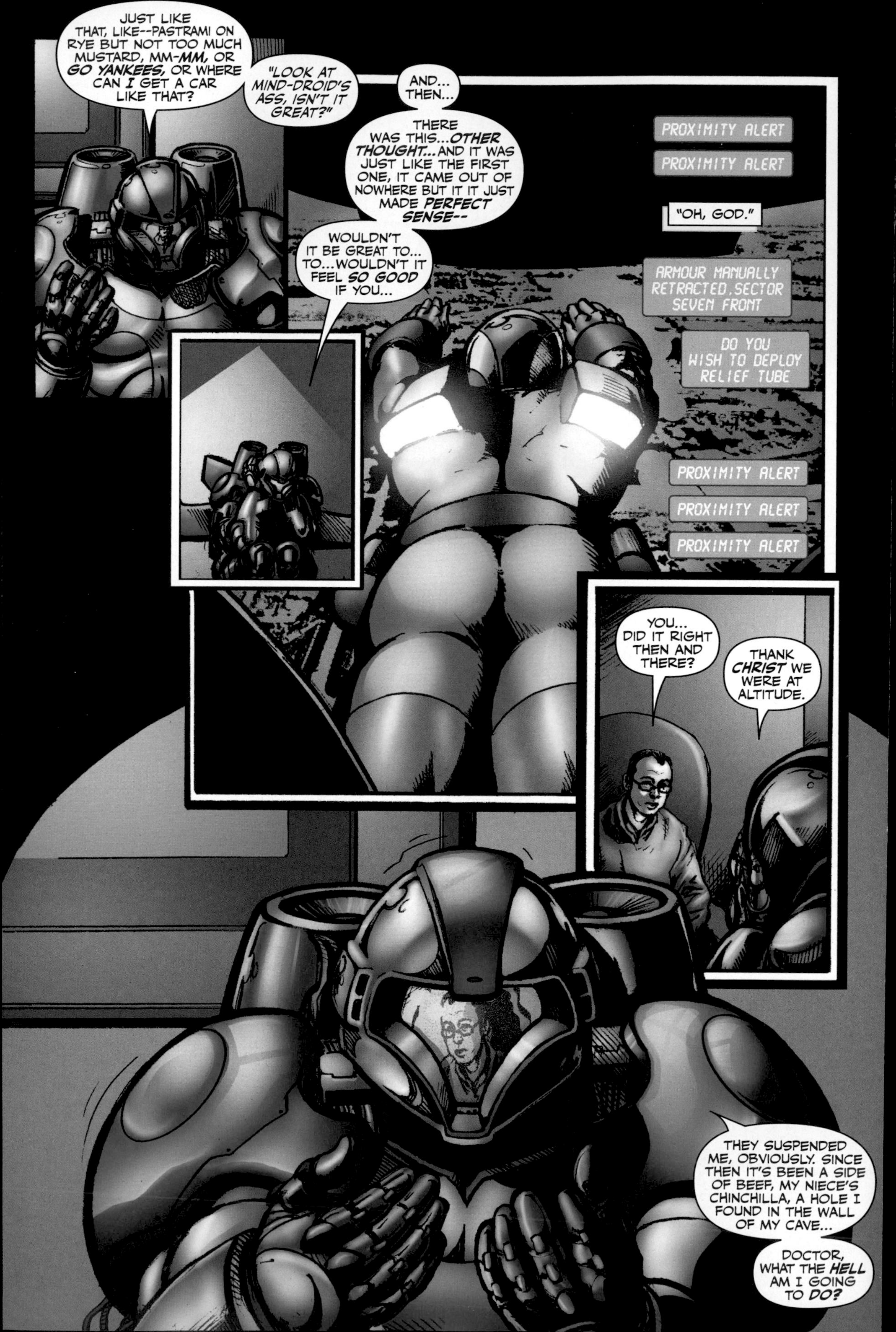
JUST LIKE THAT, LIKE--PASTRAMI ON RYE BUT NOT TOO MUCH MUSTARD, MM-*MM,* OR *GO YANKEES,* OR WHERE CAN *I* GET A CAR LIKE THAT?
"LOOK AT MIND-DROID'S ASS, ISN'T IT GREAT?"
AND... THEN...
THERE WAS THIS...*OTHER THOUGHT...* AND IT WAS JUST LIKE THE FIRST ONE, IT CAME OUT OF NOWHERE BUT IT IT JUST MADE *PERFECT SENSE--*
WOULDN'T IT BE GREAT TO... TO...WOULDN'T IT FEEL *SO GOOD* IF YOU...
PROXIMITY ALERT
PROXIMITY ALERT
"OH, GOD."
ARMOUR MANUALLY RETRACTED.SECTOR SEVEN FRONT
DO YOU WISH TO DEPLOY RELIEF TUBE
PROXIMITY ALERT
PROXIMITY ALERT
PROXIMITY ALERT
YOU... DID IT RIGHT THEN AND THERE?
THANK *CHRIST* WE WERE AT ALTITUDE.
THEY SUSPENDED ME, OBVIOUSLY. SINCE THEN IT'S BEEN A SIDE OF BEEF, MY NIECE'S CHINCHILLA, A HOLE I FOUND IN THE WALL OF MY CAVE...
DOCTOR, WHAT THE *HELL* AM I GOING TO *DO?*

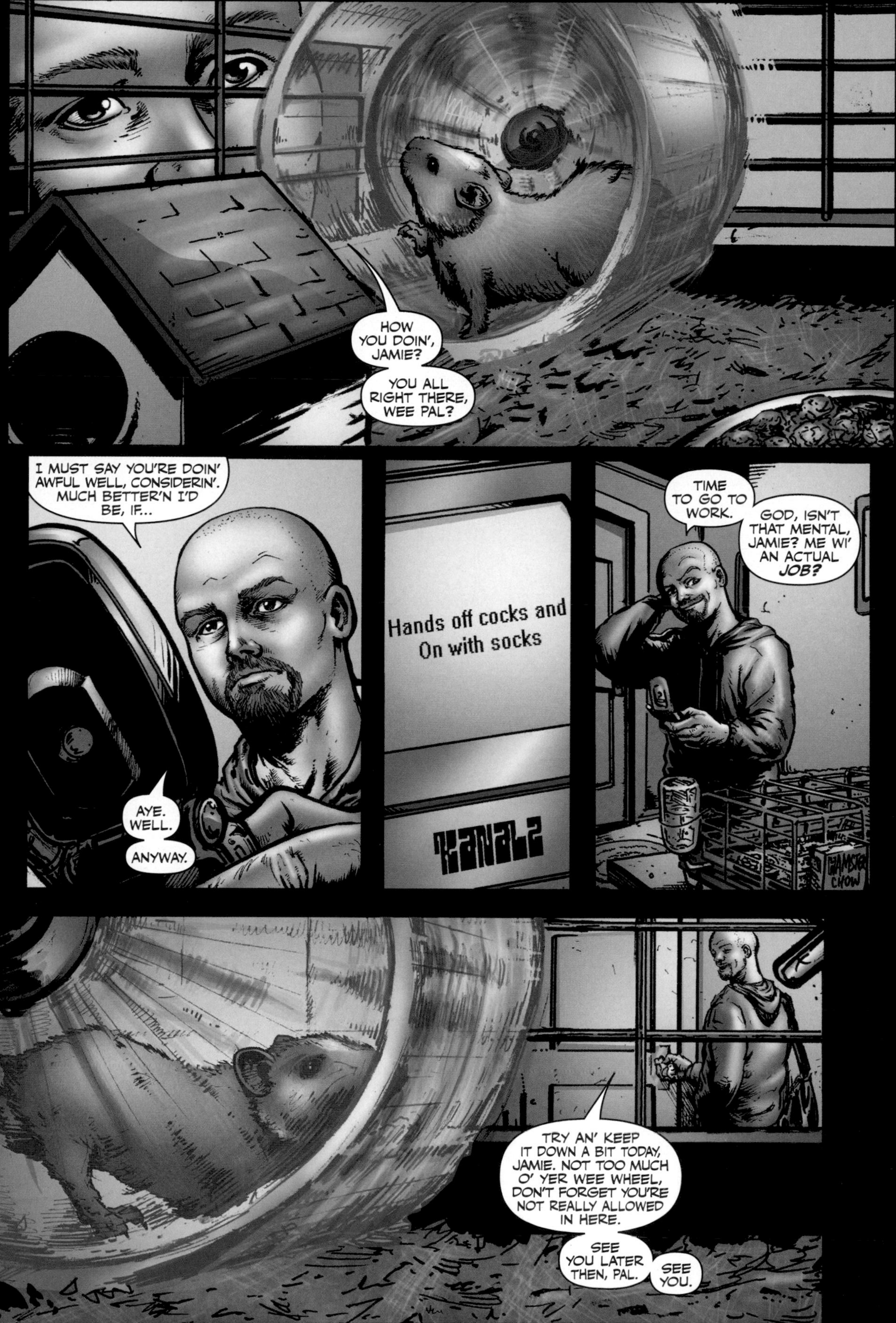
HOW YOU DOIN', JAMIE?
YOU ALL RIGHT THERE, WEE PAL?
I MUST SAY YOU'RE DOIN' AWFUL WELL, CONSIDERIN'. MUCH BETTER'N I'D BE, IF...
AYE. WELL.
ANYWAY.
Hands off cocks and On with socks
KANAL 2
TIME TO GO TO WORK.
GOD, ISN'T THAT MENTAL, JAMIE? ME WI' AN ACTUAL *JOB*?
HAMSTER CHOW
TRY AN' KEEP IT DOWN A BIT TODAY, JAMIE. NOT TOO MUCH O' YER WEE WHEEL, DON'T FORGET YOU'RE NOT REALLY ALLOWED IN HERE.
SEE YOU LATER THEN, PAL.
SEE YOU.

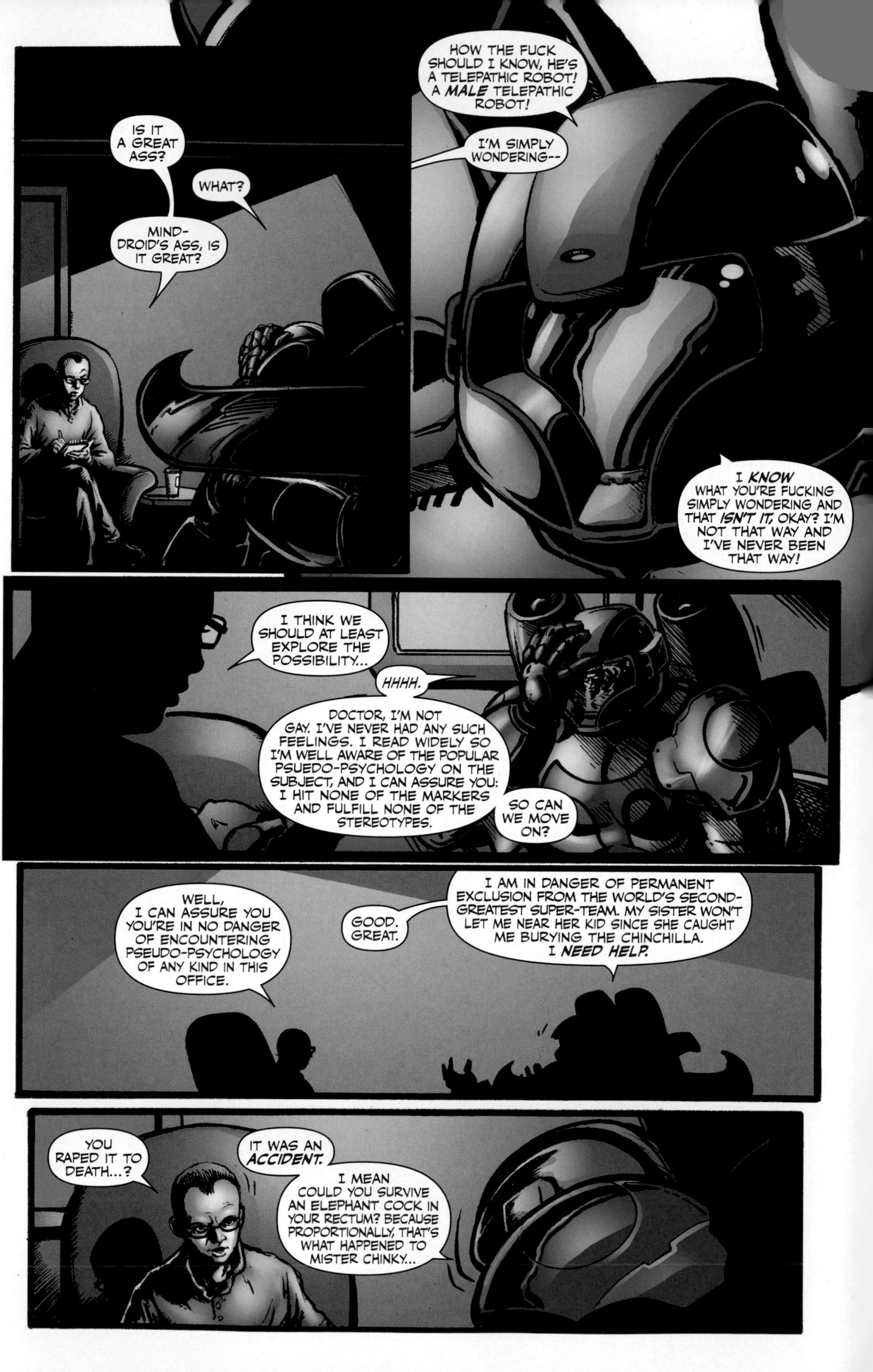
IS IT A GREAT ASS?
WHAT?
MIND-DROID'S ASS, IS IT GREAT?
HOW THE FUCK SHOULD I KNOW, HE'S A TELEPATHIC ROBOT! A MALE TELEPATHIC ROBOT!
I'M SIMPLY WONDERING--
I KNOW WHAT YOU'RE FUCKING SIMPLY WONDERING AND THAT ISN'T IT, OKAY? I'M NOT THAT WAY AND I'VE NEVER BEEN THAT WAY!
I THINK WE SHOULD AT LEAST EXPLORE THE POSSIBILITY...
HHHH.
DOCTOR, I'M NOT GAY. I'VE NEVER HAD ANY SUCH FEELINGS. I READ WIDELY SO I'M WELL AWARE OF THE POPULAR PSUEDO-PSYCHOLOGY ON THE SUBJECT, AND I CAN ASSURE YOU: I HIT NONE OF THE MARKERS AND FULFILL NONE OF THE STEREOTYPES.
SO CAN WE MOVE ON?
WELL, I CAN ASSURE YOU YOU'RE IN NO DANGER OF ENCOUNTERING PSEUDO-PSYCHOLOGY OF ANY KIND IN THIS OFFICE.
GOOD. GREAT.
I AM IN DANGER OF PERMANENT EXCLUSION FROM THE WORLD'S SECOND-GREATEST SUPER-TEAM. MY SISTER WON'T LET ME NEAR HER KID SINCE SHE CAUGHT ME BURYING THE CHINCHILLA. I NEED HELP.
YOU RAPED IT TO DEATH...?
IT WAS AN ACCIDENT.
I MEAN COULD YOU SURVIVE AN ELEPHANT COCK IN YOUR RECTUM? BECAUSE PROPORTIONALLY, THAT'S WHAT HAPPENED TO MISTER CHINKY...

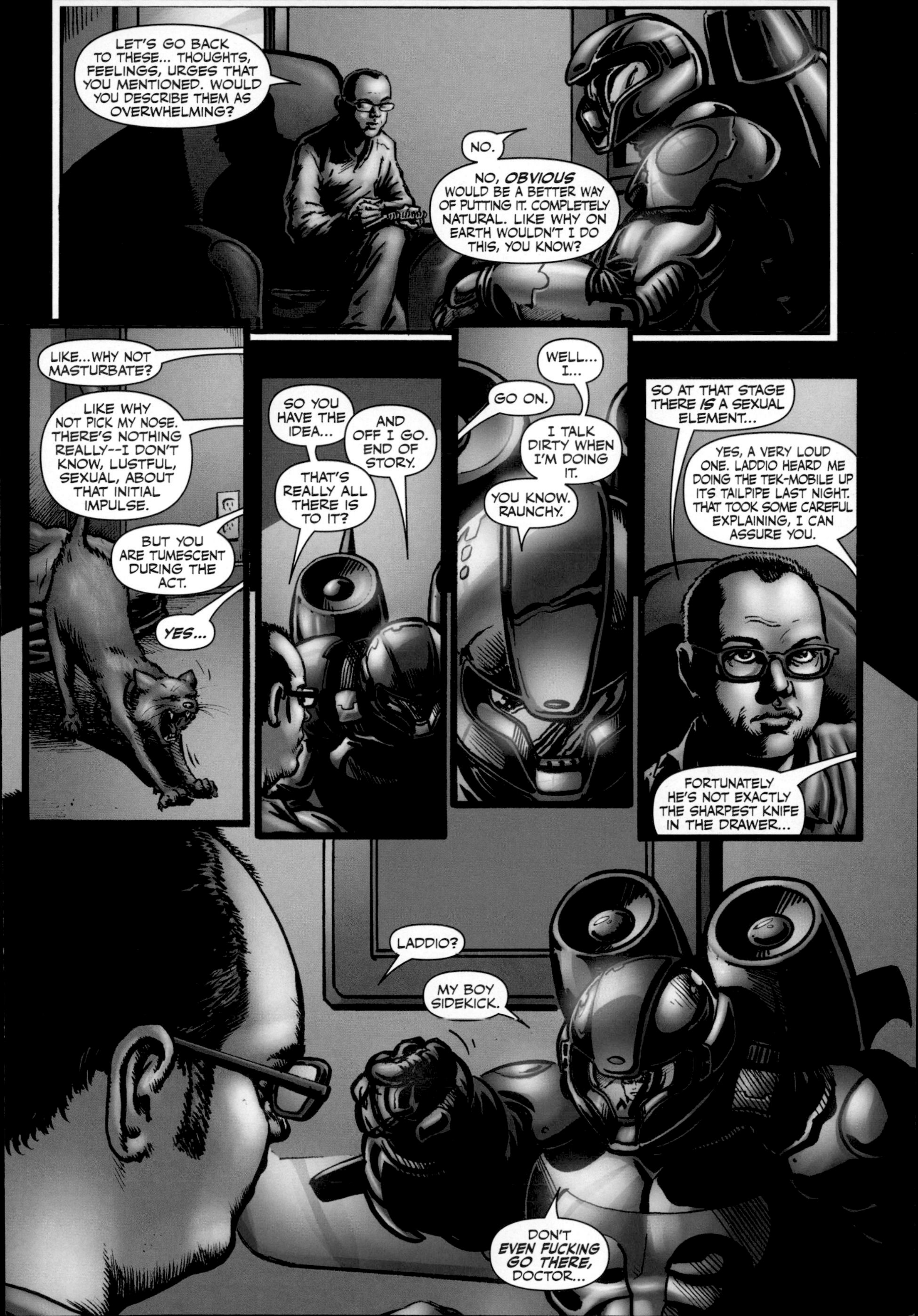

LET'S GO BACK TO THESE... THOUGHTS, FEELINGS, URGES THAT YOU MENTIONED. WOULD YOU DESCRIBE THEM AS OVERWHELMING?
NO.
NO, *OBVIOUS* WOULD BE A BETTER WAY OF PUTTING IT. COMPLETELY NATURAL. LIKE WHY ON EARTH WOULDN'T I DO THIS, YOU KNOW?
LIKE...WHY NOT MASTURBATE?
LIKE WHY NOT PICK MY NOSE. THERE'S NOTHING REALLY--I DON'T KNOW, LUSTFUL, SEXUAL, ABOUT THAT INITIAL IMPULSE.
BUT YOU ARE TUMESCENT DURING THE ACT.
YES...
SO YOU HAVE THE IDEA...
AND OFF I GO. END OF STORY.
THAT'S REALLY ALL THERE IS TO IT?
WELL... I...
GO ON.
I TALK DIRTY WHEN I'M DOING IT.
YOU KNOW. RAUNCHY.
SO AT THAT STAGE THERE *IS* A SEXUAL ELEMENT...
YES, A VERY LOUD ONE. LADDIO HEARD ME DOING THE TEK-MOBILE UP ITS TAILPIPE LAST NIGHT. THAT TOOK SOME CAREFUL EXPLAINING, I CAN ASSURE YOU.
FORTUNATELY HE'S NOT EXACTLY THE SHARPEST KNIFE IN THE DRAWER...
LADDIO?
MY BOY SIDEKICK.
DON'T *EVEN FUCKING GO THERE,* DOCTOR...

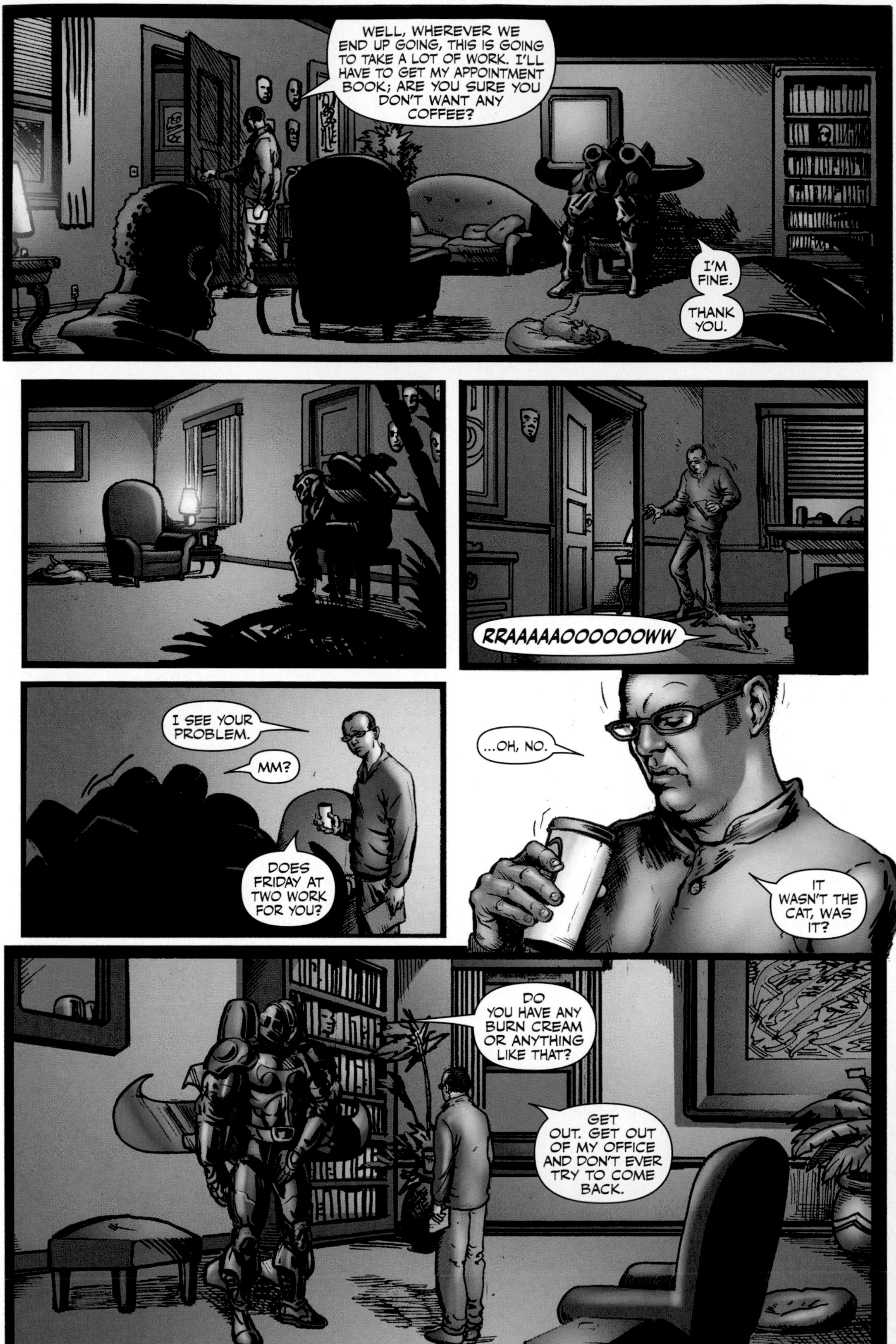
WELL, WHEREVER WE END UP GOING, THIS IS GOING TO TAKE A LOT OF WORK. I'LL HAVE TO GET MY APPOINTMENT BOOK; ARE YOU SURE YOU DON'T WANT ANY COFFEE?
I'M FINE.
THANK YOU.
RRAAAAAOOOOOOWW
I SEE YOUR PROBLEM.
MM?
DOES FRIDAY AT TWO WORK FOR YOU?
...OH, NO.
IT WASN'T THE CAT, WAS IT?
DO YOU HAVE ANY BURN CREAM OR ANYTHING LIKE THAT?
GET OUT. GET OUT OF MY OFFICE AND DON'T EVER TRY TO COME BACK.

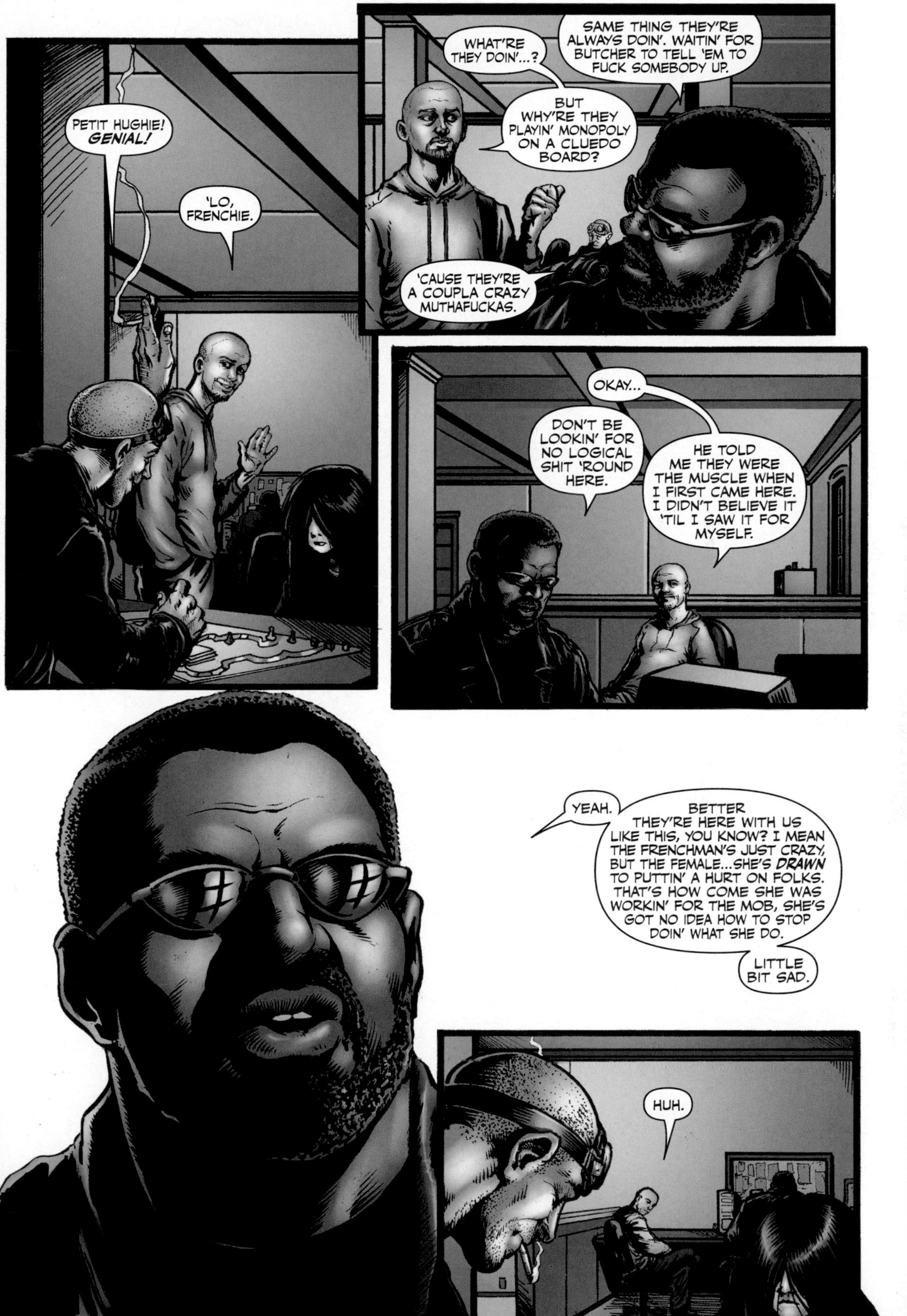
PETIT HUGHIE! *GENIAL!*
'LO, FRENCHIE.
WHAT'RE THEY DOIN'...?
SAME THING THEY'RE ALWAYS DOIN'. WAITIN' FOR BUTCHER TO TELL 'EM TO FUCK SOMEBODY UP.
BUT WHY'RE THEY PLAYIN' MONOPOLY ON A CLUEDO BOARD?
'CAUSE THEY'RE A COUPLA CRAZY MUTHAFUCKAS.
OKAY...
DON'T BE LOOKIN' FOR NO LOGICAL SHIT 'ROUND HERE.
HE TOLD ME THEY WERE THE MUSCLE WHEN I FIRST CAME HERE. I DIDN'T BELIEVE IT 'TIL I SAW IT FOR MYSELF.
YEAH.
BETTER THEY'RE HERE WITH US LIKE THIS, YOU KNOW? I MEAN THE FRENCHMAN'S JUST CRAZY, BUT THE FEMALE...SHE'S *DRAWN* TO PUTTIN' A HURT ON FOLKS. THAT'S HOW COME SHE WAS WORKIN' FOR THE MOB, SHE'S GOT NO IDEA HOW TO STOP DOIN' WHAT SHE DO.
LITTLE BIT SAD.
HUH.

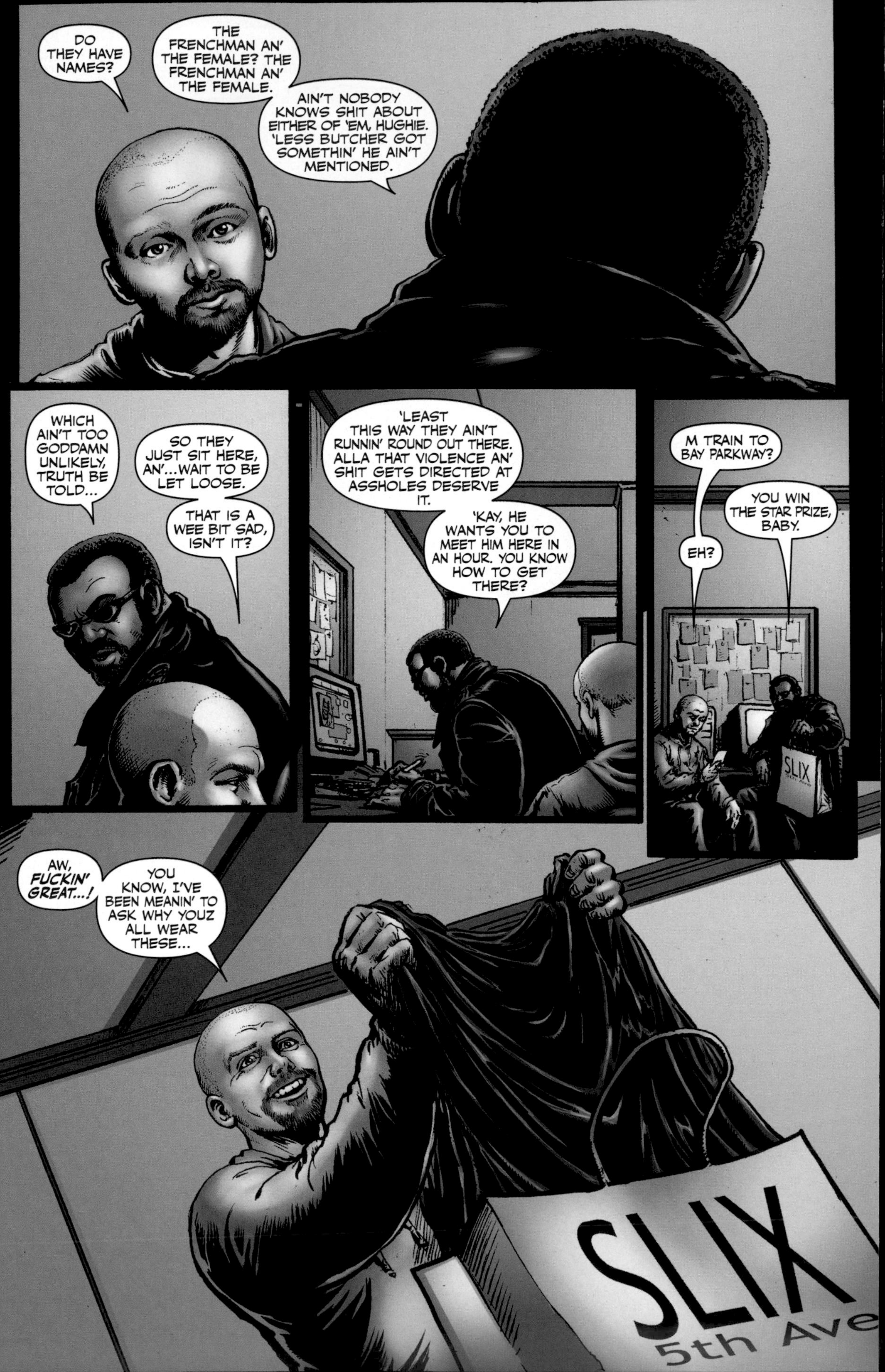
DO THEY HAVE NAMES?
THE FRENCHMAN AN' THE FEMALE? THE FRENCHMAN AN' THE FEMALE.
AIN'T NOBODY KNOWS SHIT ABOUT EITHER OF 'EM, HUGHIE. 'LESS BUTCHER GOT SOMETHIN' HE AIN'T MENTIONED.
WHICH AIN'T TOO GODDAMN UNLIKELY, TRUTH BE TOLD...
SO THEY JUST SIT HERE, AN'...WAIT TO BE LET LOOSE.
THAT IS A WEE BIT SAD, ISN'T IT?
'LEAST THIS WAY THEY AIN'T RUNNIN' ROUND OUT THERE. ALLA THAT VIOLENCE AN' SHIT GETS DIRECTED AT ASSHOLES DESERVE IT.
'KAY, HE WANTS YOU TO MEET HIM HERE IN AN HOUR. YOU KNOW HOW TO GET THERE?
M TRAIN TO BAY PARKWAY?
YOU WIN THE STAR PRIZE, BABY.
EH?
SLIX 5th Ave
AW, *FUCKIN' GREAT...!*
YOU KNOW, I'VE BEEN MEANIN' TO ASK WHY YOUZ ALL WEAR THESE...
SLIX
5th Ave

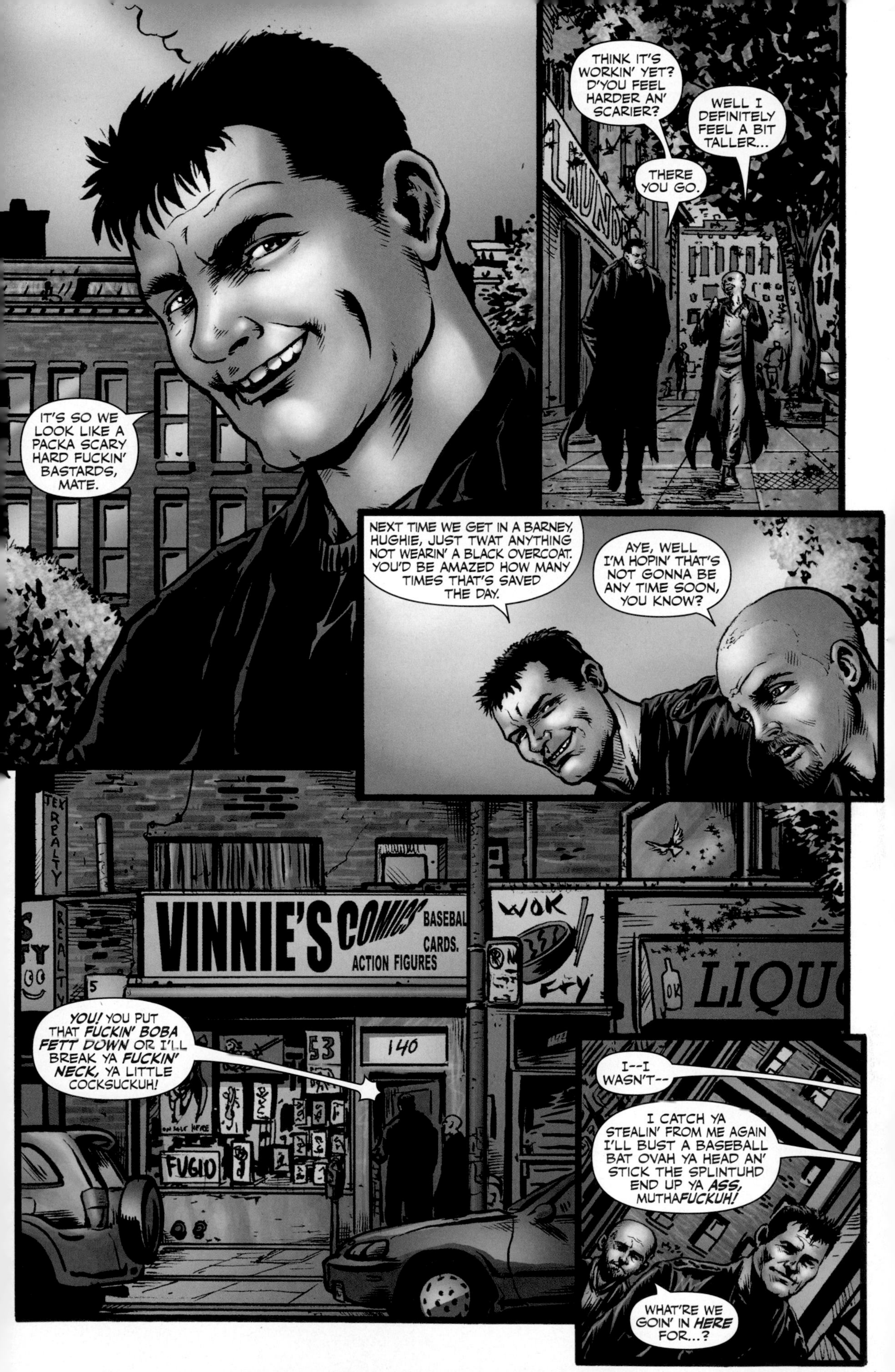
IT'S SO WE LOOK LIKE A PACKA SCARY HARD FUCKIN' BASTARDS, MATE.
THINK IT'S WORKIN' YET? D'YOU FEEL HARDER AN' SCARIER?
WELL I DEFINITELY FEEL A BIT TALLER...
THERE YOU GO.
NEXT TIME WE GET IN A BARNEY, HUGHIE, JUST TWAT ANYTHING NOT WEARIN' A BLACK OVERCOAT. YOU'D BE AMAZED HOW MANY TIMES THAT'S SAVED THE DAY.
AYE, WELL I'M HOPIN' THAT'S NOT GONNA BE ANY TIME SOON, YOU KNOW?
VINNIE'S COMICS BASEBALL CARDS. ACTION FIGURES
WOK
LIQU
140
YOU! YOU PUT THAT FUCKIN' BOBA FETT DOWN OR I'LL BREAK YA FUCKIN' NECK, YA LITTLE COCKSUCKUH!
I--I WASN'T--
I CATCH YA STEALIN' FROM ME AGAIN I'LL BUST A BASEBALL BAT OVAH YA HEAD AN' STICK THE SPLINTUHD END UP YA ASS, MUTHAFUCKUH!
WHAT'RE WE GOIN' IN HERE FOR...?

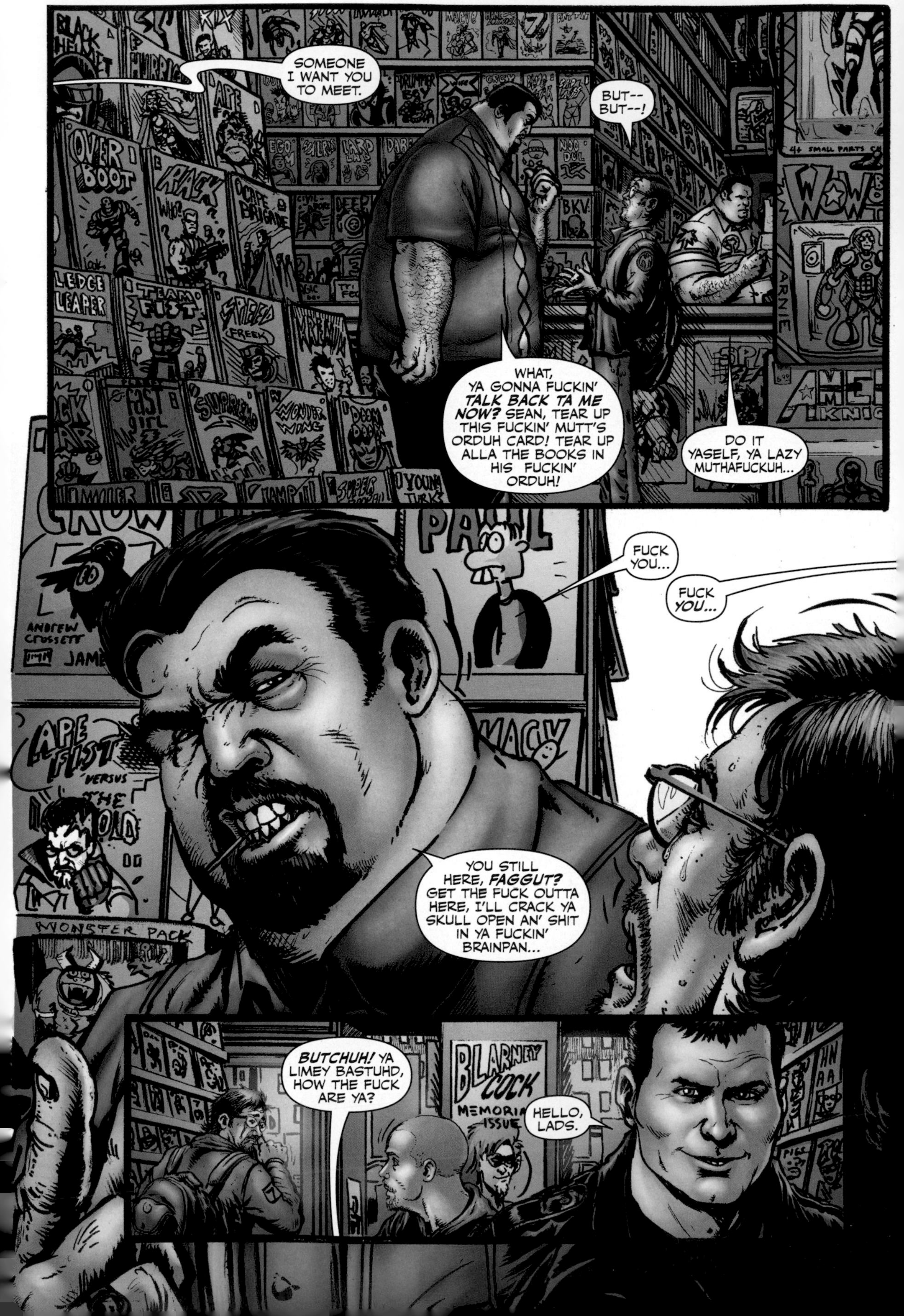
SOMEONE I WANT YOU TO MEET.
BUT-- BUT--!
WHAT, YA GONNA FUCKIN' *TALK BACK TA ME NOW?* SEAN, TEAR UP THIS FUCKIN' MUTT'S ORDUH CARD! TEAR UP ALLA THE BOOKS IN HIS FUCKIN' ORDUH!
DO IT YASELF, YA LAZY MUTHAFUCKUH...
FUCK YOU...
FUCK *YOU...*
YOU STILL HERE, *FAGGUT?* GET THE FUCK OUTTA HERE, I'LL CRACK YA SKULL OPEN AN' SHIT IN YA FUCKIN' BRAINPAN...
BUTCHUH! YA LIMEY BASTUHD, HOW THE FUCK ARE YA?
HELLO, LADS.

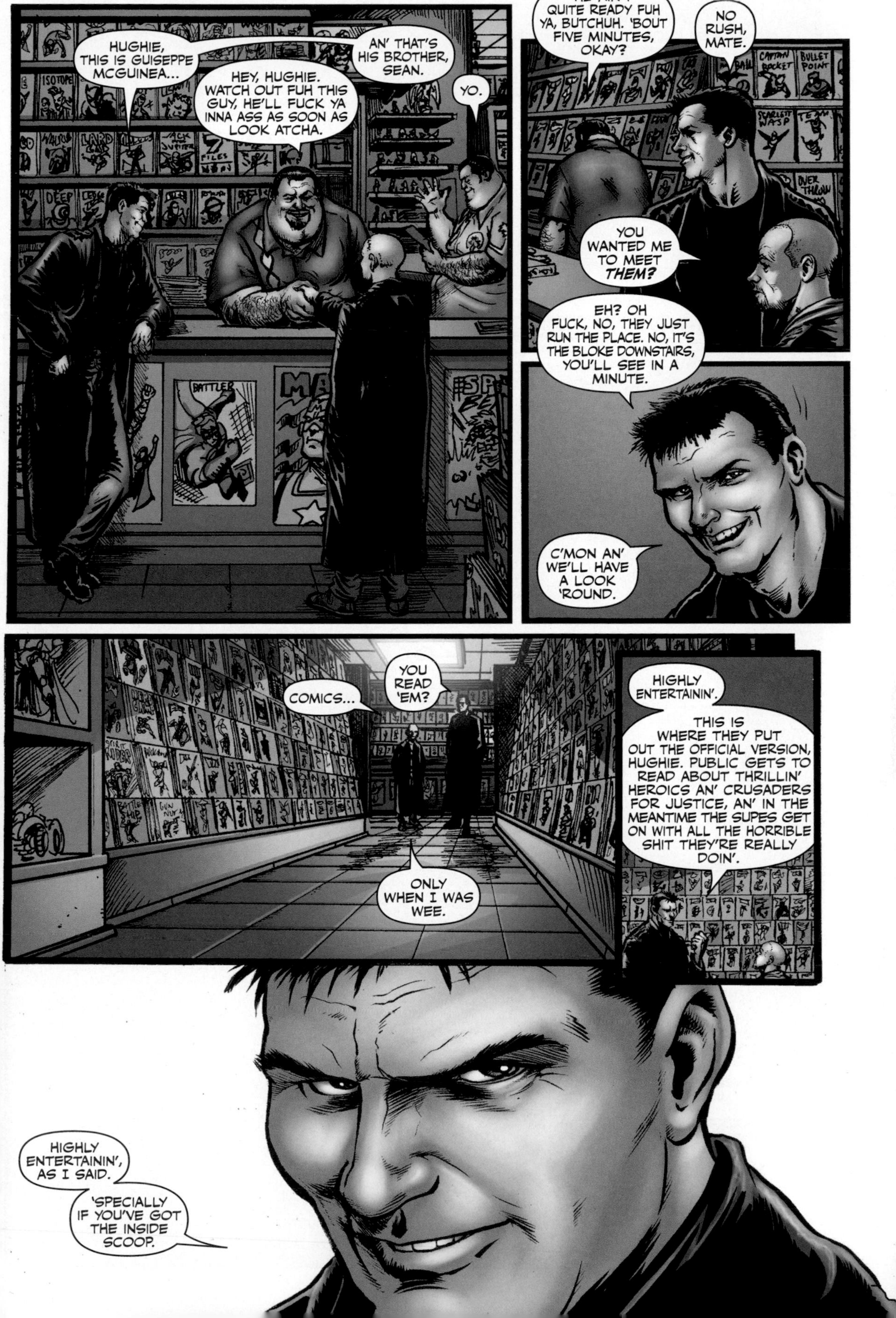
HUGHIE, THIS IS GUISEPPE MCGUINEA...
AN' THAT'S HIS BROTHER, SEAN.
HEY, HUGHIE. WATCH OUT FUH THIS GUY, HE'LL FUCK YA INNA ASS AS SOON AS LOOK ATCHA.
YO.
HE AIN'T QUITE READY FUH YA, BUTCHUH. 'BOUT FIVE MINUTES, OKAY?
NO RUSH, MATE.
YOU WANTED ME TO MEET *THEM?*
EH? OH FUCK, NO, THEY JUST RUN THE PLACE. NO, IT'S THE BLOKE DOWNSTAIRS, YOU'LL SEE IN A MINUTE.
C'MON AN' WE'LL HAVE A LOOK 'ROUND.
COMICS...
YOU READ 'EM?
ONLY WHEN I WAS WEE.
HIGHLY ENTERTAININ'.
THIS IS WHERE THEY PUT OUT THE OFFICIAL VERSION, HUGHIE. PUBLIC GETS TO READ ABOUT THRILLIN' HEROICS AN' CRUSADERS FOR JUSTICE, AN' IN THE MEANTIME THE SUPES GET ON WITH ALL THE HORRIBLE SHIT THEY'RE REALLY DOIN'.
HIGHLY ENTERTAININ', AS I SAID.
'SPECIALLY IF YOU'VE GOT THE INSIDE SCOOP.

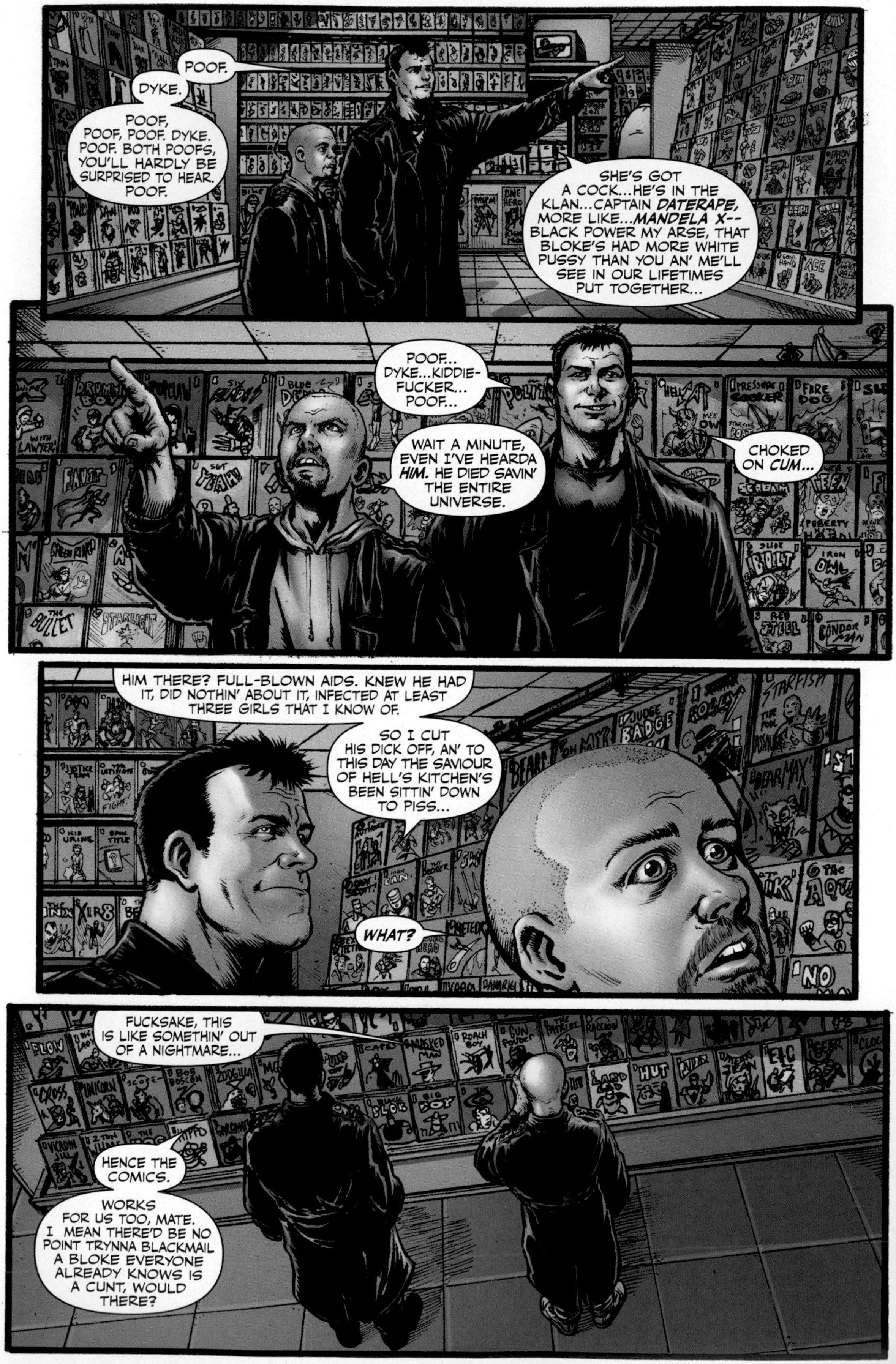
POOF.
DYKE.
POOF, POOF, POOF. DYKE. POOF. BOTH POOFS, YOU'LL HARDLY BE SURPRISED TO HEAR. POOF.
SHE'S GOT A COCK...HE'S IN THE KLAN...CAPTAIN DATERAPE, MORE LIKE...MANDELA X-- BLACK POWER MY ARSE, THAT BLOKE'S HAD MORE WHITE PUSSY THAN YOU AN' ME'LL SEE IN OUR LIFETIMES PUT TOGETHER...
POOF... DYKE...KIDDIE-FUCKER... POOF...
WAIT A MINUTE, EVEN I'VE HEARDA HIM. HE DIED SAVIN' THE ENTIRE UNIVERSE.
CHOKED ON CUM...
HIM THERE? FULL-BLOWN AIDS. KNEW HE HAD IT, DID NOTHIN' ABOUT IT, INFECTED AT LEAST THREE GIRLS THAT I KNOW OF.
SO I CUT HIS DICK OFF, AN' TO THIS DAY THE SAVIOUR OF HELL'S KITCHEN'S BEEN SITTIN' DOWN TO PISS...
WHAT?
FUCKSAKE, THIS IS LIKE SOMETHIN' OUT OF A NIGHTMARE...
HENCE THE COMICS.
WORKS FOR US TOO, MATE. I MEAN THERE'D BE NO POINT TRYNNA BLACKMAIL A BLOKE EVERYONE ALREADY KNOWS IS A CUNT, WOULD THERE?

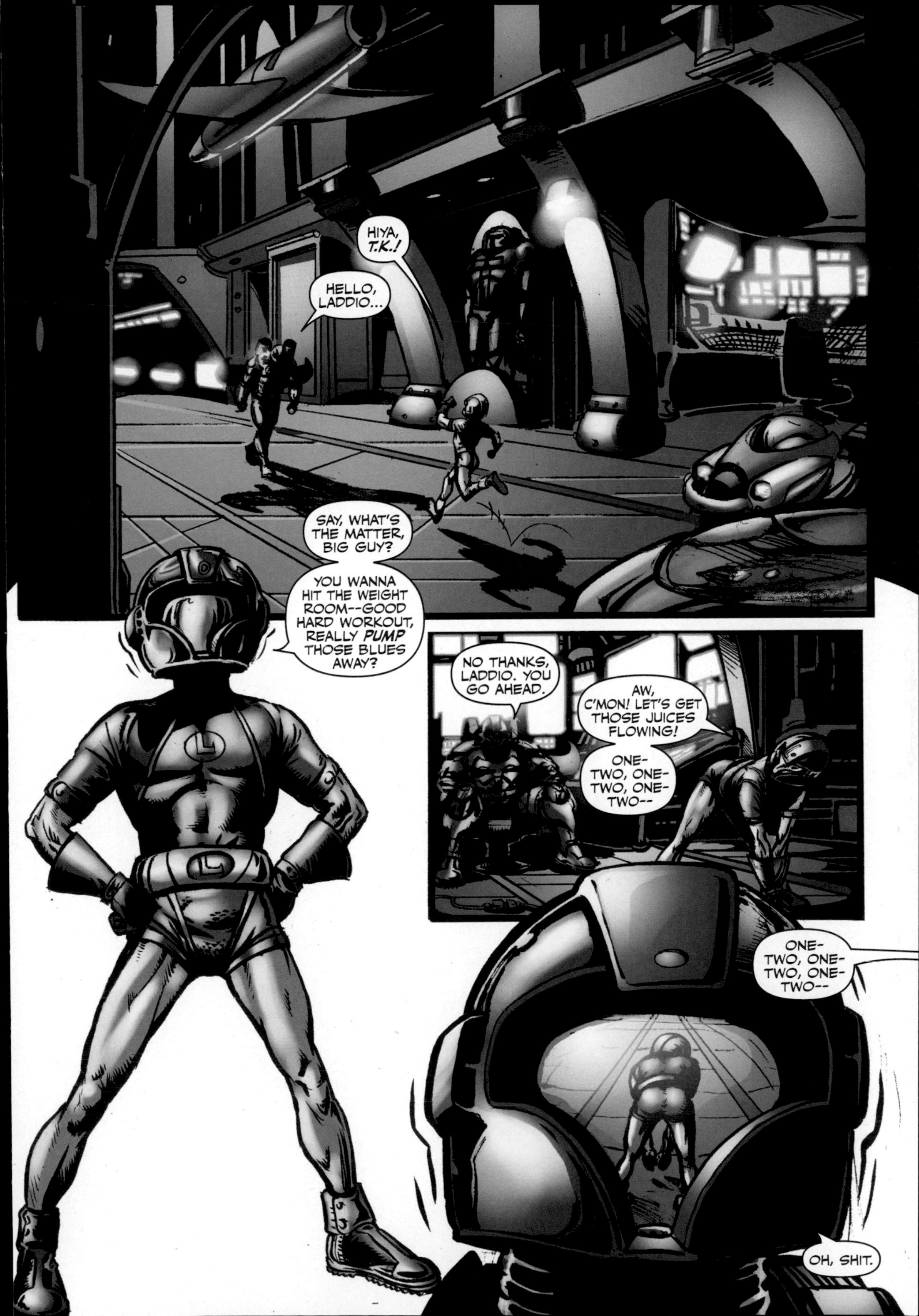
HIYA, T.K.!
HELLO, LADDIO...
SAY, WHAT'S THE MATTER, BIG GUY?
YOU WANNA HIT THE WEIGHT ROOM--GOOD HARD WORKOUT, REALLY PUMP THOSE BLUES AWAY?
NO THANKS, LADDIO. YOU GO AHEAD.
AW, C'MON! LET'S GET THOSE JUICES FLOWING!
ONE-TWO, ONE-TWO, ONE-TWO--
ONE-TWO, ONE-TWO, ONE-TWO--
OH, SHIT.

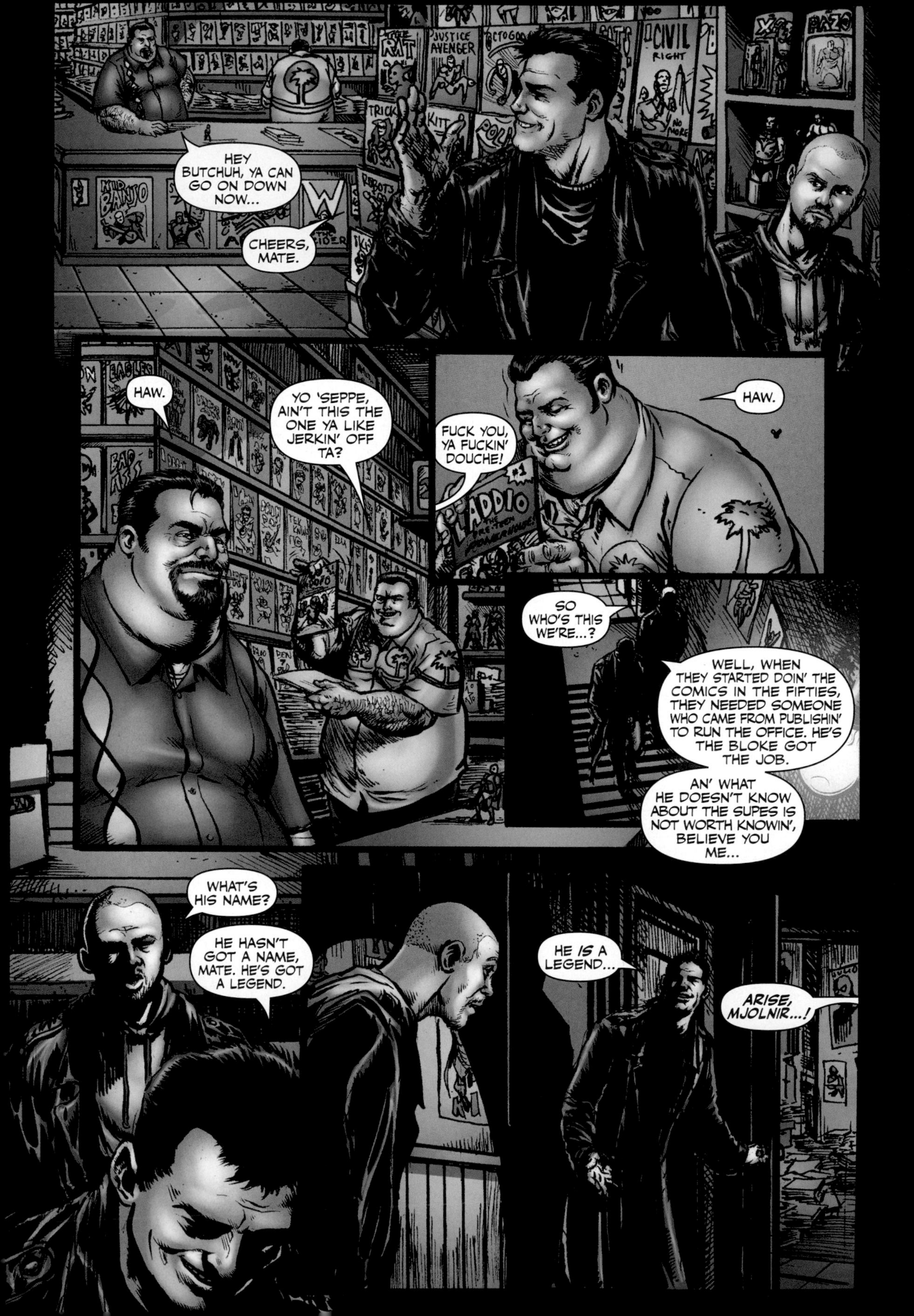
HEY BUTCHUH, YA CAN GO ON DOWN NOW...
CHEERS, MATE.
HAW.
YO 'SEPPE, AIN'T THIS THE ONE YA LIKE JERKIN' OFF TA?
HAW.
FUCK YOU, YA FUCKIN' DOUCHE!
SO WHO'S THIS WE'RE...?
WELL, WHEN THEY STARTED DOIN' THE COMICS IN THE FIFTIES, THEY NEEDED SOMEONE WHO CAME FROM PUBLISHIN' TO RUN THE OFFICE. HE'S THE BLOKE GOT THE JOB.
AN' WHAT HE DOESN'T KNOW ABOUT THE SUPES IS NOT WORTH KNOWIN', BELIEVE YOU ME...
WHAT'S HIS NAME?
HE HASN'T GOT A NAME, MATE. HE'S GOT A LEGEND.
HE *IS* A LEGEND...
ARISE, MJOLNIR...!

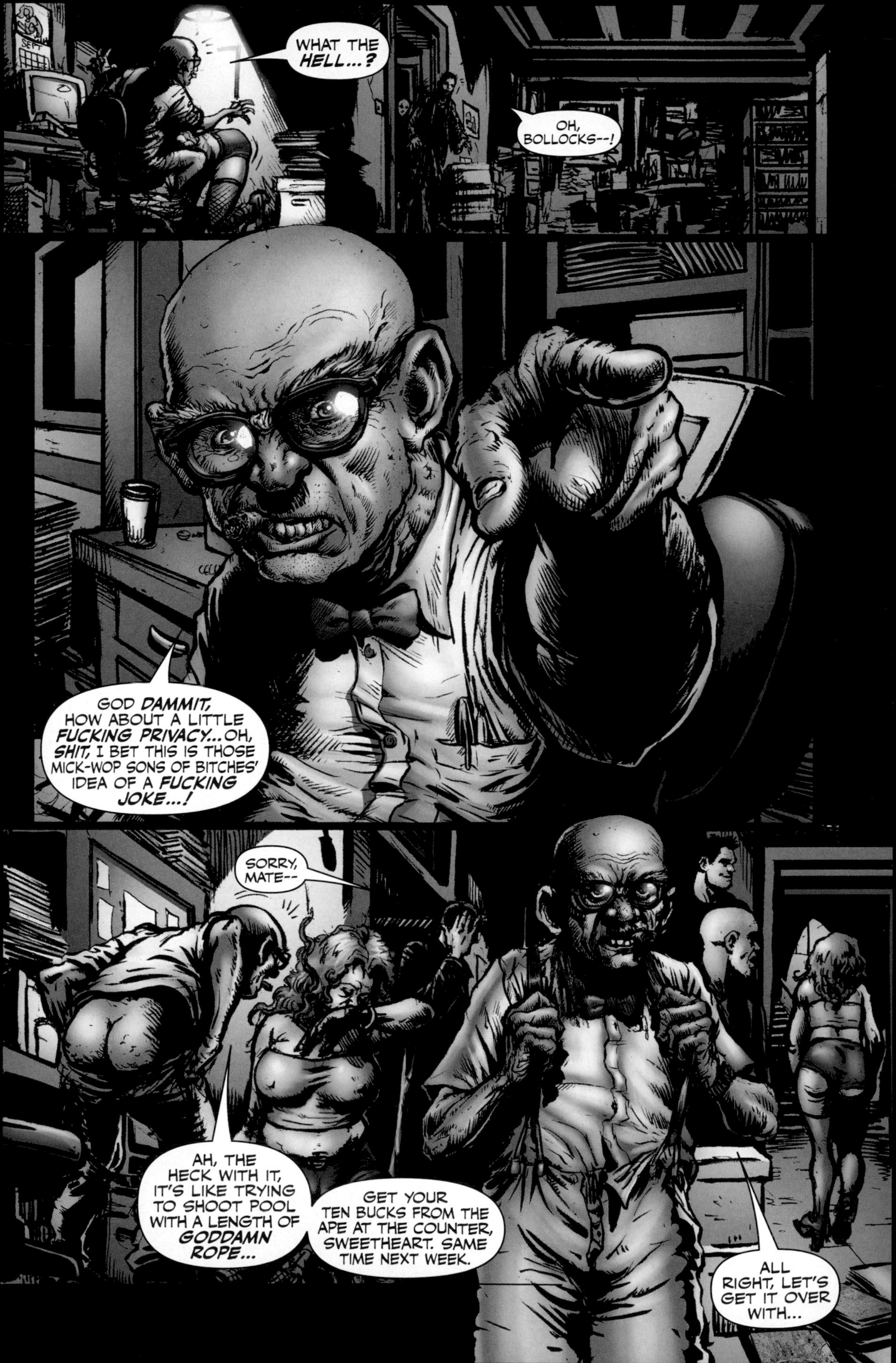
SEPT
WHAT THE HELL...?
OH, BOLLOCKS--!
GOD DAMMIT, HOW ABOUT A LITTLE FUCKING PRIVACY...OH, SHIT, I BET THIS IS THOSE MICK-WOP SONS OF BITCHES' IDEA OF A FUCKING JOKE...!
SORRY, MATE--
AH, THE HECK WITH IT, IT'S LIKE TRYING TO SHOOT POOL WITH A LENGTH OF GODDAMN ROPE...
GET YOUR TEN BUCKS FROM THE APE AT THE COUNTER, SWEETHEART. SAME TIME NEXT WEEK.
ALL RIGHT, LET'S GET IT OVER WITH...

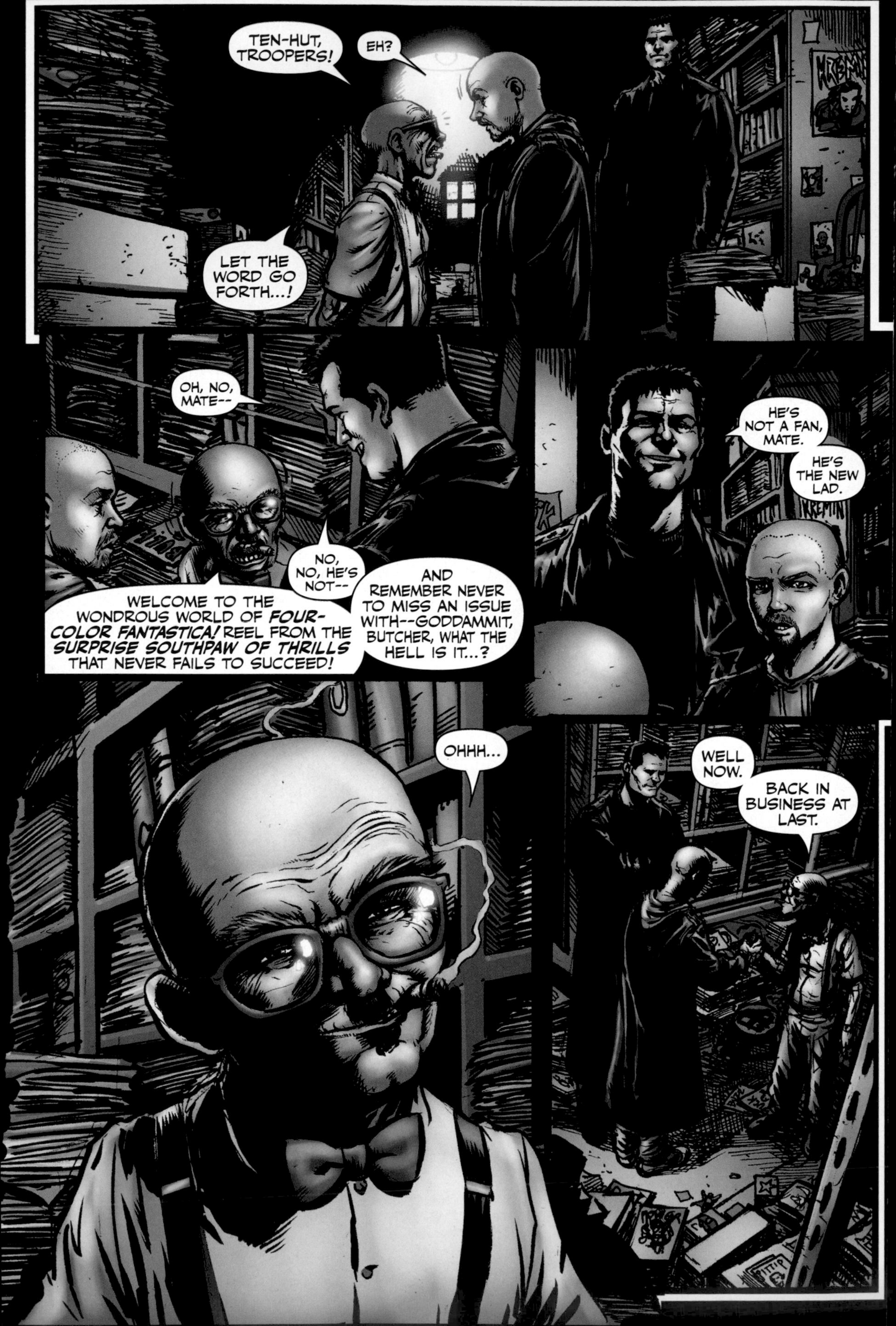
TEN-HUT, TROOPERS!
EH?
LET THE WORD GO FORTH...!
OH, NO, MATE--
NO, NO, HE'S NOT--
WELCOME TO THE WONDROUS WORLD OF *FOUR-COLOR FANTASTICA!* REEL FROM THE *SURPRISE SOUTHPAW OF THRILLS* THAT NEVER FAILS TO SUCCEED!
AND REMEMBER NEVER TO MISS AN ISSUE WITH--GODDAMMIT, BUTCHER, WHAT THE HELL IS IT...?
HE'S NOT A FAN, MATE.
HE'S THE NEW LAD.
OHHH...
WELL NOW.
BACK IN BUSINESS AT LAST.

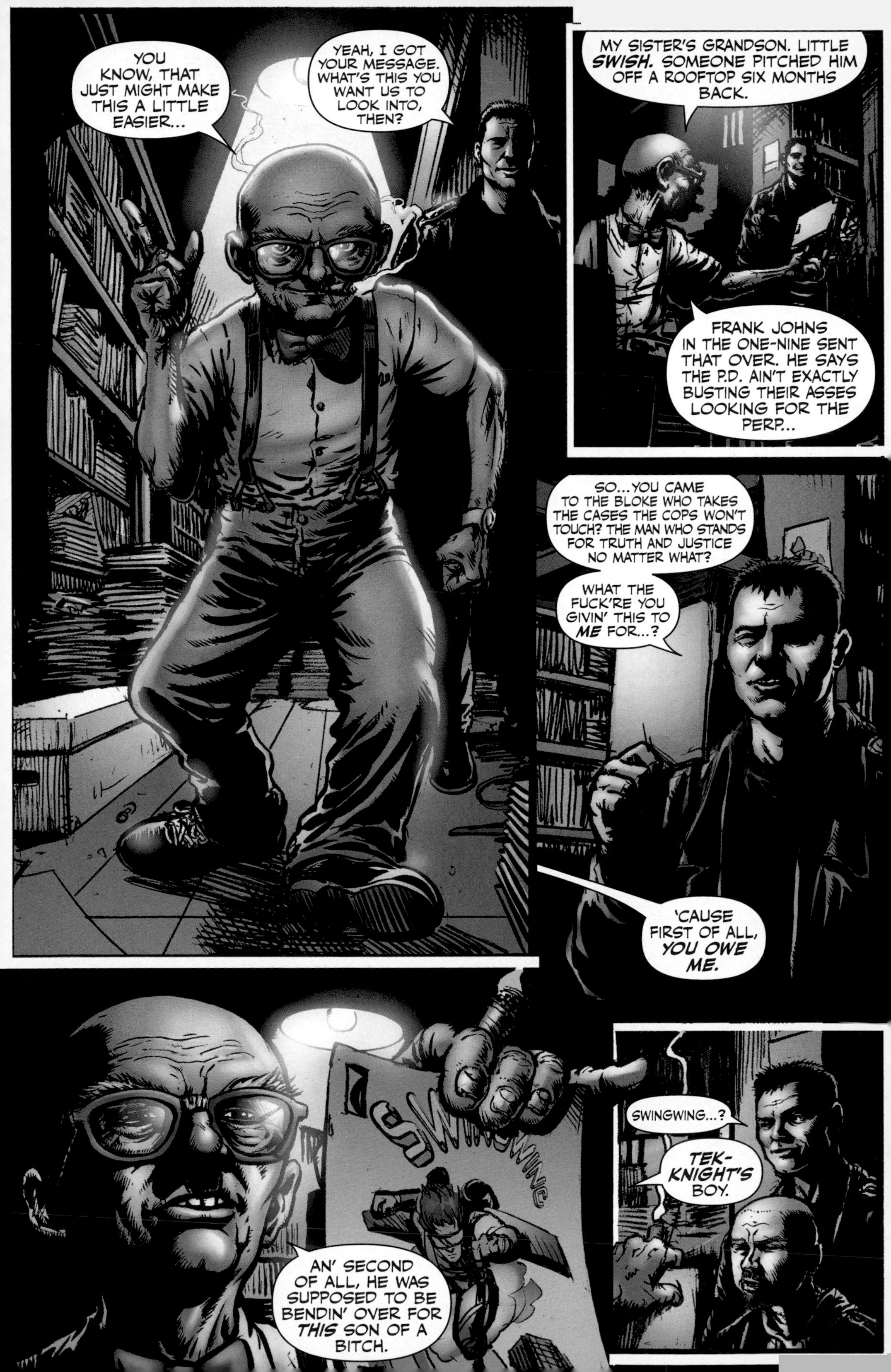
YOU KNOW, THAT JUST MIGHT MAKE THIS A LITTLE EASIER...
YEAH, I GOT YOUR MESSAGE. WHAT'S THIS YOU WANT US TO LOOK INTO, THEN?
MY SISTER'S GRANDSON. LITTLE *SWISH.* SOMEONE PITCHED HIM OFF A ROOFTOP SIX MONTHS BACK.
FRANK JOHNS IN THE ONE-NINE SENT THAT OVER. HE SAYS THE P.D. AIN'T EXACTLY BUSTING THEIR ASSES LOOKING FOR THE PERP...
SO...YOU CAME TO THE BLOKE WHO TAKES THE CASES THE COPS WON'T TOUCH? THE MAN WHO STANDS FOR TRUTH AND JUSTICE NO MATTER WHAT?
WHAT THE FUCK'RE YOU GIVIN' THIS TO *ME* FOR...?
'CAUSE FIRST OF ALL, *YOU OWE ME.*
AN' SECOND OF ALL, HE WAS SUPPOSED TO BE BENDIN' OVER FOR *THIS* SON OF A BITCH.
SWINGWING
SWINGWING...?
TEK-KNIGHT'S BOY.

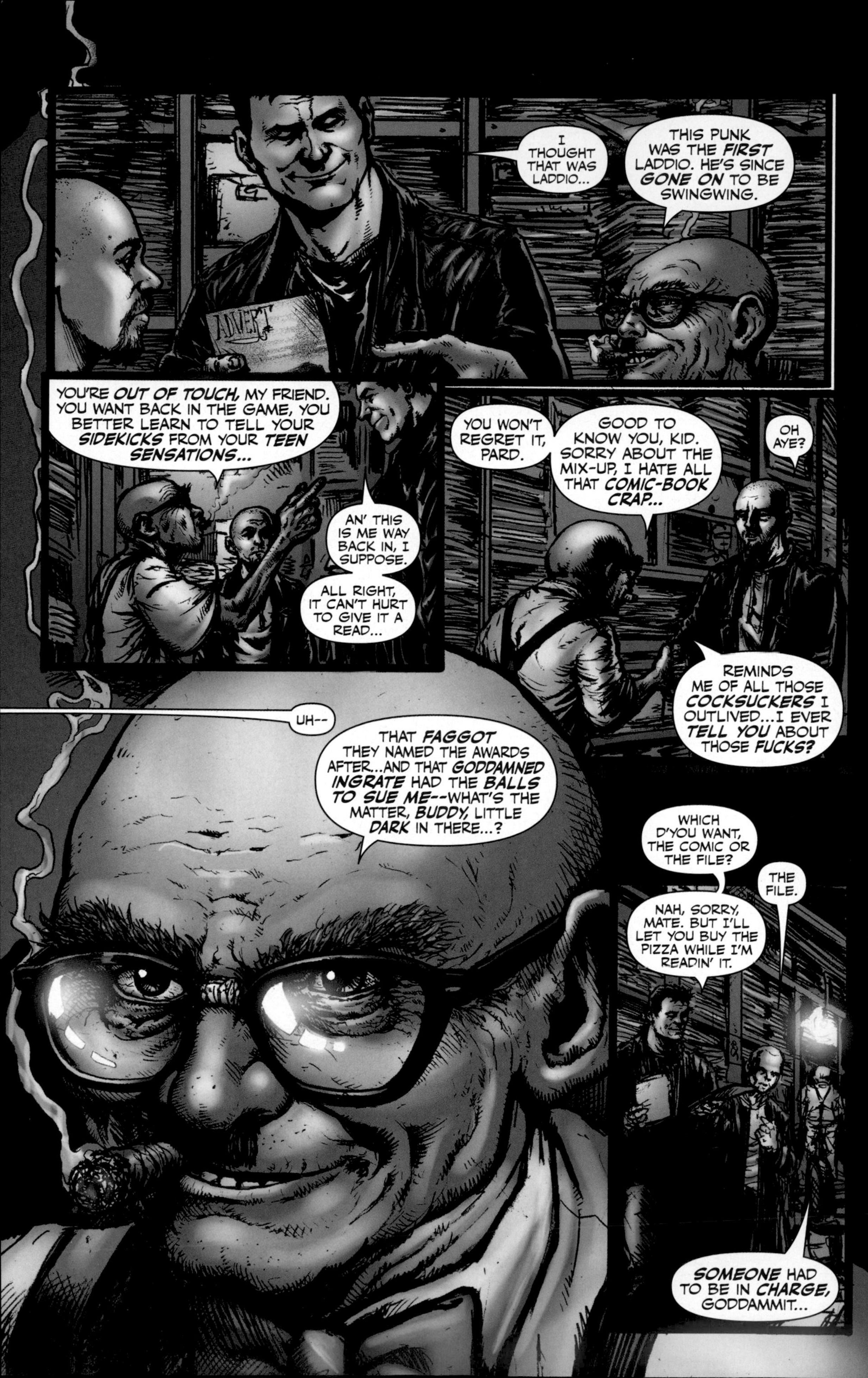
I THOUGHT THAT WAS LADDIO...
THIS PUNK WAS THE FIRST LADDIO. HE'S SINCE GONE ON TO BE SWINGWING.
ADVERT
YOU'RE OUT OF TOUCH, MY FRIEND. YOU WANT BACK IN THE GAME, YOU BETTER LEARN TO TELL YOUR SIDEKICKS FROM YOUR TEEN SENSATIONS...
AN' THIS IS ME WAY BACK IN, I SUPPOSE.
ALL RIGHT, IT CAN'T HURT TO GIVE IT A READ...
YOU WON'T REGRET IT, PARD.
GOOD TO KNOW YOU, KID. SORRY ABOUT THE MIX-UP, I HATE ALL THAT COMIC-BOOK CRAP...
OH AYE?
REMINDS ME OF ALL THOSE COCKSUCKERS I OUTLIVED...I EVER TELL YOU ABOUT THOSE FUCKS?
UH--
THAT FAGGOT THEY NAMED THE AWARDS AFTER...AND THAT GODDAMNED INGRATE HAD THE BALLS TO SUE ME--WHAT'S THE MATTER, BUDDY, LITTLE DARK IN THERE...?
WHICH D'YOU WANT, THE COMIC OR THE FILE?
THE FILE.
NAH, SORRY, MATE. BUT I'LL LET YOU BUY THE PIZZA WHILE I'M READIN' IT.
SOMEONE HAD TO BE IN CHARGE, GODDAMMIT...

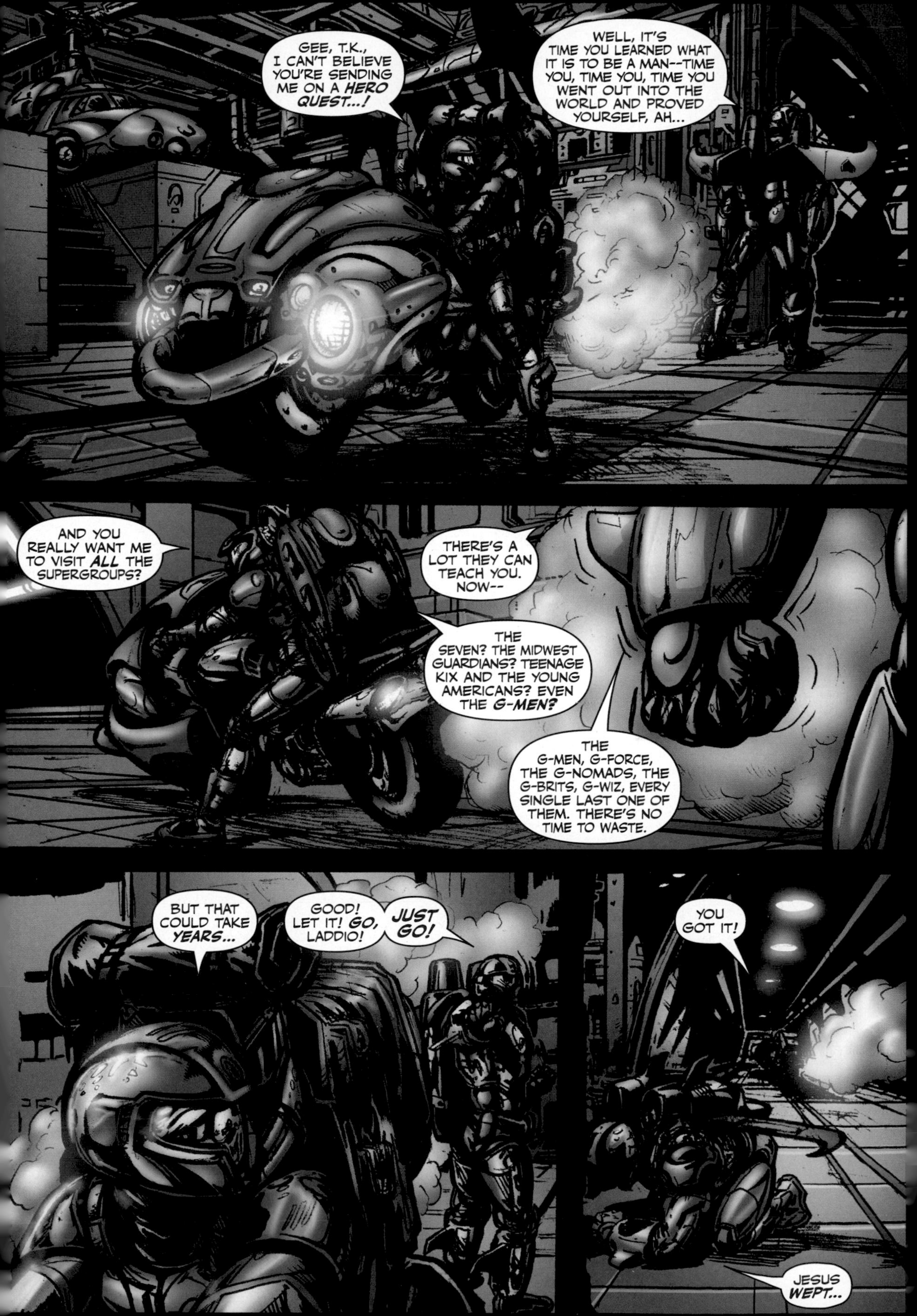

GEE, T.K., I CAN'T BELIEVE YOU'RE SENDING ME ON A HERO QUEST...!
WELL, IT'S TIME YOU LEARNED WHAT IT IS TO BE A MAN--TIME YOU, TIME YOU, TIME YOU WENT OUT INTO THE WORLD AND PROVED YOURSELF, AH...
AND YOU REALLY WANT ME TO VISIT ALL THE SUPERGROUPS?
THERE'S A LOT THEY CAN TEACH YOU. NOW--
THE SEVEN? THE MIDWEST GUARDIANS? TEENAGE KIX AND THE YOUNG AMERICANS? EVEN THE G-MEN?
THE G-MEN, G-FORCE, THE G-NOMADS, THE G-BRITS, G-WIZ, EVERY SINGLE LAST ONE OF THEM. THERE'S NO TIME TO WASTE.
BUT THAT COULD TAKE YEARS...
GOOD! LET IT! GO, LADDIO!
JUST GO!
YOU GOT IT!
JESUS WEPT...

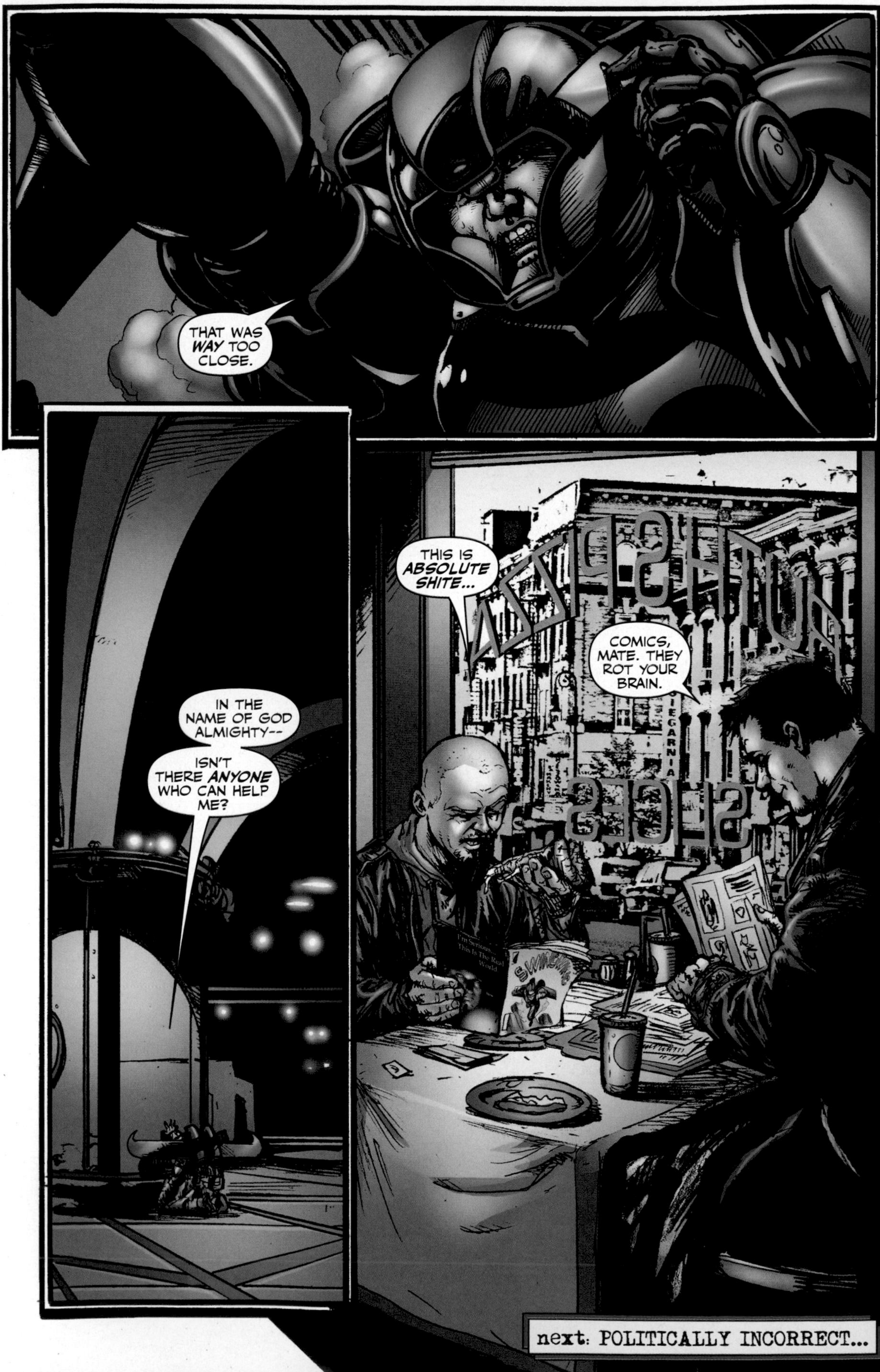
THAT WAS WAY TOO CLOSE.
IN THE NAME OF GOD ALMIGHTY--
ISN'T THERE ANYONE WHO CAN HELP ME?
THIS IS ABSOLUTE SHITE...
COMICS, MATE. THEY ROT YOUR BRAIN.
next: POLITICALLY INCORRECT...

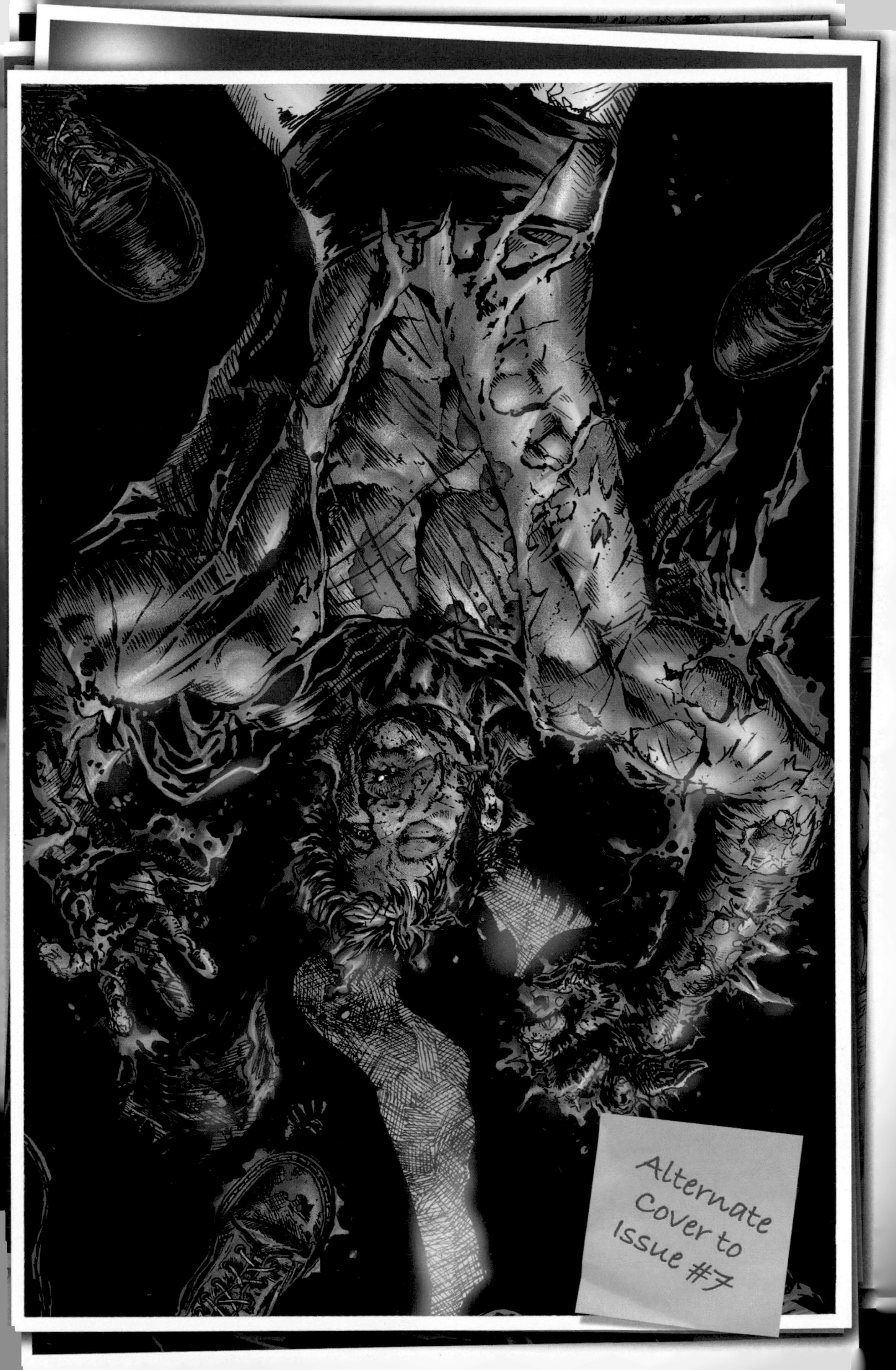
Alternate Cover to Issue #7

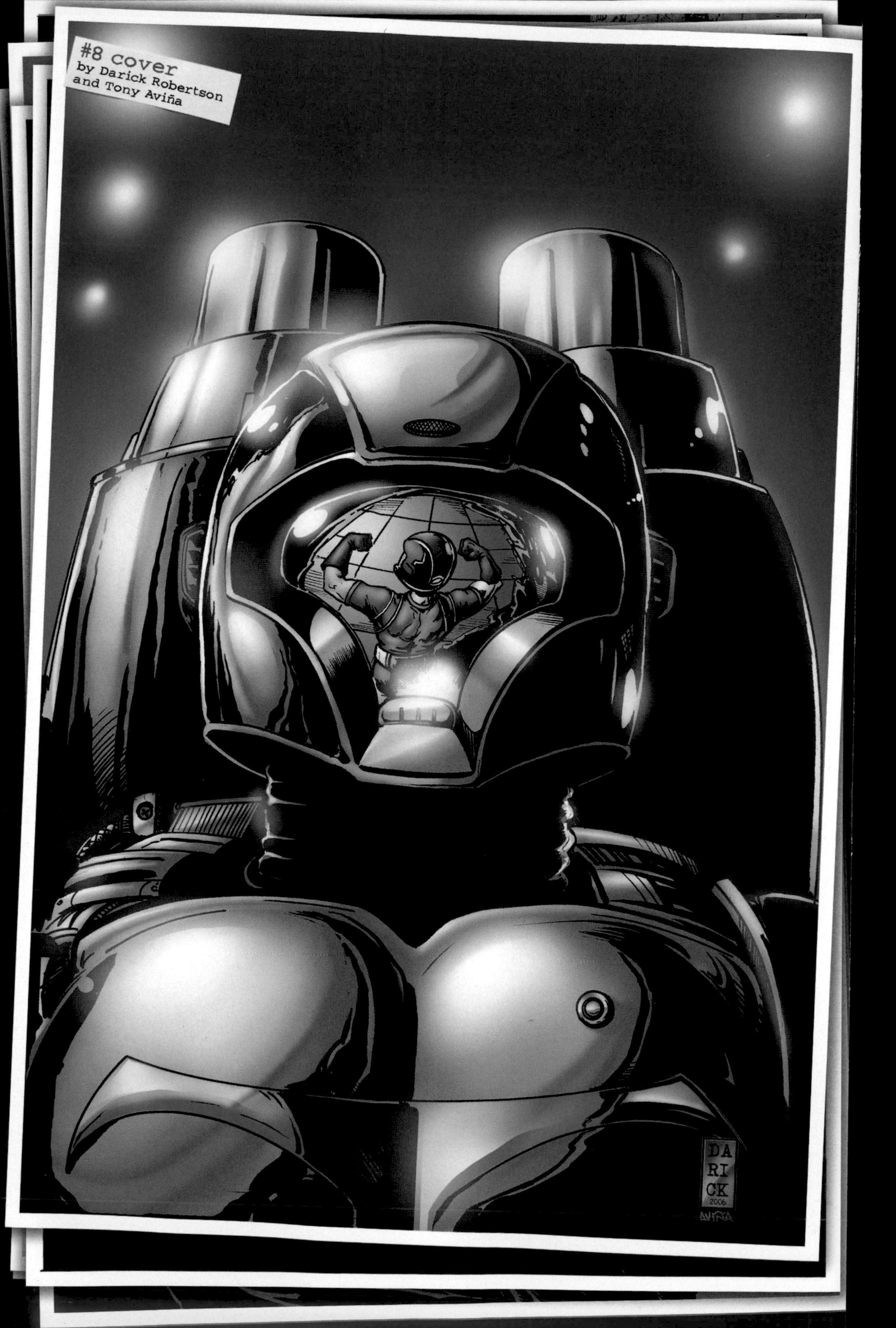
DA
RI
CK
2006
AVIÑA

#8 cover
by Darick Robertson
and Tony Aviña

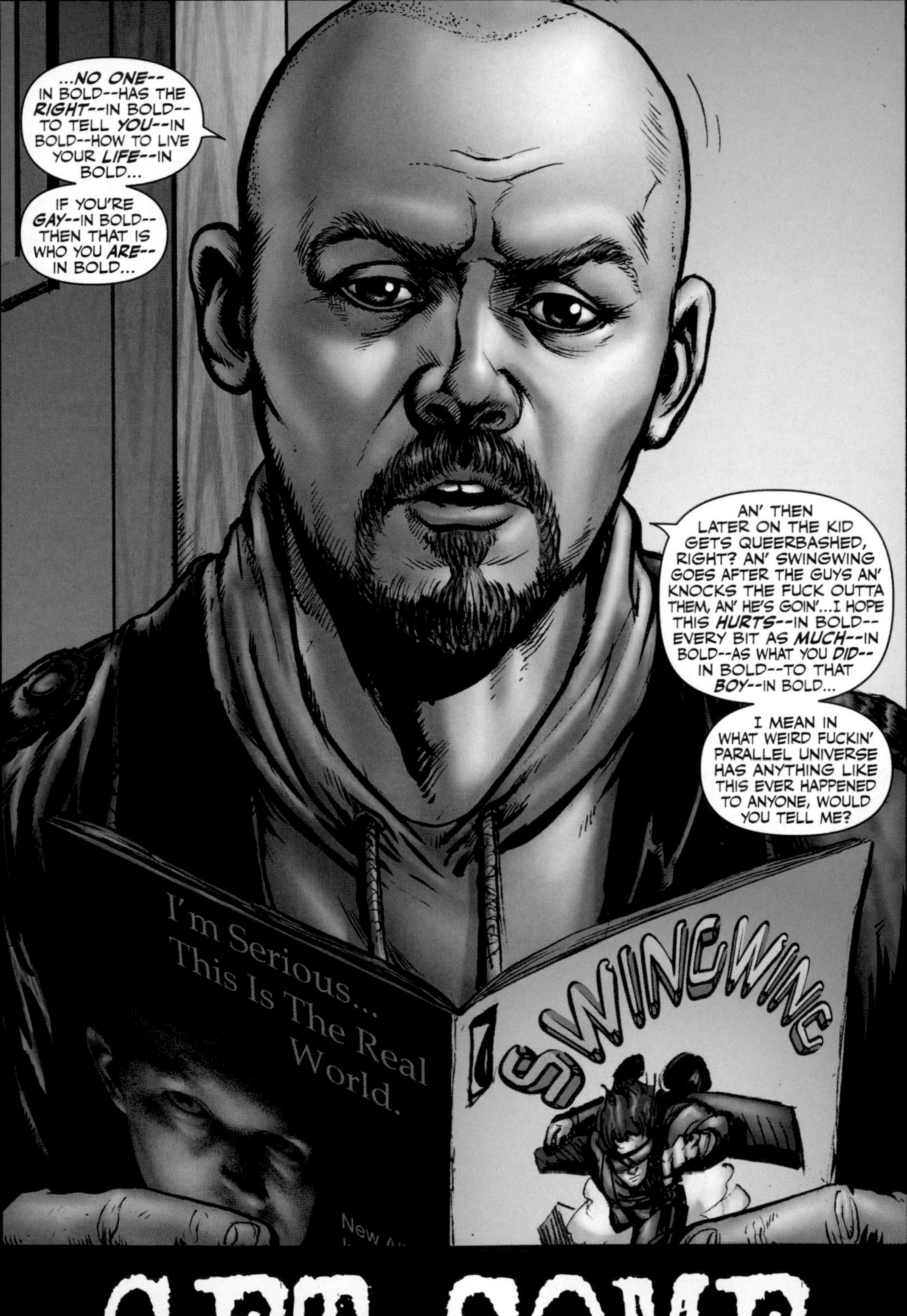
...NO ONE-- IN BOLD--HAS THE RIGHT--IN BOLD-- TO TELL YOU--IN BOLD--HOW TO LIVE YOUR LIFE--IN BOLD...
IF YOU'RE GAY--IN BOLD-- THEN THAT IS WHO YOU ARE-- IN BOLD...
AN' THEN LATER ON THE KID GETS QUEERBASHED, RIGHT? AN' SWINGWING GOES AFTER THE GUYS AN' KNOCKS THE FUCK OUTTA THEM, AN' HE'S GOIN'...I HOPE THIS HURTS--IN BOLD-- EVERY BIT AS MUCH--IN BOLD--AS WHAT YOU DID-- IN BOLD--TO THAT BOY--IN BOLD...
I MEAN IN WHAT WEIRD FUCKIN' PARALLEL UNIVERSE HAS ANYTHING LIKE THIS EVER HAPPENED TO ANYONE, WOULD YOU TELL ME?
I'm Serious... This Is The Real World.
SWINGWING

GET SOME
part two

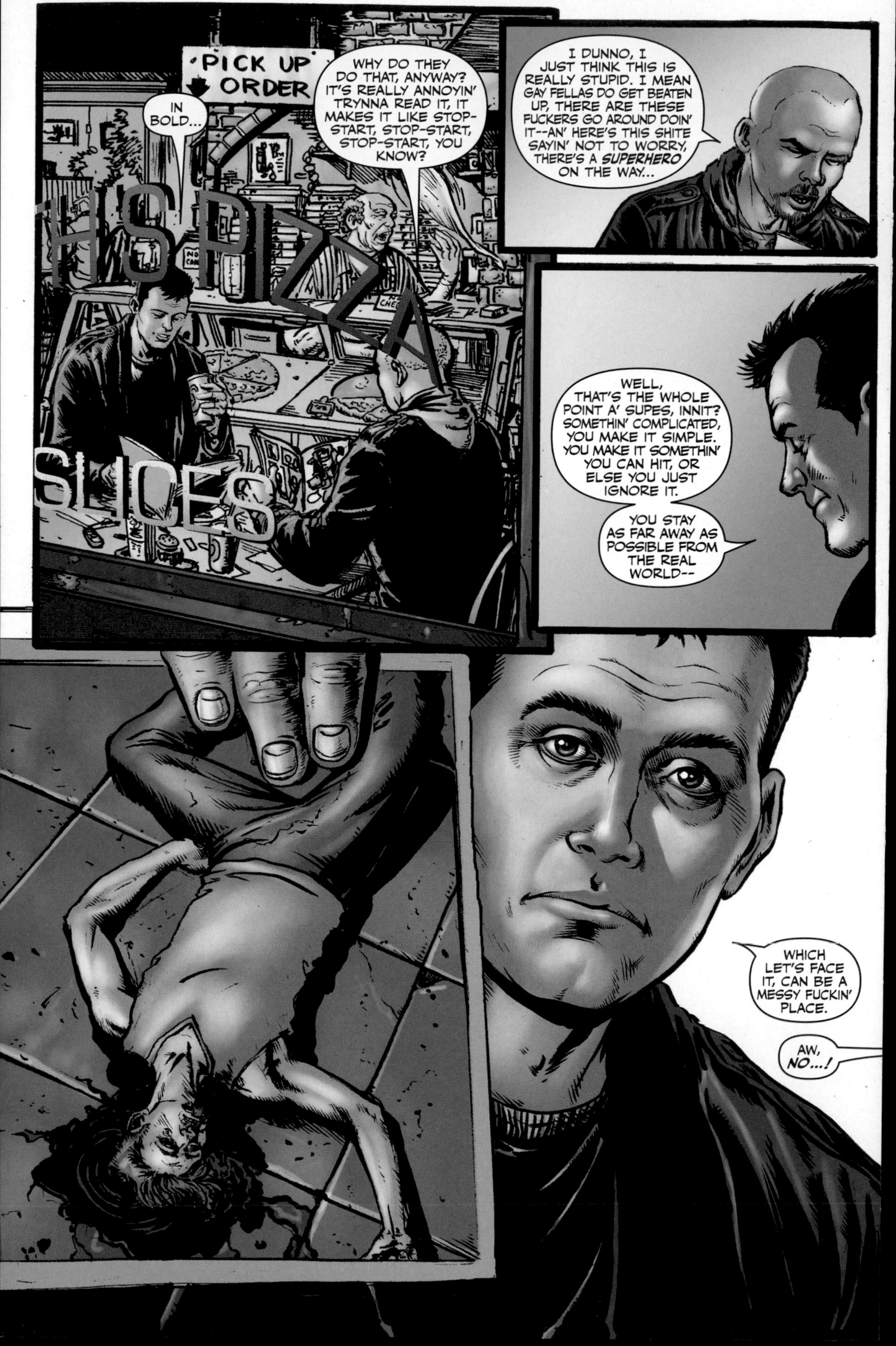
PICK UP ORDER
IN BOLD...
WHY DO THEY DO THAT, ANYWAY? IT'S REALLY ANNOYIN' TRYNNA READ IT, IT MAKES IT LIKE STOP-START, STOP-START, STOP-START, YOU KNOW?
HS PIZZA
SLICES
I DUNNO, I JUST THINK THIS IS REALLY STUPID. I MEAN GAY FELLAS DO GET BEATEN UP, THERE ARE THESE FUCKERS GO AROUND DOIN' IT--AN' HERE'S THIS SHITE SAYIN' NOT TO WORRY, THERE'S A SUPERHERO ON THE WAY...
WELL, THAT'S THE WHOLE POINT A' SUPES, INNIT? SOMETHIN' COMPLICATED, YOU MAKE IT SIMPLE. YOU MAKE IT SOMETHIN' YOU CAN HIT, OR ELSE YOU JUST IGNORE IT.
YOU STAY AS FAR AWAY AS POSSIBLE FROM THE REAL WORLD--
WHICH LET'S FACE IT, CAN BE A MESSY FUCKIN' PLACE.
AW, NO...!

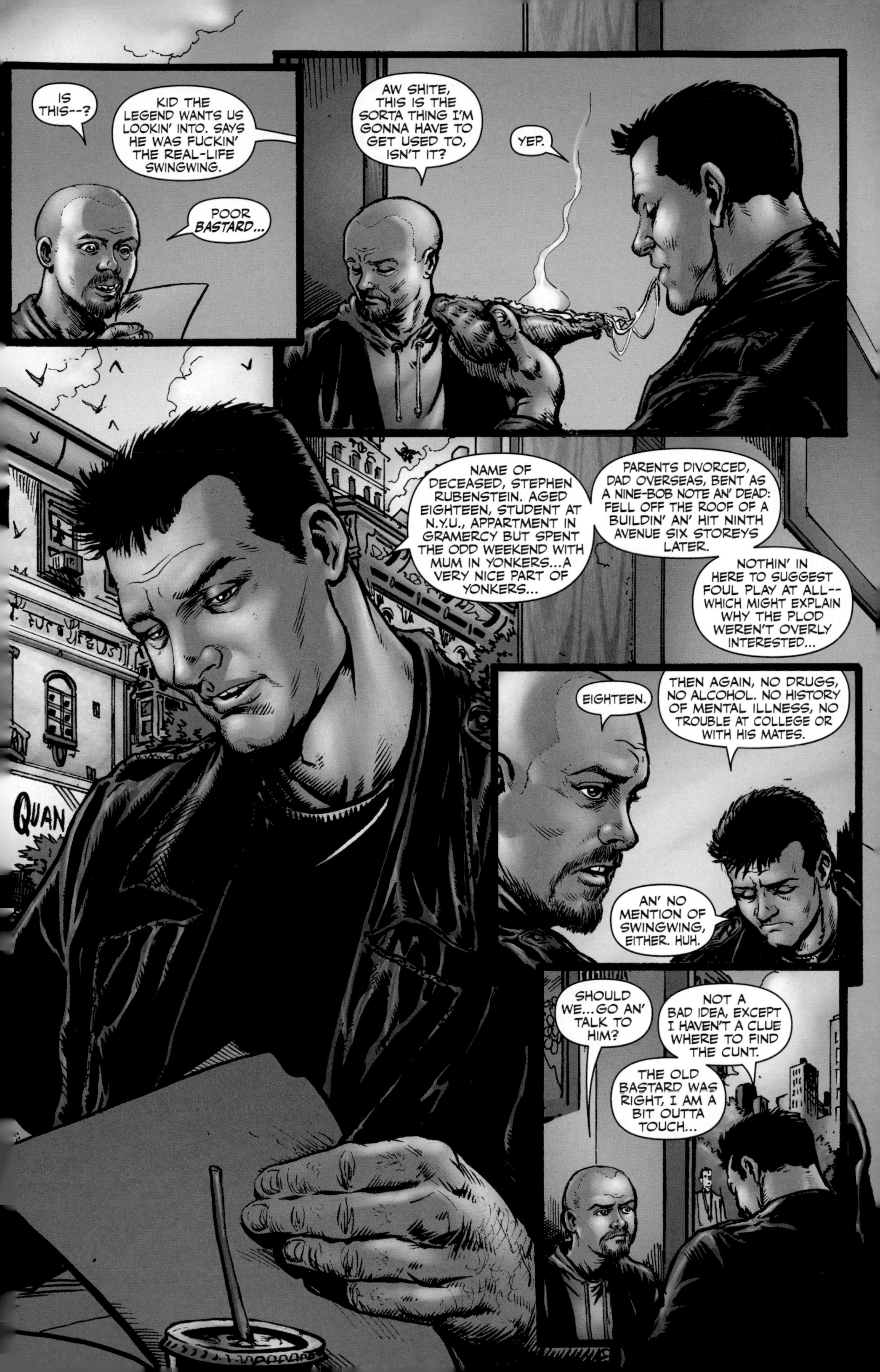

IS THIS--?
KID THE LEGEND WANTS US LOOKIN' INTO. SAYS HE WAS FUCKIN' THE REAL-LIFE SWINGWING.
POOR BASTARD...
AW SHITE, THIS IS THE SORTA THING I'M GONNA HAVE TO GET USED TO, ISN'T IT?
YEP.
NAME OF DECEASED, STEPHEN RUBENSTEIN. AGED EIGHTEEN, STUDENT AT N.Y.U., APPARTMENT IN GRAMERCY BUT SPENT THE ODD WEEKEND WITH MUM IN YONKERS...A VERY NICE PART OF YONKERS...
PARENTS DIVORCED, DAD OVERSEAS, BENT AS A NINE-BOB NOTE AN' DEAD: FELL OFF THE ROOF OF A BUILDIN' AN' HIT NINTH AVENUE SIX STOREYS LATER.
NOTHIN' IN HERE TO SUGGEST FOUL PLAY AT ALL--WHICH MIGHT EXPLAIN WHY THE PLOD WEREN'T OVERLY INTERESTED...
EIGHTEEN.
THEN AGAIN, NO DRUGS, NO ALCOHOL. NO HISTORY OF MENTAL ILLNESS, NO TROUBLE AT COLLEGE OR WITH HIS MATES.
AN' NO MENTION OF SWINGWING, EITHER. HUH.
SHOULD WE...GO AN' TALK TO HIM?
NOT A BAD IDEA, EXCEPT I HAVEN'T A CLUE WHERE TO FIND THE CUNT.
THE OLD BASTARD WAS RIGHT, I AM A BIT OUTTA TOUCH...
QUAN

THEY INTERVIEWED A FEW O' HIS PALS...

WHAT ABOUT THIS LAD DRAKE, HE'S A BIT OLDER'N THE OTHERS, ISN'T HE? HE'S *NINE* YEARS OLDER'N STEPHEN, D'YOU THINK HE'D BE WORTH TALKIN' TO?

MIGHT BE.

SAYS HE'S A BARMAN AT THIS PLACE HERE...

MM, POSSIBLE BUMCHUM. ALL RIGHT, LET'S GIVE IT A GO.

...D'YOU HAVE TO TALK ABOUT THEM LIKE THAT?

EH?

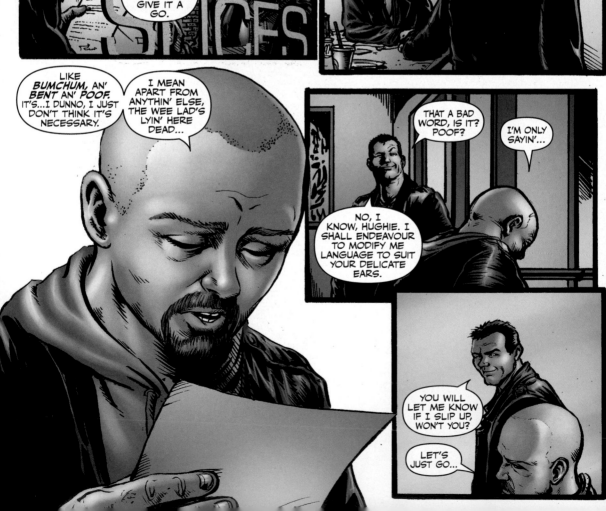

LIKE *BUMCHUM,* AN' *BENT* AN' *POOF.* IT'S...I DUNNO, I JUST DON'T THINK IT'S NECESSARY.

I MEAN APART FROM ANYTHIN' ELSE, THE WEE LAD'S LYIN' HERE DEAD...

THAT A BAD WORD, IS IT? POOF?

I'M ONLY SAYIN'...

NO, I KNOW, HUGHIE. I SHALL ENDEAVOUR TO MODIFY ME LANGUAGE TO SUIT YOUR DELICATE EARS.

YOU WILL LET ME KNOW IF I SLIP UP, WON'T YOU?

LET'S JUST GO...

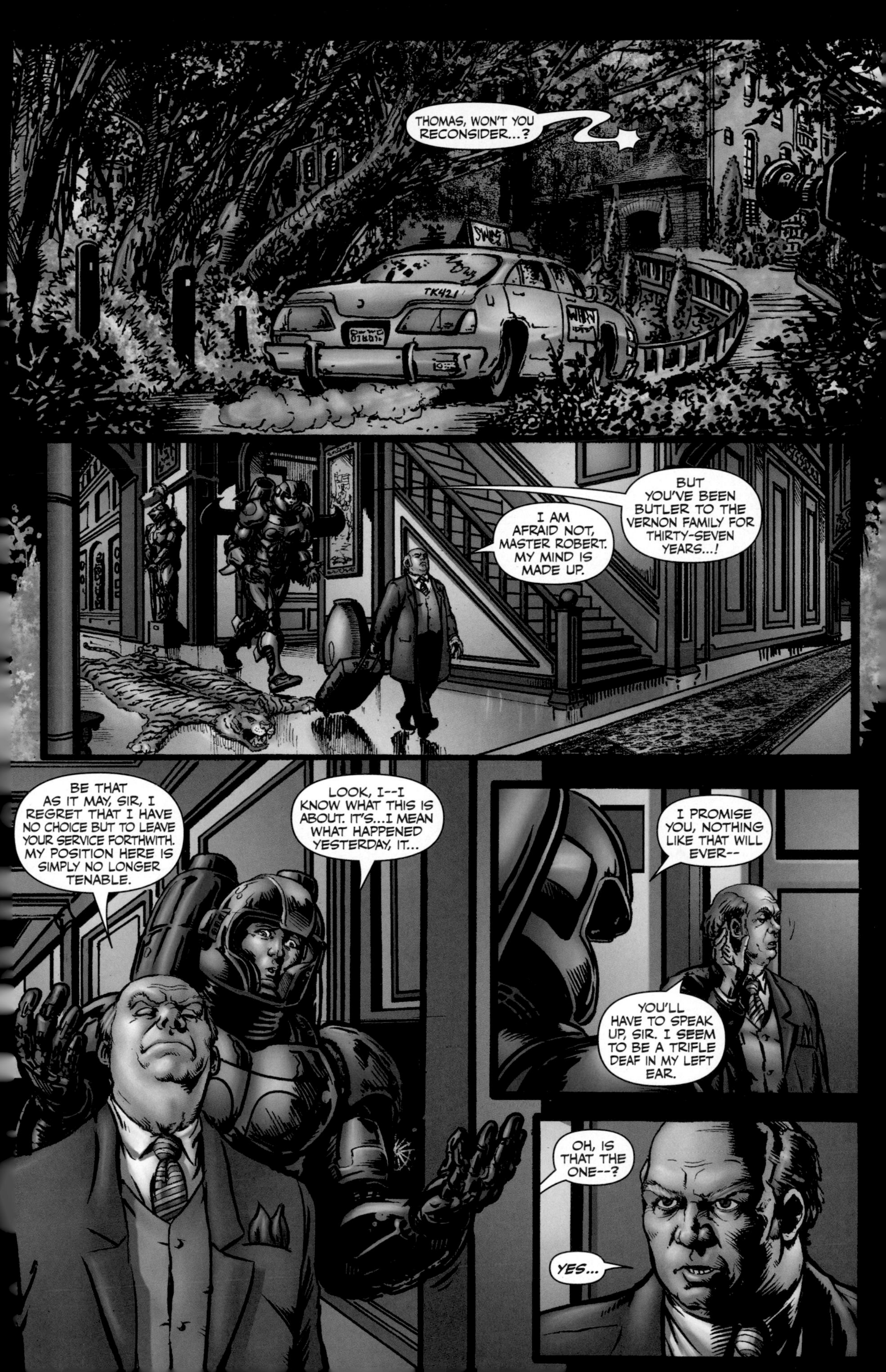
THOMAS, WON'T YOU RECONSIDER...?
BUT YOU'VE BEEN BUTLER TO THE VERNON FAMILY FOR THIRTY-SEVEN YEARS...!
I AM AFRAID NOT, MASTER ROBERT. MY MIND IS MADE UP.
BE THAT AS IT MAY, SIR, I REGRET THAT I HAVE NO CHOICE BUT TO LEAVE YOUR SERVICE FORTHWITH. MY POSITION HERE IS SIMPLY NO LONGER TENABLE.
LOOK, I--I KNOW WHAT THIS IS ABOUT. IT'S...I MEAN WHAT HAPPENED YESTERDAY, IT...
I PROMISE YOU, NOTHING LIKE THAT WILL EVER--
YOU'LL HAVE TO SPEAK UP, SIR. I SEEM TO BE A TRIFLE DEAF IN MY LEFT EAR.
OH, IS THAT THE ONE--?
YES...

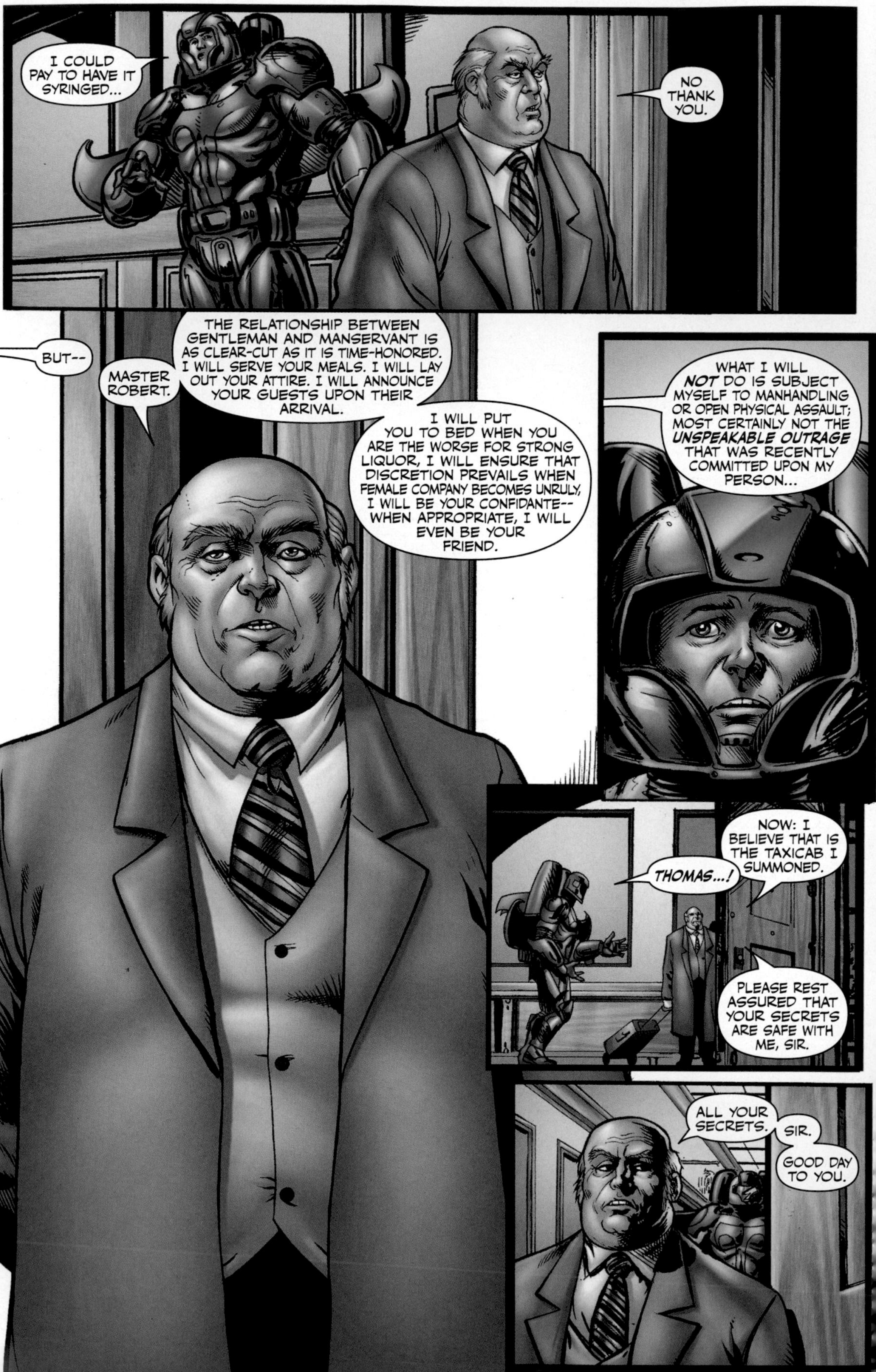
I COULD PAY TO HAVE IT SYRINGED...
NO THANK YOU.
BUT--
MASTER ROBERT.
THE RELATIONSHIP BETWEEN GENTLEMAN AND MANSERVANT IS AS CLEAR-CUT AS IT IS TIME-HONORED. I WILL SERVE YOUR MEALS. I WILL LAY OUT YOUR ATTIRE. I WILL ANNOUNCE YOUR GUESTS UPON THEIR ARRIVAL.
I WILL PUT YOU TO BED WHEN YOU ARE THE WORSE FOR STRONG LIQUOR, I WILL ENSURE THAT DISCRETION PREVAILS WHEN FEMALE COMPANY BECOMES UNRULY, I WILL BE YOUR CONFIDANTE-- WHEN APPROPRIATE, I WILL EVEN BE YOUR FRIEND.
WHAT I WILL *NOT* DO IS SUBJECT MYSELF TO MANHANDLING OR OPEN PHYSICAL ASSAULT; MOST CERTAINLY NOT THE *UNSPEAKABLE OUTRAGE* THAT WAS RECENTLY COMMITTED UPON MY PERSON...
THOMAS...!
NOW: I BELIEVE THAT IS THE TAXICAB I SUMMONED.
PLEASE REST ASSURED THAT YOUR SECRETS ARE SAFE WITH ME, SIR.
ALL YOUR SECRETS.
SIR.
GOOD DAY TO YOU.

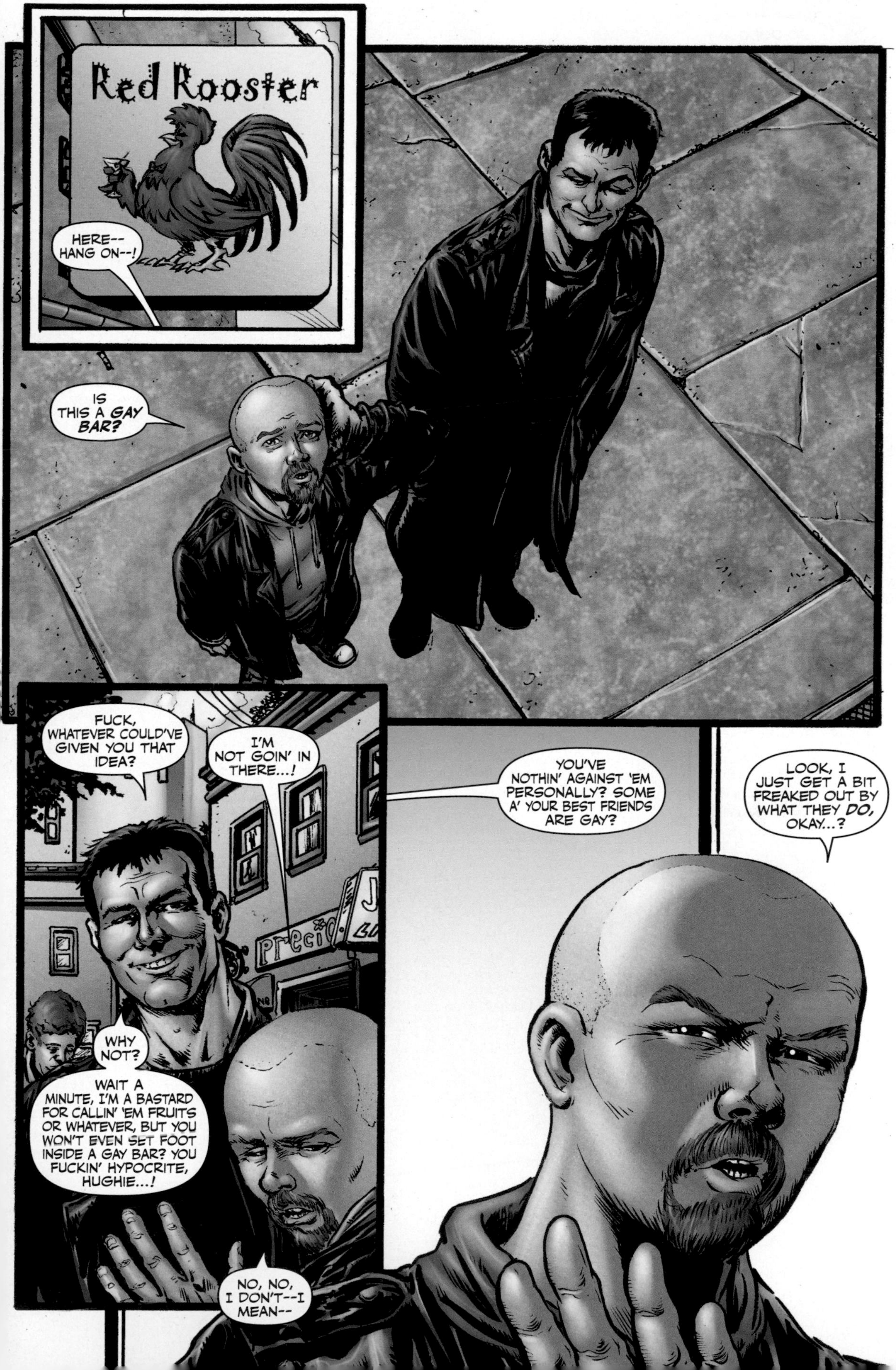
Red Rooster
HERE-- HANG ON--!
IS THIS A GAY BAR?
FUCK, WHATEVER COULD'VE GIVEN YOU THAT IDEA?
I'M NOT GOIN' IN THERE...!
WHY NOT?
WAIT A MINUTE, I'M A BASTARD FOR CALLIN' 'EM FRUITS OR WHATEVER, BUT YOU WON'T EVEN SET FOOT INSIDE A GAY BAR? YOU FUCKIN' HYPOCRITE, HUGHIE...!
NO, NO, I DON'T--I MEAN--
YOU'VE NOTHIN' AGAINST 'EM PERSONALLY? SOME A' YOUR BEST FRIENDS ARE GAY?
LOOK, I JUST GET A BIT FREAKED OUT BY WHAT THEY DO, OKAY...?

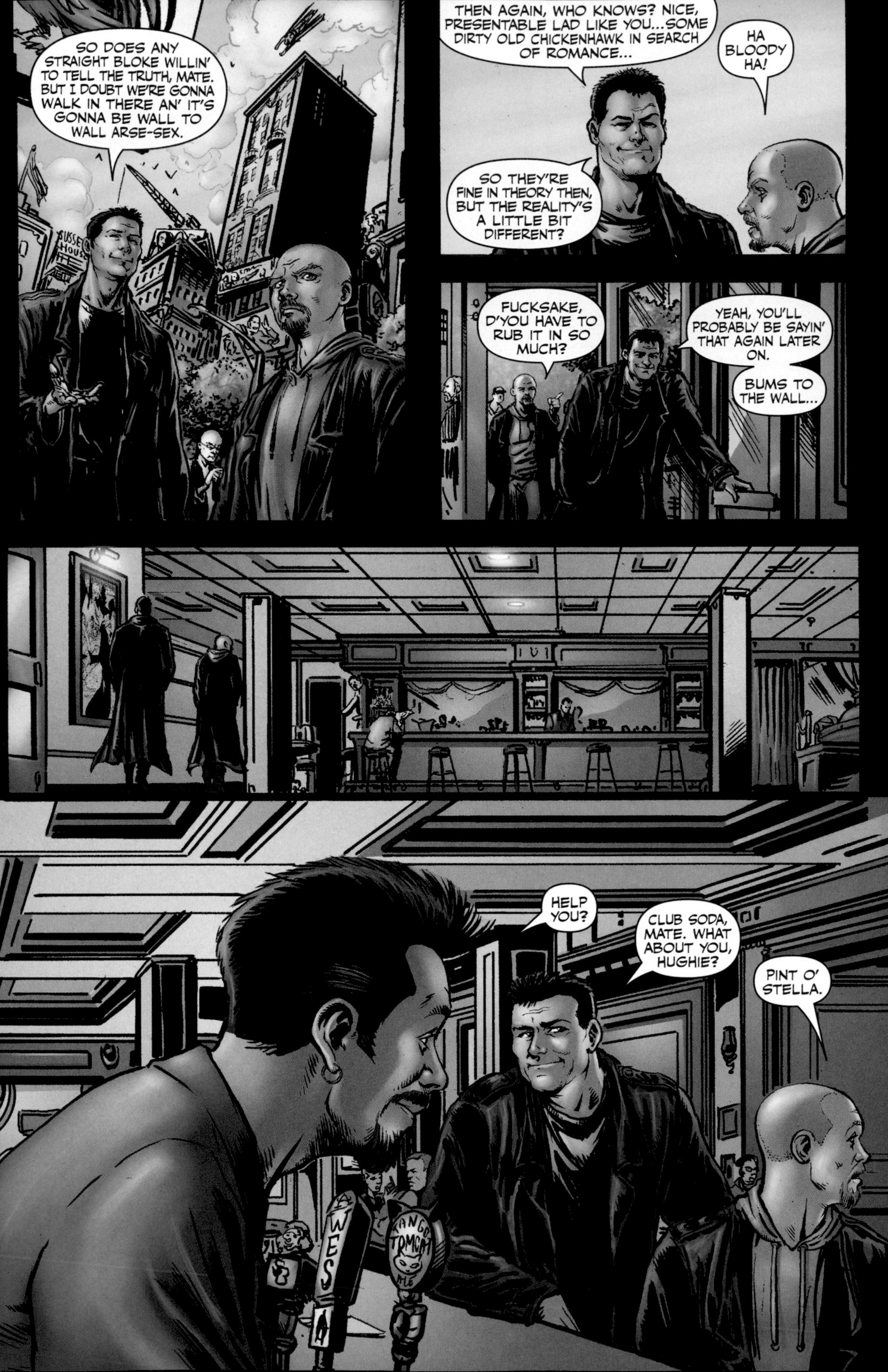
SO DOES ANY STRAIGHT BLOKE WILLIN' TO TELL THE TRUTH, MATE. BUT I DOUBT WE'RE GONNA WALK IN THERE AN' IT'S GONNA BE WALL TO WALL ARSE-SEX.
SO THEY'RE FINE IN THEORY THEN, BUT THE REALITY'S A LITTLE BIT DIFFERENT?
THEN AGAIN, WHO KNOWS? NICE, PRESENTABLE LAD LIKE YOU...SOME DIRTY OLD CHICKENHAWK IN SEARCH OF ROMANCE...
HA BLOODY HA!
FUCKSAKE, D'YOU HAVE TO RUB IT IN SO MUCH?
YEAH, YOU'LL PROBABLY BE SAYIN' THAT AGAIN LATER ON.
BUMS TO THE WALL...
HELP YOU?
CLUB SODA, MATE. WHAT ABOUT YOU, HUGHIE?
PINT O' STELLA.

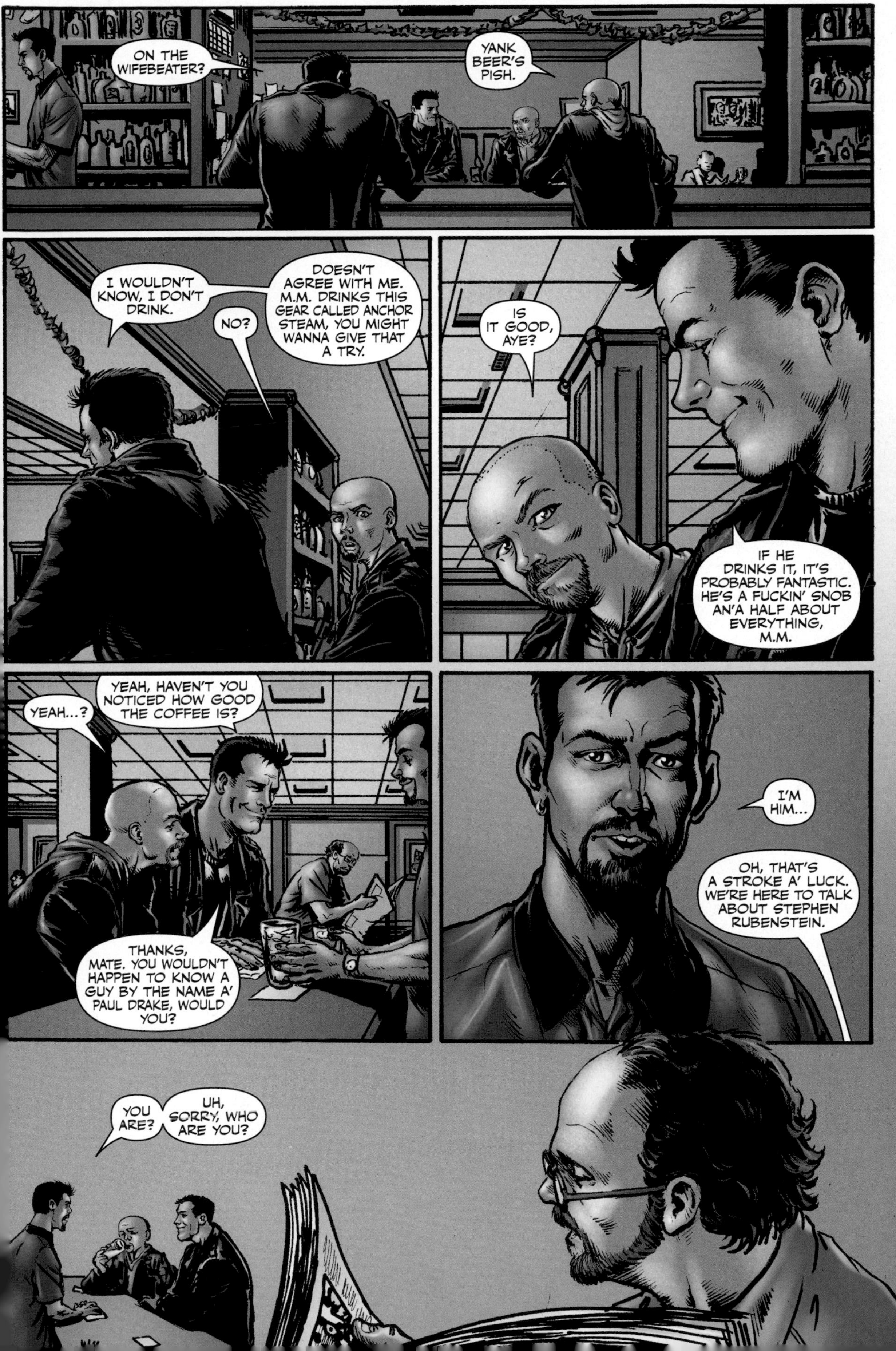
ON THE WIFEBEATER?
YANK BEER'S PISH.
I WOULDN'T KNOW, I DON'T DRINK.
NO?
DOESN'T AGREE WITH ME. M.M. DRINKS THIS GEAR CALLED ANCHOR STEAM, YOU MIGHT WANNA GIVE THAT A TRY.
IS IT GOOD, AYE?
IF HE DRINKS IT, IT'S PROBABLY FANTASTIC. HE'S A FUCKIN' SNOB AN'A HALF ABOUT EVERYTHING, M.M.
YEAH...?
YEAH, HAVEN'T YOU NOTICED HOW GOOD THE COFFEE IS?
THANKS, MATE. YOU WOULDN'T HAPPEN TO KNOW A GUY BY THE NAME A' PAUL DRAKE, WOULD YOU?
I'M HIM...
OH, THAT'S A STROKE A' LUCK. WE'RE HERE TO TALK ABOUT STEPHEN RUBENSTEIN.
YOU ARE?
UH, SORRY, WHO ARE YOU?

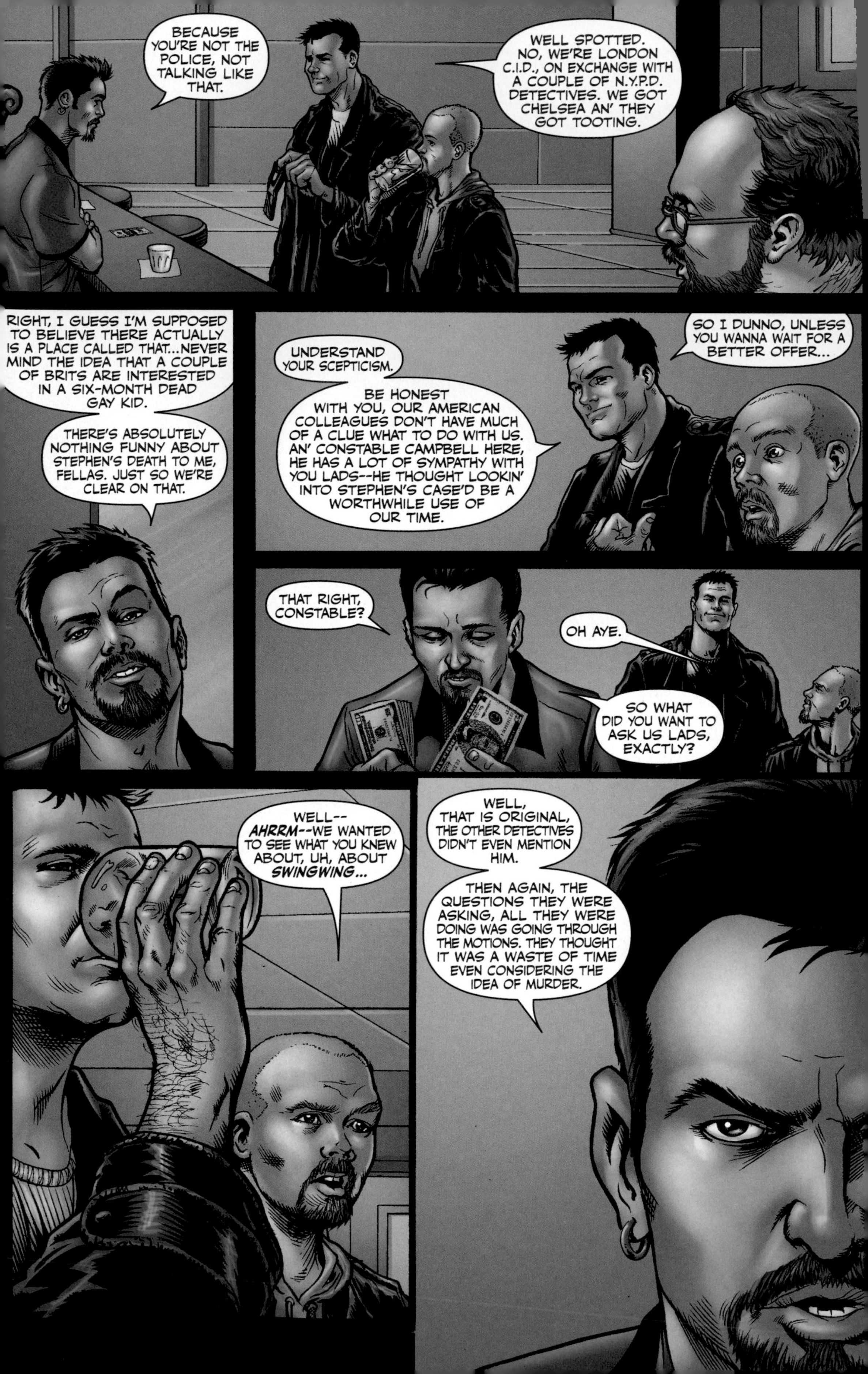
BECAUSE YOU'RE NOT THE POLICE, NOT TALKING LIKE THAT.
WELL SPOTTED. NO, WE'RE LONDON C.I.D., ON EXCHANGE WITH A COUPLE OF N.Y.P.D. DETECTIVES. WE GOT CHELSEA AN' THEY GOT TOOTING.
RIGHT, I GUESS I'M SUPPOSED TO BELIEVE THERE ACTUALLY IS A PLACE CALLED THAT...NEVER MIND THE IDEA THAT A COUPLE OF BRITS ARE INTERESTED IN A SIX-MONTH DEAD GAY KID.
THERE'S ABSOLUTELY NOTHING FUNNY ABOUT STEPHEN'S DEATH TO ME, FELLAS. JUST SO WE'RE CLEAR ON THAT.
UNDERSTAND YOUR SCEPTICISM.
BE HONEST WITH YOU, OUR AMERICAN COLLEAGUES DON'T HAVE MUCH OF A CLUE WHAT TO DO WITH US. AN' CONSTABLE CAMPBELL HERE, HE HAS A LOT OF SYMPATHY WITH YOU LADS--HE THOUGHT LOOKIN' INTO STEPHEN'S CASE'D BE A WORTHWHILE USE OF OUR TIME.
SO I DUNNO, UNLESS YOU WANNA WAIT FOR A BETTER OFFER...
THAT RIGHT, CONSTABLE?
OH AYE.
SO WHAT DID YOU WANT TO ASK US LADS, EXACTLY?
WELL-- *AHRRM*--WE WANTED TO SEE WHAT YOU KNEW ABOUT, UH, ABOUT *SWINGWING*...
WELL, THAT IS ORIGINAL, THE OTHER DETECTIVES DIDN'T EVEN MENTION HIM.
THEN AGAIN, THE QUESTIONS THEY WERE ASKING, ALL THEY WERE DOING WAS GOING THROUGH THE MOTIONS. THEY THOUGHT IT WAS A WASTE OF TIME EVEN CONSIDERING THE IDEA OF MURDER.

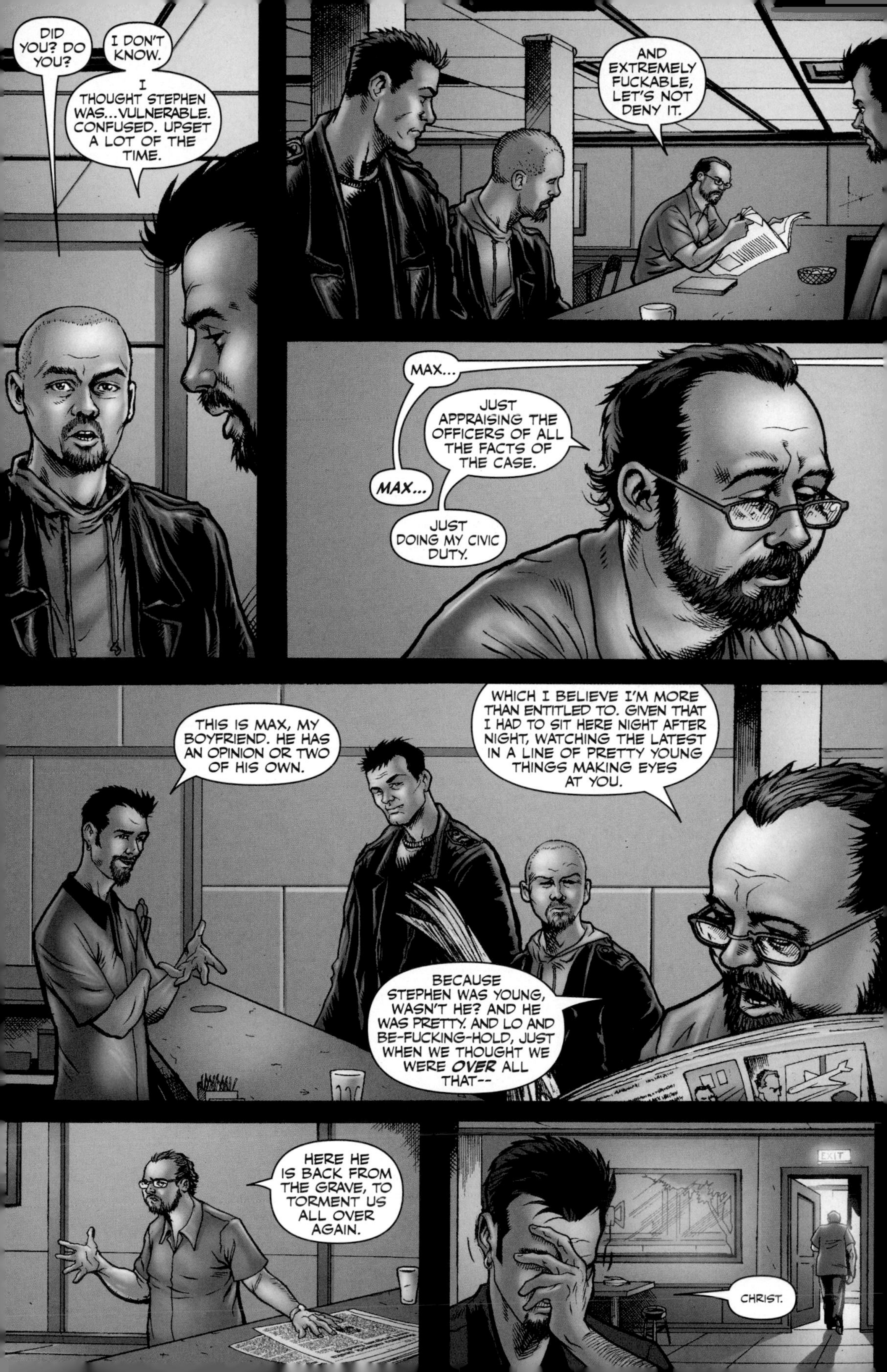

DID YOU? DO YOU?
I DON'T KNOW.
I THOUGHT STEPHEN WAS...VULNERABLE. CONFUSED. UPSET A LOT OF THE TIME.
AND EXTREMELY FUCKABLE, LET'S NOT DENY IT.
MAX...
JUST APPRAISING THE OFFICERS OF ALL THE FACTS OF THE CASE.
MAX...
JUST DOING MY CIVIC DUTY.
THIS IS MAX, MY BOYFRIEND. HE HAS AN OPINION OR TWO OF HIS OWN.
WHICH I BELIEVE I'M MORE THAN ENTITLED TO. GIVEN THAT I HAD TO SIT HERE NIGHT AFTER NIGHT, WATCHING THE LATEST IN A LINE OF PRETTY YOUNG THINGS MAKING EYES AT YOU.
BECAUSE STEPHEN WAS YOUNG, WASN'T HE? AND HE WAS PRETTY. AND LO AND BE-FUCKING-HOLD, JUST WHEN WE THOUGHT WE WERE OVER ALL THAT--
HERE HE IS BACK FROM THE GRAVE, TO TORMENT US ALL OVER AGAIN.
EXIT
CHRIST.

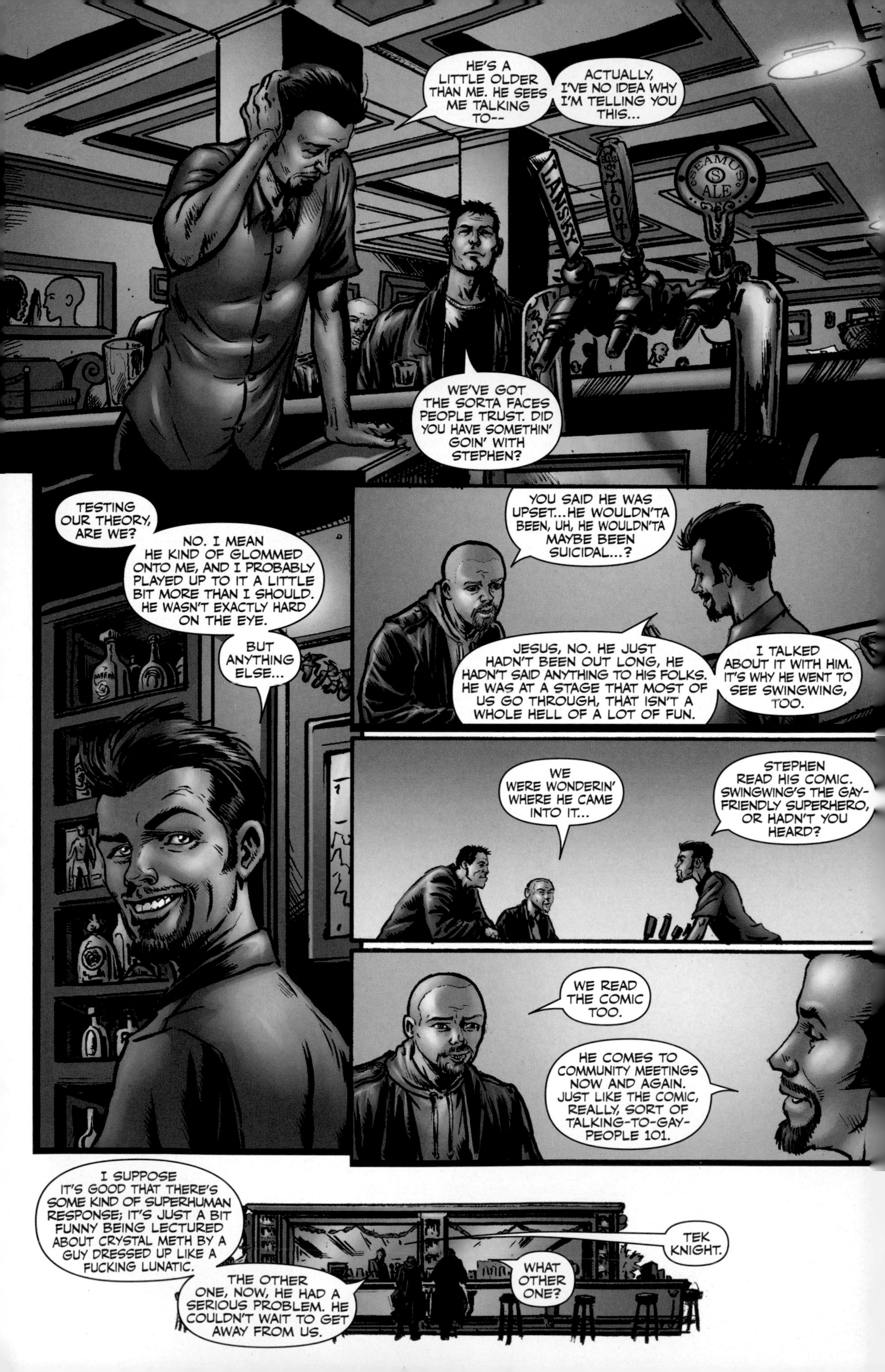
HE'S A LITTLE OLDER THAN ME. HE SEES ME TALKING TO--
ACTUALLY, I'VE NO IDEA WHY I'M TELLING YOU THIS...
LANSKY
STOUT
SEAMUS ALE
WE'VE GOT THE SORTA FACES PEOPLE TRUST. DID YOU HAVE SOMETHIN' GOIN' WITH STEPHEN?
TESTING OUR THEORY, ARE WE?
NO. I MEAN HE KIND OF GLOMMED ONTO ME, AND I PROBABLY PLAYED UP TO IT A LITTLE BIT MORE THAN I SHOULD. HE WASN'T EXACTLY HARD ON THE EYE.
BUT ANYTHING ELSE...
YOU SAID HE WAS UPSET...HE WOULDN'TA BEEN, UH, HE WOULDN'TA MAYBE BEEN SUICIDAL...?
JESUS, NO. HE JUST HADN'T BEEN OUT LONG, HE HADN'T SAID ANYTHING TO HIS FOLKS. HE WAS AT A STAGE THAT MOST OF US GO THROUGH, THAT ISN'T A WHOLE HELL OF A LOT OF FUN.
I TALKED ABOUT IT WITH HIM. IT'S WHY HE WENT TO SEE SWINGWING, TOO.
WE WERE WONDERIN' WHERE HE CAME INTO IT...
STEPHEN READ HIS COMIC. SWINGWING'S THE GAY-FRIENDLY SUPERHERO, OR HADN'T YOU HEARD?
WE READ THE COMIC TOO.
HE COMES TO COMMUNITY MEETINGS NOW AND AGAIN. JUST LIKE THE COMIC, REALLY, SORT OF TALKING-TO-GAY-PEOPLE 101.
I SUPPOSE IT'S GOOD THAT THERE'S SOME KIND OF SUPERHUMAN RESPONSE; IT'S JUST A BIT FUNNY BEING LECTURED ABOUT CRYSTAL METH BY A GUY DRESSED UP LIKE A FUCKING LUNATIC.
TEK KNIGHT.
THE OTHER ONE, NOW, HE HAD A SERIOUS PROBLEM. HE COULDN'T WAIT TO GET AWAY FROM US.
WHAT OTHER ONE?

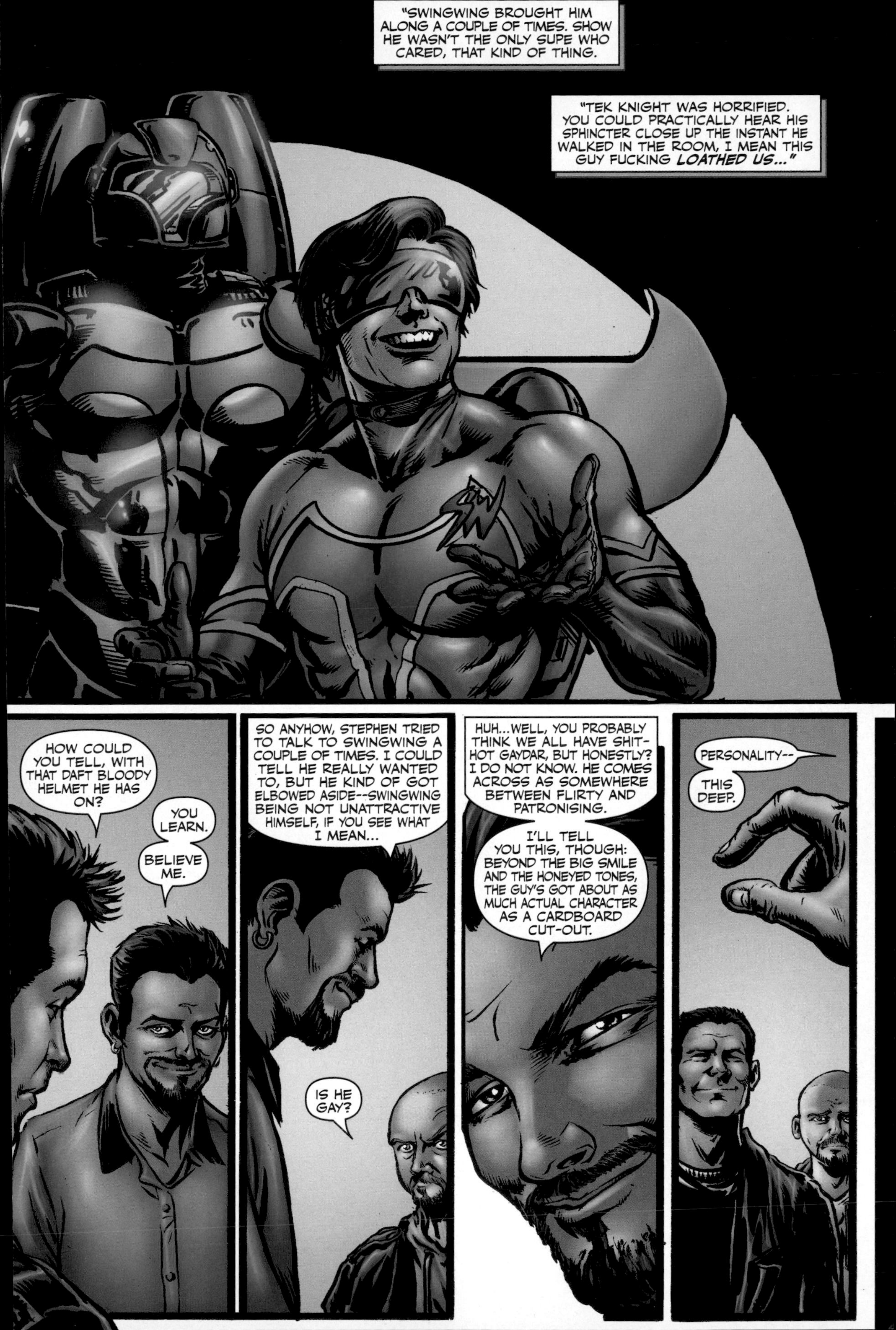
"SWINGWING BROUGHT HIM ALONG A COUPLE OF TIMES. SHOW HE WASN'T THE ONLY SUPE WHO CARED, THAT KIND OF THING.
"TEK KNIGHT WAS HORRIFIED. YOU COULD PRACTICALLY HEAR HIS SPHINCTER CLOSE UP THE INSTANT HE WALKED IN THE ROOM, I MEAN THIS GUY FUCKING *LOATHED US...*"
HOW COULD YOU TELL, WITH THAT DAFT BLOODY HELMET HE HAS ON?
YOU LEARN.
BELIEVE ME.
SO ANYHOW, STEPHEN TRIED TO TALK TO SWINGWING A COUPLE OF TIMES. I COULD TELL HE REALLY WANTED TO, BUT HE KIND OF GOT ELBOWED ASIDE--SWINGWING BEING NOT UNATTRACTIVE HIMSELF, IF YOU SEE WHAT I MEAN...
IS HE GAY?
HUH...WELL, YOU PROBABLY THINK WE ALL HAVE SHIT-HOT GAYDAR, BUT HONESTLY? I DO NOT KNOW. HE COMES ACROSS AS SOMEWHERE BETWEEN FLIRTY AND PATRONISING.
I'LL TELL YOU THIS, THOUGH: BEYOND THE BIG SMILE AND THE HONEYED TONES, THE GUY'S GOT ABOUT AS MUCH ACTUAL CHARACTER AS A CARDBOARD CUT-OUT.
PERSONALITY--
THIS DEEP.

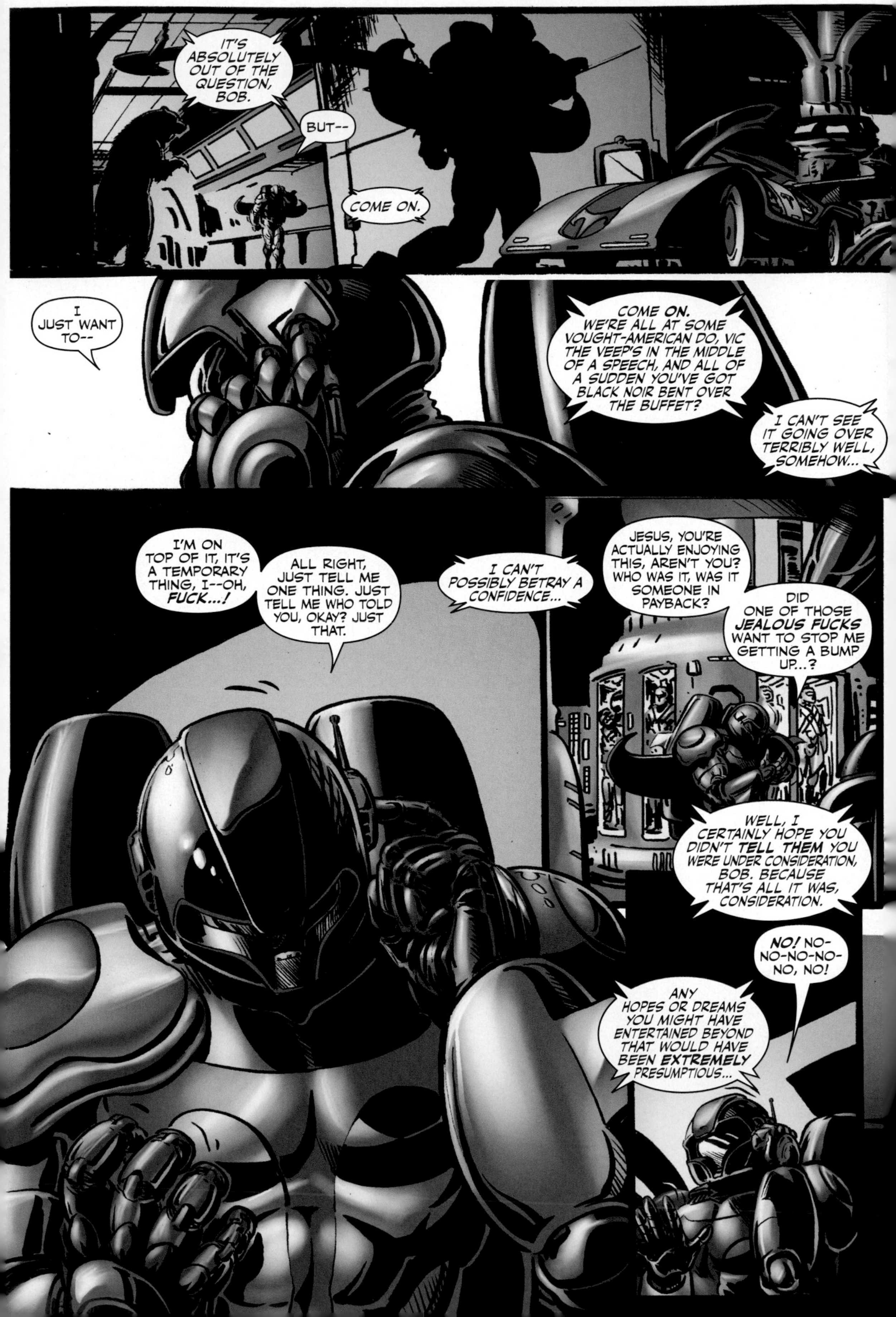
IT'S ABSOLUTELY OUT OF THE QUESTION, BOB.
BUT--
COME ON.
I JUST WANT TO--
COME ON. WE'RE ALL AT SOME VOUGHT-AMERICAN DO, VIC THE VEEP'S IN THE MIDDLE OF A SPEECH, AND ALL OF A SUDDEN YOU'VE GOT BLACK NOIR BENT OVER THE BUFFET?
I CAN'T SEE IT GOING OVER TERRIBLY WELL, SOMEHOW...
I'M ON TOP OF IT, IT'S A TEMPORARY THING, I--OH, FUCK...!
ALL RIGHT, JUST TELL ME ONE THING. JUST TELL ME WHO TOLD YOU, OKAY? JUST THAT.
I CAN'T POSSIBLY BETRAY A CONFIDENCE...
JESUS, YOU'RE ACTUALLY ENJOYING THIS, AREN'T YOU? WHO WAS IT, WAS IT SOMEONE IN PAYBACK?
DID ONE OF THOSE JEALOUS FUCKS WANT TO STOP ME GETTING A BUMP UP...?
WELL, I CERTAINLY HOPE YOU DIDN'T TELL THEM YOU WERE UNDER CONSIDERATION, BOB. BECAUSE THAT'S ALL IT WAS, CONSIDERATION.
ANY HOPES OR DREAMS YOU MIGHT HAVE ENTERTAINED BEYOND THAT WOULD HAVE BEEN EXTREMELY PRESUMPTIOUS...
NO! NO-NO-NO-NO-NO, NO!

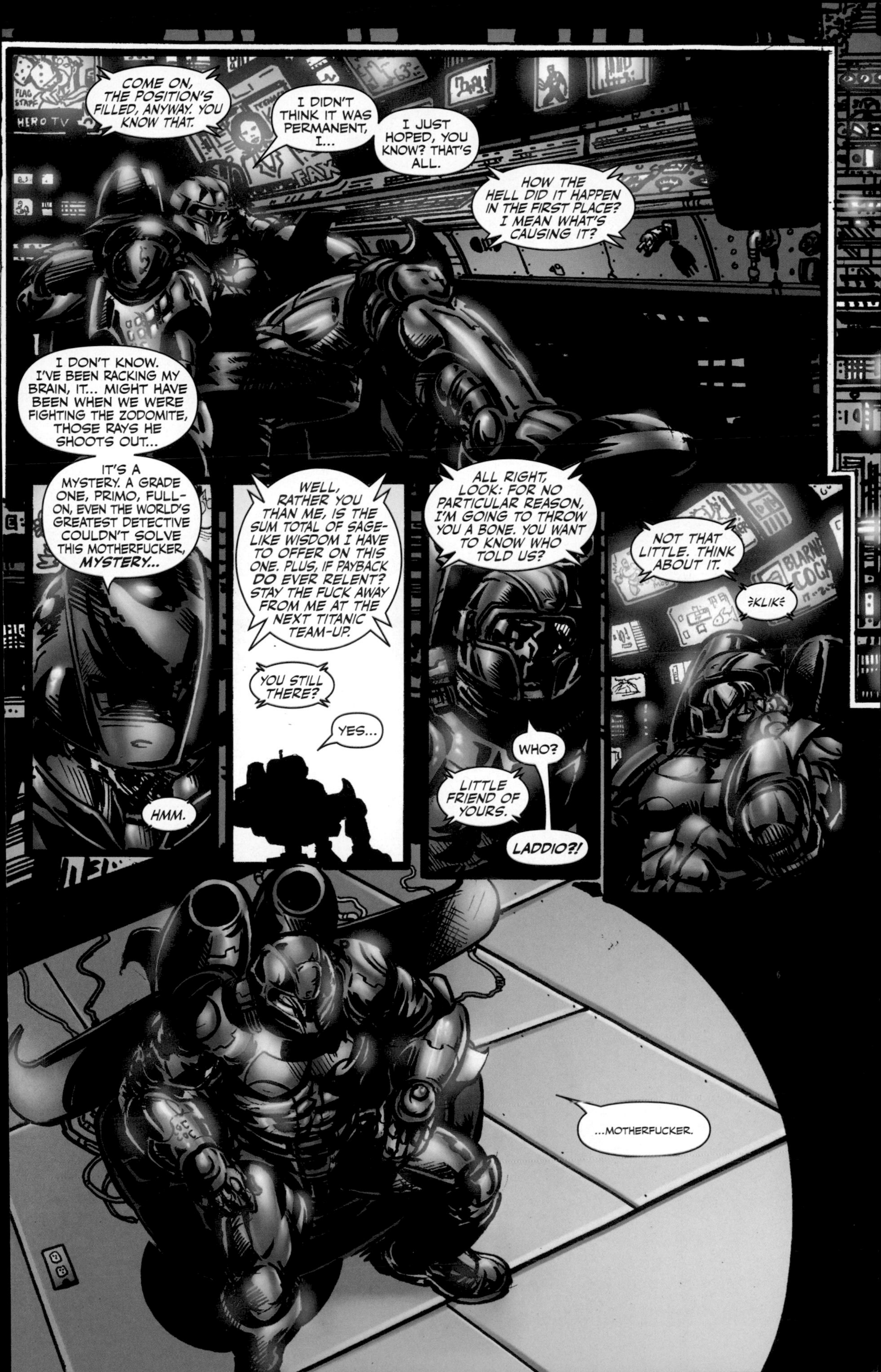

COME ON, THE POSITION'S FILLED, ANYWAY. YOU KNOW THAT.
I DIDN'T THINK IT WAS PERMANENT, I...
I JUST HOPED, YOU KNOW? THAT'S ALL.
HOW THE HELL DID IT HAPPEN IN THE FIRST PLACE? I MEAN WHAT'S CAUSING IT?
I DON'T KNOW. I'VE BEEN RACKING MY BRAIN, IT... MIGHT HAVE BEEN WHEN WE WERE FIGHTING THE ZODOMITE, THOSE RAYS HE SHOOTS OUT...
IT'S A MYSTERY. A GRADE ONE, PRIMO, FULL-ON, EVEN THE WORLD'S GREATEST DETECTIVE COULDN'T SOLVE THIS MOTHERFUCKER, MYSTERY...
HMM.
WELL, RATHER YOU THAN ME, IS THE SUM TOTAL OF SAGE-LIKE WISDOM I HAVE TO OFFER ON THIS ONE. PLUS, IF PAYBACK DO EVER RELENT? STAY THE FUCK AWAY FROM ME AT THE NEXT TITANIC TEAM-UP.
YOU STILL THERE?
YES...
ALL RIGHT, LOOK: FOR NO PARTICULAR REASON, I'M GOING TO THROW YOU A BONE. YOU WANT TO KNOW WHO TOLD US?
WHO?
LITTLE FRIEND OF YOURS.
LADDIO?!
NOT THAT LITTLE. THINK ABOUT IT.
KLIK
...MOTHERFUCKER.

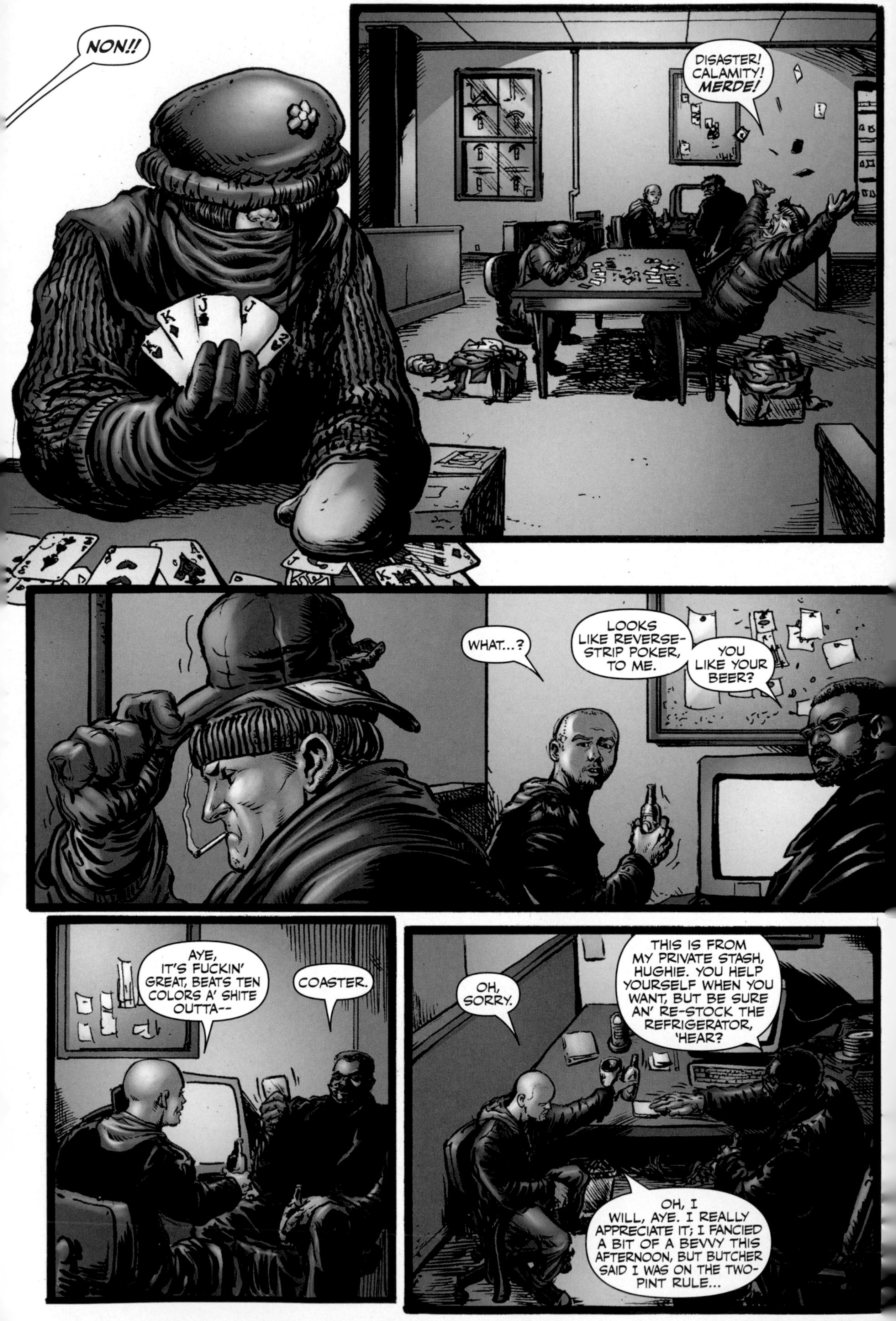
NON!!
DISASTER! CALAMITY! MERDE!
WHAT...?
LOOKS LIKE REVERSE-STRIP POKER, TO ME.
YOU LIKE YOUR BEER?
AYE, IT'S FUCKIN' GREAT, BEATS TEN COLORS A' SHITE OUTTA--
COASTER.
OH, SORRY.
THIS IS FROM MY PRIVATE STASH, HUGHIE. YOU HELP YOURSELF WHEN YOU WANT, BUT BE SURE AN' RE-STOCK THE REFRIGERATOR, 'HEAR?
OH, I WILL, AYE. I REALLY APPRECIATE IT; I FANCIED A BIT OF A BEVVY THIS AFTERNOON, BUT BUTCHER SAID I WAS ON THE TWO-PINT RULE...

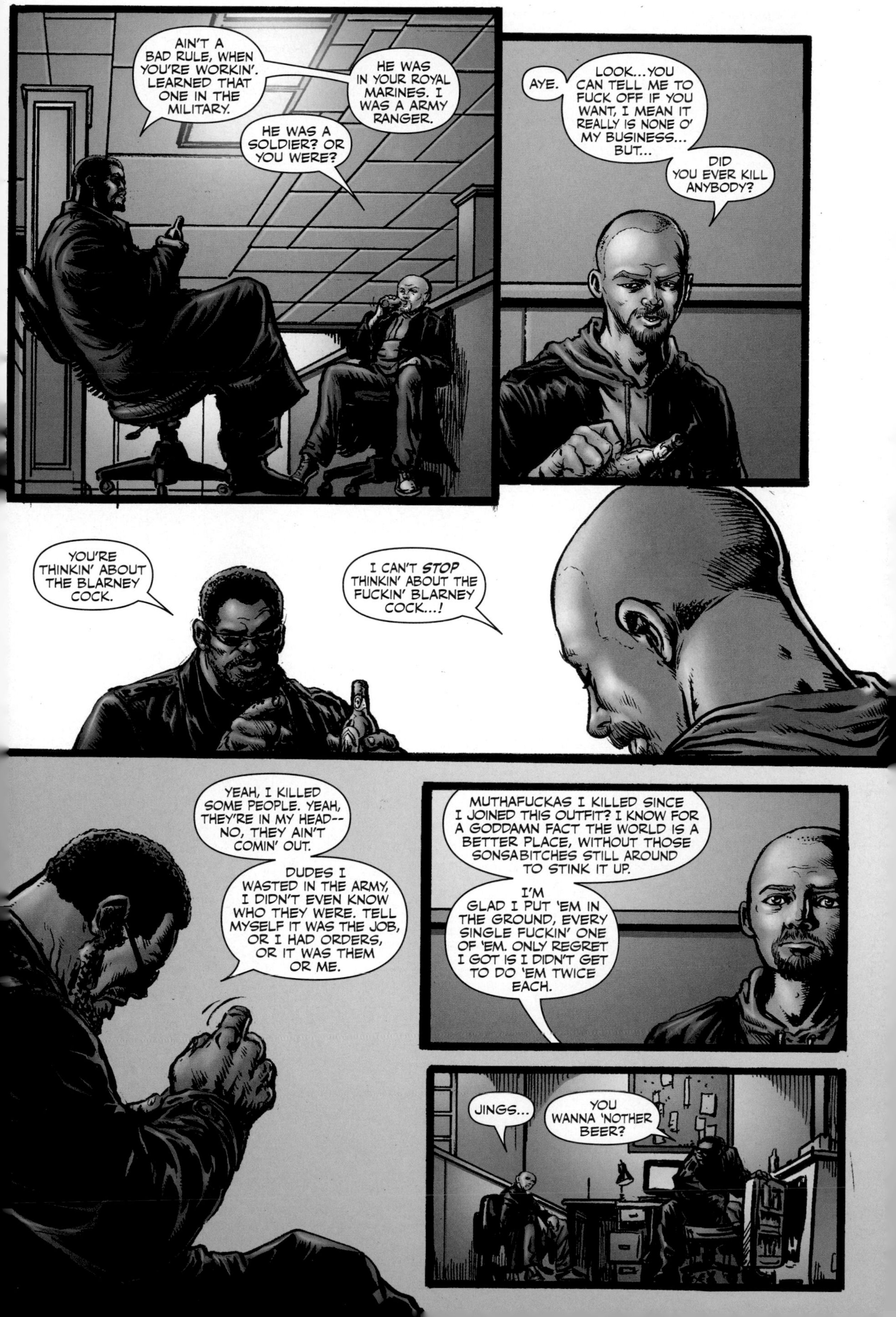
AIN'T A BAD RULE, WHEN YOU'RE WORKIN'. LEARNED THAT ONE IN THE MILITARY.
HE WAS A SOLDIER? OR YOU WERE?
HE WAS IN YOUR ROYAL MARINES. I WAS A ARMY RANGER.
AYE.
LOOK...YOU CAN TELL ME TO FUCK OFF IF YOU WANT, I MEAN IT REALLY IS NONE O' MY BUSINESS... BUT...
DID YOU EVER KILL ANYBODY?
YOU'RE THINKIN' ABOUT THE BLARNEY COCK.
I CAN'T *STOP* THINKIN' ABOUT THE FUCKIN' BLARNEY COCK...!
YEAH, I KILLED SOME PEOPLE. YEAH, THEY'RE IN MY HEAD-- NO, THEY AIN'T COMIN' OUT.
DUDES I WASTED IN THE ARMY, I DIDN'T EVEN KNOW WHO THEY WERE. TELL MYSELF IT WAS THE JOB, OR I HAD ORDERS, OR IT WAS THEM OR ME.
MUTHAFUCKAS I KILLED SINCE I JOINED THIS OUTFIT? I KNOW FOR A GODDAMN FACT THE WORLD IS A BETTER PLACE, WITHOUT THOSE SONSABITCHES STILL AROUND TO STINK IT UP.
I'M GLAD I PUT 'EM IN THE GROUND, EVERY SINGLE FUCKIN' ONE OF 'EM. ONLY REGRET I GOT IS I DIDN'T GET TO DO 'EM TWICE EACH.
JINGS...
YOU WANNA 'NOTHER BEER?

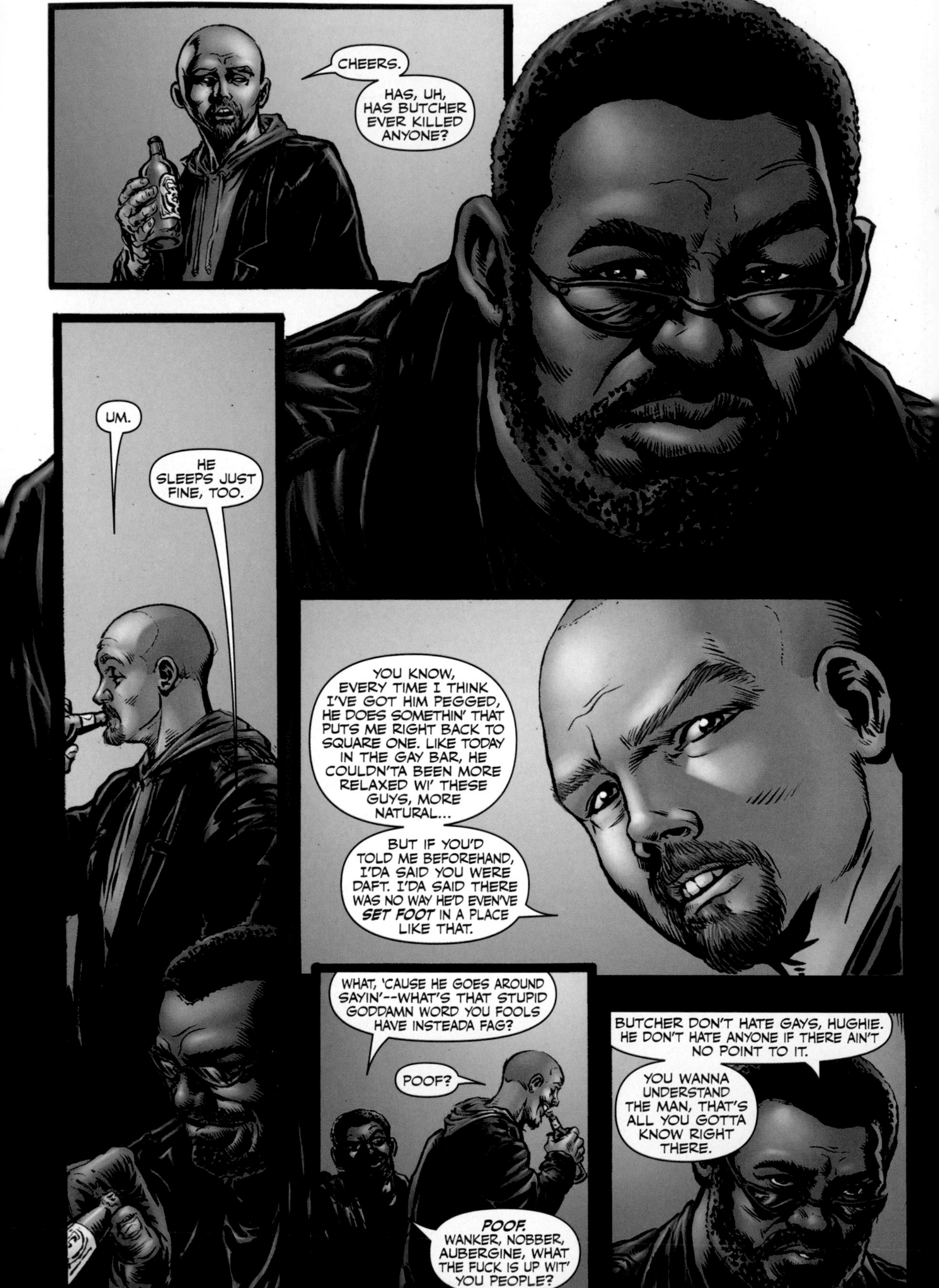
CHEERS.
HAS, UH, HAS BUTCHER EVER KILLED ANYONE?
UM.
HE SLEEPS JUST FINE, TOO.
YOU KNOW, EVERY TIME I THINK I'VE GOT HIM PEGGED, HE DOES SOMETHIN' THAT PUTS ME RIGHT BACK TO SQUARE ONE. LIKE TODAY IN THE GAY BAR, HE COULDN'TA BEEN MORE RELAXED WI' THESE GUYS, MORE NATURAL...
BUT IF YOU'D TOLD ME BEFOREHAND, I'DA SAID YOU WERE DAFT. I'DA SAID THERE WAS NO WAY HE'D EVEN'VE *SET FOOT* IN A PLACE LIKE THAT.
WHAT, 'CAUSE HE GOES AROUND SAYIN'--WHAT'S THAT STUPID GODDAMN WORD YOU FOOLS HAVE INSTEADA FAG?
POOF?
POOF. WANKER, NOBBER, AUBERGINE, WHAT THE FUCK IS UP WIT' YOU PEOPLE?
BUTCHER DON'T HATE GAYS, HUGHIE. HE DON'T HATE ANYONE IF THERE AIN'T NO POINT TO IT.
YOU WANNA UNDERSTAND THE MAN, THAT'S ALL YOU GOTTA KNOW RIGHT THERE.

UH...

CHECK IT OUT: YOU'RE EITHER A PROBLEM, OR YOU CAN HELP HIM, OR HE DON'T CARE. THERE AIN'T NO *SENSE* GETTING' PISSED AT SOMEONE 'CAUSE OF WHO THEY FUCKIN', THAT'S HOW HE SEES IT.

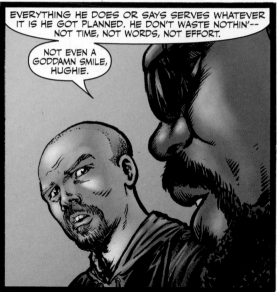

EVERYTHING HE DOES OR SAYS SERVES WHATEVER IT IS HE GOT PLANNED. HE DON'T WASTE NOTHIN'-- NOT TIME, NOT WORDS, NOT EFFORT.

NOT EVEN A GODDAMN SMILE, HUGHIE.

ME, NOW, I USEDTA HAVE A SERIOUS PROBLEM WIT' FAGS...

WHY?

PLACE I GREW UP, THAT WAS JUST HOW IT WAS.

THEY WERE WEAK. THEY WERE DISGUSTIN'. YOU HATED THE MUTHAFUCKAS, OR THERE MIGHTA BEEN SOMETHIN' WRONG WIT' YOU, TOO.

AN' THEN, ONE DAY?

I FOUND OUT WHAT HATE TRULY IS.

AN' IT AIN'T A BUNCHA LAZY-ASS FUCKIN' BULLSHIT.

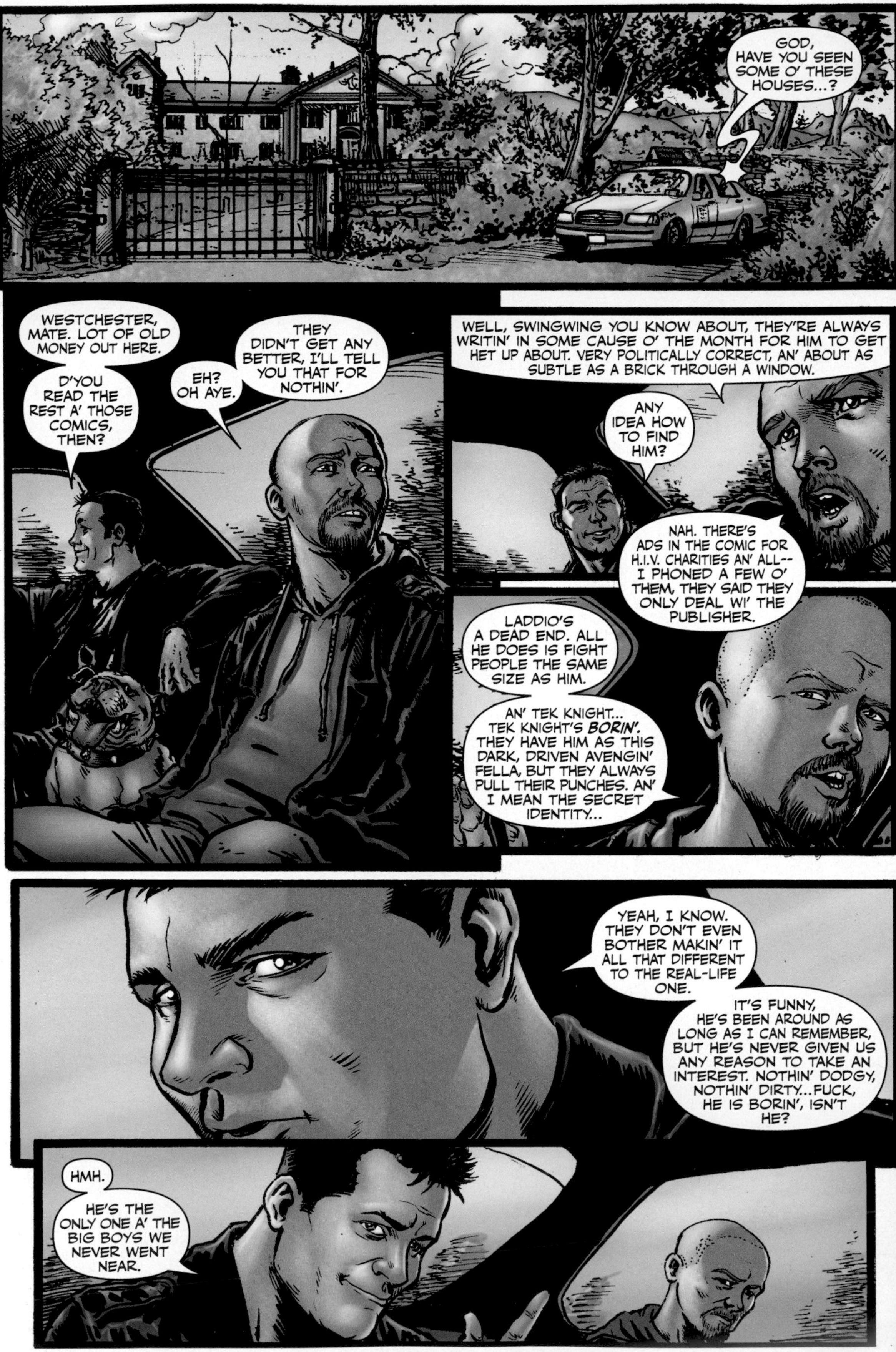
GOD, HAVE YOU SEEN SOME O' THESE HOUSES...?
WESTCHESTER, MATE. LOT OF OLD MONEY OUT HERE.
D'YOU READ THE REST A' THOSE COMICS, THEN?
EH? OH AYE.
THEY DIDN'T GET ANY BETTER, I'LL TELL YOU THAT FOR NOTHIN'.
WELL, SWINGWING YOU KNOW ABOUT, THEY'RE ALWAYS WRITIN' IN SOME CAUSE O' THE MONTH FOR HIM TO GET HET UP ABOUT. VERY POLITICALLY CORRECT, AN' ABOUT AS SUBTLE AS A BRICK THROUGH A WINDOW.
ANY IDEA HOW TO FIND HIM?
NAH. THERE'S ADS IN THE COMIC FOR H.I.V. CHARITIES AN' ALL-- I PHONED A FEW O' THEM, THEY SAID THEY ONLY DEAL WI' THE PUBLISHER.
LADDIO'S A DEAD END. ALL HE DOES IS FIGHT PEOPLE THE SAME SIZE AS HIM.
AN' TEK KNIGHT... TEK KNIGHT'S *BORIN'*. THEY HAVE HIM AS THIS DARK, DRIVEN AVENGIN' FELLA, BUT THEY ALWAYS PULL THEIR PUNCHES. AN' I MEAN THE SECRET IDENTITY...
YEAH, I KNOW. THEY DON'T EVEN BOTHER MAKIN' IT ALL THAT DIFFERENT TO THE REAL-LIFE ONE.
IT'S FUNNY, HE'S BEEN AROUND AS LONG AS I CAN REMEMBER, BUT HE'S NEVER GIVEN US ANY REASON TO TAKE AN INTEREST. NOTHIN' DODGY, NOTHIN' DIRTY...FUCK, HE IS BORIN', ISN'T HE?
HMH.
HE'S THE ONLY ONE A' THE BIG BOYS WE NEVER WENT NEAR.

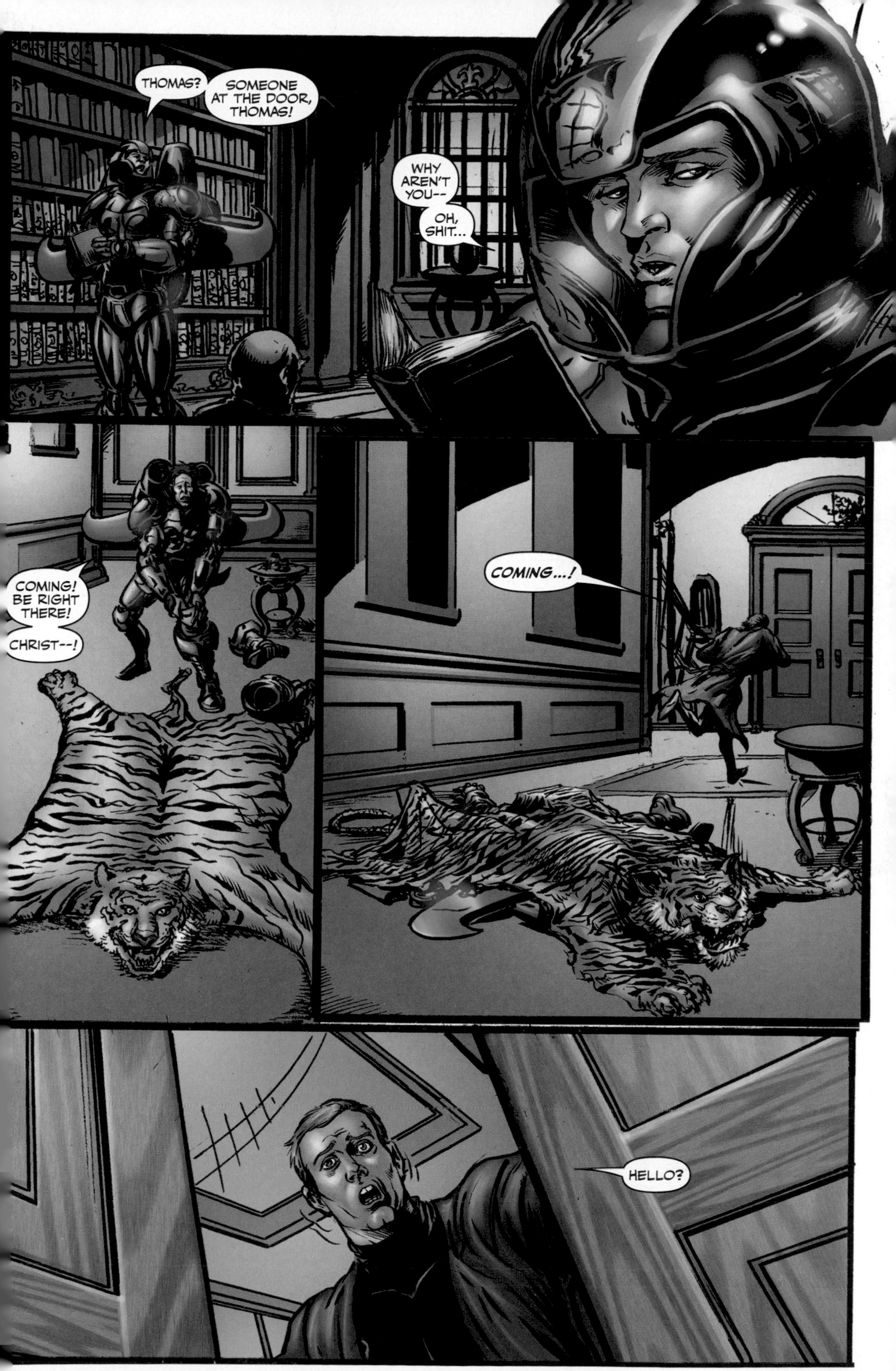
THOMAS?
SOMEONE AT THE DOOR, THOMAS!
WHY AREN'T YOU--
OH, SHIT...
COMING! BE RIGHT THERE!
CHRIST--!
COMING...!
HELLO?

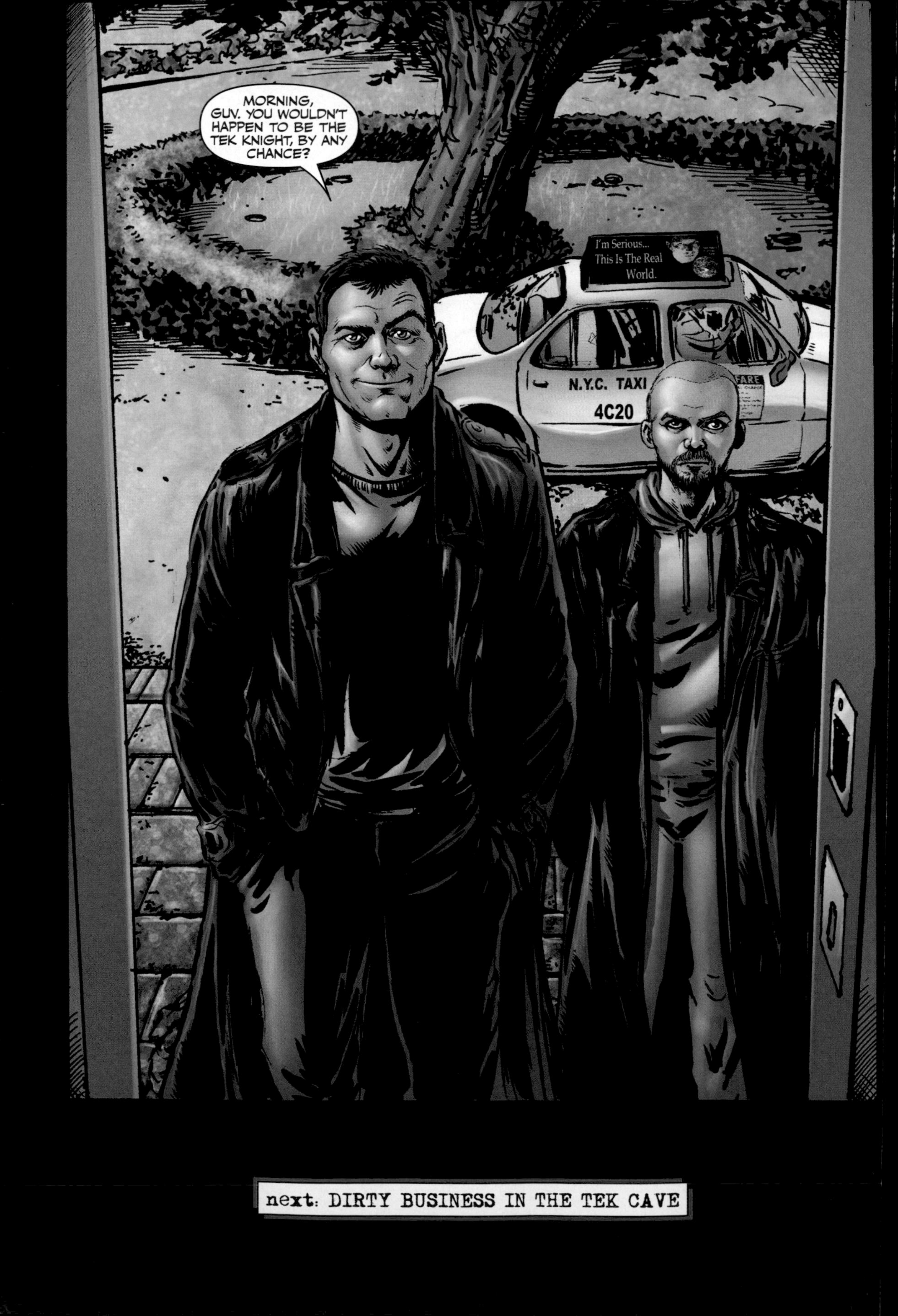
MORNING, GUV. YOU WOULDN'T HAPPEN TO BE THE TEK KNIGHT, BY ANY CHANCE?
I'm Serious... This Is The Real World.
N.Y.C. TAXI
4C20
FARE

next: DIRTY BUSINESS IN THE TEK CAVE

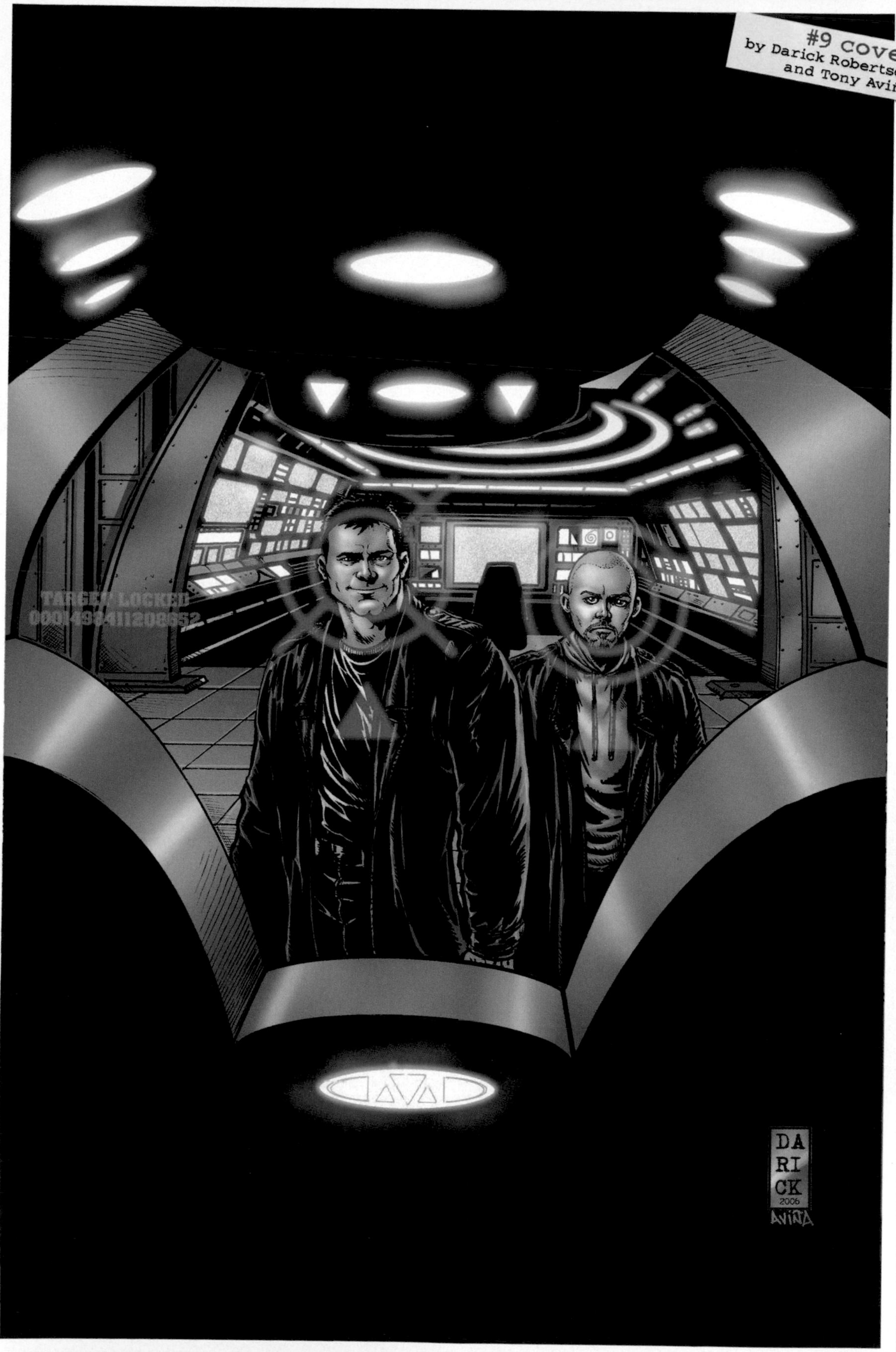
TARGET LOCKED
DARICK 2006
AVIÑA

#9 cover
by Darick Robertson
and Tony Aviña

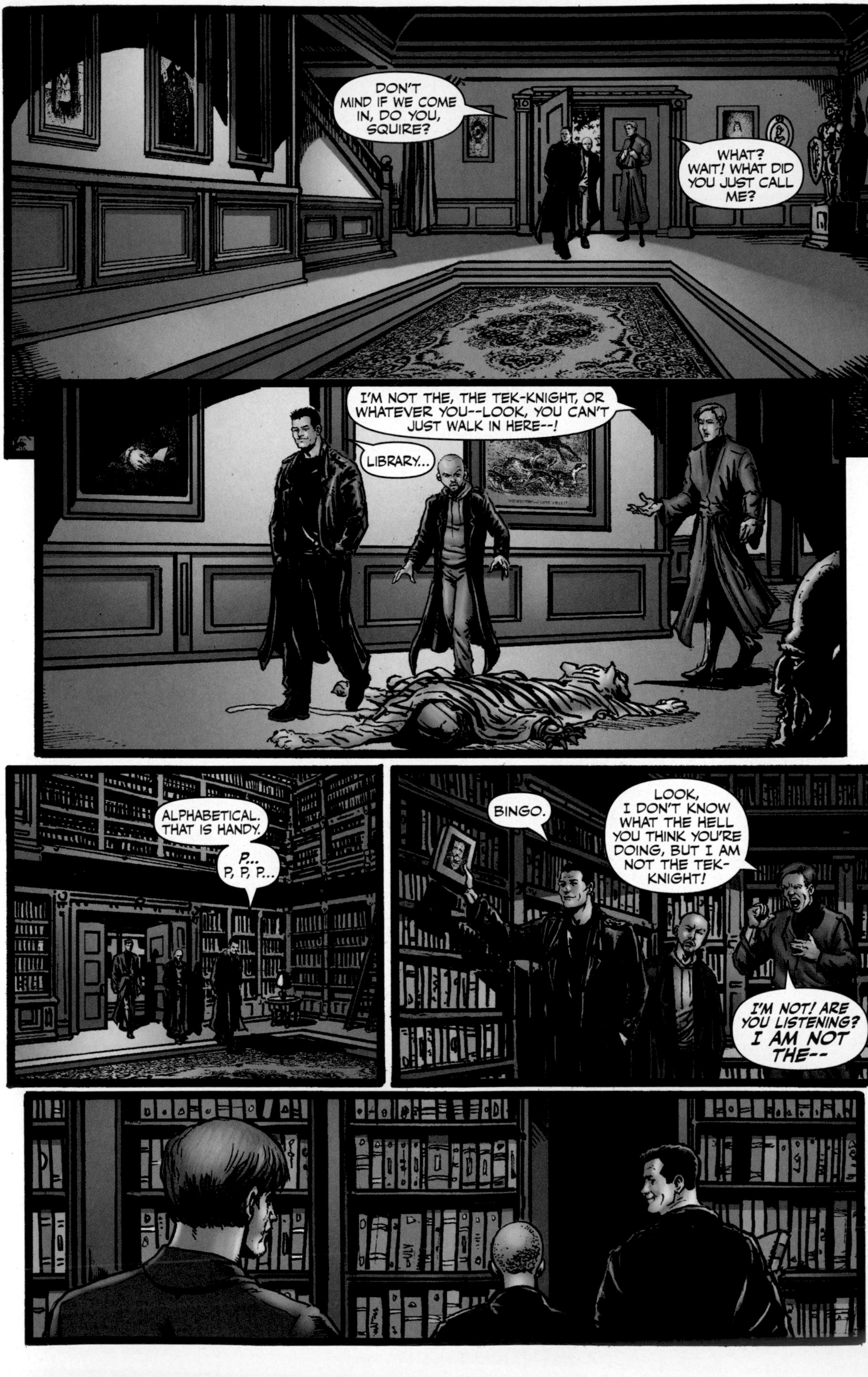
DON'T MIND IF WE COME IN, DO YOU, SQUIRE?
WHAT? WAIT! WHAT DID YOU JUST CALL ME?
I'M NOT THE, THE TEK-KNIGHT, OR WHATEVER YOU--LOOK, YOU CAN'T JUST WALK IN HERE--!
LIBRARY...
ALPHABETICAL. THAT IS HANDY.
P... P, P, P...
BINGO.
LOOK, I DON'T KNOW WHAT THE HELL YOU THINK YOU'RE DOING, BUT I AM NOT THE TEK-KNIGHT!
I'M NOT! ARE YOU LISTENING? I AM NOT THE--

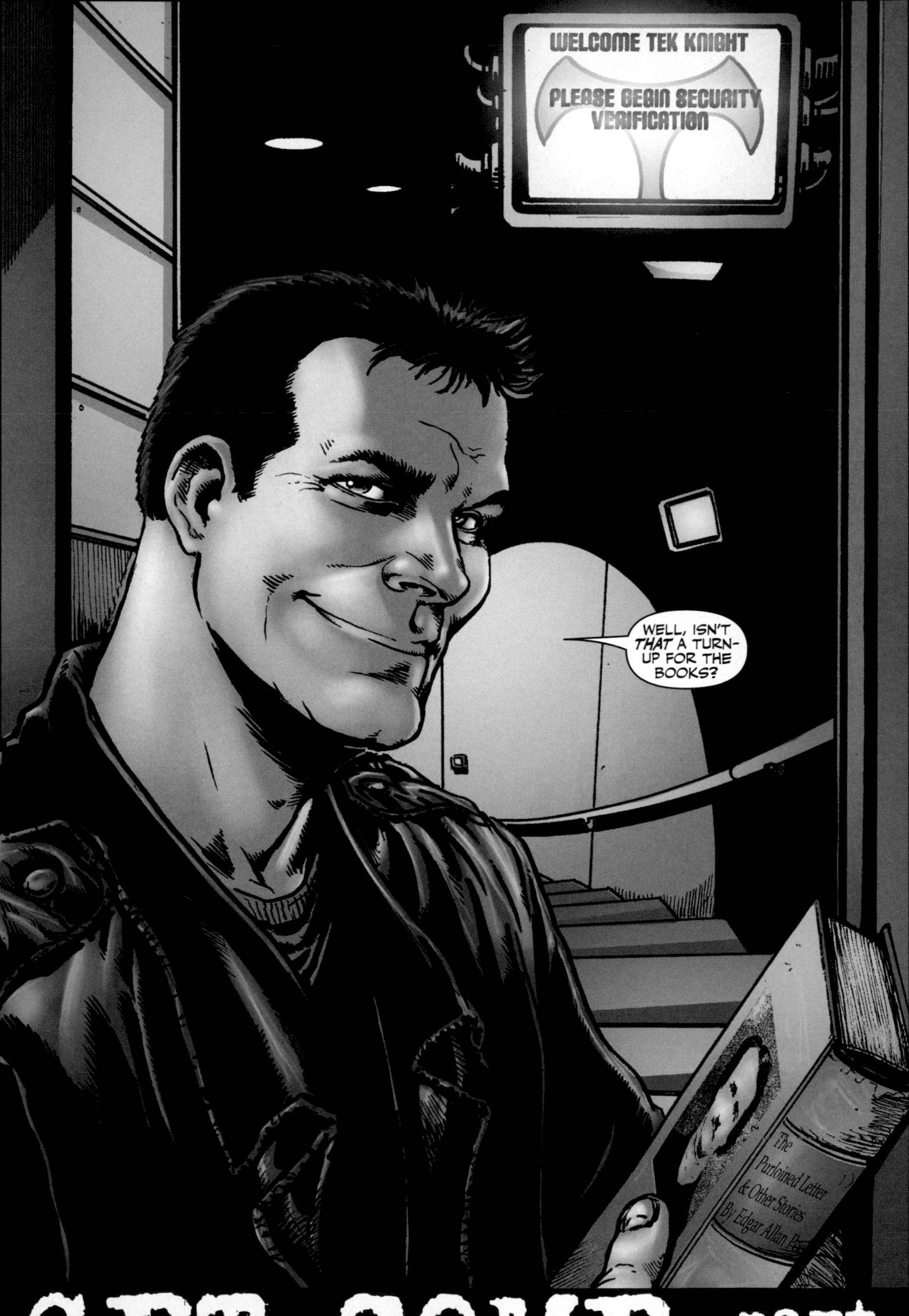
WELCOME TEK KNIGHT
PLEASE BEGIN SECURITY VERIFICATION
WELL, ISN'T *THAT* A TURN-UP FOR THE BOOKS?
The Purloined Letter & Other Stories By Edgar Allan

GET SOME part three

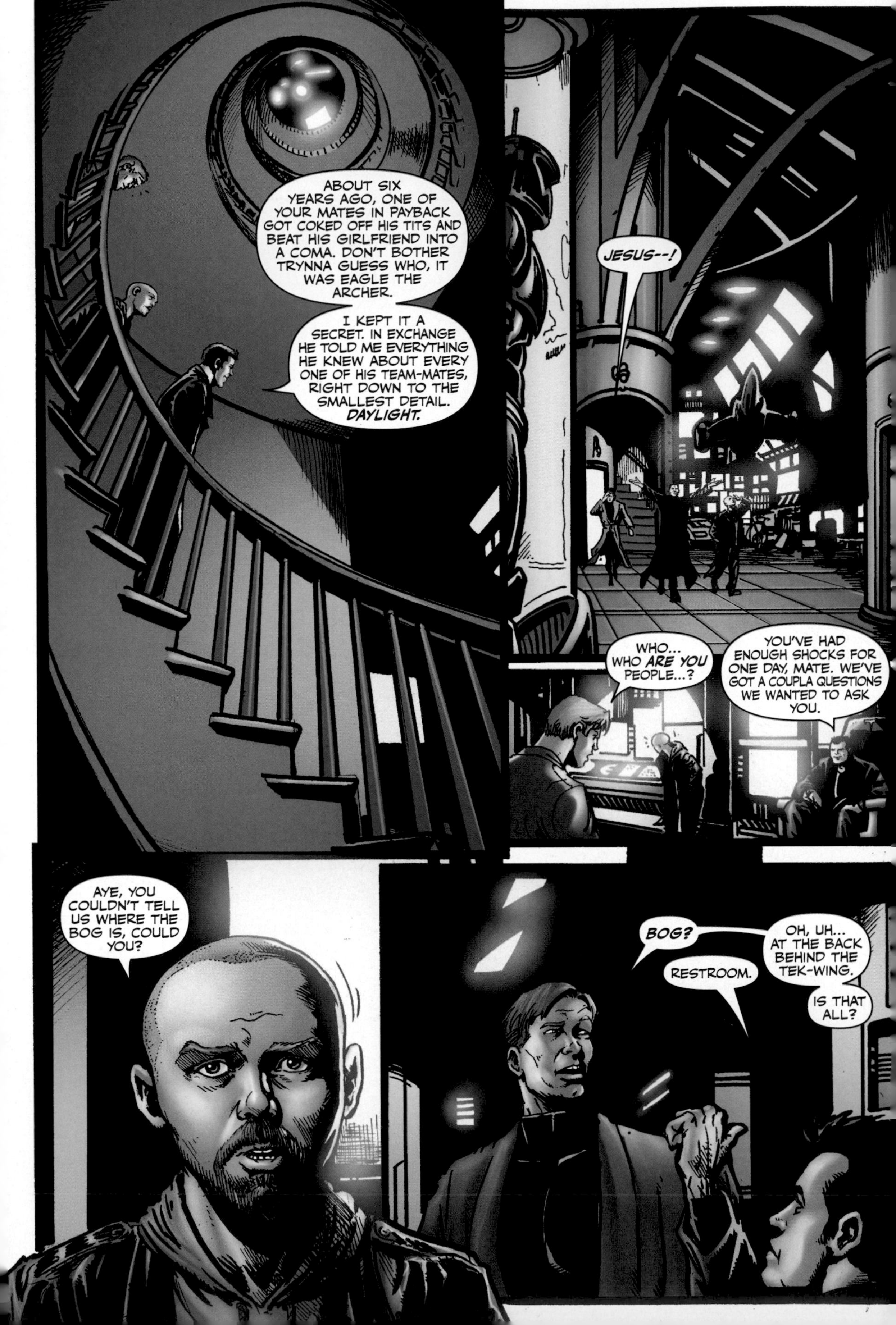

ABOUT SIX YEARS AGO, ONE OF YOUR MATES IN PAYBACK GOT COKED OFF HIS TITS AND BEAT HIS GIRLFRIEND INTO A COMA. DON'T BOTHER TRYNNA GUESS WHO, IT WAS EAGLE THE ARCHER.
I KEPT IT A SECRET. IN EXCHANGE HE TOLD ME EVERYTHING HE KNEW ABOUT EVERY ONE OF HIS TEAM-MATES, RIGHT DOWN TO THE SMALLEST DETAIL. DAYLIGHT.
JESUS--!
WHO... WHO ARE YOU PEOPLE...?
YOU'VE HAD ENOUGH SHOCKS FOR ONE DAY, MATE. WE'VE GOT A COUPLA QUESTIONS WE WANTED TO ASK YOU.
AYE, YOU COULDN'T TELL US WHERE THE BOG IS, COULD YOU?
BOG?
RESTROOM.
OH, UH... AT THE BACK BEHIND THE TEK-WING.
IS THAT ALL?

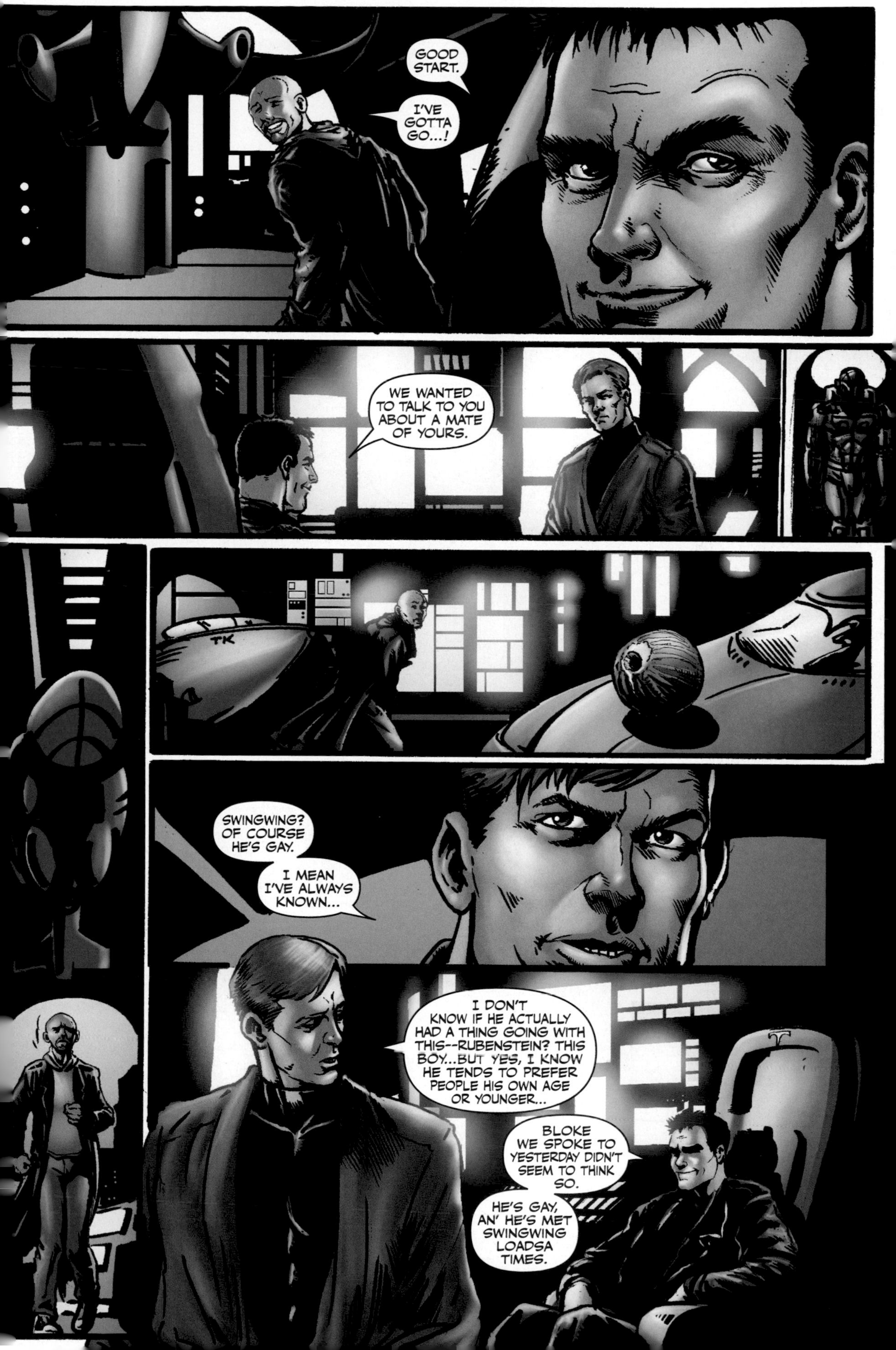
GOOD START.
I'VE GOTTA GO...!
WE WANTED TO TALK TO YOU ABOUT A MATE OF YOURS.
SWINGWING? OF COURSE HE'S GAY.
I MEAN I'VE ALWAYS KNOWN...
I DON'T KNOW IF HE ACTUALLY HAD A THING GOING WITH THIS--RUBENSTEIN? THIS BOY...BUT YES, I KNOW HE TENDS TO PREFER PEOPLE HIS OWN AGE OR YOUNGER...
BLOKE WE SPOKE TO YESTERDAY DIDN'T SEEM TO THINK SO.
HE'S GAY, AN' HE'S MET SWINGWING LOADSA TIMES.

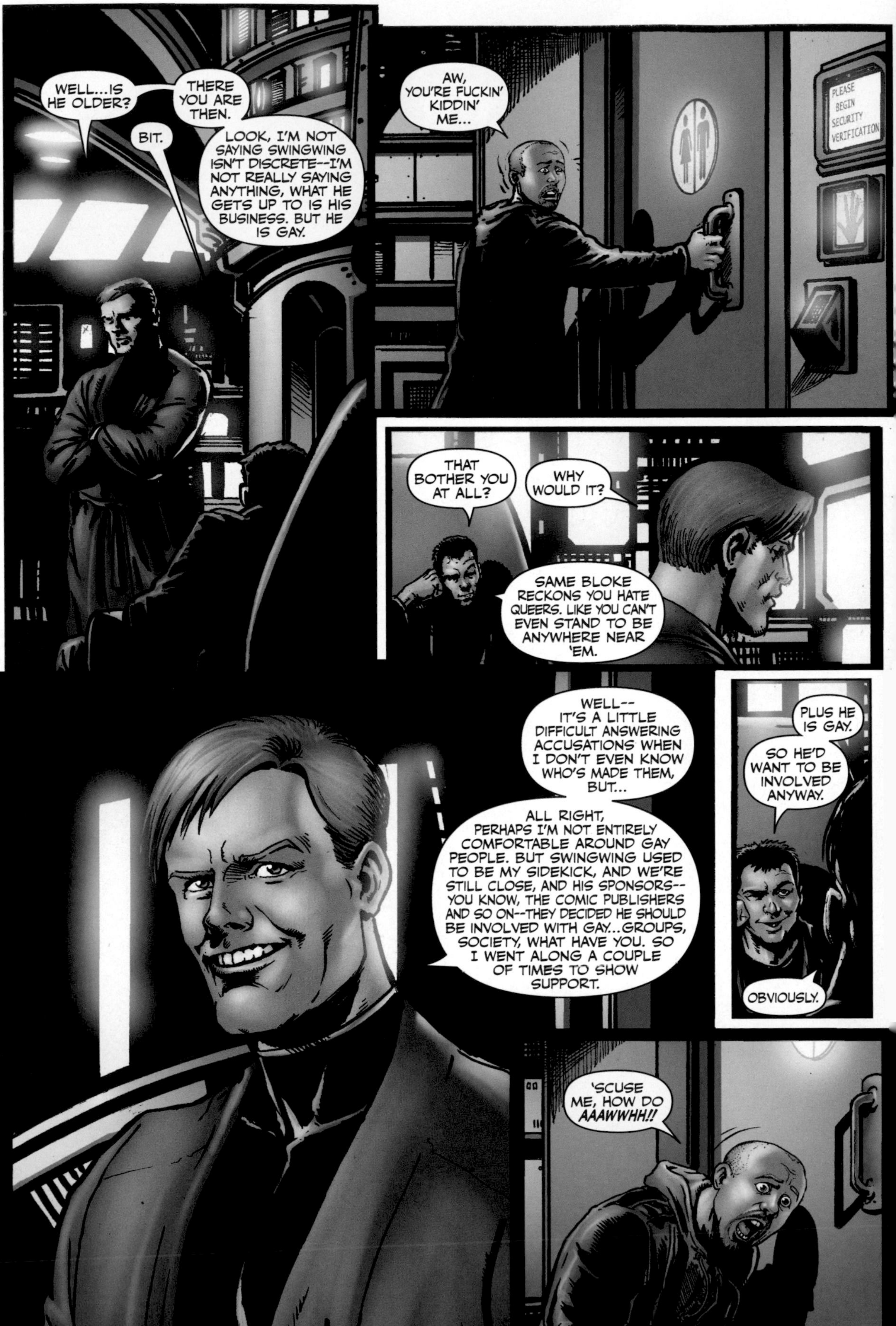
WELL...IS HE OLDER?
THERE YOU ARE THEN.
BIT.
LOOK, I'M NOT SAYING SWINGWING ISN'T DISCRETE--I'M NOT REALLY SAYING ANYTHING, WHAT HE GETS UP TO IS HIS BUSINESS. BUT HE IS GAY.
AW, YOU'RE FUCKIN' KIDDIN' ME...
PLEASE BEGIN SECURITY VERIFICATION
THAT BOTHER YOU AT ALL?
WHY WOULD IT?
SAME BLOKE RECKONS YOU HATE QUEERS. LIKE YOU CAN'T EVEN STAND TO BE ANYWHERE NEAR 'EM.
WELL-- IT'S A LITTLE DIFFICULT ANSWERING ACCUSATIONS WHEN I DON'T EVEN KNOW WHO'S MADE THEM, BUT...
ALL RIGHT, PERHAPS I'M NOT ENTIRELY COMFORTABLE AROUND GAY PEOPLE. BUT SWINGWING USED TO BE MY SIDEKICK, AND WE'RE STILL CLOSE, AND HIS SPONSORS-- YOU KNOW, THE COMIC PUBLISHERS AND SO ON--THEY DECIDED HE SHOULD BE INVOLVED WITH GAY...GROUPS, SOCIETY, WHAT HAVE YOU. SO I WENT ALONG A COUPLE OF TIMES TO SHOW SUPPORT.
PLUS HE IS GAY.
SO HE'D WANT TO BE INVOLVED ANYWAY.
OBVIOUSLY.
'SCUSE ME, HOW DO *AAAWWHH!!*

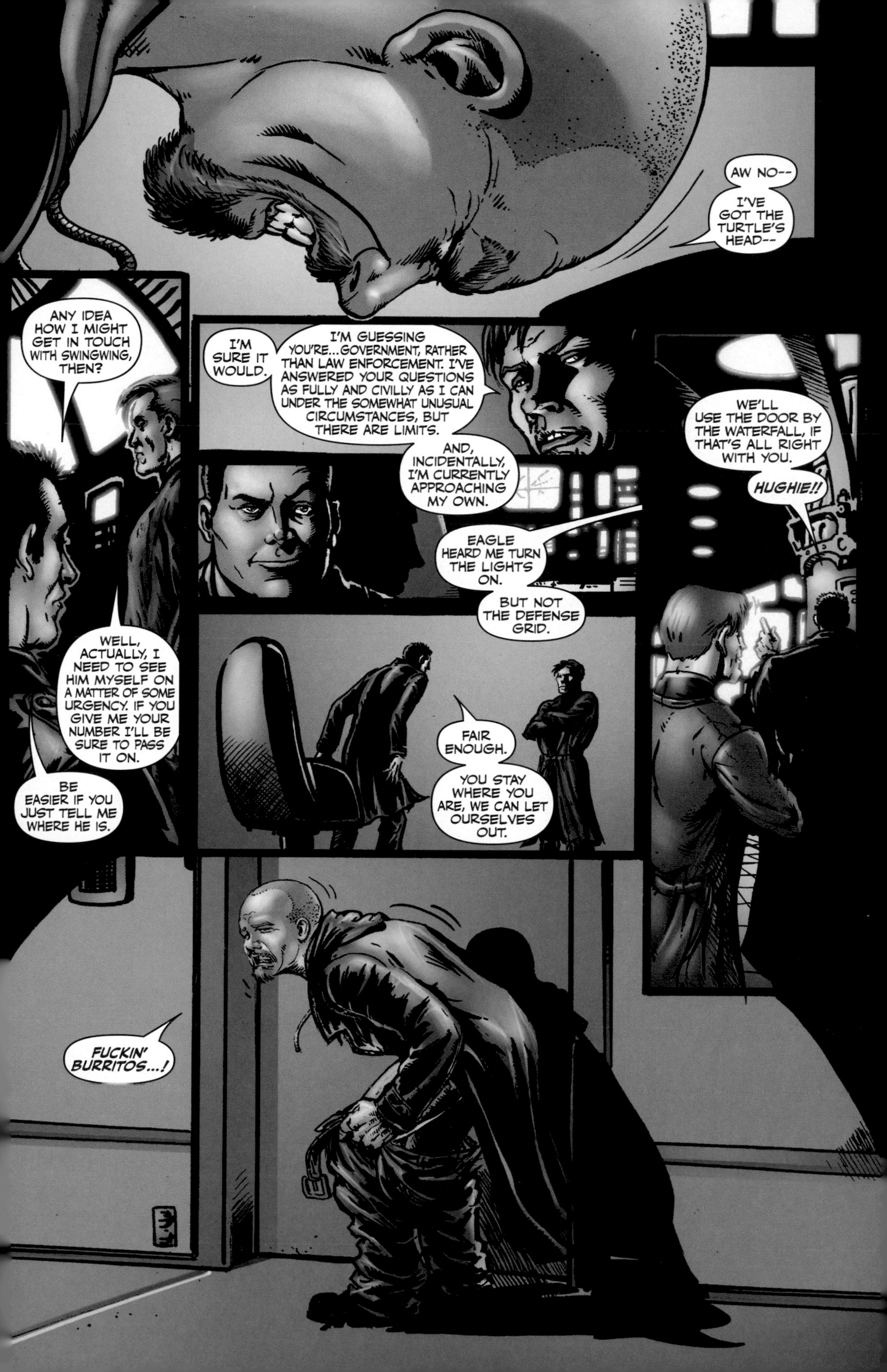
AW NO--
I'VE GOT THE TURTLE'S HEAD--
ANY IDEA HOW I MIGHT GET IN TOUCH WITH SWINGWING, THEN?
I'M SURE IT WOULD.
I'M GUESSING YOU'RE...GOVERNMENT, RATHER THAN LAW ENFORCEMENT. I'VE ANSWERED YOUR QUESTIONS AS FULLY AND CIVILLY AS I CAN UNDER THE SOMEWHAT UNUSUAL CIRCUMSTANCES, BUT THERE ARE LIMITS.
AND, INCIDENTALLY, I'M CURRENTLY APPROACHING MY OWN.
WELL, ACTUALLY, I NEED TO SEE HIM MYSELF ON A MATTER OF SOME URGENCY. IF YOU GIVE ME YOUR NUMBER I'LL BE SURE TO PASS IT ON.
BE EASIER IF YOU JUST TELL ME WHERE HE IS.
EAGLE HEARD ME TURN THE LIGHTS ON.
BUT NOT THE DEFENSE GRID.
FAIR ENOUGH.
YOU STAY WHERE YOU ARE, WE CAN LET OURSELVES OUT.
WE'LL USE THE DOOR BY THE WATERFALL, IF THAT'S ALL RIGHT WITH YOU.
HUGHIE!!
FUCKIN' BURRITOS...!

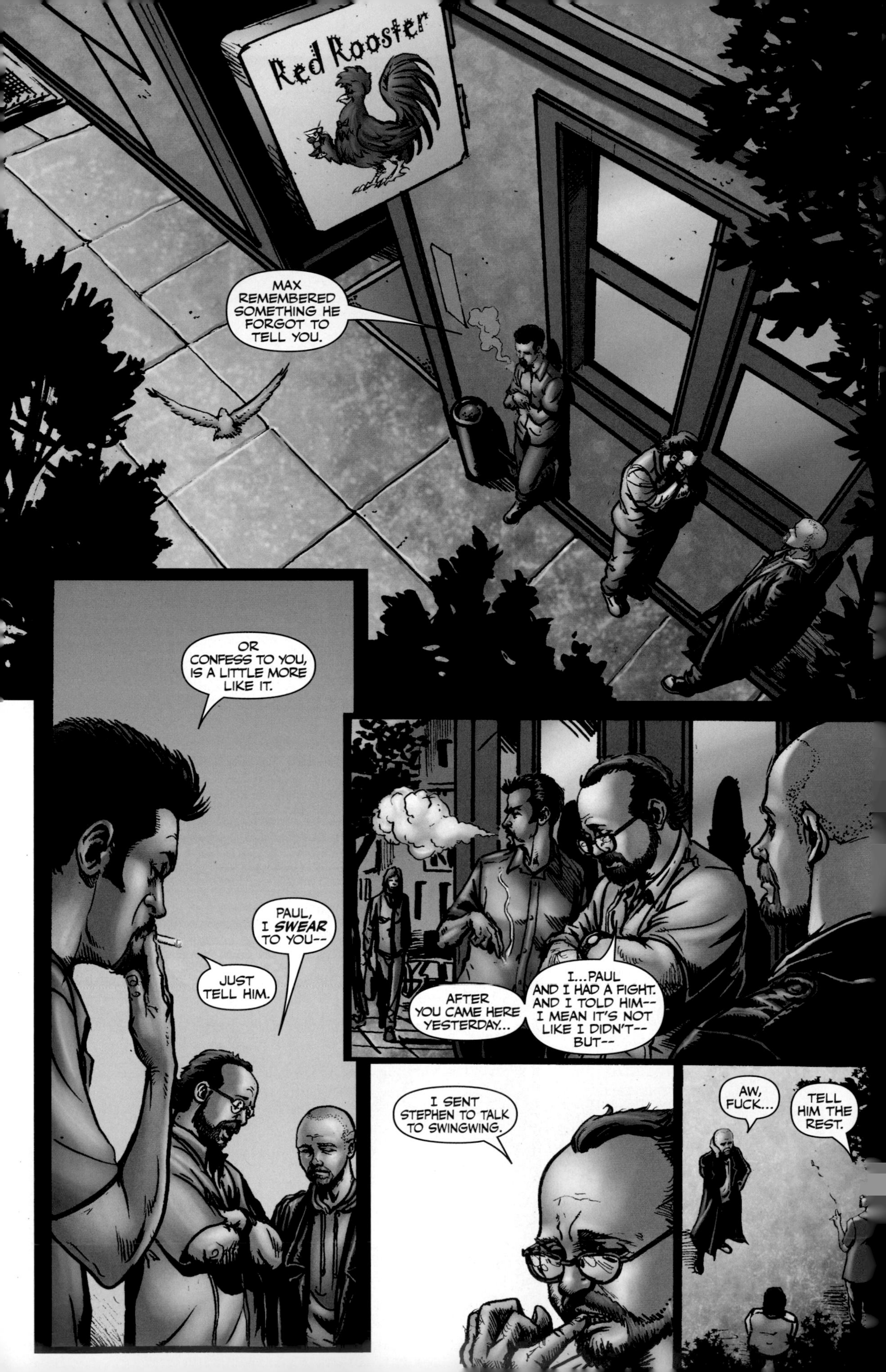
Red Rooster
MAX REMEMBERED SOMETHING HE FORGOT TO TELL YOU.
OR CONFESS TO YOU, IS A LITTLE MORE LIKE IT.
PAUL, I *SWEAR* TO YOU--
JUST TELL HIM.
AFTER YOU CAME HERE YESTERDAY...
I...PAUL AND I HAD A FIGHT. AND I TOLD HIM-- I MEAN IT'S NOT LIKE I DIDN'T-- BUT--
I SENT STEPHEN TO TALK TO SWINGWING.
AW, FUCK...
TELL HIM THE REST.

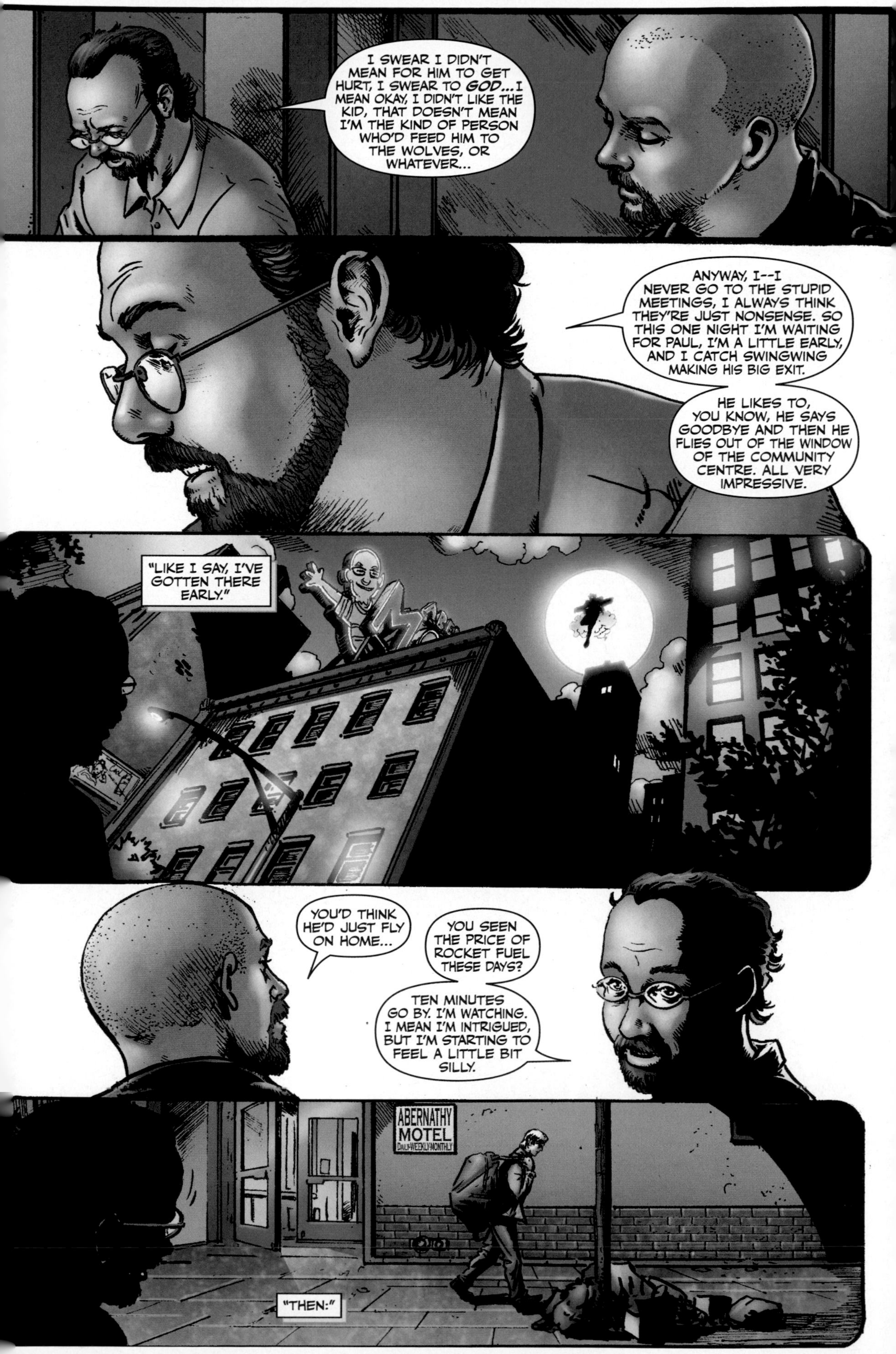
I SWEAR I DIDN'T MEAN FOR HIM TO GET HURT, I SWEAR TO GOD...I MEAN OKAY, I DIDN'T LIKE THE KID, THAT DOESN'T MEAN I'M THE KIND OF PERSON WHO'D FEED HIM TO THE WOLVES, OR WHATEVER...
ANYWAY, I--I NEVER GO TO THE STUPID MEETINGS, I ALWAYS THINK THEY'RE JUST NONSENSE. SO THIS ONE NIGHT I'M WAITING FOR PAUL, I'M A LITTLE EARLY, AND I CATCH SWINGWING MAKING HIS BIG EXIT.
HE LIKES TO, YOU KNOW, HE SAYS GOODBYE AND THEN HE FLIES OUT OF THE WINDOW OF THE COMMUNITY CENTRE. ALL VERY IMPRESSIVE.
"LIKE I SAY, I'VE GOTTEN THERE EARLY."
YOU'D THINK HE'D JUST FLY ON HOME...
YOU SEEN THE PRICE OF ROCKET FUEL THESE DAYS?
TEN MINUTES GO BY. I'M WATCHING. I MEAN I'M INTRIGUED, BUT I'M STARTING TO FEEL A LITTLE BIT SILLY.
ABERNATHY MOTEL
DAILY-WEEKLY-MONTHLY
"THEN:"

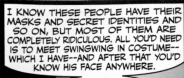

I KNOW THESE PEOPLE HAVE THEIR MASKS AND SECRET IDENTITIES AND SO ON, BUT MOST OF THEM ARE COMPLETELY RIDICULOUS. ALL YOU'D NEED IS TO MEET SWINGWING IN COSTUME-- WHICH I HAVE--AND AFTER THAT YOU'D KNOW HIS FACE ANYWHERE.

SO, A COUPLE OF NIGHTS AFTER THAT I'M HAVING A DRINK IN THE ROOSTER, AND PAUL'S BEHIND THE BAR, AND STEPHEN *WILL NOT* LEAVE HIM ALONE AND I AM *UTTERLY* SICK OF IT--

SO I TAKE HIM ASIDE AND TELL HIM WHERE HE CAN FIND SWINGWING.

I KNOW HE LIKES HIM, HE NEVER SHUTS UP ABOUT THE GUY. THE WAY I SEE IT, IF I CAN BRING HIM AND HIS IDOL TOGETHER, MAYBE HE'LL LEAVE MY MAN ALONE FOR A CHANGE.

UH-HUH.

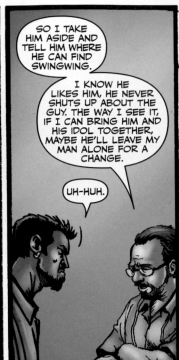

AND IF SWINGWING TURNS OUT TO BE A LITTLE OVER-PROTECTIVE OF HIS SECRET IDENTITY, WELL, I GUESS THAT'S JUST TOUGH SHIT FOR STEPHEN.

PAUL, I DIDN'T--

FUCK OFF.

I WOULDN'T HAVE WANTED THE BOY TO GET HURT, NOT IN A MILLION YEARS...I DIDN'T EVEN THINK ABOUT SWINGWING UNTIL YOU MENTIONED HIM YESTERDAY...

AYE, LOOK, I'M SORRY, PAL: BUT I HAVE GOT TO GO.

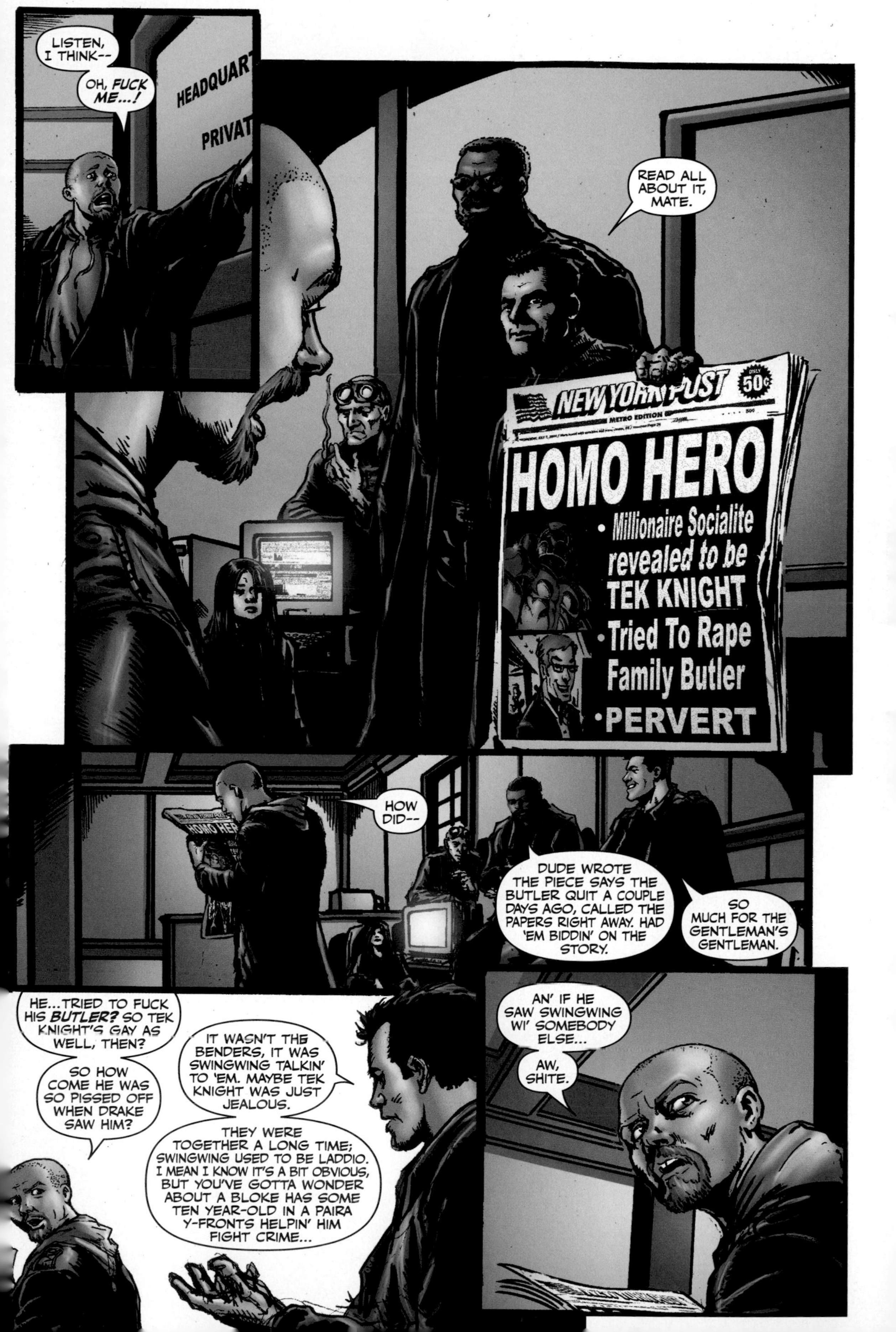
LISTEN, I THINK--
OH, FUCK ME...!
HEADQUART
PRIVAT
READ ALL ABOUT IT, MATE.
NEW YORK POST
ONLY 50¢
METRO EDITION
HOMO HERO
• Millionaire Socialite revealed to be TEK KNIGHT
• Tried To Rape Family Butler
• PERVERT
HOW DID--
DUDE WROTE THE PIECE SAYS THE BUTLER QUIT A COUPLE DAYS AGO, CALLED THE PAPERS RIGHT AWAY. HAD 'EM BIDDIN' ON THE STORY.
SO MUCH FOR THE GENTLEMAN'S GENTLEMAN.
HE...TRIED TO FUCK HIS BUTLER? SO TEK KNIGHT'S GAY AS WELL, THEN?
SO HOW COME HE WAS SO PISSED OFF WHEN DRAKE SAW HIM?
IT WASN'T THE BENDERS, IT WAS SWINGWING TALKIN' TO 'EM. MAYBE TEK KNIGHT WAS JUST JEALOUS.
THEY WERE TOGETHER A LONG TIME; SWINGWING USED TO BE LADDIO. I MEAN I KNOW IT'S A BIT OBVIOUS, BUT YOU'VE GOTTA WONDER ABOUT A BLOKE HAS SOME TEN YEAR-OLD IN A PAIRA Y-FRONTS HELPIN' HIM FIGHT CRIME...
AN' IF HE SAW SWINGWING WI' SOMEBODY ELSE...
AW, SHITE.

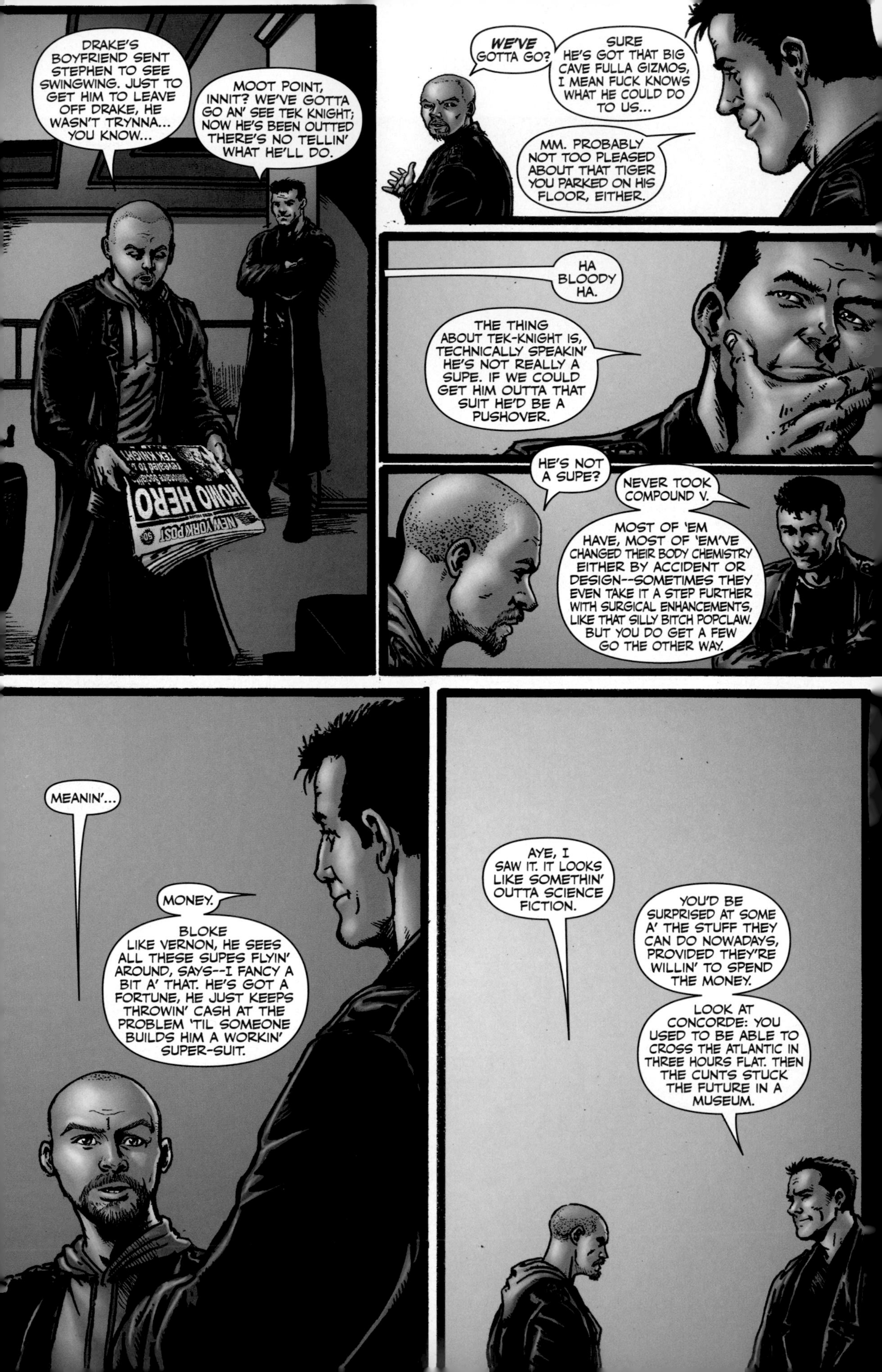
DRAKE'S BOYFRIEND SENT STEPHEN TO SEE SWINGWING. JUST TO GET HIM TO LEAVE OFF DRAKE, HE WASN'T TRYNNA... YOU KNOW...
MOOT POINT, INNIT? WE'VE GOTTA GO AN' SEE TEK KNIGHT; NOW HE'S BEEN OUTTED THERE'S NO TELLIN' WHAT HE'LL DO.
NEW YORK POST
HOMO HERO!
TEK KNIGHT
WE'VE GOTTA GO?
SURE HE'S GOT THAT BIG CAVE FULLA GIZMOS, I MEAN FUCK KNOWS WHAT HE COULD DO TO US...
MM. PROBABLY NOT TOO PLEASED ABOUT THAT TIGER YOU PARKED ON HIS FLOOR, EITHER.
HA BLOODY HA.
THE THING ABOUT TEK-KNIGHT IS, TECHNICALLY SPEAKIN' HE'S NOT REALLY A SUPE. IF WE COULD GET HIM OUTTA THAT SUIT HE'D BE A PUSHOVER.
HE'S NOT A SUPE?
NEVER TOOK COMPOUND V.
MOST OF 'EM HAVE, MOST OF 'EM'VE CHANGED THEIR BODY CHEMISTRY EITHER BY ACCIDENT OR DESIGN--SOMETIMES THEY EVEN TAKE IT A STEP FURTHER WITH SURGICAL ENHANCEMENTS, LIKE THAT SILLY BITCH POPCLAW. BUT YOU DO GET A FEW GO THE OTHER WAY.
MEANIN'...
MONEY.
BLOKE LIKE VERNON, HE SEES ALL THESE SUPES FLYIN' AROUND, SAYS--I FANCY A BIT A' THAT. HE'S GOT A FORTUNE, HE JUST KEEPS THROWIN' CASH AT THE PROBLEM 'TIL SOMEONE BUILDS HIM A WORKIN' SUPER-SUIT.
AYE, I SAW IT. IT LOOKS LIKE SOMETHIN' OUTTA SCIENCE FICTION.
YOU'D BE SURPRISED AT SOME A' THE STUFF THEY CAN DO NOWADAYS, PROVIDED THEY'RE WILLIN' TO SPEND THE MONEY.
LOOK AT CONCORDE: YOU USED TO BE ABLE TO CROSS THE ATLANTIC IN THREE HOURS FLAT. THEN THE CUNTS STUCK THE FUTURE IN A MUSEUM.

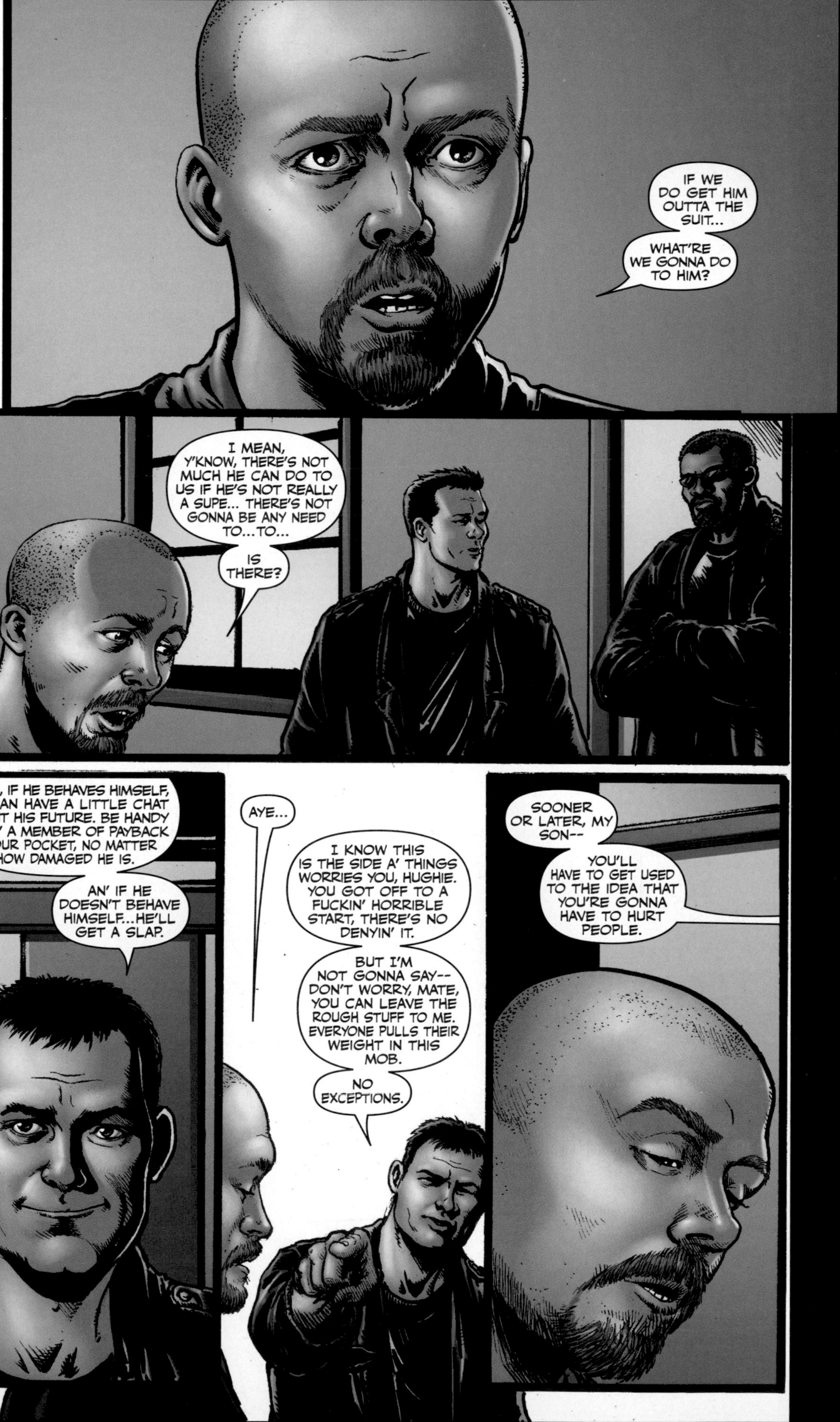
IF WE DO GET HIM OUTTA THE SUIT...
WHAT'RE WE GONNA DO TO HIM?
I MEAN, Y'KNOW, THERE'S NOT MUCH HE CAN DO TO US IF HE'S NOT REALLY A SUPE... THERE'S NOT GONNA BE ANY NEED TO...TO...
IS THERE?
WELL, IF HE BEHAVES HIMSELF, WE CAN HAVE A LITTLE CHAT ABOUT HIS FUTURE. BE HANDY HAVIN' A MEMBER OF PAYBACK IN OUR POCKET, NO MATTER HOW DAMAGED HE IS.
AN' IF HE DOESN'T BEHAVE HIMSELF...HE'LL GET A SLAP.
AYE...
I KNOW THIS IS THE SIDE A' THINGS WORRIES YOU, HUGHIE. YOU GOT OFF TO A FUCKIN' HORRIBLE START, THERE'S NO DENYIN' IT.
BUT I'M NOT GONNA SAY-- DON'T WORRY, MATE, YOU CAN LEAVE THE ROUGH STUFF TO ME. EVERYONE PULLS THEIR WEIGHT IN THIS MOB.
NO EXCEPTIONS.
SOONER OR LATER, MY SON--
YOU'LL HAVE TO GET USED TO THE IDEA THAT YOU'RE GONNA HAVE TO HURT PEOPLE.

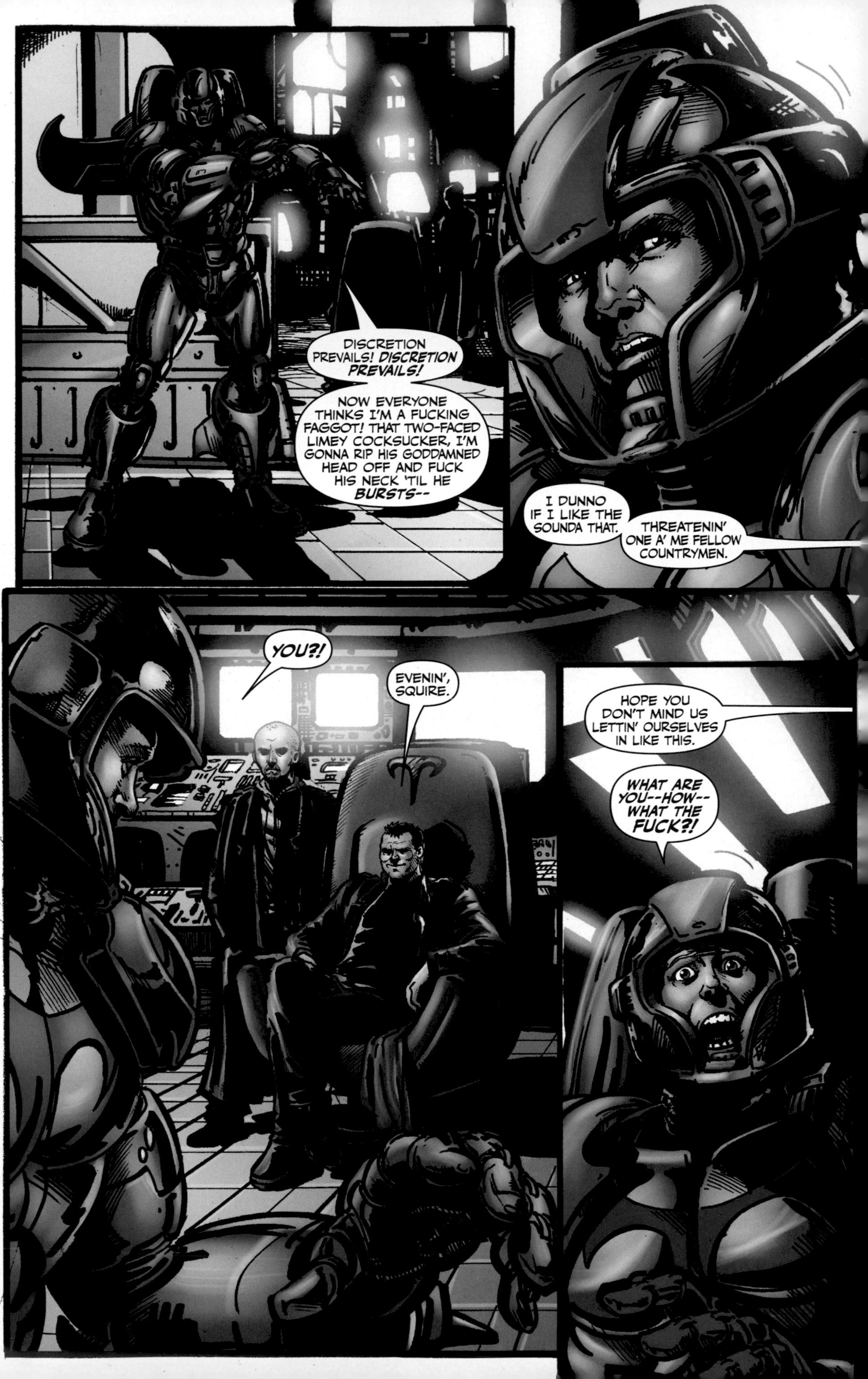
DISCRETION PREVAILS! DISCRETION PREVAILS!
NOW EVERYONE THINKS I'M A FUCKING FAGGOT! THAT TWO-FACED LIMEY COCKSUCKER, I'M GONNA RIP HIS GODDAMNED HEAD OFF AND FUCK HIS NECK 'TIL HE BURSTS--
I DUNNO IF I LIKE THE SOUNDA THAT.
THREATENIN' ONE A' ME FELLOW COUNTRYMEN.
YOU?!
EVENIN', SQUIRE.
HOPE YOU DON'T MIND US LETTIN' OURSELVES IN LIKE THIS.
WHAT ARE YOU--HOW--WHAT THE FUCK?!

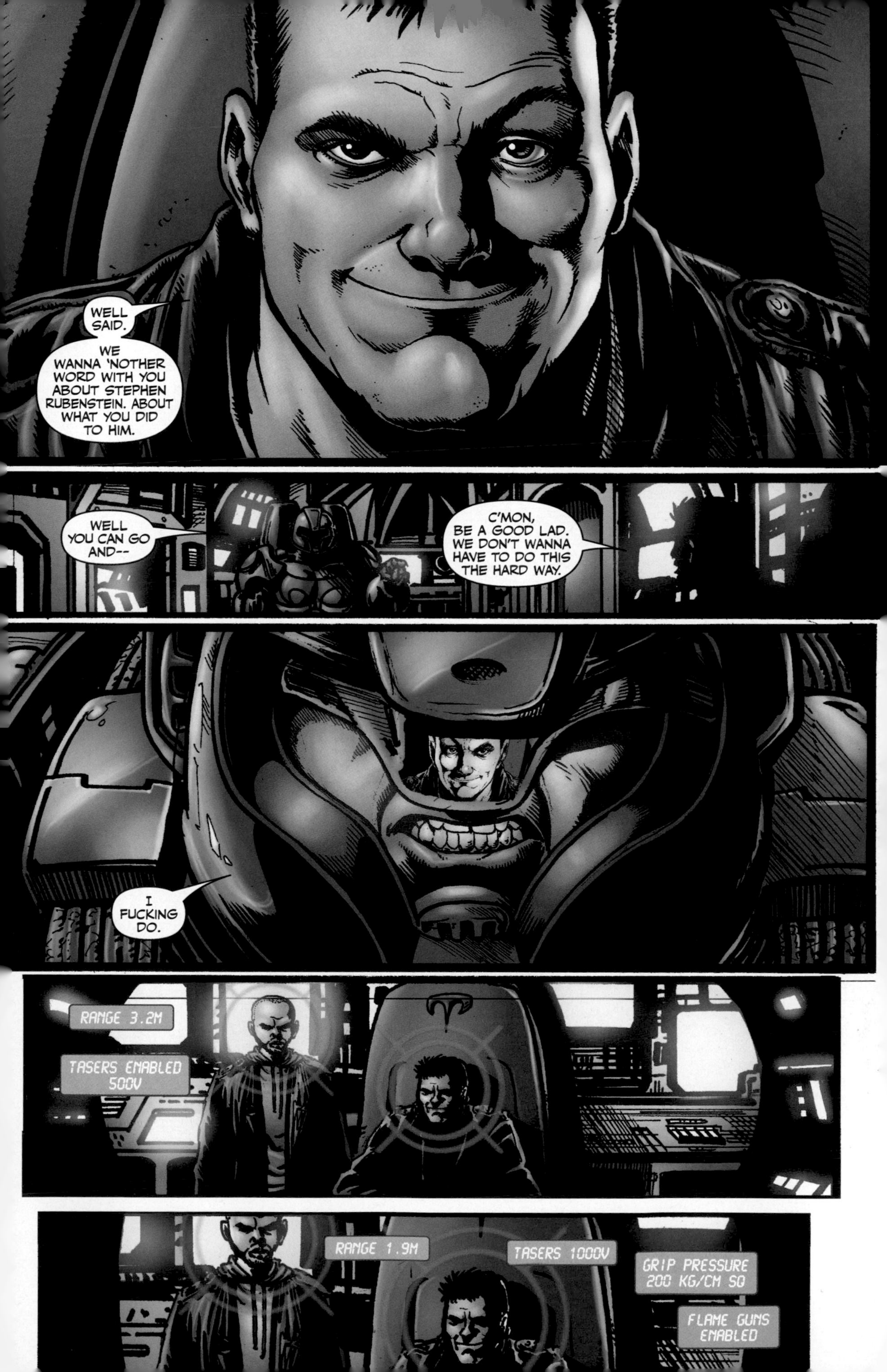
WELL SAID.
WE WANNA 'NOTHER WORD WITH YOU ABOUT STEPHEN RUBENSTEIN. ABOUT WHAT YOU DID TO HIM.
WELL YOU CAN GO AND--
C'MON, BE A GOOD LAD. WE DON'T WANNA HAVE TO DO THIS THE HARD WAY.
I FUCKING DO.
RANGE 3.2M
TASERS ENABLED 500V
RANGE 1.9M
TASERS 1000V
GRIP PRESSURE 200 KG/CM SQ
FLAME GUNS ENABLED

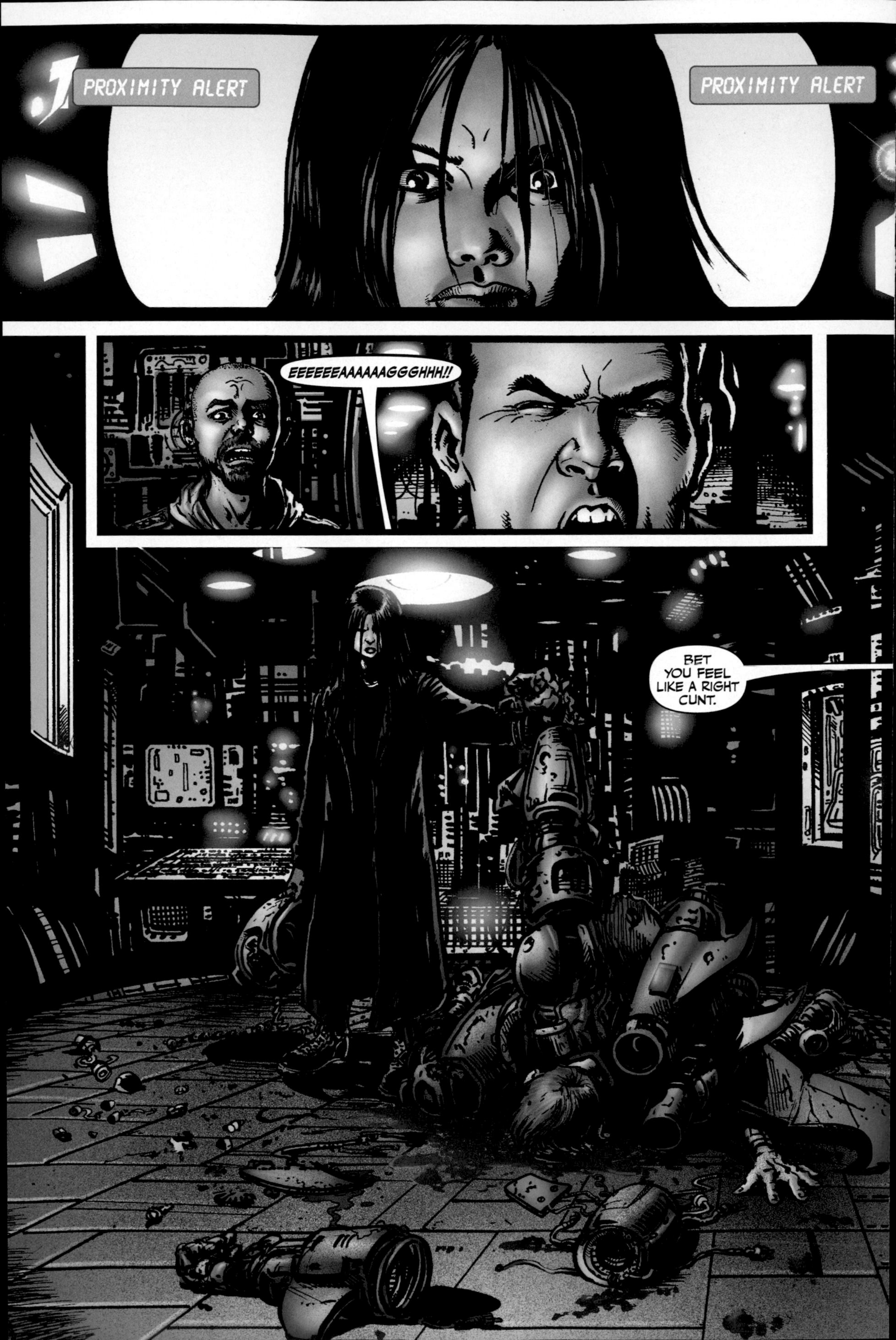
PROXIMITY ALERT
PROXIMITY ALERT
EEEEEEAAAAAAGGGHHH!!
BET YOU FEEL LIKE A RIGHT CUNT.

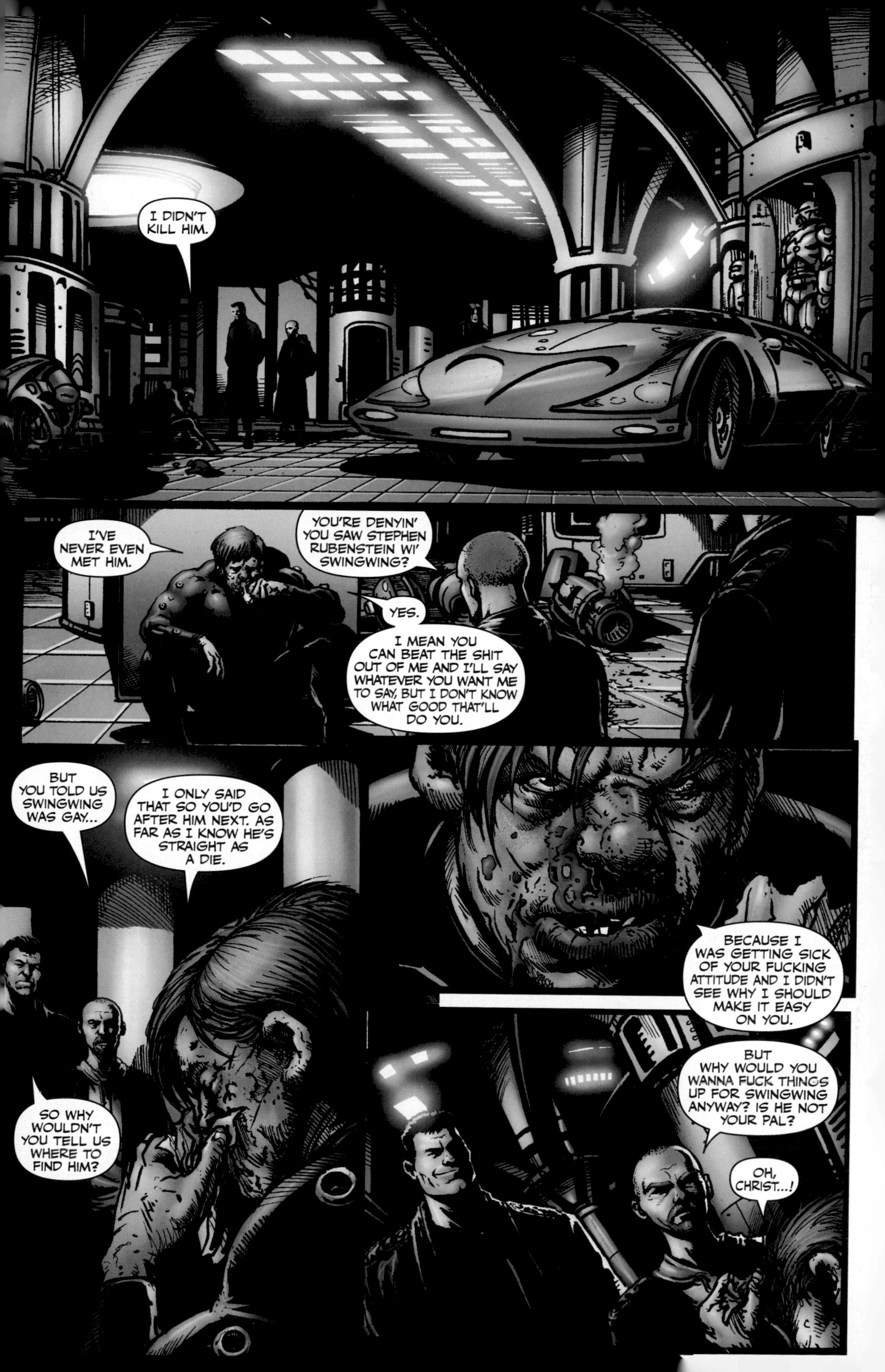
I DIDN'T KILL HIM.
I'VE NEVER EVEN MET HIM.
YOU'RE DENYIN' YOU SAW STEPHEN RUBENSTEIN WI' SWINGWING?
YES.
I MEAN YOU CAN BEAT THE SHIT OUT OF ME AND I'LL SAY WHATEVER YOU WANT ME TO SAY, BUT I DON'T KNOW WHAT GOOD THAT'LL DO YOU.
BUT YOU TOLD US SWINGWING WAS GAY...
I ONLY SAID THAT SO YOU'D GO AFTER HIM NEXT. AS FAR AS I KNOW HE'S STRAIGHT AS A DIE.
SO WHY WOULDN'T YOU TELL US WHERE TO FIND HIM?
BECAUSE I WAS GETTING SICK OF YOUR FUCKING ATTITUDE AND I DIDN'T SEE WHY I SHOULD MAKE IT EASY ON YOU.
BUT WHY WOULD YOU WANNA FUCK THINGS UP FOR SWINGWING ANYWAY? IS HE NOT YOUR PAL?
OH, CHRIST...!

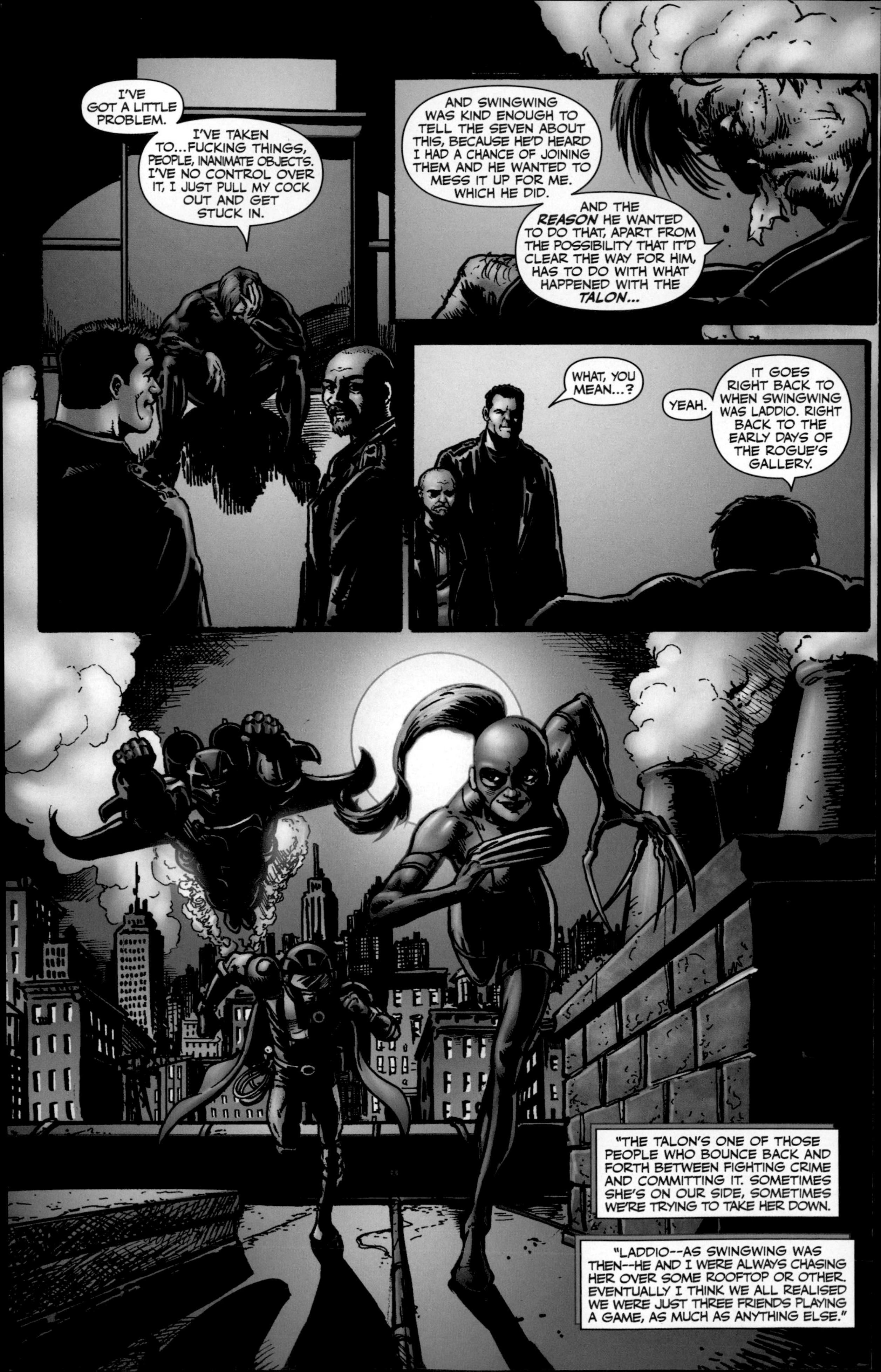
I'VE GOT A LITTLE PROBLEM.
I'VE TAKEN TO...FUCKING THINGS, PEOPLE, INANIMATE OBJECTS. I'VE NO CONTROL OVER IT, I JUST PULL MY COCK OUT AND GET STUCK IN.
AND SWINGWING WAS KIND ENOUGH TO TELL THE SEVEN ABOUT THIS, BECAUSE HE'D HEARD I HAD A CHANCE OF JOINING THEM AND HE WANTED TO MESS IT UP FOR ME. WHICH HE DID.
AND THE REASON HE WANTED TO DO THAT, APART FROM THE POSSIBILITY THAT IT'D CLEAR THE WAY FOR HIM, HAS TO DO WITH WHAT HAPPENED WITH THE TALON...
WHAT, YOU MEAN...?
YEAH.
IT GOES RIGHT BACK TO WHEN SWINGWING WAS LADDIO. RIGHT BACK TO THE EARLY DAYS OF THE ROGUE'S GALLERY.
"THE TALON'S ONE OF THOSE PEOPLE WHO BOUNCE BACK AND FORTH BETWEEN FIGHTING CRIME AND COMMITTING IT. SOMETIMES SHE'S ON OUR SIDE, SOMETIMES WE'RE TRYING TO TAKE HER DOWN.
"LADDIO--AS SWINGWING WAS THEN--HE AND I WERE ALWAYS CHASING HER OVER SOME ROOFTOP OR OTHER. EVENTUALLY I THINK WE ALL REALISED WE WERE JUST THREE FRIENDS PLAYING A GAME, AS MUCH AS ANYTHING ELSE."

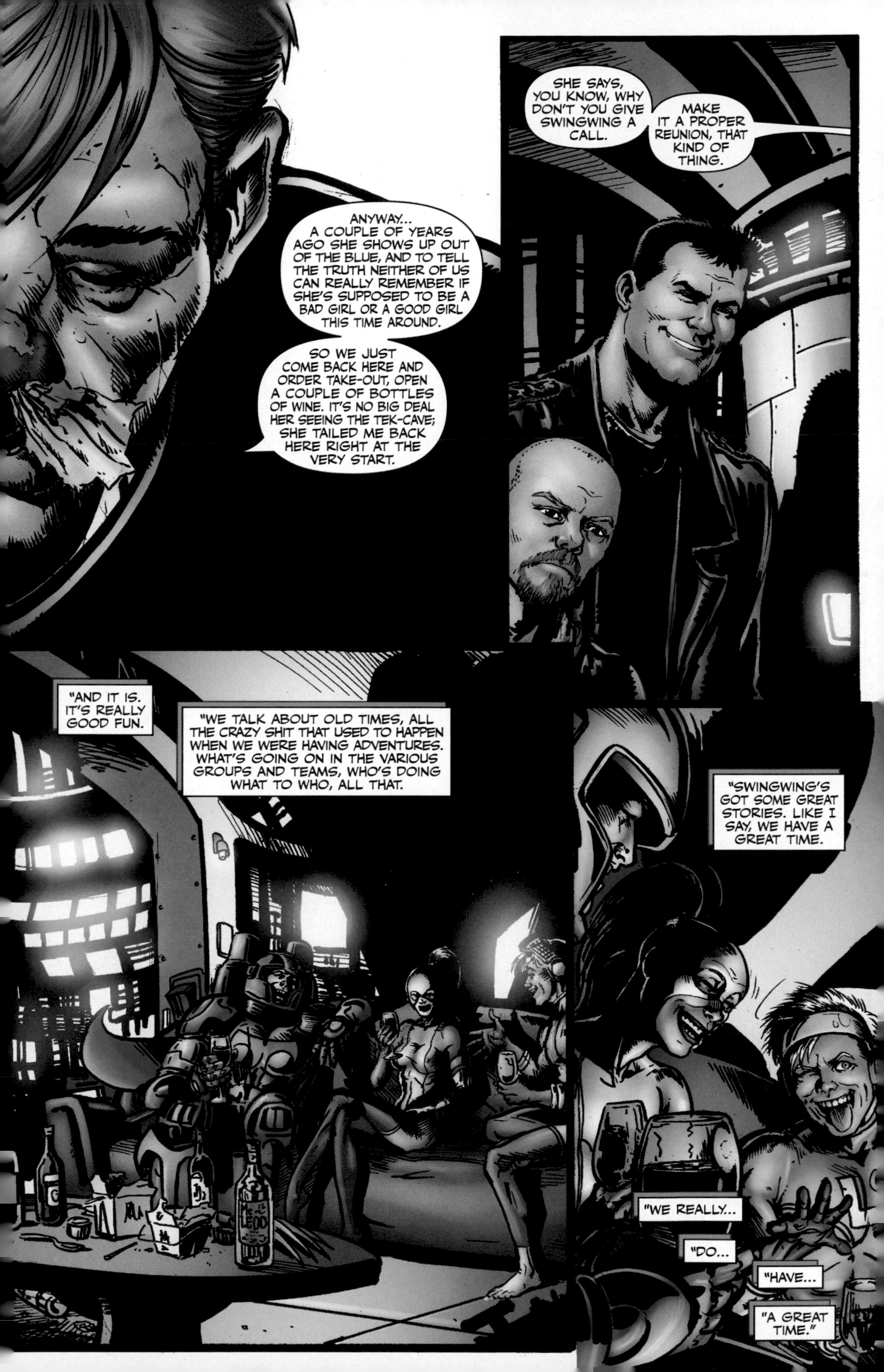
ANYWAY... A COUPLE OF YEARS AGO SHE SHOWS UP OUT OF THE BLUE, AND TO TELL THE TRUTH NEITHER OF US CAN REALLY REMEMBER IF SHE'S SUPPOSED TO BE A BAD GIRL OR A GOOD GIRL THIS TIME AROUND.
SO WE JUST COME BACK HERE AND ORDER TAKE-OUT, OPEN A COUPLE OF BOTTLES OF WINE. IT'S NO BIG DEAL HER SEEING THE TEK-CAVE; SHE TAILED ME BACK HERE RIGHT AT THE VERY START.
SHE SAYS, YOU KNOW, WHY DON'T YOU GIVE SWINGWING A CALL.
MAKE IT A PROPER REUNION, THAT KIND OF THING.
"AND IT IS. IT'S REALLY GOOD FUN.
"WE TALK ABOUT OLD TIMES, ALL THE CRAZY SHIT THAT USED TO HAPPEN WHEN WE WERE HAVING ADVENTURES. WHAT'S GOING ON IN THE VARIOUS GROUPS AND TEAMS, WHO'S DOING WHAT TO WHO, ALL THAT.
"SWINGWING'S GOT SOME GREAT STORIES. LIKE I SAY, WE HAVE A GREAT TIME.
"WE REALLY...
"DO...
"HAVE...
"A GREAT TIME."

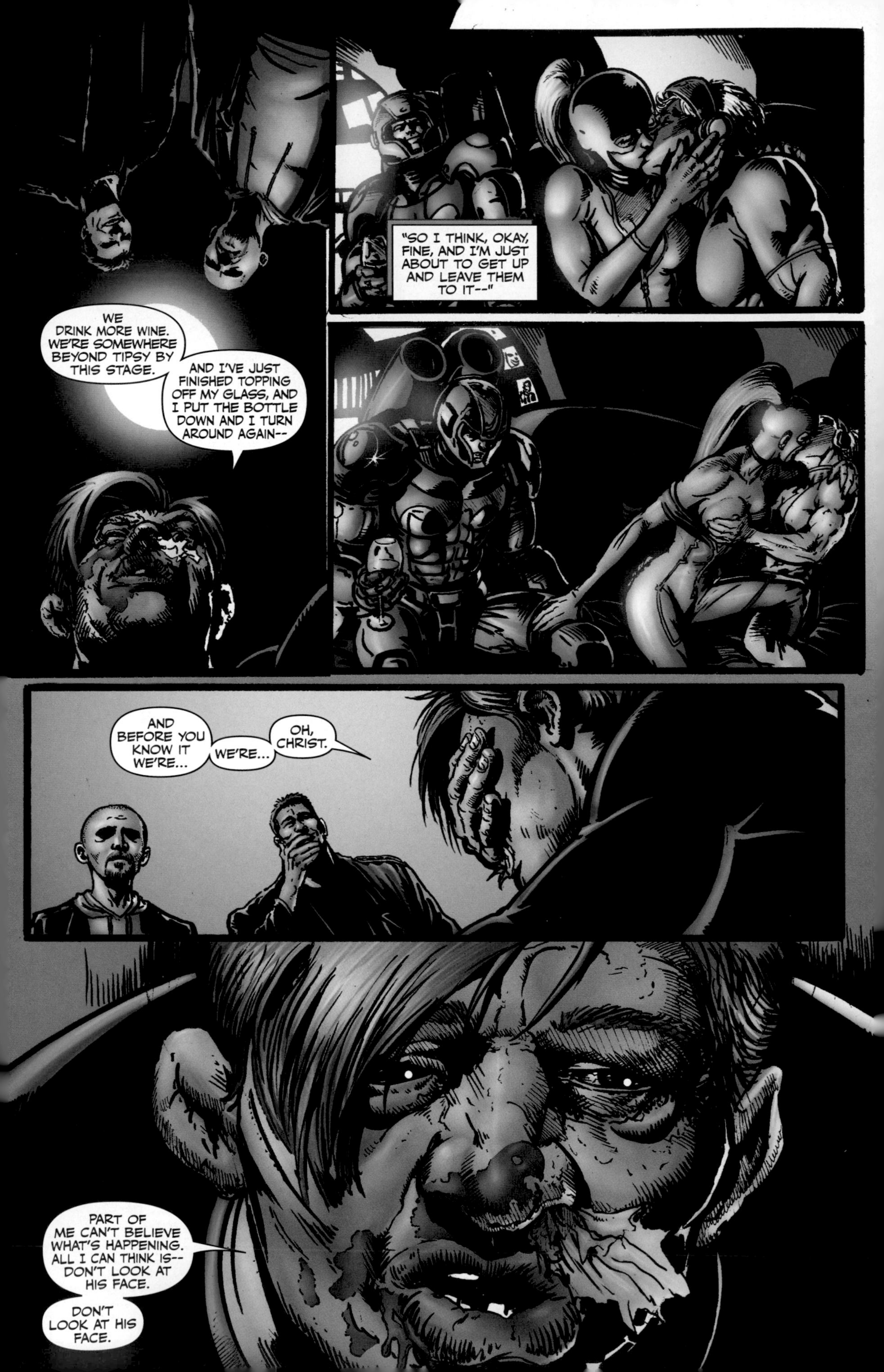
"SO I THINK, OKAY, FINE, AND I'M JUST ABOUT TO GET UP AND LEAVE THEM TO IT--"
WE DRINK MORE WINE. WE'RE SOMEWHERE BEYOND TIPSY BY THIS STAGE.
AND I'VE JUST FINISHED TOPPING OFF MY GLASS, AND I PUT THE BOTTLE DOWN AND I TURN AROUND AGAIN--
AND BEFORE YOU KNOW IT WE'RE...
WE'RE...
OH, CHRIST.
PART OF ME CAN'T BELIEVE WHAT'S HAPPENING. ALL I CAN THINK IS-- DON'T LOOK AT HIS FACE.
DON'T LOOK AT HIS FACE.

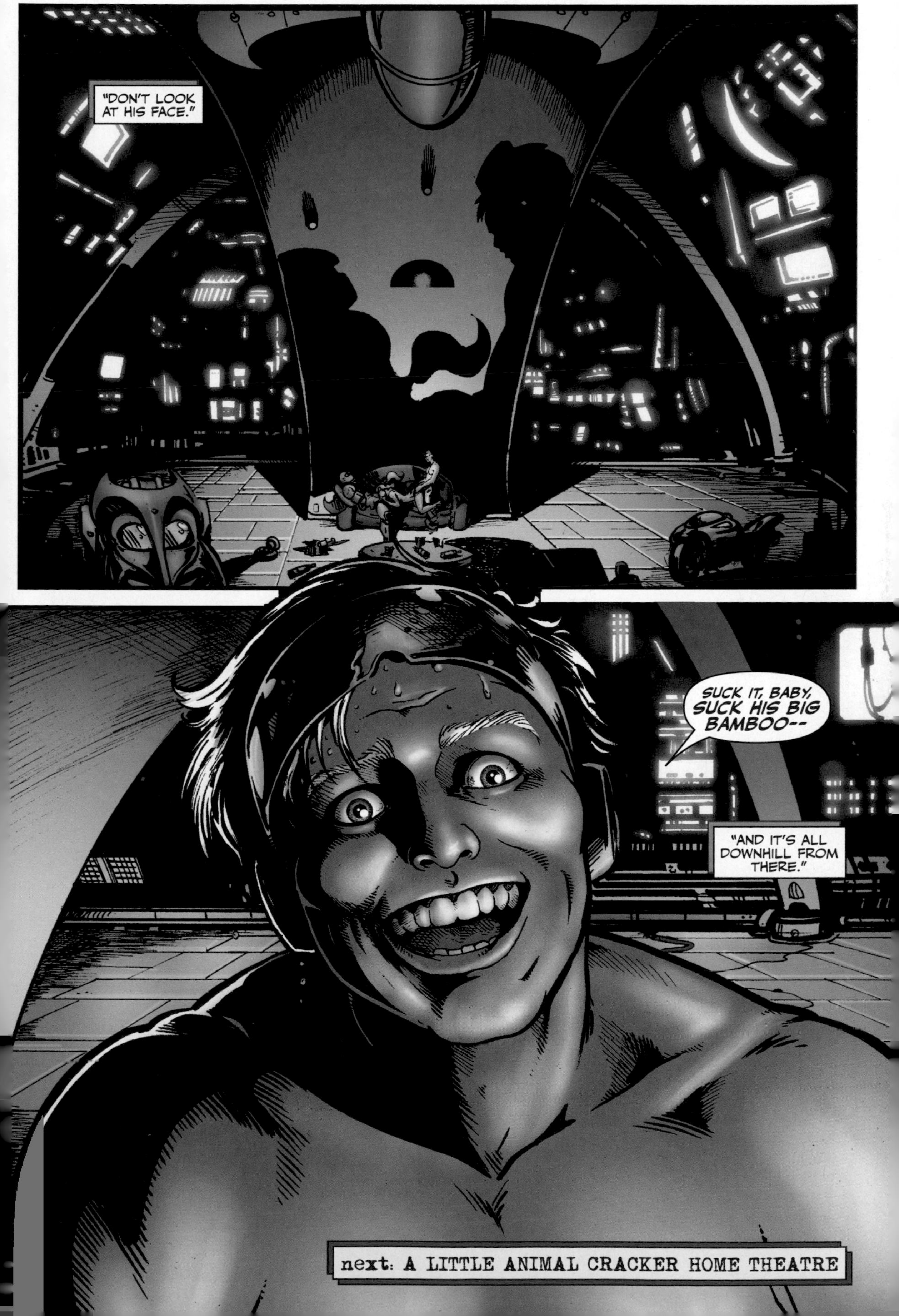
"DON'T LOOK AT HIS FACE."
SUCK IT, BABY, SUCK HIS BIG BAMBOO--
"AND IT'S ALL DOWNHILL FROM THERE."
next: A LITTLE ANIMAL CRACKER HOME THEATRE

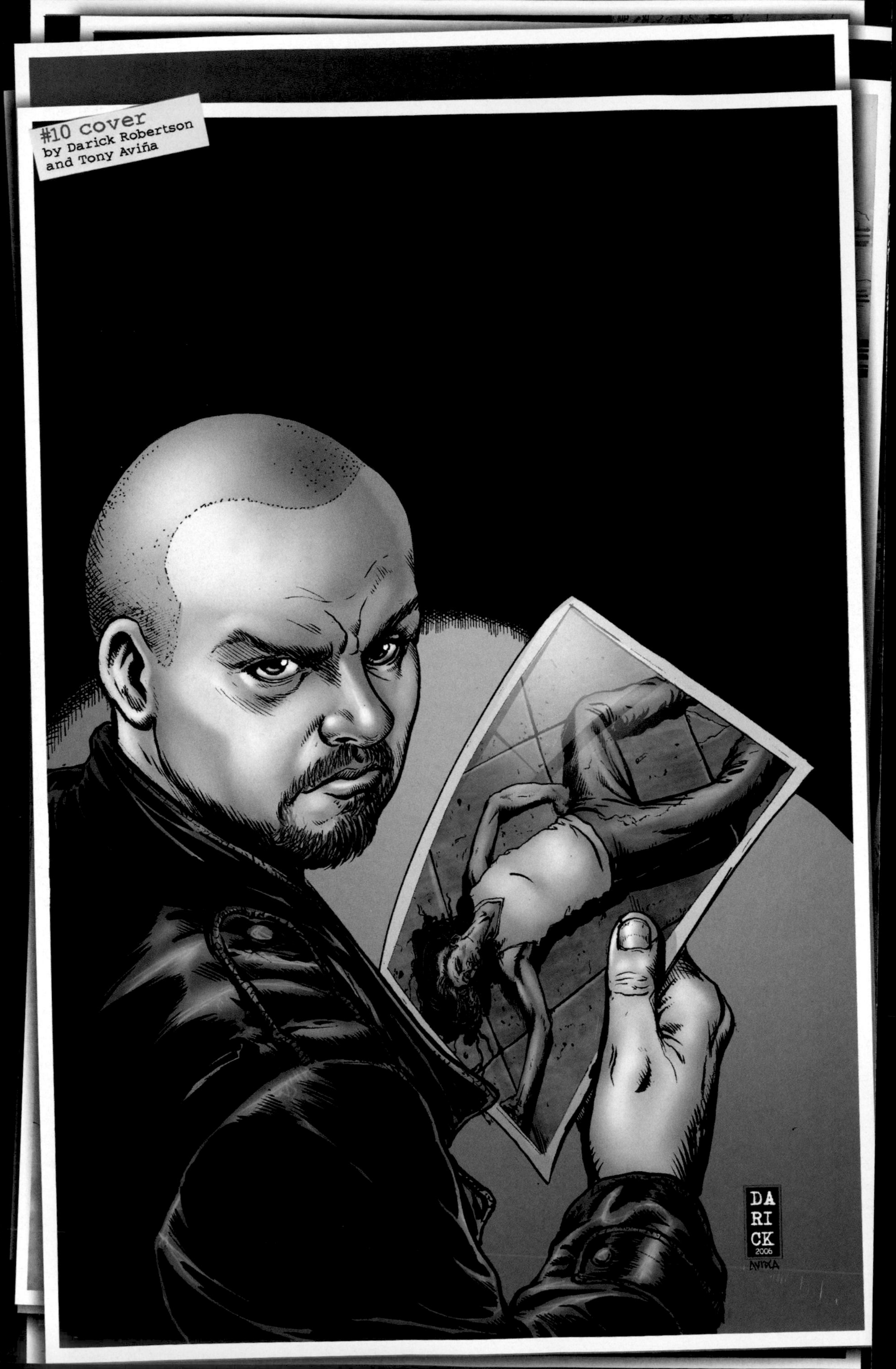
DA
RI
CK
2006

#10 cover
by Darick Robertson
and Tony Aviña

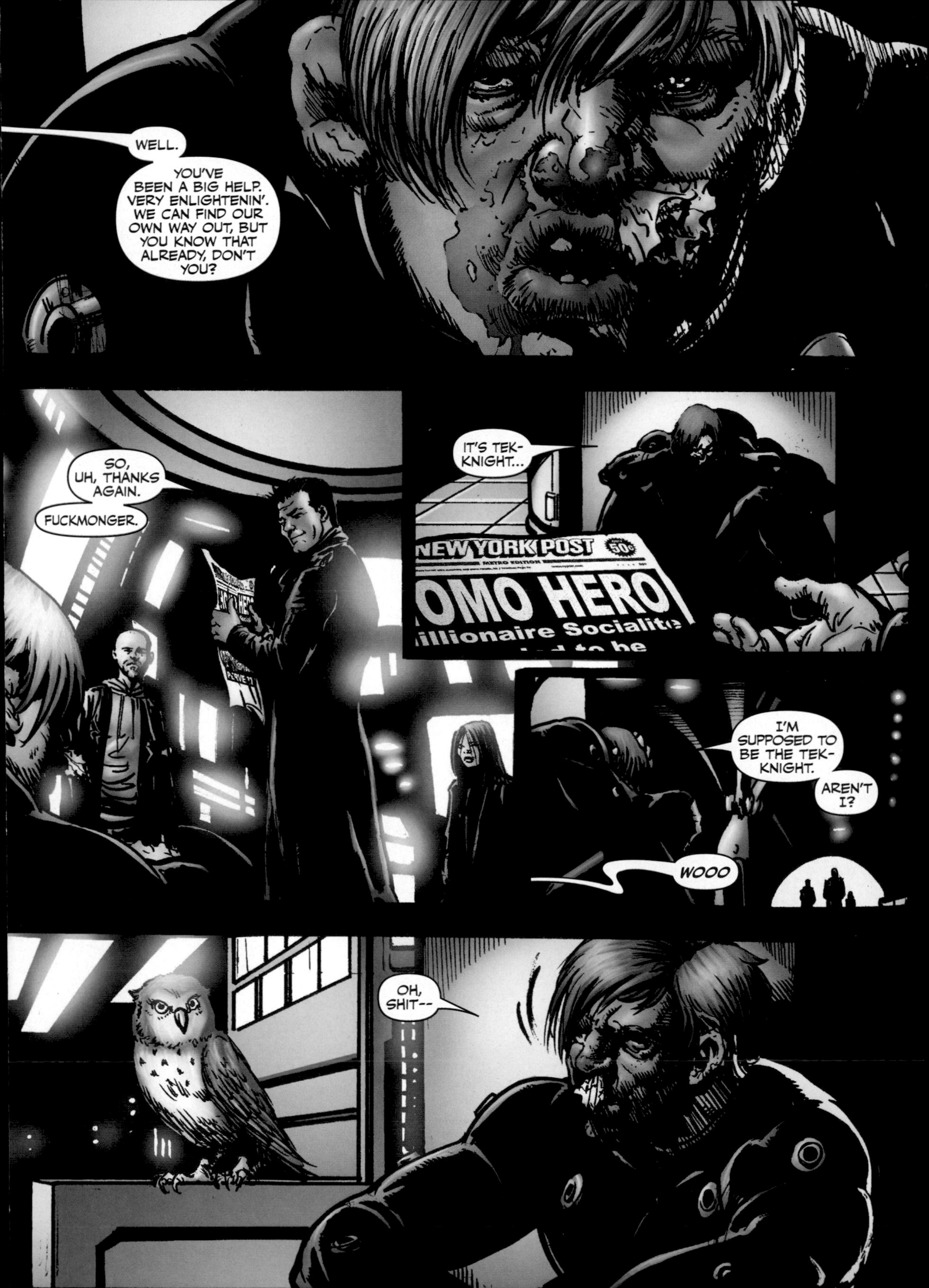
WELL.
YOU'VE BEEN A BIG HELP. VERY ENLIGHTENIN'. WE CAN FIND OUR OWN WAY OUT, BUT YOU KNOW THAT ALREADY, DON'T YOU?
SO, UH, THANKS AGAIN.
FUCKMONGER.
IT'S TEK-KNIGHT...
NEW YORK POST
50¢
OMO HERO
illionaire Socialite
I'M SUPPOSED TO BE THE TEK-KNIGHT.
AREN'T I?
WOOO
OH, SHIT--

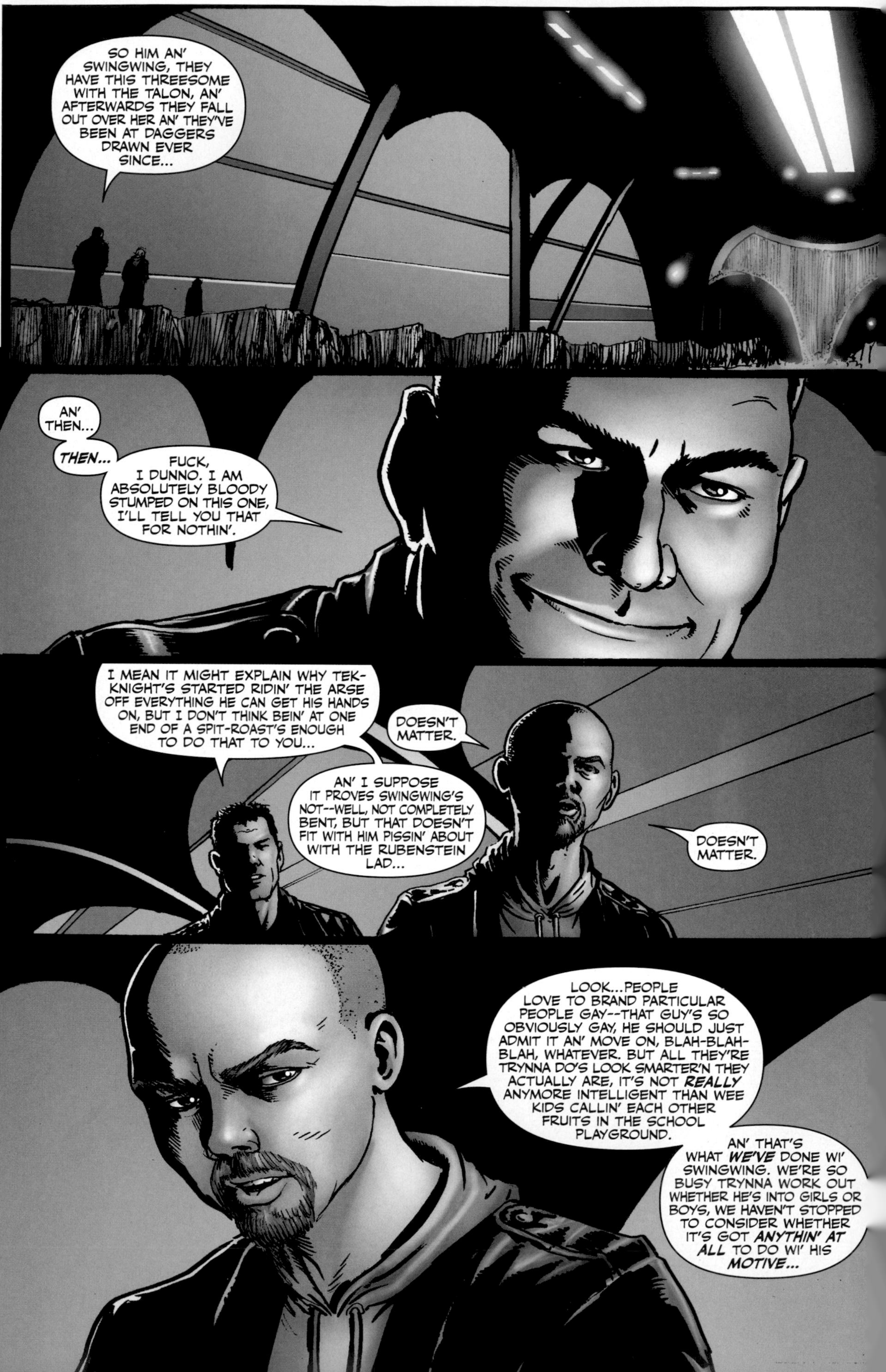
SO HIM AN' SWINGWING, THEY HAVE THIS THREESOME WITH THE TALON, AN' AFTERWARDS THEY FALL OUT OVER HER AN' THEY'VE BEEN AT DAGGERS DRAWN EVER SINCE...
AN' THEN...
THEN...
FUCK, I DUNNO. I AM ABSOLUTELY BLOODY STUMPED ON THIS ONE, I'LL TELL YOU THAT FOR NOTHIN'.
I MEAN IT MIGHT EXPLAIN WHY TEK-KNIGHT'S STARTED RIDIN' THE ARSE OFF EVERYTHING HE CAN GET HIS HANDS ON, BUT I DON'T THINK BEIN' AT ONE END OF A SPIT-ROAST'S ENOUGH TO DO THAT TO YOU...
DOESN'T MATTER.
AN' I SUPPOSE IT PROVES SWINGWING'S NOT--WELL, NOT COMPLETELY BENT, BUT THAT DOESN'T FIT WITH HIM PISSIN' ABOUT WITH THE RUBENSTEIN LAD...
DOESN'T MATTER.
LOOK...PEOPLE LOVE TO BRAND PARTICULAR PEOPLE GAY--THAT GUY'S SO OBVIOUSLY GAY, HE SHOULD JUST ADMIT IT AN' MOVE ON, BLAH-BLAH-BLAH, WHATEVER. BUT ALL THEY'RE TRYNNA DO'S LOOK SMARTER'N THEY ACTUALLY ARE, IT'S NOT REALLY ANYMORE INTELLIGENT THAN WEE KIDS CALLIN' EACH OTHER FRUITS IN THE SCHOOL PLAYGROUND.
AN' THAT'S WHAT WE'VE DONE WI' SWINGWING. WE'RE SO BUSY TRYNNA WORK OUT WHETHER HE'S INTO GIRLS OR BOYS, WE HAVEN'T STOPPED TO CONSIDER WHETHER IT'S GOT ANYTHIN' AT ALL TO DO WI' HIS MOTIVE...

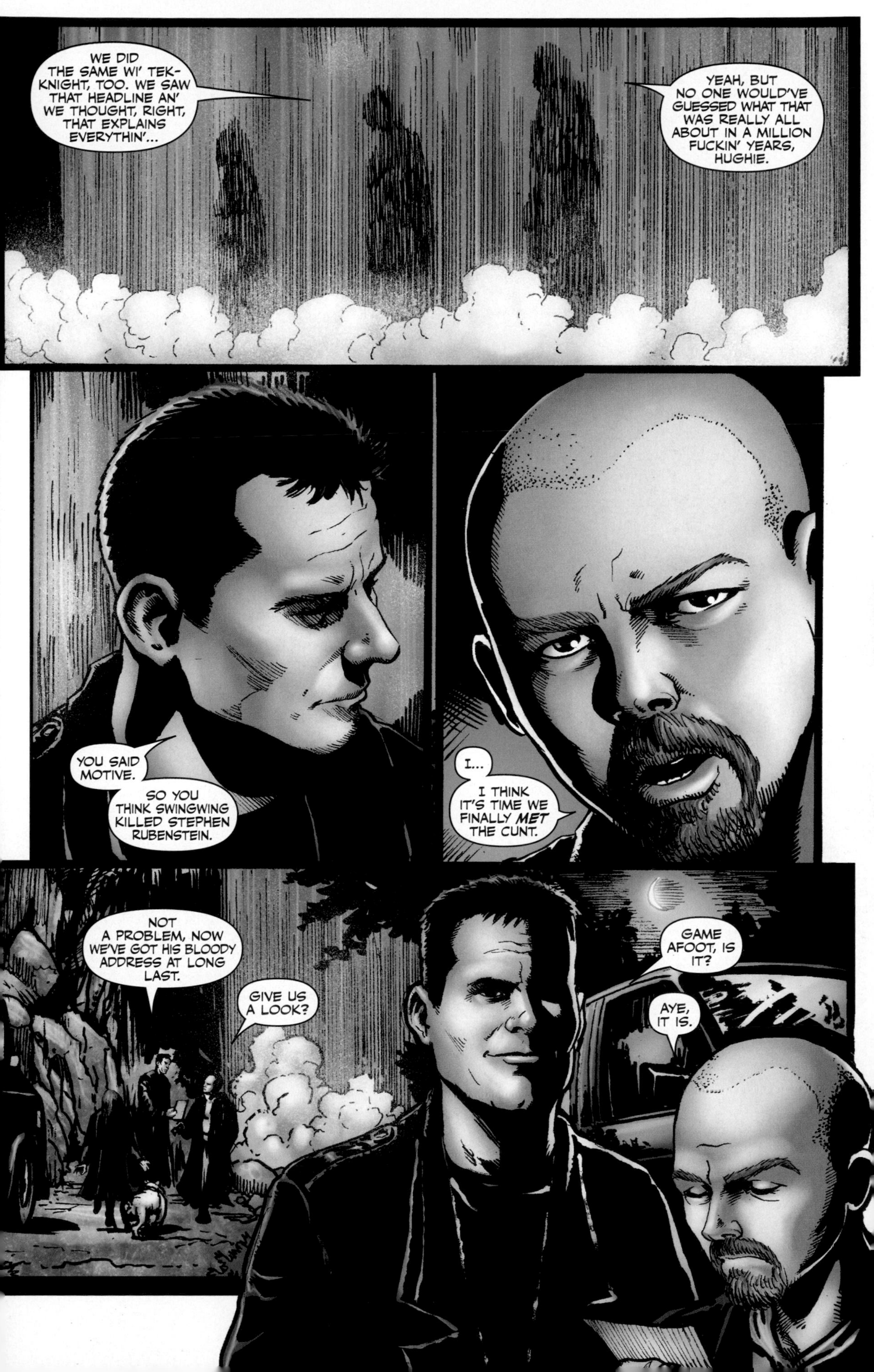
WE DID THE SAME WI' TEK-KNIGHT, TOO. WE SAW THAT HEADLINE AN' WE THOUGHT, RIGHT, THAT EXPLAINS EVERYTHIN'...
YEAH, BUT NO ONE WOULD'VE GUESSED WHAT THAT WAS REALLY ALL ABOUT IN A MILLION FUCKIN' YEARS, HUGHIE.
YOU SAID MOTIVE.
SO YOU THINK SWINGWING KILLED STEPHEN RUBENSTEIN.
I...
I THINK IT'S TIME WE FINALLY *MET* THE CUNT.
NOT A PROBLEM, NOW WE'VE GOT HIS BLOODY ADDRESS AT LONG LAST.
GIVE US A LOOK?
GAME AFOOT, IS IT?
AYE, IT IS.

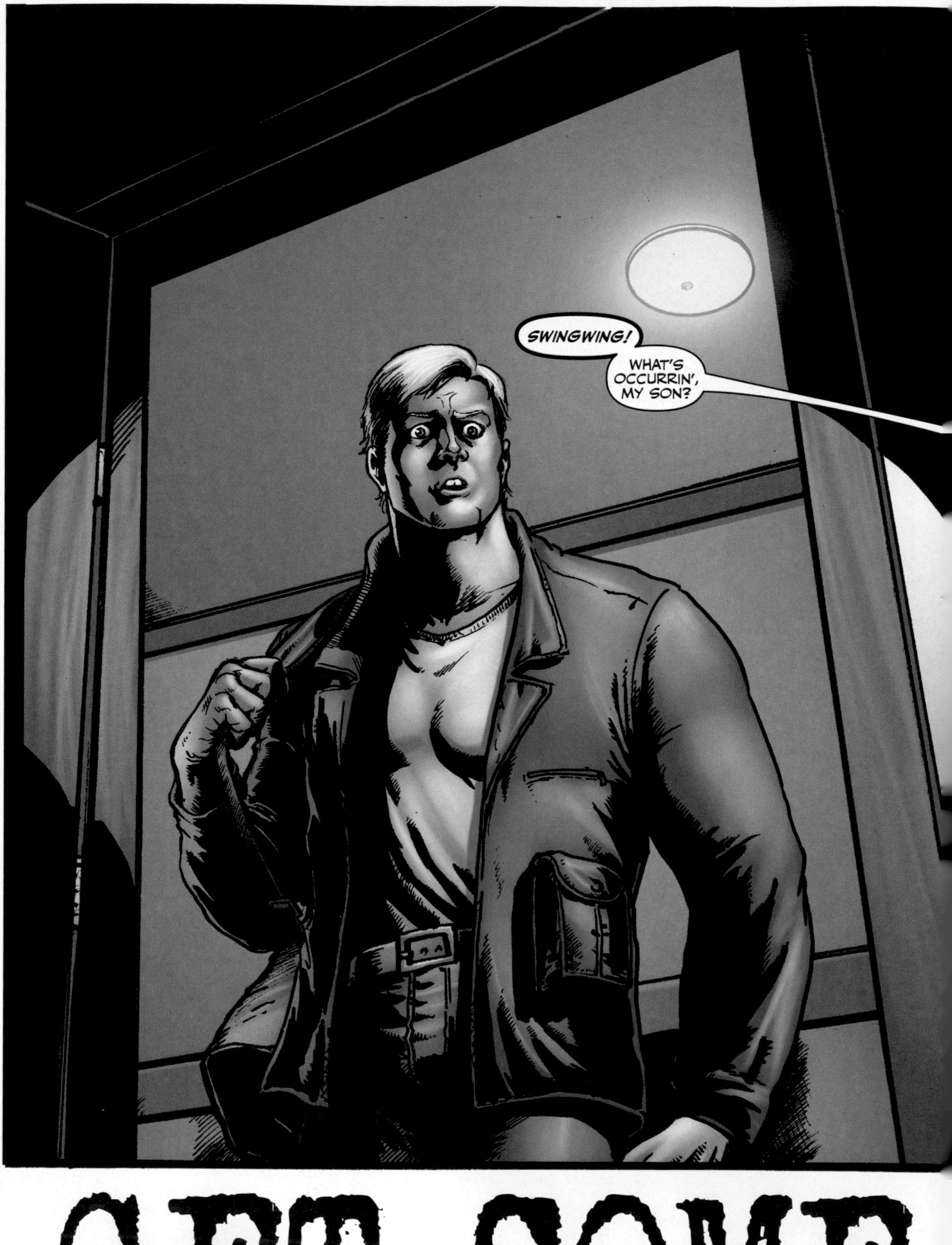
SWINGWING!
WHAT'S OCCURRIN', MY SON?

GET SOME

conclusion

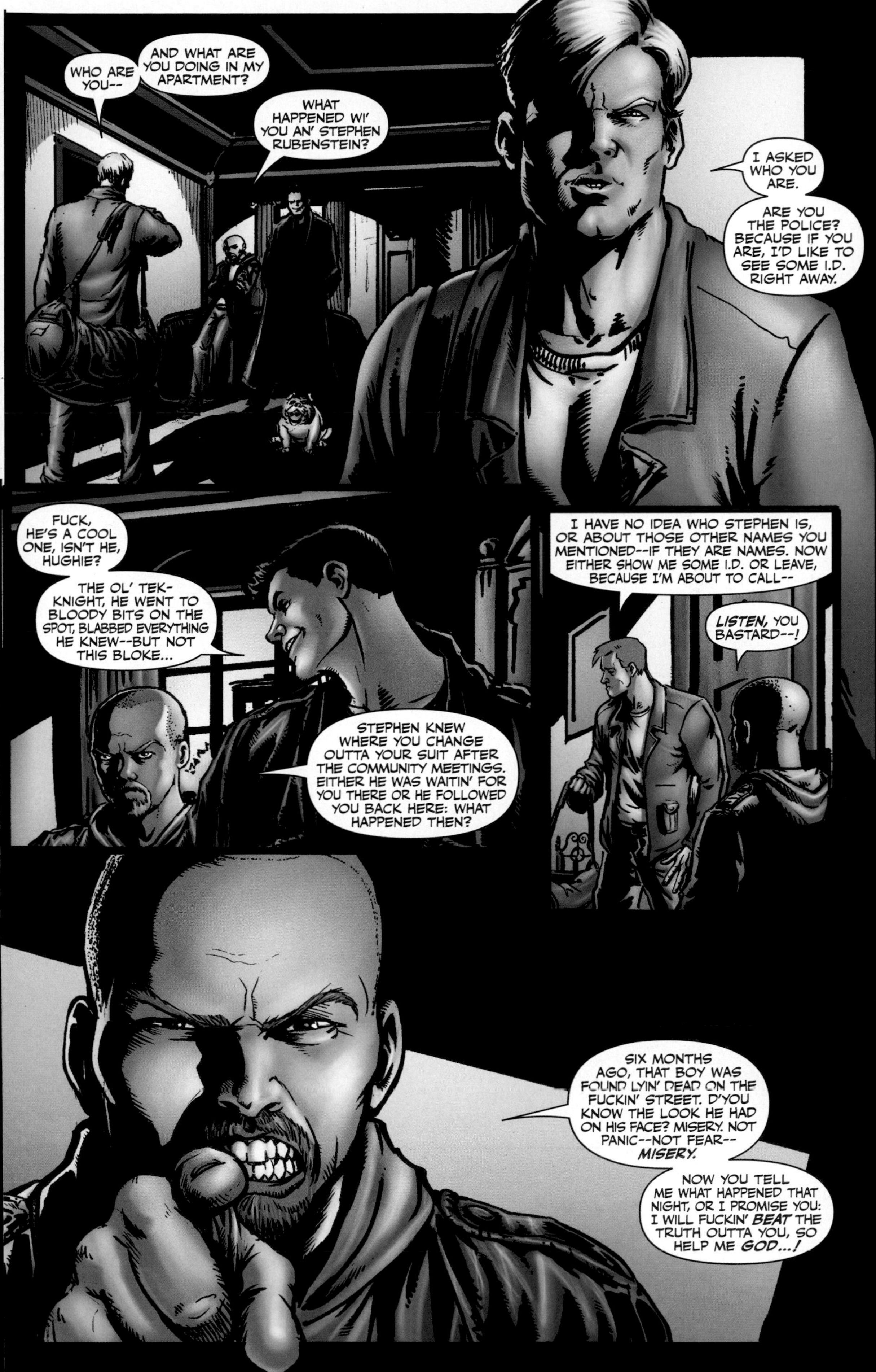
WHO ARE YOU--
AND WHAT ARE YOU DOING IN MY APARTMENT?
WHAT HAPPENED WI' YOU AN' STEPHEN RUBENSTEIN?
I ASKED WHO YOU ARE.
ARE YOU THE POLICE? BECAUSE IF YOU ARE, I'D LIKE TO SEE SOME I.D. RIGHT AWAY.
FUCK, HE'S A COOL ONE, ISN'T HE, HUGHIE?
THE OL' TEK-KNIGHT, HE WENT TO BLOODY BITS ON THE SPOT, BLABBED EVERYTHING HE KNEW--BUT NOT THIS BLOKE...
STEPHEN KNEW WHERE YOU CHANGE OUTTA YOUR SUIT AFTER THE COMMUNITY MEETINGS. EITHER HE WAS WAITIN' FOR YOU THERE OR HE FOLLOWED YOU BACK HERE: WHAT HAPPENED THEN?
I HAVE NO IDEA WHO STEPHEN IS, OR ABOUT THOSE OTHER NAMES YOU MENTIONED--IF THEY ARE NAMES. NOW EITHER SHOW ME SOME I.D. OR LEAVE, BECAUSE I'M ABOUT TO CALL--
LISTEN, YOU BASTARD--!
SIX MONTHS AGO, THAT BOY WAS FOUND LYIN' DEAD ON THE FUCKIN' STREET. D'YOU KNOW THE LOOK HE HAD ON HIS FACE? MISERY. NOT PANIC--NOT FEAR-- MISERY.
NOW YOU TELL ME WHAT HAPPENED THAT NIGHT, OR I PROMISE YOU: I WILL FUCKIN' BEAT THE TRUTH OUTTA YOU, SO HELP ME GOD...!

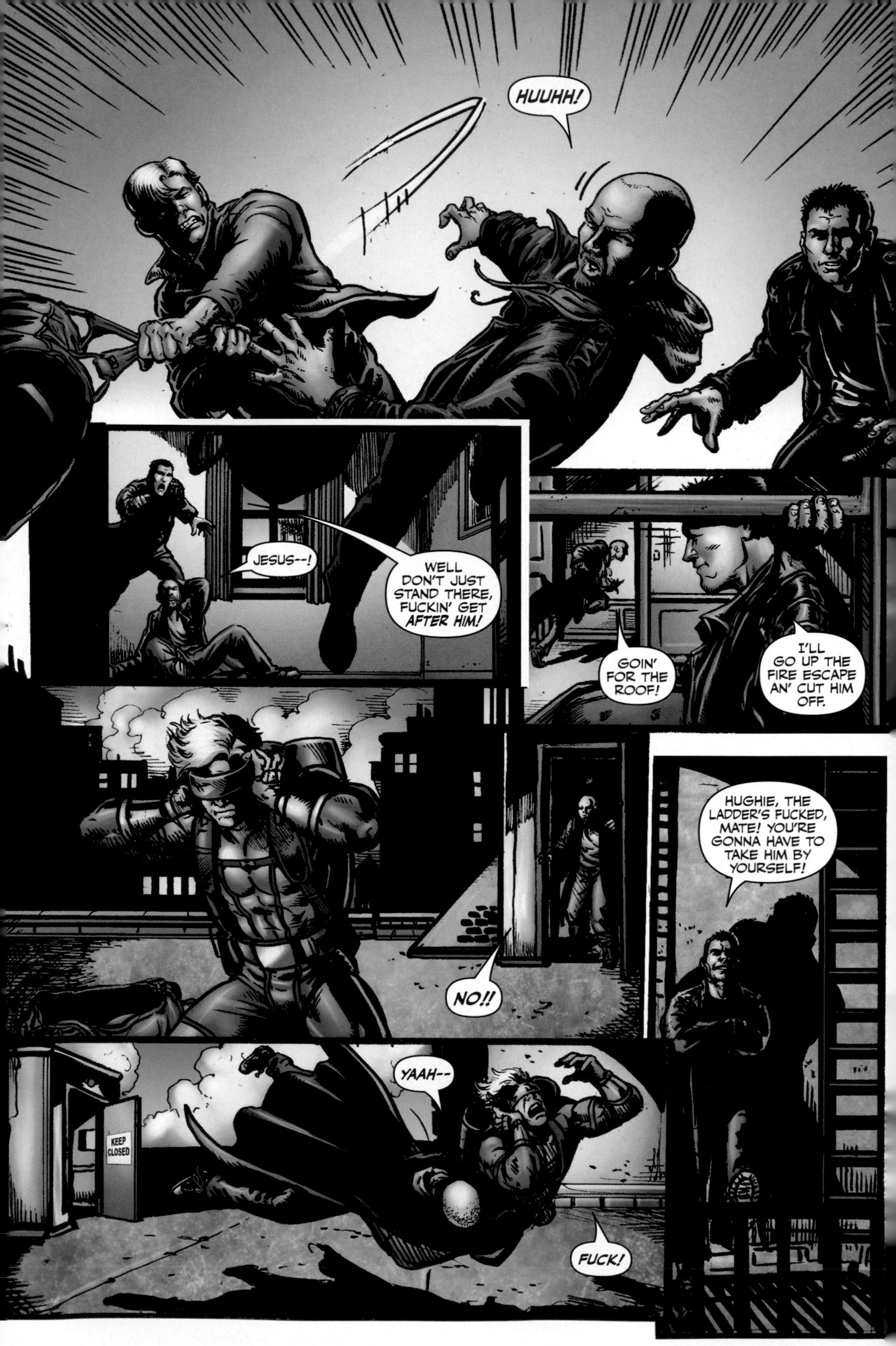
HUUUHH!
JESUS--!
WELL DON'T JUST STAND THERE, FUCKIN' GET AFTER HIM!
GOIN' FOR THE ROOF!
I'LL GO UP THE FIRE ESCAPE AN' CUT HIM OFF.
NO!!
HUGHIE, THE LADDER'S FUCKED, MATE! YOU'RE GONNA HAVE TO TAKE HIM BY YOURSELF!
KEEP CLOSED
YAAH--
FUCK!

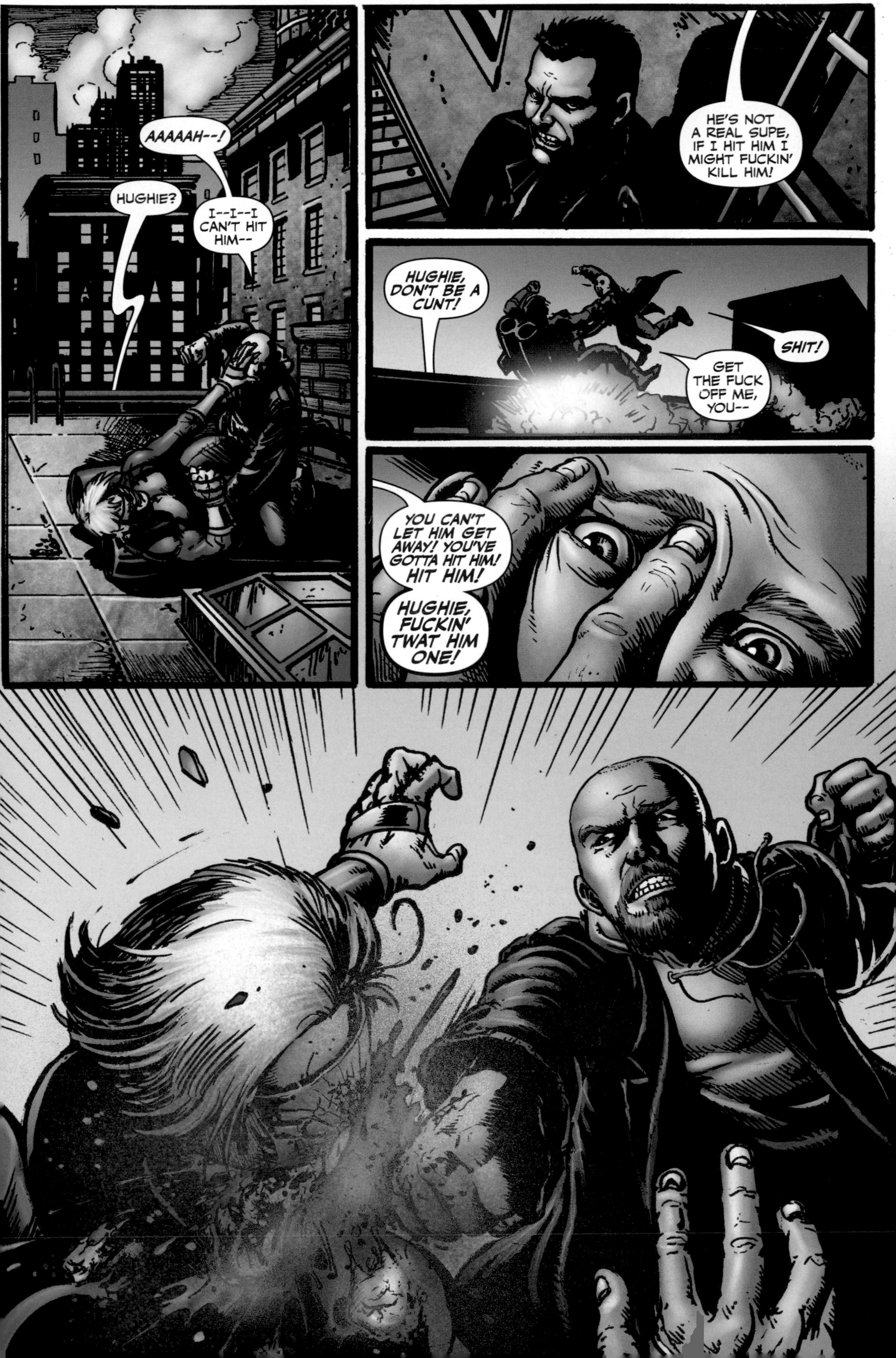
AAAAAH--!
HUGHIE?
I--I--I CAN'T HIT HIM--
HE'S NOT A REAL SUPE, IF I HIT HIM I MIGHT FUCKIN' KILL HIM!
HUGHIE, DON'T BE A CUNT!
SHIT!
GET THE FUCK OFF ME, YOU--
YOU CAN'T LET HIM GET AWAY! YOU'VE GOTTA HIT HIM! HIT HIM!
HUGHIE, FUCKIN' TWAT HIM ONE!

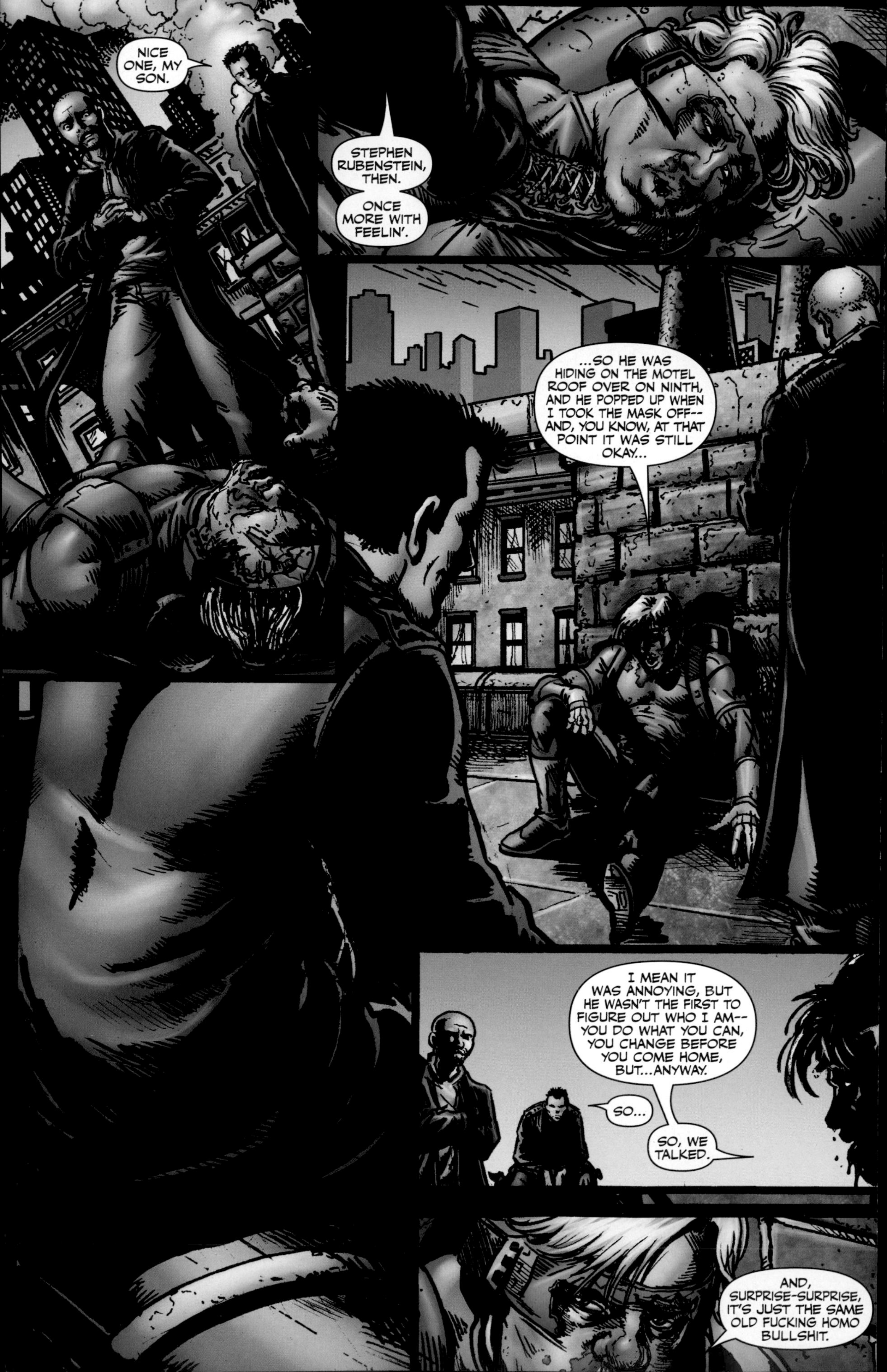
NICE ONE, MY SON.
STEPHEN RUBENSTEIN, THEN.
ONCE MORE WITH FEELIN'.
...SO HE WAS HIDING ON THE MOTEL ROOF OVER ON NINTH, AND HE POPPED UP WHEN I TOOK THE MASK OFF-- AND, YOU KNOW, AT THAT POINT IT WAS STILL OKAY...
I MEAN IT WAS ANNOYING, BUT HE WASN'T THE FIRST TO FIGURE OUT WHO I AM-- YOU DO WHAT YOU CAN, YOU CHANGE BEFORE YOU COME HOME, BUT...ANYWAY.
SO...
SO, WE TALKED.
AND, SURPRISE-SURPRISE, IT'S JUST THE SAME OLD FUCKING HOMO BULLSHIT.

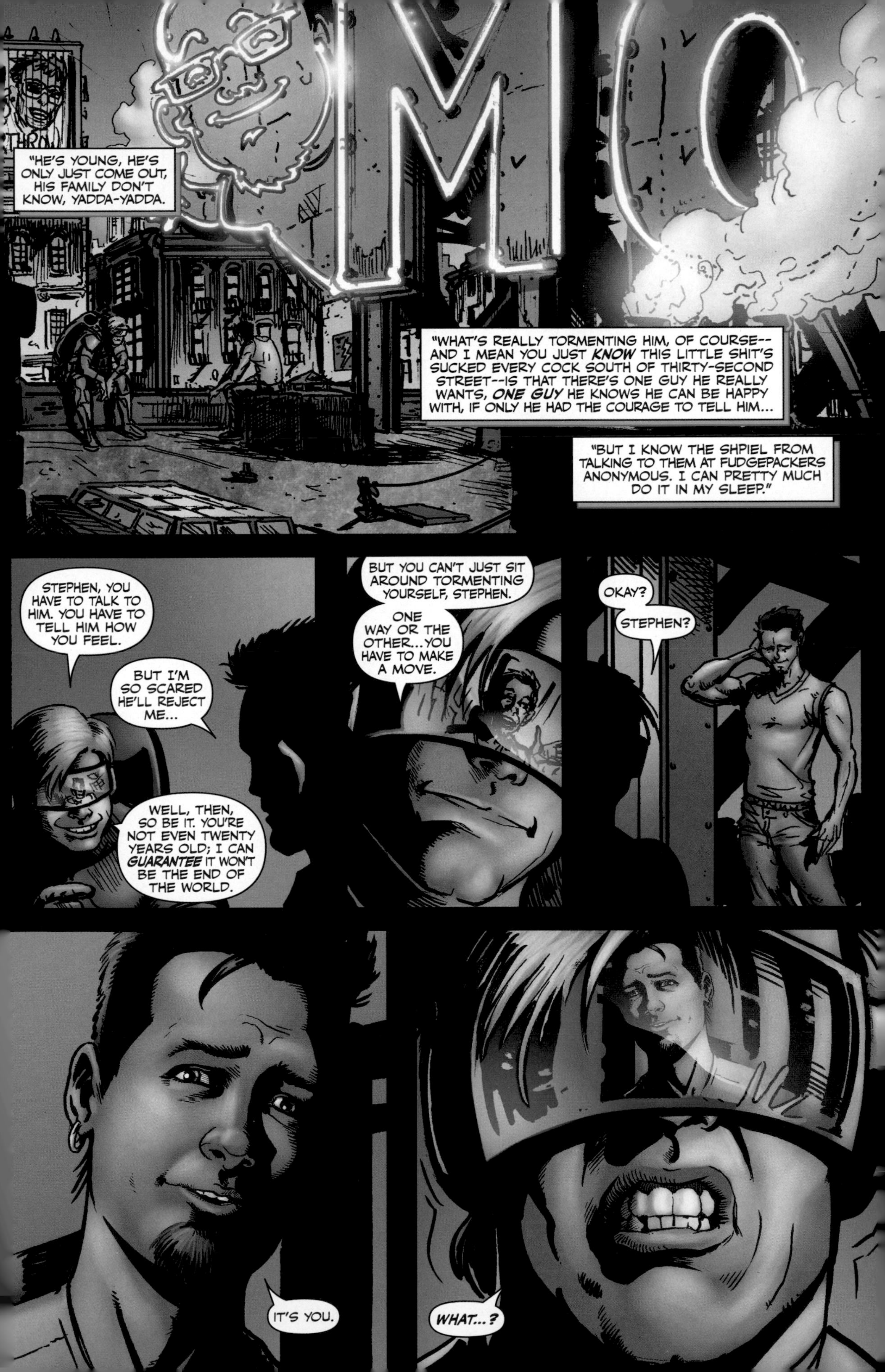
"HE'S YOUNG, HE'S ONLY JUST COME OUT, HIS FAMILY DON'T KNOW, YADDA-YADDA.
"WHAT'S REALLY TORMENTING HIM, OF COURSE-- AND I MEAN YOU JUST KNOW THIS LITTLE SHIT'S SUCKED EVERY COCK SOUTH OF THIRTY-SECOND STREET--IS THAT THERE'S ONE GUY HE REALLY WANTS, ONE GUY HE KNOWS HE CAN BE HAPPY WITH, IF ONLY HE HAD THE COURAGE TO TELL HIM...
"BUT I KNOW THE SHPIEL FROM TALKING TO THEM AT FUDGEPACKERS ANONYMOUS. I CAN PRETTY MUCH DO IT IN MY SLEEP."
STEPHEN, YOU HAVE TO TALK TO HIM. YOU HAVE TO TELL HIM HOW YOU FEEL.
BUT I'M SO SCARED HE'LL REJECT ME...
WELL, THEN, SO BE IT. YOU'RE NOT EVEN TWENTY YEARS OLD; I CAN GUARANTEE IT WON'T BE THE END OF THE WORLD.
BUT YOU CAN'T JUST SIT AROUND TORMENTING YOURSELF, STEPHEN.
ONE WAY OR THE OTHER...YOU HAVE TO MAKE A MOVE.
OKAY?
STEPHEN?
IT'S YOU.
WHAT...?

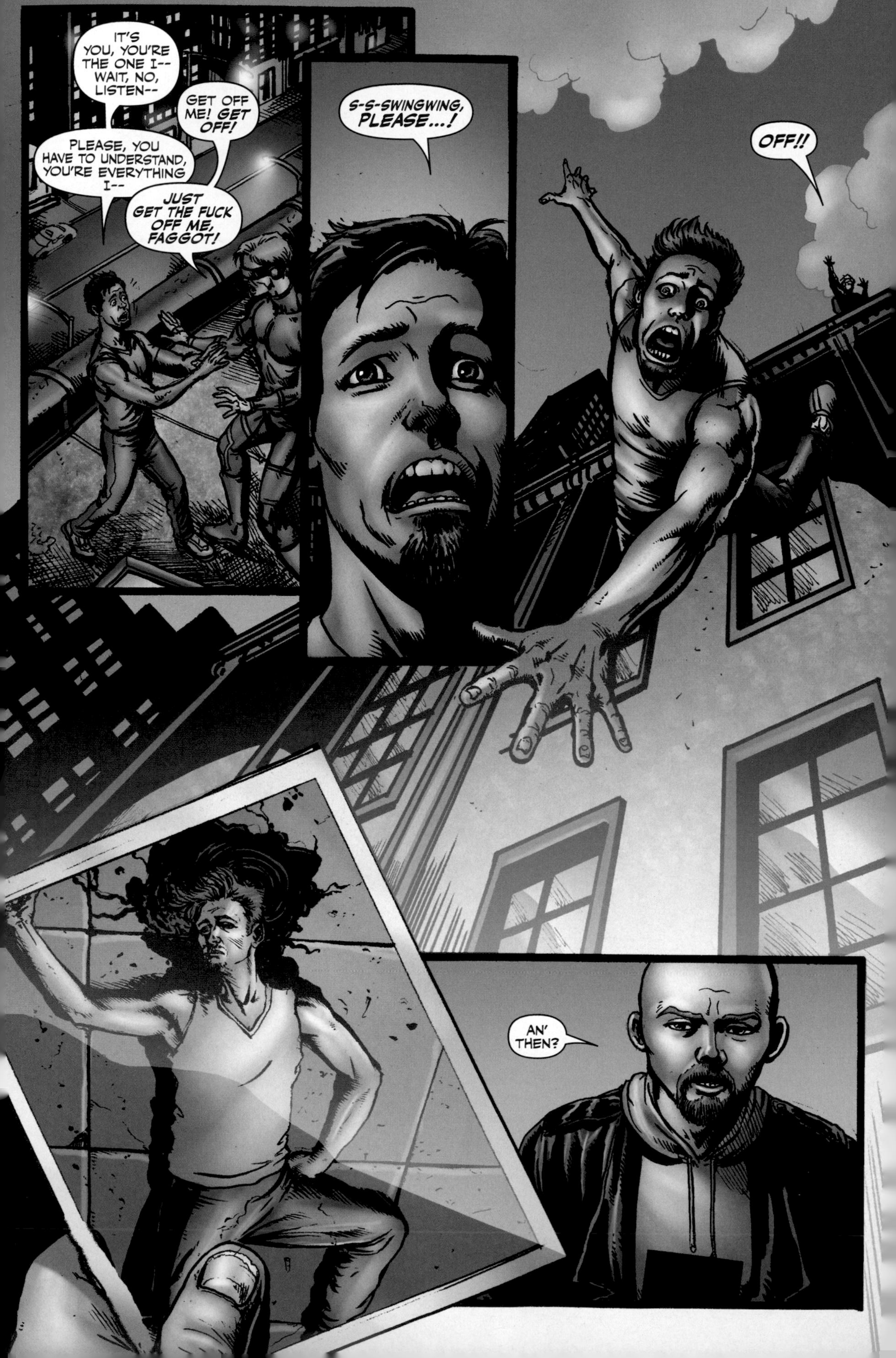
IT'S YOU, YOU'RE THE ONE I-- WAIT, NO, LISTEN--
GET OFF ME! GET OFF!
PLEASE, YOU HAVE TO UNDERSTAND, YOU'RE EVERYTHING I--
JUST GET THE FUCK OFF ME, FAGGOT!
S-S-SWINGWING, PLEASE...!
OFF!!
AN' THEN?

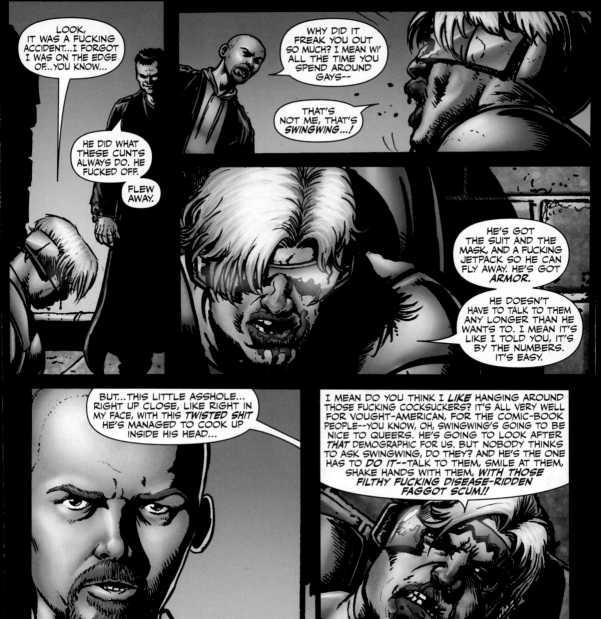

LOOK, IT WAS A FUCKING ACCIDENT...I FORGOT I WAS ON THE EDGE OF...YOU KNOW...

WHY DID IT FREAK YOU OUT SO MUCH? I MEAN WI' ALL THE TIME YOU SPEND AROUND GAYS--

THAT'S NOT ME, THAT'S *SWINGWING*...!

HE DID WHAT THESE CUNTS ALWAYS DO. HE FUCKED OFF.

FLEW AWAY.

HE'S GOT THE SUIT AND THE MASK, AND A FUCKING JETPACK SO HE CAN FLY AWAY. HE'S GOT *ARMOR*.

HE DOESN'T HAVE TO TALK TO THEM ANY LONGER THAN HE WANTS TO. I MEAN IT'S LIKE I TOLD YOU, IT'S BY THE NUMBERS. IT'S EASY.

BUT...THIS LITTLE ASSHOLE... RIGHT UP CLOSE, LIKE RIGHT IN MY FACE, WITH THIS *TWISTED SHIT* HE'S MANAGED TO COOK UP INSIDE HIS HEAD...

I MEAN DO YOU THINK I *LIKE* HANGING AROUND THOSE FUCKING COCKSUCKERS? IT'S ALL VERY WELL FOR VOUGHT-AMERICAN, FOR THE COMIC-BOOK PEOPLE--YOU KNOW, OH, SWINGWING'S GOING TO BE NICE TO QUEERS. HE'S GOING TO LOOK AFTER *THAT* DEMOGRAPHIC FOR US. BUT NOBODY THINKS TO ASK SWINGWING, DO THEY? AND HE'S THE ONE HAS TO *DO IT*--TALK TO THEM, SMILE AT THEM, SHAKE HANDS WITH THEM, *WITH THOSE FILTHY FUCKING DISEASE-RIDDEN FAGGOT SCUM!!*

BLIMEY, MATE, TELL US HOW YOU REALLY FEEL.

GET UP.

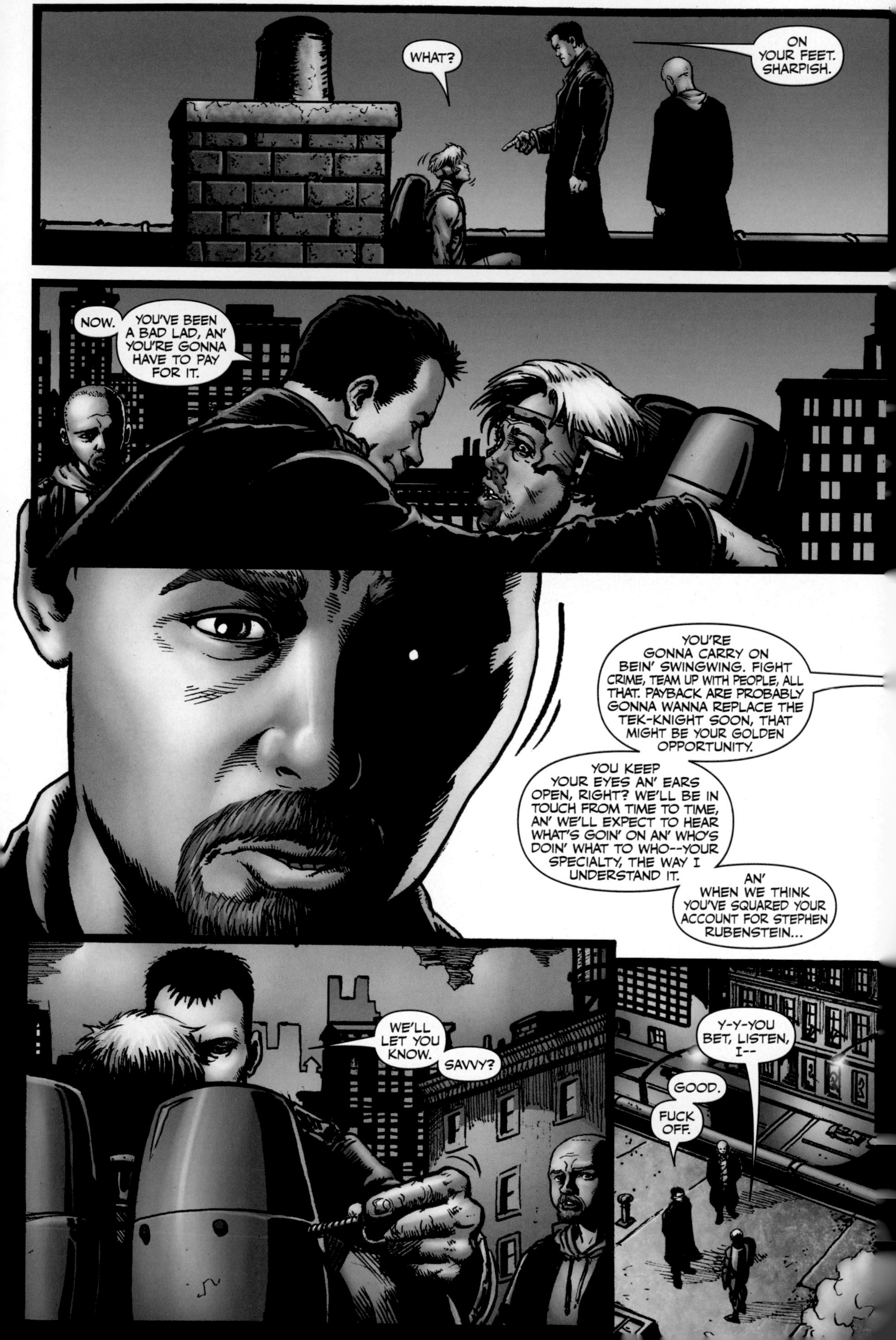
WHAT?
ON YOUR FEET. SHARPISH.
NOW.
YOU'VE BEEN A BAD LAD, AN' YOU'RE GONNA HAVE TO PAY FOR IT.
YOU'RE GONNA CARRY ON BEIN' SWINGWING. FIGHT CRIME, TEAM UP WITH PEOPLE, ALL THAT. PAYBACK ARE PROBABLY GONNA WANNA REPLACE THE TEK-KNIGHT SOON, THAT MIGHT BE YOUR GOLDEN OPPORTUNITY.
YOU KEEP YOUR EYES AN' EARS OPEN, RIGHT? WE'LL BE IN TOUCH FROM TIME TO TIME, AN' WE'LL EXPECT TO HEAR WHAT'S GOIN' ON AN' WHO'S DOIN' WHAT TO WHO--YOUR SPECIALTY, THE WAY I UNDERSTAND IT.
AN' WHEN WE THINK YOU'VE SQUARED YOUR ACCOUNT FOR STEPHEN RUBENSTEIN...
WE'LL LET YOU KNOW.
SAVVY?
Y-Y-YOU BET, LISTEN, I--
GOOD.
FUCK OFF.

CHRIST, I FEEL LIKE I COULD SLEEP FOR A FUCKIN' WEEK...

NOT HUNGRY?

S'POSE NOT.

SURPRISED I LET THE WANKER OFF SO LIGHTLY?

I DON'T THINK YOU DID LET HIM OFF LIGHTLY. I KNOW YOU'RE GONNA MAKE HIS LIFE A LIVIN' HELL, AN' MORE POWER TO YOU: A PART O' ME'S HOPIN' I GET TO TURN A COUPLA THE SCREWS MYSELF.

BUT...NO, I'M NOT SURPRISED. AN' THAT'S THE THING.

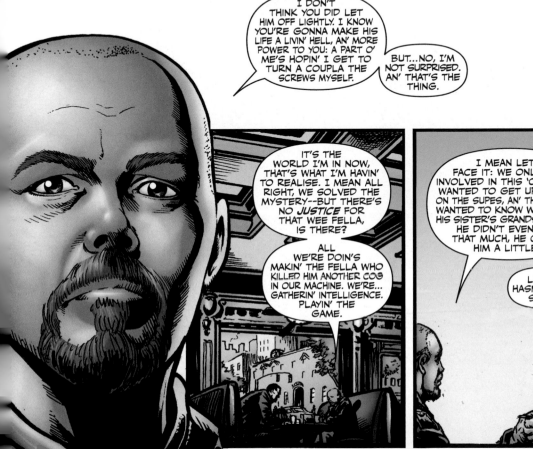

IT'S THE WORLD I'M IN NOW, THAT'S WHAT I'M HAVIN' TO REALISE. I MEAN ALL RIGHT, WE SOLVED THE MYSTERY--BUT THERE'S NO *JUSTICE* FOR THAT WEE FELLA, IS THERE?

ALL WE'RE DOIN'S MAKIN' THE FELLA WHO KILLED HIM ANOTHER COG IN OUR MACHINE. WE'RE... GATHERIN' INTELLIGENCE. PLAYIN' THE GAME.

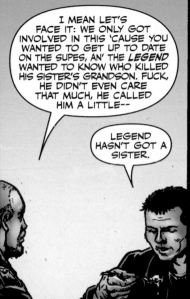

I MEAN LET'S FACE IT: WE ONLY GOT INVOLVED IN THIS 'CAUSE YOU WANTED TO GET UP TO DATE ON THE SUPES, AN' THE *LEGEND* WANTED TO KNOW WHO KILLED HIS SISTER'S GRANDSON. FUCK, HE DIDN'T EVEN CARE THAT MUCH, HE CALLED HIM A LITTLE--

LEGEND HASN'T GOT A SISTER.

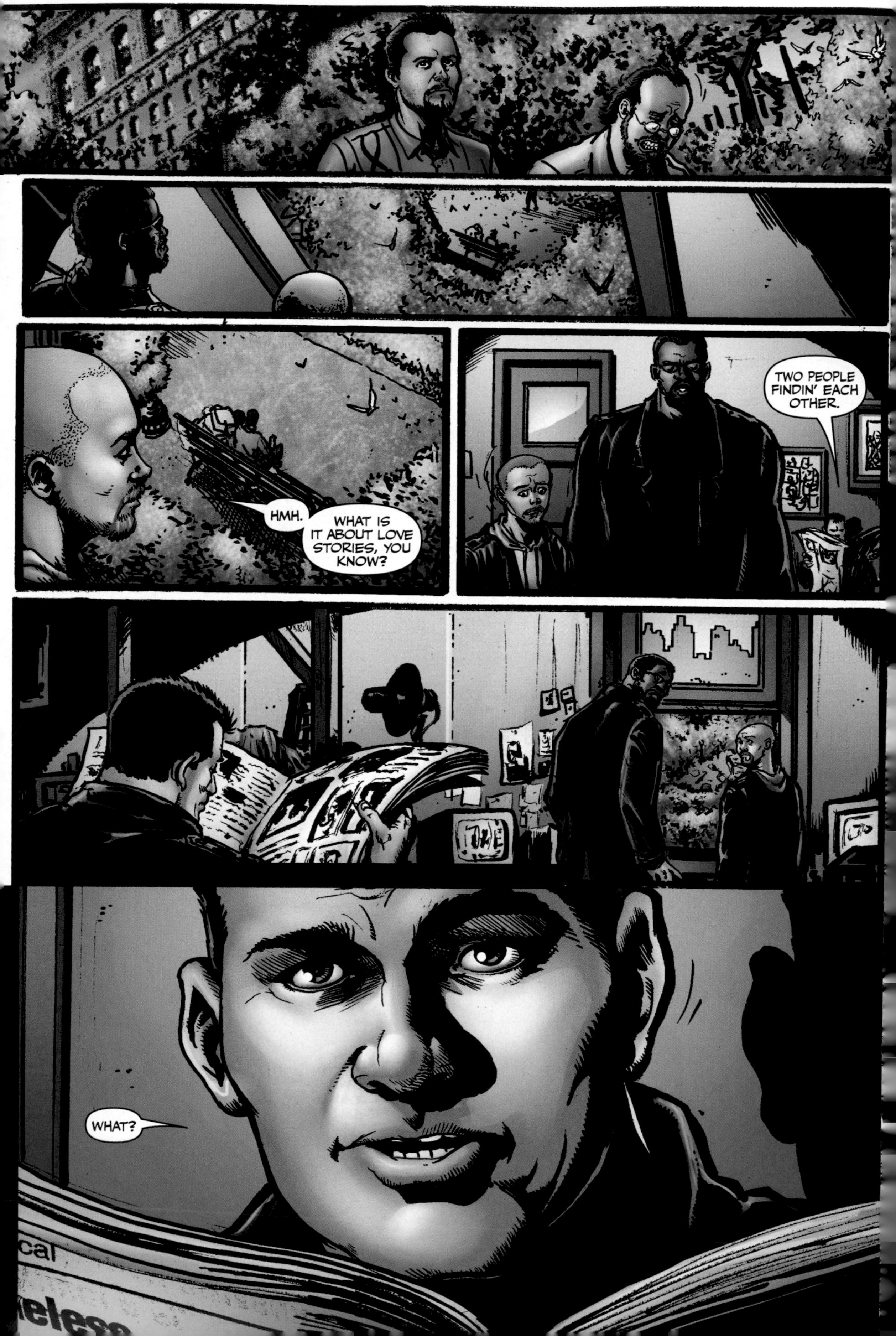
HMH.
WHAT IS IT ABOUT LOVE STORIES, YOU KNOW?
TWO PEOPLE FINDIN' EACH OTHER.
WHAT?

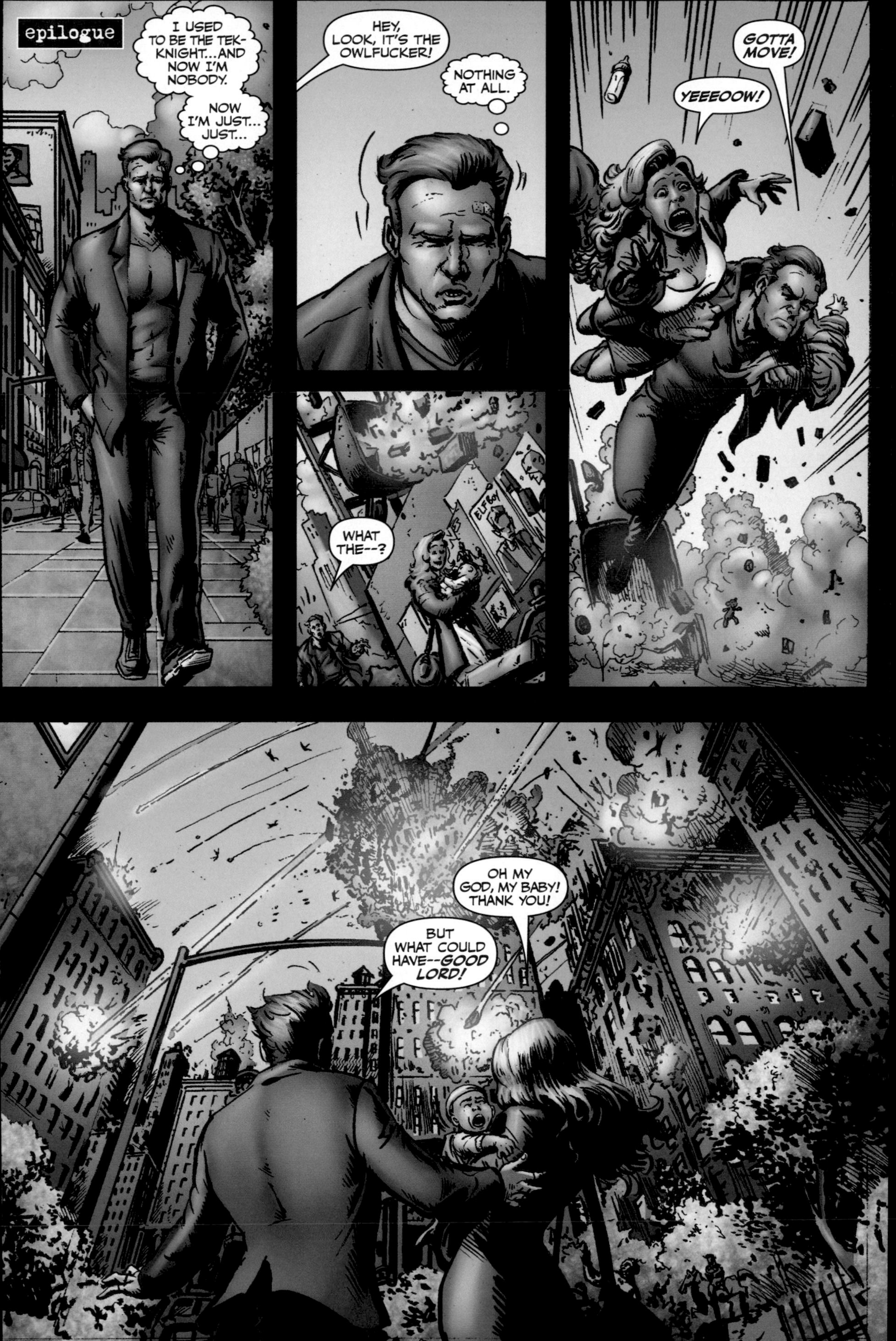
epilogue
I USED TO BE THE TEK-KNIGHT...AND NOW I'M NOBODY.
NOW I'M JUST... JUST...
HEY, LOOK, IT'S THE OWLFUCKER!
NOTHING AT ALL.
WHAT THE--?
GOTTA MOVE!
YEEEOOW!
ELF BOY
OH MY GOD, MY BABY! THANK YOU!
BUT WHAT COULD HAVE--GOOD LORD!

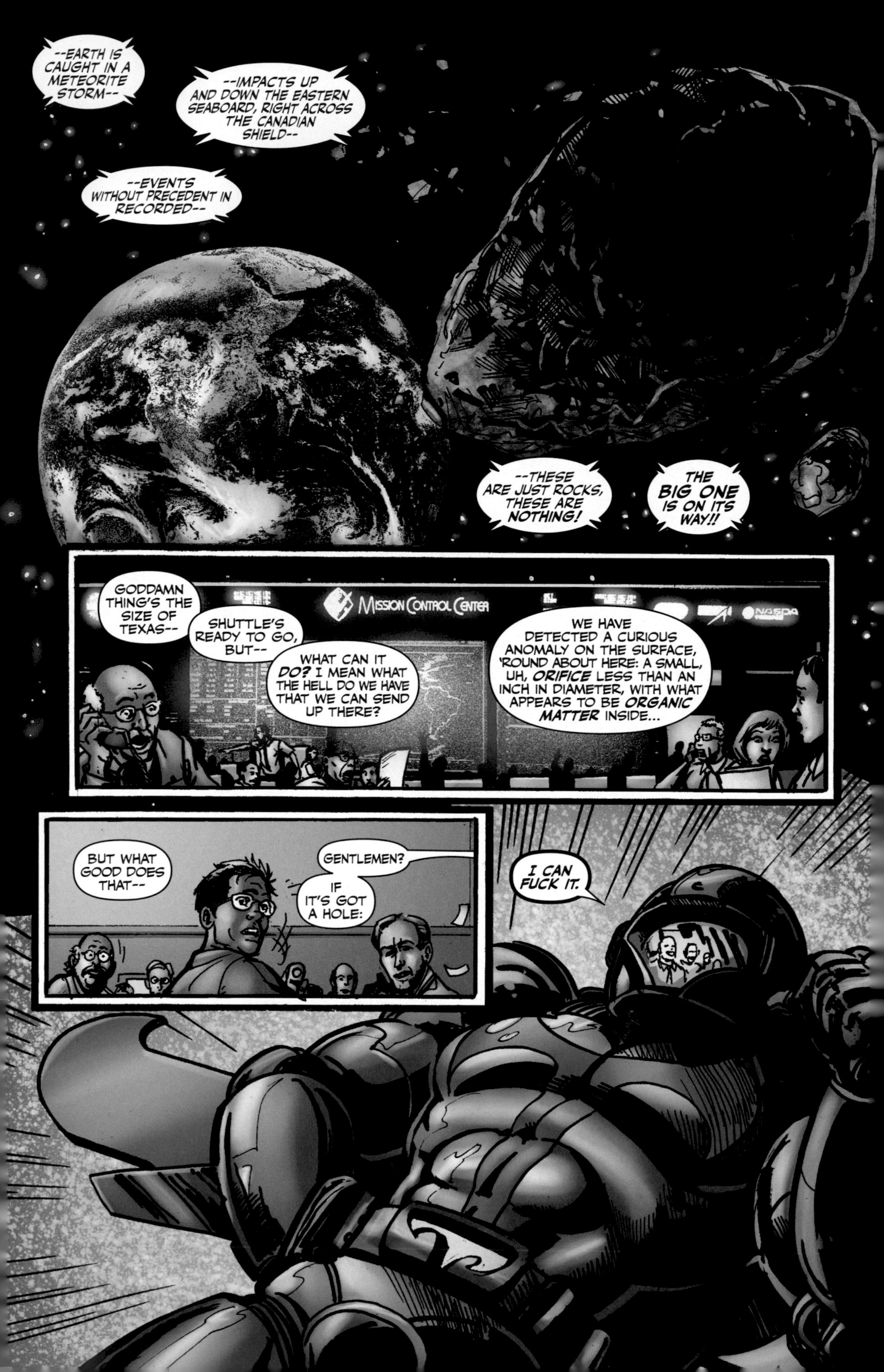
--EARTH IS CAUGHT IN A METEORITE STORM--
--IMPACTS UP AND DOWN THE EASTERN SEABOARD, RIGHT ACROSS THE CANADIAN SHIELD--
--EVENTS WITHOUT PRECEDENT IN RECORDED--
--THESE ARE JUST ROCKS, THESE ARE NOTHING!
THE BIG ONE IS ON ITS WAY!!
MISSION CONTROL CENTER
GODDAMN THING'S THE SIZE OF TEXAS--
SHUTTLE'S READY TO GO, BUT--
WHAT CAN IT DO? I MEAN WHAT THE HELL DO WE HAVE THAT WE CAN SEND UP THERE?
WE HAVE DETECTED A CURIOUS ANOMALY ON THE SURFACE, 'ROUND ABOUT HERE: A SMALL, UH, ORIFICE LESS THAN AN INCH IN DIAMETER, WITH WHAT APPEARS TO BE ORGANIC MATTER INSIDE...
BUT WHAT GOOD DOES THAT--
GENTLEMEN?
IF IT'S GOT A HOLE:
I CAN FUCK IT.

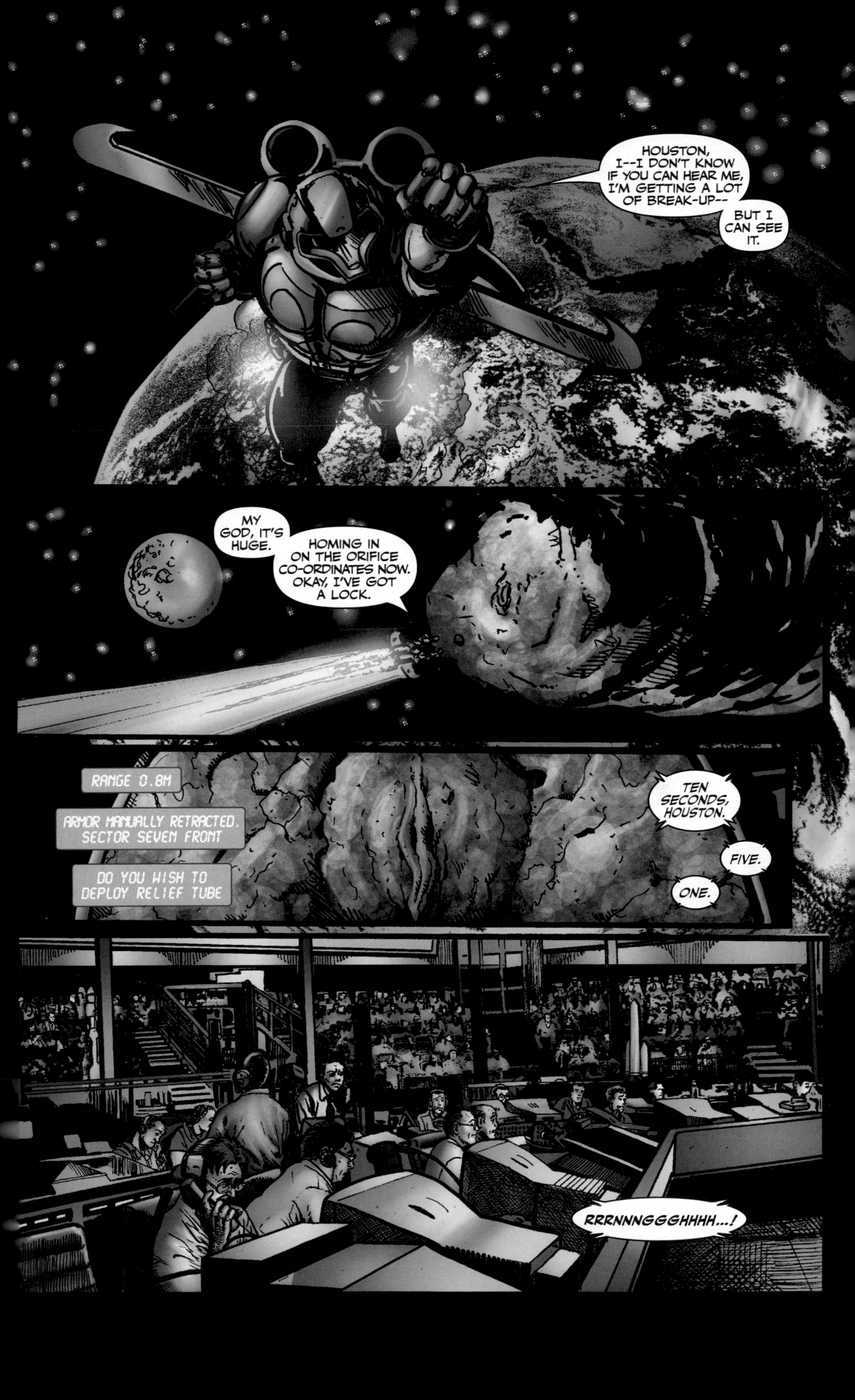
HOUSTON, I--I DON'T KNOW IF YOU CAN HEAR ME, I'M GETTING A LOT OF BREAK-UP--
BUT I CAN SEE IT.
MY GOD, IT'S HUGE.
HOMING IN ON THE ORIFICE CO-ORDINATES NOW. OKAY, I'VE GOT A LOCK.
RANGE 0.8M
ARMOR MANUALLY RETRACTED. SECTOR SEVEN FRONT
DO YOU WISH TO DEPLOY RELIEF TUBE
TEN SECONDS, HOUSTON.
FIVE.
ONE.
RRRNNNGGGHHHH...!

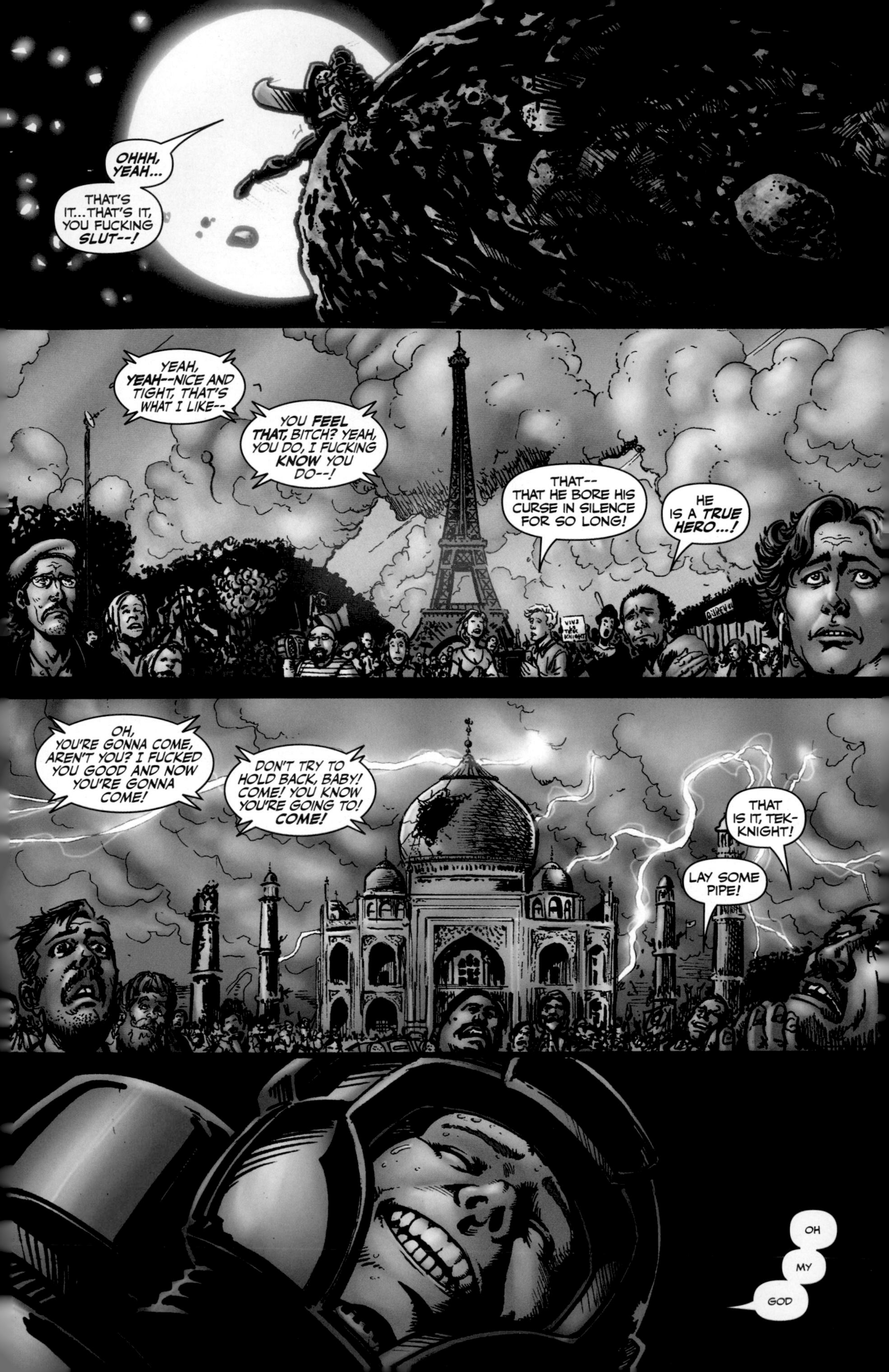
OHHH, YEAH...
THAT'S IT...THAT'S IT, YOU FUCKING SLUT--!
YEAH, YEAH--NICE AND TIGHT, THAT'S WHAT I LIKE--
YOU FEEL THAT, BITCH? YEAH, YOU DO, I FUCKING KNOW YOU DO--!
THAT-- THAT HE BORE HIS CURSE IN SILENCE FOR SO LONG!
HE IS A TRUE HERO...!
OH, YOU'RE GONNA COME, AREN'T YOU? I FUCKED YOU GOOD AND NOW YOU'RE GONNA COME!
DON'T TRY TO HOLD BACK, BABY! COME! YOU KNOW YOU'RE GOING TO! COME!
THAT IS IT, TEK-KNIGHT!
LAY SOME PIPE!
OH
MY
GOD

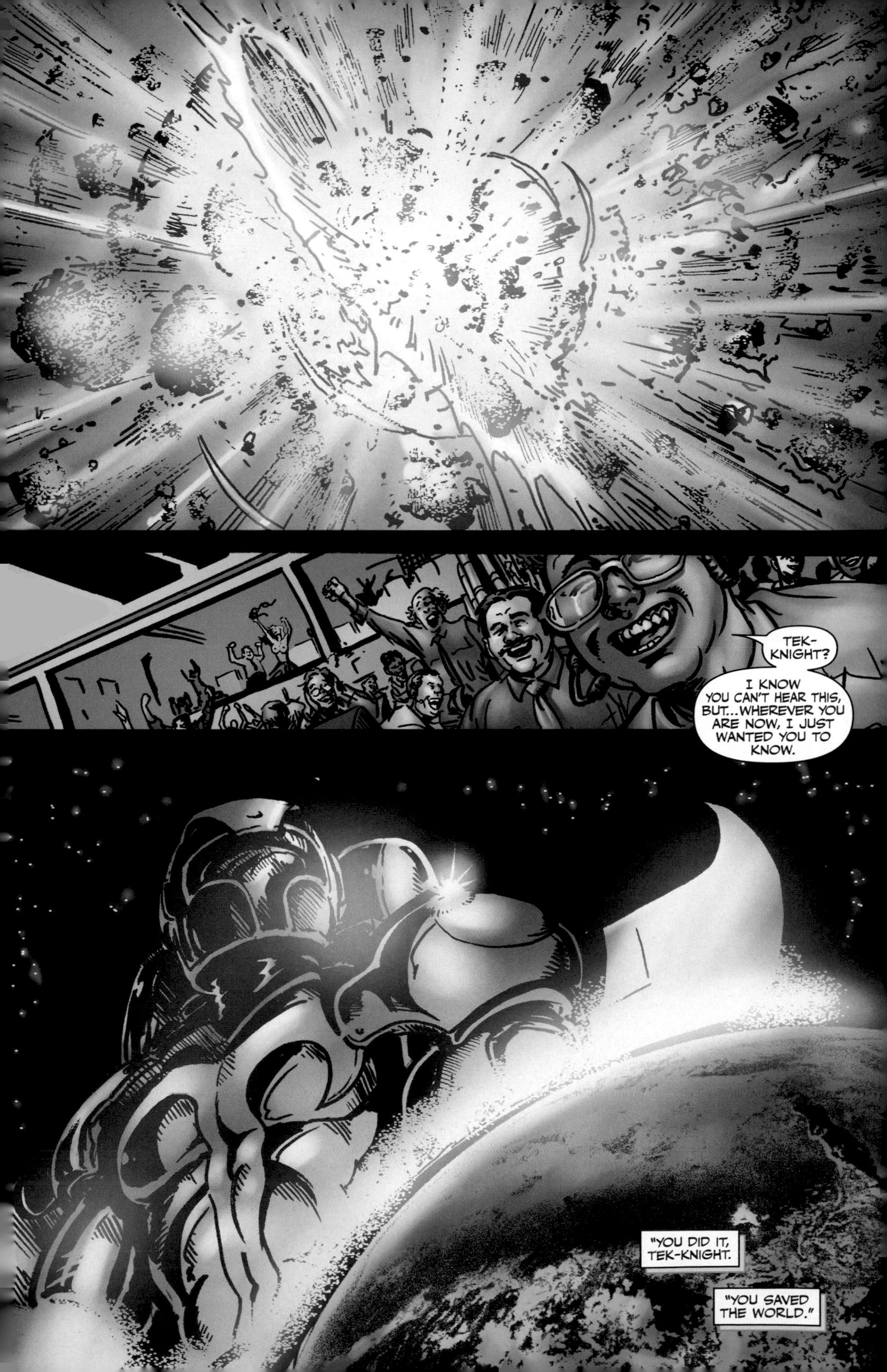
TEK-KNIGHT?
I KNOW YOU CAN'T HEAR THIS, BUT...WHEREVER YOU ARE NOW, I JUST WANTED YOU TO KNOW.
"YOU DID IT, TEK-KNIGHT.
"YOU SAVED THE WORLD."

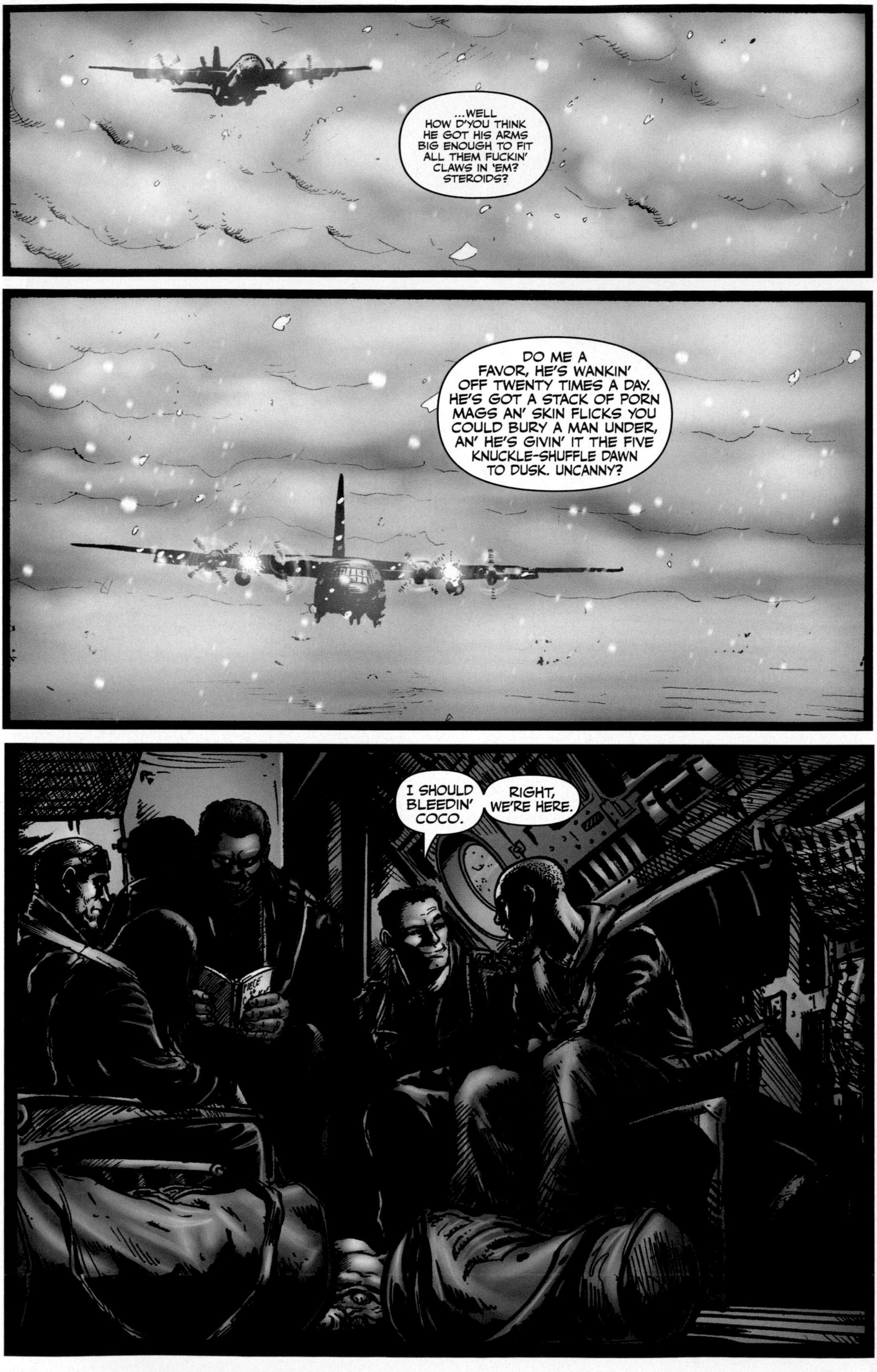
...WELL HOW D'YOU THINK HE GOT HIS ARMS BIG ENOUGH TO FIT ALL THEM FUCKIN' CLAWS IN 'EM? STEROIDS?
DO ME A FAVOR, HE'S WANKIN' OFF TWENTY TIMES A DAY. HE'S GOT A STACK OF PORN MAGS AN' SKIN FLICKS YOU COULD BURY A MAN UNDER, AN' HE'S GIVIN' IT THE FIVE KNUCKLE-SHUFFLE DAWN TO DUSK. UNCANNY?
I SHOULD BLEEDIN' COCO.
RIGHT, WE'RE HERE.

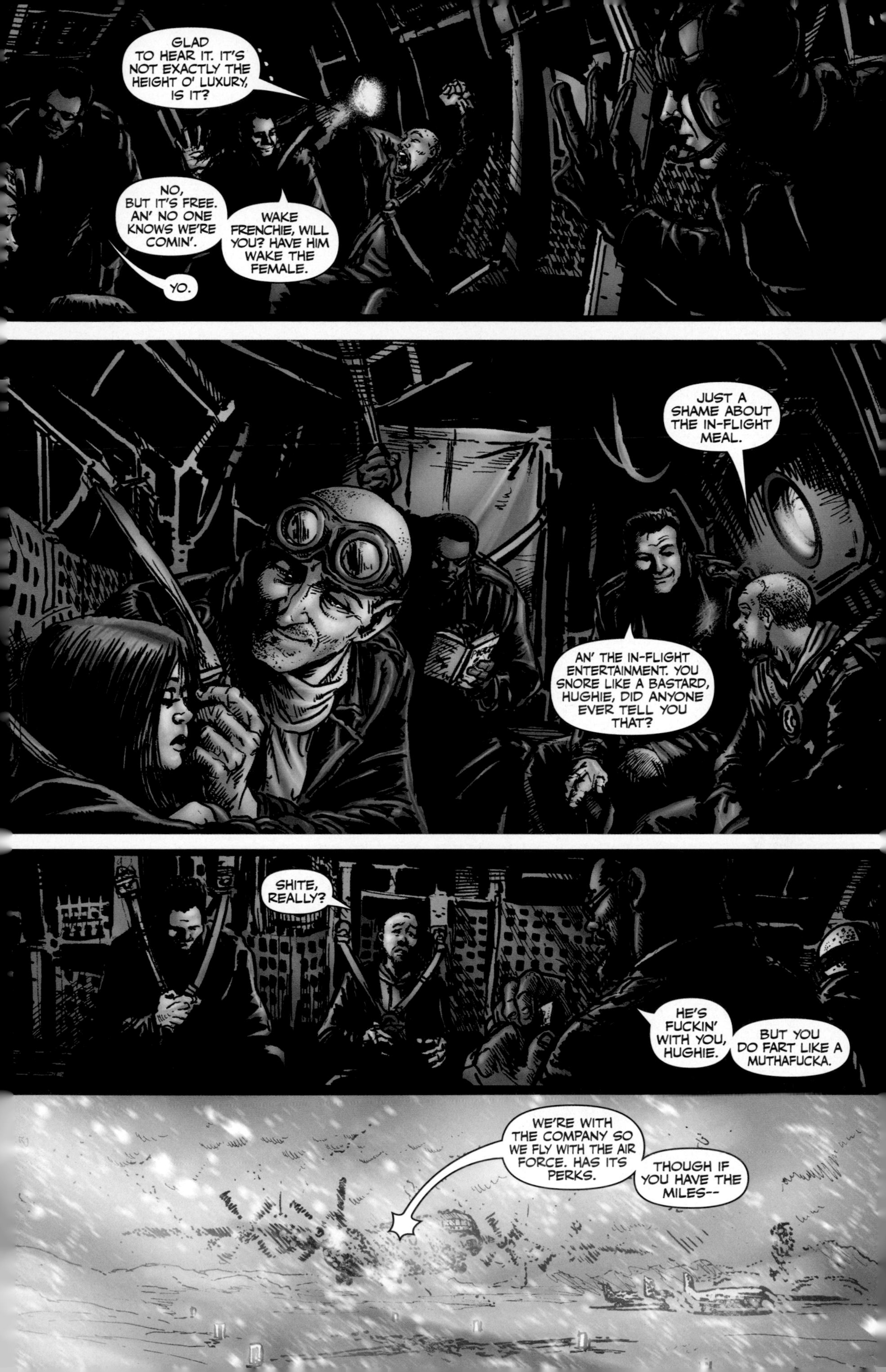
GLAD TO HEAR IT. IT'S NOT EXACTLY THE HEIGHT O' LUXURY, IS IT?
NO, BUT IT'S FREE. AN' NO ONE KNOWS WE'RE COMIN'.
WAKE FRENCHIE, WILL YOU? HAVE HIM WAKE THE FEMALE.
YO.
JUST A SHAME ABOUT THE IN-FLIGHT MEAL.
AN' THE IN-FLIGHT ENTERTAINMENT. YOU SNORE LIKE A BASTARD, HUGHIE, DID ANYONE EVER TELL YOU THAT?
SHITE, REALLY?
HE'S FUCKIN' WITH YOU, HUGHIE.
BUT YOU DO FART LIKE A MUTHAFUCKA.
WE'RE WITH THE COMPANY SO WE FLY WITH THE AIR FORCE. HAS ITS PERKS.
THOUGH IF YOU HAVE THE MILES--

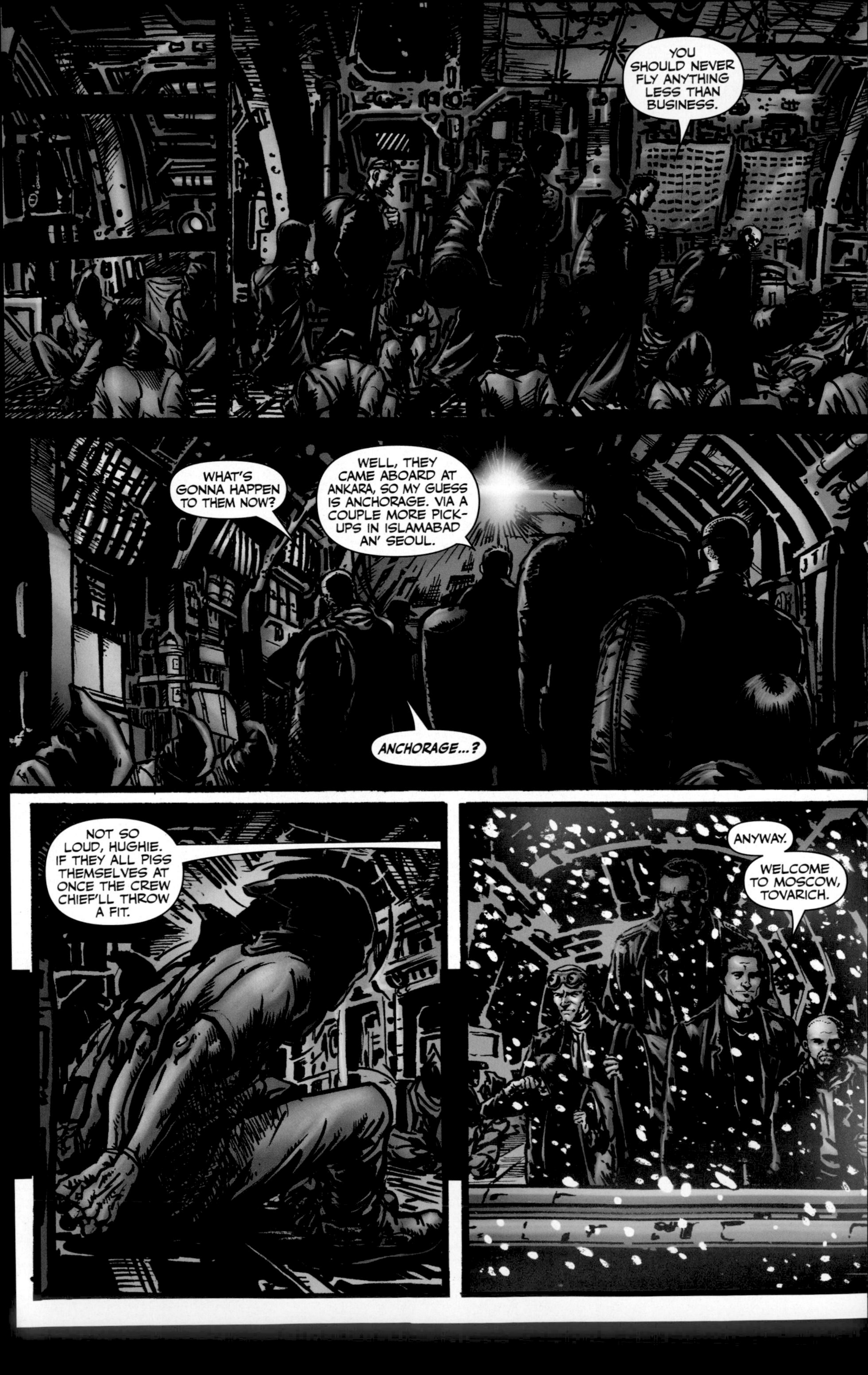
YOU SHOULD NEVER FLY ANYTHING LESS THAN BUSINESS.
WHAT'S GONNA HAPPEN TO THEM NOW?
WELL, THEY CAME ABOARD AT ANKARA, SO MY GUESS IS ANCHORAGE. VIA A COUPLE MORE PICK-UPS IN ISLAMABAD AN' SEOUL.
ANCHORAGE...?
NOT SO LOUD, HUGHIE. IF THEY ALL PISS THEMSELVES AT ONCE THE CREW CHIEF'LL THROW A FIT.
ANYWAY.
WELCOME TO MOSCOW, TOVARICH.

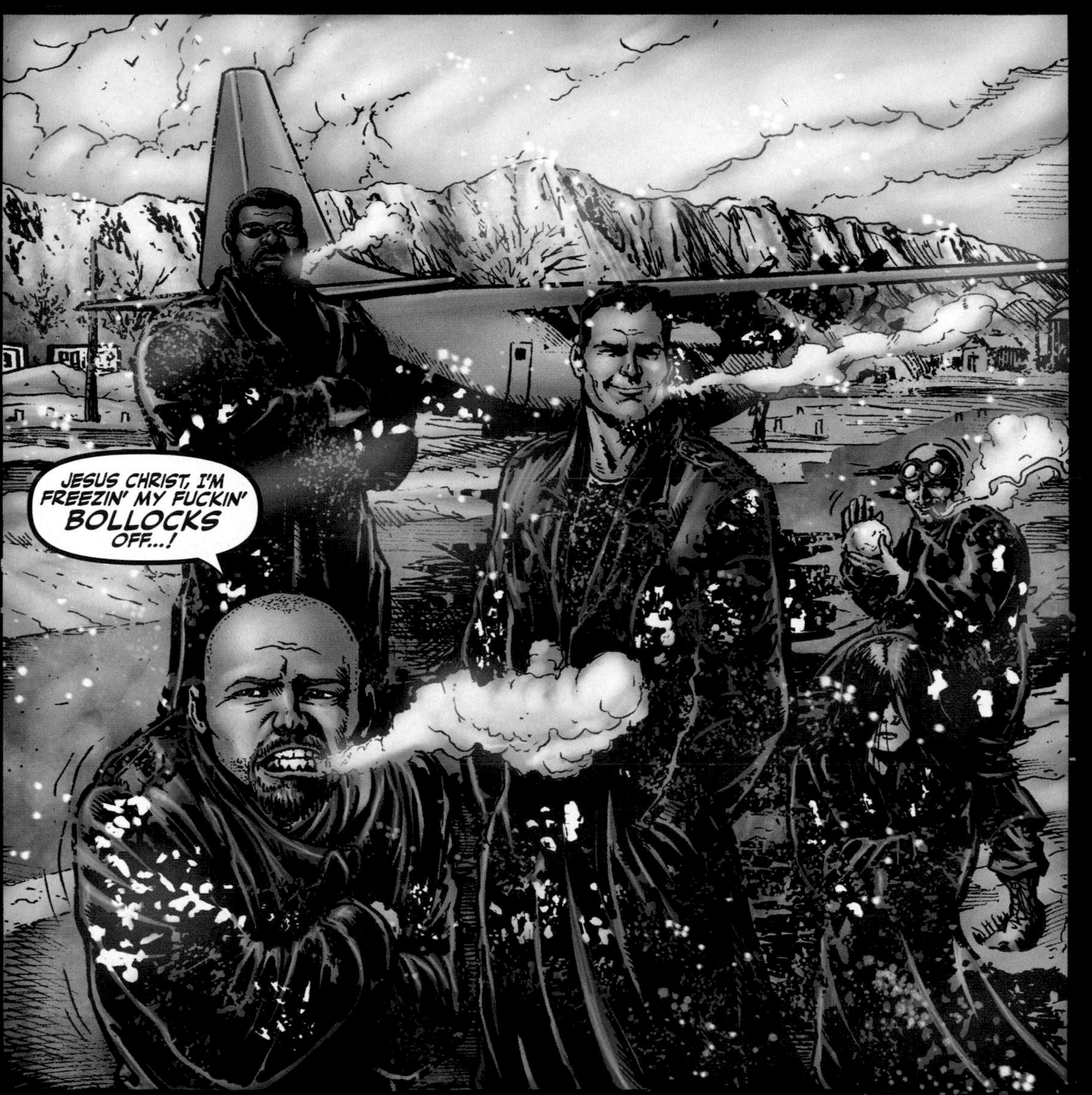
JESUS CHRIST, I'M FREEZIN' MY FUCKIN' BOLLOCKS OFF...!

GLORIOUS FIVE YEAR PLAN

part one

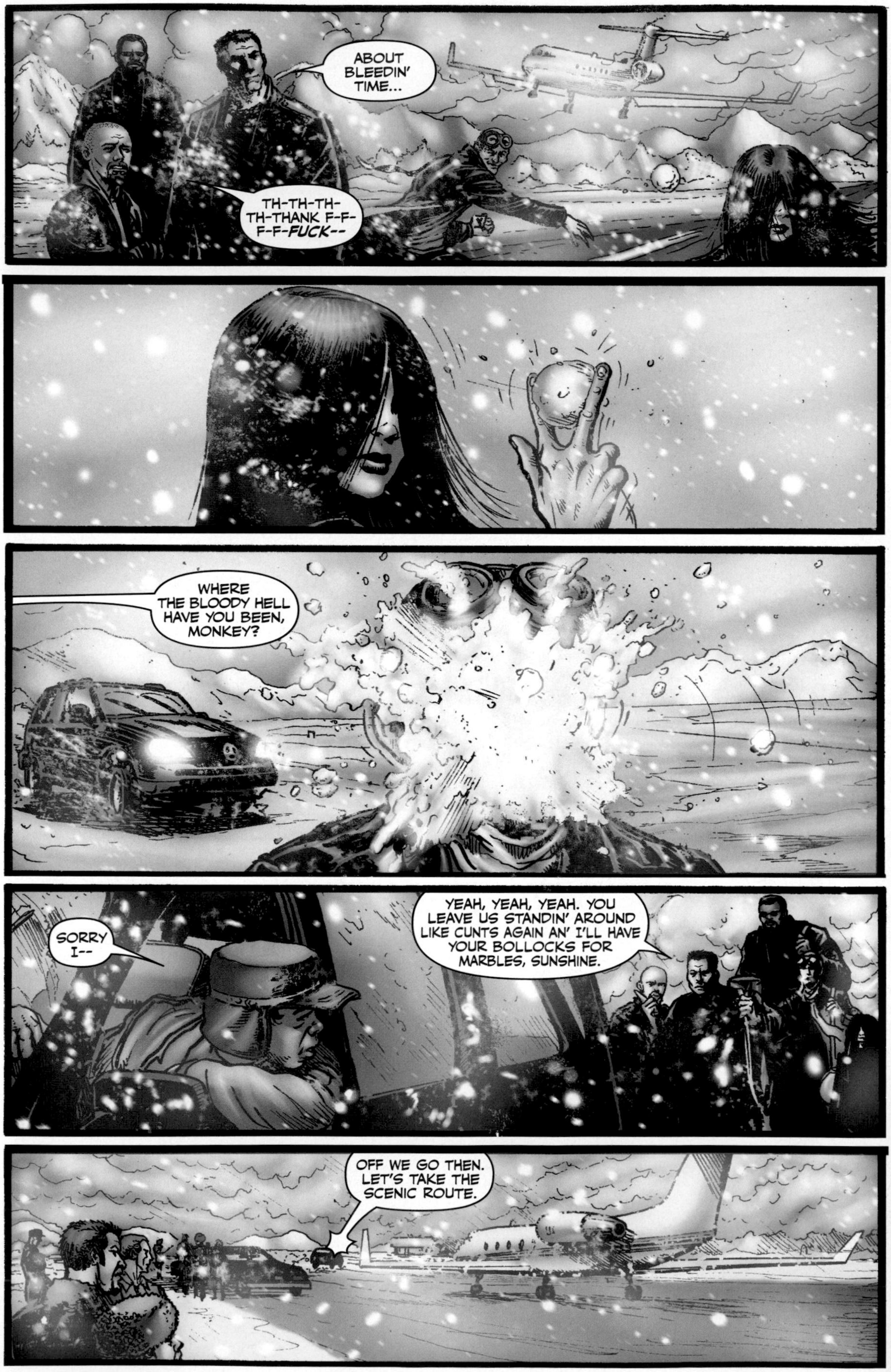
ABOUT BLEEDIN' TIME...
TH-TH-TH-TH-THANK F-F-F-F-FUCK--
WHERE THE BLOODY HELL HAVE YOU BEEN, MONKEY?
SORRY I--
YEAH, YEAH, YEAH. YOU LEAVE US STANDIN' AROUND LIKE CUNTS AGAIN AN' I'LL HAVE YOUR BOLLOCKS FOR MARBLES, SUNSHINE.
OFF WE GO THEN. LET'S TAKE THE SCENIC ROUTE.

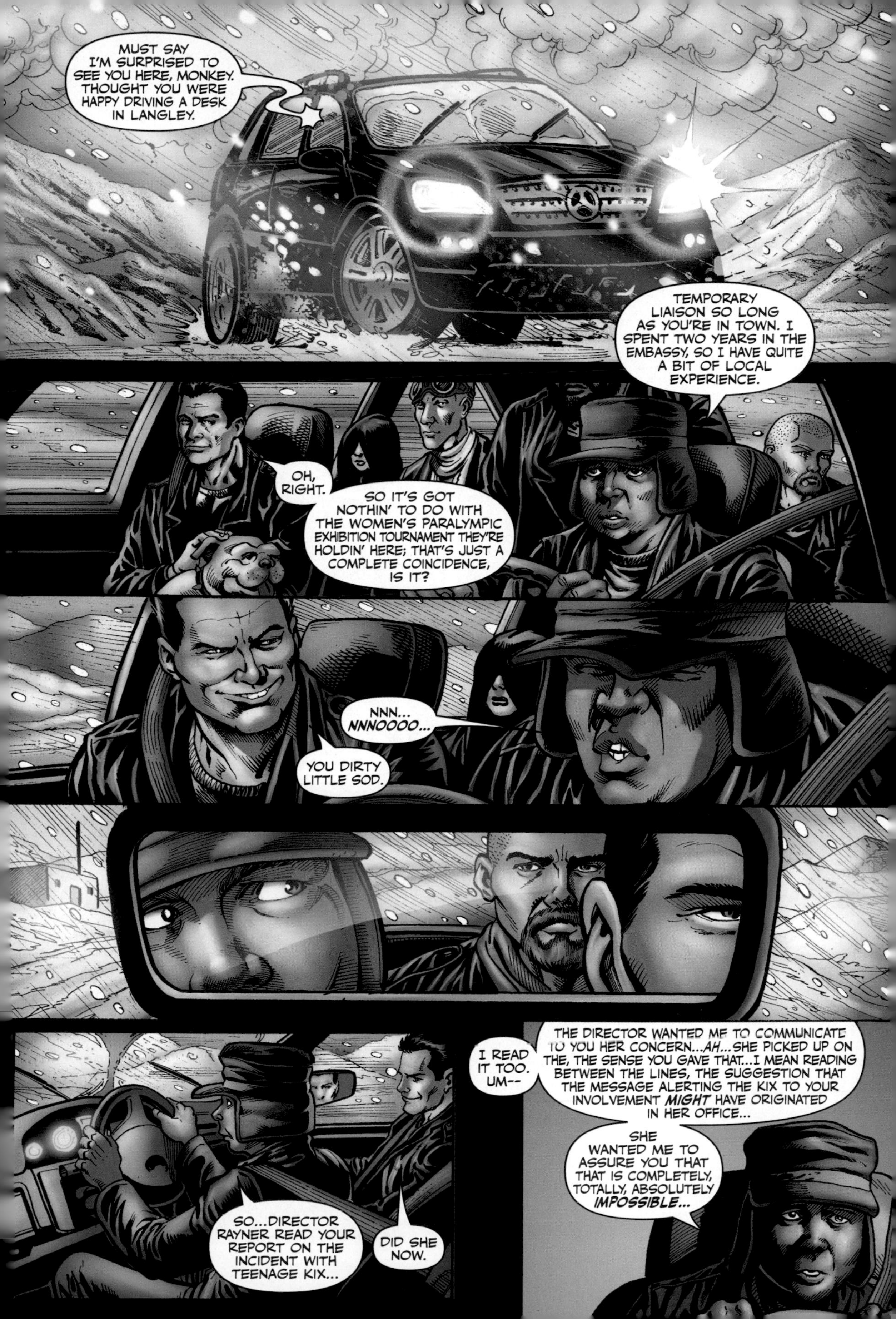
MUST SAY I'M SURPRISED TO SEE YOU HERE, MONKEY. THOUGHT YOU WERE HAPPY DRIVING A DESK IN LANGLEY.
TEMPORARY LIAISON SO LONG AS YOU'RE IN TOWN. I SPENT TWO YEARS IN THE EMBASSY, SO I HAVE QUITE A BIT OF LOCAL EXPERIENCE.
OH, RIGHT.
SO IT'S GOT NOTHIN' TO DO WITH THE WOMEN'S PARALYMPIC EXHIBITION TOURNAMENT THEY'RE HOLDIN' HERE; THAT'S JUST A COMPLETE COINCIDENCE, IS IT?
NNN... NNNOOOO...
YOU DIRTY LITTLE SOD.
SO...DIRECTOR RAYNER READ YOUR REPORT ON THE INCIDENT WITH TEENAGE KIX...
DID SHE NOW.
I READ IT TOO. UM--
THE DIRECTOR WANTED ME TO COMMUNICATE TO YOU HER CONCERN...AH...SHE PICKED UP ON THE, THE SENSE YOU GAVE THAT...I MEAN READING BETWEEN THE LINES, THE SUGGESTION THAT THE MESSAGE ALERTING THE KIX TO YOUR INVOLVEMENT MIGHT HAVE ORIGINATED IN HER OFFICE...
SHE WANTED ME TO ASSURE YOU THAT THAT IS COMPLETELY, TOTALLY, ABSOLUTELY IMPOSSIBLE...

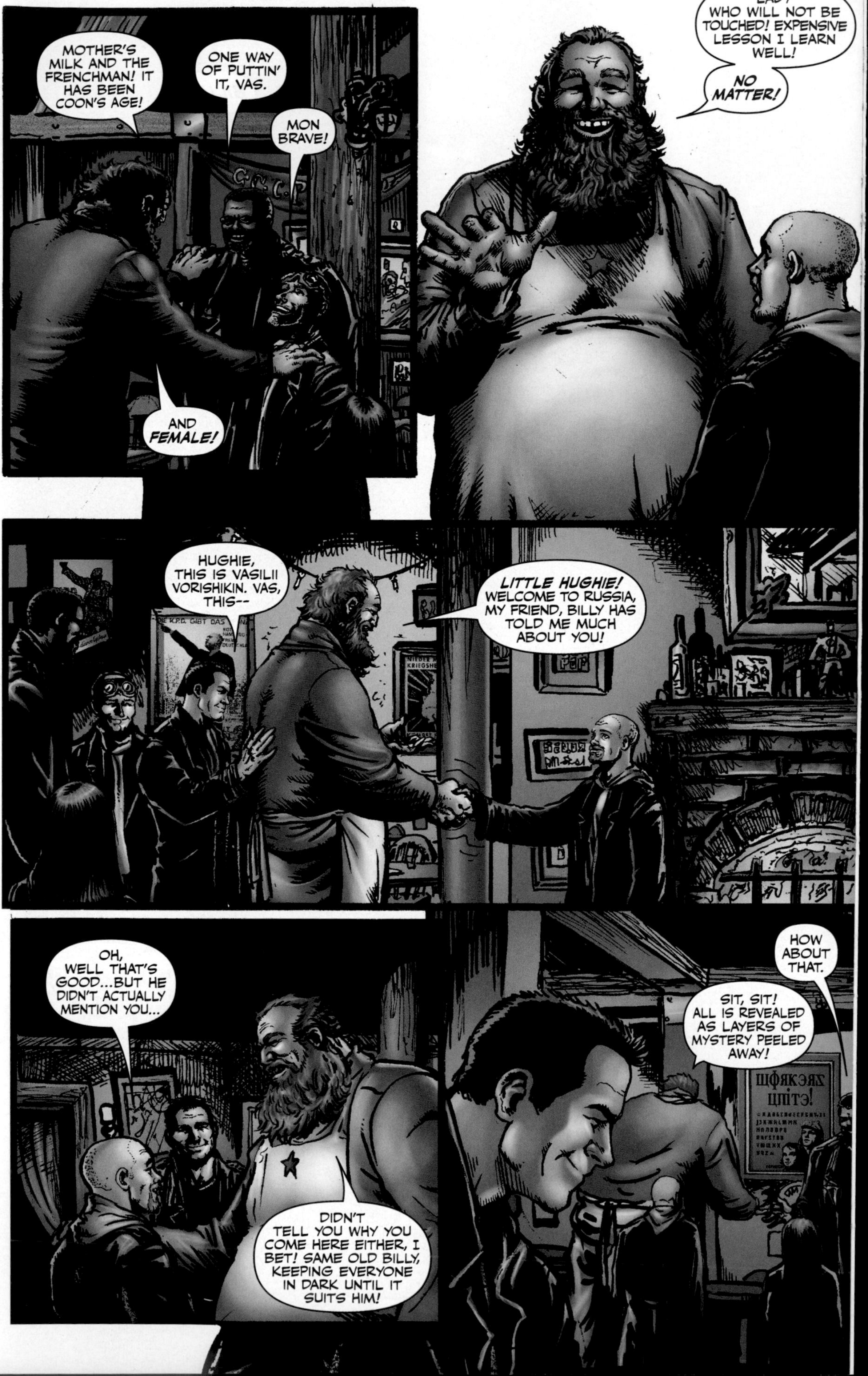
MOTHER'S MILK AND THE FRENCHMAN! IT HAS BEEN COON'S AGE!
ONE WAY OF PUTTIN' IT, VAS.
MON BRAVE!
AND FEMALE!
LADY WHO WILL NOT BE TOUCHED! EXPENSIVE LESSON I LEARN WELL!
NO MATTER!
HUGHIE, THIS IS VASILII VORISHIKIN. VAS, THIS--
LITTLE HUGHIE! WELCOME TO RUSSIA, MY FRIEND, BILLY HAS TOLD ME MUCH ABOUT YOU!
OH, WELL THAT'S GOOD...BUT HE DIDN'T ACTUALLY MENTION YOU...
DIDN'T TELL YOU WHY YOU COME HERE EITHER, I BET! SAME OLD BILLY, KEEPING EVERYONE IN DARK UNTIL IT SUITS HIM!
HOW ABOUT THAT.
SIT, SIT! ALL IS REVEALED AS LAYERS OF MYSTERY PEELED AWAY!

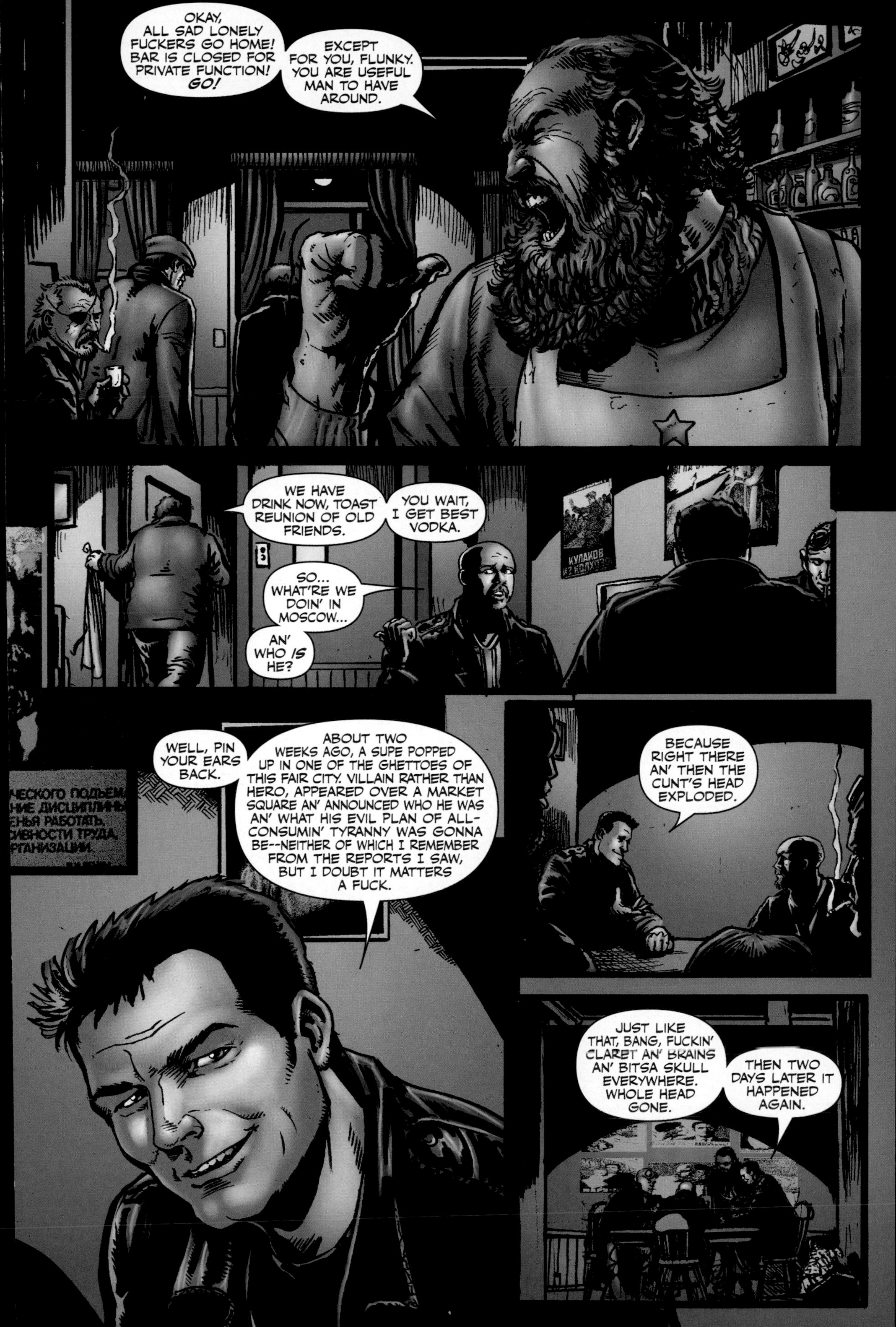

OKAY, ALL SAD LONELY FUCKERS GO HOME! BAR IS CLOSED FOR PRIVATE FUNCTION! *GO!*
EXCEPT FOR YOU, FLUNKY. YOU ARE USEFUL MAN TO HAVE AROUND.
WE HAVE DRINK NOW, TOAST REUNION OF OLD FRIENDS.
YOU WAIT, I GET BEST VODKA.
SO... WHAT'RE WE DOIN' IN MOSCOW...
AN' WHO *IS* HE?
КУЛАКОВ
WELL, PIN YOUR EARS BACK.
ABOUT TWO WEEKS AGO, A SUPE POPPED UP IN ONE OF THE GHETTOES OF THIS FAIR CITY. VILLAIN RATHER THAN HERO, APPEARED OVER A MARKET SQUARE AN' ANNOUNCED WHO HE WAS AN' WHAT HIS EVIL PLAN OF ALL-CONSUMIN' TYRANNY WAS GONNA BE--NEITHER OF WHICH I REMEMBER FROM THE REPORTS I SAW, BUT I DOUBT IT MATTERS A FUCK.
BECAUSE RIGHT THERE AN' THEN THE CUNT'S HEAD EXPLODED.
JUST LIKE THAT, BANG, FUCKIN' CLARET AN' BRAINS AN' BITSA SKULL EVERYWHERE. WHOLE HEAD GONE.
THEN TWO DAYS LATER IT HAPPENED AGAIN.

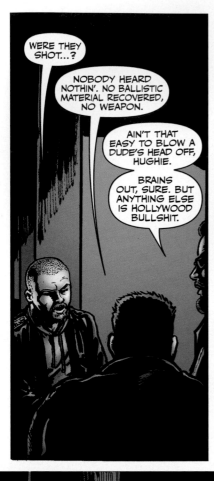

WERE THEY SHOT...?

NOBODY HEARD NOTHIN'. NO BALLISTIC MATERIAL RECOVERED, NO WEAPON.

AIN'T THAT EASY TO BLOW A DUDE'S HEAD OFF, HUGHIE.

BRAINS OUT, SURE. BUT ANYTHING ELSE IS HOLLYWOOD BULLSHIT.

FIFTY CALIBER, AVEC SILENCIEUX? TWELVE POINT SEVEN MILLI?

VAS IS GETTING' US INTO THE MORGUE THIS AFTERNOON, FRENCHIE. YOU CAN HAVE A PROPER DEKKO THEN, ALL RIGHT?

BACK IN THE EARLY NINETIES, I READ ABOUT SOME EGGHEAD HAVIN' A GO AT A BOOSTED VERSION OF COMPOUND V— BOOSTED PAST THE POINT IT STOPPED BEIN' STABLE, APPARENTLY.

IDEA WAS, YOU COULD INJECT THIS STUFF INTO A SUPE AN' IT'D BE LIKE A CHEMICAL TIME BOMB. GET THE DOSE RIGHT AN' THE BODY'D TEAR ITSELF APART. COMPLETELY UNTRACEABLE, THE TWATS'RE ALL SHOT FULL OF V TO BEGIN WITH.

BUT WHY WOULD ANYONE WANT TO...

KILL SUPES? I HAVEN'T THE SLIGHTEST IDEA, MATE.

IT DIDN'T WORK.

NO. TOO UNSTABLE. THEY SHOT IT INTO V'ED UP CHIMPS, AN' HALF THE TIME NOTHIN' HAPPENED AT ALL.

THE OTHER HALF, YOU COULDN'T PREDICT WHEN IT WAS GONNA GO OFF. ONE EXPLODED *TWO YEARS* AFTER INJECTION, WHEN IT'D BEEN SOLD TO A FUCKIN' ZOO...

WE DRINK!

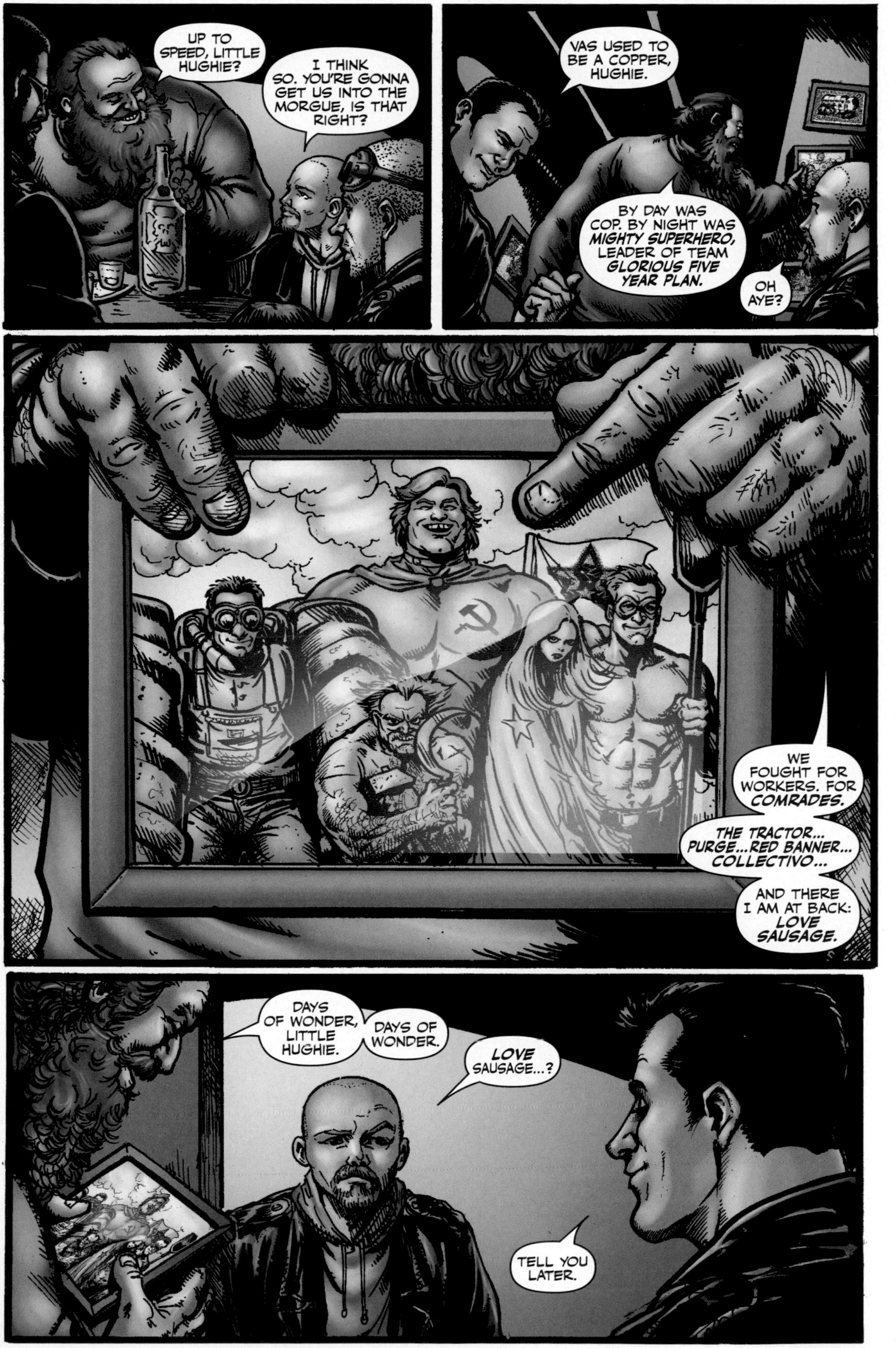
UP TO SPEED, LITTLE HUGHIE?
I THINK SO. YOU'RE GONNA GET US INTO THE MORGUE, IS THAT RIGHT?
VAS USED TO BE A COPPER, HUGHIE.
BY DAY WAS COP. BY NIGHT WAS MIGHTY SUPERHERO, LEADER OF TEAM GLORIOUS FIVE YEAR PLAN.
OH AYE?
WE FOUGHT FOR WORKERS. FOR COMRADES.
THE TRACTOR... PURGE...RED BANNER... COLLECTIVO...
AND THERE I AM AT BACK: LOVE SAUSAGE.
DAYS OF WONDER, LITTLE HUGHIE.
DAYS OF WONDER.
LOVE SAUSAGE...?
TELL YOU LATER.

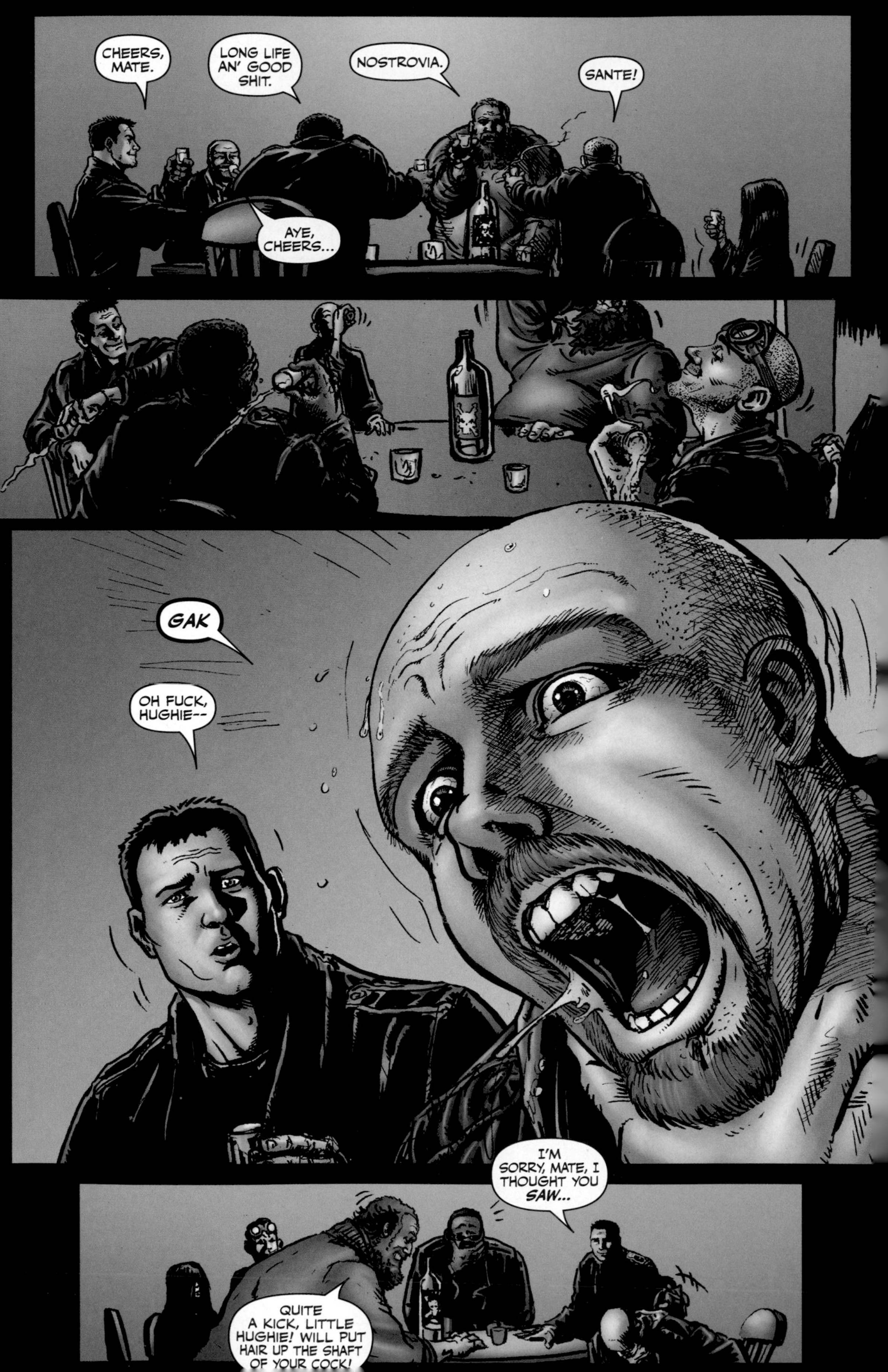
CHEERS, MATE.
LONG LIFE AN' GOOD SHIT.
NOSTROVIA.
SANTE!
AYE, CHEERS...
GAK
OH FUCK, HUGHIE--
I'M SORRY, MATE, I THOUGHT YOU SAW...
QUITE A KICK, LITTLE HUGHIE! WILL PUT HAIR UP THE SHAFT OF YOUR COCK!

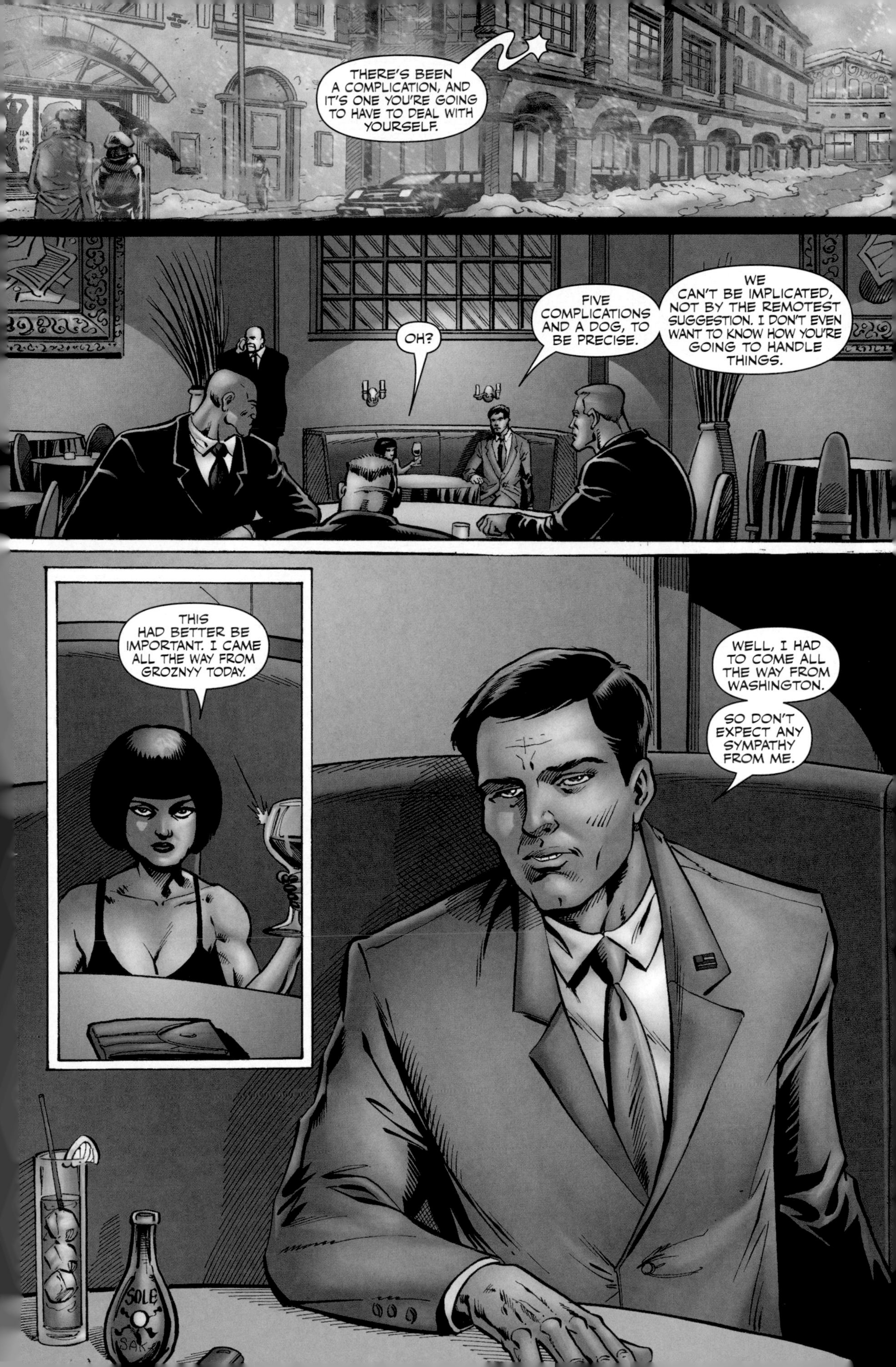
THERE'S BEEN A COMPLICATION, AND IT'S ONE YOU'RE GOING TO HAVE TO DEAL WITH YOURSELF.
OH?
FIVE COMPLICATIONS AND A DOG, TO BE PRECISE.
WE CAN'T BE IMPLICATED, NOT BY THE REMOTEST SUGGESTION. I DON'T EVEN WANT TO KNOW HOW YOU'RE GOING TO HANDLE THINGS.
THIS HAD BETTER BE IMPORTANT. I CAME ALL THE WAY FROM GROZNYY TODAY.
WELL, I HAD TO COME ALL THE WAY FROM WASHINGTON.
SO DON'T EXPECT ANY SYMPATHY FROM ME.
SOLE

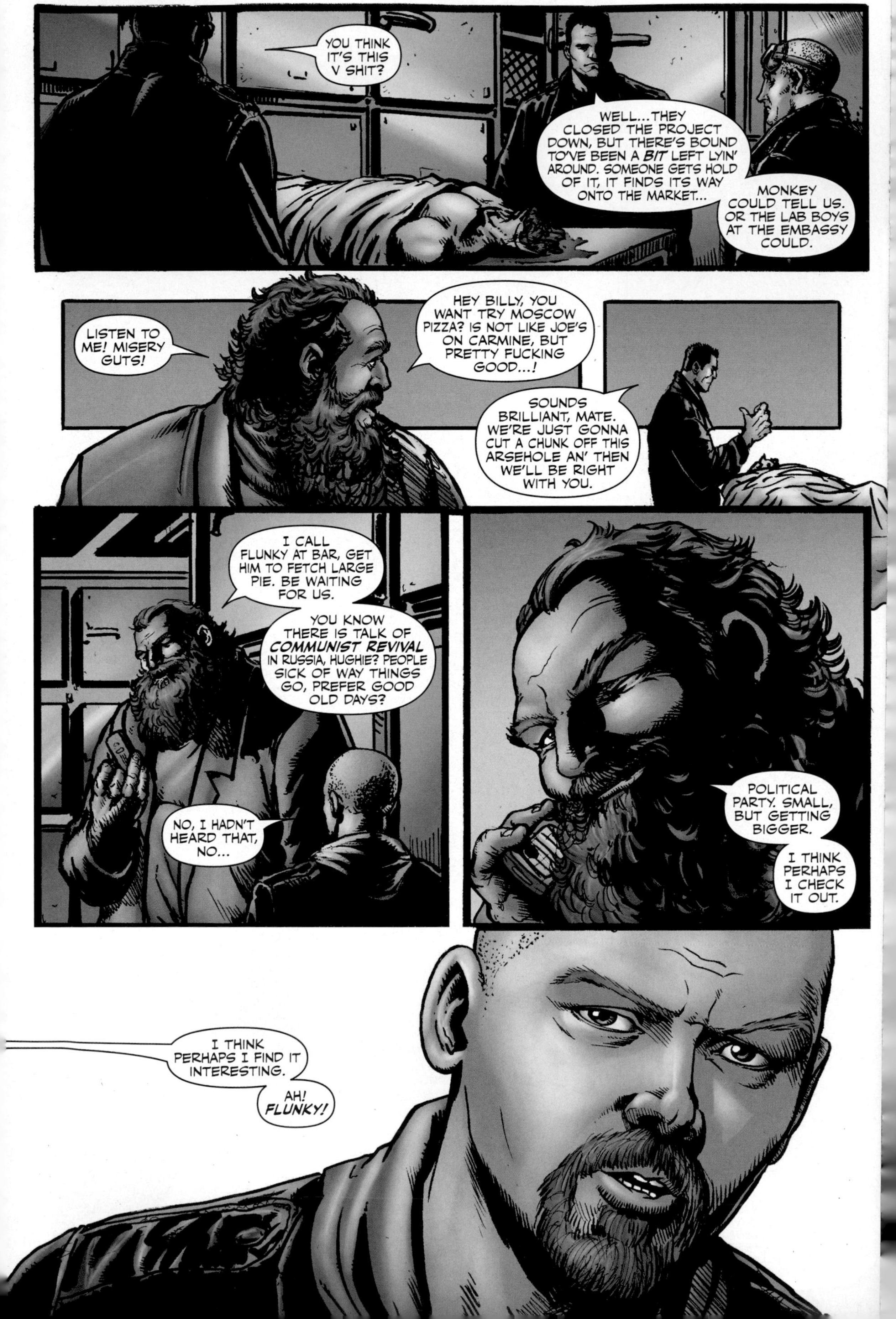
YOU THINK IT'S THIS V SHIT?
WELL...THEY CLOSED THE PROJECT DOWN, BUT THERE'S BOUND TO'VE BEEN A *BIT* LEFT LYIN' AROUND. SOMEONE GETS HOLD OF IT, IT FINDS ITS WAY ONTO THE MARKET...
MONKEY COULD TELL US. OR THE LAB BOYS AT THE EMBASSY COULD.
LISTEN TO ME! MISERY GUTS!
HEY BILLY, YOU WANT TRY MOSCOW PIZZA? IS NOT LIKE JOE'S ON CARMINE, BUT PRETTY FUCKING GOOD...!
SOUNDS BRILLIANT, MATE. WE'RE JUST GONNA CUT A CHUNK OFF THIS ARSEHOLE AN' THEN WE'LL BE RIGHT WITH YOU.
I CALL FLUNKY AT BAR, GET HIM TO FETCH LARGE PIE. BE WAITING FOR US.
YOU KNOW THERE IS TALK OF ***COMMUNIST REVIVAL*** IN RUSSIA, HUGHIE? PEOPLE SICK OF WAY THINGS GO, PREFER GOOD OLD DAYS?
NO, I HADN'T HEARD THAT, NO...
POLITICAL PARTY. SMALL, BUT GETTING BIGGER.
I THINK PERHAPS I CHECK IT OUT.
I THINK PERHAPS I FIND IT INTERESTING.
AH! ***FLUNKY!***

WHERE THE HELL IS FLUNKY?

SHOULD BE HERE BY NOW. WITH PIZZA.

PATHETIC COCKROACH.

STALINGRAD

NOT LIKE THIS IN OLD DAYS... NO...

SO VAS USED TO BE A SUPE, THEN?

THAT'S RIGHT, YEAH.

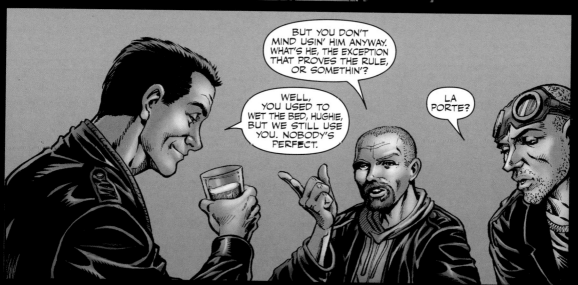

BUT YOU DON'T MIND USIN' HIM ANYWAY. WHAT'S HE, THE EXCEPTION THAT PROVES THE RULE, OR SOMETHIN'?

WELL, YOU USED TO WET THE BED, HUGHIE, BUT WE STILL USE YOU. NOBODY'S PERFECT.

LA PORTE?

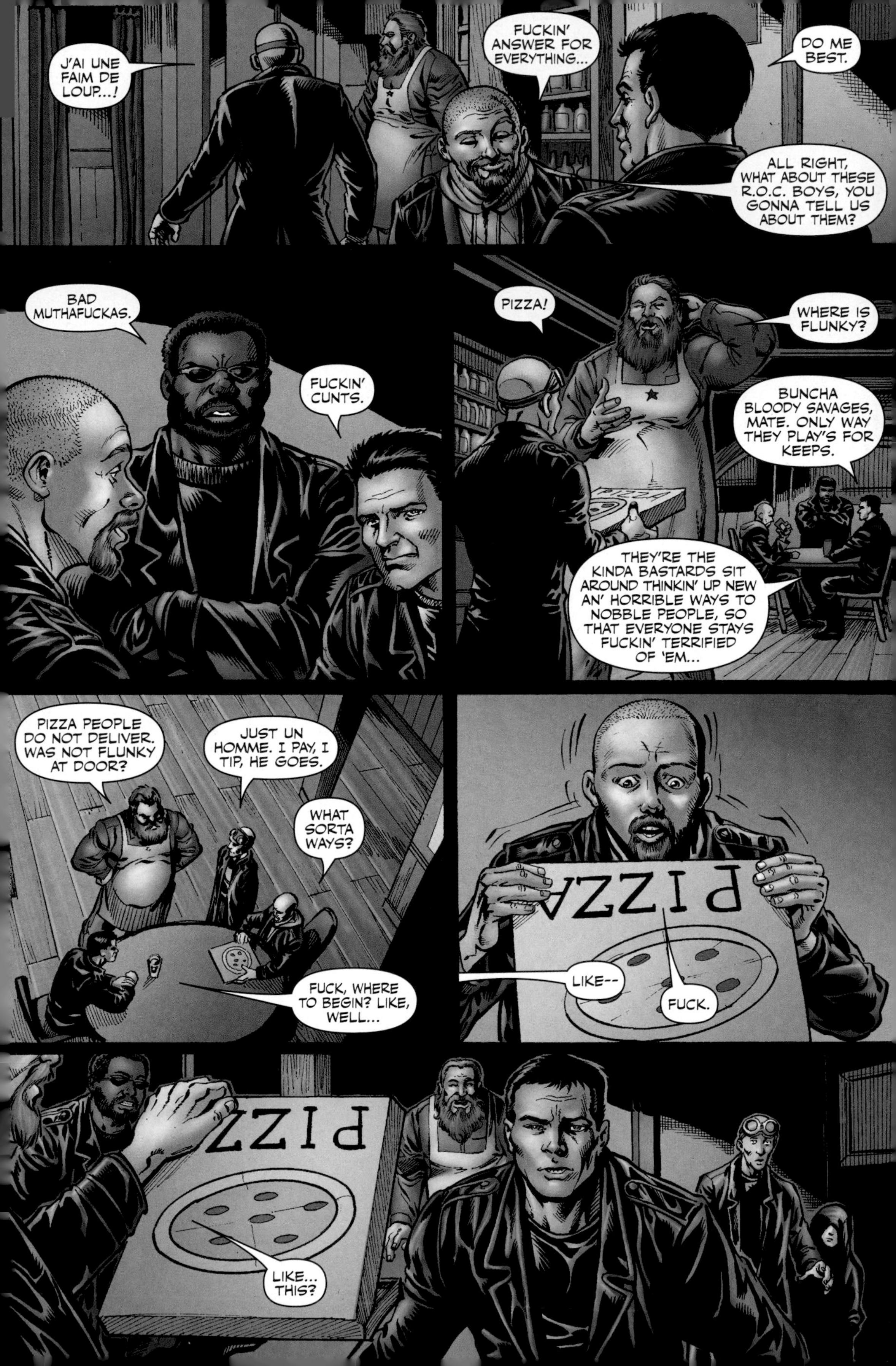
J'AI UNE FAIM DE LOUP...!
FUCKIN' ANSWER FOR EVERYTHING...
DO ME BEST.
ALL RIGHT, WHAT ABOUT THESE R.O.C. BOYS, YOU GONNA TELL US ABOUT THEM?
BAD MUTHAFUCKAS.
FUCKIN' CUNTS.
PIZZA!
WHERE IS FLUNKY?
BUNCHA BLOODY SAVAGES, MATE. ONLY WAY THEY PLAY'S FOR KEEPS.
THEY'RE THE KINDA BASTARDS SIT AROUND THINKIN' UP NEW AN' HORRIBLE WAYS TO NOBBLE PEOPLE, SO THAT EVERYONE STAYS FUCKIN' TERRIFIED OF 'EM...
PIZZA PEOPLE DO NOT DELIVER. WAS NOT FLUNKY AT DOOR?
JUST UN HOMME. I PAY, I TIP, HE GOES.
WHAT SORTA WAYS?
FUCK, WHERE TO BEGIN? LIKE, WELL...
PIZZA
LIKE--
FUCK.
PIZZ
LIKE... THIS?

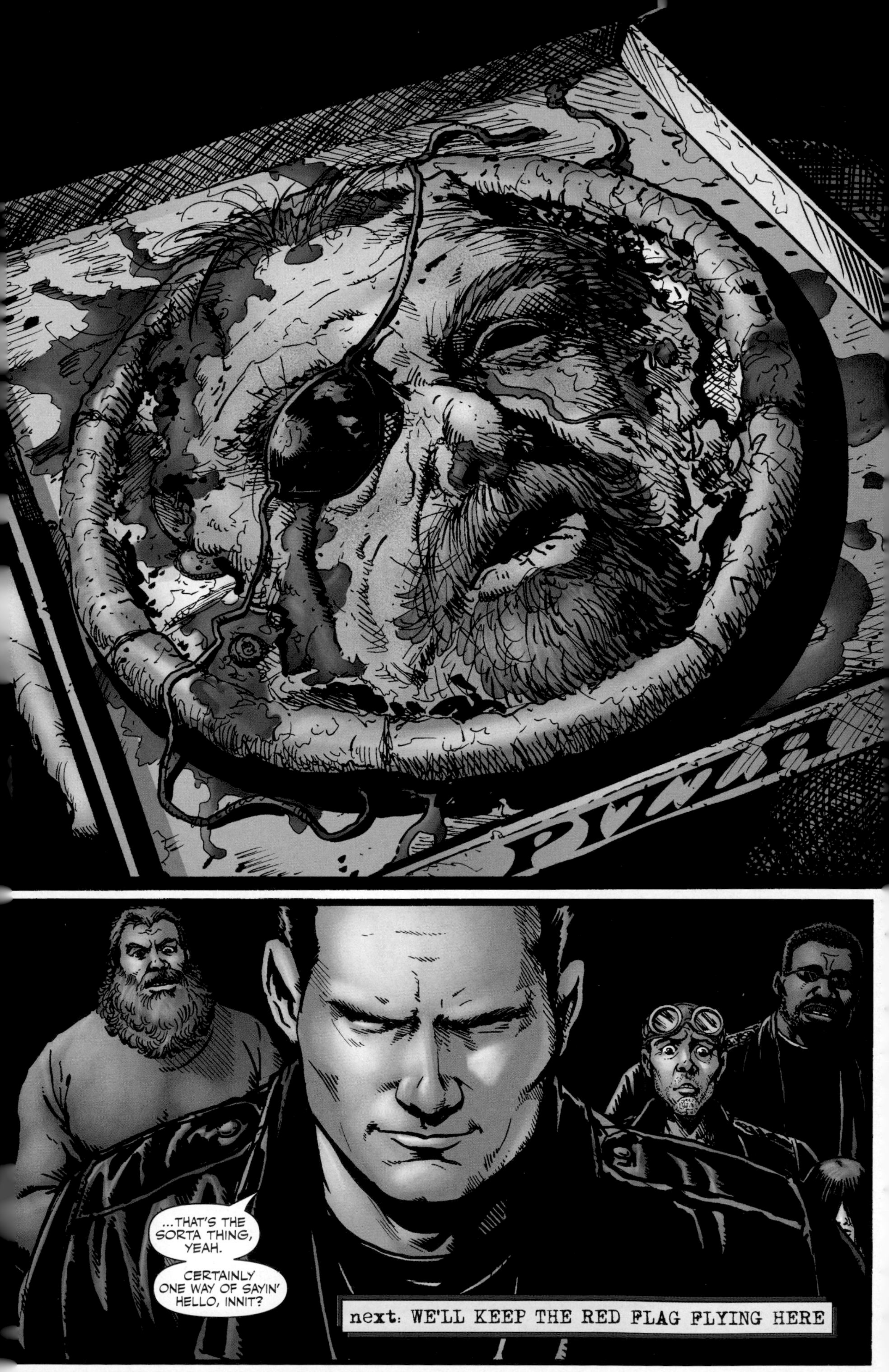
...THAT'S THE SORTA THING, YEAH.
CERTAINLY ONE WAY OF SAYIN' HELLO, INNIT?
next: WE'LL KEEP THE RED FLAG FLYING HERE

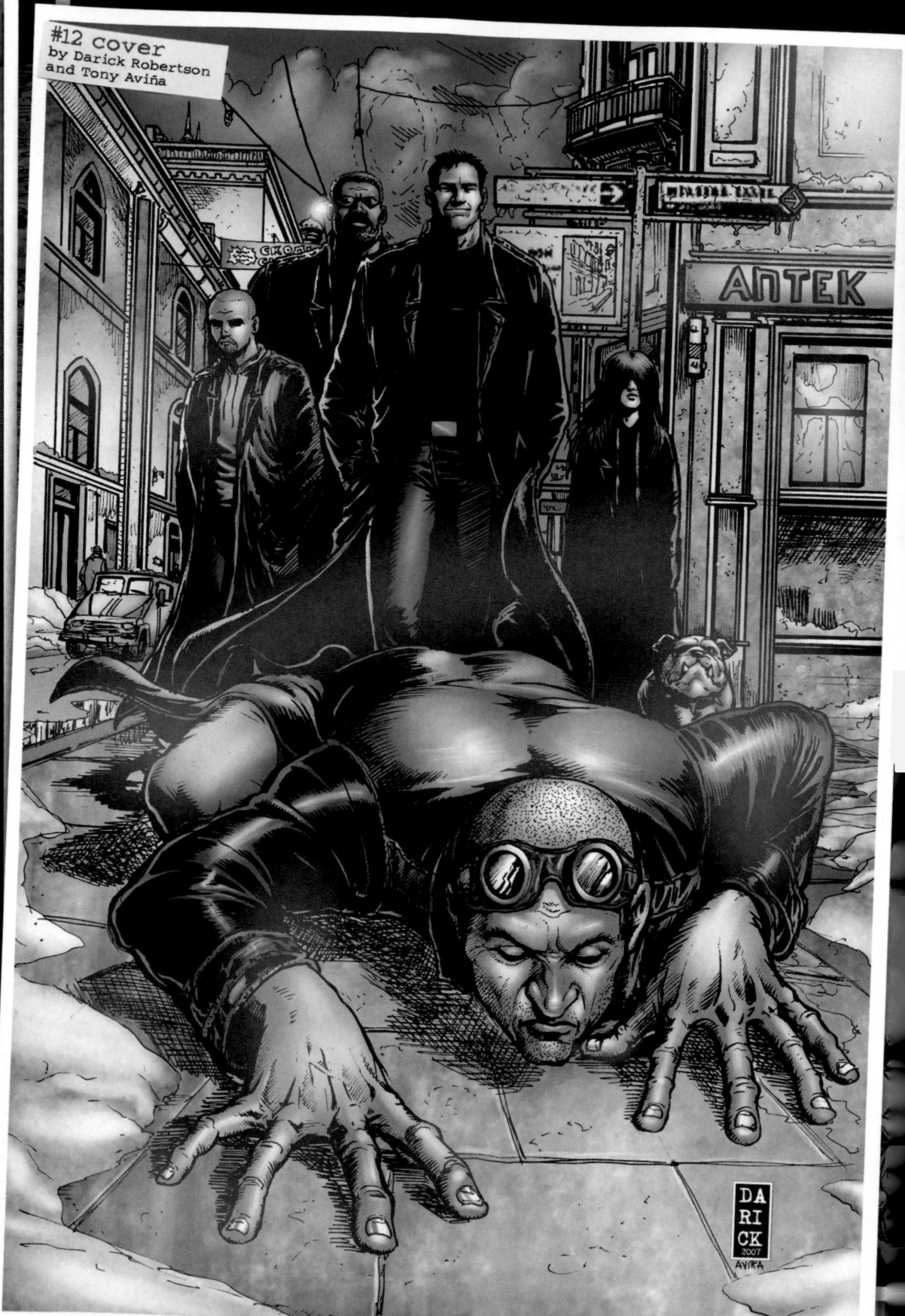
АПТЕК
DA
RI
CK
2007

#12 cover
by Darick Robertson
and Tony Aviña

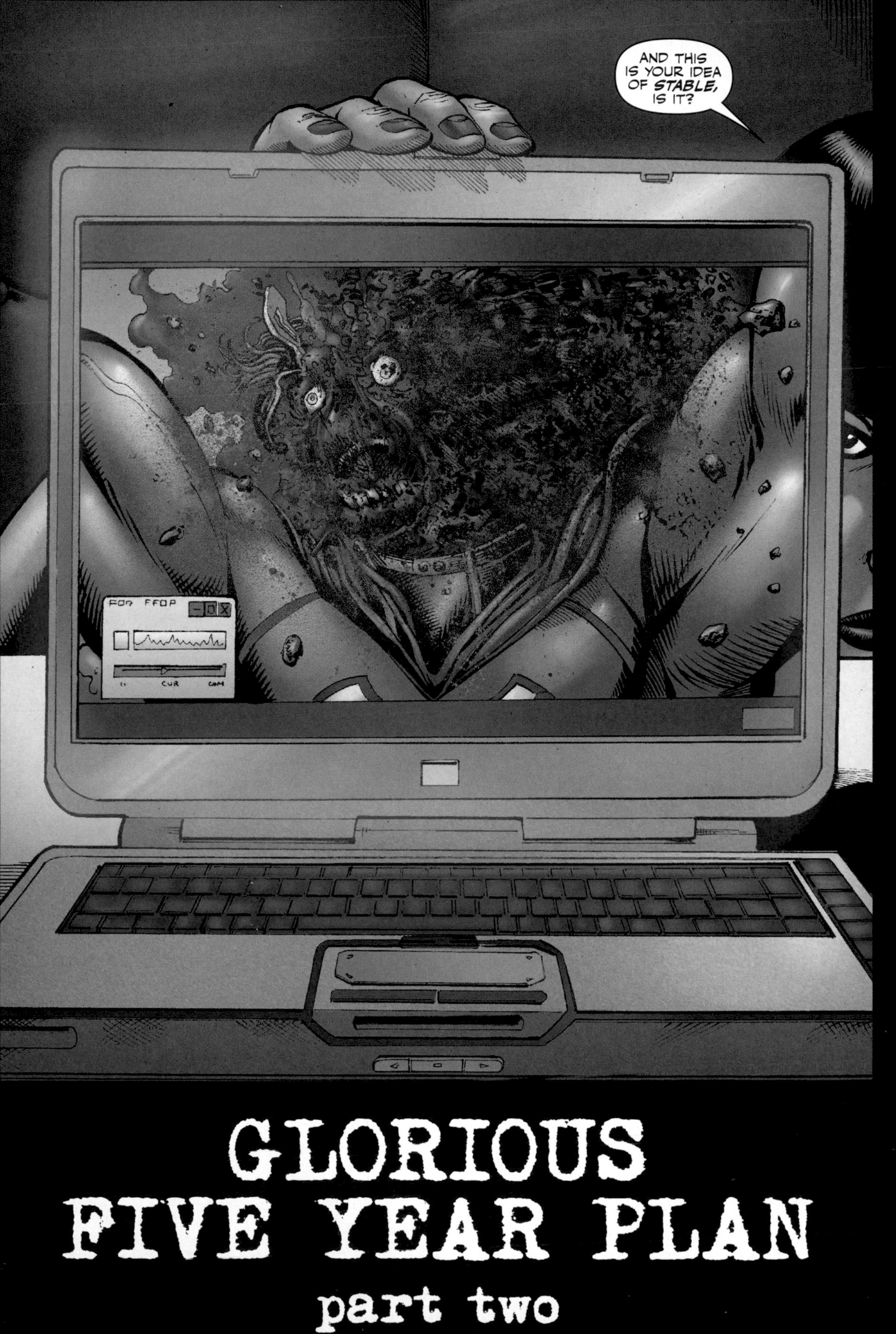
AND THIS IS YOUR IDEA OF STABLE, IS IT?

GLORIOUS FIVE YEAR PLAN

part two

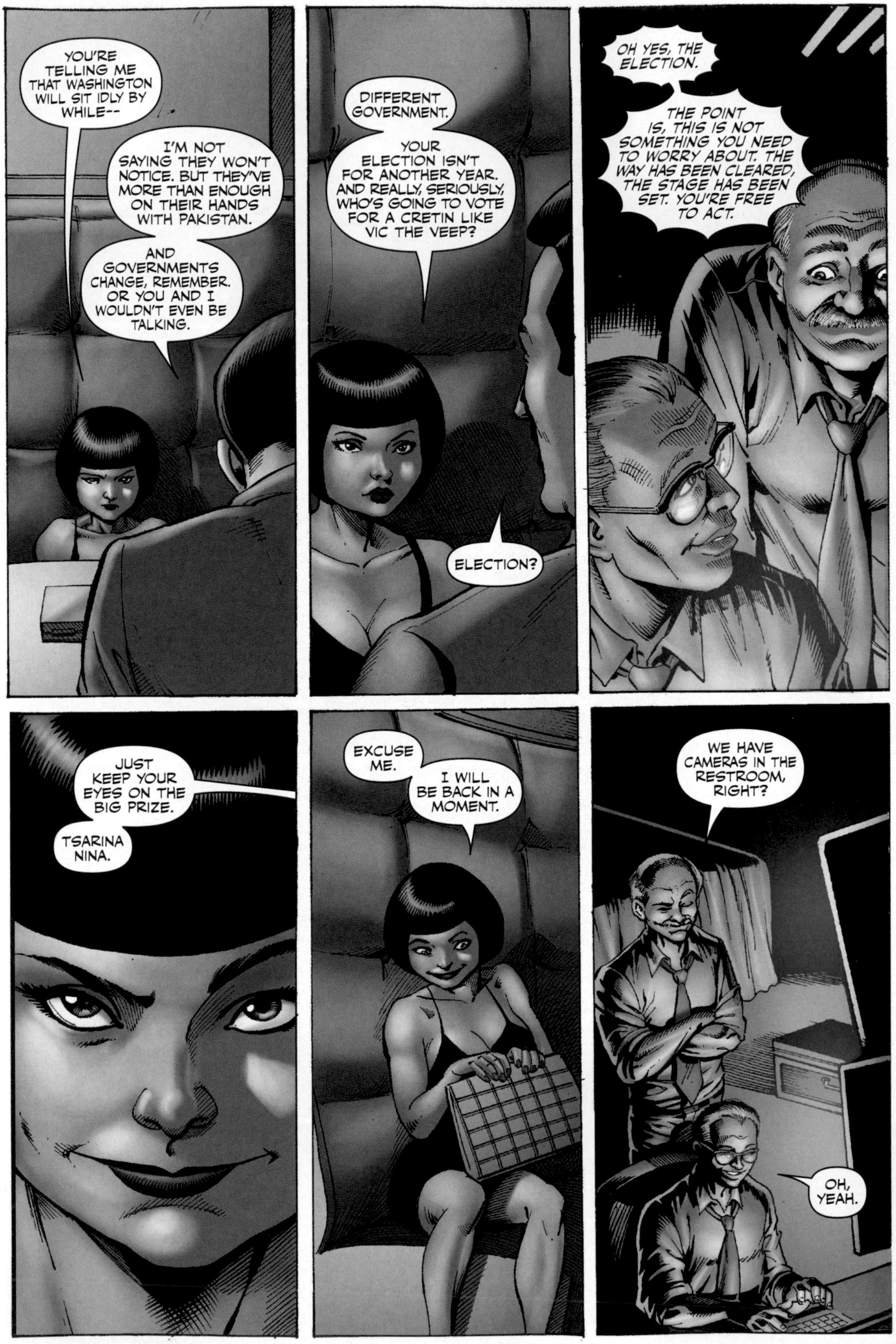

YOU'RE TELLING ME THAT WASHINGTON WILL SIT IDLY BY WHILE--
I'M NOT SAYING THEY WON'T NOTICE. BUT THEY'VE MORE THAN ENOUGH ON THEIR HANDS WITH PAKISTAN.
AND GOVERNMENTS CHANGE, REMEMBER. OR YOU AND I WOULDN'T EVEN BE TALKING.
DIFFERENT GOVERNMENT.
YOUR ELECTION ISN'T FOR ANOTHER YEAR. AND REALLY, SERIOUSLY, WHO'S GOING TO VOTE FOR A CRETIN LIKE VIC THE VEEP?
ELECTION?
OH YES, THE ELECTION.
THE POINT IS, THIS IS NOT SOMETHING YOU NEED TO WORRY ABOUT. THE WAY HAS BEEN CLEARED, THE STAGE HAS BEEN SET. YOU'RE FREE TO ACT.
JUST KEEP YOUR EYES ON THE BIG PRIZE.
TSARINA NINA.
EXCUSE ME.
I WILL BE BACK IN A MOMENT.
WE HAVE CAMERAS IN THE RESTROOM, RIGHT?
OH, YEAH.

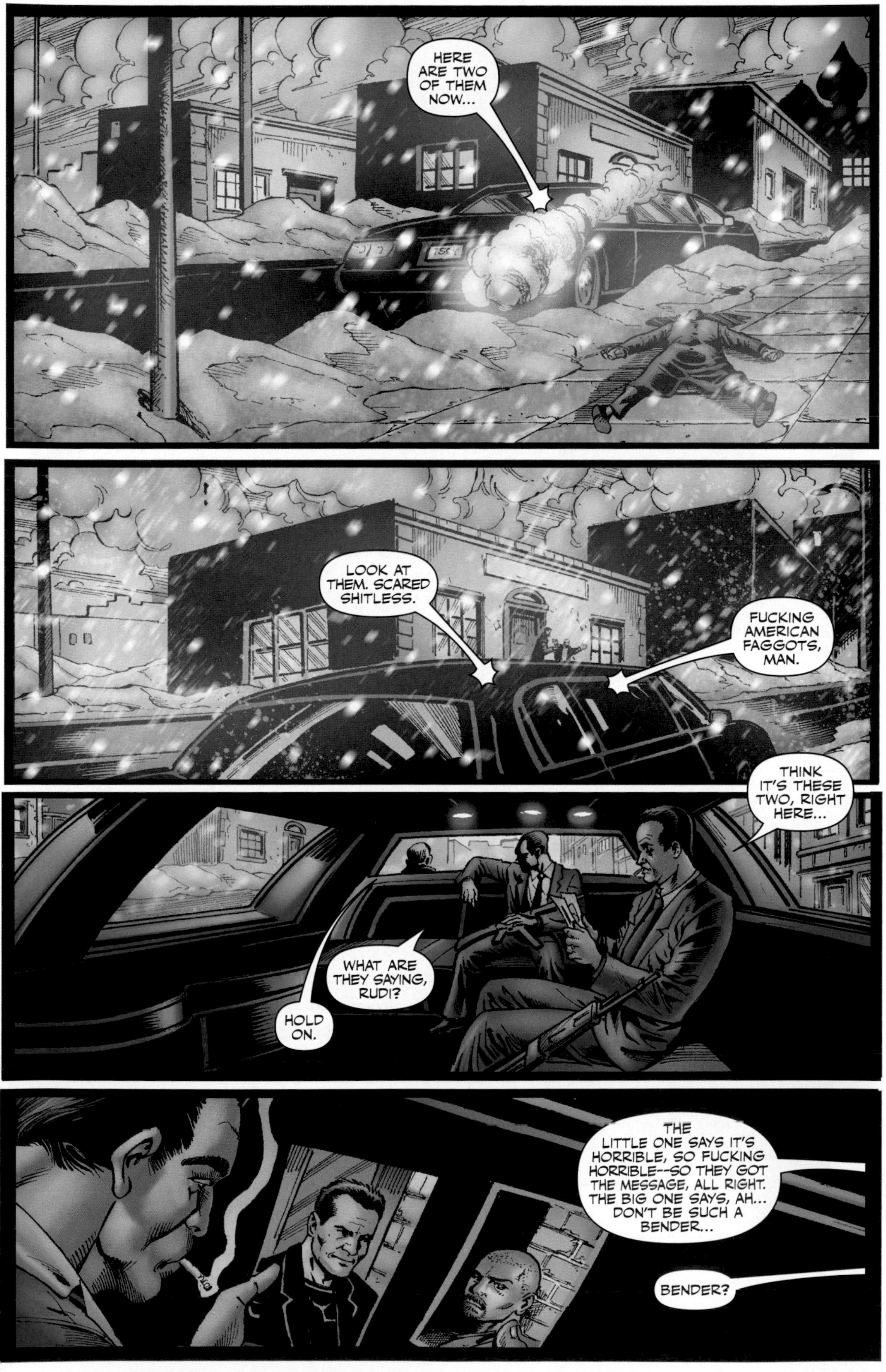
HERE ARE TWO OF THEM NOW...
LOOK AT THEM. SCARED SHITLESS.
FUCKING AMERICAN FAGGOTS, MAN.
THINK IT'S THESE TWO, RIGHT HERE...
WHAT ARE THEY SAYING, RUDI?
HOLD ON.
THE LITTLE ONE SAYS IT'S HORRIBLE, SO FUCKING HORRIBLE--SO THEY GOT THE MESSAGE, ALL RIGHT. THE BIG ONE SAYS, AH... DON'T BE SUCH A BENDER...
BENDER?

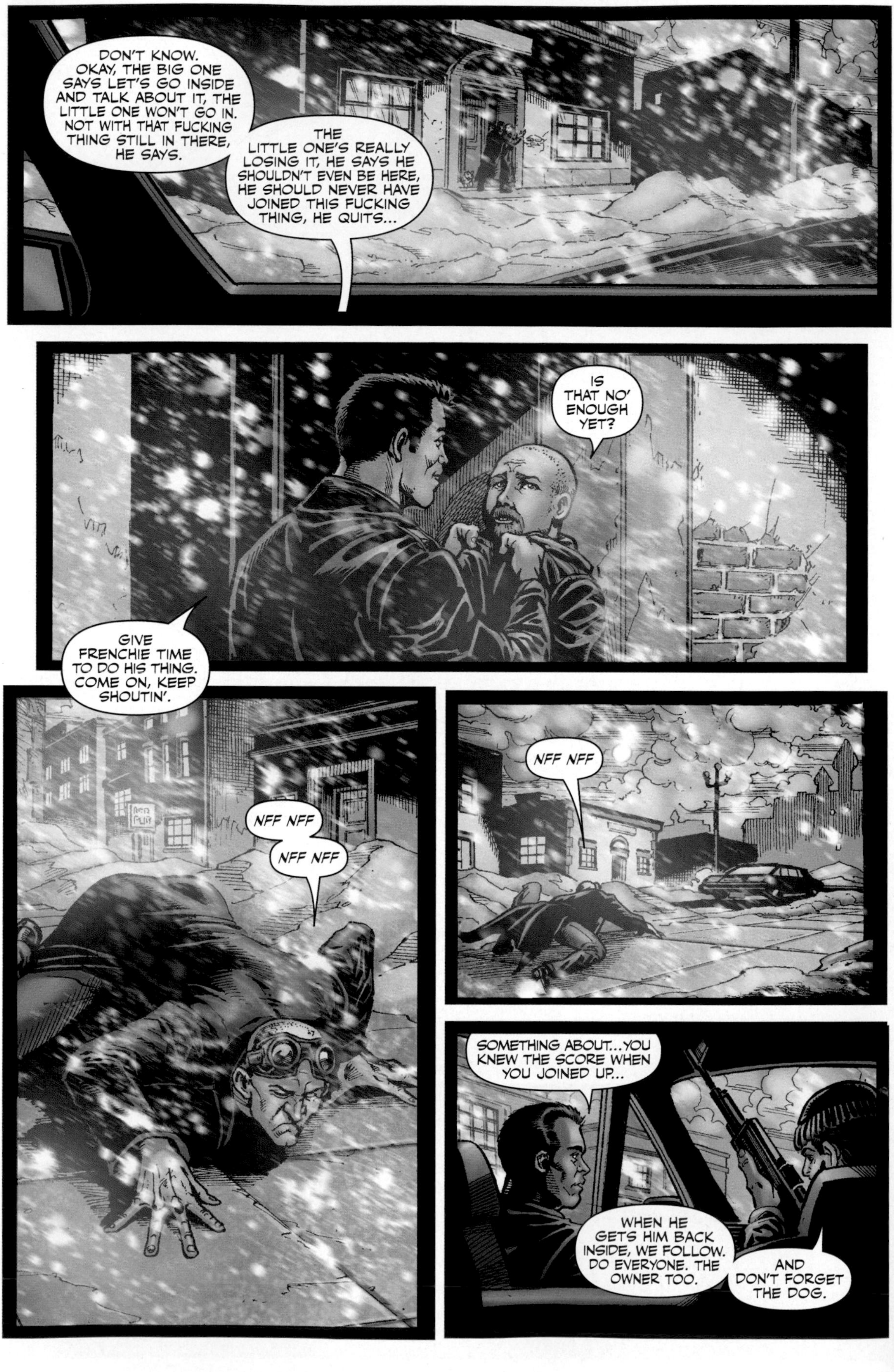
DON'T KNOW. OKAY, THE BIG ONE SAYS LET'S GO INSIDE AND TALK ABOUT IT, THE LITTLE ONE WON'T GO IN. NOT WITH THAT FUCKING THING STILL IN THERE, HE SAYS.
THE LITTLE ONE'S REALLY LOSING IT, HE SAYS HE SHOULDN'T EVEN BE HERE, HE SHOULD NEVER HAVE JOINED THIS FUCKING THING, HE QUITS...
IS THAT NO' ENOUGH YET?
GIVE FRENCHIE TIME TO DO HIS THING. COME ON, KEEP SHOUTIN'.
NFF NFF
NFF NFF
NFF NFF
SOMETHING ABOUT...YOU KNEW THE SCORE WHEN YOU JOINED UP...
WHEN HE GETS HIM BACK INSIDE, WE FOLLOW. DO EVERYONE. THE OWNER TOO.
AND DON'T FORGET THE DOG.

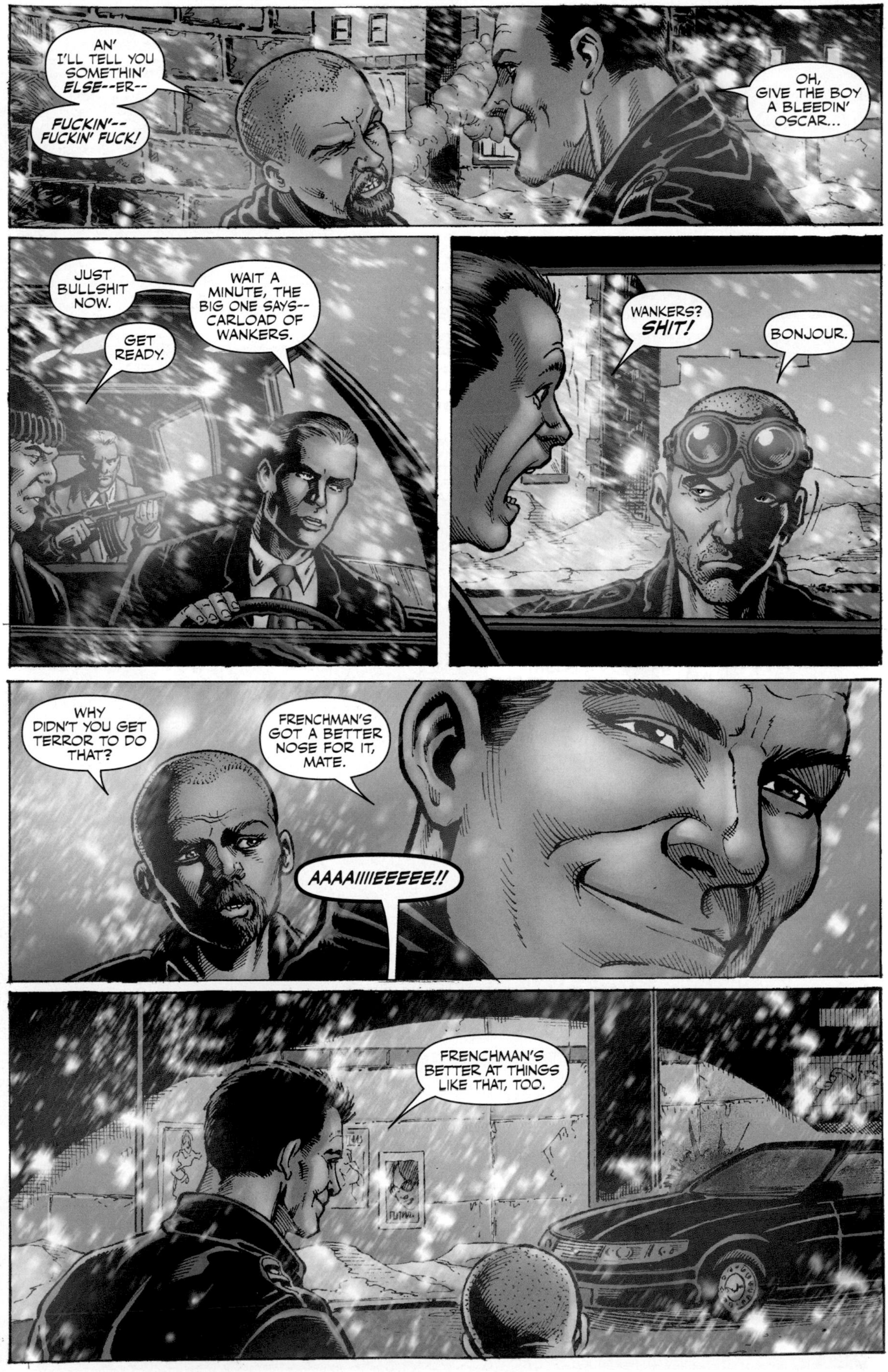
AN' I'LL TELL YOU SOMETHIN' ELSE--ER--
FUCKIN'-- FUCKIN' FUCK!
OH, GIVE THE BOY A BLEEDIN' OSCAR...
JUST BULLSHIT NOW.
WAIT A MINUTE, THE BIG ONE SAYS-- CARLOAD OF WANKERS.
GET READY.
WANKERS? SHIT!
BONJOUR.
WHY DIDN'T YOU GET TERROR TO DO THAT?
FRENCHMAN'S GOT A BETTER NOSE FOR IT, MATE.
AAAAIIIIIEEEEE!!
FRENCHMAN'S BETTER AT THINGS LIKE THAT, TOO.

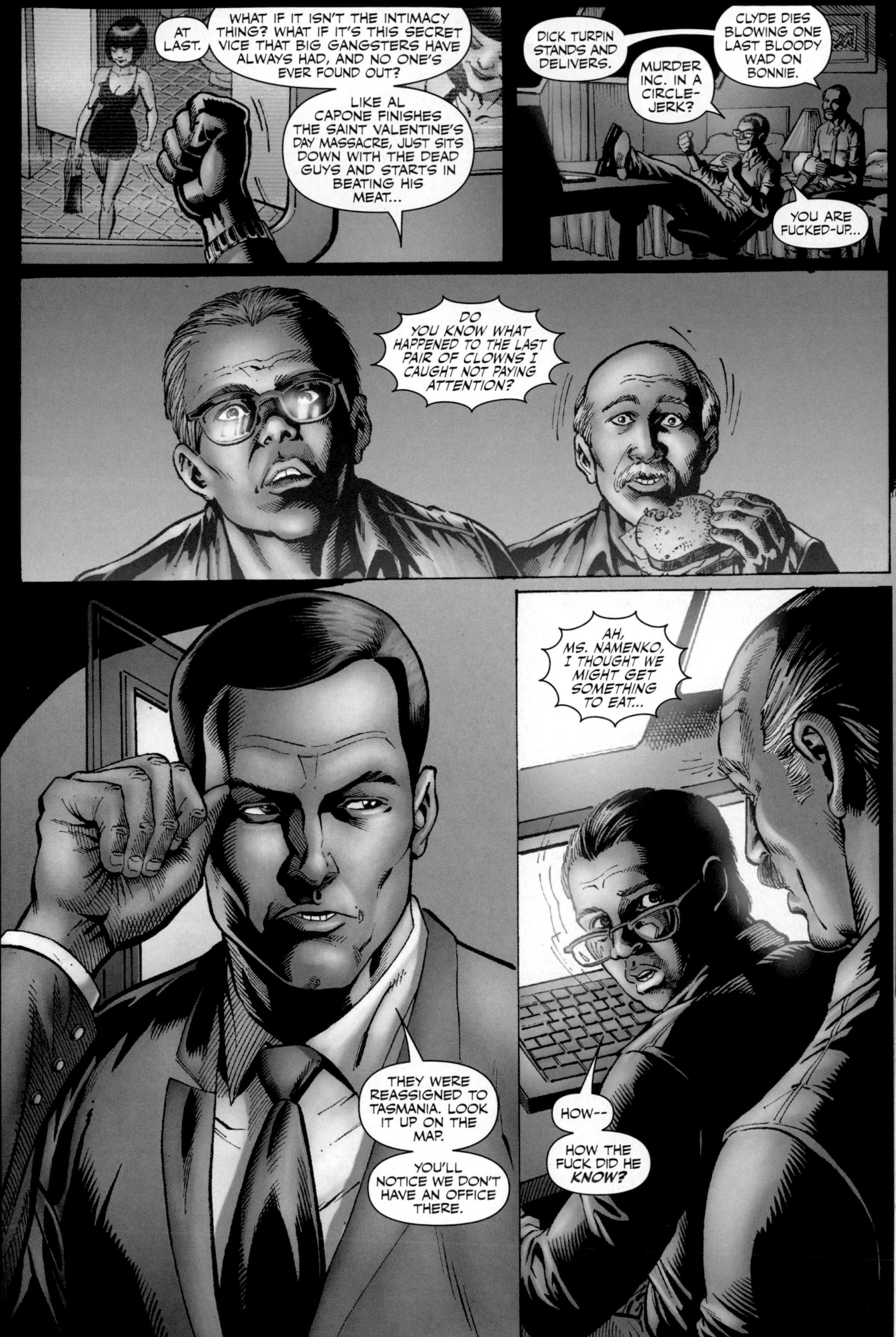

AT LAST.
WHAT IF IT ISN'T THE INTIMACY THING? WHAT IF IT'S THIS SECRET VICE THAT BIG GANGSTERS HAVE ALWAYS HAD, AND NO ONE'S EVER FOUND OUT?
LIKE AL CAPONE FINISHES THE SAINT VALENTINE'S DAY MASSACRE, JUST SITS DOWN WITH THE DEAD GUYS AND STARTS IN BEATING HIS MEAT...
DICK TURPIN STANDS AND DELIVERS.
MURDER INC. IN A CIRCLE-JERK?
CLYDE DIES BLOWING ONE LAST BLOODY WAD ON BONNIE.
YOU ARE FUCKED-UP...
DO YOU KNOW WHAT HAPPENED TO THE LAST PAIR OF CLOWNS I CAUGHT NOT PAYING ATTENTION?
THEY WERE REASSIGNED TO TASMANIA. LOOK IT UP ON THE MAP.
YOU'LL NOTICE WE DON'T HAVE AN OFFICE THERE.
AH, MS. NAMENKO, I THOUGHT WE MIGHT GET SOMETHING TO EAT...
HOW--
HOW THE FUCK DID HE *KNOW?*

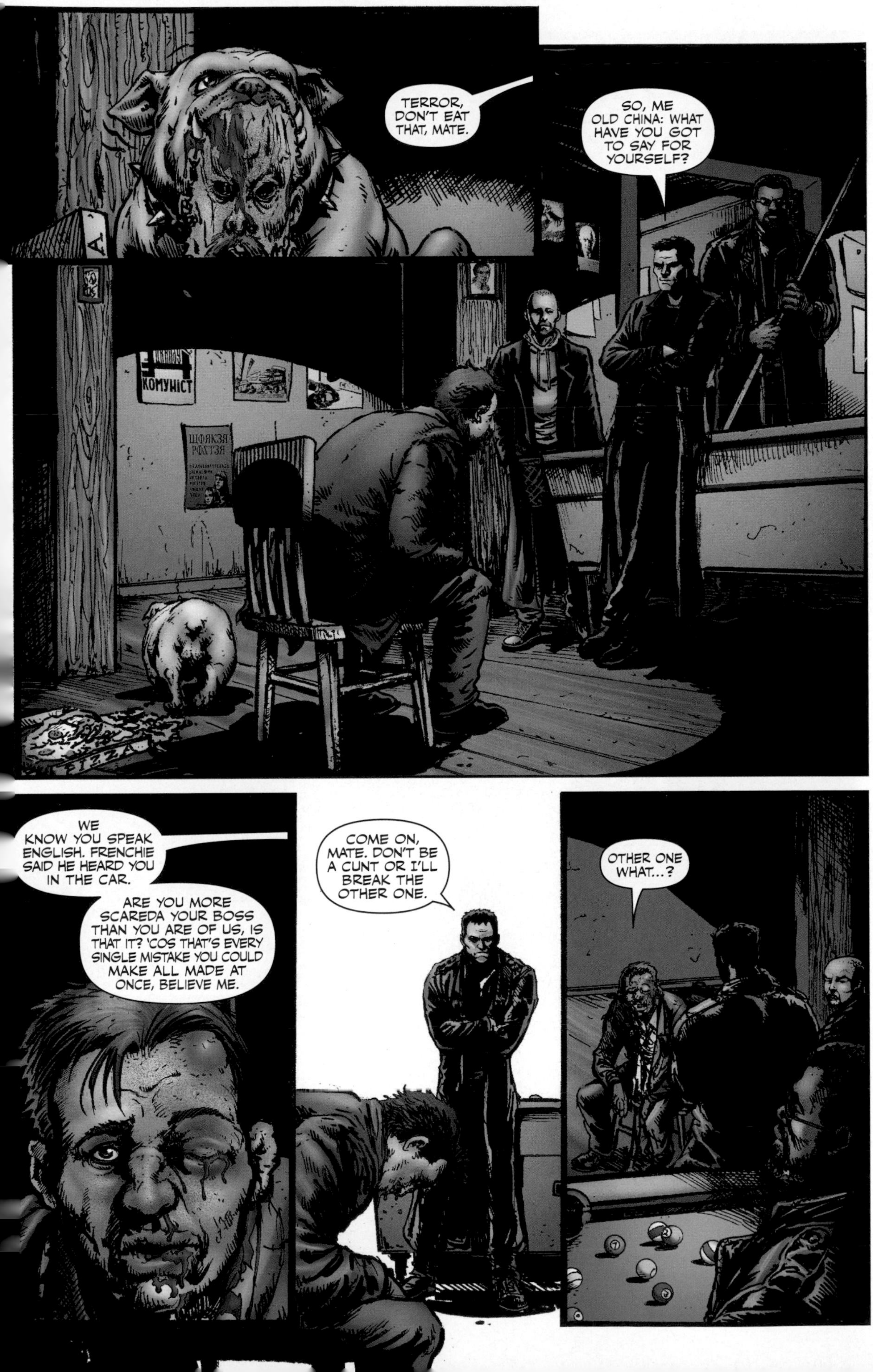
TERROR, DON'T EAT THAT, MATE.
SO, ME OLD CHINA: WHAT HAVE YOU GOT TO SAY FOR YOURSELF?
КОМУНІСТ
WE KNOW YOU SPEAK ENGLISH. FRENCHIE SAID HE HEARD YOU IN THE CAR.
ARE YOU MORE SCAREDA YOUR BOSS THAN YOU ARE OF US, IS THAT IT? 'COS THAT'S EVERY SINGLE MISTAKE YOU COULD MAKE ALL MADE AT ONCE, BELIEVE ME.
COME ON, MATE. DON'T BE A CUNT OR I'LL BREAK THE OTHER ONE.
OTHER ONE WHAT...?

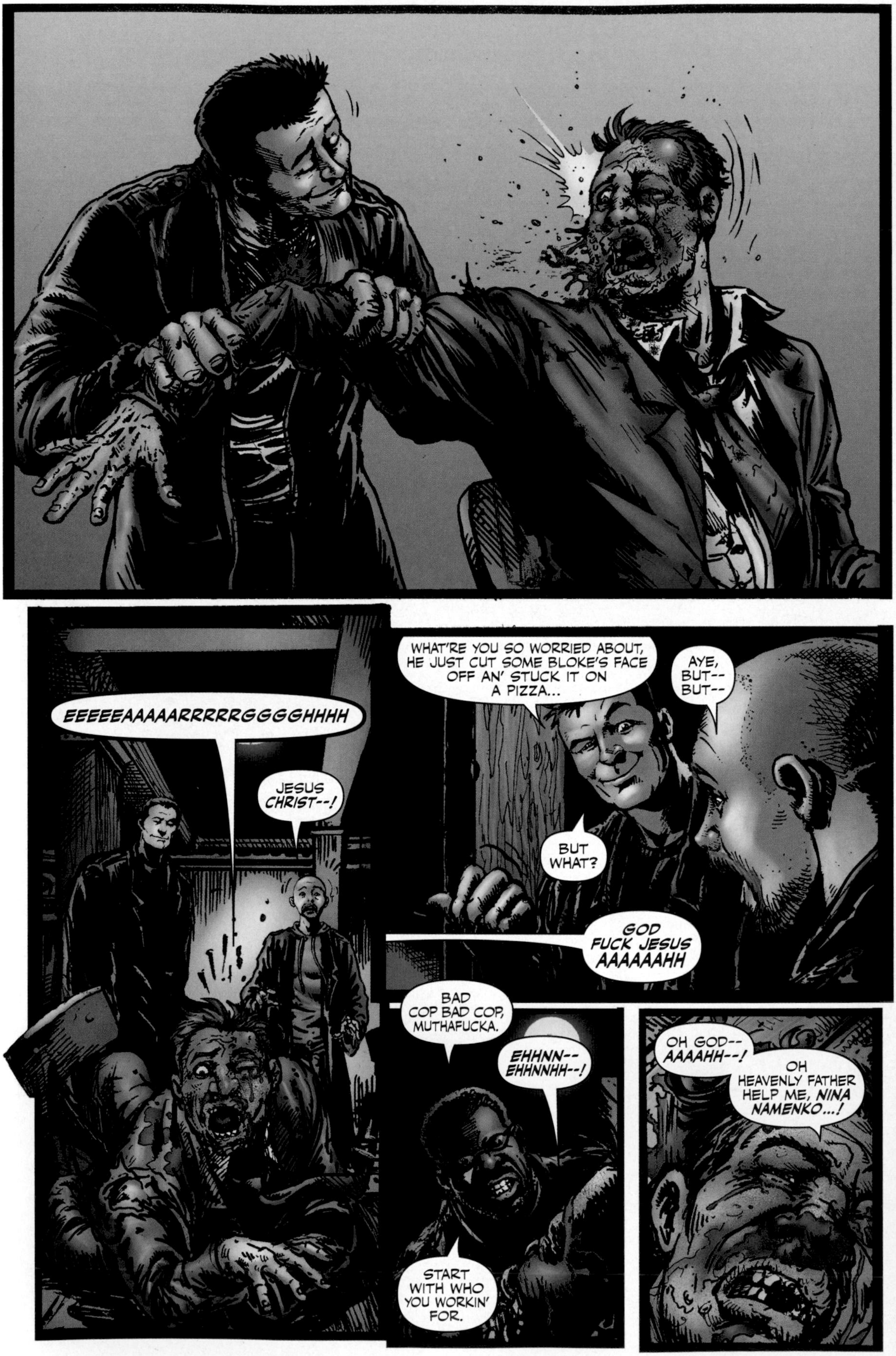
EEEEEAAAAARRRRRGGGGHHHH
JESUS CHRIST--!
WHAT'RE YOU SO WORRIED ABOUT, HE JUST CUT SOME BLOKE'S FACE OFF AN' STUCK IT ON A PIZZA...
AYE, BUT-- BUT--
BUT WHAT?
GOD FUCK JESUS AAAAAAHH
BAD COP BAD COP, MUTHAFUCKA.
EHHNN-- EHHNNHH--!
START WITH WHO YOU WORKIN' FOR.
OH GOD-- AAAAHH--!
OH HEAVENLY FATHER HELP ME, NINA NAMENKO...!

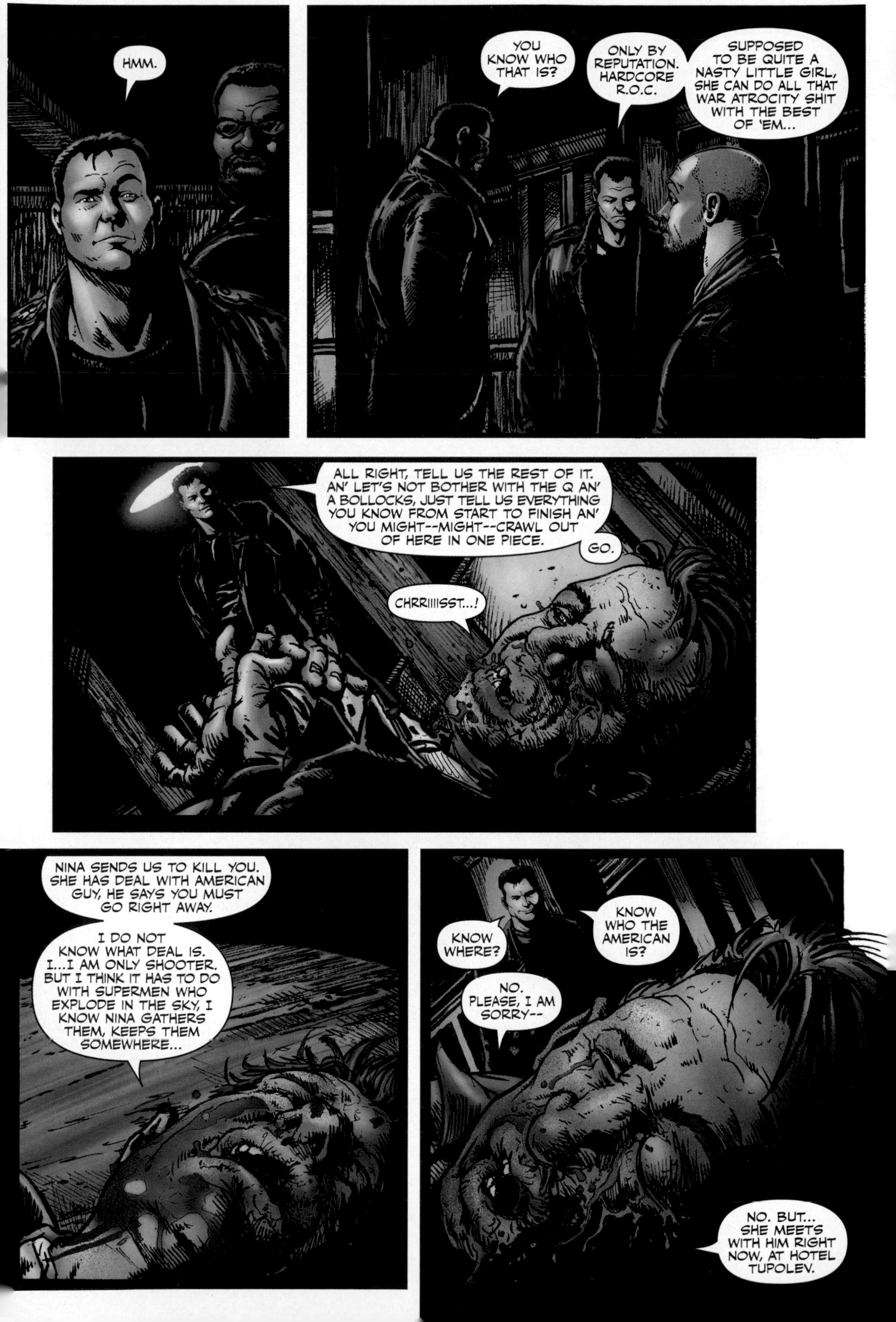
HMM.
YOU KNOW WHO THAT IS?
ONLY BY REPUTATION. HARDCORE R.O.C.
SUPPOSED TO BE QUITE A NASTY LITTLE GIRL, SHE CAN DO ALL THAT WAR ATROCITY SHIT WITH THE BEST OF 'EM...
ALL RIGHT, TELL US THE REST OF IT. AN' LET'S NOT BOTHER WITH THE Q AN' A BOLLOCKS, JUST TELL US EVERYTHING YOU KNOW FROM START TO FINISH AN' YOU MIGHT--MIGHT--CRAWL OUT OF HERE IN ONE PIECE.
GO.
CHRRIIIISST...!
NINA SENDS US TO KILL YOU. SHE HAS DEAL WITH AMERICAN GUY, HE SAYS YOU MUST GO RIGHT AWAY.
I DO NOT KNOW WHAT DEAL IS. I...I AM ONLY SHOOTER. BUT I THINK IT HAS TO DO WITH SUPERMEN WHO EXPLODE IN THE SKY, I KNOW NINA GATHERS THEM, KEEPS THEM SOMEWHERE...
KNOW WHO THE AMERICAN IS?
KNOW WHERE?
NO. PLEASE, I AM SORRY--
NO. BUT... SHE MEETS WITH HIM RIGHT NOW, AT HOTEL TUPOLEV.

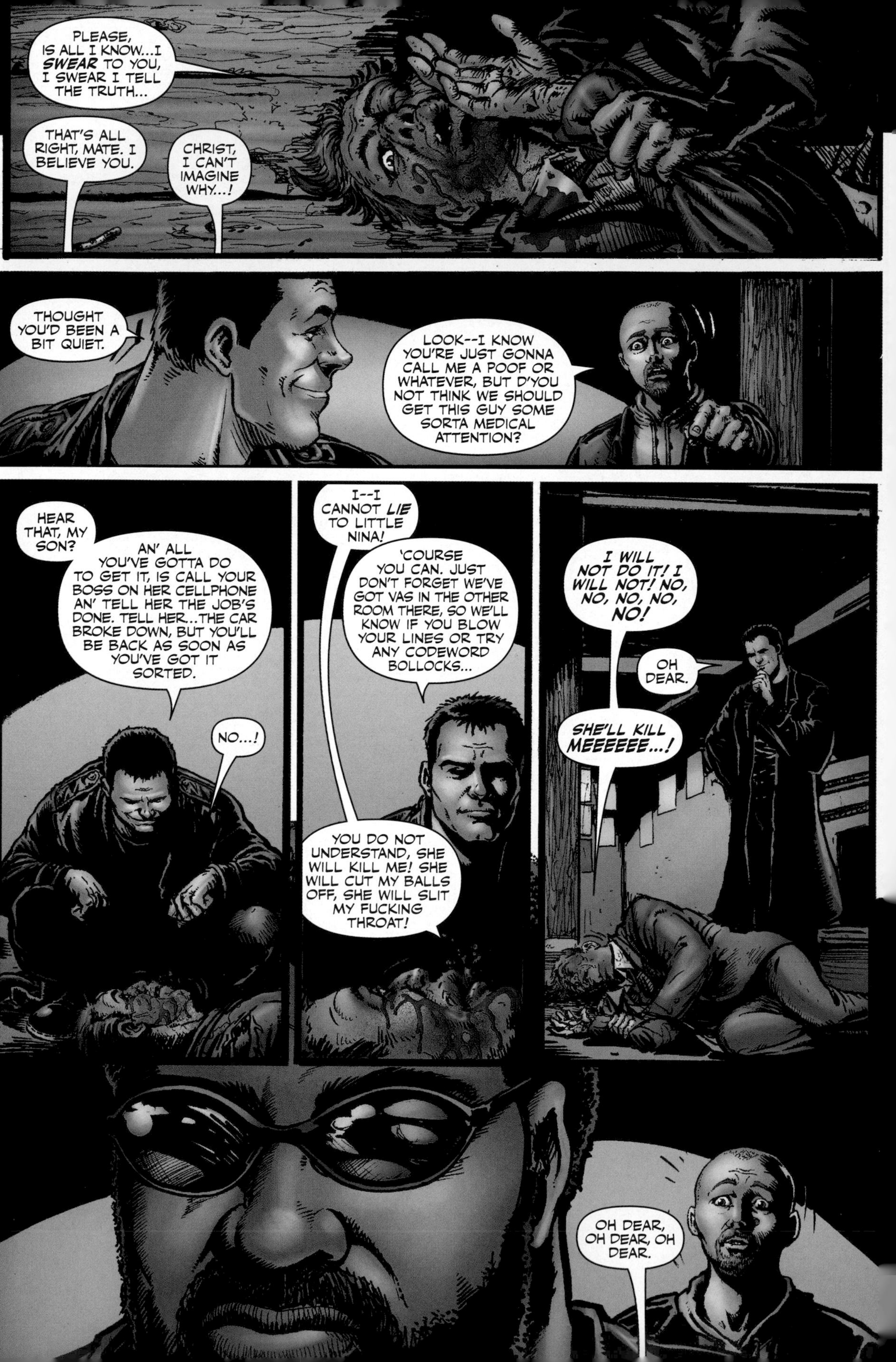
PLEASE, IS ALL I KNOW...I SWEAR TO YOU, I SWEAR I TELL THE TRUTH...
THAT'S ALL RIGHT, MATE. I BELIEVE YOU.
CHRIST, I CAN'T IMAGINE WHY...!
THOUGHT YOU'D BEEN A BIT QUIET.
LOOK--I KNOW YOU'RE JUST GONNA CALL ME A POOF OR WHATEVER, BUT D'YOU NOT THINK WE SHOULD GET THIS GUY SOME SORTA MEDICAL ATTENTION?
HEAR THAT, MY SON?
AN' ALL YOU'VE GOTTA DO TO GET IT, IS CALL YOUR BOSS ON HER CELLPHONE AN' TELL HER THE JOB'S DONE. TELL HER...THE CAR BROKE DOWN, BUT YOU'LL BE BACK AS SOON AS YOU'VE GOT IT SORTED.
NO...!
I--I CANNOT LIE TO LITTLE NINA!
'COURSE YOU CAN. JUST DON'T FORGET WE'VE GOT VAS IN THE OTHER ROOM THERE, SO WE'LL KNOW IF YOU BLOW YOUR LINES OR TRY ANY CODEWORD BOLLOCKS...
YOU DO NOT UNDERSTAND, SHE WILL KILL ME! SHE WILL CUT MY BALLS OFF, SHE WILL SLIT MY FUCKING THROAT!
I WILL NOT DO IT! I WILL NOT! NO, NO, NO, NO, NO!
OH DEAR.
SHE'LL KILL MEEEEEE...!
OH DEAR, OH DEAR, OH DEAR.

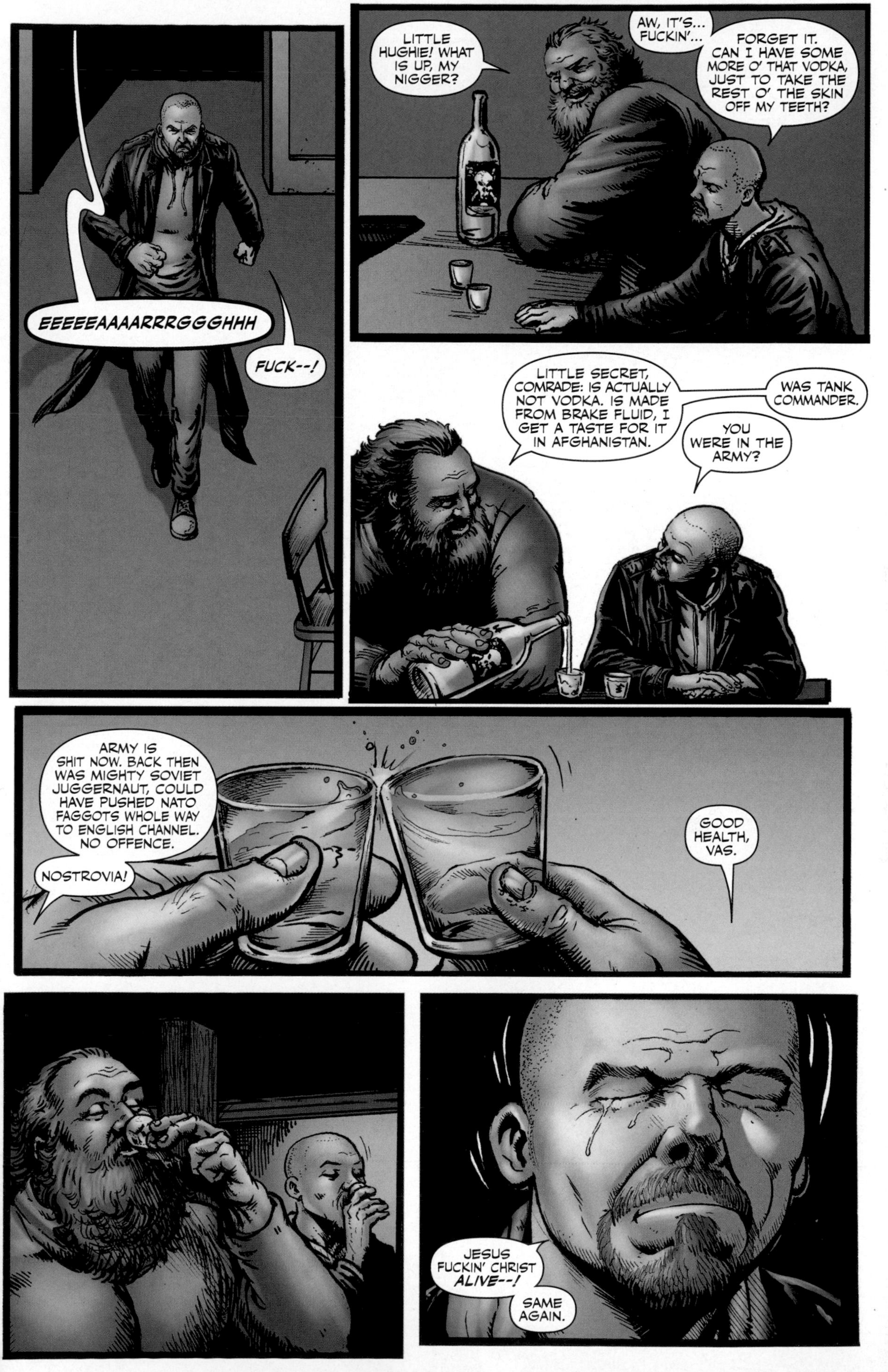
EEEEEAAAARRRGGGHHH
FUCK--!
LITTLE HUGHIE! WHAT IS UP, MY NIGGER?
AW, IT'S... FUCKIN'...
FORGET IT. CAN I HAVE SOME MORE O' THAT VODKA, JUST TO TAKE THE REST O' THE SKIN OFF MY TEETH?
LITTLE SECRET, COMRADE: IS ACTUALLY NOT VODKA. IS MADE FROM BRAKE FLUID, I GET A TASTE FOR IT IN AFGHANISTAN.
YOU WERE IN THE ARMY?
WAS TANK COMMANDER.
ARMY IS SHIT NOW. BACK THEN WAS MIGHTY SOVIET JUGGERNAUT, COULD HAVE PUSHED NATO FAGGOTS WHOLE WAY TO ENGLISH CHANNEL. NO OFFENCE.
NOSTROVIA!
GOOD HEALTH, VAS.
JESUS FUCKIN' CHRIST *ALIVE*--!
SAME AGAIN.

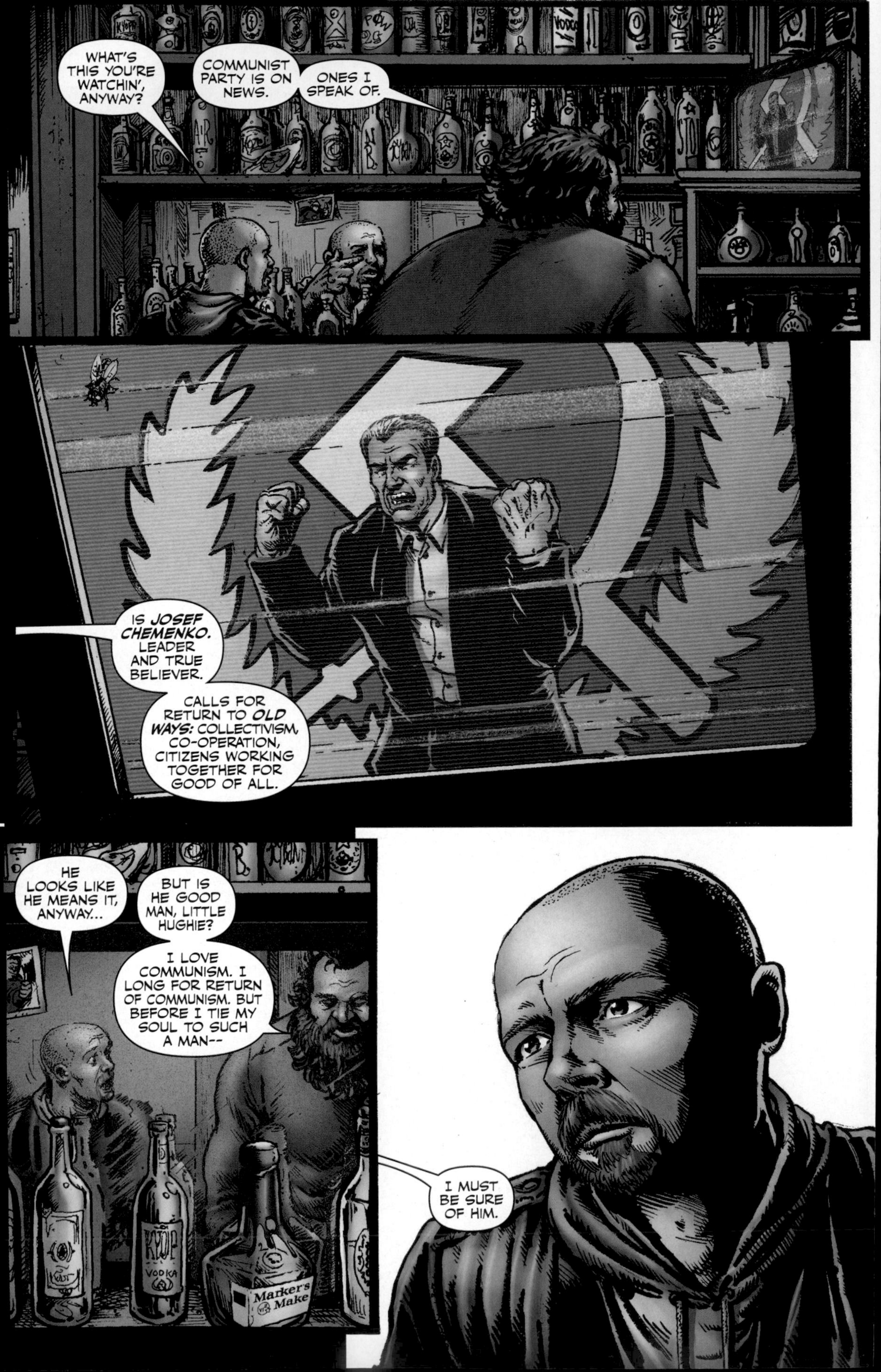
WHAT'S THIS YOU'RE WATCHIN', ANYWAY?
COMMUNIST PARTY IS ON NEWS.
ONES I SPEAK OF.
IS JOSEF CHEMENKO. LEADER AND TRUE BELIEVER.
CALLS FOR RETURN TO OLD WAYS: COLLECTIVISM, CO-OPERATION, CITIZENS WORKING TOGETHER FOR GOOD OF ALL.
HE LOOKS LIKE HE MEANS IT, ANYWAY...
BUT IS HE GOOD MAN, LITTLE HUGHIE?
I LOVE COMMUNISM. I LONG FOR RETURN OF COMMUNISM. BUT BEFORE I TIE MY SOUL TO SUCH A MAN--
I MUST BE SURE OF HIM.

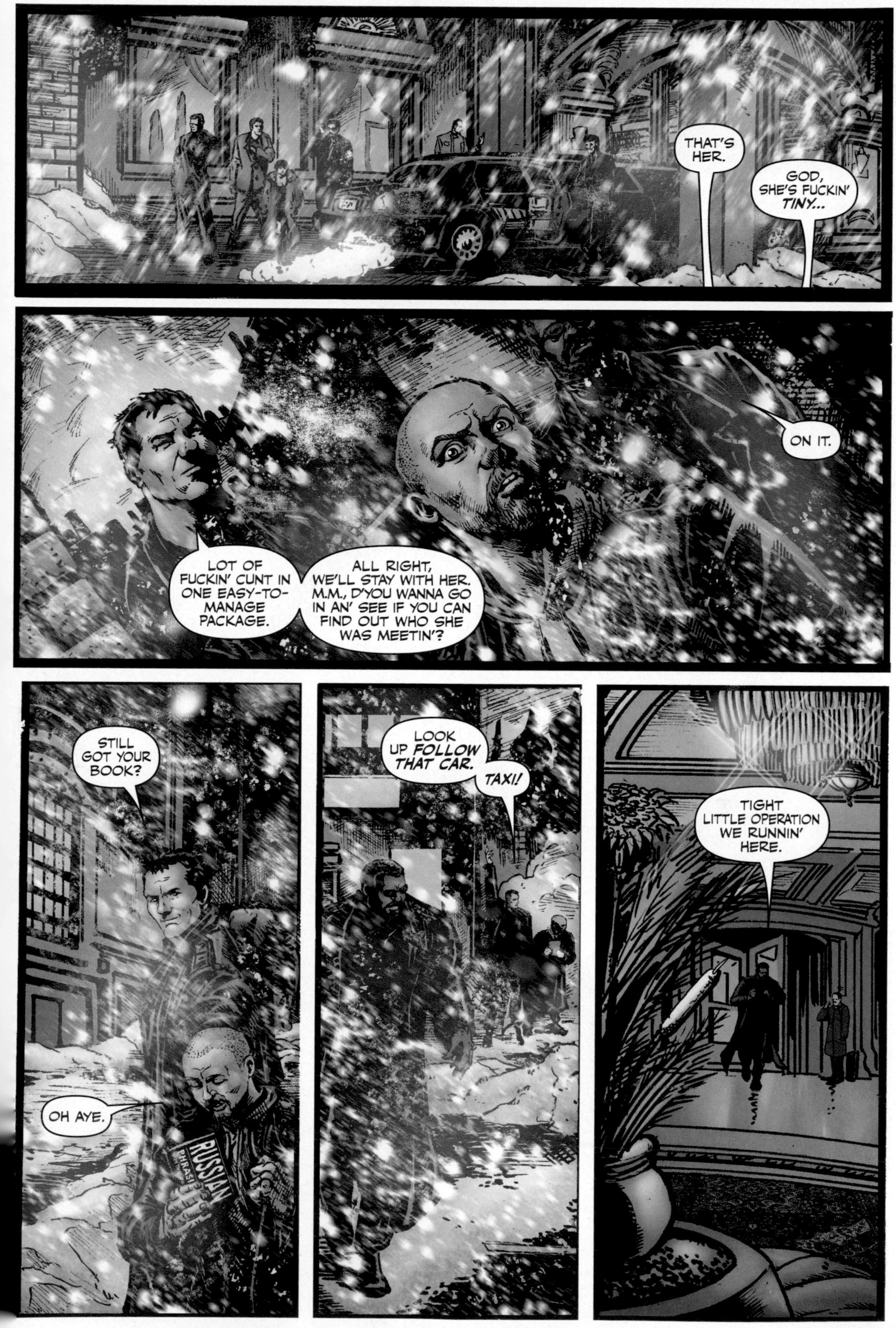
THAT'S HER.
GOD, SHE'S FUCKIN' *TINY...*
ON IT.
LOT OF FUCKIN' CUNT IN ONE EASY-TO-MANAGE PACKAGE.
ALL RIGHT, WE'LL STAY WITH HER. M.M., D'YOU WANNA GO IN AN' SEE IF YOU CAN FIND OUT WHO SHE WAS MEETIN'?
STILL GOT YOUR BOOK?
OH AYE.
RUSSIAN
LOOK UP *FOLLOW THAT CAR.*
TAXI!
TIGHT LITTLE OPERATION WE RUNNIN' HERE.

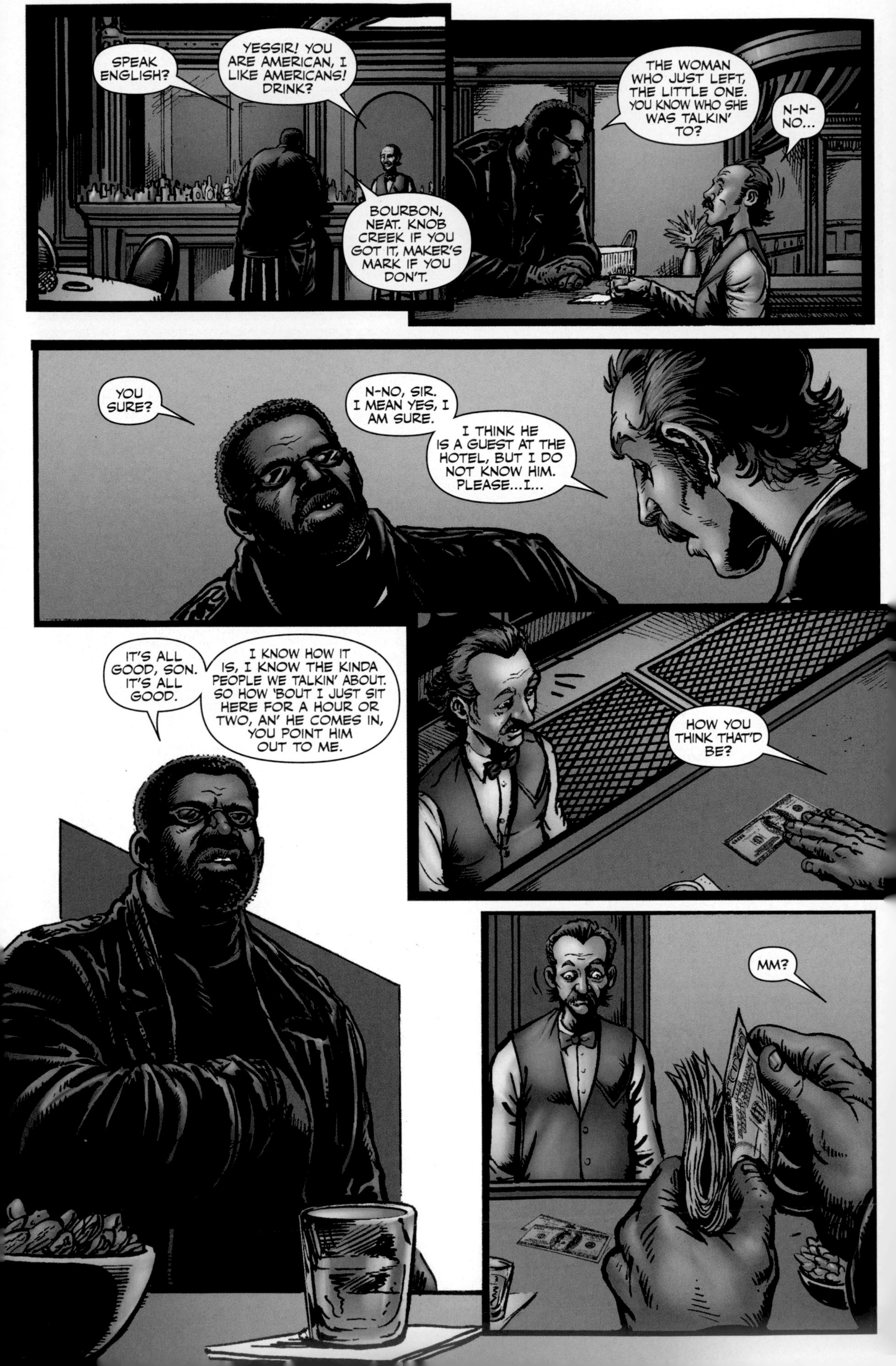
SPEAK ENGLISH?
YESSIR! YOU ARE AMERICAN, I LIKE AMERICANS! DRINK?
BOURBON, NEAT. KNOB CREEK IF YOU GOT IT, MAKER'S MARK IF YOU DON'T.
THE WOMAN WHO JUST LEFT, THE LITTLE ONE. YOU KNOW WHO SHE WAS TALKIN' TO?
N-N-NO...
YOU SURE?
N-NO, SIR. I MEAN YES, I AM SURE.
I THINK HE IS A GUEST AT THE HOTEL, BUT I DO NOT KNOW HIM. PLEASE...I...
IT'S ALL GOOD, SON. IT'S ALL GOOD.
I KNOW HOW IT IS, I KNOW THE KINDA PEOPLE WE TALKIN' ABOUT. SO HOW 'BOUT I JUST SIT HERE FOR A HOUR OR TWO, AN' HE COMES IN, YOU POINT HIM OUT TO ME.
HOW YOU THINK THAT'D BE?
MM?

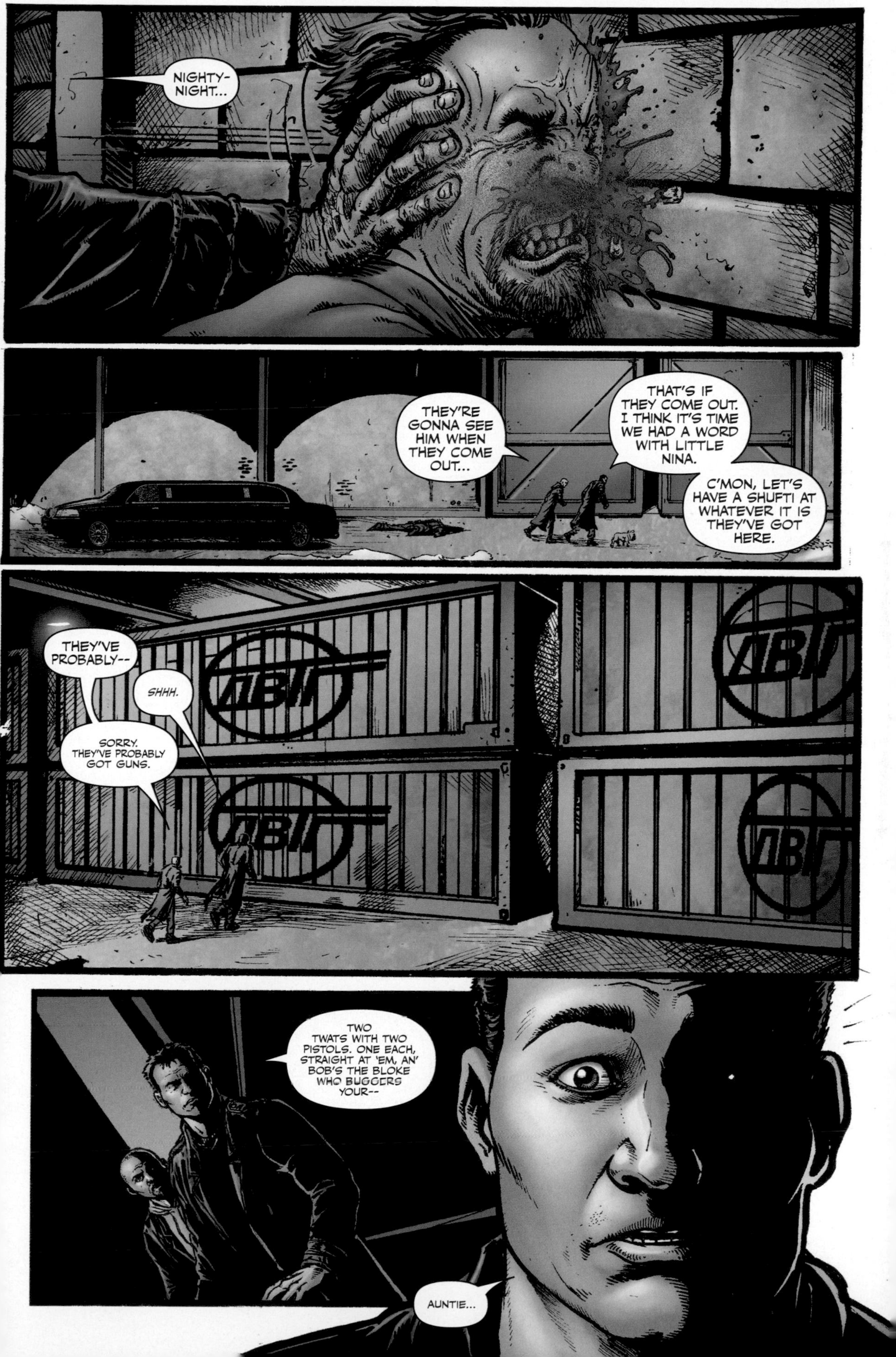
NIGHTY-NIGHT...
THEY'RE GONNA SEE HIM WHEN THEY COME OUT...
THAT'S IF THEY COME OUT. I THINK IT'S TIME WE HAD A WORD WITH LITTLE NINA.
C'MON, LET'S HAVE A SHUFTI AT WHATEVER IT IS THEY'VE GOT HERE.
THEY'VE PROBABLY--
SHHH.
SORRY. THEY'VE PROBABLY GOT GUNS.
TWO TWATS WITH TWO PISTOLS. ONE EACH, STRAIGHT AT 'EM, AN' BOB'S THE BLOKE WHO BUGGERS YOUR--
AUNTIE...

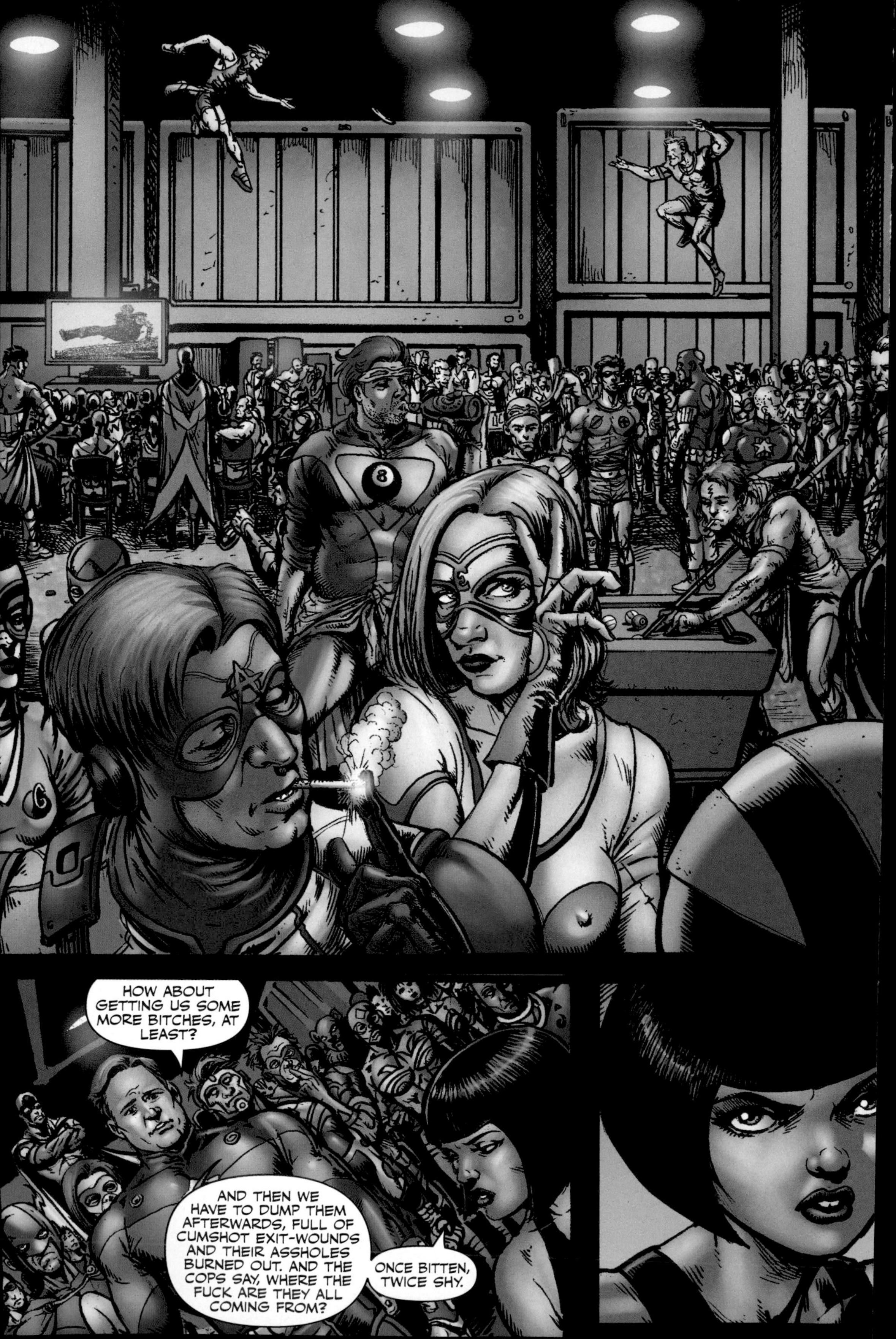
HOW ABOUT GETTING US SOME MORE BITCHES, AT LEAST?
AND THEN WE HAVE TO DUMP THEM AFTERWARDS, FULL OF CUMSHOT EXIT-WOUNDS AND THEIR ASSHOLES BURNED OUT. AND THE COPS SAY, WHERE THE FUCK ARE THEY ALL COMING FROM?
ONCE BITTEN, TWICE SHY.

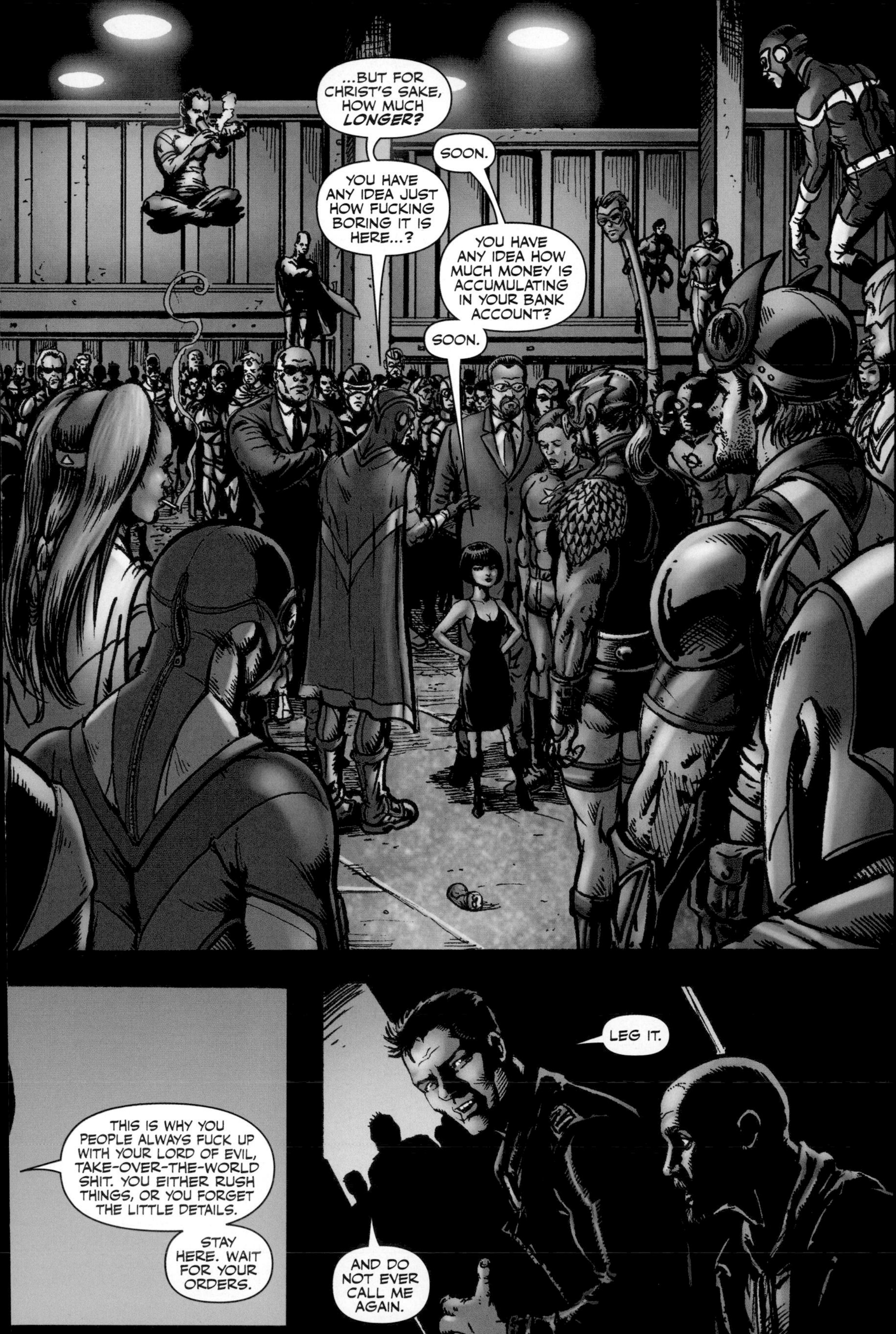

...BUT FOR CHRIST'S SAKE, HOW MUCH **LONGER?**
YOU HAVE ANY IDEA JUST HOW FUCKING BORING IT IS HERE...?
SOON.
YOU HAVE ANY IDEA HOW MUCH MONEY IS ACCUMULATING IN YOUR BANK ACCOUNT?
SOON.
THIS IS WHY YOU PEOPLE ALWAYS FUCK UP WITH YOUR LORD OF EVIL, TAKE-OVER-THE-WORLD SHIT. YOU EITHER RUSH THINGS, OR YOU FORGET THE LITTLE DETAILS.
STAY HERE. WAIT FOR YOUR ORDERS.
LEG IT.
AND DO NOT EVER CALL ME AGAIN.

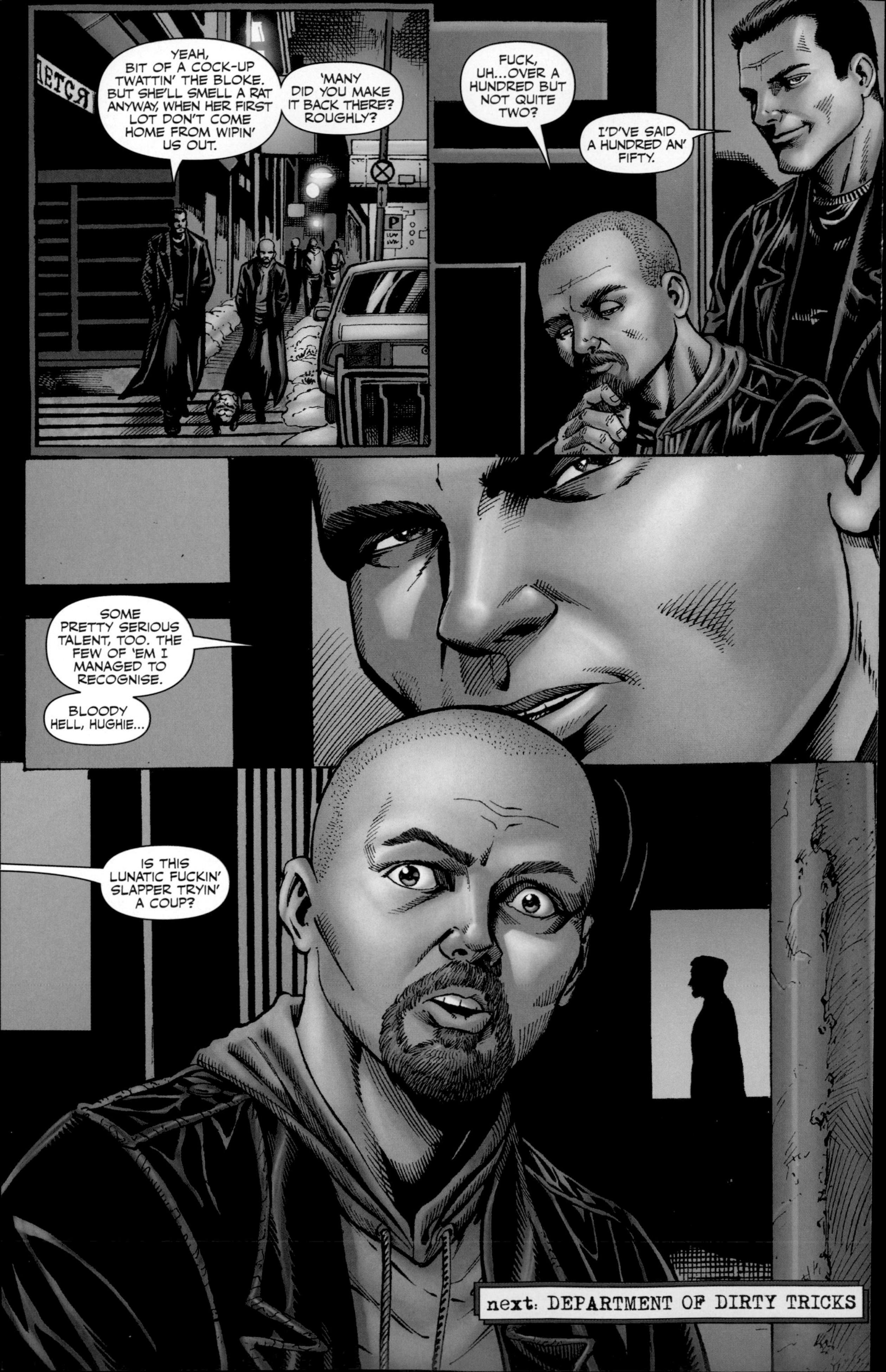
YEAH, BIT OF A COCK-UP TWATTIN' THE BLOKE. BUT SHE'LL SMELL A RAT ANYWAY, WHEN HER FIRST LOT DON'T COME HOME FROM WIPIN' US OUT.
'MANY DID YOU MAKE IT BACK THERE? ROUGHLY?
FUCK, UH...OVER A HUNDRED BUT NOT QUITE TWO?
I'D'VE SAID A HUNDRED AN' FIFTY.
SOME PRETTY SERIOUS TALENT, TOO. THE FEW OF 'EM I MANAGED TO RECOGNISE.
BLOODY HELL, HUGHIE...
IS THIS LUNATIC FUCKIN' SLAPPER TRYIN' A COUP?
next: DEPARTMENT OF DIRTY TRICKS

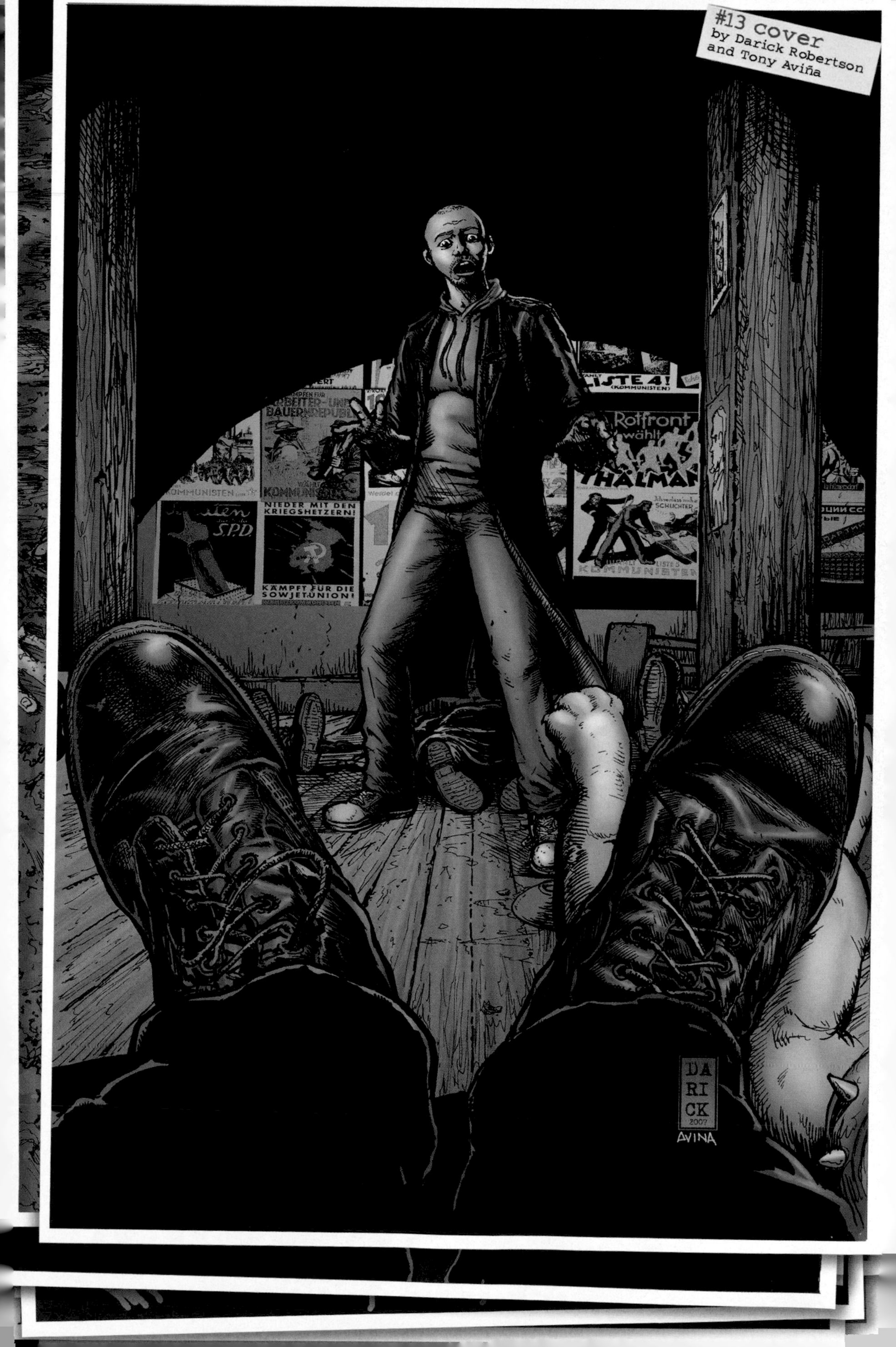
LISTE 4!
(KOMMUNISTEN)
Rotfront
wählt
THÄLMAN
NIEDER MIT DEN
KRIEGSHETZERN!
KÄMPFT FÜR DIE
SOWJETUNION!
S.P.D.
KOMMUNISTEN
DA
RI
CK
2007
AVINA

#13 cover
by Darick Robertson
and Tony Aviña

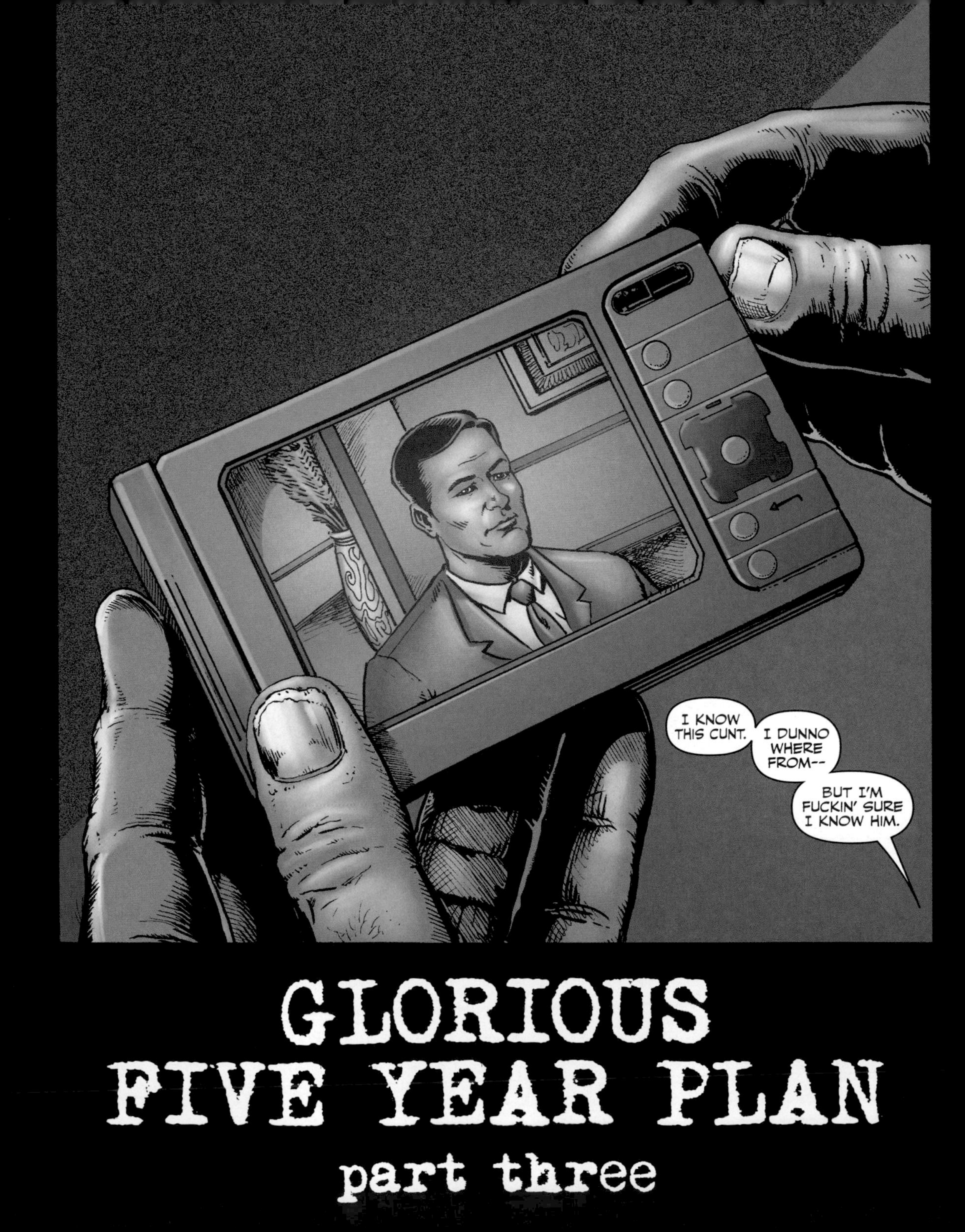
I KNOW THIS CUNT.
I DUNNO WHERE FROM--
BUT I'M FUCKIN' SURE I KNOW HIM.

GLORIOUS FIVE YEAR PLAN

part three

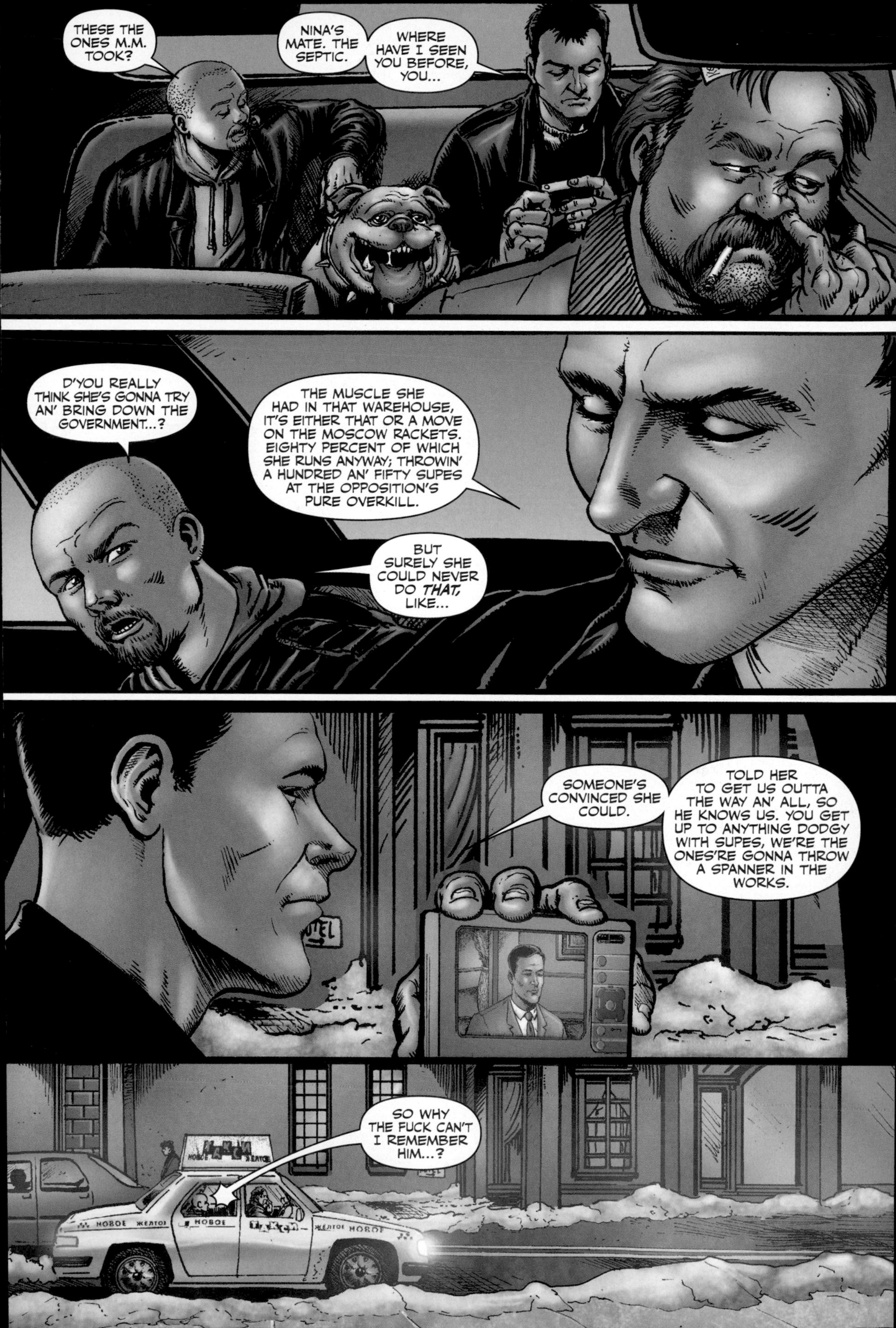
THESE THE ONES M.M. TOOK?
NINA'S MATE. THE SEPTIC.
WHERE HAVE I SEEN YOU BEFORE, YOU...
D'YOU REALLY THINK SHE'S GONNA TRY AN' BRING DOWN THE GOVERNMENT...?
THE MUSCLE SHE HAD IN THAT WAREHOUSE, IT'S EITHER THAT OR A MOVE ON THE MOSCOW RACKETS. EIGHTY PERCENT OF WHICH SHE RUNS ANYWAY; THROWIN' A HUNDRED AN' FIFTY SUPES AT THE OPPOSITION'S PURE OVERKILL.
BUT SURELY SHE COULD NEVER DO *THAT,* LIKE...
SOMEONE'S CONVINCED SHE COULD.
TOLD HER TO GET US OUTTA THE WAY AN' ALL, SO HE KNOWS US. YOU GET UP TO ANYTHING DODGY WITH SUPES, WE'RE THE ONES'RE GONNA THROW A SPANNER IN THE WORKS.
SO WHY THE FUCK CAN'T I REMEMBER HIM...?

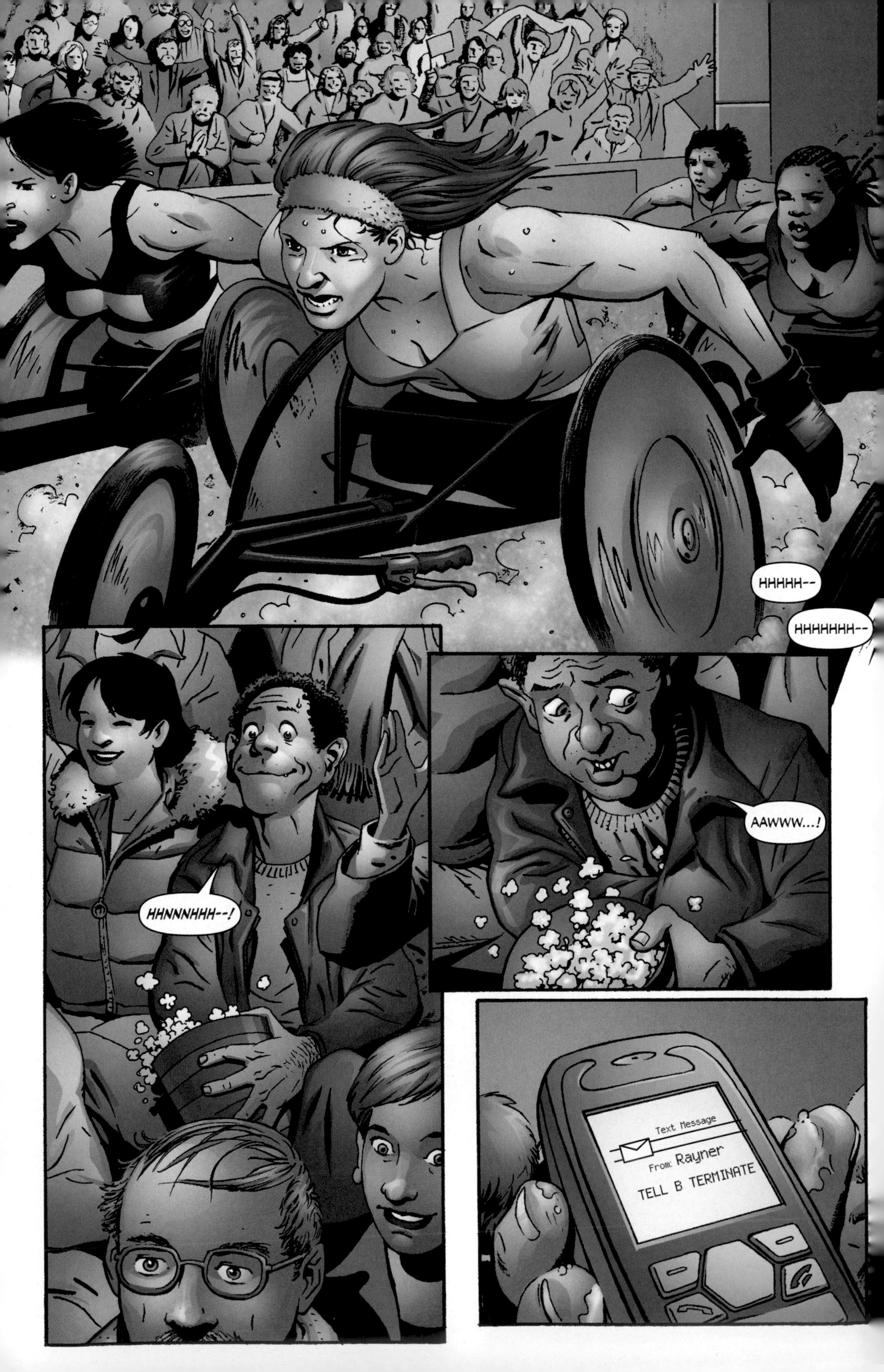
HHHHH--
HHHHHHH--
HHNNNHHH--!
AAWWW...!
Text Message
From: Rayner
TELL B TERMINATE

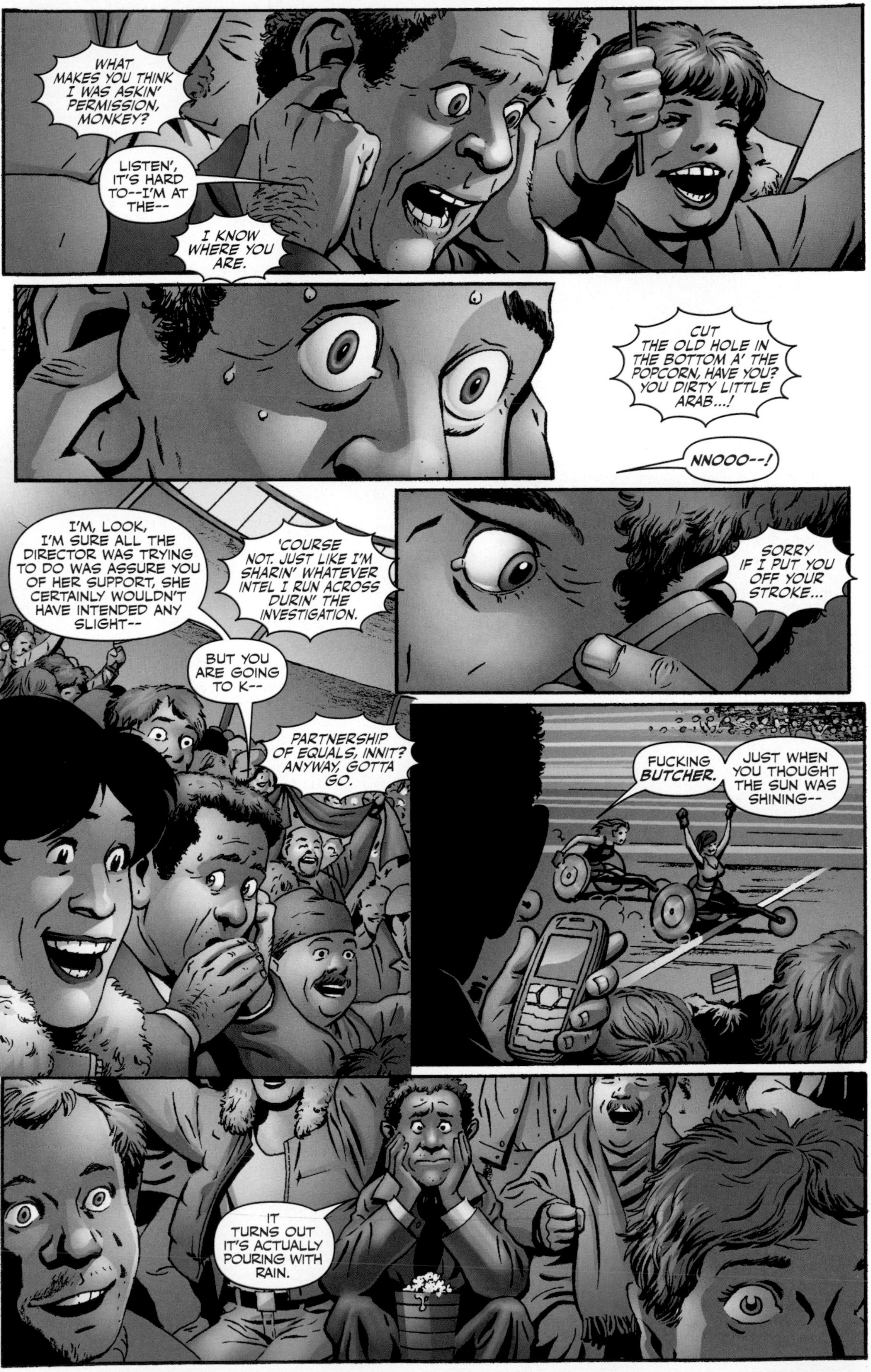
WHAT MAKES YOU THINK I WAS ASKIN' PERMISSION, MONKEY?
LISTEN', IT'S HARD TO--I'M AT THE--
I KNOW WHERE YOU ARE.
CUT THE OLD HOLE IN THE BOTTOM A' THE POPCORN, HAVE YOU? YOU DIRTY LITTLE ARAB...!
NNOOO--!
I'M, LOOK, I'M SURE ALL THE DIRECTOR WAS TRYING TO DO WAS ASSURE YOU OF HER SUPPORT, SHE CERTAINLY WOULDN'T HAVE INTENDED ANY SLIGHT--
'COURSE NOT. JUST LIKE I'M SHARIN' WHATEVER INTEL I RUN ACROSS DURIN' THE INVESTIGATION.
BUT YOU ARE GOING TO K--
PARTNERSHIP OF EQUALS, INNIT? ANYWAY, GOTTA GO.
SORRY IF I PUT YOU OFF YOUR STROKE...
FUCKING BUTCHER.
JUST WHEN YOU THOUGHT THE SUN WAS SHINING--
IT TURNS OUT IT'S ACTUALLY POURING WITH RAIN.

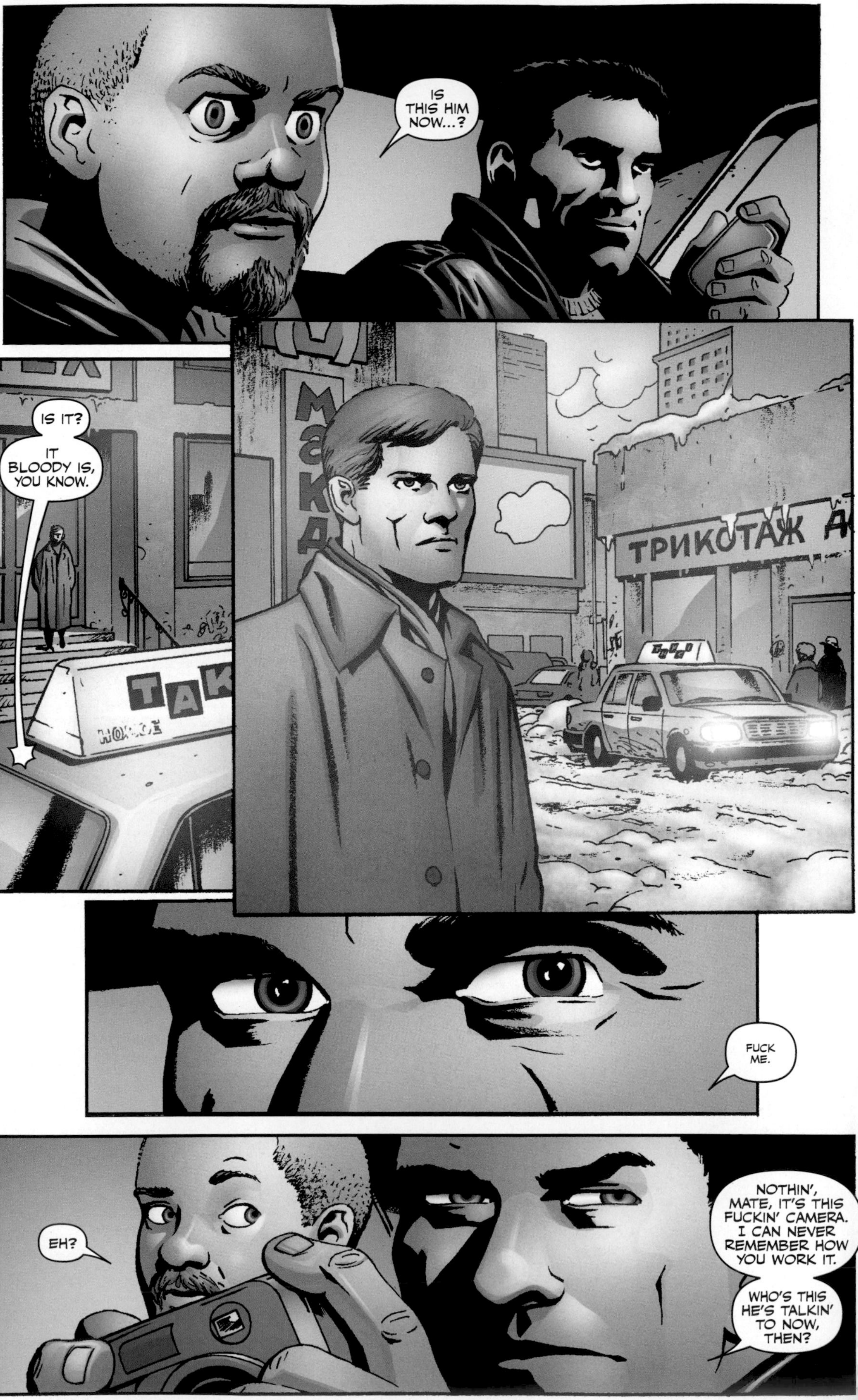
IS THIS HIM NOW...?
IS IT?
IT BLOODY IS, YOU KNOW.
ТАК
ТРИКОТАЖ
FUCK ME.
EH?
NOTHIN', MATE, IT'S THIS FUCKIN' CAMERA. I CAN NEVER REMEMBER HOW YOU WORK IT.
WHO'S THIS HE'S TALKIN' TO NOW, THEN?

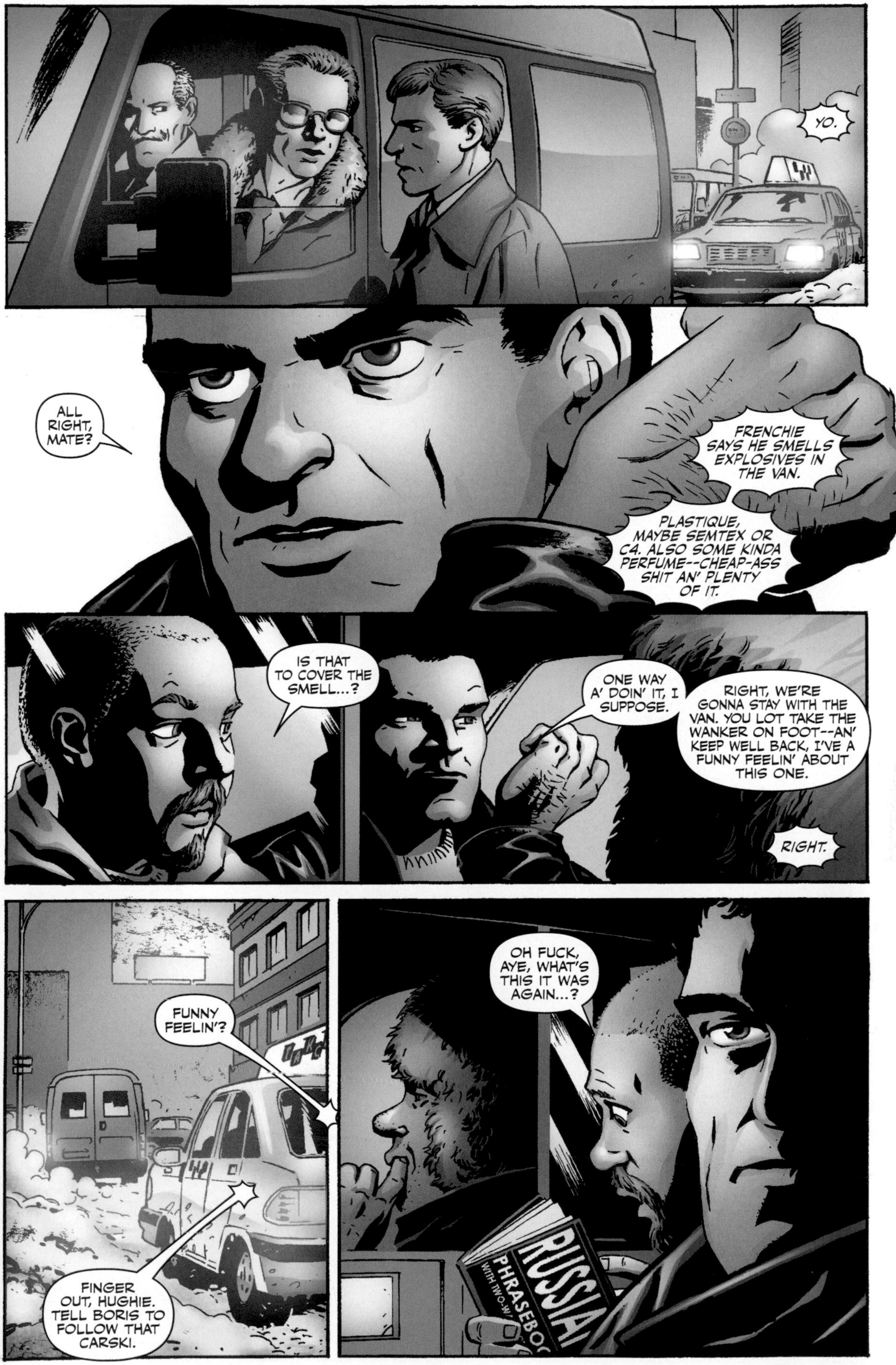
YO.
ALL RIGHT, MATE?
FRENCHIE SAYS HE SMELLS EXPLOSIVES IN THE VAN.
PLASTIQUE, MAYBE SEMTEX OR C4. ALSO SOME KINDA PERFUME--CHEAP-ASS SHIT AN' PLENTY OF IT.
IS THAT TO COVER THE SMELL...?
ONE WAY A' DOIN' IT, I SUPPOSE.
RIGHT, WE'RE GONNA STAY WITH THE VAN. YOU LOT TAKE THE WANKER ON FOOT--AN' KEEP WELL BACK, I'VE A FUNNY FEELIN' ABOUT THIS ONE.
RIGHT.
FUNNY FEELIN'?
FINGER OUT, HUGHIE. TELL BORIS TO FOLLOW THAT CARSKI.
OH FUCK, AYE, WHAT'S THIS IT WAS AGAIN...?
RUSSIAN
PHRASEBO

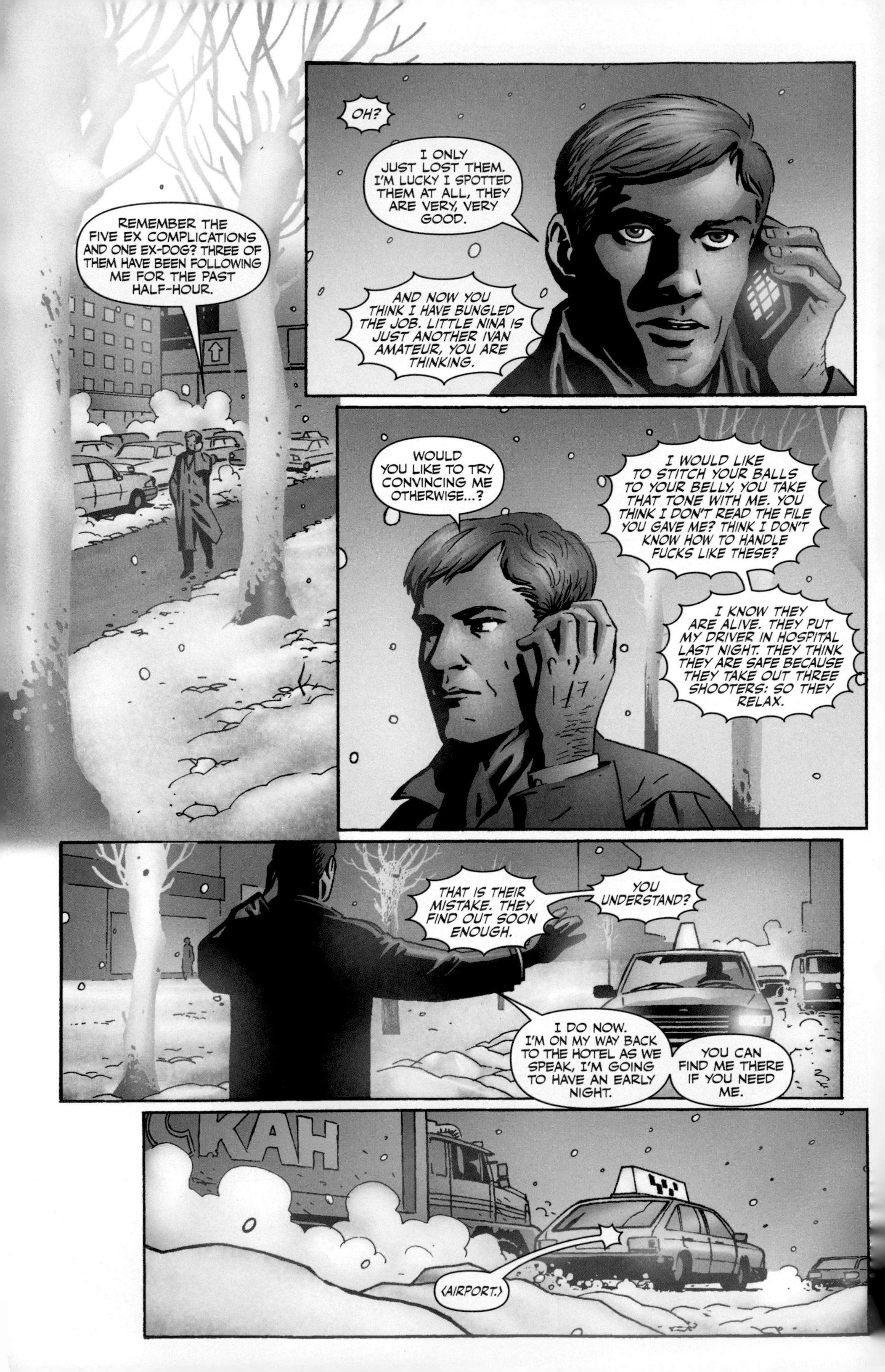
REMEMBER THE FIVE EX COMPLICATIONS AND ONE EX-DOG? THREE OF THEM HAVE BEEN FOLLOWING ME FOR THE PAST HALF-HOUR.
OH?
I ONLY JUST LOST THEM. I'M LUCKY I SPOTTED THEM AT ALL, THEY ARE VERY, VERY GOOD.
AND NOW YOU THINK I HAVE BUNGLED THE JOB. LITTLE NINA IS JUST ANOTHER IVAN AMATEUR, YOU ARE THINKING.
WOULD YOU LIKE TO TRY CONVINCING ME OTHERWISE...?
I WOULD LIKE TO STITCH YOUR BALLS TO YOUR BELLY, YOU TAKE THAT TONE WITH ME. YOU THINK I DON'T READ THE FILE YOU GAVE ME? THINK I DON'T KNOW HOW TO HANDLE FUCKS LIKE THESE?
I KNOW THEY ARE ALIVE. THEY PUT MY DRIVER IN HOSPITAL LAST NIGHT. THEY THINK THEY ARE SAFE BECAUSE THEY TAKE OUT THREE SHOOTERS: SO THEY RELAX.
THAT IS THEIR MISTAKE. THEY FIND OUT SOON ENOUGH.
YOU UNDERSTAND?
I DO NOW. I'M ON MY WAY BACK TO THE HOTEL AS WE SPEAK, I'M GOING TO HAVE AN EARLY NIGHT.
YOU CAN FIND ME THERE IF YOU NEED ME.
KAH
<AIRPORT.>

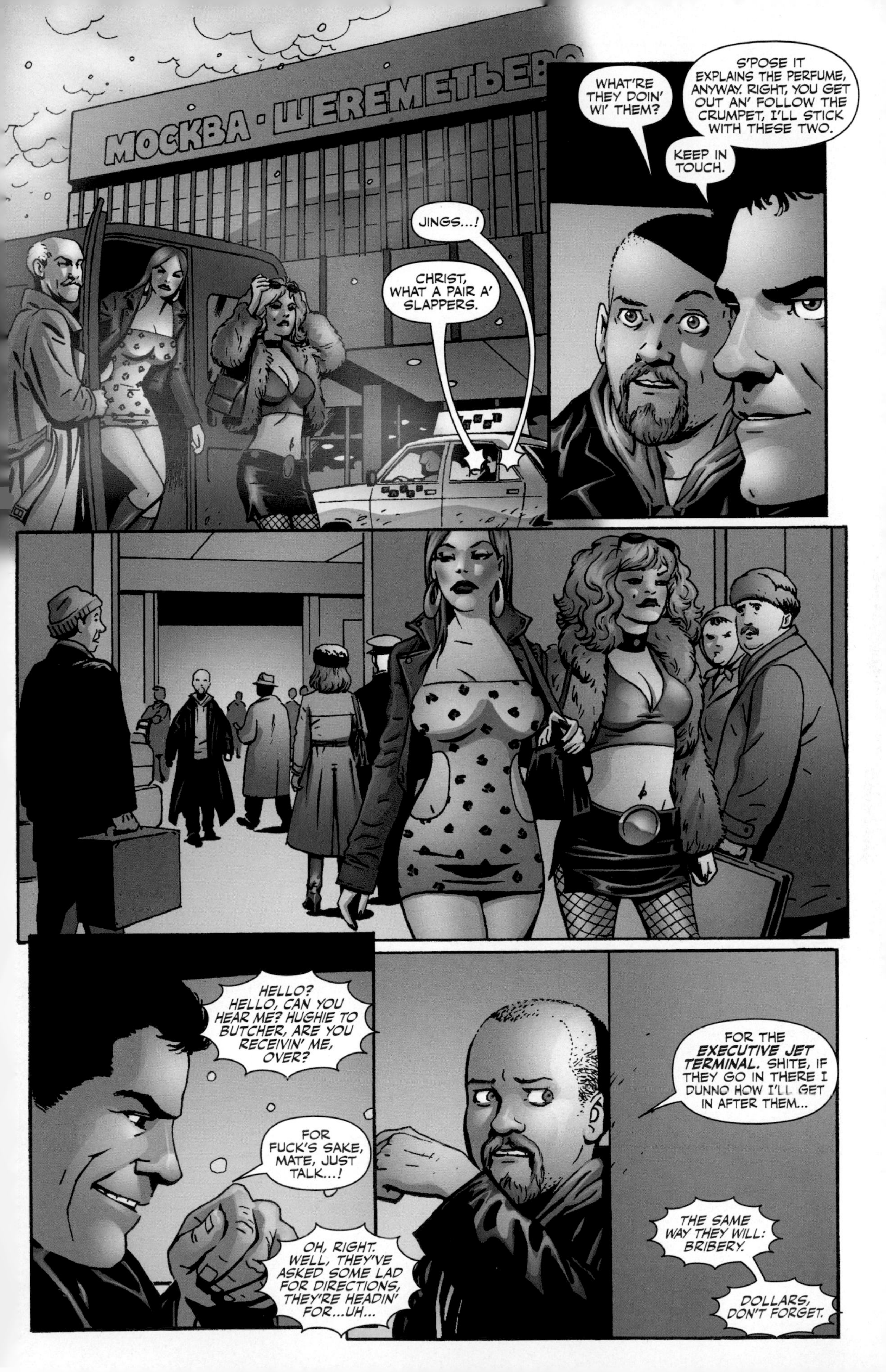
МОСКВА · ШЕРЕМЕТЬЕВО
JINGS...!
CHRIST, WHAT A PAIR A' SLAPPERS.
WHAT'RE THEY DOIN' WI' THEM?
S'POSE IT EXPLAINS THE PERFUME, ANYWAY. RIGHT, YOU GET OUT AN' FOLLOW THE CRUMPET, I'LL STICK WITH THESE TWO.
KEEP IN TOUCH.
HELLO? HELLO, CAN YOU HEAR ME? HUGHIE TO BUTCHER, ARE YOU RECEIVIN' ME, OVER?
FOR FUCK'S SAKE, MATE, JUST TALK...!
OH, RIGHT. WELL, THEY'VE ASKED SOME LAD FOR DIRECTIONS, THEY'RE HEADIN' FOR...UH...
FOR THE EXECUTIVE JET TERMINAL. SHITE, IF THEY GO IN THERE I DUNNO HOW I'LL GET IN AFTER THEM...
THE SAME WAY THEY WILL: BRIBERY.
DOLLARS, DON'T FORGET.

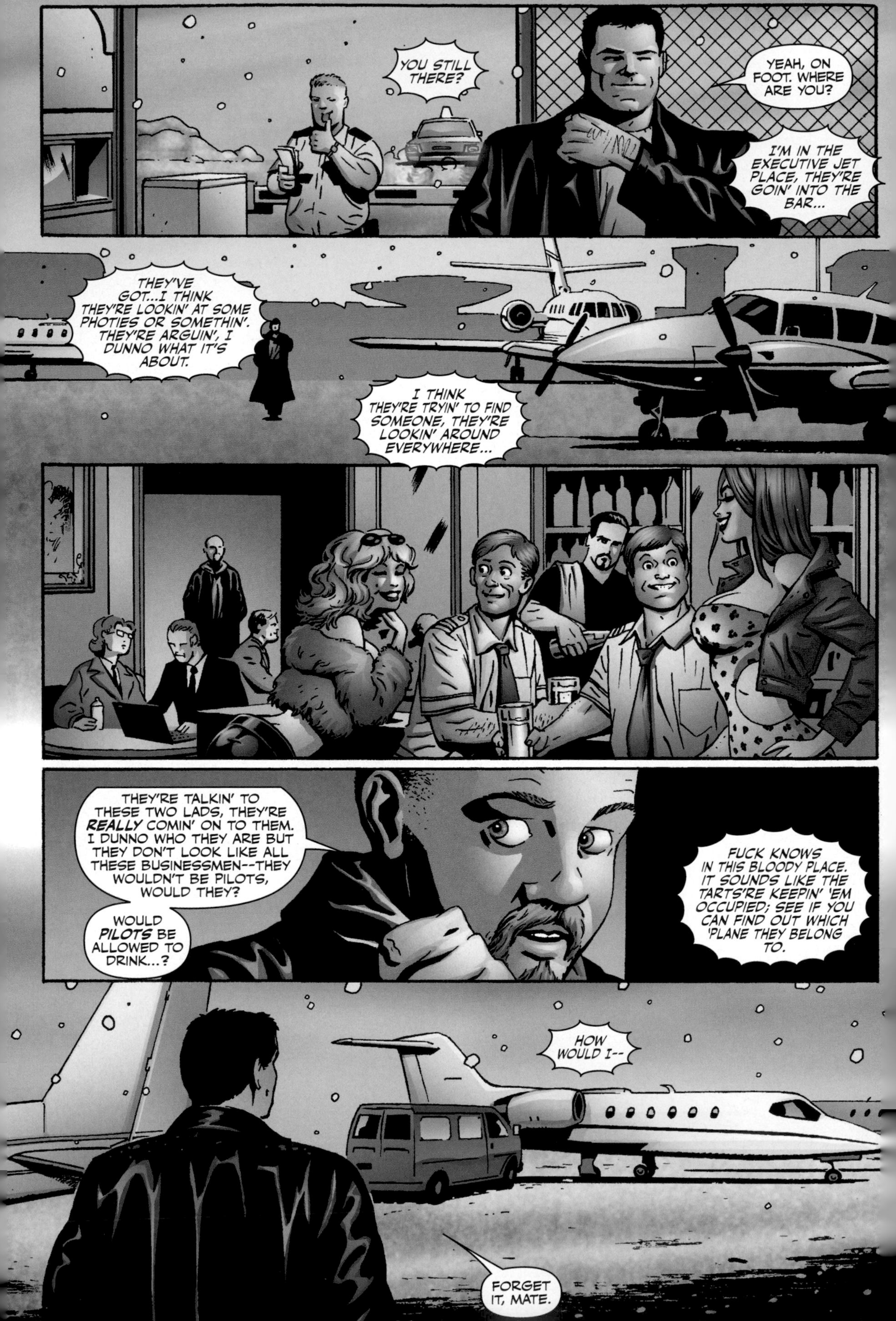
YOU STILL THERE?
YEAH, ON FOOT. WHERE ARE YOU?
I'M IN THE EXECUTIVE JET PLACE, THEY'RE GOIN' INTO THE BAR...
THEY'VE GOT...I THINK THEY'RE LOOKIN' AT SOME PHOTIES OR SOMETHIN'. THEY'RE ARGUIN', I DUNNO WHAT IT'S ABOUT.
I THINK THEY'RE TRYIN' TO FIND SOMEONE, THEY'RE LOOKIN' AROUND EVERYWHERE...
THEY'RE TALKIN' TO THESE TWO LADS, THEY'RE REALLY COMIN' ON TO THEM. I DUNNO WHO THEY ARE BUT THEY DON'T LOOK LIKE ALL THESE BUSINESSMEN--THEY WOULDN'T BE PILOTS, WOULD THEY?
WOULD PILOTS BE ALLOWED TO DRINK...?
FUCK KNOWS IN THIS BLOODY PLACE. IT SOUNDS LIKE THE TARTS'RE KEEPIN' 'EM OCCUPIED; SEE IF YOU CAN FIND OUT WHICH 'PLANE THEY BELONG TO.
HOW WOULD I--
FORGET IT, MATE.

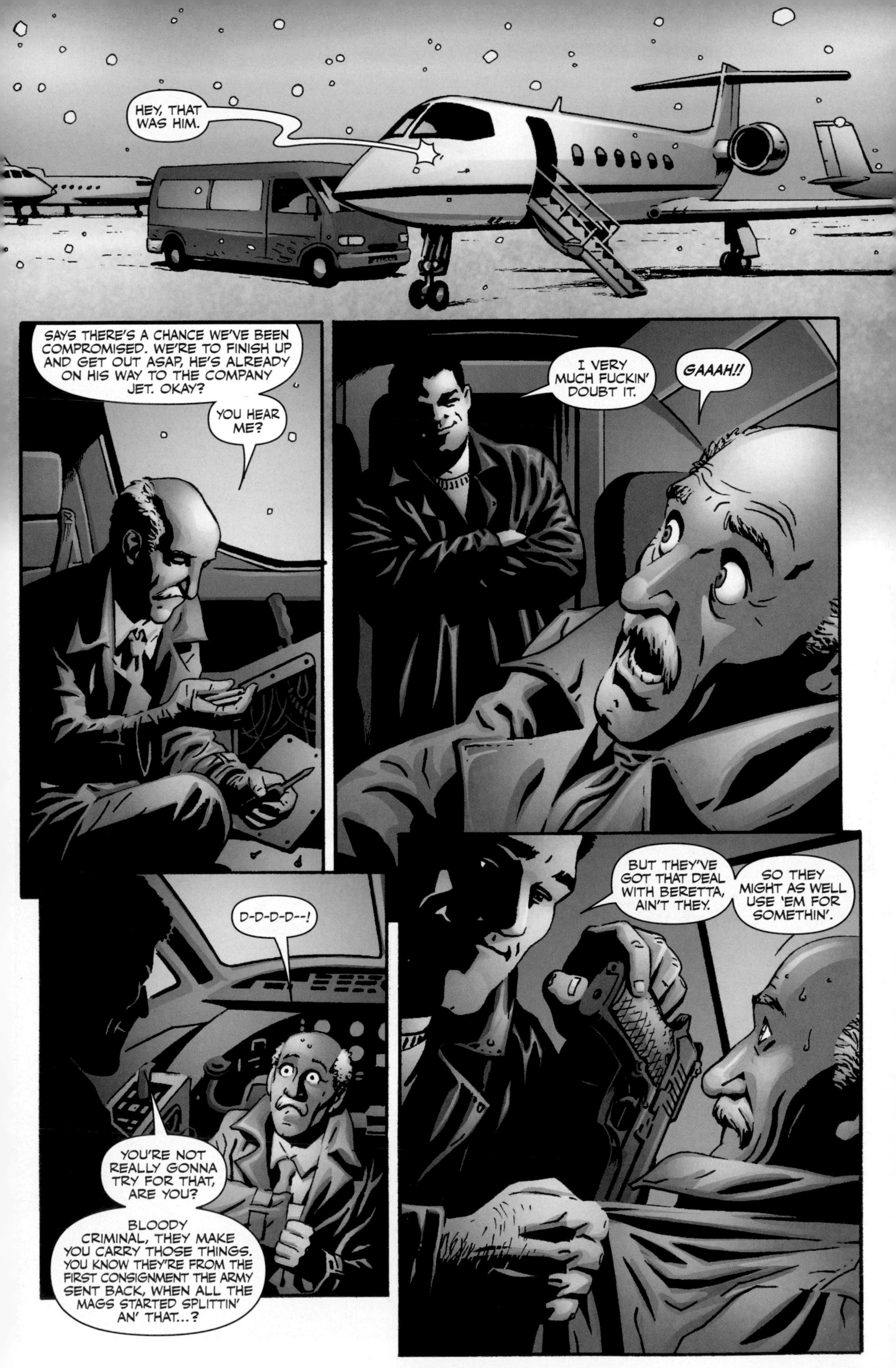
HEY, THAT WAS HIM.
SAYS THERE'S A CHANCE WE'VE BEEN COMPROMISED. WE'RE TO FINISH UP AND GET OUT ASAP, HE'S ALREADY ON HIS WAY TO THE COMPANY JET. OKAY?
YOU HEAR ME?
I VERY MUCH FUCKIN' DOUBT IT.
GAAAH!!
D-D-D-D--!
YOU'RE NOT REALLY GONNA TRY FOR THAT, ARE YOU?
BLOODY CRIMINAL, THEY MAKE YOU CARRY THOSE THINGS. YOU KNOW THEY'RE FROM THE FIRST CONSIGNMENT THE ARMY SENT BACK, WHEN ALL THE MAGS STARTED SPLITTIN' AN' THAT...?
BUT THEY'VE GOT THAT DEAL WITH BERETTA, AIN'T THEY.
SO THEY MIGHT AS WELL USE 'EM FOR SOMETHIN'.

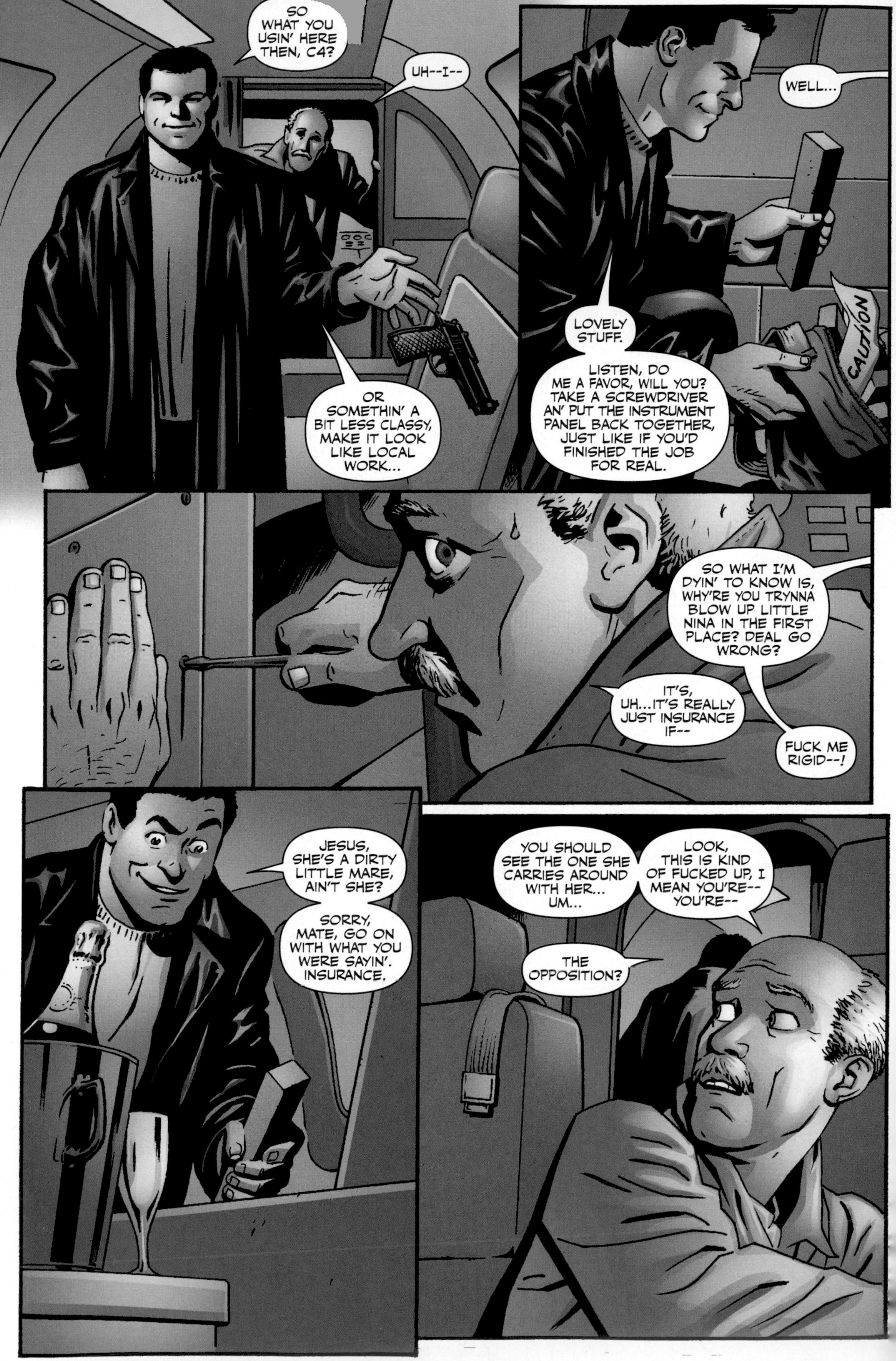
SO WHAT YOU USIN' HERE THEN, C4?
UH--I--
OR SOMETHIN' A BIT LESS CLASSY, MAKE IT LOOK LIKE LOCAL WORK...
WELL...
LOVELY STUFF.
LISTEN, DO ME A FAVOR, WILL YOU? TAKE A SCREWDRIVER AN' PUT THE INSTRUMENT PANEL BACK TOGETHER, JUST LIKE IF YOU'D FINISHED THE JOB FOR REAL.
CAUTION
SO WHAT I'M DYIN' TO KNOW IS, WHY'RE YOU TRYNNA BLOW UP LITTLE NINA IN THE FIRST PLACE? DEAL GO WRONG?
IT'S, UH...IT'S REALLY JUST INSURANCE IF--
FUCK ME RIGID--!
JESUS, SHE'S A DIRTY LITTLE MARE, AIN'T SHE?
SORRY, MATE, GO ON WITH WHAT YOU WERE SAYIN'. INSURANCE.
YOU SHOULD SEE THE ONE SHE CARRIES AROUND WITH HER... UM...
LOOK, THIS IS KIND OF FUCKED UP, I MEAN YOU'RE-- YOU'RE--
THE OPPOSITION?

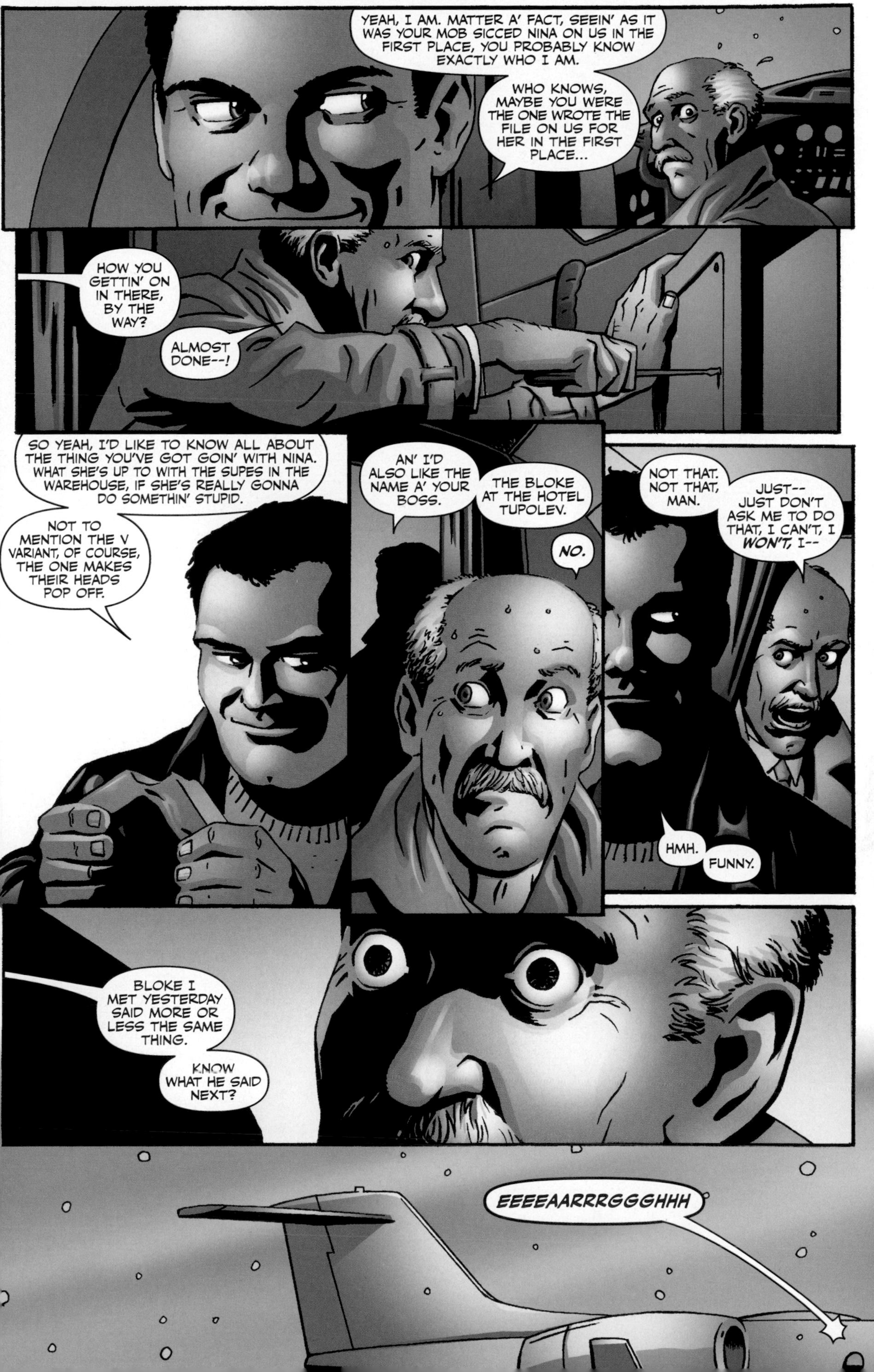
YEAH, I AM. MATTER A' FACT, SEEIN' AS IT WAS YOUR MOB SICCED NINA ON US IN THE FIRST PLACE, YOU PROBABLY KNOW EXACTLY WHO I AM.
WHO KNOWS, MAYBE YOU WERE THE ONE WROTE THE FILE ON US FOR HER IN THE FIRST PLACE...
HOW YOU GETTIN' ON IN THERE, BY THE WAY?
ALMOST DONE--!
SO YEAH, I'D LIKE TO KNOW ALL ABOUT THE THING YOU'VE GOT GOIN' WITH NINA. WHAT SHE'S UP TO WITH THE SUPES IN THE WAREHOUSE, IF SHE'S REALLY GONNA DO SOMETHIN' STUPID.
NOT TO MENTION THE V VARIANT, OF COURSE, THE ONE MAKES THEIR HEADS POP OFF.
AN' I'D ALSO LIKE THE NAME A' YOUR BOSS.
THE BLOKE AT THE HOTEL TUPOLEV.
NO.
NOT THAT. NOT THAT, MAN.
JUST-- JUST DON'T ASK ME TO DO THAT, I CAN'T, I WON'T, I--
HMH.
FUNNY.
BLOKE I MET YESTERDAY SAID MORE OR LESS THE SAME THING.
KNOW WHAT HE SAID NEXT?
EEEEAARRRGGGHHH

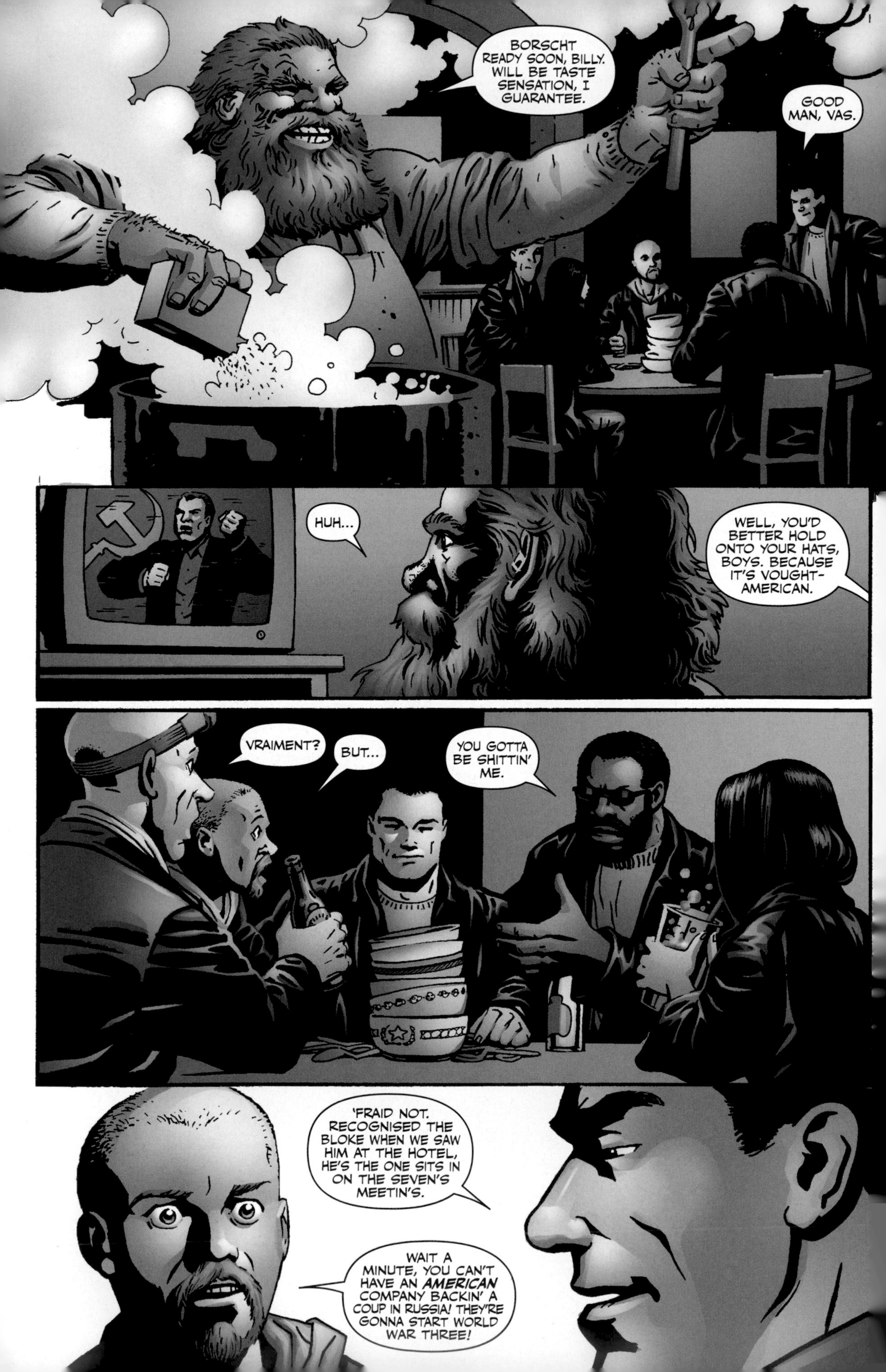
BORSCHT READY SOON, BILLY. WILL BE TASTE SENSATION, I GUARANTEE.
GOOD MAN, VAS.
HUH...
WELL, YOU'D BETTER HOLD ONTO YOUR HATS, BOYS. BECAUSE IT'S VOUGHT-AMERICAN.
VRAIMENT?
BUT...
YOU GOTTA BE SHITTIN' ME.
'FRAID NOT. RECOGNISED THE BLOKE WHEN WE SAW HIM AT THE HOTEL, HE'S THE ONE SITS IN ON THE SEVEN'S MEETIN'S.
WAIT A MINUTE, YOU CAN'T HAVE AN *AMERICAN* COMPANY BACKIN' A COUP IN RUSSIA! THEY'RE GONNA START WORLD WAR THREE!

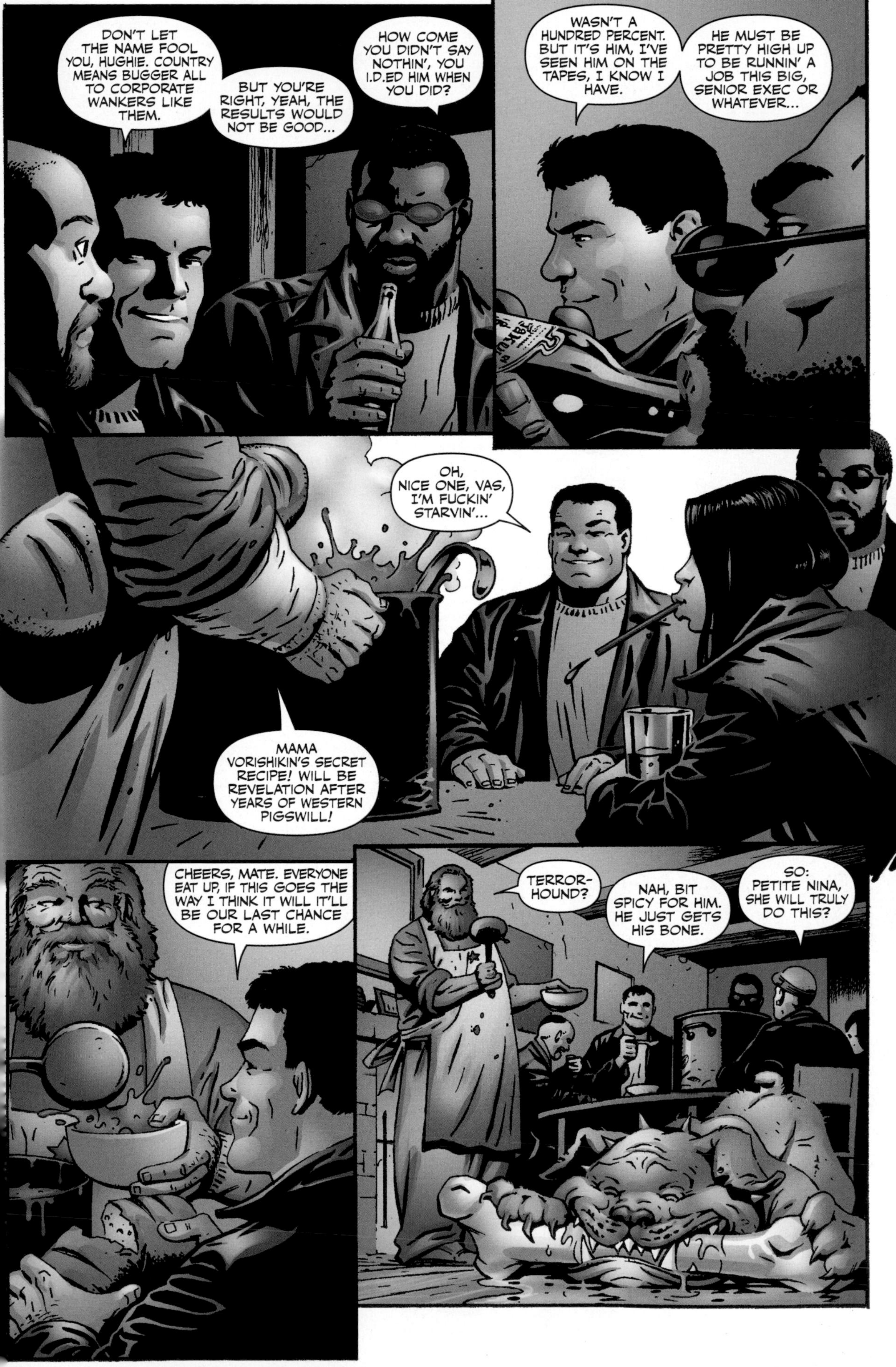
DON'T LET THE NAME FOOL YOU, HUGHIE. COUNTRY MEANS BUGGER ALL TO CORPORATE WANKERS LIKE THEM.
BUT YOU'RE RIGHT, YEAH, THE RESULTS WOULD NOT BE GOOD...
HOW COME YOU DIDN'T SAY NOTHIN', YOU I.D.ED HIM WHEN YOU DID?
WASN'T A HUNDRED PERCENT. BUT IT'S HIM, I'VE SEEN HIM ON THE TAPES, I KNOW I HAVE.
HE MUST BE PRETTY HIGH UP TO BE RUNNIN' A JOB THIS BIG, SENIOR EXEC OR WHATEVER...
OH, NICE ONE, VAS, I'M FUCKIN' STARVIN'...
MAMA VORISHIKIN'S SECRET RECIPE! WILL BE REVELATION AFTER YEARS OF WESTERN PIGSWILL!
CHEERS, MATE. EVERYONE EAT UP, IF THIS GOES THE WAY I THINK IT WILL IT'LL BE OUR LAST CHANCE FOR A WHILE.
TERROR-HOUND?
NAH, BIT SPICY FOR HIM. HE JUST GETS HIS BONE.
SO: PETITE NINA, SHE WILL TRULY DO THIS?

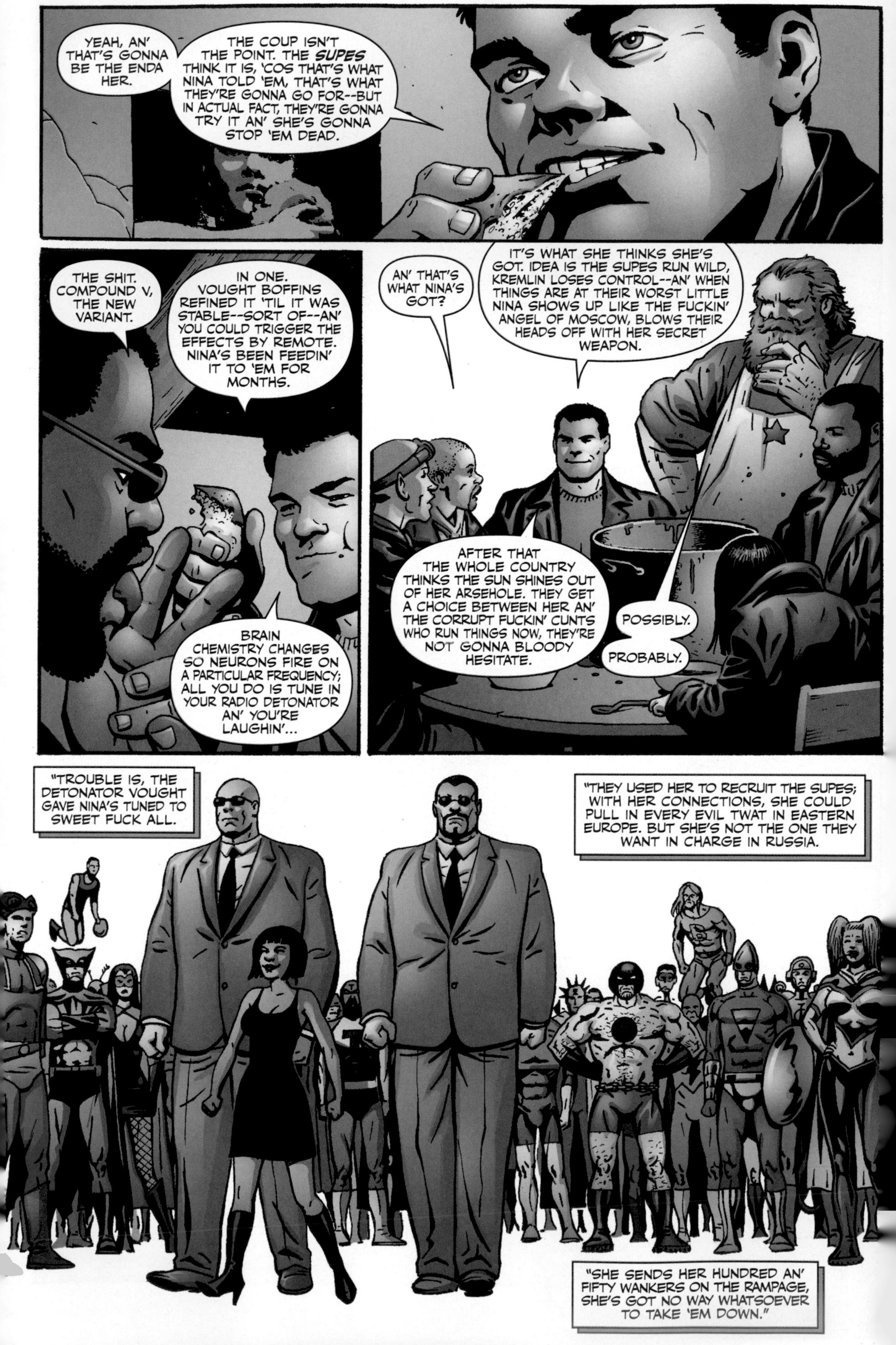
YEAH, AN' THAT'S GONNA BE THE ENDA HER.
THE COUP ISN'T THE POINT. THE *SUPES* THINK IT IS, 'COS THAT'S WHAT NINA TOLD 'EM, THAT'S WHAT THEY'RE GONNA GO FOR--BUT IN ACTUAL FACT, THEY'RE GONNA TRY IT AN' SHE'S GONNA STOP 'EM DEAD.
THE SHIT. COMPOUND V, THE NEW VARIANT.
IN ONE. VOUGHT BOFFINS REFINED IT 'TIL IT WAS STABLE--SORT OF--AN' YOU COULD TRIGGER THE EFFECTS BY REMOTE. NINA'S BEEN FEEDIN' IT TO 'EM FOR MONTHS.
BRAIN CHEMISTRY CHANGES SO NEURONS FIRE ON A PARTICULAR FREQUENCY; ALL YOU DO IS TUNE IN YOUR RADIO DETONATOR AN' YOU'RE LAUGHIN'...
AN' THAT'S WHAT NINA'S GOT?
IT'S WHAT SHE THINKS SHE'S GOT. IDEA IS THE SUPES RUN WILD, KREMLIN LOSES CONTROL--AN' WHEN THINGS ARE AT THEIR WORST LITTLE NINA SHOWS UP LIKE THE FUCKIN' ANGEL OF MOSCOW, BLOWS THEIR HEADS OFF WITH HER SECRET WEAPON.
AFTER THAT THE WHOLE COUNTRY THINKS THE SUN SHINES OUT OF HER ARSEHOLE. THEY GET A CHOICE BETWEEN HER AN' THE CORRUPT FUCKIN' CUNTS WHO RUN THINGS NOW, THEY'RE NOT GONNA BLOODY HESITATE.
POSSIBLY.
PROBABLY.
"TROUBLE IS, THE DETONATOR VOUGHT GAVE NINA'S TUNED TO SWEET FUCK ALL.
"THEY USED HER TO RECRUIT THE SUPES; WITH HER CONNECTIONS, SHE COULD PULL IN EVERY EVIL TWAT IN EASTERN EUROPE. BUT SHE'S NOT THE ONE THEY WANT IN CHARGE IN RUSSIA.
"SHE SENDS HER HUNDRED AN' FIFTY WANKERS ON THE RAMPAGE, SHE'S GOT NO WAY WHATSOEVER TO TAKE 'EM DOWN."

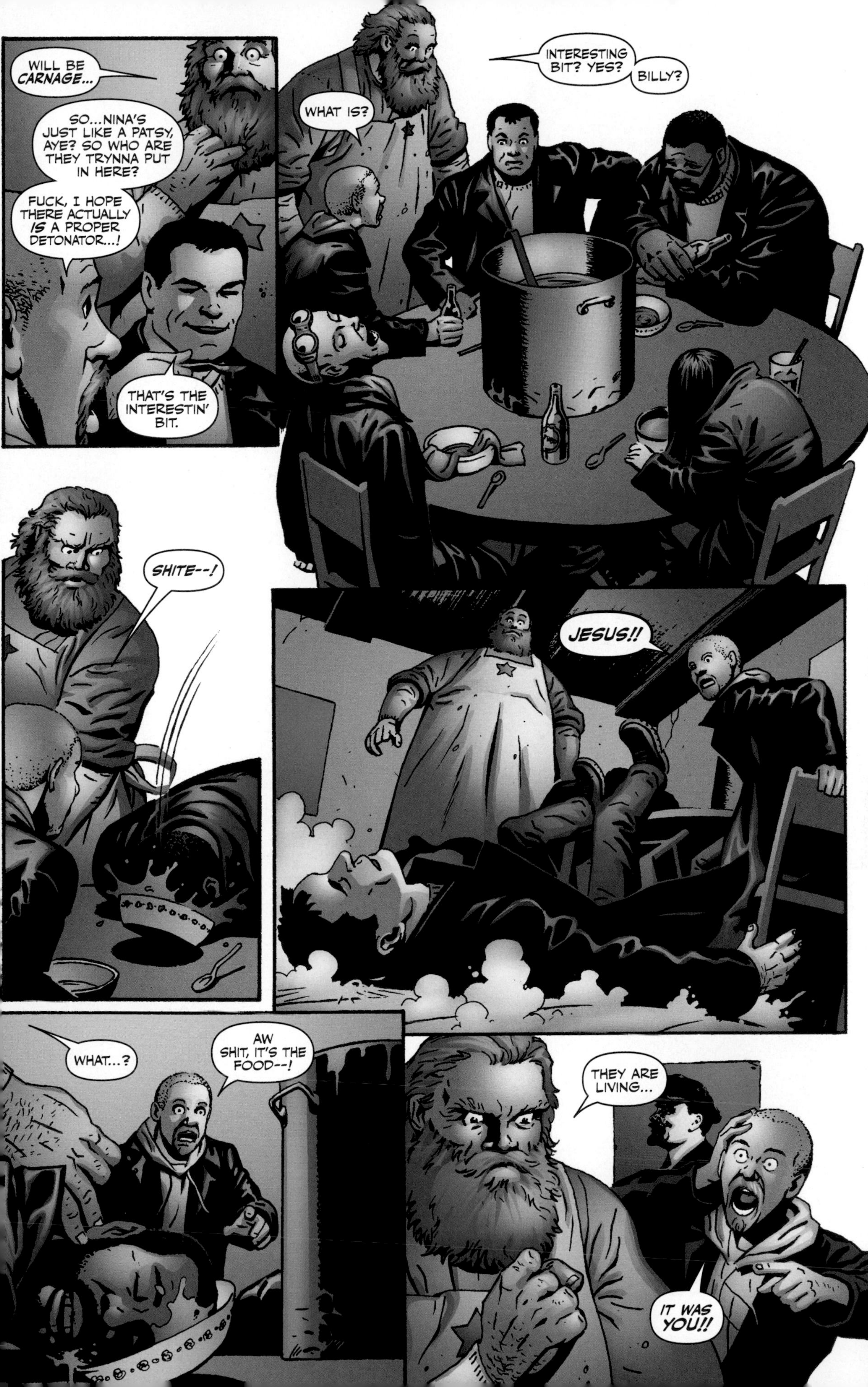
WILL BE CARNAGE...
SO...NINA'S JUST LIKE A PATSY, AYE? SO WHO ARE THEY TRYNNA PUT IN HERE?
FUCK, I HOPE THERE ACTUALLY IS A PROPER DETONATOR...!
THAT'S THE INTERESTIN' BIT.
WHAT IS?
INTERESTING BIT? YES?
BILLY?
SHITE--!
JESUS!!
WHAT...?
AW SHIT, IT'S THE FOOD--!
THEY ARE LIVING...
IT WAS YOU!!

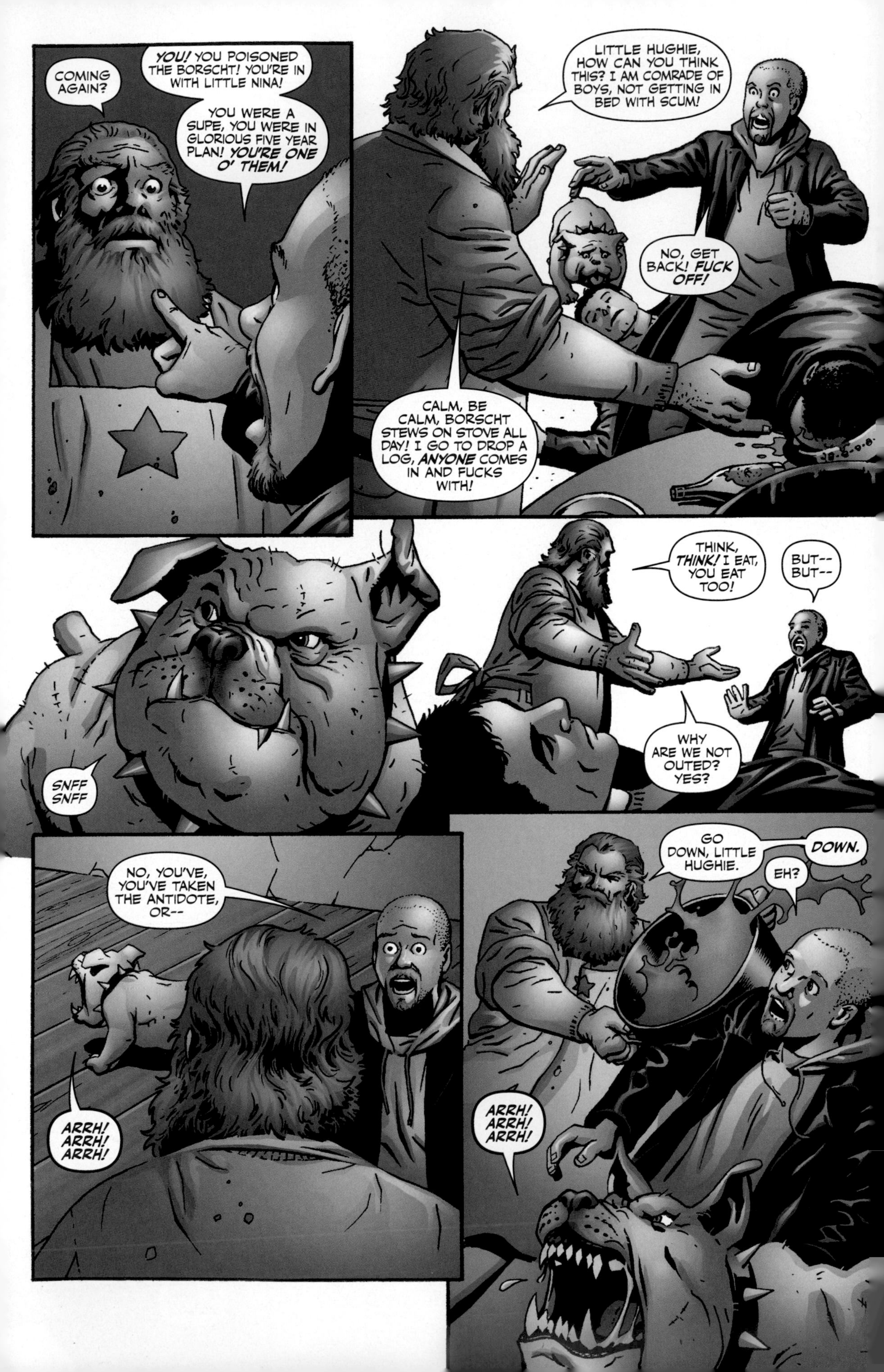
COMING AGAIN?
YOU! YOU POISONED THE BORSCHT! YOU'RE IN WITH LITTLE NINA!
YOU WERE A SUPE, YOU WERE IN GLORIOUS FIVE YEAR PLAN! YOU'RE ONE O' THEM!
LITTLE HUGHIE, HOW CAN YOU THINK THIS? I AM COMRADE OF BOYS, NOT GETTING IN BED WITH SCUM!
NO, GET BACK! FUCK OFF!
CALM, BE CALM, BORSCHT STEWS ON STOVE ALL DAY! I GO TO DROP A LOG, ANYONE COMES IN AND FUCKS WITH!
SNFF SNFF
THINK, THINK! I EAT, YOU EAT TOO!
BUT-- BUT--
WHY ARE WE NOT OUTED? YES?
NO, YOU'VE, YOU'VE TAKEN THE ANTIDOTE, OR--
ARRH! ARRH! ARRH!
GO DOWN, LITTLE HUGHIE.
DOWN.
EH?
ARRH! ARRH! ARRH!

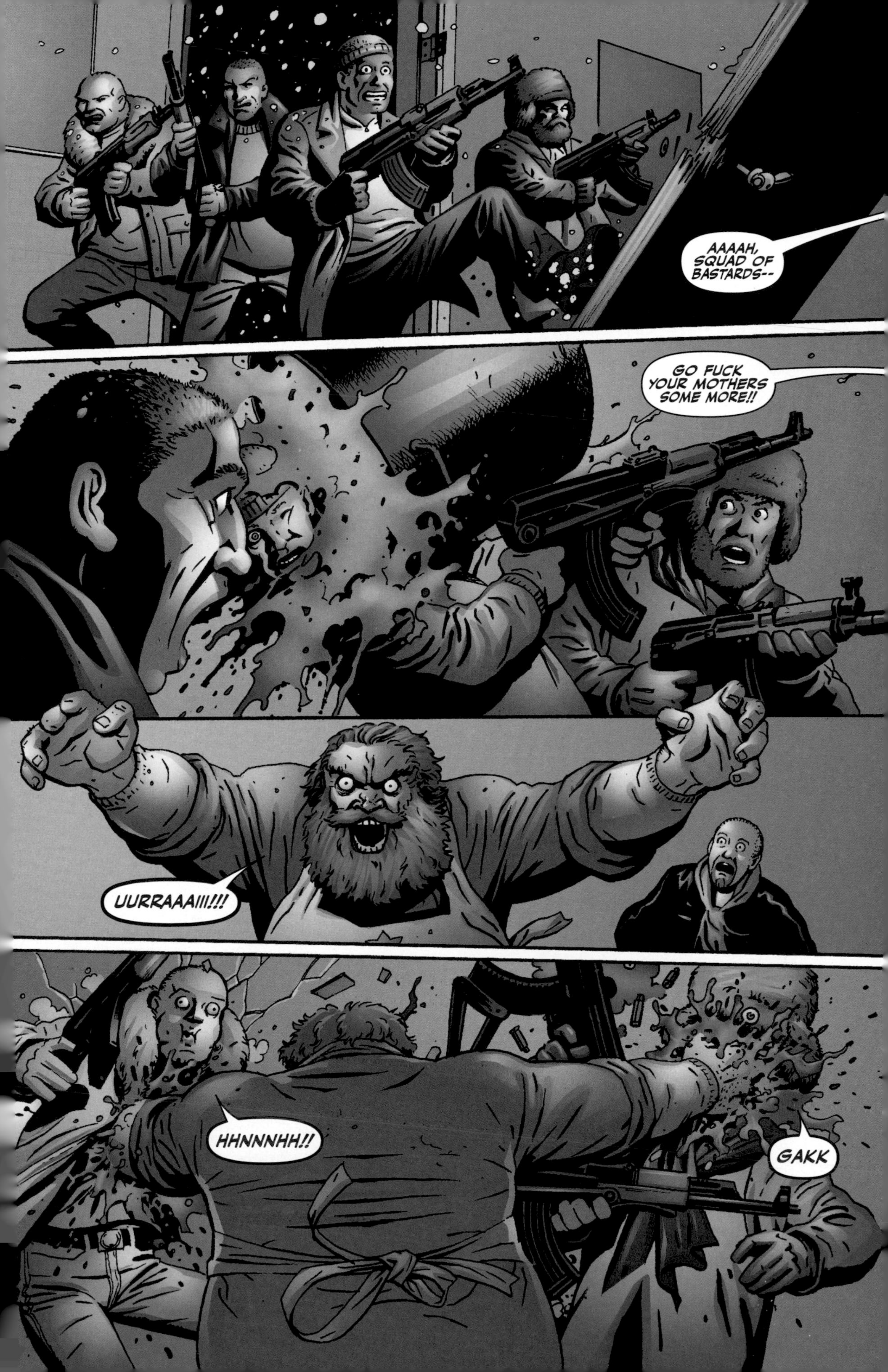
AAAAH, SQUAD OF BASTARDS--
GO FUCK YOUR MOTHERS SOME MORE!!
UURRAAAIII!!!
HHNNNHH!!
GAKK

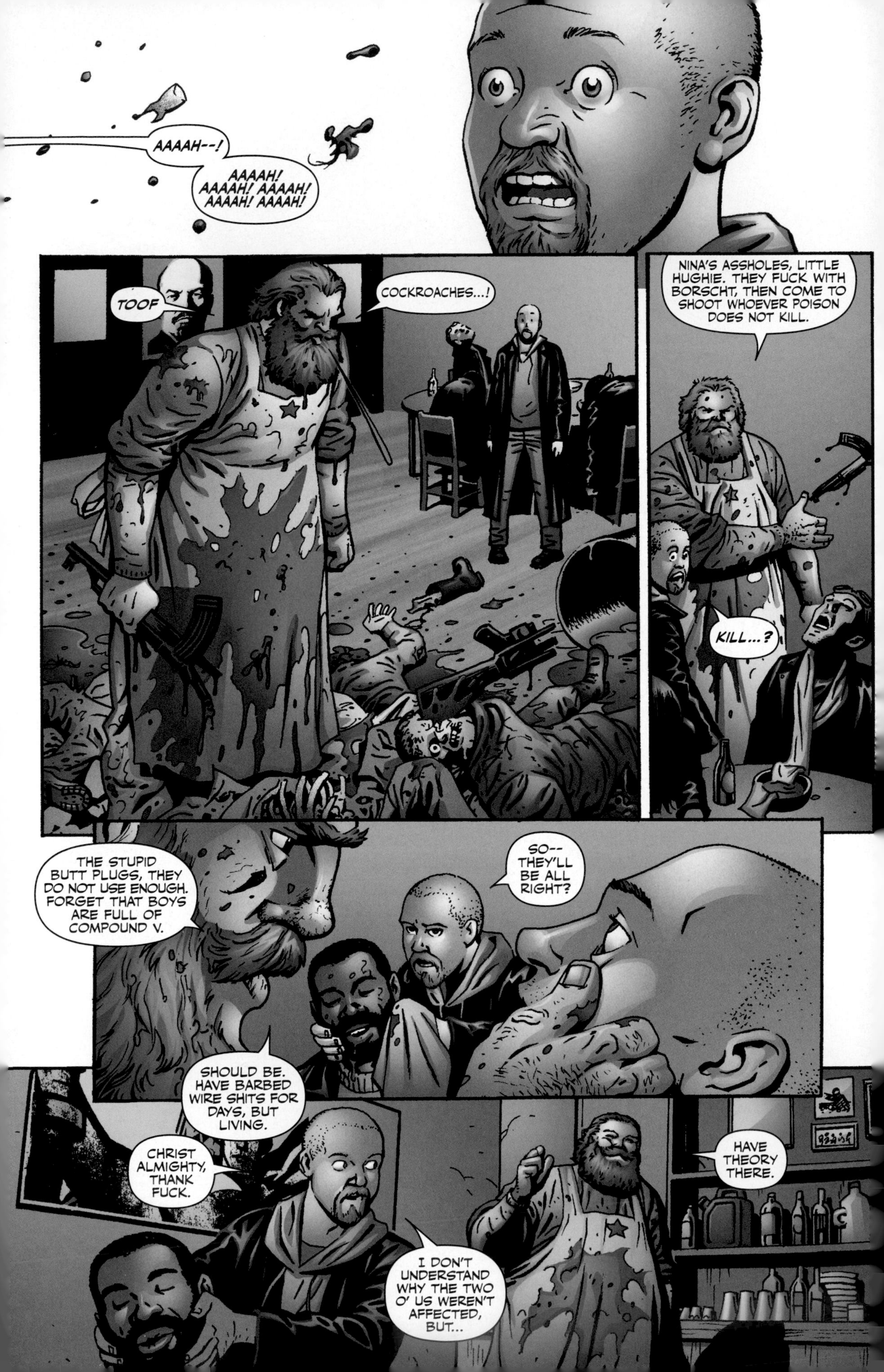
AAAAH--!
AAAAH! AAAAH! AAAAH! AAAAH! AAAAH!
TOOF
COCKROACHES...!
NINA'S ASSHOLES, LITTLE HUGHIE. THEY FUCK WITH BORSCHT, THEN COME TO SHOOT WHOEVER POISON DOES NOT KILL.
KILL...?
THE STUPID BUTT PLUGS, THEY DO NOT USE ENOUGH. FORGET THAT BOYS ARE FULL OF COMPOUND V.
SO-- THEY'LL BE ALL RIGHT?
SHOULD BE. HAVE BARBED WIRE SHITS FOR DAYS, BUT LIVING.
CHRIST ALMIGHTY, THANK FUCK.
I DON'T UNDERSTAND WHY THE TWO O' US WEREN'T AFFECTED, BUT...
HAVE THEORY THERE.

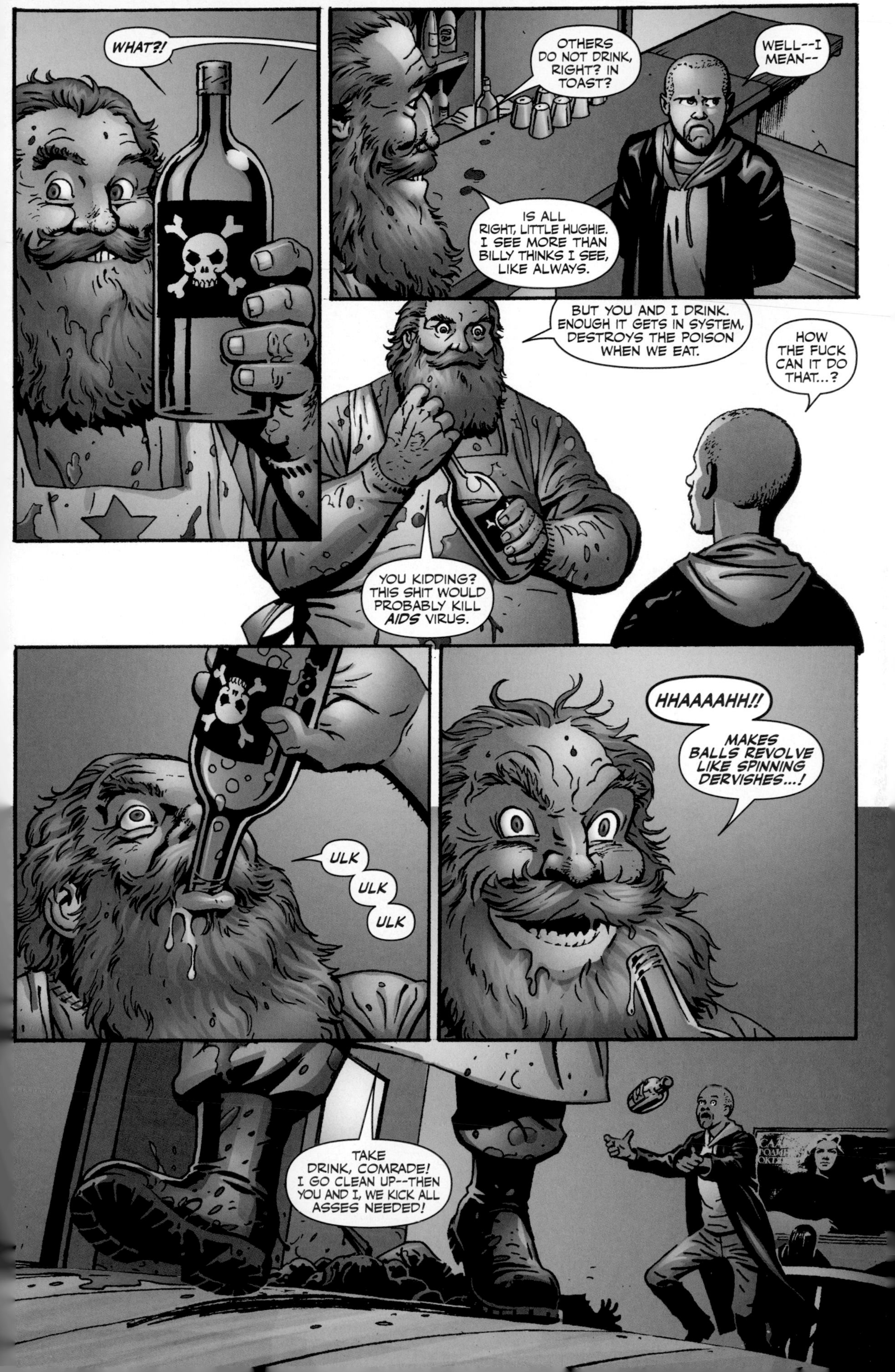
WHAT?!
OTHERS DO NOT DRINK, RIGHT? IN TOAST?
WELL--I MEAN--
IS ALL RIGHT, LITTLE HUGHIE. I SEE MORE THAN BILLY THINKS I SEE, LIKE ALWAYS.
BUT YOU AND I DRINK. ENOUGH IT GETS IN SYSTEM, DESTROYS THE POISON WHEN WE EAT.
HOW THE FUCK CAN IT DO THAT...?
YOU KIDDING? THIS SHIT WOULD PROBABLY KILL AIDS VIRUS.
ULK
ULK
ULK
HHAAAAHH!!
MAKES BALLS REVOLVE LIKE SPINNING DERVISHES...!
TAKE DRINK, COMRADE! I GO CLEAN UP--THEN YOU AND I, WE KICK ALL ASSES NEEDED!

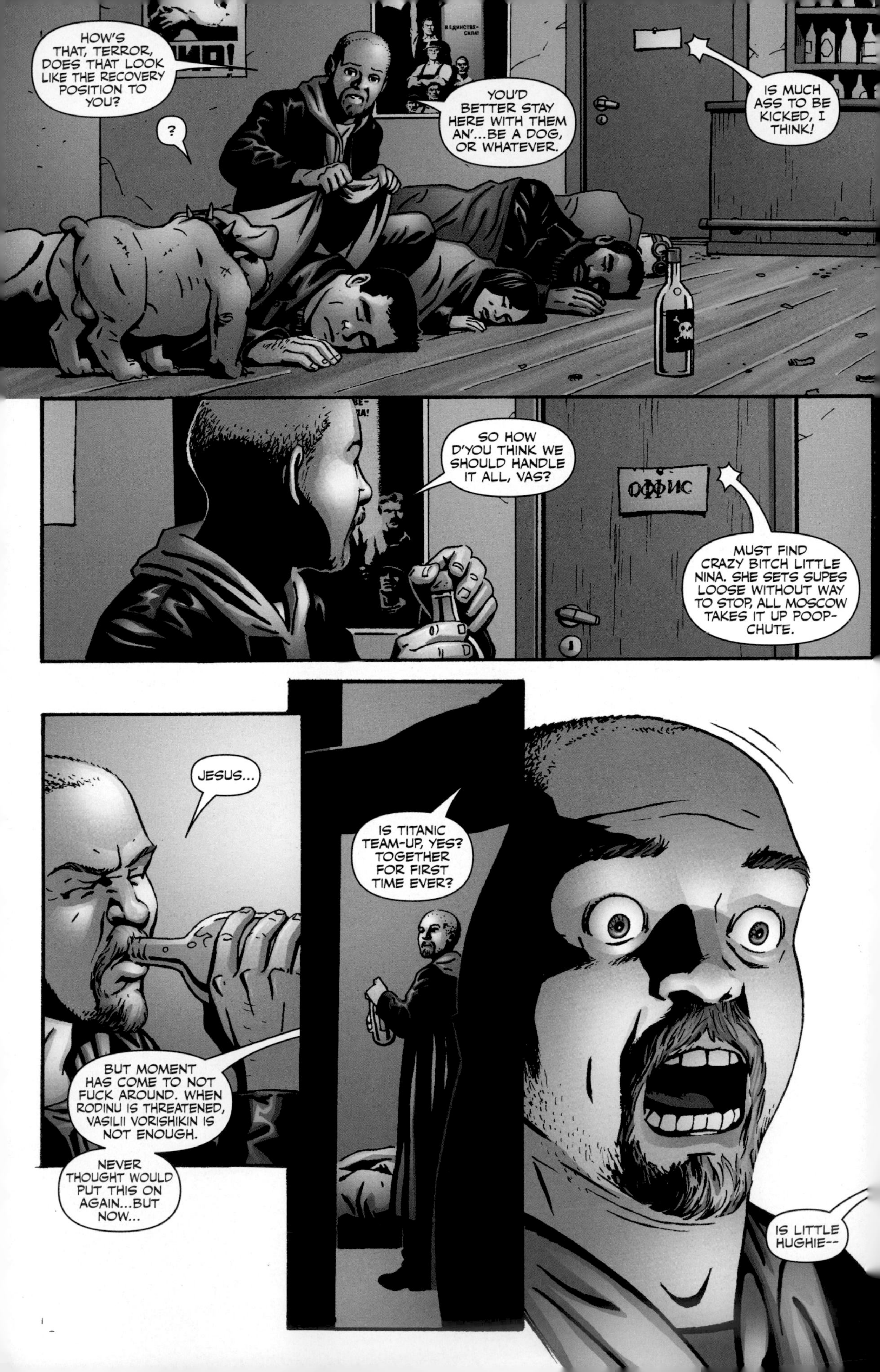
HOW'S THAT, TERROR, DOES THAT LOOK LIKE THE RECOVERY POSITION TO YOU?
?
YOU'D BETTER STAY HERE WITH THEM AN'...BE A DOG, OR WHATEVER.
IS MUCH ASS TO BE KICKED, I THINK!
SO HOW D'YOU THINK WE SHOULD HANDLE IT ALL, VAS?
ОФФИС
MUST FIND CRAZY BITCH LITTLE NINA. SHE SETS SUPES LOOSE WITHOUT WAY TO STOP, ALL MOSCOW TAKES IT UP POOP-CHUTE.
JESUS...
BUT MOMENT HAS COME TO NOT FUCK AROUND. WHEN RODINU IS THREATENED, VASILII VORISHIKIN IS NOT ENOUGH.
NEVER THOUGHT WOULD PUT THIS ON AGAIN...BUT NOW...
IS TITANIC TEAM-UP, YES? TOGETHER FOR FIRST TIME EVER?
IS LITTLE HUGHIE--

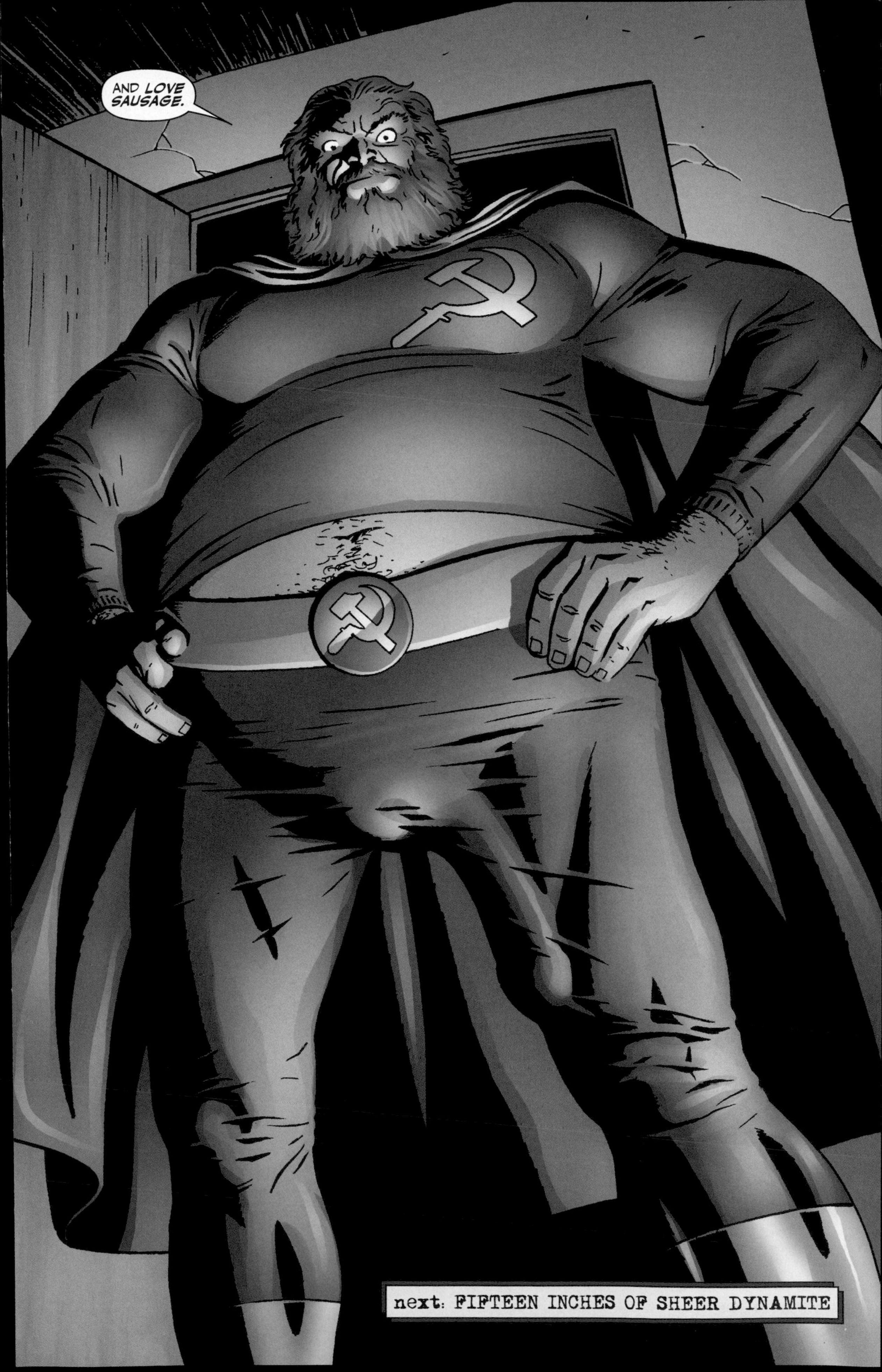
AND LOVE SAUSAGE.
next: FIFTEEN INCHES OF SHEER DYNAMITE

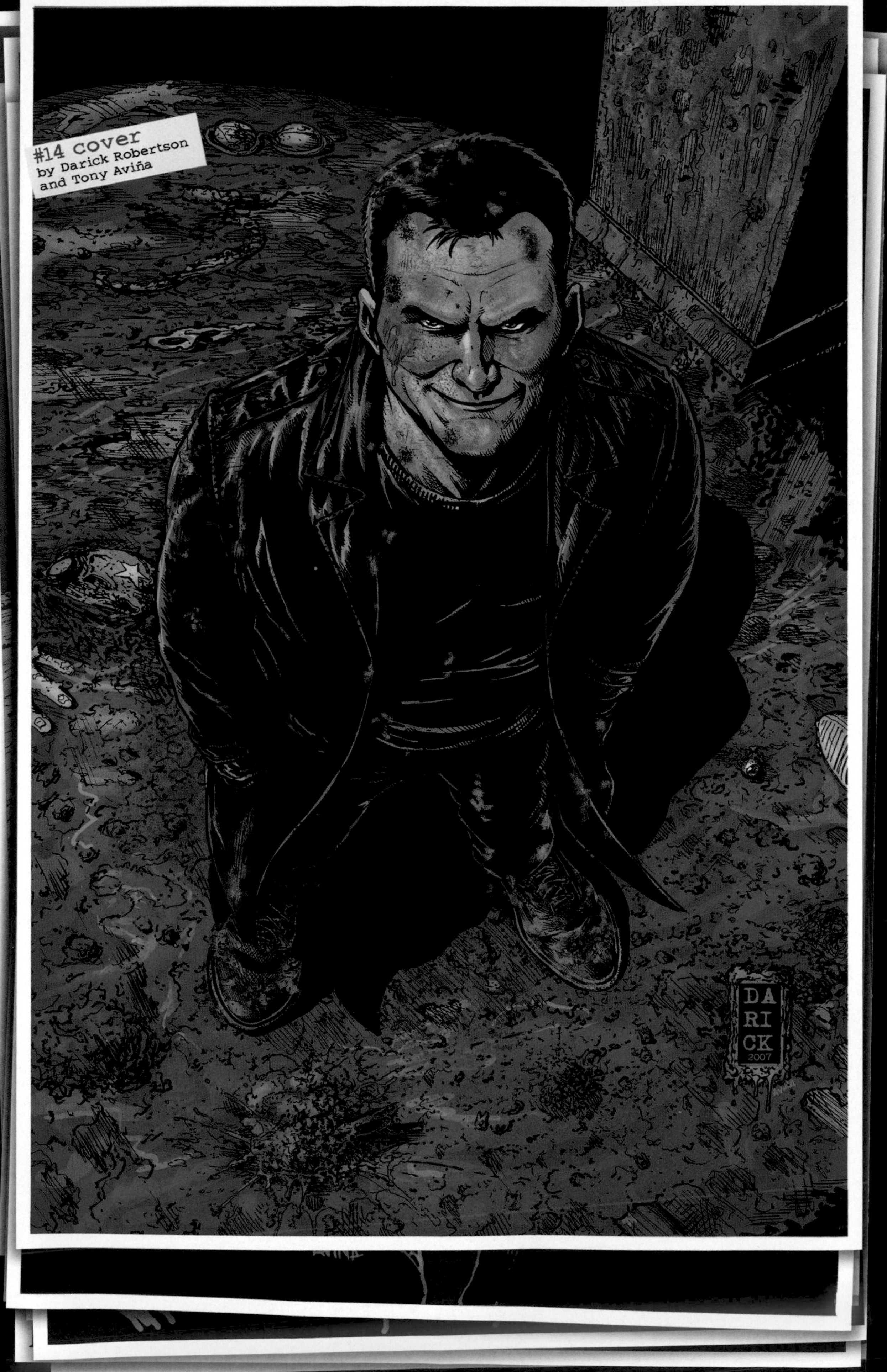
DA
RI
CK
2007

#14 cover
by Darick Robertson
and Tony Aviña

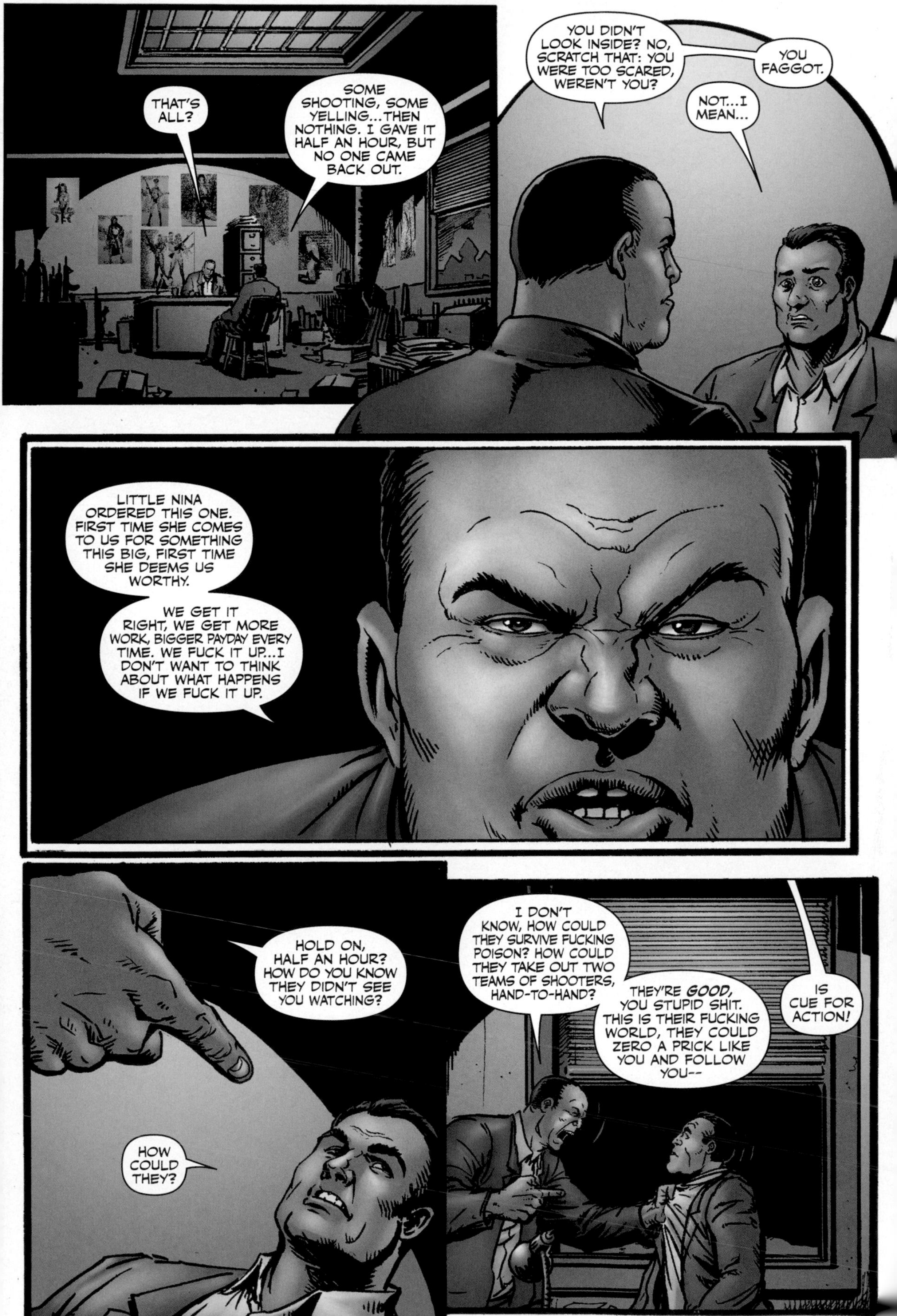
THAT'S ALL?
SOME SHOOTING, SOME YELLING...THEN NOTHING. I GAVE IT HALF AN HOUR, BUT NO ONE CAME BACK OUT.
YOU DIDN'T LOOK INSIDE? NO, SCRATCH THAT: YOU WERE TOO SCARED, WEREN'T YOU?
YOU FAGGOT.
NOT...I MEAN...
LITTLE NINA ORDERED THIS ONE. FIRST TIME SHE COMES TO US FOR SOMETHING THIS BIG, FIRST TIME SHE DEEMS US WORTHY.
WE GET IT RIGHT, WE GET MORE WORK, BIGGER PAYDAY EVERY TIME. WE FUCK IT UP...I DON'T WANT TO THINK ABOUT WHAT HAPPENS IF WE FUCK IT UP.
HOLD ON, HALF AN HOUR? HOW DO YOU KNOW THEY DIDN'T SEE YOU WATCHING?
HOW COULD THEY?
I DON'T KNOW, HOW COULD THEY SURVIVE FUCKING POISON? HOW COULD THEY TAKE OUT TWO TEAMS OF SHOOTERS, HAND-TO-HAND?
THEY'RE *GOOD*, YOU STUPID SHIT. THIS IS THEIR FUCKING WORLD, THEY COULD ZERO A PRICK LIKE YOU AND FOLLOW YOU--
IS CUE FOR ACTION!

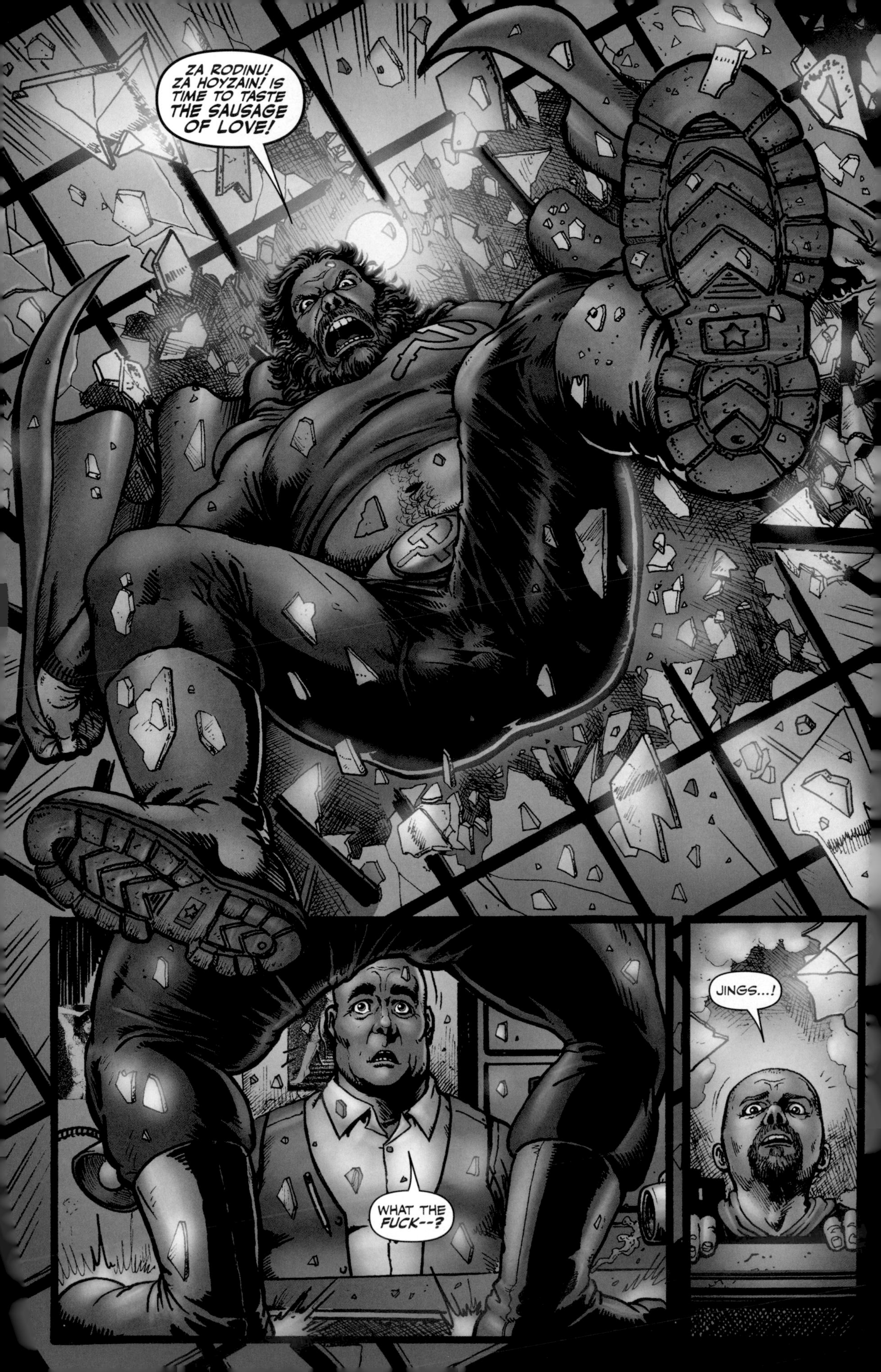
ZA RODINU! ZA HOYZAIN! IS TIME TO TASTE THE SAUSAGE OF LOVE!
WHAT THE FUCK--?
JINGS...!

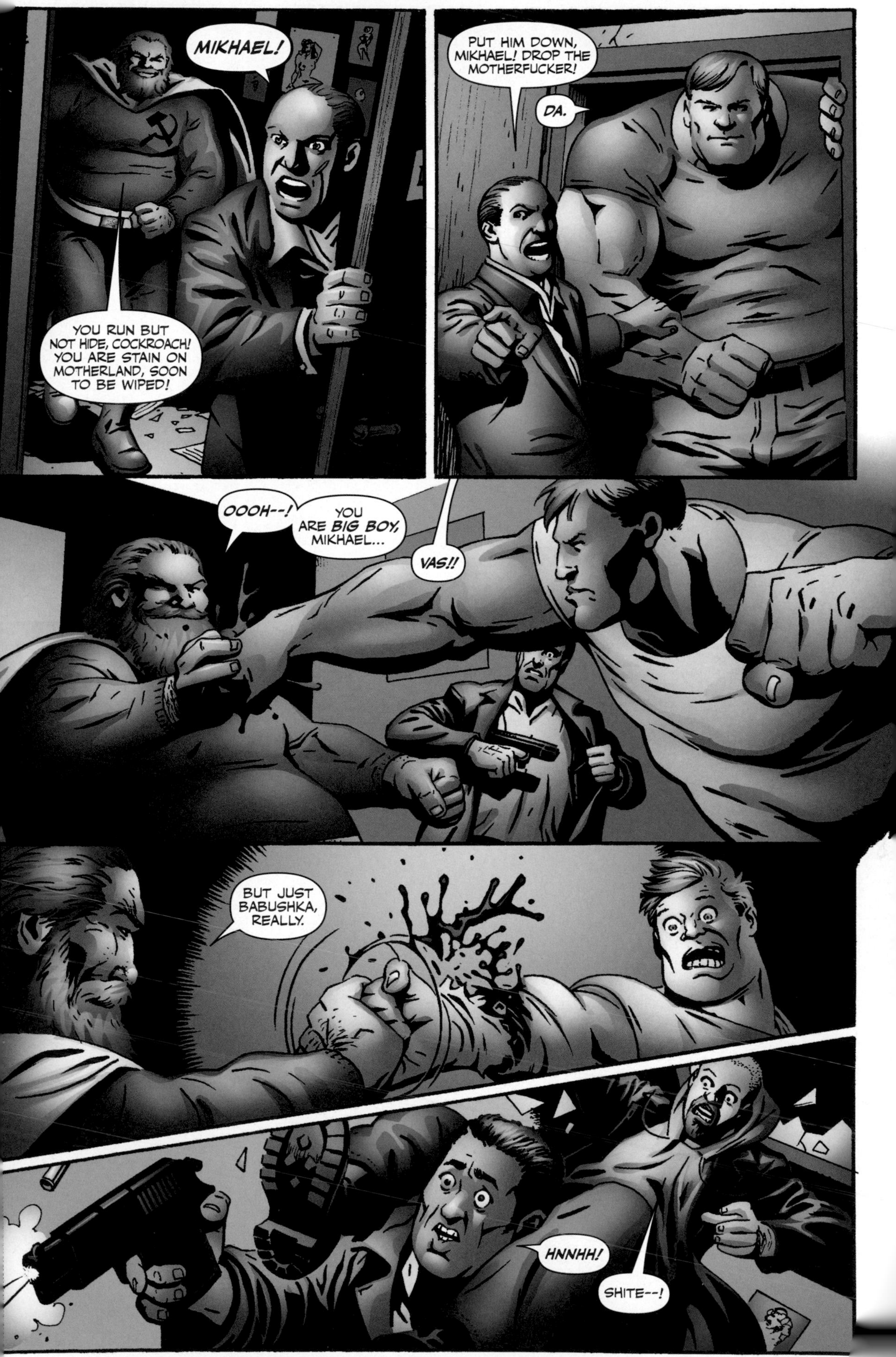
MIKHAEL!
YOU RUN BUT NOT HIDE, COCKROACH! YOU ARE STAIN ON MOTHERLAND, SOON TO BE WIPED!
PUT HIM DOWN, MIKHAEL! DROP THE MOTHERFUCKER!
DA.
OOOH--!
YOU ARE BIG BOY, MIKHAEL...
VAS!!
BUT JUST BABUSHKA, REALLY.
HNNHH!
SHITE--!

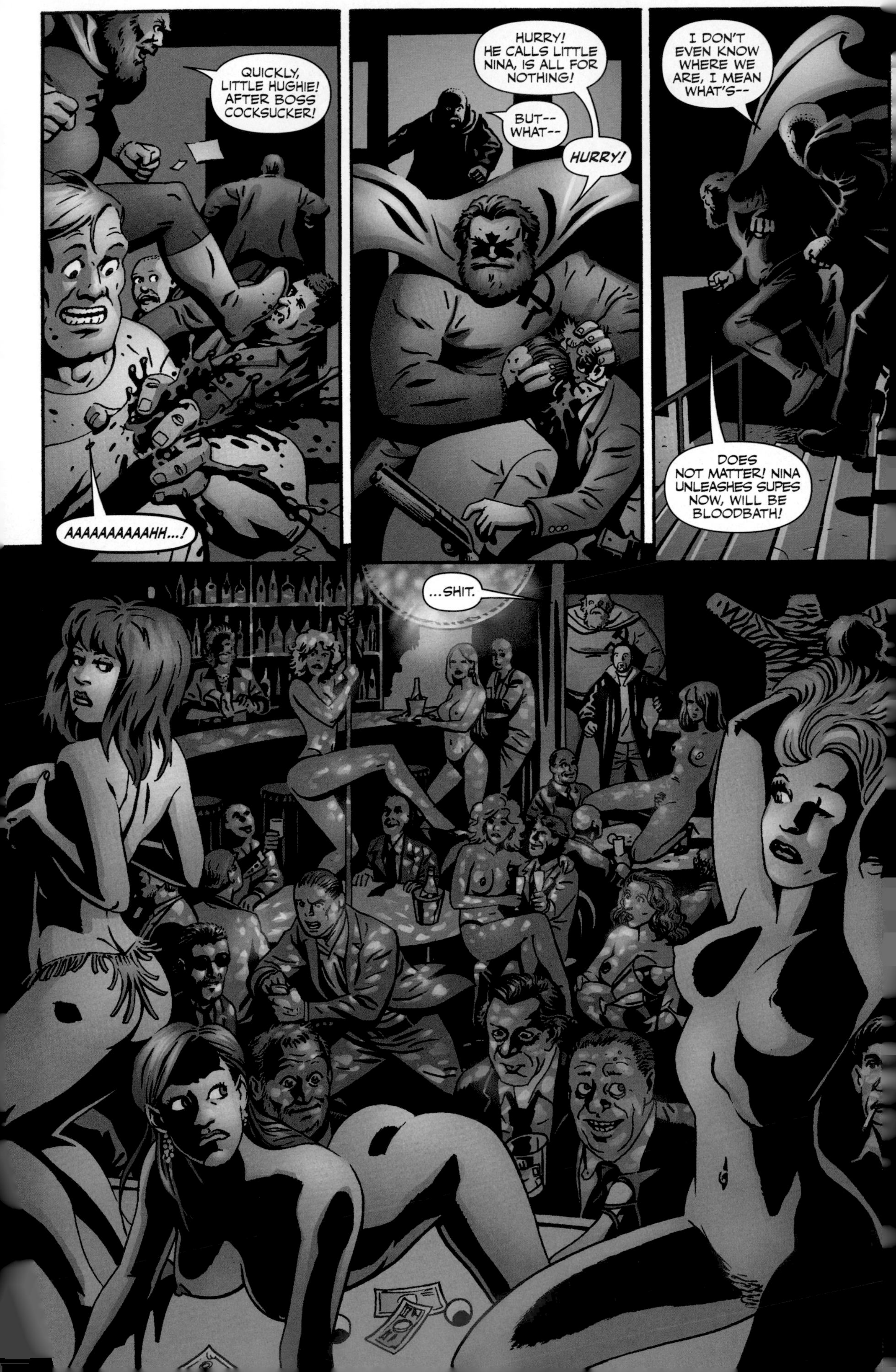

QUICKLY, LITTLE HUGHIE! AFTER BOSS COCKSUCKER!
AAAAAAAAAAAH...!
HURRY! HE CALLS LITTLE NINA, IS ALL FOR NOTHING!
BUT-- WHAT--
HURRY!
I DON'T EVEN KNOW WHERE WE ARE, I MEAN WHAT'S--
DOES NOT MATTER! NINA UNLEASHES SUPES NOW, WILL BE BLOODBATH!
...SHIT.

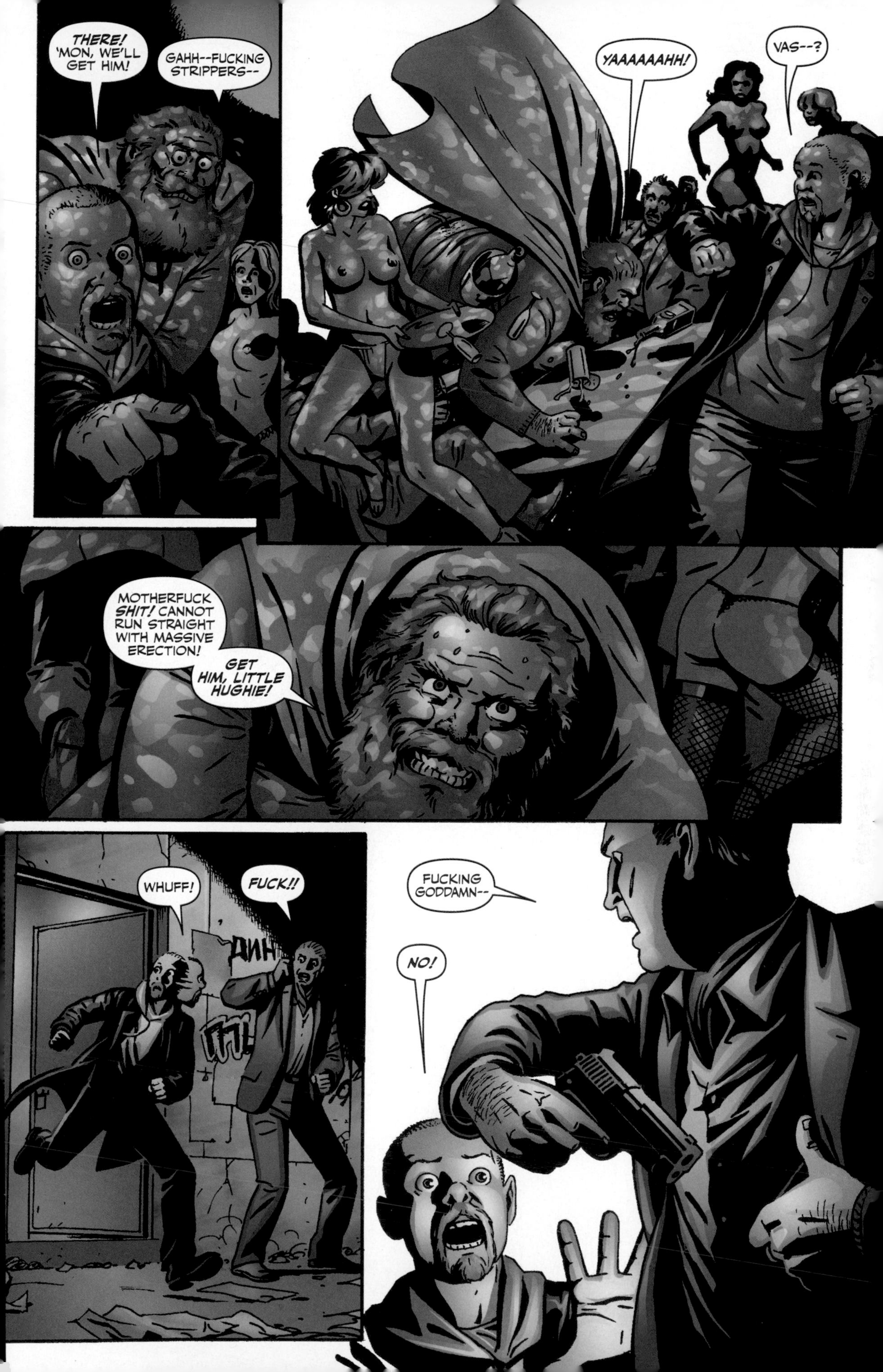
THERE! 'MON, WE'LL GET HIM!
GAHH--FUCKING STRIPPERS--
YAAAAAAHH!
VAS--?
MOTHERFUCK SHIT! CANNOT RUN STRAIGHT WITH MASSIVE ERECTION!
GET HIM, LITTLE HUGHIE!
WHUFF!
FUCK!!
FUCKING GODDAMN--
NO!

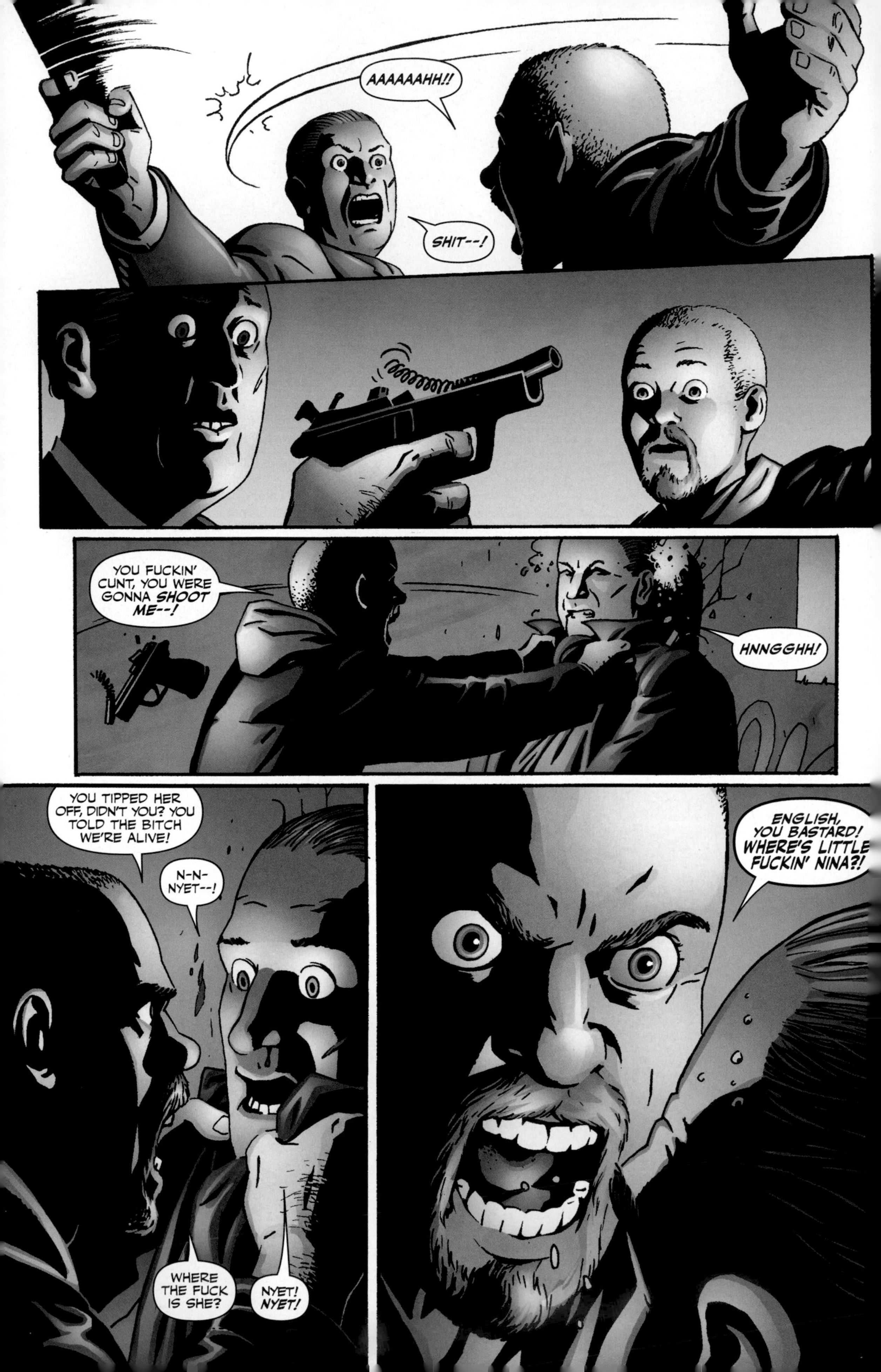
AAAAAAHH!!
SHIT--!
YOU FUCKIN' CUNT, YOU WERE GONNA SHOOT ME--!
HNNGGHH!
YOU TIPPED HER OFF, DIDN'T YOU? YOU TOLD THE BITCH WE'RE ALIVE!
N-N-NYET--!
WHERE THE FUCK IS SHE?
NYET! NYET!
ENGLISH, YOU BASTARD! WHERE'S LITTLE FUCKIN' NINA?!

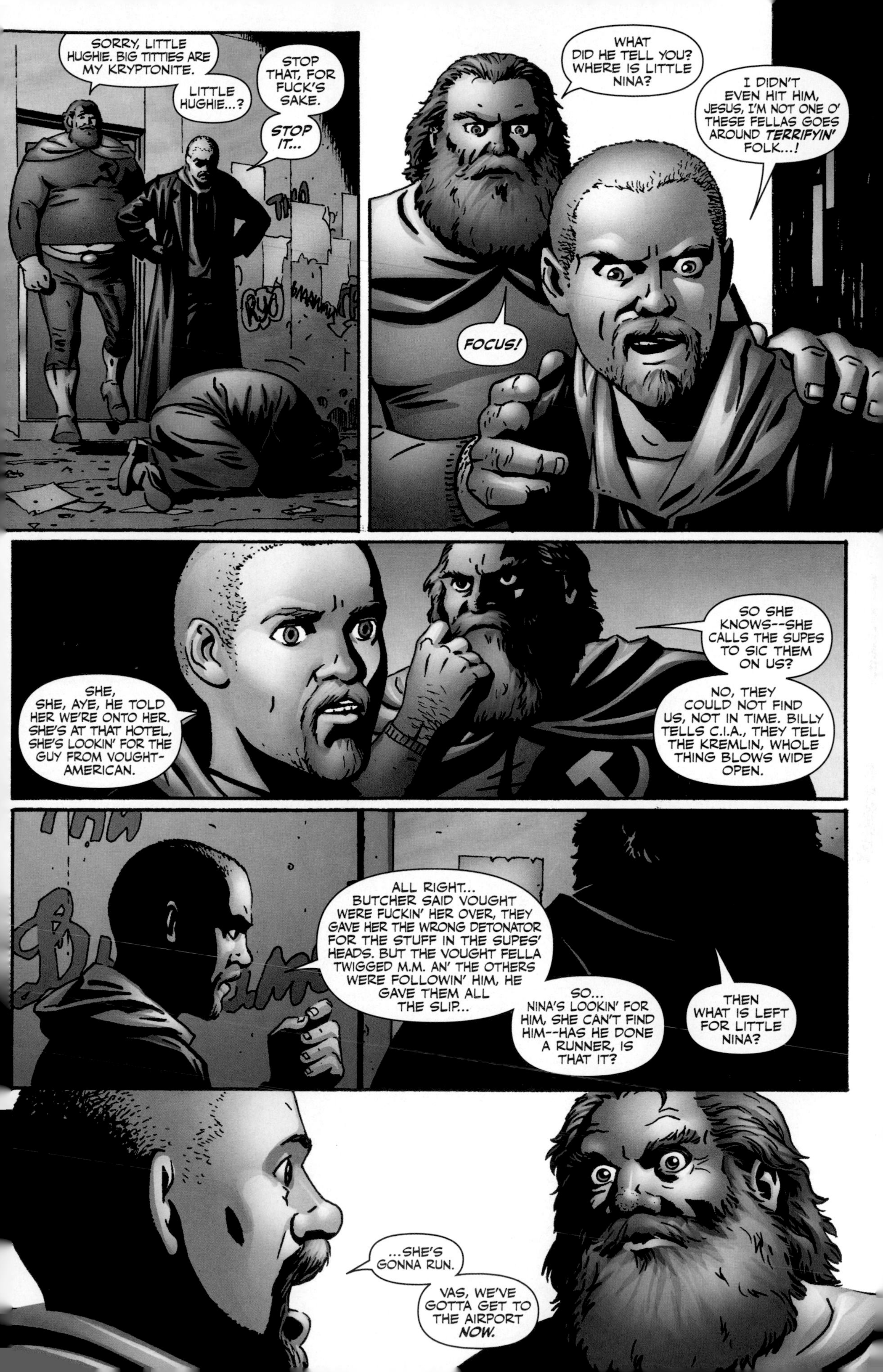
SORRY, LITTLE HUGHIE. BIG TITTIES ARE MY KRYPTONITE.
LITTLE HUGHIE...?
STOP THAT, FOR FUCK'S SAKE.
STOP IT...
WHAT DID HE TELL YOU? WHERE IS LITTLE NINA?
I DIDN'T EVEN HIT HIM, JESUS, I'M NOT ONE O' THESE FELLAS GOES AROUND TERRIFYIN' FOLK...!
FOCUS!
SHE, SHE, AYE, HE TOLD HER WE'RE ONTO HER. SHE'S AT THAT HOTEL, SHE'S LOOKIN' FOR THE GUY FROM VOUGHT-AMERICAN.
SO SHE KNOWS--SHE CALLS THE SUPES TO SIC THEM ON US?
NO, THEY COULD NOT FIND US, NOT IN TIME. BILLY TELLS C.I.A., THEY TELL THE KREMLIN, WHOLE THING BLOWS WIDE OPEN.
ALL RIGHT... BUTCHER SAID VOUGHT WERE FUCKIN' HER OVER, THEY GAVE HER THE WRONG DETONATOR FOR THE STUFF IN THE SUPES' HEADS. BUT THE VOUGHT FELLA TWIGGED M.M. AN' THE OTHERS WERE FOLLOWIN' HIM, HE GAVE THEM ALL THE SLIP...
SO... NINA'S LOOKIN' FOR HIM, SHE CAN'T FIND HIM--HAS HE DONE A RUNNER, IS THAT IT?
THEN WHAT IS LEFT FOR LITTLE NINA?
...SHE'S GONNA RUN.
VAS, WE'VE GOTTA GET TO THE AIRPORT NOW.

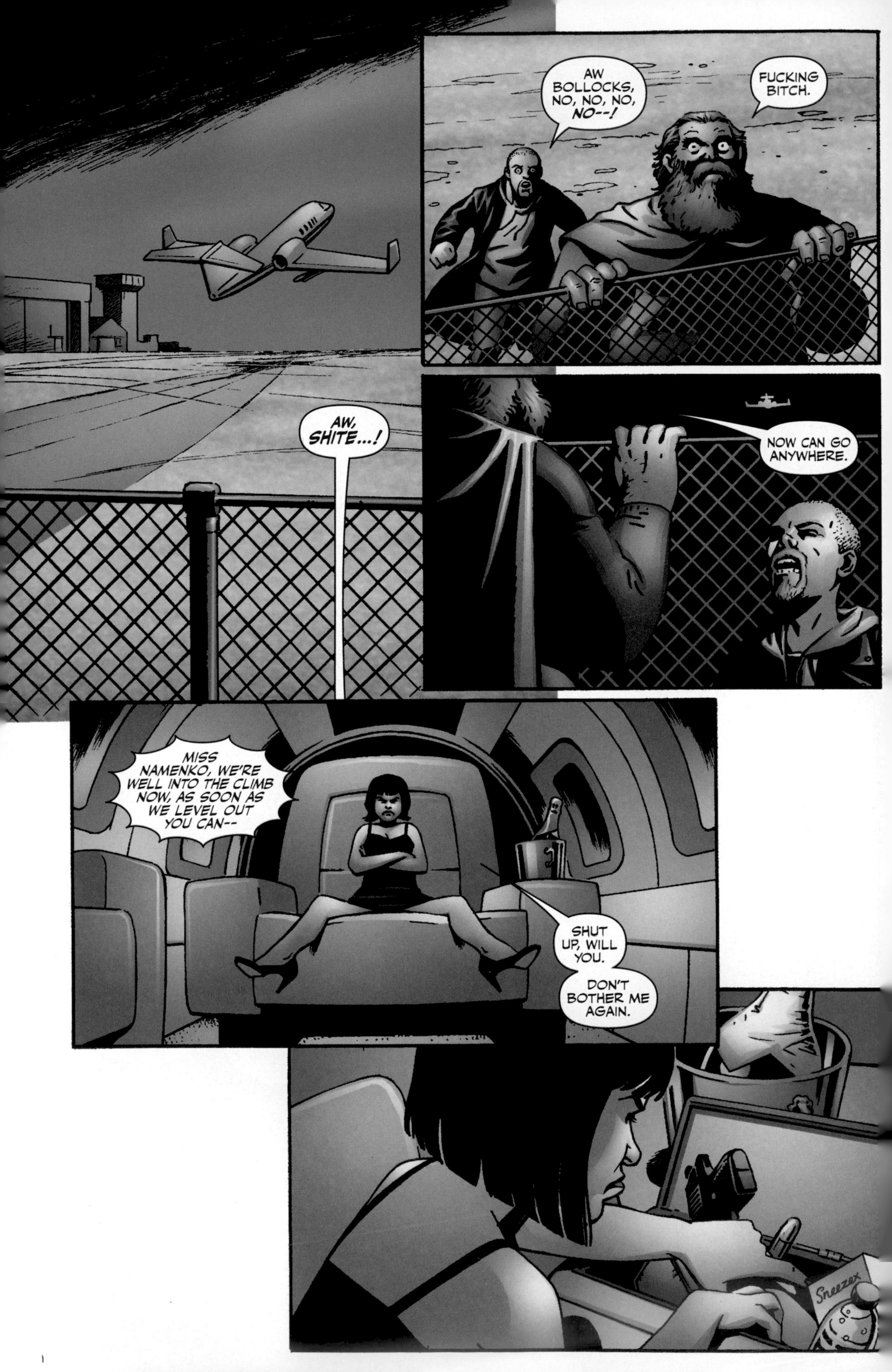
AW BOLLOCKS, NO, NO, NO, NO--!
FUCKING BITCH.
AW, SHITE...!
NOW CAN GO ANYWHERE.
MISS NAMENKO, WE'RE WELL INTO THE CLIMB NOW, AS SOON AS WE LEVEL OUT YOU CAN--
SHUT UP, WILL YOU.
DON'T BOTHER ME AGAIN.
Sneezex

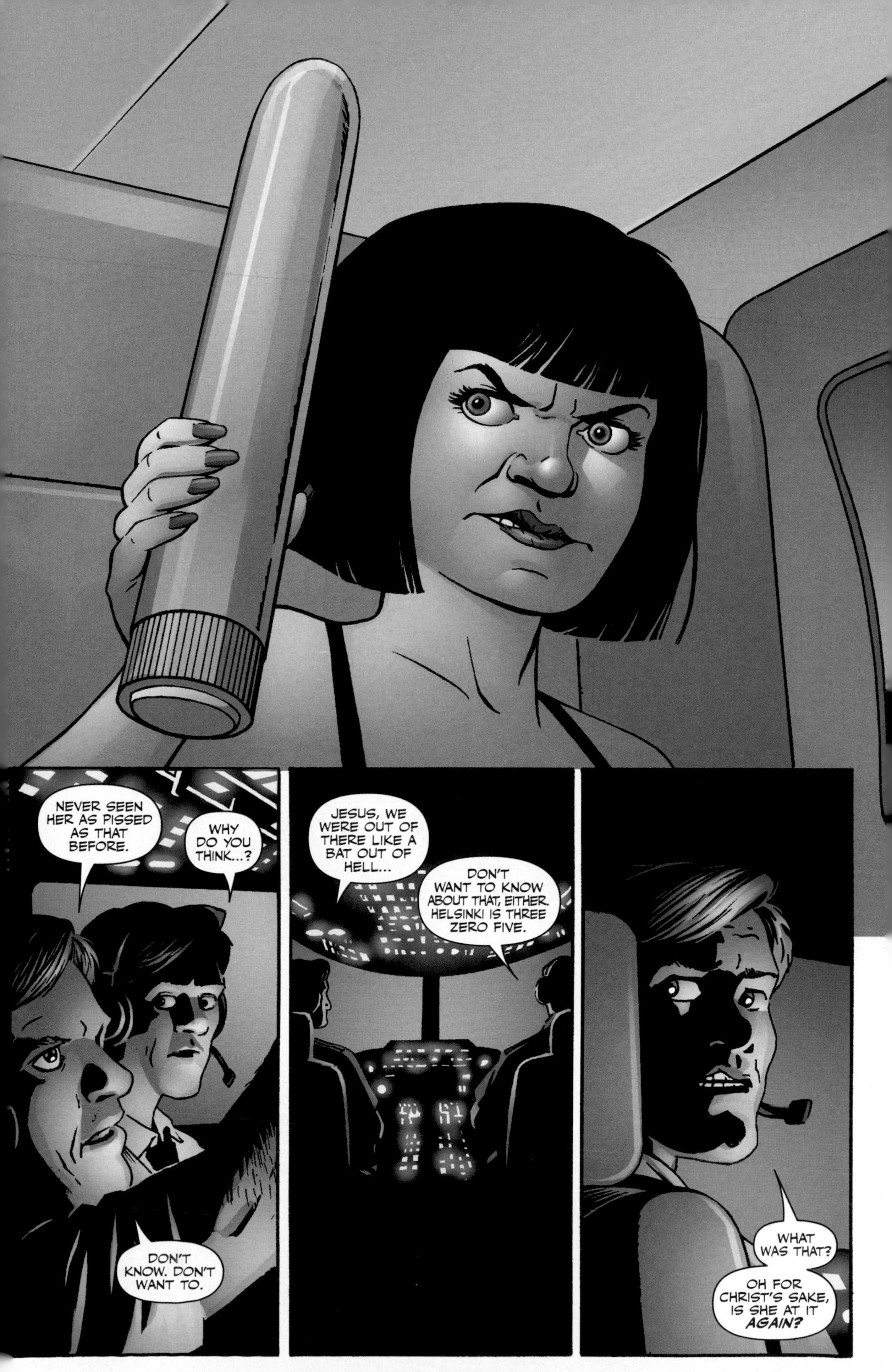
NEVER SEEN HER AS PISSED AS THAT BEFORE.
WHY DO YOU THINK...?
DON'T KNOW. DON'T WANT TO.
JESUS, WE WERE OUT OF THERE LIKE A BAT OUT OF HELL...
DON'T WANT TO KNOW ABOUT THAT, EITHER. HELSINKI IS THREE ZERO FIVE.
WHAT WAS THAT?
OH FOR CHRIST'S SAKE, IS SHE AT IT *AGAIN?*

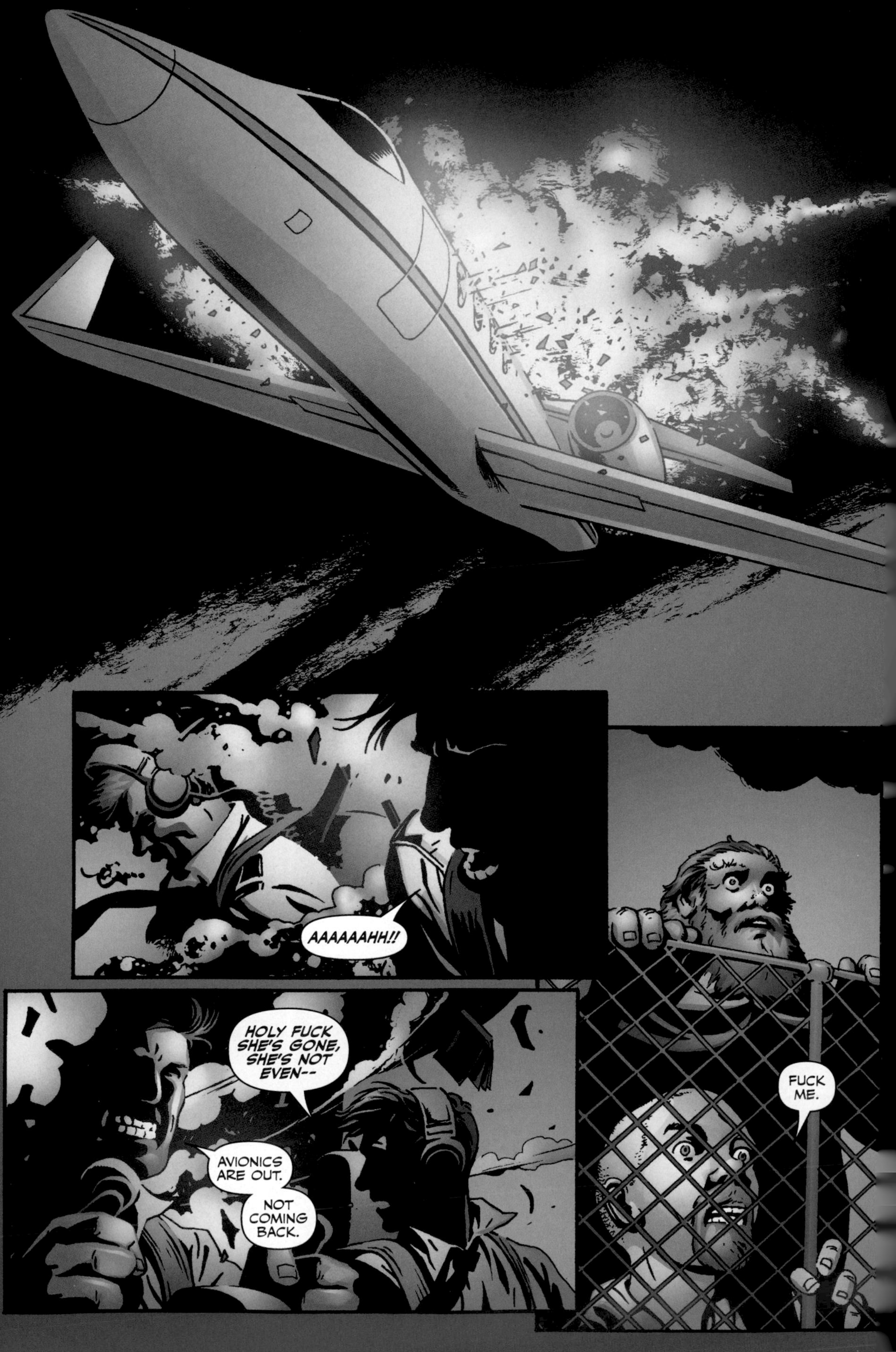
AAAAAAHH!!
HOLY FUCK SHE'S GONE, SHE'S NOT EVEN--
AVIONICS ARE OUT.
NOT COMING BACK.
FUCK ME.

YOU PUT A *BOMB* IN HER *VIBRATOR...?*

KEEP IT DOWN A BIT, WILL YOU, HUGHIE? WE GOT FUCKIN' POISONED LAST NIGHT, WE'RE JUST TRYNNA DIE IN PEACE.

BUT-- BUT--BUT--

WHY...?

WELL THE VOUGHT-AMERICAN CUNTS WERE GONNA STICK ONE IN THE COCKPIT, WEREN'T THEY? I THOUGHT FUCKIN' HELL, LET'S BY ALL MEANS GET RIDDA LITTLE NINA, BUT WHAT IF THE BLOODY THING COMES DOWN ON SOMEBODY'S HOUSE?

'LEAST THIS WAY THE PILOTS HAD A CHANCE TO LAND IT SOMEWHERE SAFE...

AYE, WELL YOU'LL BE PLEASED TO HEAR THEY LANDED IT INTO THE SIDE OF A MOUNTAIN.

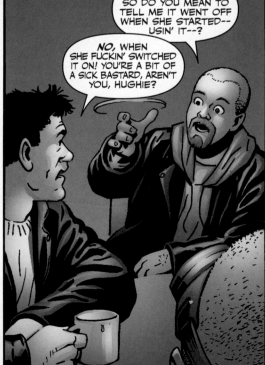

SO DO YOU MEAN TO TELL ME IT WENT OFF WHEN SHE STARTED-- USIN' IT--?

NO, WHEN SHE FUCKIN' SWITCHED IT ON! YOU'RE A BIT OF A SICK BASTARD, AREN'T YOU, HUGHIE?

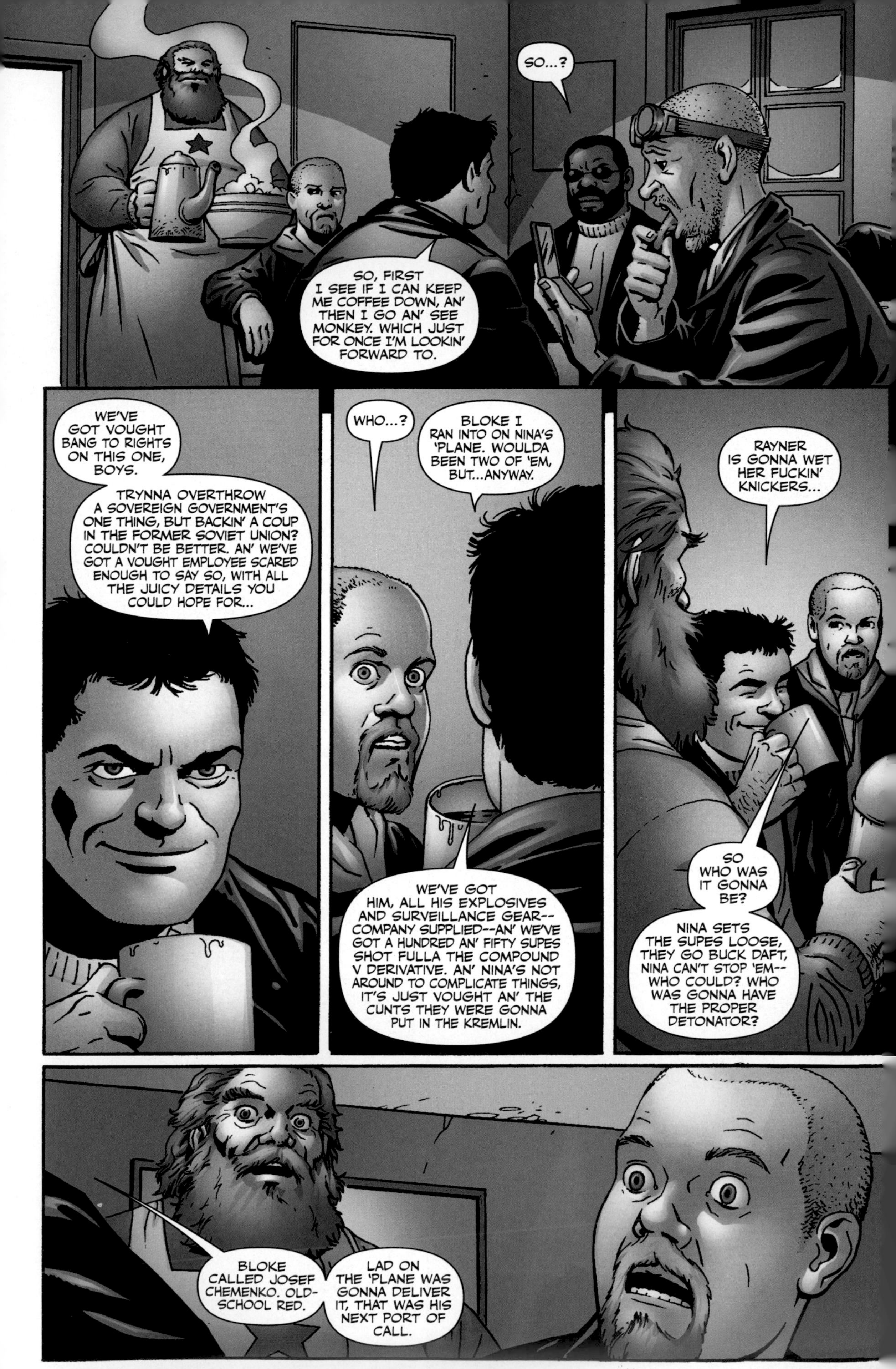
SO...?
SO, FIRST I SEE IF I CAN KEEP ME COFFEE DOWN, AN' THEN I GO AN' SEE MONKEY. WHICH JUST FOR ONCE I'M LOOKIN' FORWARD TO.
WE'VE GOT VOUGHT BANG TO RIGHTS ON THIS ONE, BOYS.
TRYNNA OVERTHROW A SOVEREIGN GOVERNMENT'S ONE THING, BUT BACKIN' A COUP IN THE FORMER SOVIET UNION? COULDN'T BE BETTER. AN' WE'VE GOT A VOUGHT EMPLOYEE SCARED ENOUGH TO SAY SO, WITH ALL THE JUICY DETAILS YOU COULD HOPE FOR...
WHO...?
BLOKE I RAN INTO ON NINA'S 'PLANE. WOULDA BEEN TWO OF 'EM, BUT...ANYWAY.
WE'VE GOT HIM, ALL HIS EXPLOSIVES AND SURVEILLANCE GEAR--COMPANY SUPPLIED--AN' WE'VE GOT A HUNDRED AN' FIFTY SUPES SHOT FULLA THE COMPOUND V DERIVATIVE. AN' NINA'S NOT AROUND TO COMPLICATE THINGS, IT'S JUST VOUGHT AN' THE CUNTS THEY WERE GONNA PUT IN THE KREMLIN.
RAYNER IS GONNA WET HER FUCKIN' KNICKERS...
SO WHO WAS IT GONNA BE?
NINA SETS THE SUPES LOOSE, THEY GO BUCK DAFT, NINA CAN'T STOP 'EM--WHO COULD? WHO WAS GONNA HAVE THE PROPER DETONATOR?
BLOKE CALLED JOSEF CHEMENKO. OLD-SCHOOL RED.
LAD ON THE 'PLANE WAS GONNA DELIVER IT, THAT WAS HIS NEXT PORT OF CALL.

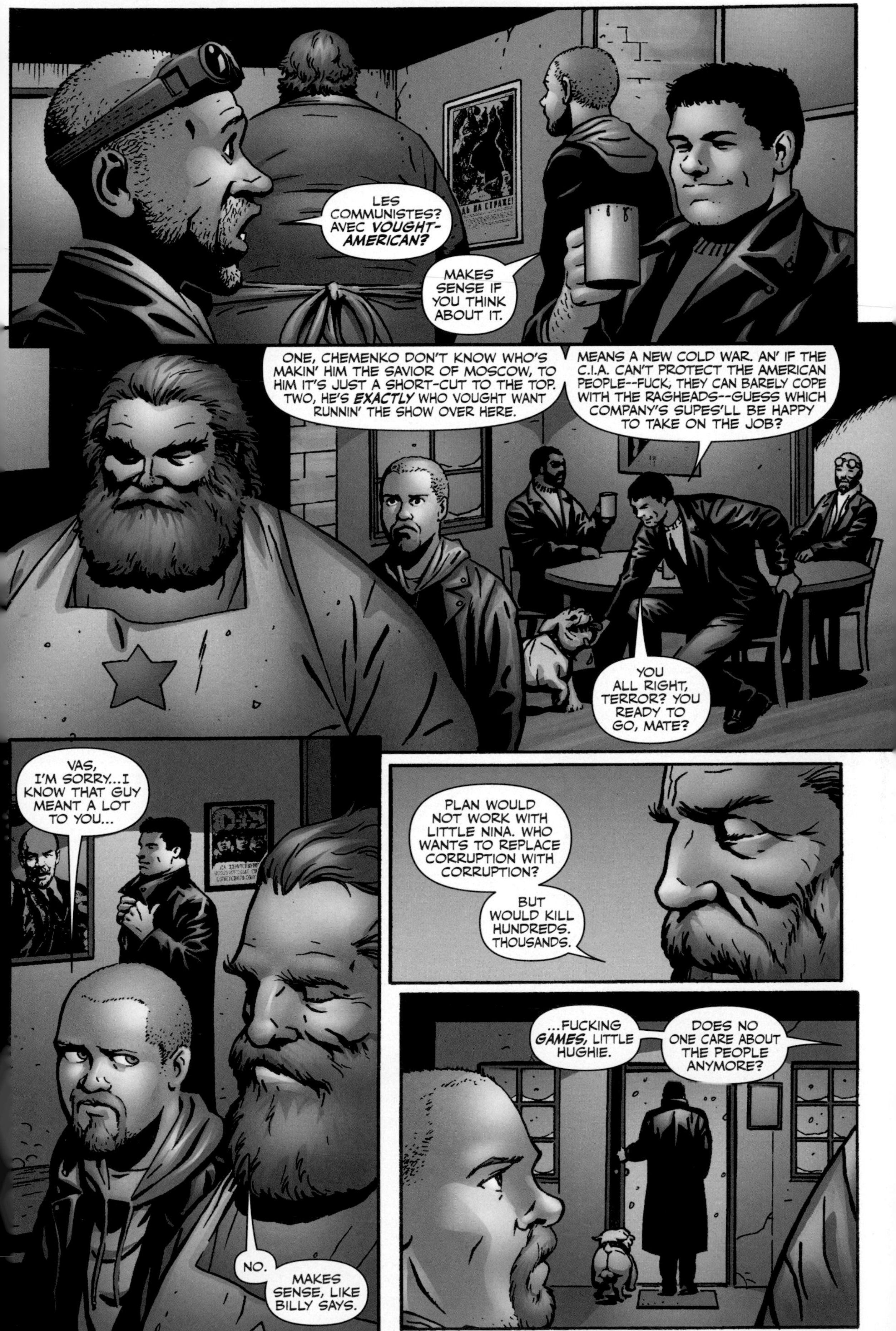
LES COMMUNISTES? AVEC VOUGHT-AMERICAN?
MAKES SENSE IF YOU THINK ABOUT IT.
ONE, CHEMENKO DON'T KNOW WHO'S MAKIN' HIM THE SAVIOR OF MOSCOW, TO HIM IT'S JUST A SHORT-CUT TO THE TOP. TWO, HE'S EXACTLY WHO VOUGHT WANT RUNNIN' THE SHOW OVER HERE.
MEANS A NEW COLD WAR. AN' IF THE C.I.A. CAN'T PROTECT THE AMERICAN PEOPLE--FUCK, THEY CAN BARELY COPE WITH THE RAGHEADS--GUESS WHICH COMPANY'S SUPES'LL BE HAPPY TO TAKE ON THE JOB?
YOU ALL RIGHT, TERROR? YOU READY TO GO, MATE?
VAS, I'M SORRY...I KNOW THAT GUY MEANT A LOT TO YOU...
NO.
MAKES SENSE, LIKE BILLY SAYS.
PLAN WOULD NOT WORK WITH LITTLE NINA. WHO WANTS TO REPLACE CORRUPTION WITH CORRUPTION?
BUT WOULD KILL HUNDREDS. THOUSANDS.
...FUCKING GAMES, LITTLE HUGHIE.
DOES NO ONE CARE ABOUT THE PEOPLE ANYMORE?

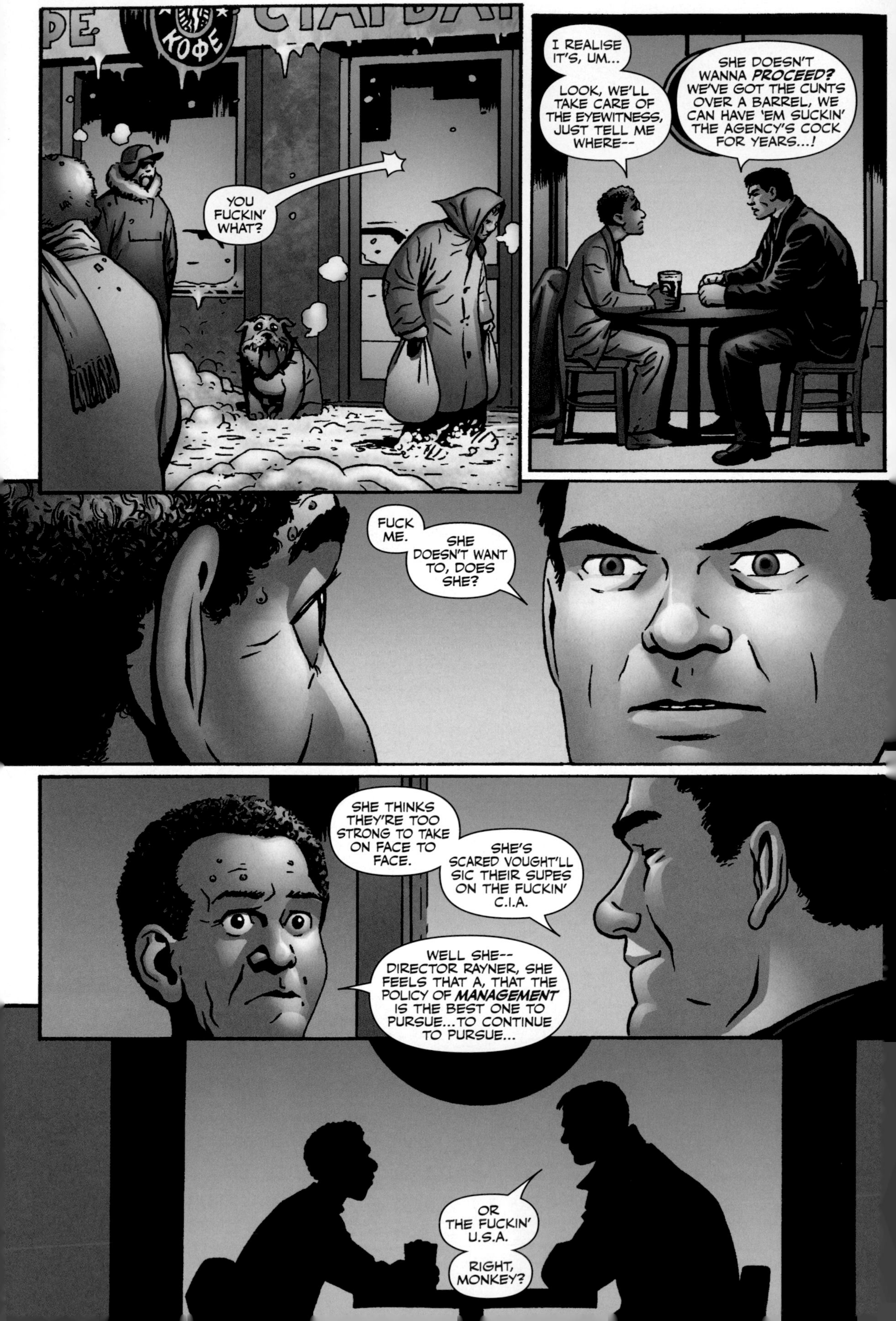
КОФЕ
YOU FUCKIN' WHAT?
I REALISE IT'S, UM...
LOOK, WE'LL TAKE CARE OF THE EYEWITNESS, JUST TELL ME WHERE--
SHE DOESN'T WANNA *PROCEED?* WE'VE GOT THE CUNTS OVER A BARREL, WE CAN HAVE 'EM SUCKIN' THE AGENCY'S COCK FOR YEARS...!
FUCK ME.
SHE DOESN'T WANT TO, DOES SHE?
SHE THINKS THEY'RE TOO STRONG TO TAKE ON FACE TO FACE.
SHE'S SCARED VOUGHT'LL SIC THEIR SUPES ON THE FUCKIN' C.I.A.
WELL SHE-- DIRECTOR RAYNER, SHE FEELS THAT A, THAT THE POLICY OF ***MANAGEMENT*** IS THE BEST ONE TO PURSUE...TO CONTINUE TO PURSUE...
OR THE FUCKIN' U.S.A.
RIGHT, MONKEY?

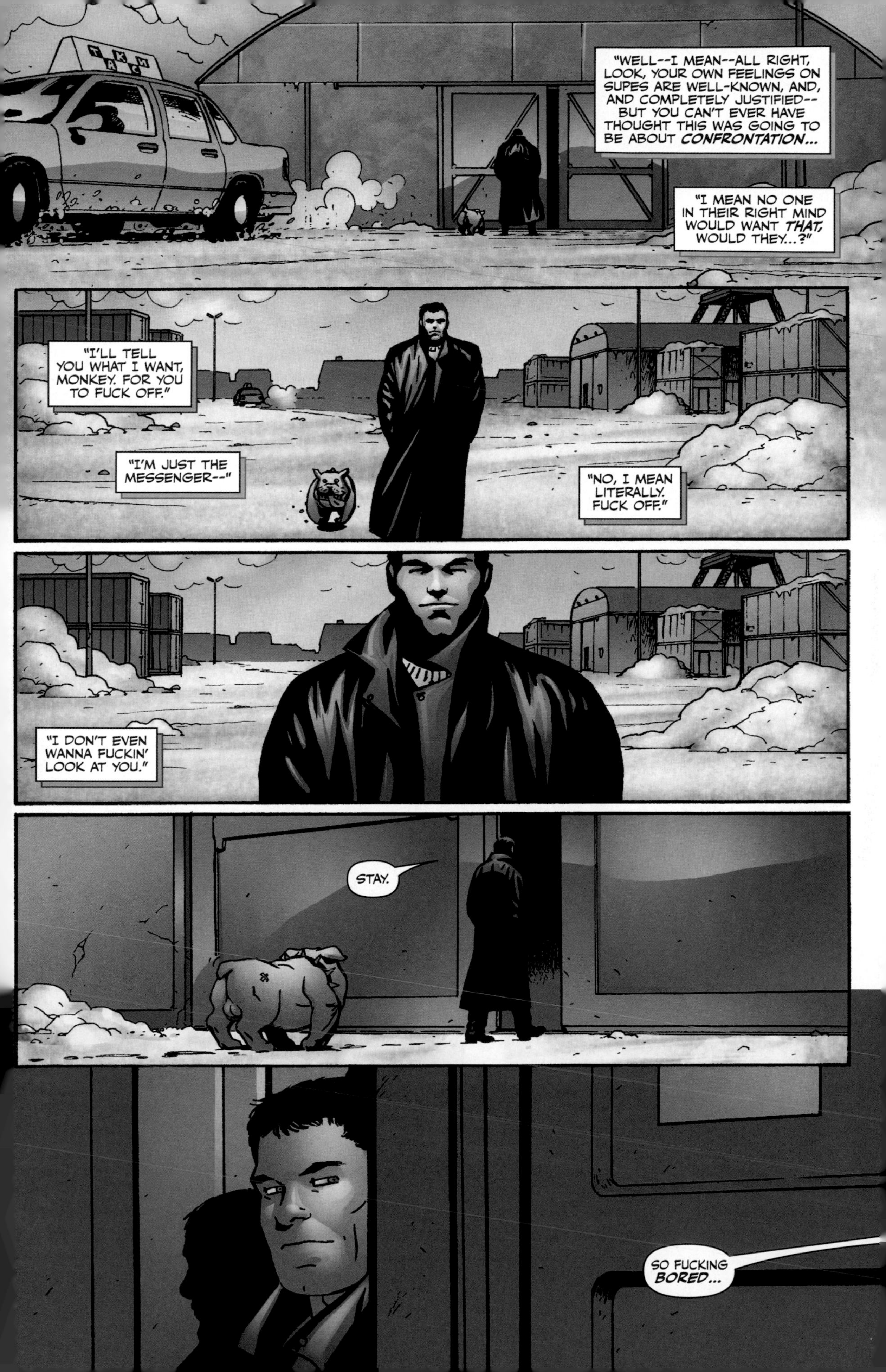
"WELL--I MEAN--ALL RIGHT, LOOK, YOUR OWN FEELINGS ON SUPES ARE WELL-KNOWN, AND, AND COMPLETELY JUSTIFIED--BUT YOU CAN'T EVER HAVE THOUGHT THIS WAS GOING TO BE ABOUT CONFRONTATION...
"I MEAN NO ONE IN THEIR RIGHT MIND WOULD WANT THAT, WOULD THEY...?"
"I'LL TELL YOU WHAT I WANT, MONKEY. FOR YOU TO FUCK OFF."
"I'M JUST THE MESSENGER--"
"NO, I MEAN LITERALLY. FUCK OFF."
"I DON'T EVEN WANNA FUCKIN' LOOK AT YOU."
STAY.
SO FUCKING BORED...

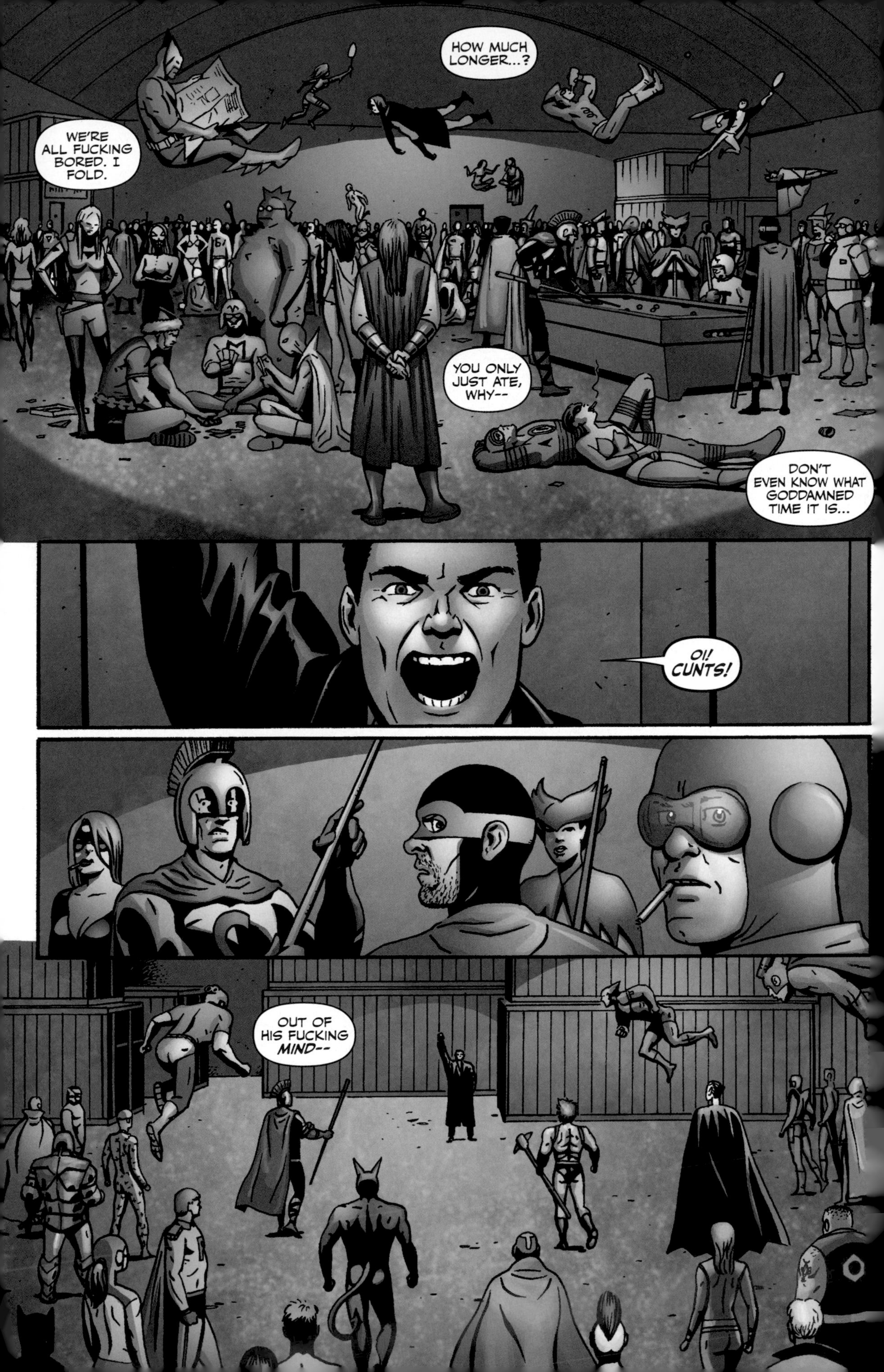
HOW MUCH LONGER...?
WE'RE ALL FUCKING BORED. I FOLD.
YOU ONLY JUST ATE, WHY--
DON'T EVEN KNOW WHAT GODDAMNED TIME IT IS...
OI! CUNTS!
OUT OF HIS FUCKING MIND--

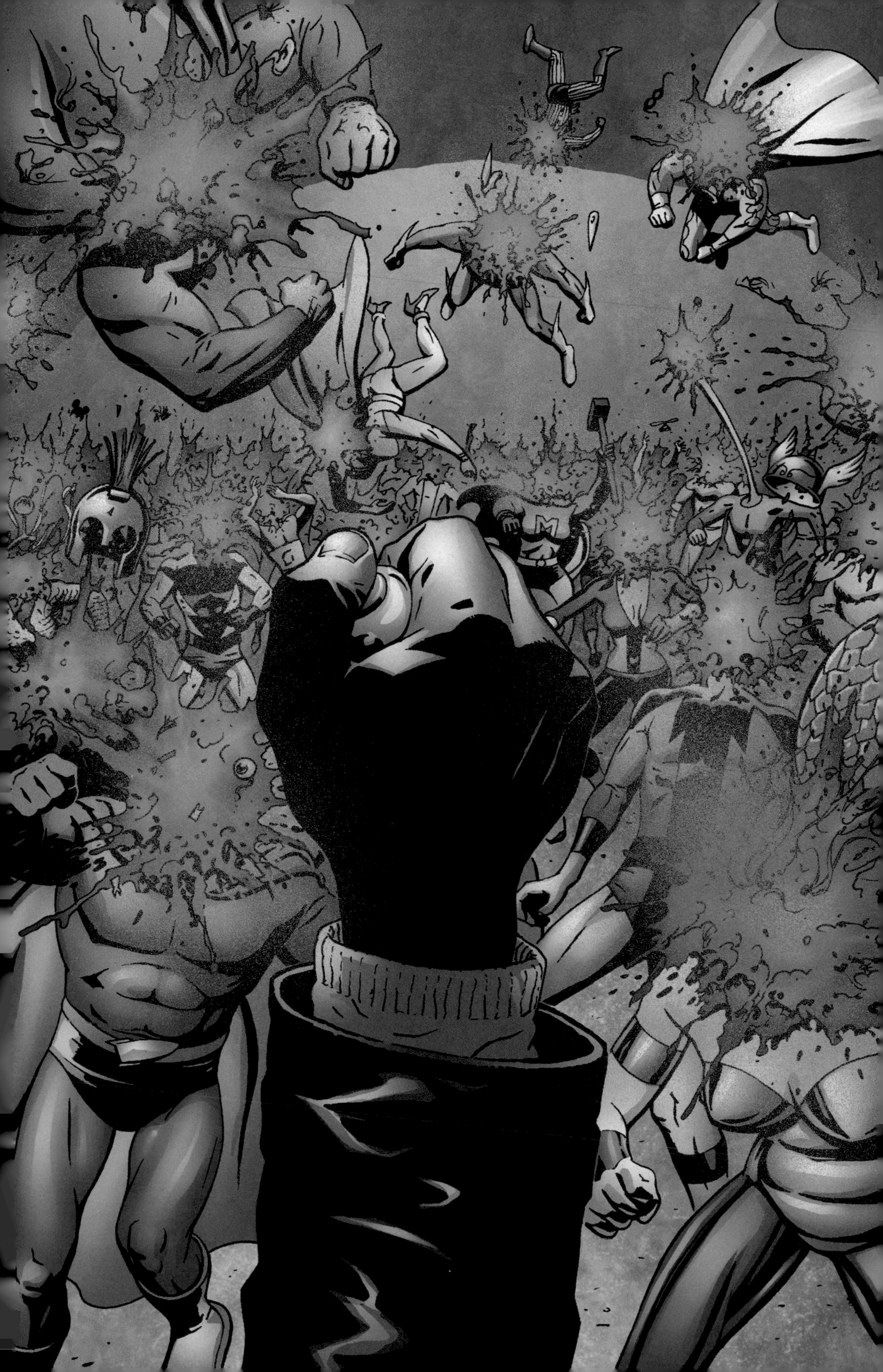

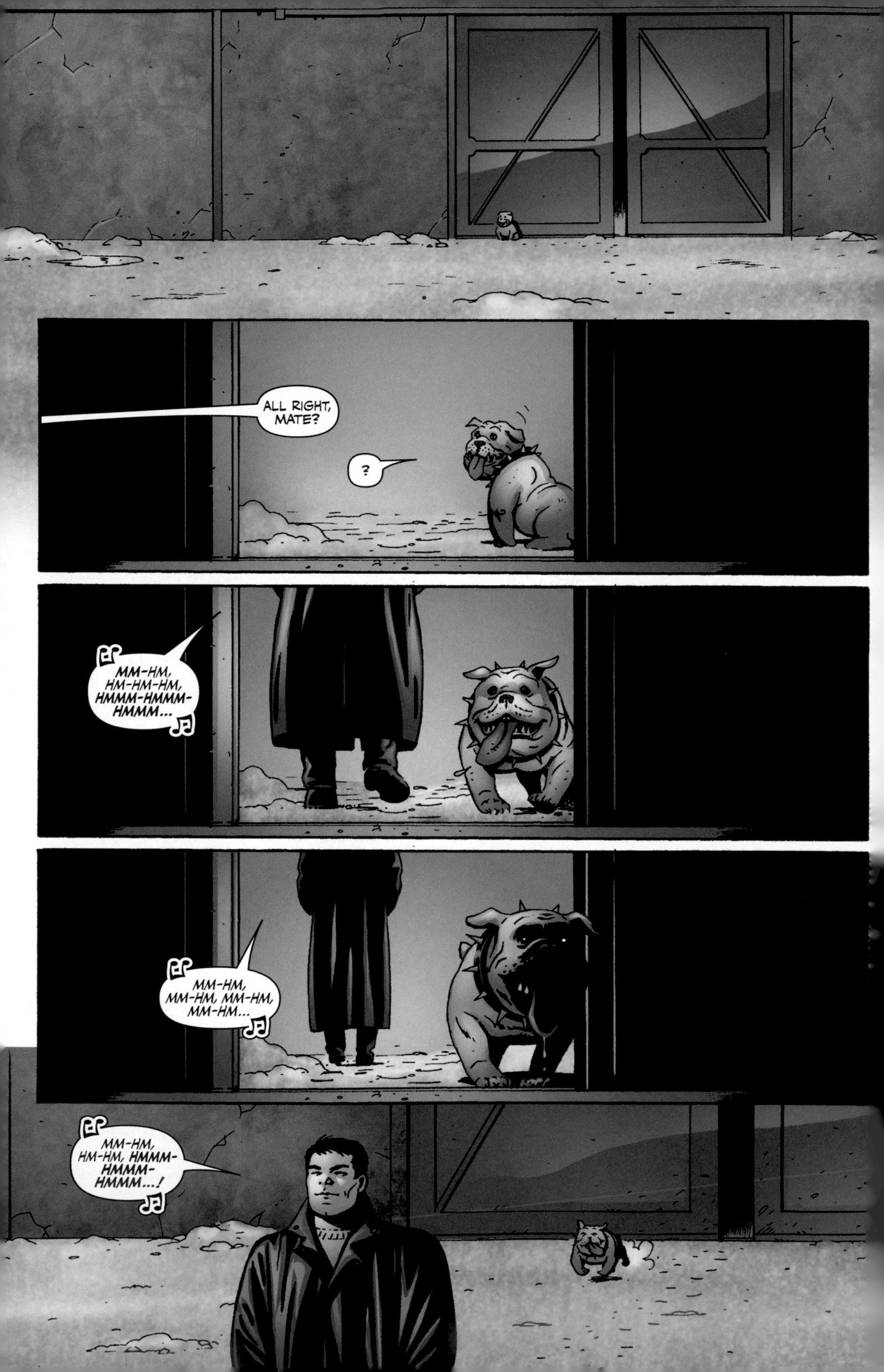
ALL RIGHT, MATE?
?
MM-HM, HM-HM-HM, HMMM-HMMM-HMMM...
MM-HM, MM-HM, MM-HM, MM-HM...
MM-HM, HM-HM, HMMM-HMMM-HMMM...!

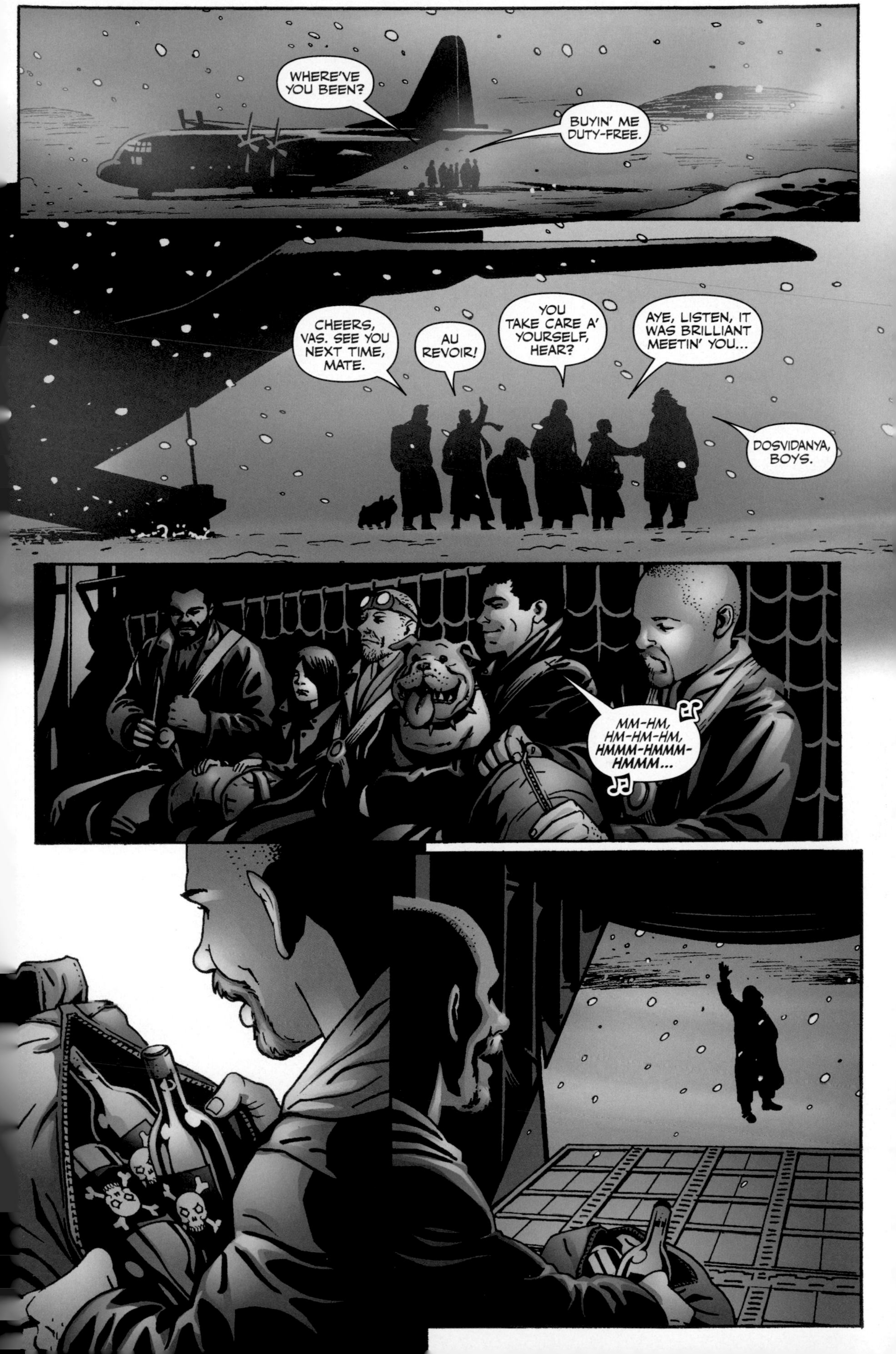
WHERE'VE YOU BEEN?
BUYIN' ME DUTY-FREE.
CHEERS, VAS. SEE YOU NEXT TIME, MATE.
AU REVOIR!
YOU TAKE CARE A' YOURSELF, HEAR?
AYE, LISTEN, IT WAS BRILLIANT MEETIN' YOU...
DOSVIDANYA, BOYS.
MM-HM, HM-HM-HM, HMMM-HMMM-HMMM...

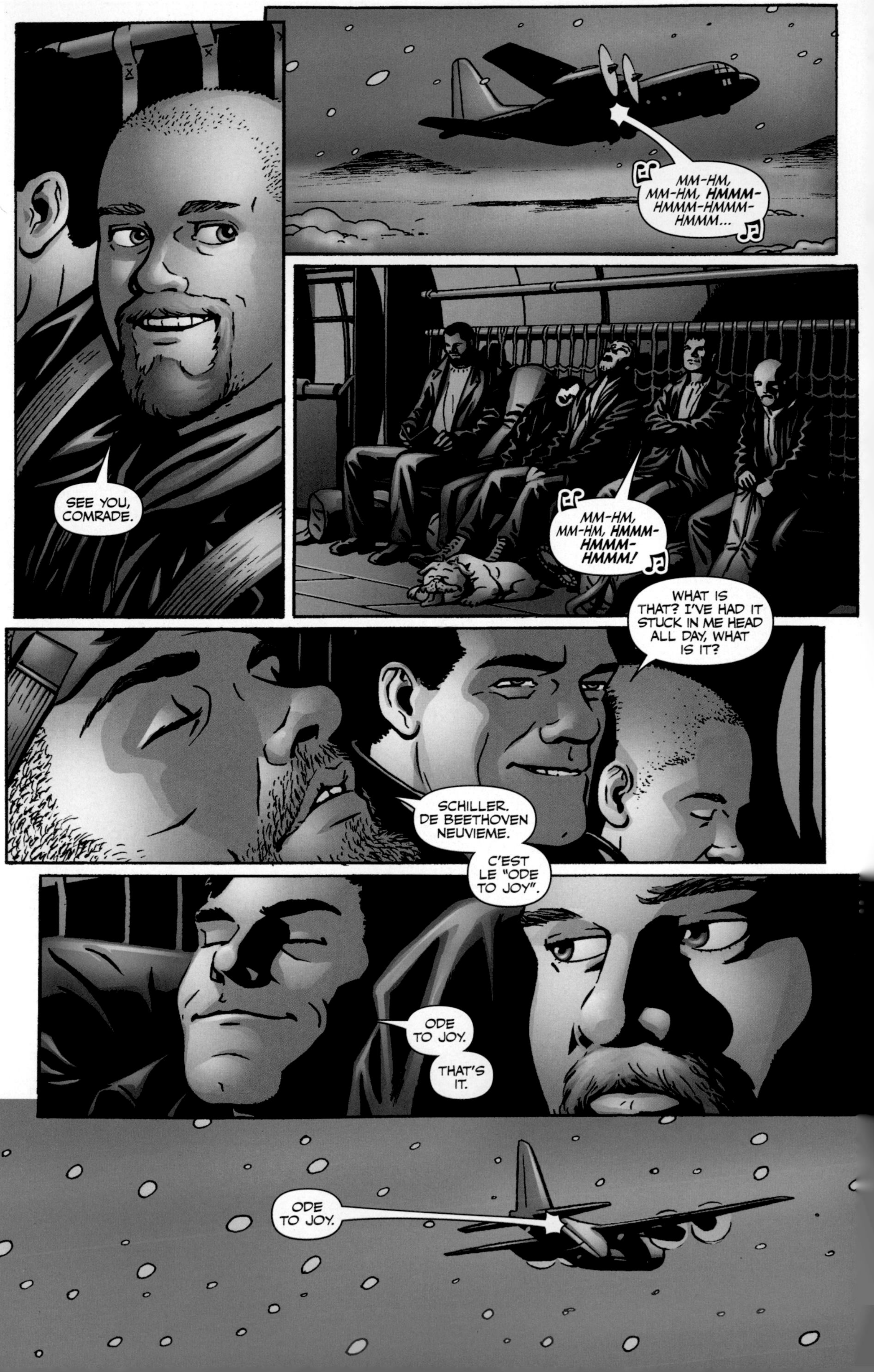

MM-HM, MM-HM, HMMM-HMMM-HMMM-HMMM...
SEE YOU, COMRADE.
MM-HM, MM-HM, HMMM-HMMM-HMMM!
WHAT IS THAT? I'VE HAD IT STUCK IN ME HEAD ALL DAY, WHAT IS IT?
SCHILLER. DE BEETHOVEN NEUVIEME.
C'EST LE "ODE TO JOY".
ODE TO JOY.
THAT'S IT.
ODE TO JOY.

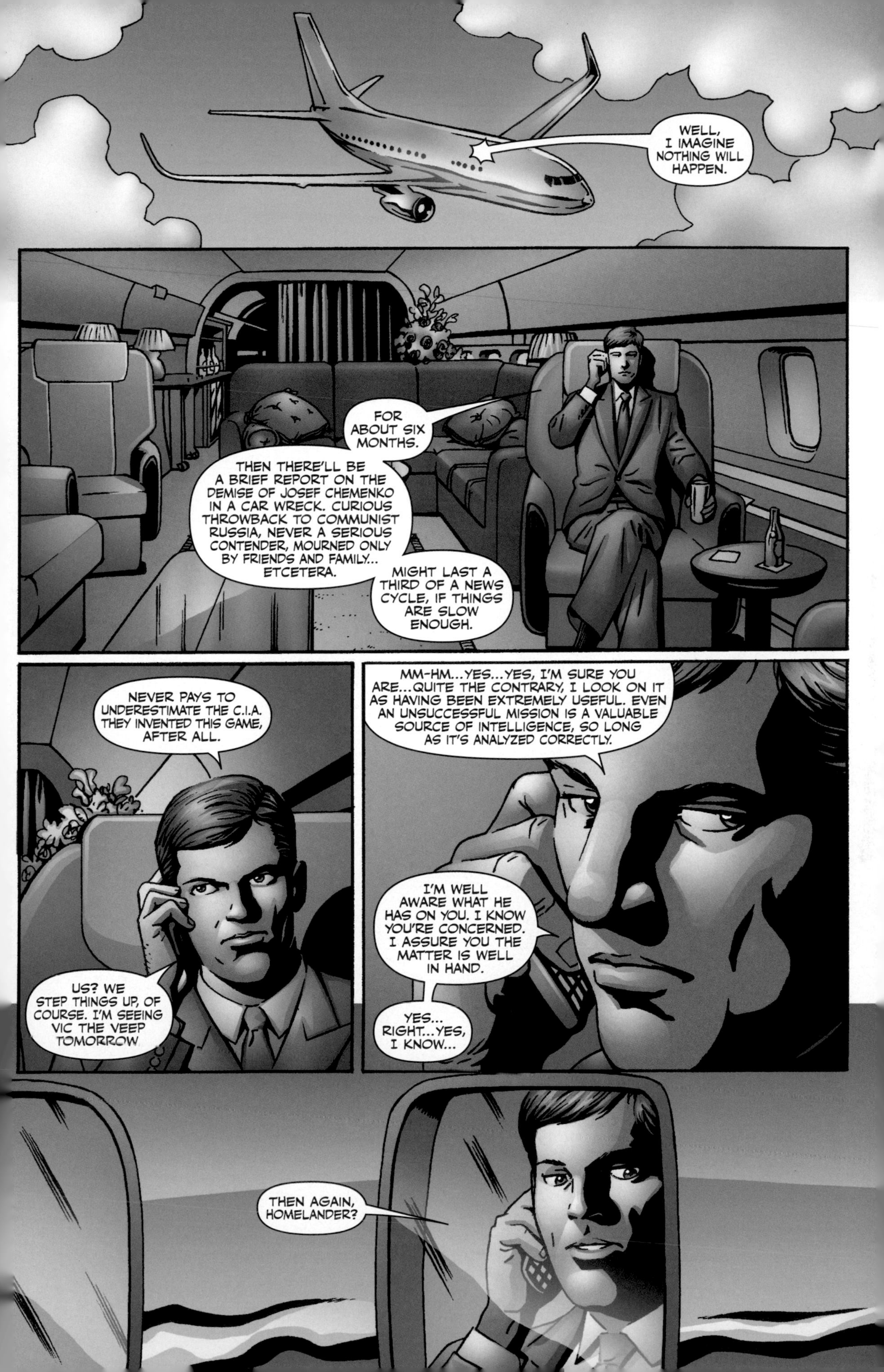
WELL, I IMAGINE NOTHING WILL HAPPEN.
FOR ABOUT SIX MONTHS.
THEN THERE'LL BE A BRIEF REPORT ON THE DEMISE OF JOSEF CHEMENKO IN A CAR WRECK. CURIOUS THROWBACK TO COMMUNIST RUSSIA, NEVER A SERIOUS CONTENDER, MOURNED ONLY BY FRIENDS AND FAMILY... ETCETERA.
MIGHT LAST A THIRD OF A NEWS CYCLE, IF THINGS ARE SLOW ENOUGH.
NEVER PAYS TO UNDERESTIMATE THE C.I.A. THEY INVENTED THIS GAME, AFTER ALL.
US? WE STEP THINGS UP, OF COURSE. I'M SEEING VIC THE VEEP TOMORROW.
MM-HM...YES...YES, I'M SURE YOU ARE...QUITE THE CONTRARY, I LOOK ON IT AS HAVING BEEN EXTREMELY USEFUL. EVEN AN UNSUCCESSFUL MISSION IS A VALUABLE SOURCE OF INTELLIGENCE, SO LONG AS IT'S ANALYZED CORRECTLY.
I'M WELL AWARE WHAT HE HAS ON YOU. I KNOW YOU'RE CONCERNED. I ASSURE YOU THE MATTER IS WELL IN HAND.
YES... RIGHT...YES, I KNOW...
THEN AGAIN, HOMELANDER?

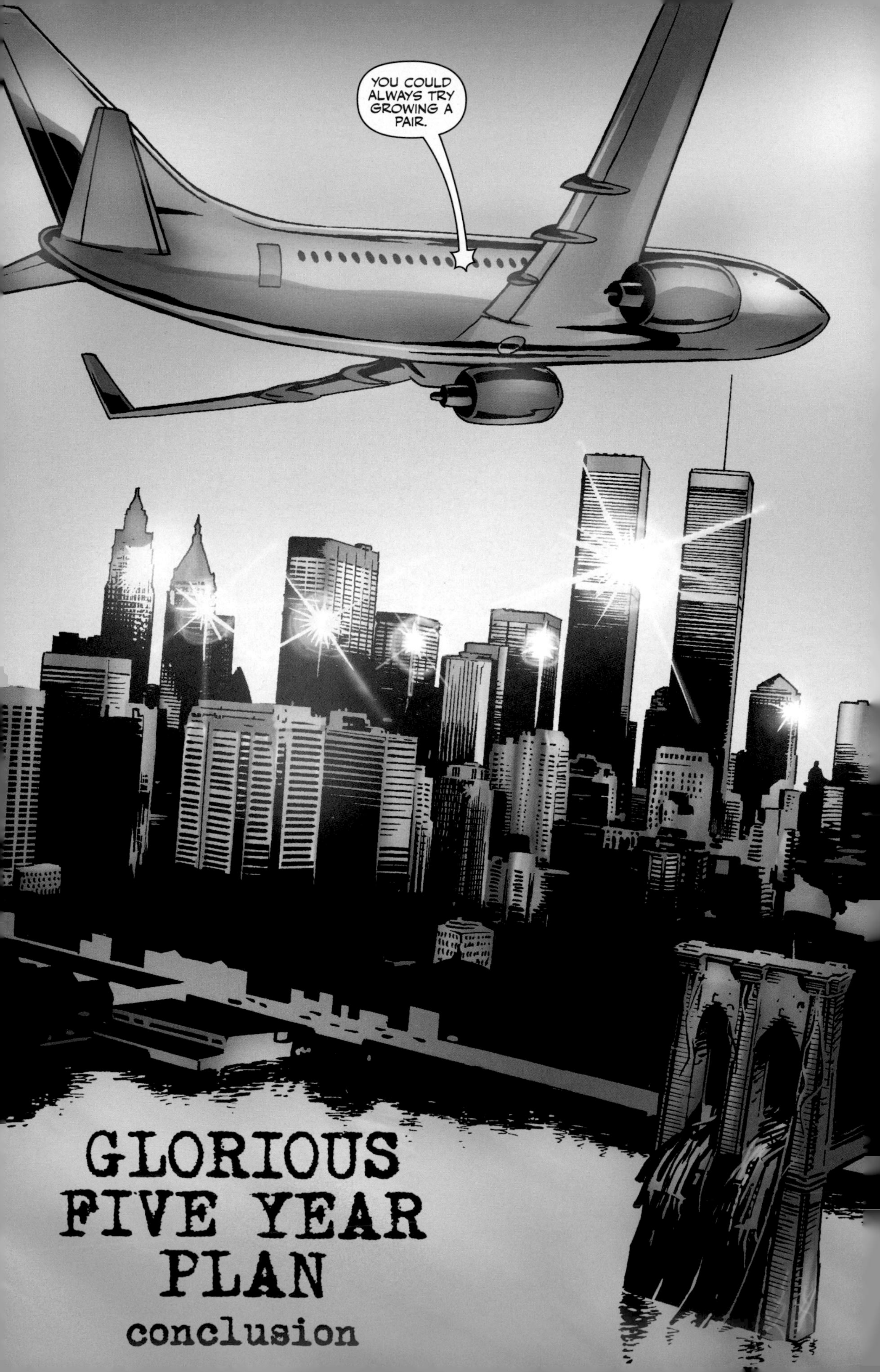
YOU COULD ALWAYS TRY GROWING A PAIR.
GLORIOUS FIVE YEAR PLAN
conclusion

OMNIBUS
BONUS MATERIAL

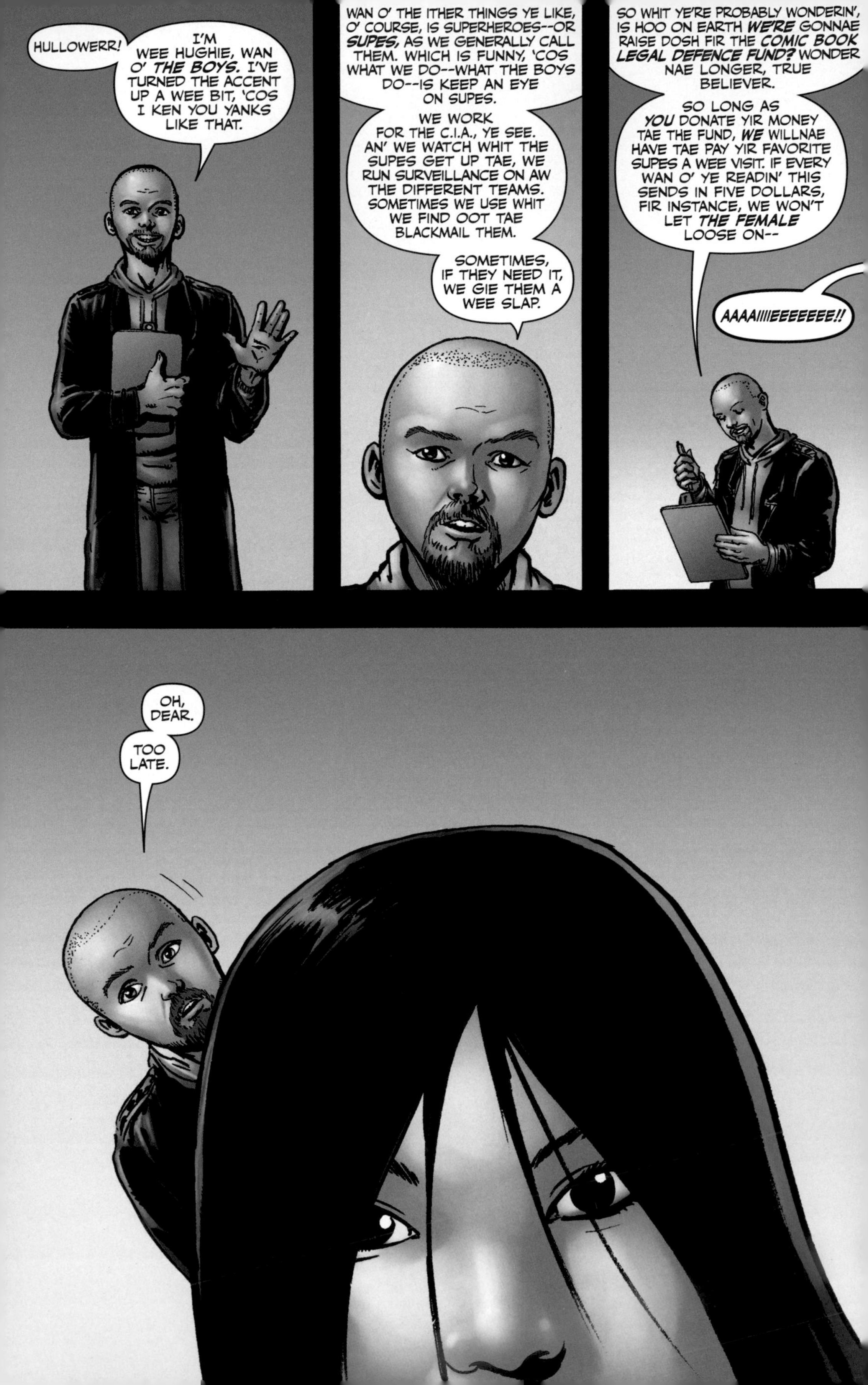
HULLOWERR!
I'M WEE HUGHIE, WAN O' THE BOYS. I'VE TURNED THE ACCENT UP A WEE BIT, 'COS I KEN YOU YANKS LIKE THAT.
WAN O' THE ITHER THINGS YE LIKE, O' COURSE, IS SUPERHEROES--OR SUPES, AS WE GENERALLY CALL THEM. WHICH IS FUNNY, 'COS WHAT WE DO--WHAT THE BOYS DO--IS KEEP AN EYE ON SUPES.
WE WORK FOR THE C.I.A., YE SEE. AN' WE WATCH WHIT THE SUPES GET UP TAE, WE RUN SURVEILLANCE ON AW THE DIFFERENT TEAMS. SOMETIMES WE USE WHIT WE FIND OOT TAE BLACKMAIL THEM.
SOMETIMES, IF THEY NEED IT, WE GIE THEM A WEE SLAP.
SO WHIT YE'RE PROBABLY WONDERIN', IS HOO ON EARTH WE'RE GONNAE RAISE DOSH FIR THE COMIC BOOK LEGAL DEFENCE FUND? WONDER NAE LONGER, TRUE BELIEVER.
SO LONG AS YOU DONATE YIR MONEY TAE THE FUND, WE WILLNAE HAVE TAE PAY YIR FAVORITE SUPES A WEE VISIT. IF EVERY WAN O' YE READIN' THIS SENDS IN FIVE DOLLARS, FIR INSTANCE, WE WON'T LET THE FEMALE LOOSE ON--
AAAAIIIIIEEEEEEE!!
OH, DEAR.
TOO LATE.

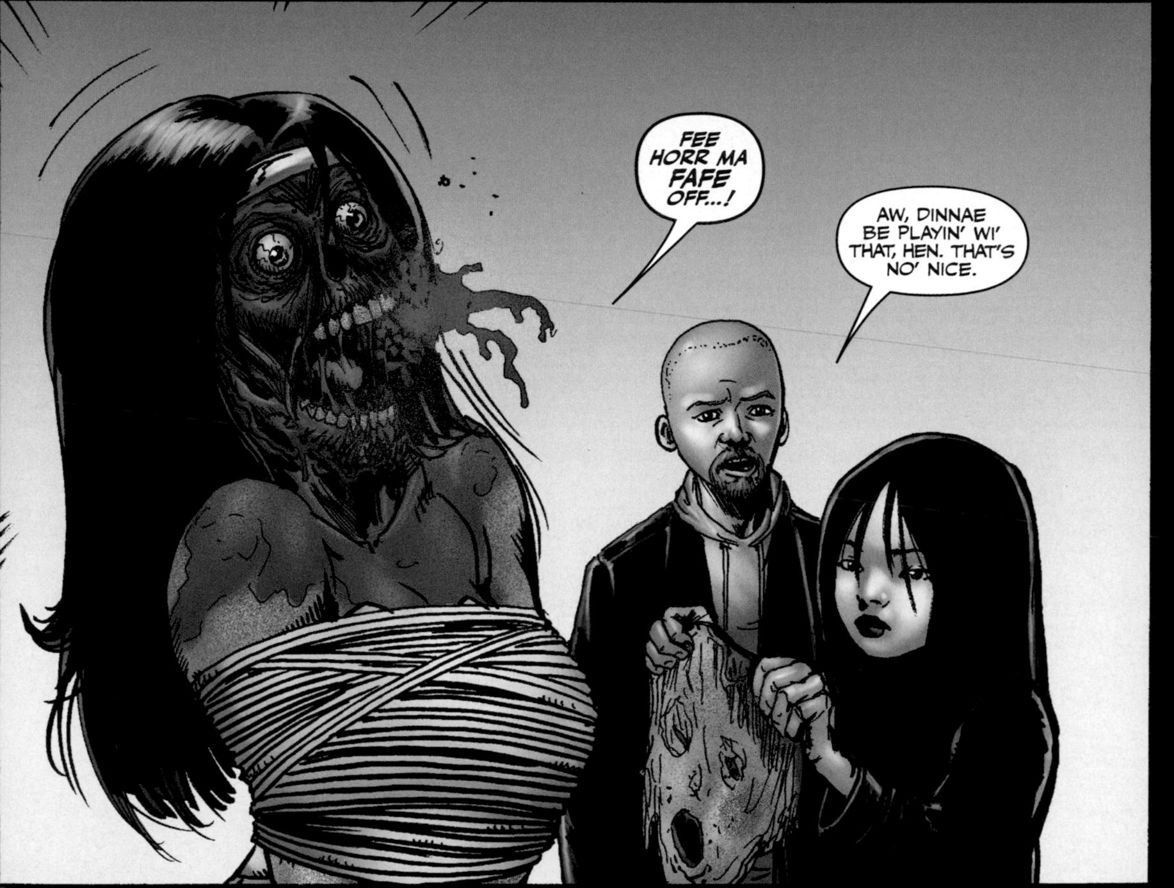
FEE HORR MA FAFE OFF...!
AW, DINNAE BE PLAYIN' WI' THAT, HEN. THAT'S NO' NICE.

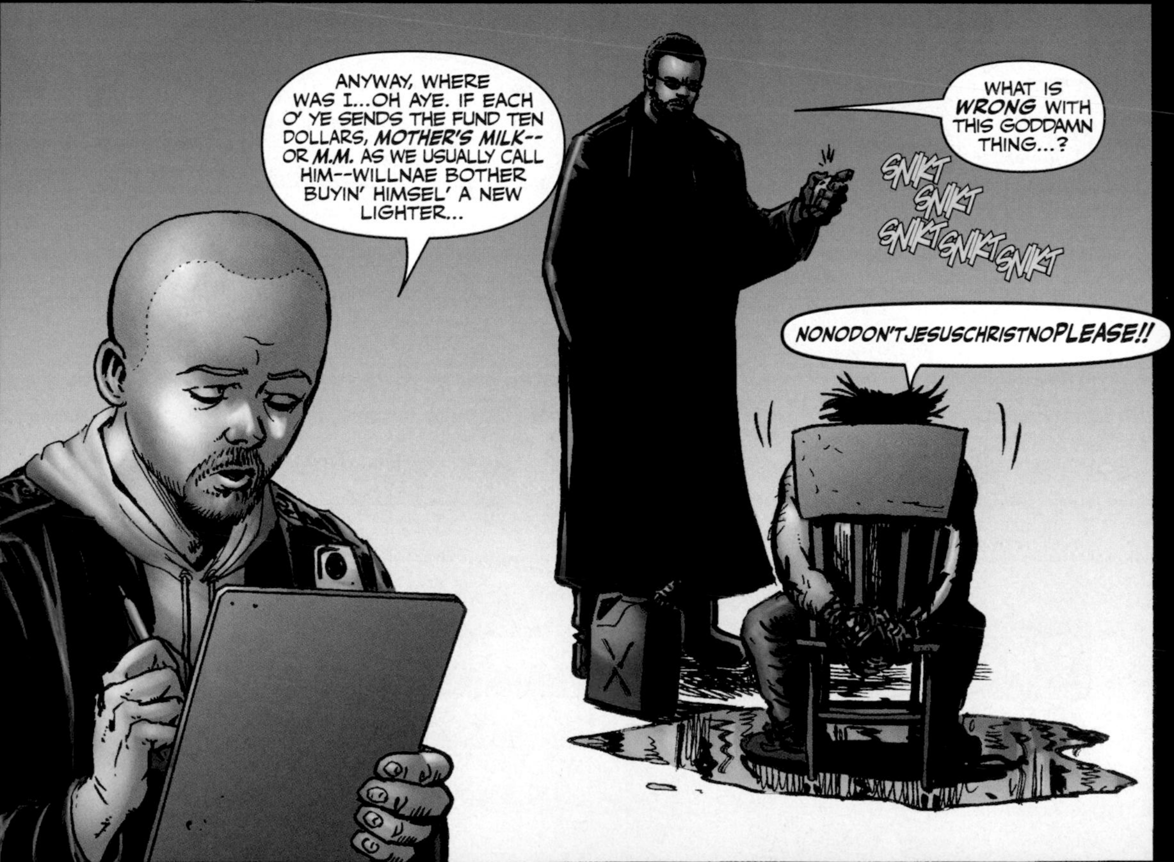
ANYWAY, WHERE WAS I...OH AYE. IF EACH O' YE SENDS THE FUND TEN DOLLARS, MOTHER'S MILK-- OR M.M. AS WE USUALLY CALL HIM--WILLNAE BOTHER BUYIN' HIMSEL' A NEW LIGHTER...
WHAT IS WRONG WITH THIS GODDAMN THING...?
SNIKT SNIKT SNIKT SNIKT SNIKT
NONODON'TJESUSCHRISTNOPLEASE!!

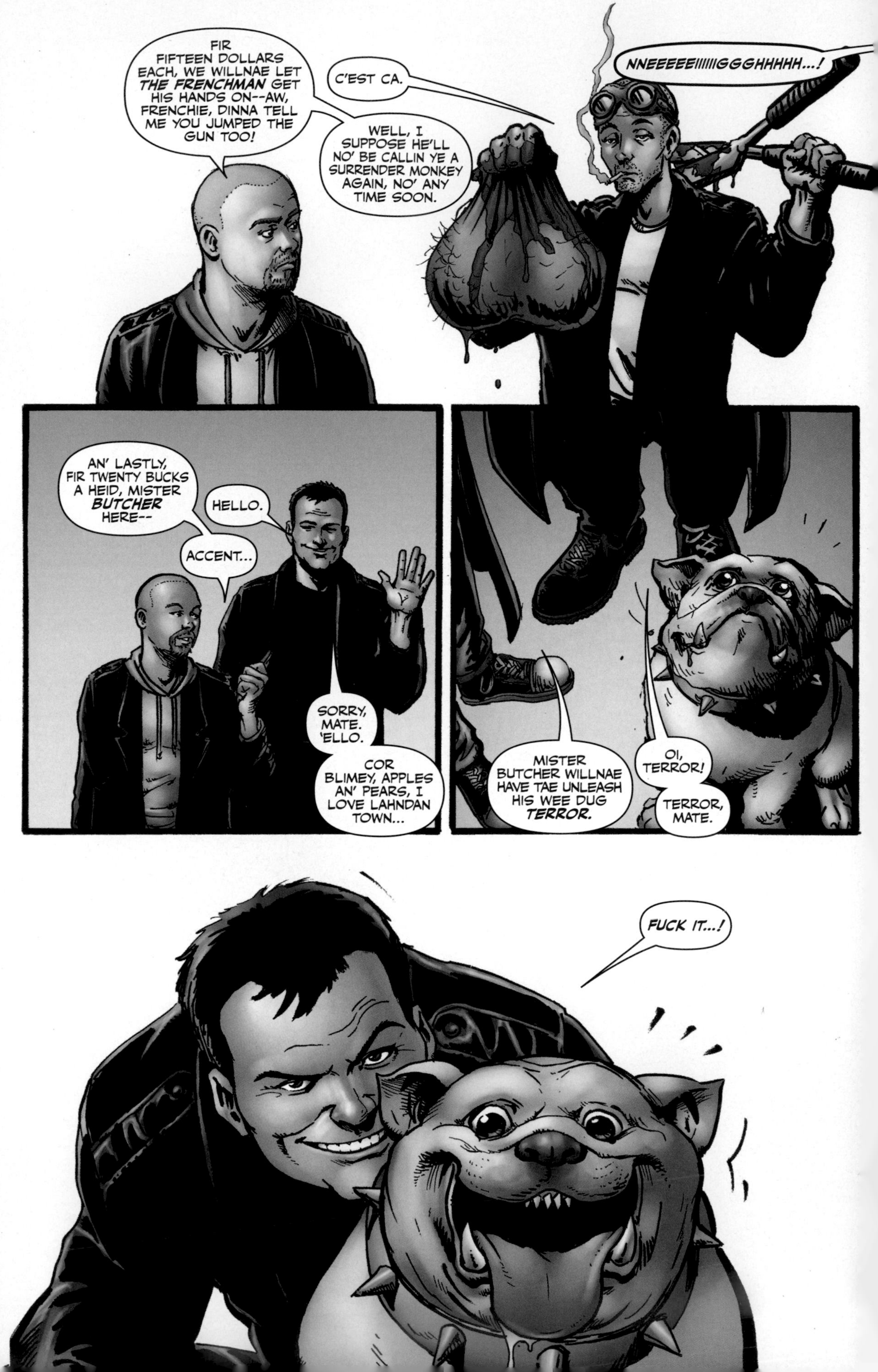
FIR FIFTEEN DOLLARS EACH, WE WILLNAE LET THE FRENCHMAN GET HIS HANDS ON--AW, FRENCHIE, DINNA TELL ME YOU JUMPED THE GUN TOO!
C'EST CA.
NNEEEEEIIIIIIGGGHHHHH...!
WELL, I SUPPOSE HE'LL NO' BE CALLIN YE A SURRENDER MONKEY AGAIN, NO' ANY TIME SOON.
AN' LASTLY, FIR TWENTY BUCKS A HEID, MISTER BUTCHER HERE--
HELLO.
ACCENT...
SORRY, MATE. 'ELLO.
COR BLIMEY, APPLES AN' PEARS, I LOVE LAHNDAN TOWN...
MISTER BUTCHER WILLNAE HAVE TAE UNLEASH HIS WEE DUG TERROR.
OI, TERROR!
TERROR, MATE.
FUCK IT...!

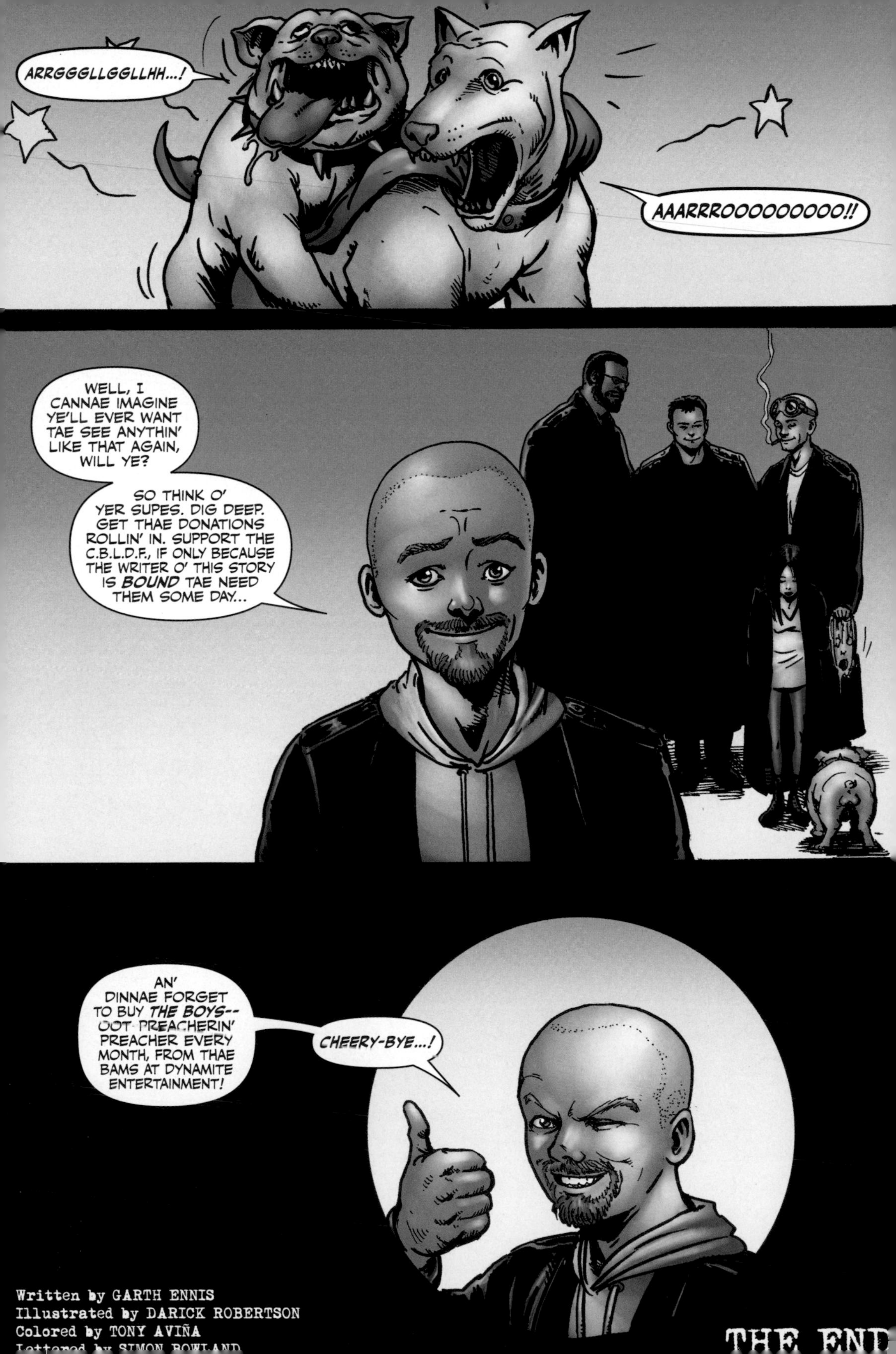
ARRGGGLLGGLLHH...!
AAARRROOOOOOOOO!!
WELL, I CANNAE IMAGINE YE'LL EVER WANT TAE SEE ANYTHIN' LIKE THAT AGAIN, WILL YE?
SO THINK O' YER SUPES. DIG DEEP. GET THAE DONATIONS ROLLIN' IN. SUPPORT THE C.B.L.D.F., IF ONLY BECAUSE THE WRITER O' THIS STORY IS *BOUND* TAE NEED THEM SOME DAY...
AN' DINNAE FORGET TO BUY *THE BOYS*--OOT PREACHERIN' PREACHER EVERY MONTH, FROM THAE BAMS AT DYNAMITE ENTERTAINMENT!
CHEERY-BYE...!
Written by GARTH ENNIS
Illustrated by DARICK ROBERTSON
Colored by TONY AVIÑA
Lettered by SIMON BOWLAND
THE END

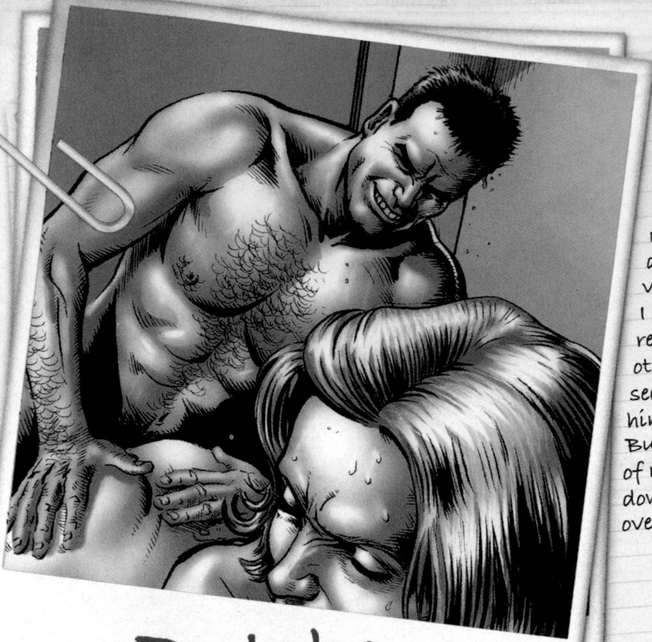

Butcher

BUTCHER

Originally conceived as "Savage", Garth later changed the name to "Butcher". I had a hard time wrapping my head around a character as brutal as Butcher without imagining another version of Nick Fury or Frank Castle. I entertained signature cigars and requisite stubble on his iron jaw but other than a gleeful smile, I wasn't seeing the character as Garth wanted him. Only until Garth described Billy Butcher as having a "dark, cruel smile of malicious intent" - that got me to sit down and draw Butcher's face over and over until I got it right.

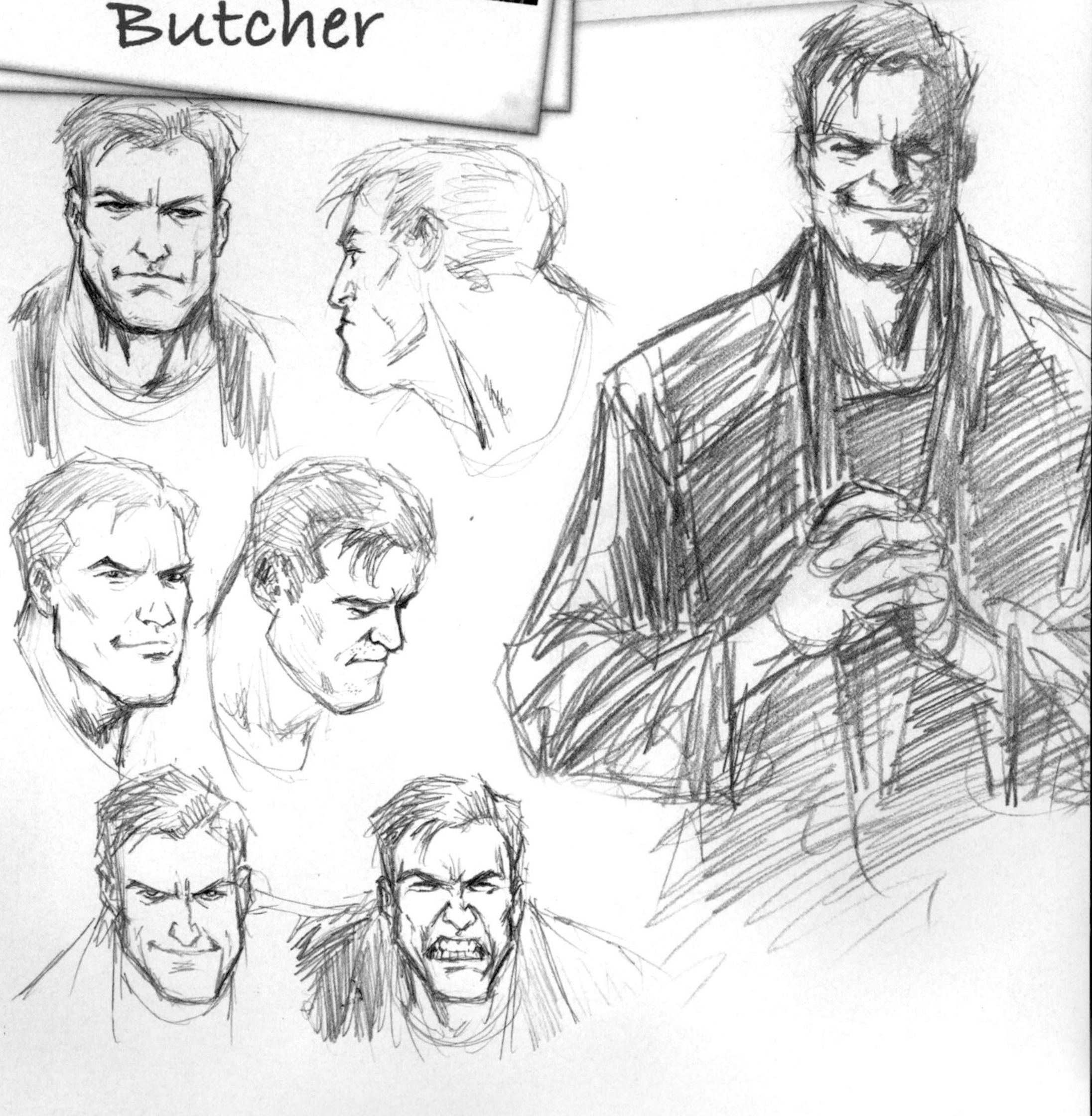

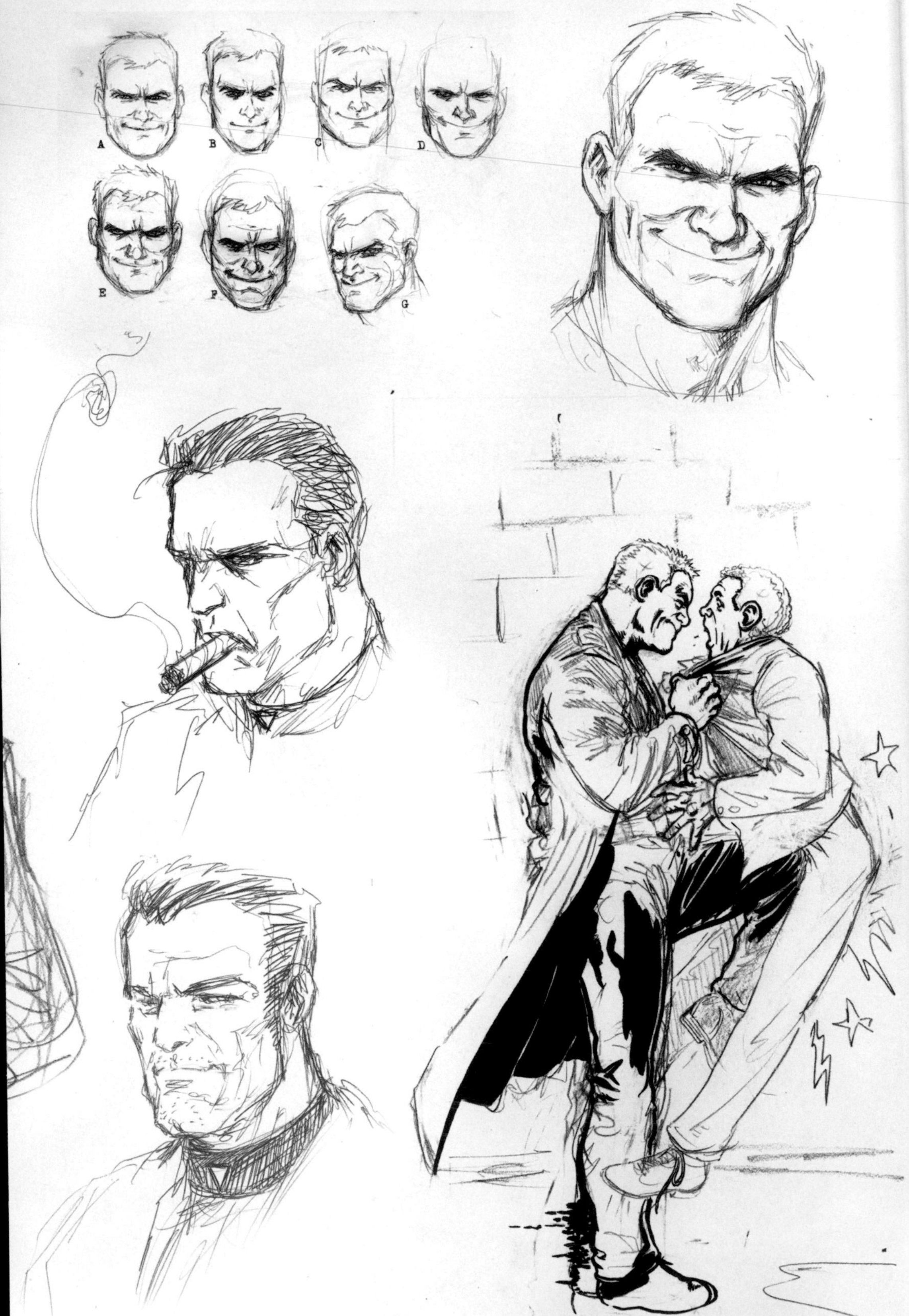
A
B
C
D
E
F
G

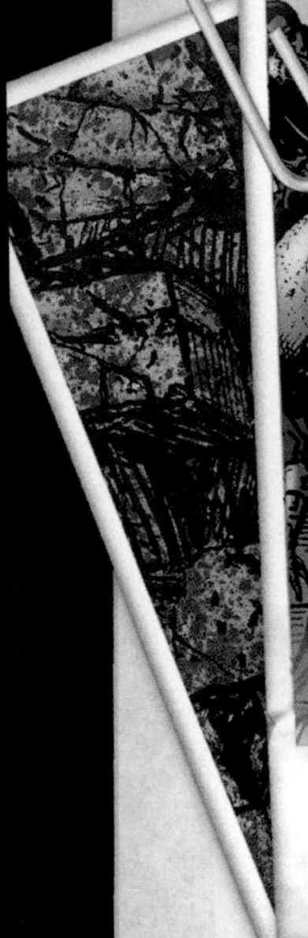

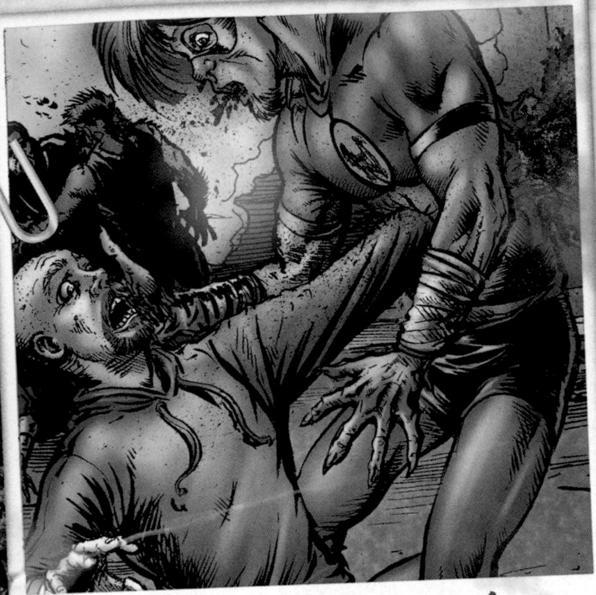

"Wee" Hughie

Rob
girlfriend - deceas

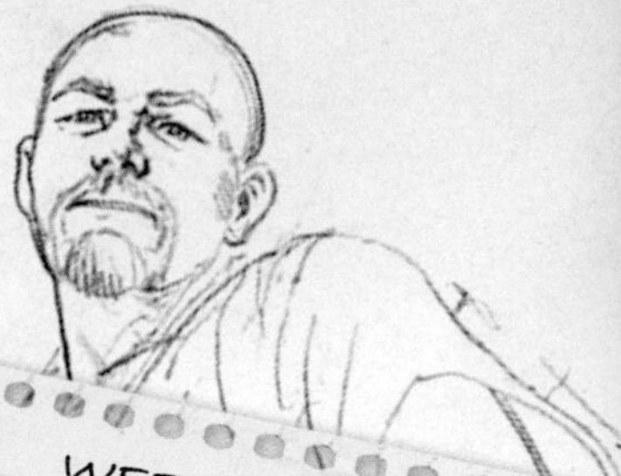

WEE HUGHIE

Wee Hughie was inspired by an old friend of Garth's. Garth emphasized that it was important to capture an innocence but tough determination in Hughie. Two things that seemed to contradict each other, and somehow, in early sketches, he kept looking too old.

When I saw Simon Pegg in 'Spaced' I thought he captured that balance perfectly, and "Shaun" nailed that home. I never thought the reference would get so much attention, but I was thrilled when Simon contacted me and showed us such support! Wee Hughie has become my favorite character in the book to draw, since that balance in his nature is always a challenge and when I feel I get it, I have the most satisfaction accomplishing that.

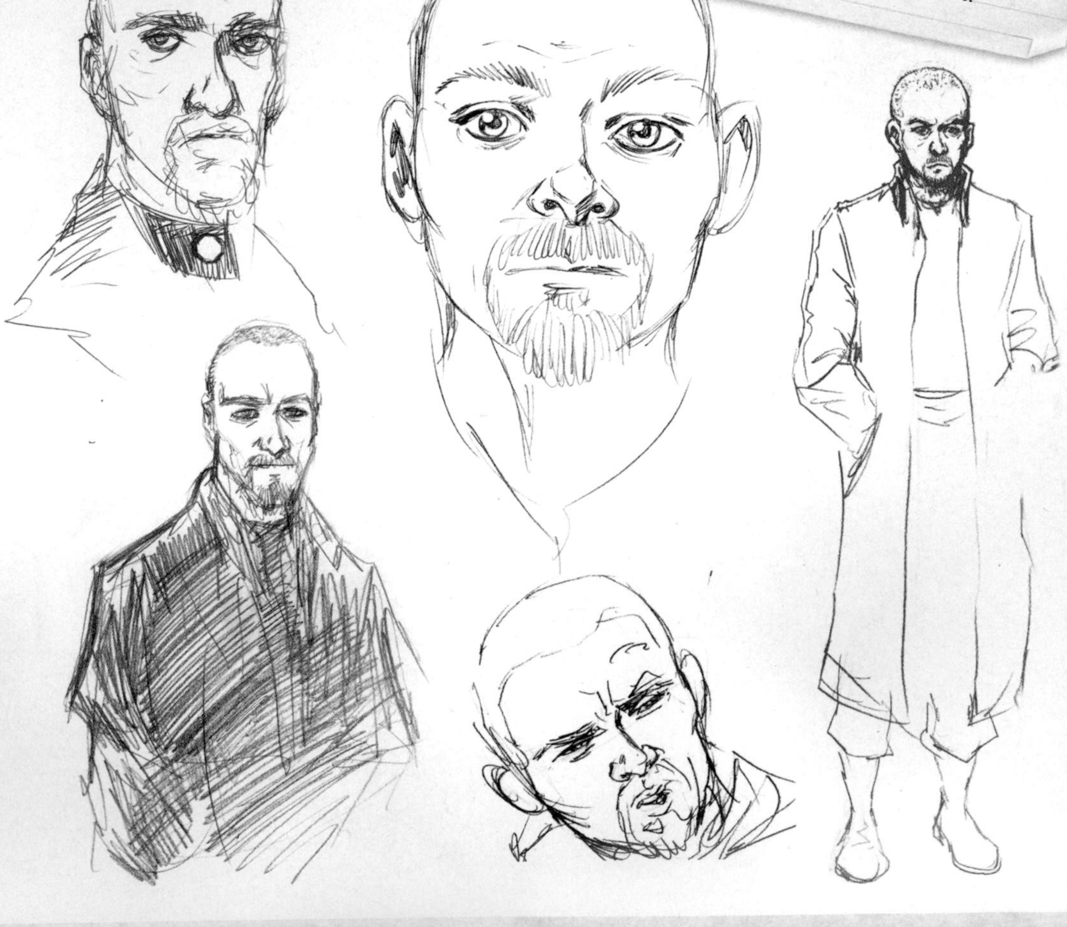

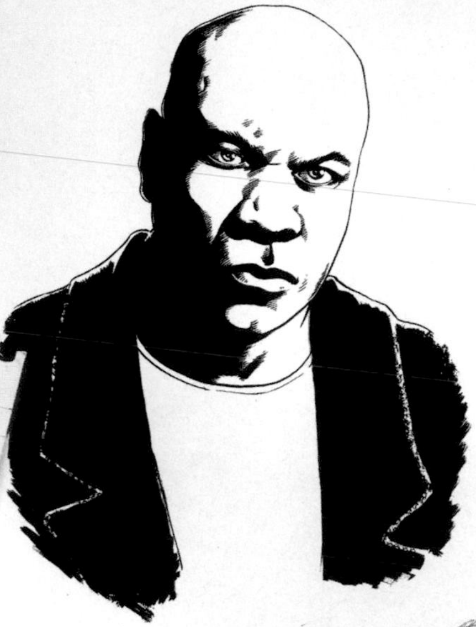

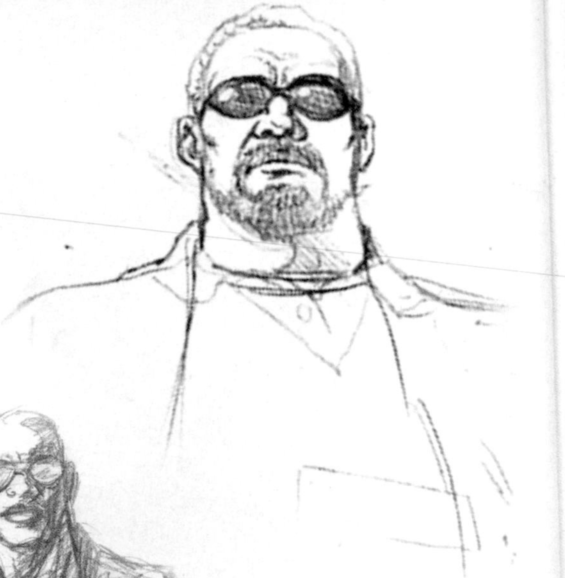

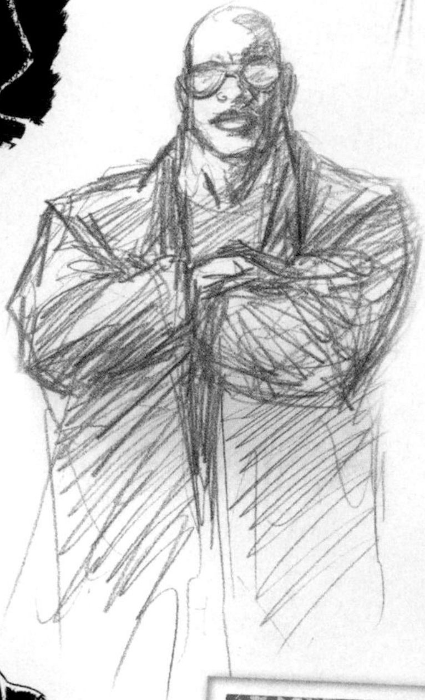

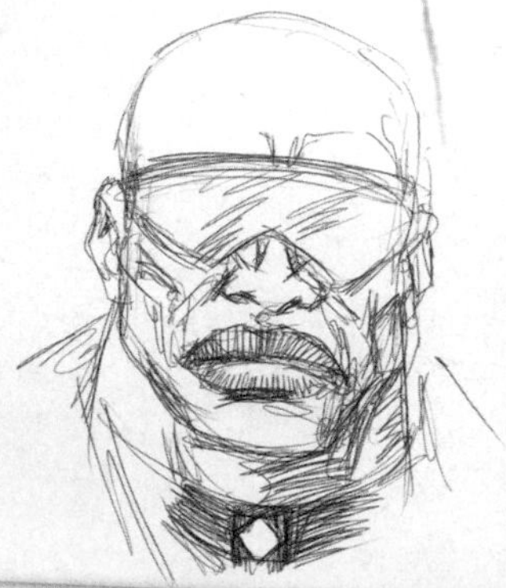

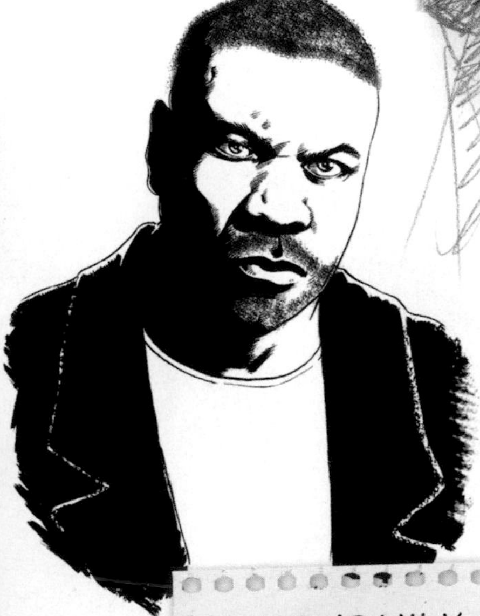

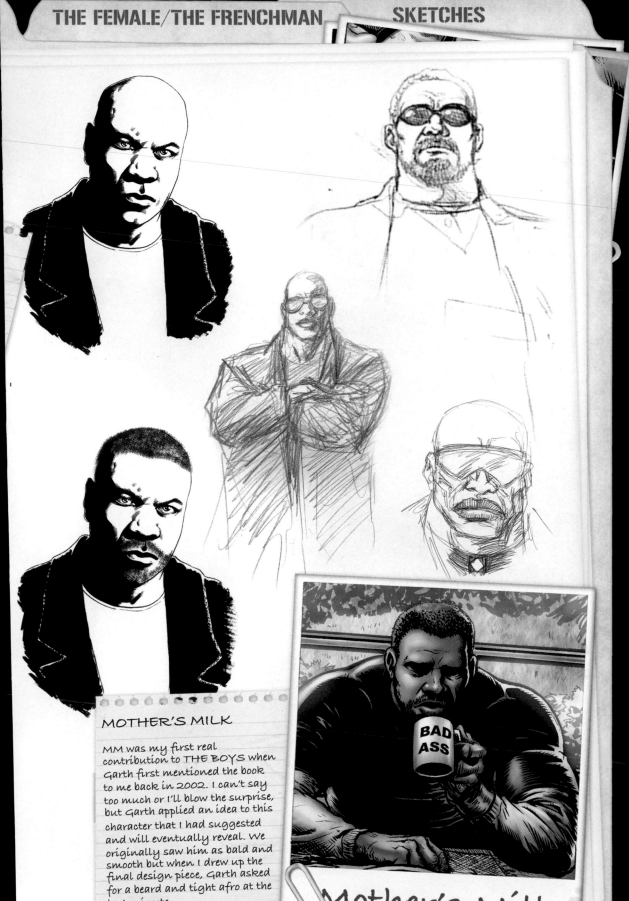

MOTHER'S MILK

MM was my first real contribution to THE BOYS when Garth first mentioned the book to me back in 2002. I can't say too much or I'll blow the surprise, but Garth applied an idea to this character that I had suggested and will eventually reveal. We originally saw him as bald and smooth but when I drew up the final design piece, Garth asked for a beard and tight afro at the last minute.

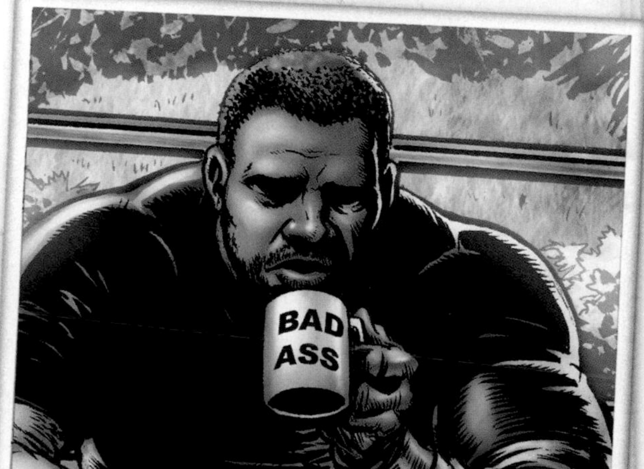
BAD
ASS

Mother's Milk

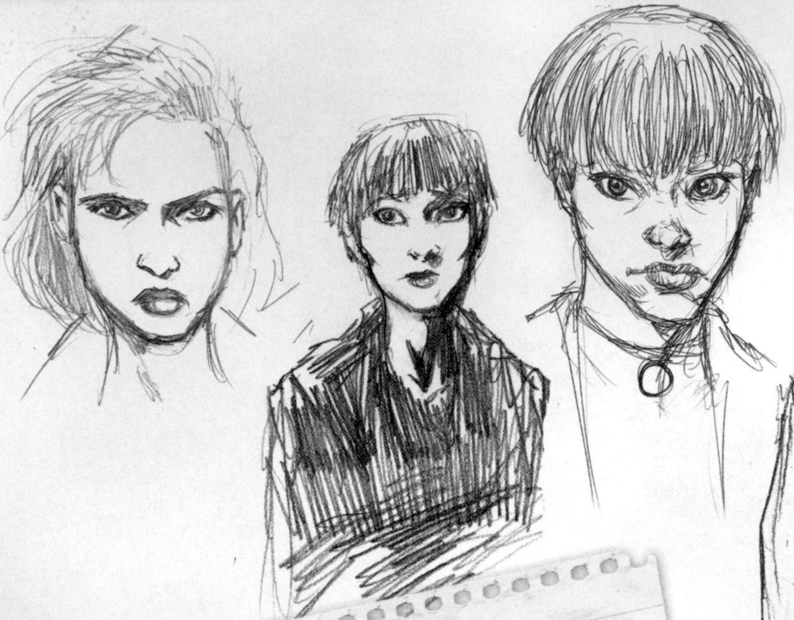

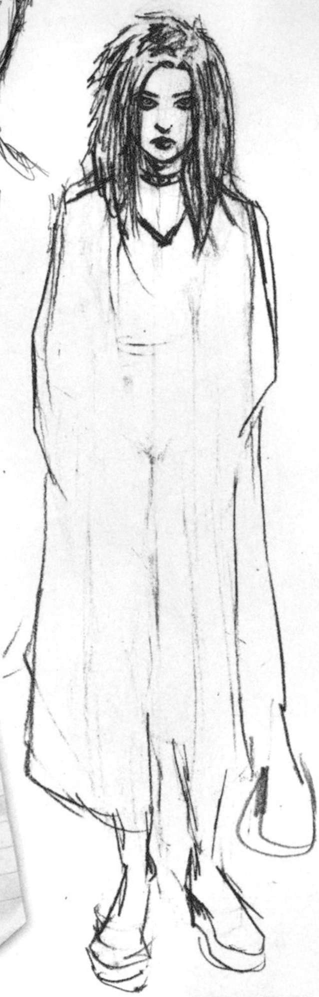

THE FEMALE

The point was to make her small and insane. In the years leading up to actually having scripts to see these characters in action, I didn't fully realize what Garth was going for, and I think my instinct was to go for sexy, like a 'Kill Bill' Tarantino-esque character.

In a later sketch, I tried making her Japanese and that's when the character came to life for me. When I suggested the change in nationality to Garth, he lit up, and embraced the idea. I can't wait for the origin story he said the change inspired.

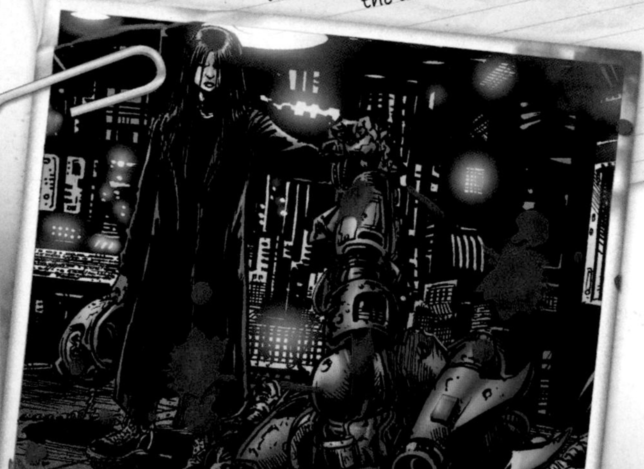

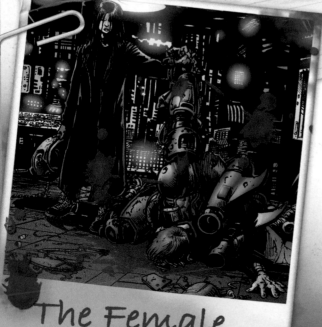

The Female

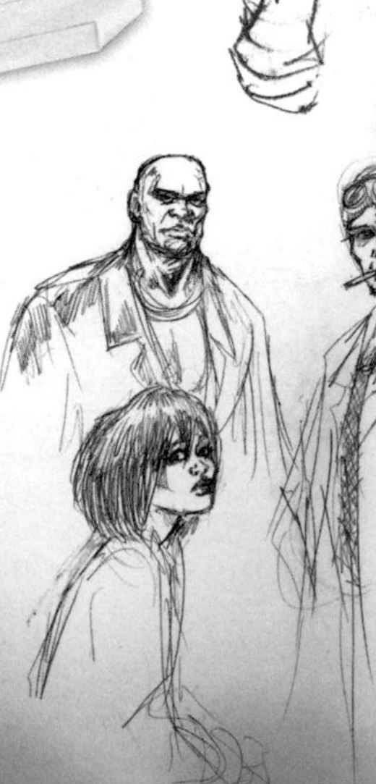

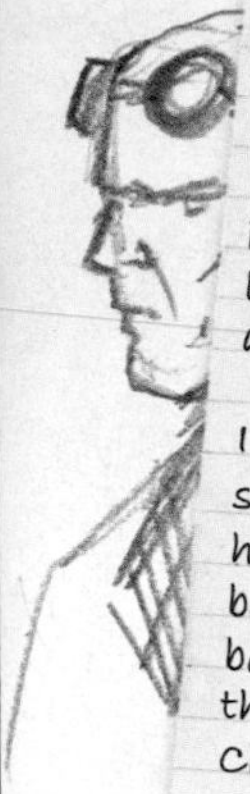

THE FRENCHMAN

The earliest character I played with when sketching, I imagined him in action from the beginning. Rolling off of Transmetropolitan, it was important not to make him too much like Spider Jerusalem, since he's skinny, bald and smokes and has goggles on all the time.

I felt it was important at first to give the BOYS some sort of logo, or symbol. I imagined them having their place in the super hero world and being more public figures. I designed a symbol for their coats and little collars for what I thought would be super suits beneath, ala the Challengers of the Unknown or Fantastic 4.

The key to The Boys is how otherwise normal they look aside from their signature boots and trench coats. Less is more.

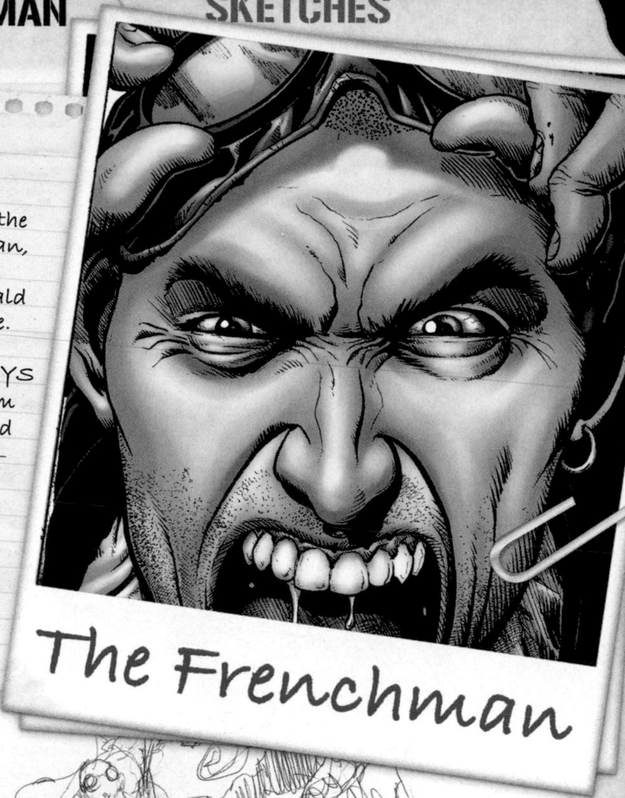

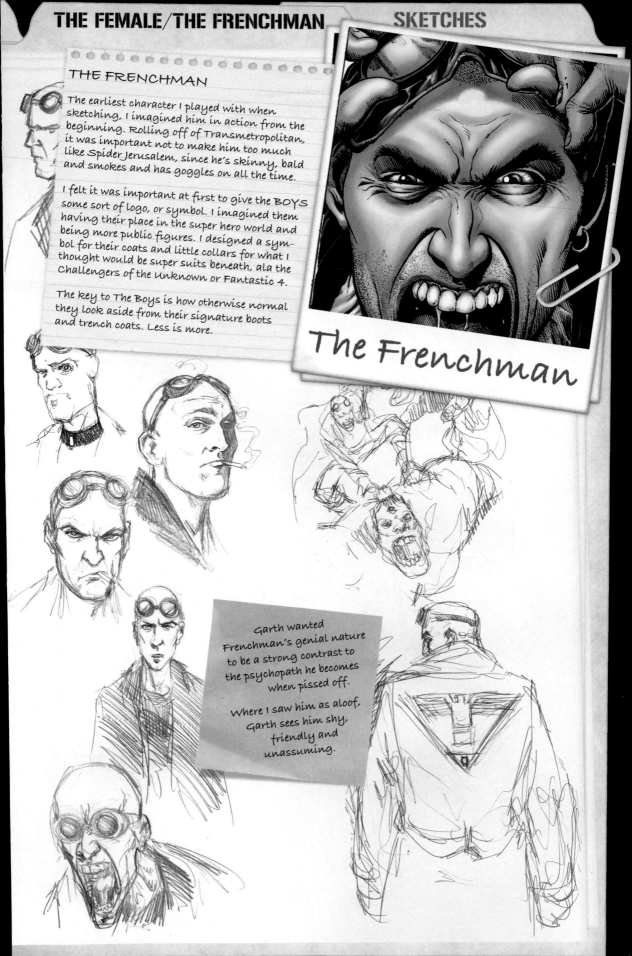

The Frenchman

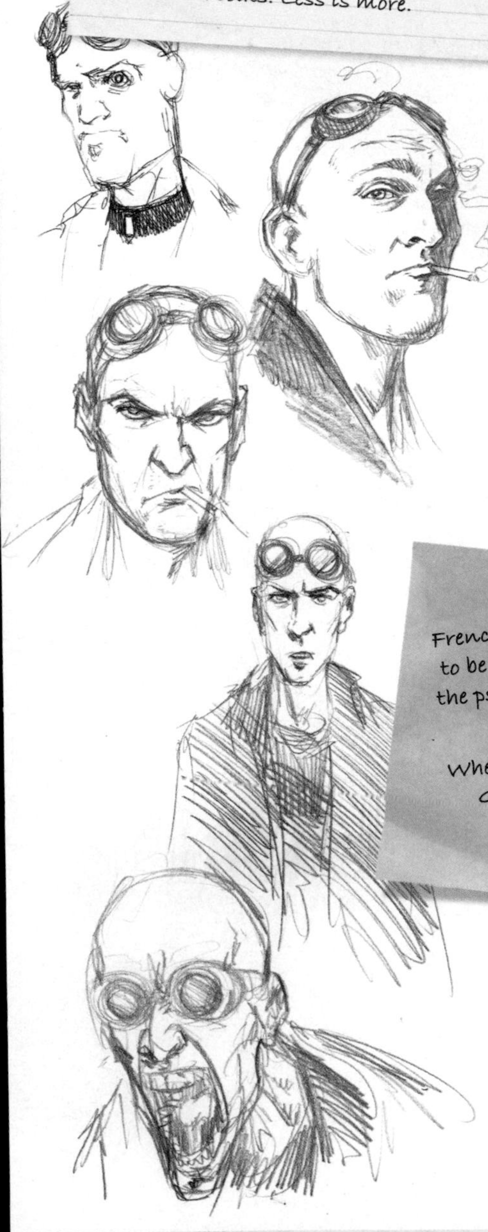

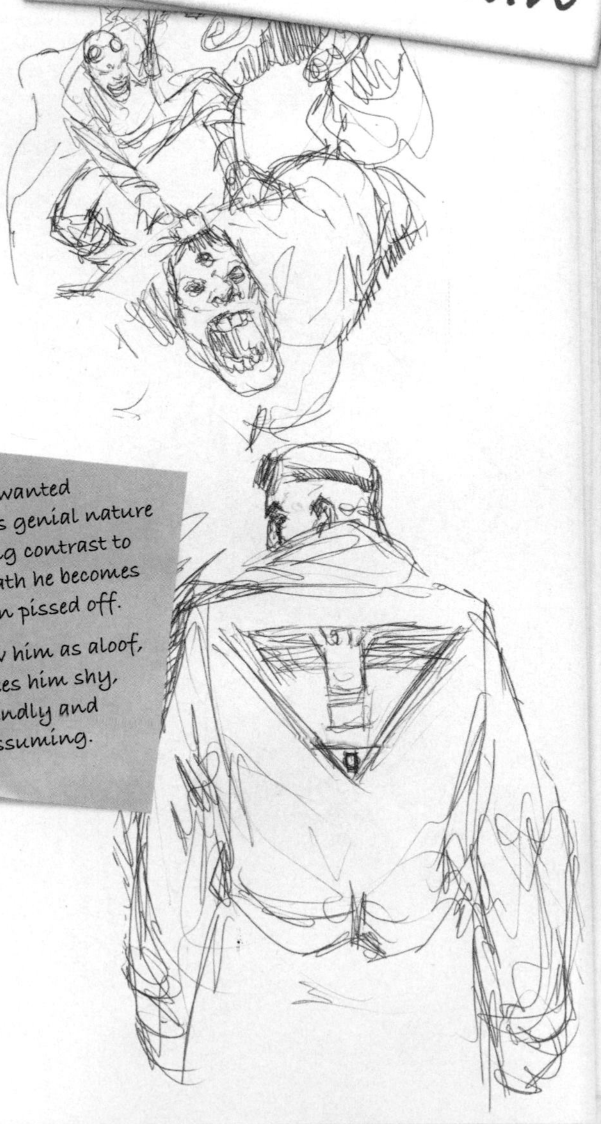

Garth wanted Frenchman's genial nature to be a strong contrast to the psychopath he becomes when pissed off.

Where I saw him as aloof, Garth sees him shy, friendly and unassuming.

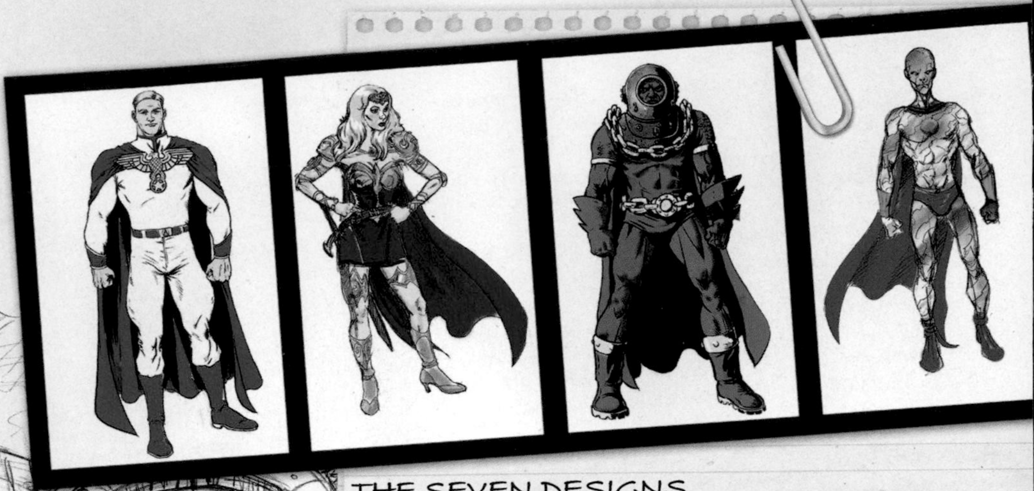

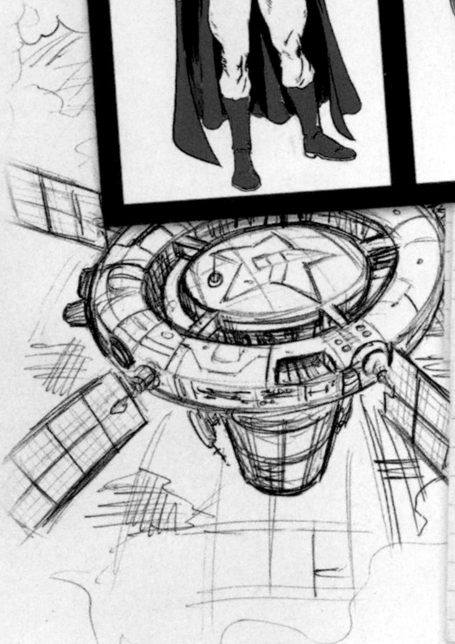

THE SEVEN DESIGNS

- Homelander round one: I liked the Nazi overtones, but we agreed it was a little too overt. There was something appealing about the white suit that I still like.
- Queen Maeve went through a few rounds back and forth. The early ones were far more Celtic in theme.
- The Seven's headquarters appeared almost exactly the way I sketched it out in this drawing from my sketch book.
- That Ass hal 'A-Train' was right there from the start.
- Starlight's costume was all about covering her up, and making her sweet and innocent so when the Seven gets a hold of her, the contrast would be clear.

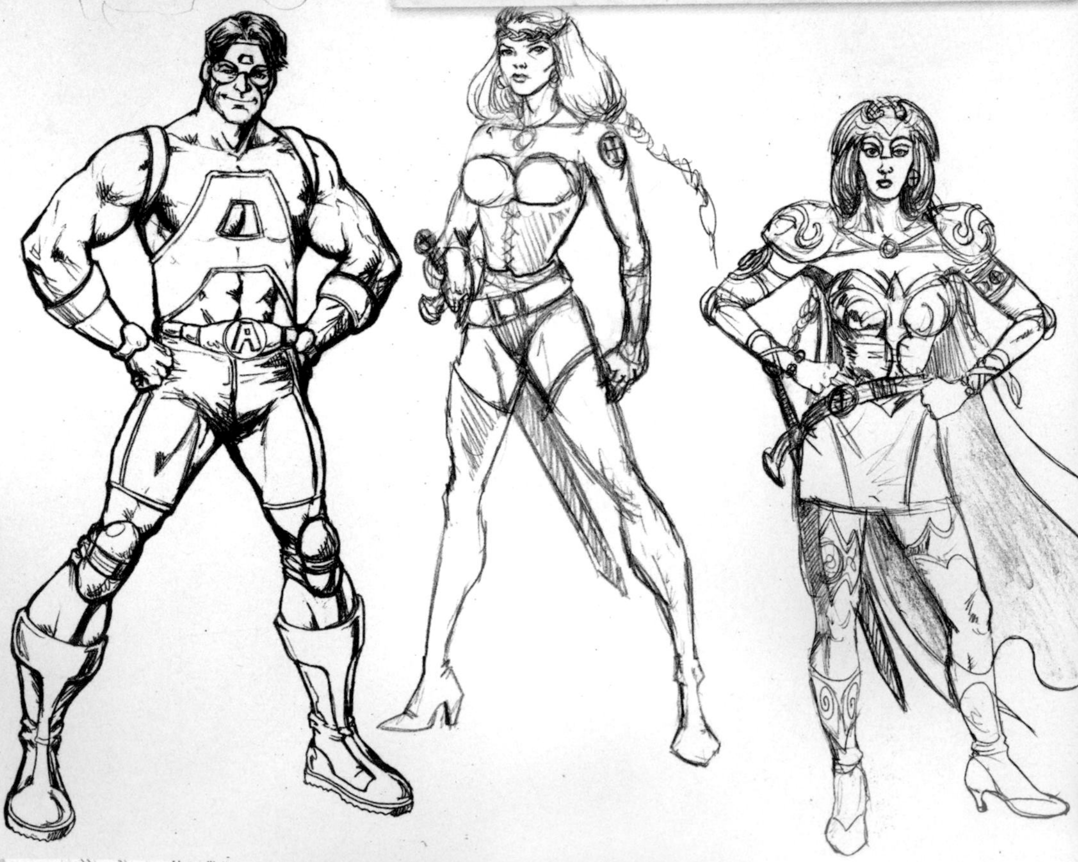

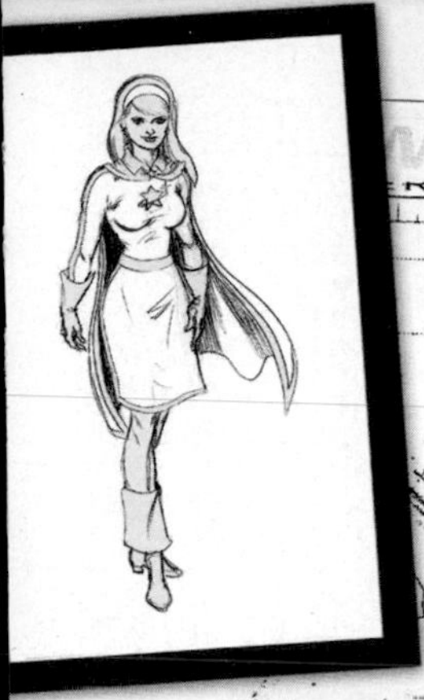

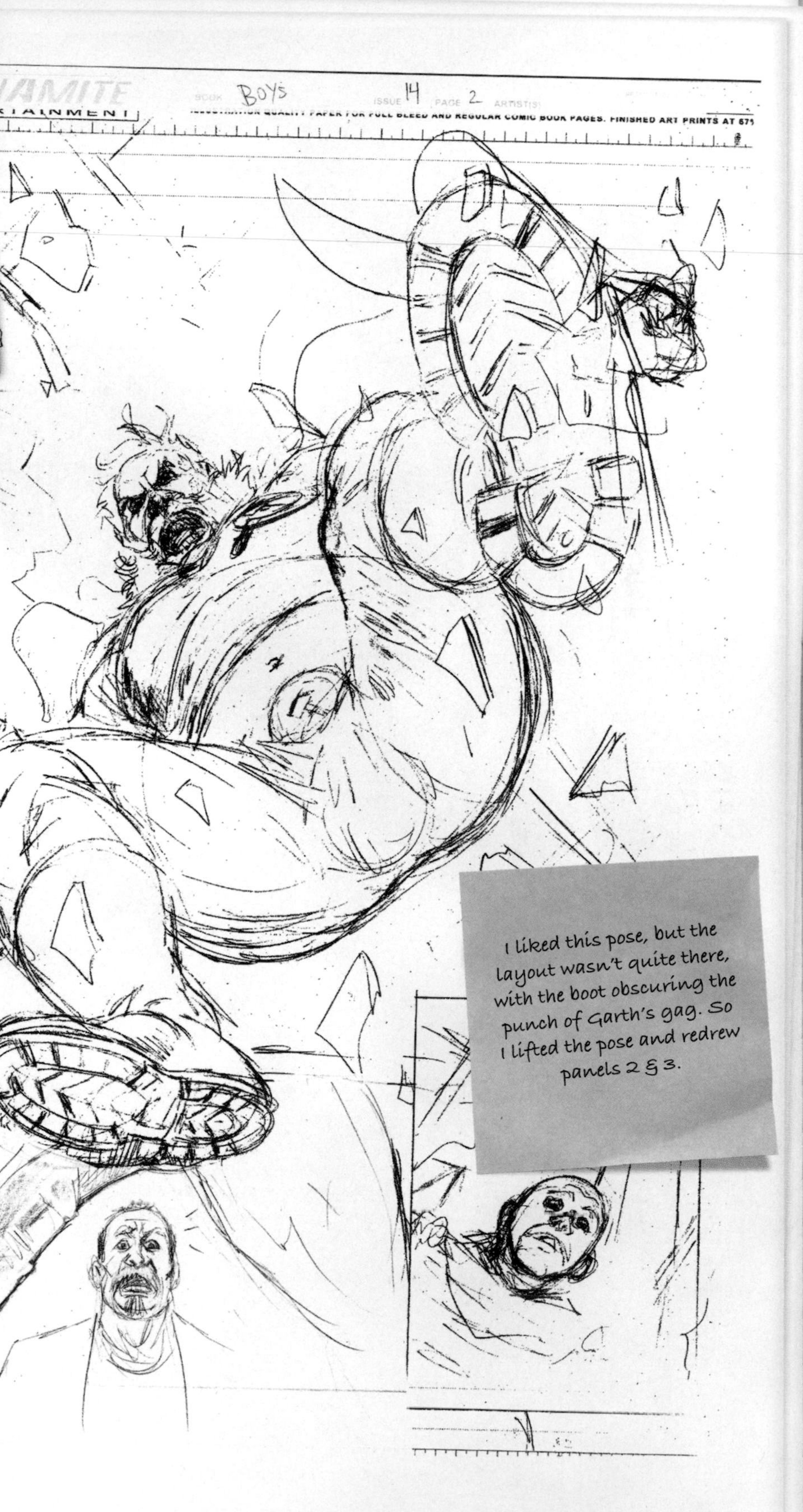
BOOK Boys ISSUE 14 PAGE 2 ARTIST(S)

I liked this pose, but the layout wasn't quite there, with the boot obscuring the punch of Garth's gag. So I lifted the pose and redrew panels 2 & 3.

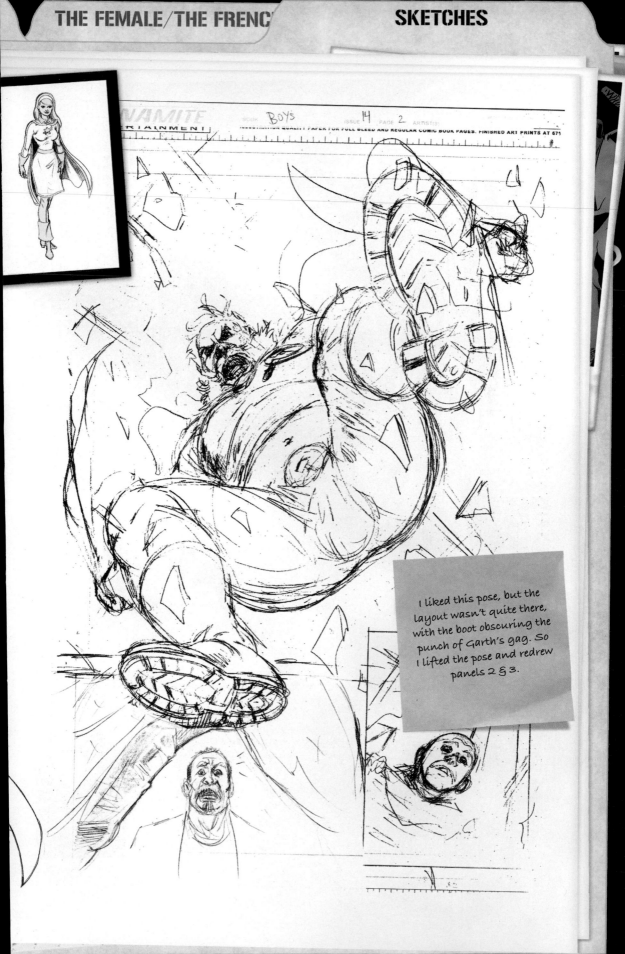

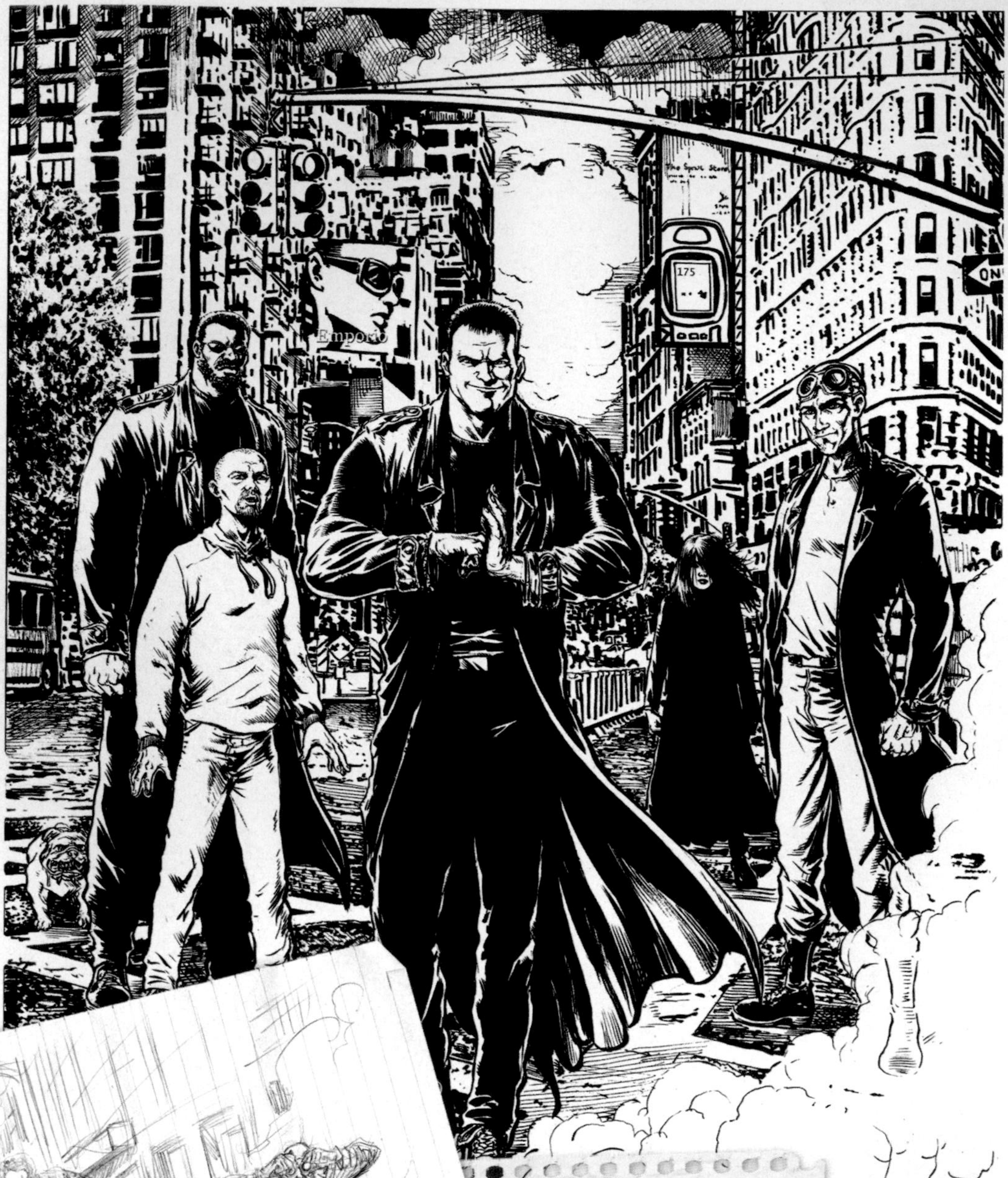
Emporio
175

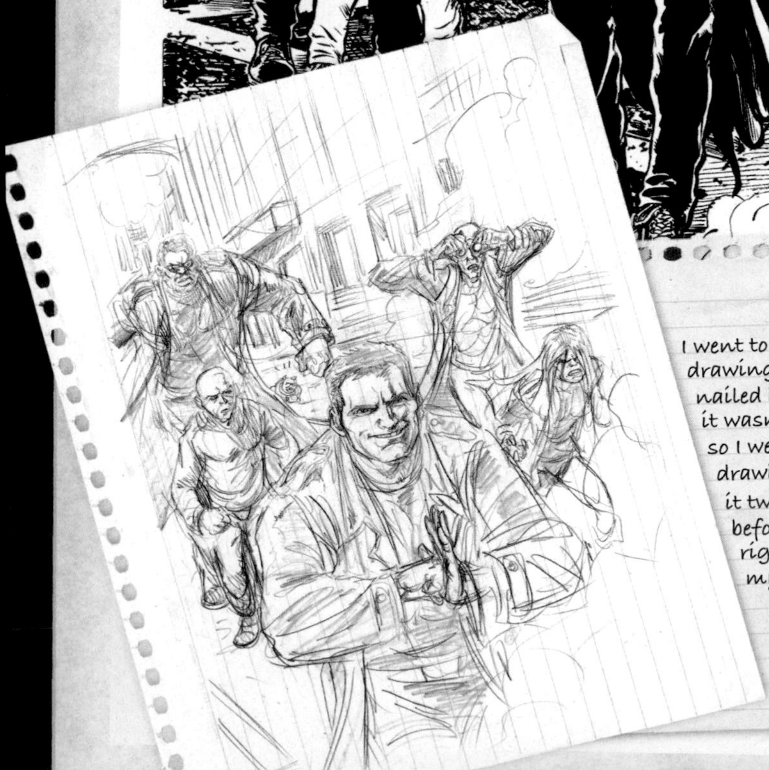

I went to town on this drawing and thought I'd nailed it. Problem was, it wasn't working for Garth, so I went back to the drawing board and drew it two more times before it came out just right. I did get to use my background though.

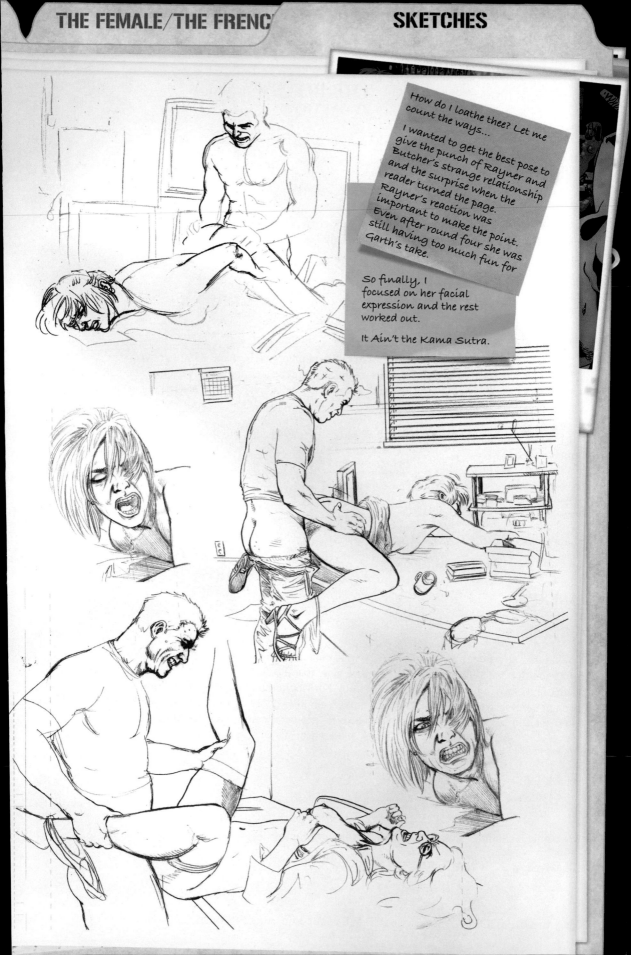

How do I loathe thee? Let me count the ways...

I wanted to get the best pose to give the punch of Rayner and Butcher's strange relationship and the surprise when the reader turned the page. Rayner's reaction was important to make the point. Even after round four she was still having too much fun for Garth's take.

So finally, I focused on her facial expression and the rest worked out.

It Ain't the Kama Sutra.

THE BOYS 4
BY GARTH ENNIS

PAGE ONE

1.

Night. Exterior a large, three storey house on the edge of the interstate, somewhere in the endless hinterland of Jersey. Strip mall central. Neon signs. Traffic roaring by on the road further back. The house is an old-fashioned red brick structure, kind of stuck out on its own. Looks a bit odd with no other residential buildings in the area.

House: **CHANGE!**

2.

Inside, in a wide upstairs hallway, six out of eight members of Teenage Kix run out of six different doorways. They're all naked except for their masks- maybe a couple have kept their boots on too. Very excited, laughing their asses off. Not that we see the details, but a couple are jerking off as they run. Absent are Gunpowder and Popclaw.

The place is a pretty obvious Brothel: dark red carpet, wallpaper and drapes, erotic prints on the walls, lamps turned down low.

Whack Job: **HA HA HA HA**

Jetstreak: **MOVE**, DUDE--!

Blarney Cock: **HA HA HA HA HA!**

PAGE TWO

1.

Dogknott is now banging a hooker doggy style on a large, luxurious bed with dark red satin sheets- rooms are decorated much like the hallways. Note that the curtains are not pulled. The girl doesn't seem to be enjoying it much, gritting her teeth, but Dogknott's laughing his ass off. Behind them, seen through the doorway and across the hall through another doorway (all the doors are kept open), Whack Job is fucking another hooker on another bed- missionary position, just for variety.

Dogknott: **HA HA HA HA HA--!**

Whack Job: FUCKIN' **YEAH—**

2.

Big Game's banging another hooker, suddenly turns and yells.

Big Game: **CHANGE!**

3.

They rush from room to room across the hall again. Long shot this time.

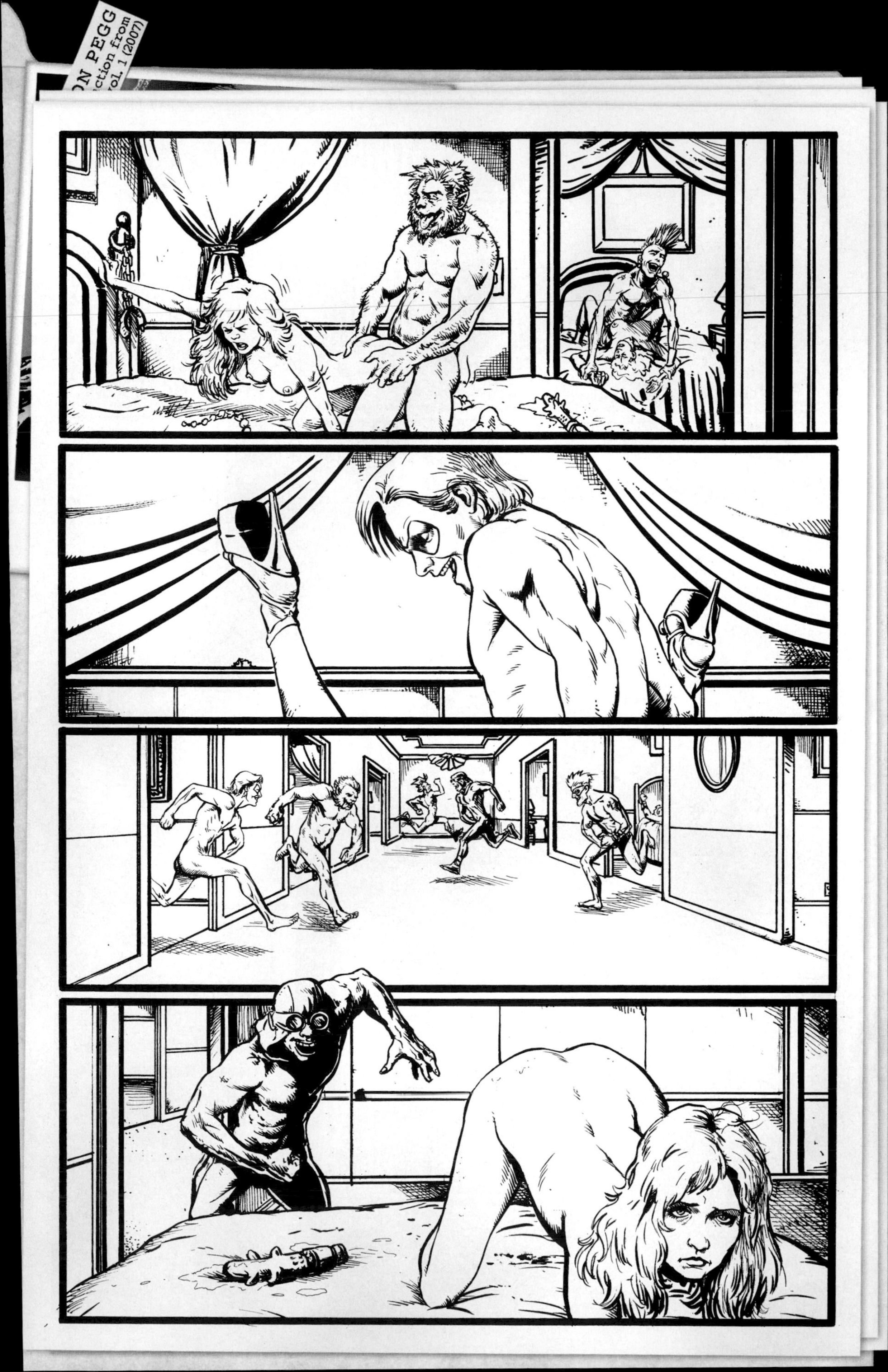

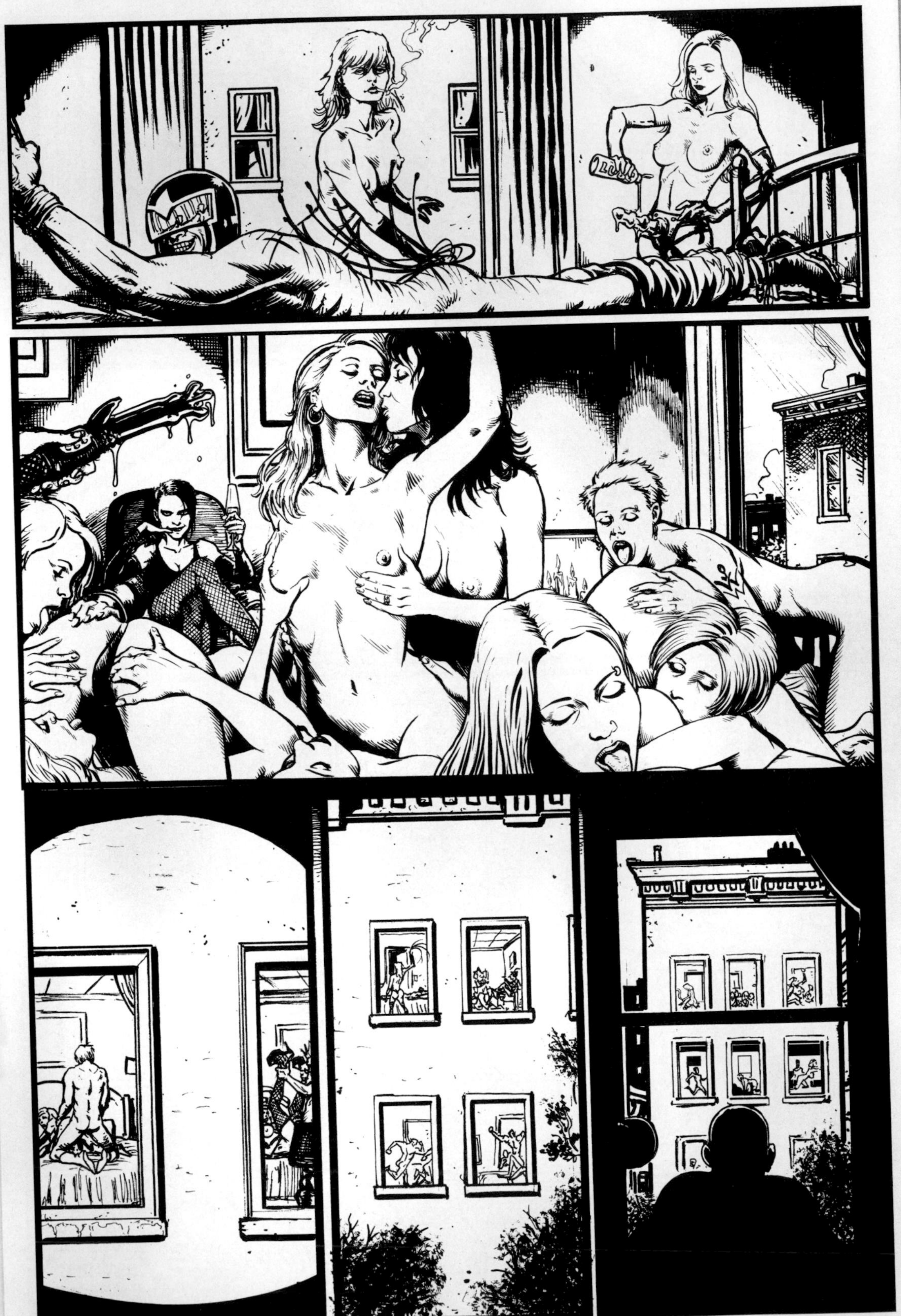

Whack Job: **HA HA HA HA HA—**

4.

The hooker Dogknott was banging waits with a gloomy, pissed off look on her face and her ass in the air as Shout Out charges into the room, intentions obvious.

Shout Out: **TEENAGE KIX ARE COMIN' <u>ATCHA!!</u>**

Door;   HA HA HA HA HA

PAGE THREE

1.

Another room. Gunpowder- mask on, pants pulled down- is tied to a bed, belly down, with a bored-looking hooker whipping the hell out of him with a cat o'nine tails. He grits his teeth in agony, she's drawing quite a bit of blood. Further back another hooker, pours oil over the huge strap-on she's wearing. Make sure we can see the window- curtains not pulled.

Gunpowder: **HURT ME**, YOU FUCKING CUNT, JUST BE MY FUCKING
               PUNISHER—

2.

View past an all-girl orgy at Popclaw, wearing her costume, sipping champagne as she watches the action intently, Looks like a critic examining a work of art rather than someone getting off. All we see of the orgy is an upraised leg with a hand coming in from offshot to pull it back by the ankle. Pretty close on Popclaw.

Popclaw: IN HER ASS NOW.

"   "   THAT'S IT.

3.

Now a through-binoculars shot of the exterior of the house: focussing on one window with a partial view of the next tone, two of the Kix visible fucking hookers, one seen through each window.

Jag: **CHANGE!**

4.

Pull back, no binocs anymore. From this far we can see through two windows on the second floor, where the two guys leave the hookers and run for the doors, and two windows on the third, where Gunpowder and Popclaw are up to their shenanigans.

Jag: HA HA HA HA HA

5.

Back a little further. Sane view but from the window of another building. Dark in here. Two different guys fucking the girls on the second floor here.

Jag: HA HA HA HA **HA--**

PAGE FOUR

1.

Wee Hughie peers out the window at us, stunned, no idea what to think. In front of him, set up on a tripod, are the large pair of hi-power binocs he's just looked up from. Next to those, also on a tripod, is a camera with a huge telephoto lens. Gloomy in here. Some shitty motel room, styrene cups, half eaten pizza. Butcher sits behind Hughie, laughing quietly to himself as he reads the New York Times by the light of a little lamp. Terror's asleep. There's also a large, technical looking radio receiver set up on a table.

Hughie: JINGS…!

Radio(jag):   **CHANGE!**

Title: **CHERRY** part two

And credits.

PAGE FIVE

1.

The Seven's meeting room on their floating HQ. Night outside, if we can see out the windows. They sit around the table, the Homelander addressing them. Also present is a guy in a suit, sitting further back in a chair on his own. Arms folded, legs crossed, listening calmly but intently. Looks like a corporate officer, which in fact he is.

We've already met Queen Maeve, A-Train, Black Noir and Annie (pretty subdued here, looking bleakly at the table)- the other two are The Deep and Jack From Jupiter.

The Deep wears a dark green cape and outfit, with a bright golden helmet like the ones deep sea divers used to wear. The front is cut away so we can see his face- big black guy with grim, heavy features, head shaved. Heavy gold chain around his neck.

Jack from Jupiter wears only a tight speedo and boots; his entire body is marked like the surface of the planet Jupiter- the swirling yellow and brown clouds, and a huge dark red spot like a giant bruise on his chest. Note that the "clouds" don't actually move, it's really just an all-over tattoo. Bald and skinny. No body hair, not even eyebrows or eyelashes. Each team member has a little plaque in front of them with their name on it- try to draw them in the first time you do a close up on each character. Annie's reads STARLIGHT

Homelander: … AND I HEREBY BRING THIS MEETING OF **THE SEVEN** TO
                 ORDER.

2.

The Homelander addresses us with the guy in the suit watching behind him. He's calm and polite here, behaving very properly. Not mocking or sleazy, like last ep. never happened.

Homelander: FIRST ITEM ON THE AGENDA IS TO WELCOME OUR NEW
                 MEMBER, **STARLIGHT**, WHO'LL BE SERVING IN PLACE OF THE
                 LAMPLIGHTER DURING HIS ABSENCE. YOU'VE EACH MET HER
                 INDIVIDUALLY OVER THE LAST COUPLE OF DAYS, BUT THIS IS

                 HER FIRST APPEARANCE AT AN OFFICIAL MEETING.

"   "   STARLIGHT, WOULD YOU LIKE TO SAY A FEW WORDS BY
                 WAY OF INTRODUCING YOURSELF?

3.

Annie looks up, slightly startled. Suddenly under the spotlight, wasn't expecting it. Awkward.

Annie: OH.

PAGE SIX

1.

Annie nervously gets to her feet, no idea what to say or where to look. Aware everyone's looking at her.

Annie: I, AH…

"   "   I…

2.

The Homelander smiles encouragingly at her- he's gone back to being the sweet guy who met her on her arrival last ep. Nearer us Queen Maeve loses interest, lights a cigarette.

Homelander: IT'S ALL RIGHT, DON'T BE INTIMIDATED. YOU'RE AMONG
                 FRIENDS HERE.

3.

Annie just looks sad. Lowers her gaze. Remembering what happened.

Annie: WELL, I JUST… I WANTED TO SAY HOW PR—

"   "   **AHRRRM**

"   "   HOW PROUD I AM TO BE HERE, I GUESS.

Off: **SHLP SHLP SHLP SHLP**

4.

A-Train is miming a blow-job, jerking his fist towards his mouth and sticking his tongue hard into his cheek. Nasty sneer. He doesn't actually look at Annie- view past her here, no view of her face. Anyone else in shot doesn't react.

A-Train: **SHLP SHLP SHLP SHLP**

5.

Annie looks stricken, lost. Right on the edge of tears. Further back the Homelander continues, polite and proper, not missing a beat.

Homelander: THANK YOU, STARLIGHT. I KNOW WE'LL ALL DO OUR
                UTMOST TO HELP YOU SETTLE IN.

"   "   I BELIEVE THE **DEEP** HAD A QUESTION HE WANTED TO
                RAISE…?

PAGE SEVEN

1.

The Deep, grim.

Deep: A QUESTION OF **MERCHANDISING**.

"   "   I WOULD LIKE TO KNOW WHY THE HOMELANDER, BLACK NOIR
                AND QUEEN MAEVE ARE ON A **FULL ONE PERCENT EACH**,
                COMPARED TO THE REST OF US ON **POINT SEVEN FIVE.**

2.

The Homelander answers calmly- Maeve and Black Noir sit either side of him, by the way.

Homelander: BECAUSE WE'RE THE BIG THREE. WE ALWAYS HAVE BEEN.
                LOOK AT THE SALES OF OUR INDIVIDUALLY TRADEMARKED
                MATERIAL NEXT TO YOURS, IF YOU DON'T UNDERSTAND THE
                DISTINCTION.

3.

Deep isn't impressed, quite icy. Jack glances at Maeve's ample bosom nearest, sneers.

Deep: I DID NOT SEE THE **BIG THREE** MENTIONED ANYWHERE IN
                THE CONTRACT; AS A MATTER OF FACT, I HAVE NEVER
                HEARD IT USED EXCEPT IN THE MOST **INFORMAL CONTEXT**…

Jack: LOOKS TO ME LIKE MAEVE'S GOT THE BIG **TWO** GOING ON
                ALL ON HER LONESOME HERE.

4.

Maeve coolly blows smoke over Jack, who hacks and coughs. The Deep's not letting up.

Jack:	**ICCHA- ICCH**
Deep:	INDIVIDUAL POPULARITY IS BESIDE THE POINT. IT WAS A GROUP DECISION TO SIGN; IT FOLLOWS THAT ANY REMUNERATION SHOULD BE DIVIDED EQUALLY AMONG THE **GROUP**.

5.

Annie only, watching and listening, getting a bit edgy. Not what she expected at all.

Off:	LOOK, WE ALL HAD AN OPPORTUNITY TO EXAMINE THE CONTRACT IN DEPTH: IF ANYBODY'S LAWYER FOUND ANY KIND OF CAUSE FOR CONCERN, **THAT** WOULD HAVE BEEN THE TIME TO DRAW ATTENTION TO IT.
Off 2:	**I** WAS NOT INFORMED THAT INVOLVING A LAWYER WOULD BE **NECESSARY**…
Off 3:	NOR WAS I. BUT I MANAGED TO FIGURE IT OUT FOR MYSELF.
Off 4:	LISTEN, SO LONG AS WE'RE TALKING ABOUT THE CONTRACT--

PAGE EIGHT

1.

View through the binoculars, the Kix still up to their tricks.

Off:	THIS IS **BABYLONIAN**…

2.

Hughie looks through the binocs, face twisting. Behind him Butcher relaxes, puts his feet up on the bed.

Hughie:	I MEAN DO THEY DO THIS STUFF ALL THE TIME…?
Butcher:	THEY'RE CELEBRATIN'. THEY PUT THE FEARSOME FOURSOME BACK IN RIKER'S LAST WEEK.
" "	YOU KNOW THE BIT WHERE SOMEONE CRACKS A FUNNY AN' THEY ALL PISS THEMSELVES LAUGHIN' AN' THE SCREEN FREEZES? WELL, THIS IS WHAT USUALLY HAPPENS NEXT.

3.

Hughie looks up, curious.

Hughie:	ARE THEY ALL AT IT?
Butcher:	THE SUPES? SOME ARE, SOME AREN'T. MOST OF 'EM HAVE SOME KINK OR OTHER.

4.

View past Hughie as he goes back to his binocs. We can see various activities continuing at the windows of the brothel.

Off: THIS IS THE ONLY KNOCKIN' SHOP ON THE EAST COAST THAT OPENS ITS DOORS TO THESE ARSEHOLES. YOU CAN USUALLY RELY ON SOMEONE IMPORTANT BEIN' HERE.

Hughie: THE ONLY ONE?

Off: NEVER ENOUGH TARTS, MATE. HIGH TURNOVER. I MEAN THE MONEY'S GOOD--

5.

Through binocs shot of a naked hooker in the bathroom, sat on the commode. She winces with pain as she holds up her fingers to examine them- covered in blood.

Off: BUT GETTIN' A LENGTH OFF A SUPE IS NO JOKE.

PAGE NINE

1.

Hughie peers through the binoculars. Butcher gets up to go, pulls his coat on.

Hughie: I SEE WHAT YOU MEAN. THERE'S THREE LASSIES IN THE KITCHEN DOIN' A FUCKIN' TON OF BLOW.

Butcher: KEEPS 'EM GOIN'.

2.

Through binocs shot of three of the hookers in the brothel's kitchen, one snorting lines of powder, another chopping out more lines with a credit card, a third anxiously waiting her turn. Huge pile of powder- which, on closer examination, is actually pale blue. The girls wear robes, the anxious one is just naked.

Off: HARD TO KEEP UP WITH ABLOKE WHO CAN OUTRUN A LEOPARD.

"   "   NUMBS 'EM, TOO.

3.

Hughie turns to Butcher, curious. Butcher calls to Terror, who wakes up.

Hughie: ISN'T THE OWNER TAKIN' A BIT OF A RISK, LETTIN' US BUG THE PLACE AN' ALL?

Butcher: NOT AS BIG A RISK AS SAYIN' NO TO ME, MATE. HE KNOWS WHAT'S GOOD FOR HIM, DON'T YOU WORRY.

"   "   TOMORROW AT SIX, ALL RIGHT? TERROR!

4.

Butcher opens the door, Terror at his heels. Nearer us Hughie goes back to the binocs.

Hughie: A   YE, ALL RIGHT. I'LL TAKE A FEW MORE PHOTIES LATER.

"   "   HERE…

5.

Hughie looks up again, bewildered. The door shuts behind him, Butcher's gone.

Hughie: THAT'S NO' COKE.

"   "   THAT'S **BLUE.**

PAGE TEN

1.

Night. Exterior the Seven's HQ.

From in: **AAWH--!**

2.

Inside, in a corridor, A-Train squirms on the floor holding his stomach, face twisting in agony. The Homelander stands over him, pissed off. No one else present.

Homelander: WHAT WAS THAT SHIT IN THERE SUPPOSED TO BE? THAT
                 STUPID FUCKING SLURPING, WHAT WAS THAT?

A-Train: JESUS—I WAS ONLY—

"   "   I WAS **KIDDING**, FOR CHRIST'S SAKE…!

3.

Annie's walking towards a bend in the corridor with a glass of water when she stops, puzzled.

Bend: YOU WERE KIDDING. THAT'S BRILLIANT.

"   "   THAT WAS AN **OFFICIAL MEETING OF THE SEVEN**—THAT
                 MEANS **PLAYTIME OVER**, DO YOU UNDERSTAND?

4.

A-Train cringes a bit, grimacing with resentment as he raises a hand to protect his face.

Homelander: **DO YOU?**

A-Train: **YES…!**

5.

Annie peers carefully around the corner.

Off: A-TRAIN—

"   "   DID YOU JUST RAISE YOUR HAND TO ME?

PAGE ELEVEN

1.

The Homelander only, icy cold. His eyes gleam with red light. Red steam rises from them.

Down: **NO! <u>NO!</u> HOMELANDER, I SWEAR TO GOD I DIDN'T! PLEASE!**

2.

View past the Homelander's legs at the cringing A-Train, who gazes fearfully up at him.

Homelander: HHHH.

"   "   TRY AND GET IT INTO YOUR SHIT-FILLED HEAD, YOU LITTLE
                   PRICK: THAT MAN IN THERE IS FROM VOUGHT-AMERICAN.
                   THAT MEANS HE'S THE MONEY.

3.

Close as the Homelander leans down to stick his face in A-Train's, deadly serious, grim as hell. Eyes
back to normal, though. A-Train is riveted.

Homelander: AND WE **DON'T** FUCK AROUND IN FRONT OF THE MONEY,
                   GOT ME?

A-Train: YES--!

4.

The Homelander only, cold.

Homelander: GLAD TO HEAR IT.

"   "   YOU'RE IN THE SEVEN NOW. THE BIG LEAGUES. SO START
                   ACTING LIKE IT—

5.

A-Train, stunned.

Off: OR YOU CAN FUCK OFF BACK TO THE KIX.

6.

Annie stands nearest us, back against the wall, deeply troubled. Mind awhirl, more shit about her ex-
heroes to deal with. Around the corner A-Train watches the Homelander stride off down the corridor.

Homelander: DON'T GET UP UNTIL I'M LONG GONE.

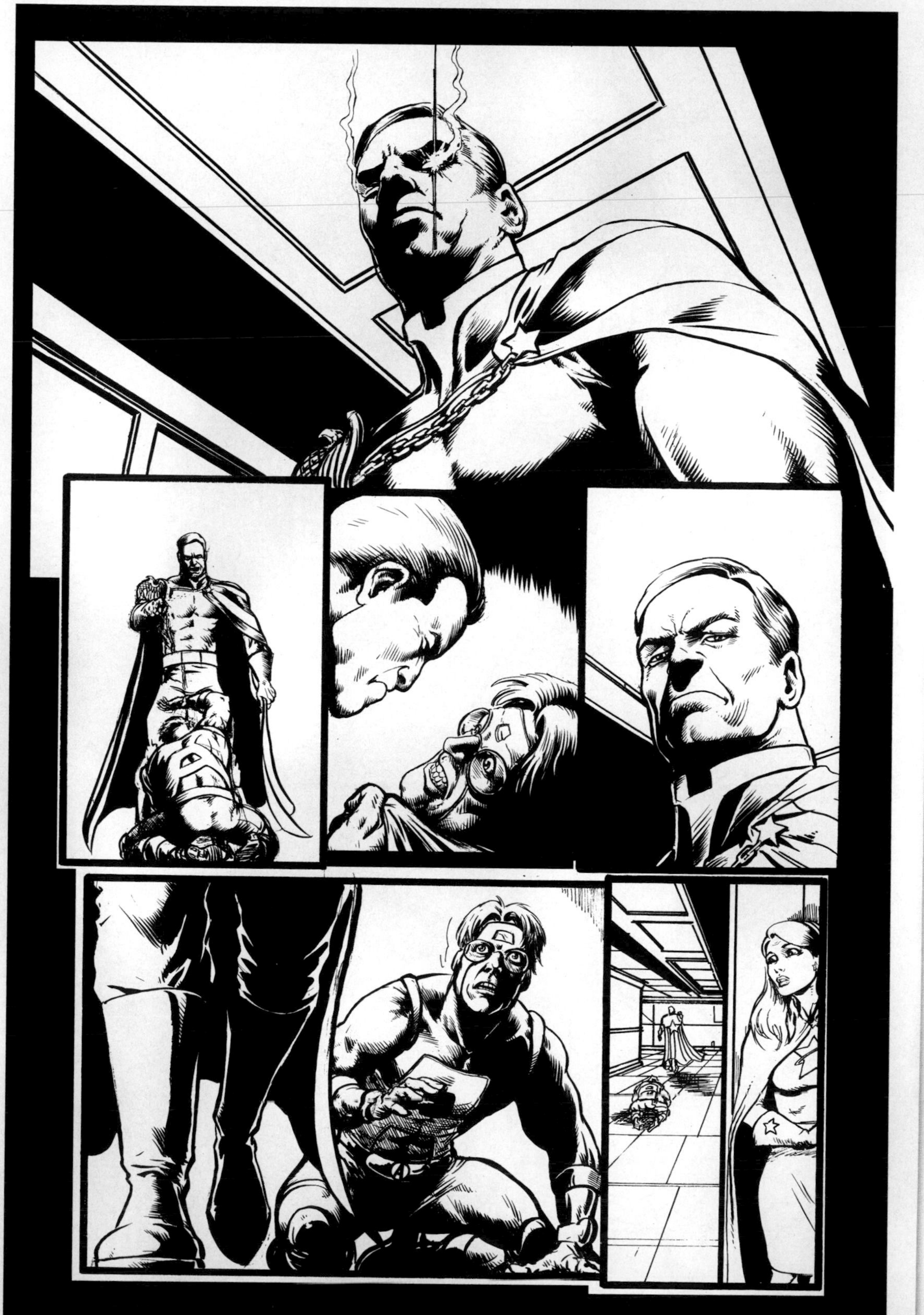

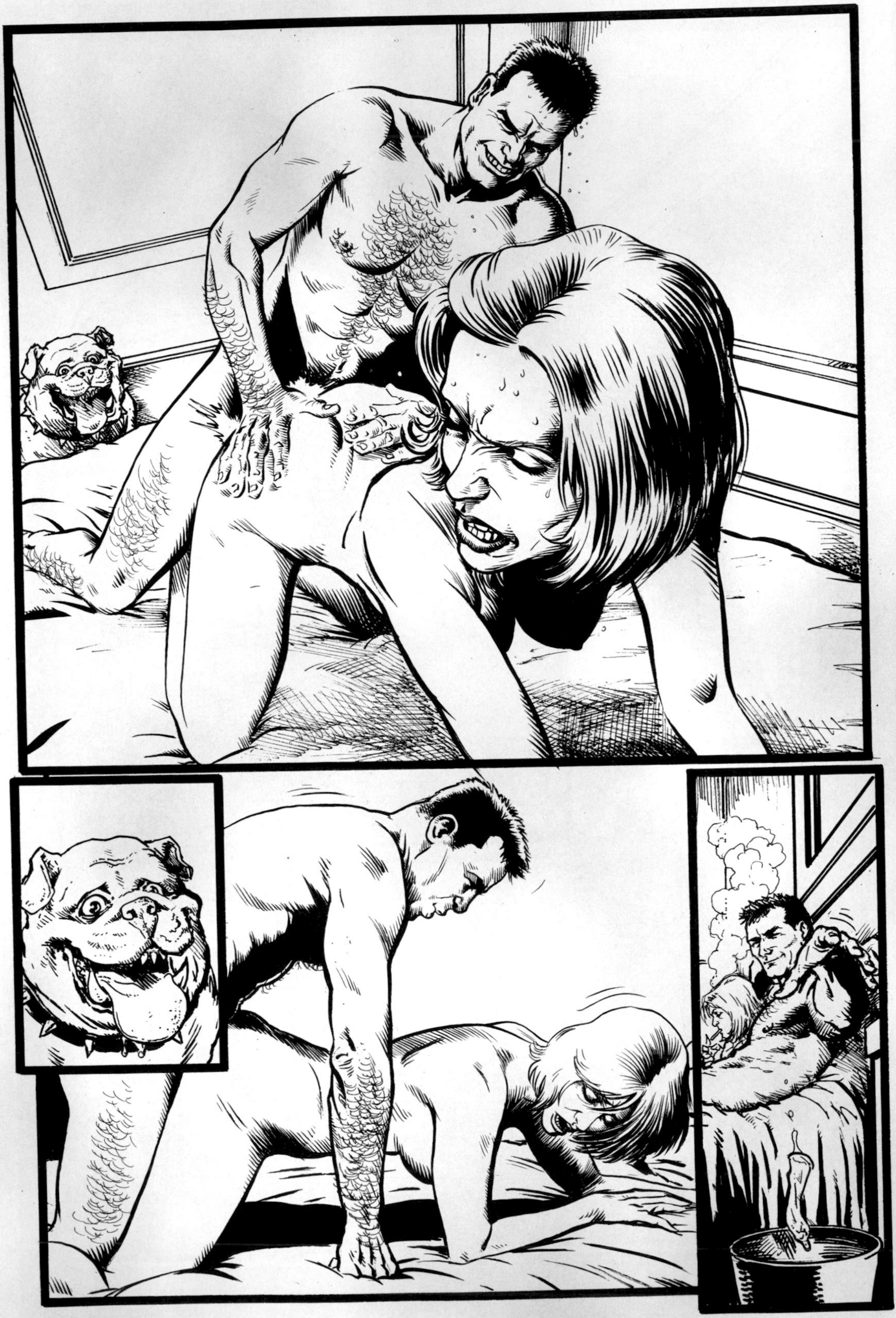

PAGE TWELVE

1.

A posh hotel room. Clothes scattered about the room, Butcher is fucking Rayner doggy style, laughing nastily as he hits her a good hard slap on the ass. She turns her head to scream hatefully at him, livid.

Rayner: **AAOW! YOU PIECE OF SHIT, HOW FUCKING DARE YOU, I RUN THE C.I.A.!**

Butcher: YOU **LOVE IT,** YOU SLAG--!

2.

Terror only, watching enthusiastically.

Off: **OH YOU FUCKING BASTARD AAAAAAAAHHH**

3.

Rayner's face goes slack in the throes of orgasm. Butcher smiles, obviously just come himself, seems pleasantly surprised. Sags forward a little, holds himself up on her back.

Butcher: WHOOF. WELL.

"   "   THAT WAS BETTER OUT THAN IN.

4.

Rayner reaches for her cigarettes, obviously disgusted with herself. Butcher shrugs nearest us, drops his condom into the wastepaper bin.

Rayner: IT IS A FUCKING MYSTERY TO ME WHY I PUT MYSELF THROUGH THIS SHIT…

Butcher: SAME REASON AS ME, LUV. YOU LIKE SCREWING SOMEONE WHO CAN'T STAND YOU.

PAGE THIRTEEN

1.

Butcher looks round, curious. Rayner lights her ciggy, still pretty resentful.

Butcher: SO WHERE'S THE…?

Rayner: MY PURSE. YOU HAVE TO SIGN FOR IT.

2.

Butcher has taken a small metal box about six inches long out of Rayner's purse, nonchalantly flips it in the air. Rayner glares at him.

Rayner: BUTCHER--!

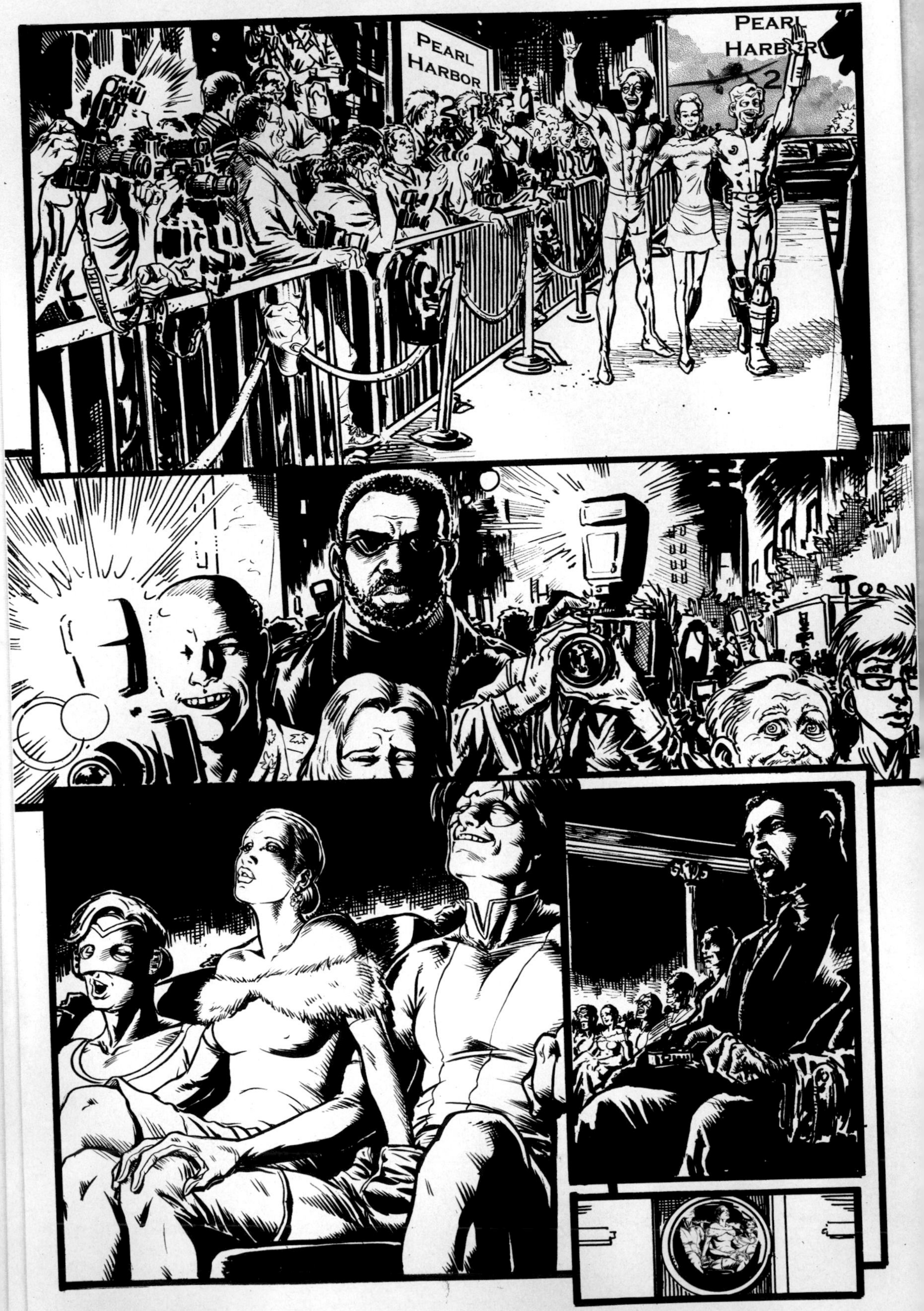
PEARL HARBOR 2
PEARL HARBOR 2

"   "   JESUS CHRIST, DO YOU KNOW HOW MUCH THAT COST?

Butcher: WELL IF I DON'T, WHO DOES?

3.

Close up as he opens it: contains a hypodermic syringe wrapped in plastic, filled with blue liquid- same shade of glue as the powder the hookers were snorting.

Off;   OH, YES, THIS OUGHT TO DO NICELY…

Off 2:   IT BETTER. EVEN GETTING THAT MUCH TOOK A COUPLE OF FORESTS' WORTH OF PAPERWORK.

"   "   HERE.

4.

Butcher signs a form, smiling to himself.

Butcher: CAN'T DO THE JOB WITHOUT IT, LUV. ALL RIGHT, RECEIVED FROM DIRECTOR RAYNER, TWELVE… SEVEN… OH-SIX.

"   "   RIGHT! I'VE GIVEN MESELF THE NIGHT OFF, SO WHAT ABOUT A BLOW-JOB WHILE I'M ON THE PHONE TO ROOM SERVICE?

5.

Rayner peers at us with eyes narrowed, somewhere between disbelief and disgust.

Rayner: …

"   "   YOU THINK YOU'RE **STAYING?**

6.

Butcher grins darkly, holds up the phone.

Butcher: I THINK YOU CAME ALL THE WAY FROM D.C IN PERSON, AN' IT WASN'T TO HAND-DELIVER THE GEAR.

"   "   WHAT YOU WANT ON YOUR SANDWICH, MADAM DIRECTOR?

PAGE FOURTEEN

1.

A movie premiere, press gathered to see the stars on the red carpet. Cameras flash as a certain empty-headed blond socialite stands with her arms around Big Game and Jetstreak, who are both in costume. Big smiles. Other stars in tuxes and dresses further back. Movie title over the theatre entrance PEARL HARBOUR 2 and GRAND PREMIERE

2.

MM stands amongst the press pack, watching carefully as the flashes blaze. Clearly legible press pass pinned to the front of his coat.

3.

In the darkened theatre, the socialite has a hand down the crotch of both supes' costumes- they sit either side of her. All smiling. No one else sees what they're up to, all watching the movie.

4.

Without bothering to look, MM takes a photo with a tiny camera, the kind spies have in movies. He sits at the end of the row, carefully holding the camera low to shoot past us. The person next to him's enjoying the movie, doesn't see what he's doing.

PAGE FIFTEEN

1.

The Blarney Cock and Whack Job (in costume) are visiting a children's hospital- Whack Job clowns around to entertain the kids, who love him. Some kids are on portable IV drips, some have no hair, one's on crutches. The nurses look on approvingly.

2.

The Blarney Cock smiles, keeping a careful eye out as he fills a plastic bag with dozens of jars of pills, obviously in some storage area of the hospital. Doesn't see the Frenchman watching him from above through a ceiling panel he's slid aside.

3.

Close up. Big Game making out with Shout Out, in costume.

4.

Big Game smoking crack as Dogknott blows him- seen from behind. They're in a bathroom- not a public one, a posh one in an apartment.

5.

Hughie with headphones on, carefully adjusting dials on a radio receiver.

PAGE SIXTEEN

1.

Popclaw sits in her bedroom, in costume. Posters for Goth bands, black wallpaper etc. Gloomy, but we can see she's extended her claws: two long, vicious looking blades extended from her wrist, gleaming as she thoughtfully examines them.

2.

Close. She's pulled up one sleeve and is using one claw to cut herself- a two inch cut to join the others already there, scabbed over in a neat row. New one bleeds. She looks furtive here, edgy.

3.

Now she rolls her sleeve up, bit surly and resentful, glancing around to be sure she's alone. Doesn't see the Female at the window behind her, only appearing from the eyes up. First full shot of the window, by the way.

4.

A hand holding a b+w photo of 2. above, but seen from the angle of the window. More photos spread out below, showing all the shit from the last three pages- think about the angles they'll be taken from, eg. Looking down on the Blarney Cock as he steals the pills.

5.

Butcher puts it down with the rest, smiles darkly to himself, pleased. Somewhere gloomy.

Butcher: LOVELY.

PAGE SEVENTEEN

1.

Night. Butcher opens the back door of a van outside an upper East Side apartment, right next to the Park. Balances a cup of coffee on top of another. No one around.

Butcher: ALL RIGHT, MATE? WHAT'S THE SCORE?

2.

Inside the van, Butcher hands one of the coffees to Hughie as he pulls the door closed. Hughie sits next to the radio receiver, headphones round his neck.

Hughie: AW, CHEERS.

" " NOTHIN' NEW SINCE YESTERDAY, REALLY. I'VE BEEN
TRYNNA WORK OUT IF SHOUT OUT **KNOWS** BIG GAME'S
SHAGGIN' DOGKNOTT AS WELL AS HIM…

Butcher: SO YOU'RE ENJOYIN' YOURSELF?

3.

Hughie smiles, a bit embarrassed. Butcher is amused.

Hughie: I HAVE TO ADMIT THERE'S A SORT OF HORRIBLE
FASCINATION TO IT. THE WEE BASTARDS ARE INTO STUFF
I NEVER EVEN KNEW WAS POSSIBLE.

" " BLOODY NICE PLACE THEY'VE GOT, TOO. I HAD A WEE LOOK
AROUND WHILE THE FRENCHMAN WAS PUTTIN' THE BUGS IN.

Butcher: GAP PAYS FOR MOST OF IT. MODELLIN' CONTRACT.

4.

Butcher puts his coffee down, reaches into his coat. Hughie's sipping his coffee, looking over the radio gear.

Butcher: GEAR WORKIN' OKAY?

Hughie: OH AYE, NO BOTHER AT ALL. IT'S PISS-EASY ONCE YOU KNOW WHAT YOU'RE DOIN'.

5.

Butcher only, examining something carefully.

Butcher: SOUNDS LIKE YOU'RE A NATURAL.

"   "   HERE, LEAN FORWARD A MINUTE, WILL YOU?

PAGE EIGHTEEN

1.

Big, close. Hughie leans forward and Butcher takes hold of the back of his head with one hand, slams the hypo needle into the back of his neck with the other. Hughie yelps with shock.

Hughie: WHY? **AAAAH!!**

2.

Hughie's freaking out, but Butcher hold shim steady as he coolly depresses the plunger, emptying the blue stuff into his neck.

Hughie: **FUCK, CHRIST, WHAT IS THAT--?**

Butcher: COMPOUND V. HOLD STILL A SECOND—

"   "   THERE YOU GO.

3.

Butcher sets down the syringe. Hughie turns to gape at him, holding the back of his neck.

Hughie: WHAT THE FUCK D'YOU DO **THAT** FOR?

Butcher: BOOST YOUR SYSTEM. SO YOU'RE TOUGH ENOUGH TO GO UP AGAINST THE SUPES.

Hughie: **JESUS CHRIST, IS IT FUCKIN' PERMANENT?!**

4.

Butcher only. Not amused now, not mocking, just being honest and reasonable.

Butcher: IT IS IN ITS PURE FORM, YEAH. BUT MOST OF THE STUFF OUT THERE'S CUT, EFFECTS ONLY LAST FOR A COUPLE OF DAYS.

"   "   THE SLAGS AT THE WHOREHOUSE, THAT'S WHAT THEY WERE ON. HELP 'EM STAND THE PACE AN' THAT.

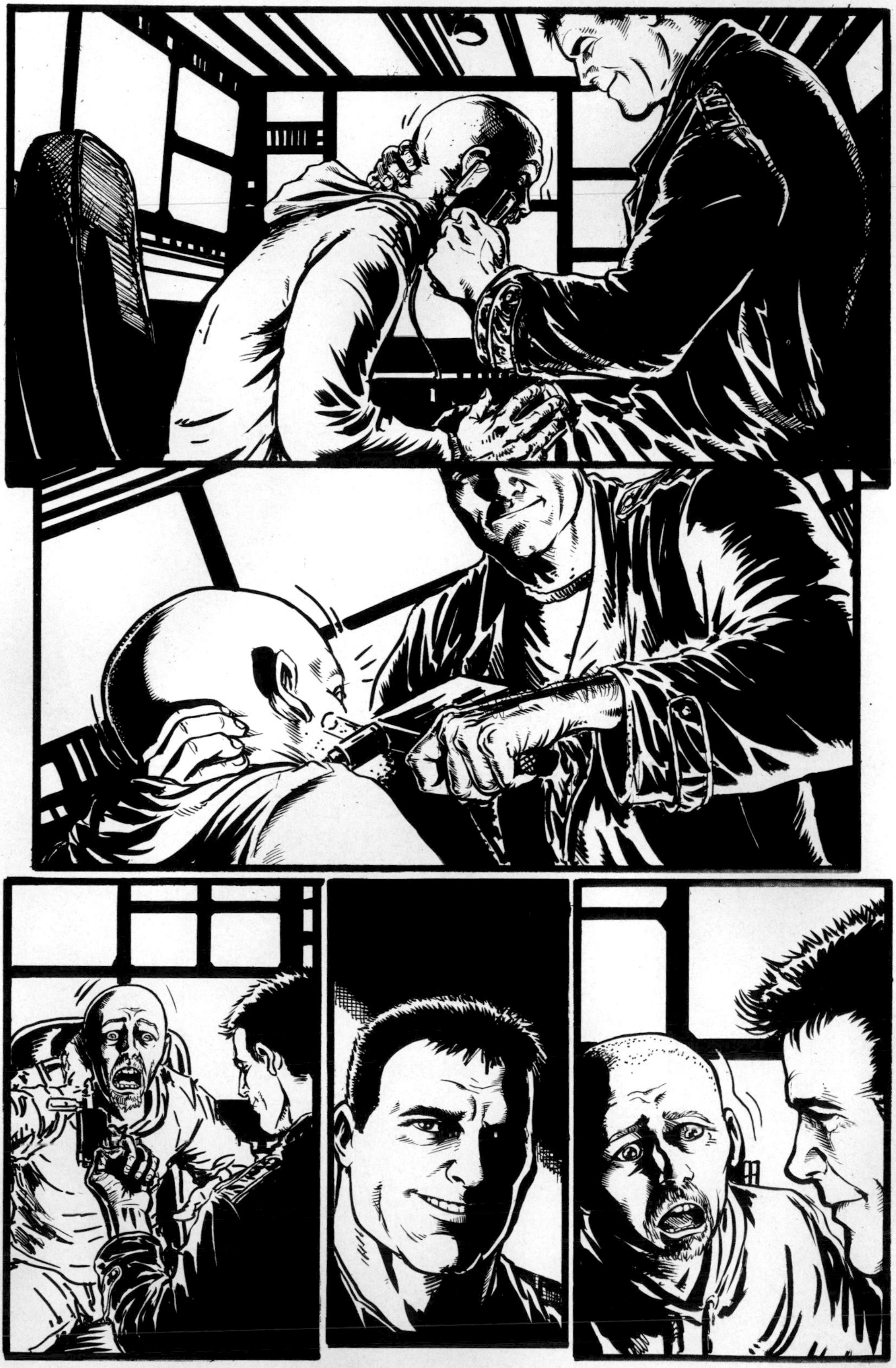

5.

Side view as Hughie stares at Butcher, quietly terrified. Butcher smiles nonchalantly.

Hughie: WH… WHAT ARE THE SIDE EFFECTS…?

Butcher: TURNS YOUR SHIT BLUE.

"   "   THAT'S IT.

PAGE NINETEEN

1.

Hughie turns away, still aghast. Butcher tries to be reasonable.

Hughie: I CAN'T BELIEVE YOU FUCKIN' DID THAT…!

Butcher: WE'VE ALL TAKEN IT, MATE. CAN'T OPERATE WITHOUT IT.

"   "   'CAUSE OTHERWISE, YOU GET INTO A BARNEY WITH ONE OF
          THESE CUNTS AN' HE PUNCHES YOU IN THE FACE, HE'S
          GONNA TAKE YOUR WHOLE HEAD OFF…

2.

Butcher holds up the syringe, serious.

Butcher: SEE, THIS IS WHY THE SUPES **ARE** SUPES. SOME JERRY CAME
          UP WITH IT IN THE THIRTIES, STARTED TRIALS ON PEOPLE.

"   "   IT ALTERS D.N.A., SO YOU CAN INHERIT IT, OR SOMETIMES IT
          JUST SHOWS UP IN THE FOOD CHAIN. NOW AN' AGAIN SOME
          ARSEHOLE GETS HIS HANDS ON SOME OF THE PURE STUFF.

3.

Butcher puts the syringe down again, sips his coffee. Hughie is not reassured at all.

Butcher: ALL THAT DYING BLOKE IN A SPACESHIP GAVE ME POWERS,
          NUKE TESTS MADE ME INTO A MONSTER BOLLOCKS—THAT'S
          ALL IT IS, REALLY.

"   "   BOLLOCKS.

Hughie: WAIT A MINUTE, WAIT A MINUTES, **ALTERS D.N.A.?** WHAT
          THE FUCK'S GONNA HAPPEN TO ME?

4.

Butcher is weary, like Hughie's a drama queen. Hughie shouts, alarmed and indignant.

Butcher: YOU'LL… BE ABOUT FIFTEEN TO TWENTY TIMES STRONGER.

SHOULD TAKE ABOUT A DAY TO KICK IN.

Hughie: **AN' YOU FUCKIN' DID THIS TO ME AN' YOU DIDN'T EVEN ASK?**

5.

Butcher smiles in disbelief. Hughie yells, furious.

Butcher; HUGHIE, YOU'RE GONNA **NEED IT…**

Hughie: **SHITE! FUCK OFF! I NEVER SAID I WAS GONNA JOIN YOUR GANG OF HEAD-THE-BALLS! I NEVER FUCKIN'S SAID!**

PAGE TWENTY

1.

Butcher tries to be reasonable. Hughie angrily wrenches open the van door.

Butcher: COME ON, MATE, IT'S OVER A WEEK SINCE YOU GOT HERE…

Hughie: OH, AN' THAT WAS TO HELP ME MAKE MY MIND UP, WAS IT?

Butcher: IF I'D TOLD YOU UP FRONT YOU'D'VE WANTED TO THINK IT OVER FOR FUCK KNOWS HOW LONG. WHAT HAPPENS IF THE KIX TWIG WHAT WE'RE UP TO WHILE YOU'RE STILL UMMIN' AN' AHHIN'?

2.

Hughie rolls his eyes in angry disbelief. Butcher folds his arms, regretful look about him.

Hughie: SO WHAT, IT WAS FOR MY OWN **FUCKIN' GOOD…?**

Butcher: IT WAS BECAUSE THIS IS WHERE YOU BELONG, HUGHIE. WHERE YOU CAN DO SOMETHIN' ABOUT ALL THOSE FUCKIN' TOSSERS.

3.

Hughie rounds on Butcher, points angrily at him. Butcher almost looks sad.

Hughie: **FUCK OFF!** AN' DON'T BRING UP ROBIN, DO NOT FUCKIN' **DARE** BRING UP ROBIN!

" " YOU PUT THAT BLUE SHITE IN ME, YOU BASTARD! YOU TURNED ME INTO A FUCKIN' **FREAK** AN' YOU NEVER GIMME A CHOICE!

4.

View past Butcher watching Hughie exit the van.

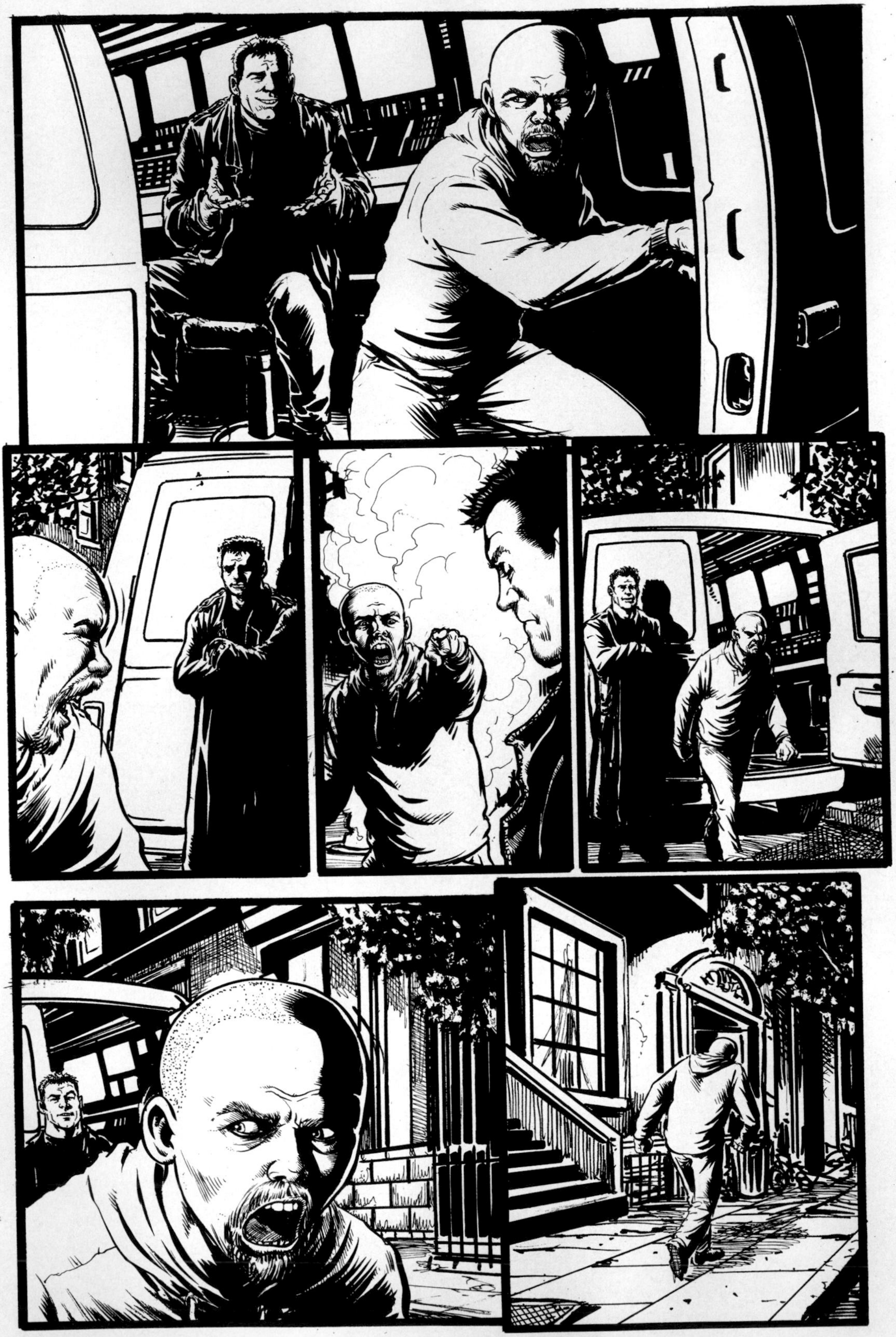

Butcher:	WHERE YOU GOIN'?
Hughie:	**HOME**.
Butcher:	YEAH, ALL RIGHT, MATE. SLEEP ON IT.

5.

Butcher watches Hughie angrily stomp off down the street towards us. Butcher rolls his eyes a bit, slightly amused. Doesn't for one second believe Hughie's serious.

Hughie:	HOME TO FUCKIN' GLASGOW.

6.

Hughie only, stomping along, furious and desperate. Sheer frustration, like he doesn't know what to do or think.

Off:	HUGHIE…!

PAGE TWENTY-ONE

1.

Exterior Hughie's God-awful hotel. Mr. Mad Bastard can just be seen stumbling along the sidewalk again. Night.

Mr. M.B:	LUNCH
" "	LUNCH
" "	LUNCH
" "	LUNCH

2.

Hughie in his shitty little room: single bed, little bedside table and lamp (on), chair, sink. Still dressed. His backpack is on the bed and he's grimly stuffing clothes into it.

3.

Hughie snatches his airline ticket and passport out of the drawer in the bedside table.

4.

Close up on the passport and ticket in his hand. The passport's a UK one.

5.

Headshot on Hughie. Fuming with frustration, just can't make his kind up.

6.

Pull back as he sits down on the bed, pissed off but completely lost.

PAGE TWENTY-TWO

1.

Close up. The passport and ticket are back in the drawer, next to the US passport Butcher gave him. Hughie's hand is sliding the drawer shut.

2.

Pull back. Hughie switches the light off. He's in bed now, clothes dumped next to his backpack. Just looks sad now, troubled.

3.

Hughie lies in the gloom and gazes at the ceiling. Sad and troubled. No idea what to do.

4.

He turns to look offshot, puzzled.

Off: **UUNNNGGHHH**

5.

Hughie sits up and puts the light on, peers down at the floor, face twisting in confusion. Nearest us, pooled at the bottom of the door, is about half a pint of dubious, cloudy white fluid with large flecks of blood in it. Inch gap at the bottom of the door, more than enough space.

6.

Close. Hughie's face falls in weary misery as he realises what it is.

Hughie: **AW, NO...!**

7.

Pull back. Light off again, Hughie lies in bed and stares at the ceiling. Couldn't be more miserable, more beaten.

NEXT: LIFE AMONG THE SEPTICS

SIMON PEGG
introduction from
The Boys vol. 1 (2007)

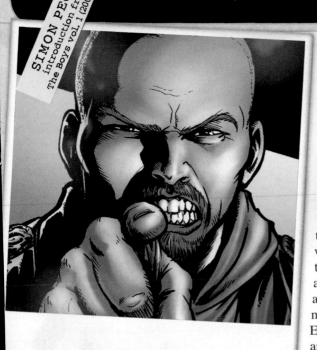

As an actor, auditions are a necessary evil. An appointment is made; script pages are received, a line reading takes place in front of several dispassionates and an ominous little DV cam. Sometimes, an offer will arrive without condition, requiring a straight yes or no. You never get a part without knowing about it. You never switch on the TV or settle down in the cinema to watch something you are unaware stars you. Seeing yourself acting in scenes you don't recall performing would surely be extremely disconcerting. Although I can't say I was anything less than thrilled when I opened the first issue of *The Boys* and came face to face with a young man called Wee Hughie, it wasn't a total surprise. A few months earlier I had received an email from a colleague informing me that an artist called Darick Robertson had appropriated my likeness for a new comic book written by Garth Ennis. Had I not been a comic book fan, or indeed an admirer of Garth's previous works, I might have been a little pissed off, but the fact is I was chuffed to bits. Apparently Robertson had seen episodes of a sitcom called *Spaced*, which I had co-written and appeared in, around the turn of the millennium and figured I was a ringer for the plucky little Scot in Ennis's darkly funny tale of extreme hero bashing. I guess Darick assumed I would forever be consigned to culty British television and would never emerge into the mainstream enough for me or anyone else to make the connection. I don't hold that against him, I thought much the same at the time. As it turned out, a cricket bat and a zombie outbreak in Crouch End, North London put paid to that speculation in 2004, and before long I discovered with a huge amount of geekish joy that, in likeness at least, I was being conscripted by a hard bitten team of "hero police", hell-bent on dishing out bloody justice to those corrupted by the burden of super-humanity.

I bought my first proper comic at the age of seven. A Marvel UK title called *The Incredible Hulk Weekly*. Aside from its title character, who was enjoying a resurgence of mainstream popularity thanks to Bill Bixby and Lou Ferrigno, the comic featured stories such as Alan Moore's dark precursor to V, *Night Raven*, and our own super flag flier *Captain Britain*. Every week I would pore over the pages, studying each panel, getting lost in the stories. I soon learned to appreciate the relationship between writer and artist and how the maxim "being on the same page" was never more fitting than when describing this vital symbiosis. Thrills, scares, jokes and dramas are made and broken by the effectiveness of this connection. The titles I have most enjoyed over the years have seen writers and artists tossing set ups and pay offs between each other like unpinned hand grenades, sharing the responsibilities of storytelling and truly exploiting the medium. With *The Boys*, Ennis' signature gleeful moral depravity is brilliantly realized by Robertson's sly graphics. Sick, funny and disturbing, this rather marvellous collaboration answers an old question, "who watches the Watchmen?" *The Boys*, of course, and they kick the living, fucking shit out of them to boot.

Hell, I'm in.

Simon Pegg
2007-03-29 (for *The Boys Vol. 1: The Name of The Game*)

Simon John Pegg is an English stand-up comedian, writer and film and television actor. He is perhaps best known for his title roles in *Shaun of the Dead* and *Hot Fuzz*, the British sitcom *Spaced* and more recently in the *Star Trek*, *Star Wars* and *Mission Impossible* franchises. Much of his major work has been in collaboration with some combination of Jessica Stevenson, Edgar Wright and Nick Frost.

GARTH ENNIS

Garth Ennis has been writing comics since 1989. Credits include *Preacher*, *Hitman*, *Crossed*, *Rover Red Charlie*, *Code Pru*, *Caliban*, *War Stories*, *A Walk Through Hell* and *Sara*, and successful runs on *The Punisher* and *Fury* for Marvel Comics. Originally from Northern Ireland, Ennis now resides in New York City with his wife, Ruth.

DARICK ROBERTSON

Darick Robertson is an American comic book artist, writer and creator with a decades long career in the industry. Born and raised in the Northern California Bay Area and self trained as an artist, his notable works include co-creating the award winning *Transmetropolitan*, *The Boys*, *Happy!*, and *Oliver* with Gary Whitta for Image Comics, debuting in January 2019. Darick has illustrated for both Marvel and DC Comics on characters including Batman, The Justice League, Wolverine, The Punisher, and Spider-man.

PETER SNEJBJERG

Peter Snejbjerg is a Danish comic book artist perhaps best-known for his work with writer James Robison on *Starman* at DC Comics and *Battlefields: Dear Billy* with writer Garth Ennis for Dynamite.

TONY AVIÑA

Tony Aviña got his start as an in-house colorist at WIldwtorm. His credits include *Sleeper*, *Stormwatch: Team Achilles*, *Authority: Prime*, *Battlefields*, *The Boys*, *Sherlock Holmes*, *Green Lantern*, *Justice League*, *Batman '66*, *Wonder Woman '77*, and *Suicide Squad: Hell to Pay*. He currently lives in St. Louis, which, contrary to popular belief, isn't one big farm (it's actually three or four moderately sized farms).

SIMON BOWLAND

Simon Bowland has been lettering comics since 2004, and in that time has worked for all of the mainstream publishers. Born and bred in the UK, Simon still lives there today alongside Pippa, his partner, and Jess, their tabby cat.

GREG THOMAS

Greg Thomas is a letterer and writer best known for his work lettering the *Boys* (#1-6) and *Supernatural*, as well as writing for *Scooby Doo* at DC/Wildstorm. He is also the co-creator/writer/letterer of *Hero Camp* for Image Comics.

COLLECT THE COMPLETE SERIES!

FROM THE EISNER AWARD-WINNING CREATOR OF PREACHER
ENNIS • ROBERTSON • SNEJBJERG
THE BOYS
omnibus VOLUME ONE

THE BOYS
OMNIBUS VOL. 1 TP
978-1-5241-1097-0
Ennis, Robertson,
Snejbjerg

FROM THE EISNER AWARD-WINNING CREATOR OF PREACHER
ENNIS • ROBERTSON • HIGGINS
THE BOYS
omnibus VOLUME TWO

THE BOYS
OMNIBUS VOL. 2 TP
978-1-5241-1098-7
Ennis, Robertson,
Higgins

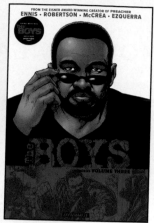

FROM THE EISNER AWARD-WINNING CREATOR OF PREACHER
ENNIS • ROBERTSON • McCREA • EZQUERRA
THE BOYS
omnibus VOLUME THREE

THE BOYS
OMNIBUS VOL. 3 TP
978-1-5241-1099-4
Ennis, Robertson
McCrea, Ezquerra

FROM THE EISNER AWARD-WINNING CREATOR OF PREACHER
ENNIS • BRAUN • McCREA
BURNS • CLARK • ROBERTSON
THE BOYS
omnibus VOLUME FOUR

THE BOYS
OMNIBUS VOL. 4 TP
978-1-5241-1100-7
Ennis, Braun, McCrea,
Burns, Clark, Robertson

FROM THE EISNER AWARD-WINNING CREATOR OF PREACHER
ENNIS • BRAUN • McCREA
BURNS • ROBERTSON
THE BOYS
omnibus VOLUME FIVE

THE BOYS
OMNIBUS VOL. 5 TP
978-1-5241-1101-4
Ennis. Braun, McCrea,
Burns, Robertson

FROM THE EISNER AWARD-WINNING CREATOR OF PREACHER
ENNIS • BRAUN • McCREA
BURNS • CLARK • ROBERTSON
THE BOYS
omnibus VOLUME SIX

THE BOYS
OMNIBUS VOL. 6 TP
978-1-5241-1102-1
Ennis, Braun, McCrea,
Burns, Clark, Robertson

ALSO AVAILABLE FROM GARTH ENNIS & DYNAMITE:

THE COMPLETE BATTLEFIELDS VOL. 1 TP 978-1-60690-0255-4
THE COMPLETE BATTLEFIELDS VOL. 2 TP 978-1-5241-0385-9
THE COMPLETE BATTLEFIELDS VOL. 3 TP 978-1-5241-0474-0

RED TEAM VOL. 1 TP 978-1-6069-0443-5
RED TEAM VOL. 2: DOUBLE TAP, CENTER MASS TP 978-1-5241-0395-8

A TRAIN CALLED LOVE TP 978-1-5241-0168-8
JENNIFER BLOOD VOL. 1: A WOMEN'S WORK IS NEVER DONE TP 978-1-6069-0261-5

VISIT WWW.DYNAMITE.COM FOR A FULL LIST!